Original Copyright ©1996   Revised 2000

N&N Publishing Company, Inc.

18 Montgomery Street   Middletown, New York 10940
phone: 1 800 NN 4 TEXT   email: nn4text@aol.com

Cat # 906 Hard Cover Edition: ISBN # 0-935487 23 9
Cat # 900 Soft Cover Edition: ISBN # 0-935487 28 X

2 3 4 5 6 7 8 9 BMP 2005 2004 2003 2001 2000

Printed in the United States of America, Book-mart Press, NJ

SAN # 216 - 4221

ECONOMICS

ASSESSMENT OF THE AMERICAN DREAM

Hard work and education once insured achieving the American Dream – equality of opportunity, comfort, and success. While not everyone shared equally, the Dream became a guideline for our culture. Today, in a world filled with doubt and uncertainty, the Dream appears to be in jeopardy.

Authors:

Paul Stich

George Habib

Editor:

Wayne Garnsey

Cover Design, Illustrations, and Artwork:

Eugene B. Fairbanks
Granville, New York

N&N Publishing Company, Inc.
18 Montgomery Street
Middletown, New York 10940
phone: 1 800 NN 4 TEXT   email: nn4text@aol.com

Special Appreciation

Dedicated to our students, with the sincere hope that
ECONOMICS – Assessment of the American Dream
will further enhance their education and better prepare them
to participate in the world's economic systems.

Special Credits

To the many teachers who have contributed their knowledge, skills,
and years of experience to the making of our text, we thank you.

To these others, our researchers and readers, our deepest appreciation
for their assistance in the preparation of this manuscript.

David Bennett
John Farrell
Fran Harrison
Maureen Stich

Cindy Fairbanks
Kenneth Garnsey
Joanne Stich
Gloria Tonkinson

To the directors, librarians, and research staffs of these fine NY libraries
we extend our gratitude for their cooperation, excellence, and professionalism.

East Fishkill Public Library, Hopewell Junction
John Jay High School Library, Hopewell Junction
State University Library, Albany
Thrall Library, Middletown
Vassar College Library, Poughkeepsie

ECONOMICS – Assessment of the American Dream was produced on a Macintosh Quadra 840AV. Microsoft *Word* and *Canvas* by Deneba were used to produce text, graphics, and illustrations. Original line drawings and photos were reproduced with a Microtek MSF-300zs, scanned and modified with Adobe *Photoshop*. The format, special designs, graphic incorporation, and page layout were accomplished with *QuarkXPress*. High resolution scans and film were produced by John Spear, Spear Printing, Washingtonville, New York. Special technical assistance was provided by Frank Valenza and Len Genesee of Newburgh, New York. To all, thank you for your excellent software, hardware, and technical support.

TABLE OF CONTENTS

LONG-RANGE PROJECTS

ISSUE 1   WHAT IS HAPPENING TO THE AMERICAN DREAM?

ISSUE 2   WHY MUST CHOICES BE MADE?

ISSUE 3   WHY ARE THERE DIFFERENT ECONOMIC SYSTEMS?

ISSUE 4   HOW DOES THE PRICE SYSTEM OPERATE?

ISSUE 5   HOW DO PEOPLE ORGANIZE IN A MARKET?

ISSUE 6   CAN WORKERS SURVIVE?

ISSUE 7   HOW DO PEOPLE USE MONEY, CREDIT, AND BANKING?

PREFACE
THE AMERICAN DREAM
AND ECONOMIC LITERACY

We live in a new world filled with doubt and uncertainty. Substantial changes occur every year. Once, it seemed hard work and education insured achieving the American Dream of equality of opportunity, comfort, and success. Historically, not everyone shared in the equality factor. Still, it became a guideline for our culture. We seem to judge our progress by the Dream.

Today, the simple requirements for the Dream have changed significantly. Some observers of American life claim it is impossible for the upcoming generation to achieve the level of prosperity experienced by the working class thirty years ago. Others honestly believe the Dream is dead. Success is always elusive. No matter what age one might be, the Dream can be well in hand one moment and gone the next.

Sid Wilkins, the president of a California job placement service, said recently, "The first thing you have to learn is that nothing is forever anymore ... There is no such thing as job security ... The stress of being fired has been replaced with the fear of never being rehired." (New York *Times*. 5 September 1993, A13)

Dismal as that may sound, Wilkins and other experts agree there is hope, but the path to success has some new twists. Workers need new skills and a deeper understanding of how our economic system works. The study of economics was once the province of a few academics. Now, it is necessary to become economically literate to survive, prosper, and keep the American Dream in reach.

Almost all aspects of life call for economic decision-making. Sometimes decisions are made on global or national levels, and people must live with them. In American society, most decisions are made on a personal level. The average person does not use graphs and charts. Still, on the typical kitchen table, one often finds papers with calculations. The brain has to be engaged to make important responses to economic challenges. Making the right choices leads to success.

This book attempts to present a common sense look at economics. It aims at making the reader literate and functional in a changing economic environment. The material is neither too theoretical nor difficult. The authors' aim is to prepare the reader for participation in a different world requiring different skills to achieve the American Dream.

INTRODUCTION TO FRAMEWORKS
THE USE OF FRAMEWORKS IN SHAPING THE AMERICAN DREAM

ECONOMICS – Assessment of the American Dream presents a fresh approach to learning for both students and teachers. Underlying the text are two frameworks to meet contemporary instructional needs:

- The **Learning Standards Framework** correlates basic learning objectives.

- The **Assessment Framework** provides a system of measuring learning objectives.

These frameworks support the total learning process. They define tasks to help students grasp the underlying meaning of each issue. They provide tools to dissect and analyze complex relationships. Spending some time understanding these frameworks will make the economics course more meaningful and rewarding.

©PhotoDisc

LEARNING STANDARDS FRAMEWORK

As American education undergoes broad changes, much attention centers on the *process* of learning. Often, traditional instruction concentrates heavily on content study. Many educators now recommend that basic learning standards and outcomes should be the focal point of the classroom. The substance and activities of learning spring from these learning standards. The standards that are the basis for the questions, skill activities, and assessments of this text are as follows:

Learners should be able to:

(1) understand that while different socioeconomic (as well as national, ethnic, religious, racial, and gender) groups have varied perspectives, values, and diverse practices and traditions, they face the same global economic challenges.

(2) understand that interdependence requires personal and collective responsibility for the local and global environment.

(3) understand that the ideals of democracy and human rights constantly evolve in the light of global economic realities.

(4) understand that civic values and socially responsible behavior are required of members of school groups, local, state, national, and global communities.

(5) analyze problems and evaluate decisions about the economic effects on society and the individual caused by human, technological, and natural activities.

(6) present their ideas both in writing and orally in clear, concise, and properly accepted fashion.

(7) employ a variety of information from written, graphic, and multimedia sources.

(8) monitor, reflect upon, and improve their own and others' work.

(9) work cooperatively and show respect for the rights of others to think, act, and speak differently from themselves within the context of democratic principles and social justice.

ASSESSMENT FRAMEWORK

"The primary purpose of the social studies is to help young people develop the ability to make informed and reasoned decisions for the public good as citizens of a culturally diverse, democratic society in an interdependent world."

– National Council of Social Studies, 1993

As schools redefine their mission, social studies instruction demands new ways of assessing academic performance. Schools require more than on-demand multiple choice testing. Constant performance analysis calls for assessments that are intrinsic as opposed to disembodied testing events. Assessments must encourage active, in-depth understanding and application of knowledge in new and complex situations. Instead of numerical ratings, newer directions call for cumulative course portfolios that have long-range diagnostic use.

PHILOSOPHY OF ASSESSMENT

While *ECONOMICS – Assessment of the American Dream* contains traditional measurements such as open-ended questions, brief essays, and cooperative learning activities, each issue concludes with a short-term performance assessment project. Content instruction is important, but a learning standards framework requires broader methods of evaluation. With this in mind, the authors and editors developed an assessment framework based on the following assumptions:

Assessments should:

- … be based on learning standards determined by the educational institution's over arching goals. The assessments offered here reflect universal goals and can be easily modified to meet the goals that local communities and states establish for their students.

- … be learner-centered. When students can construct their answers and apply skills, they demonstrate inherent knowledge as opposed to luck or guesswork.

- … be varied. The assessments offer a wide array of opportunities to show learning (e.g., oral presentations, research writing, role playing, debates, community participation).

- … be as authentic as possible. The assessments allow for application of life skills, knowledge, and strategies. The assessments place students in contact with community resources.

- … develop students' abilities. The assessments enhance conceptual analysis and communication skills.

- … allow for individual differences. The assessments are flexible, permitting instructors to build on students' differing experiences, backgrounds, and capacities.

By embodying the ideas listed above, the performance assessments in *ECONOMICS – Assessment of the American Dream* are not just measures of student achievement and mechanisms for public accountability. The assessments provide opportunities to explore many dimensions of knowledge. They measure the extent to which students can manage and organize data and make linkages between that data and larger issues. The assessments determine how students view issues from multiple perspectives, solve problems, and think critically. In combination, the assessments constitute performance portfolio work that can give evidence to what students *know* and can *do*.

FLEXIBLE, MULTI-LEVEL ASSESSMENT SYSTEM

ECONOMICS – Assessment of the American Dream has a multi-level framework of assessment tasks. It is essential to overview this system at the beginning of the course to allow for practical selection and longer-range planning. Certain assessment designs, such as the Interscholastic Economic Summit, require preliminary work before examining the chapter itself within the normal course progression.

THREE TYPES OF PERFORMANCE ASSESSMENT OPPORTUNITIES

The design of the individual student's performance portfolio depends on many factors – state, school, department, and teacher requirements, student ability, mixture of quiz, test, and project elements, and other subjective and objective evaluations. Appropriate selection also depends on classifying tasks as to completion time and level of effort. All activities and performance tasks are classified by the symbols – ⊕ (clocks representing time) and the ⚹ (figures representing effort). A key to the symbols is as follows:

Estimated Completion Time:

⊕ = designed to be done in 1 sitting (1 class or 1 evening's homework)

⊕ ⊕ = designed to be done in 2-4 sittings (several classes or evenings' homework)

⊕ ⊕ ⊕ = designed to be done over several weeks (8-10 classes or evenings' homework)

⊕ ⊕ ⊕ ⊕ = designed to be done over two months or more (10 weeks or more)

Estimated Effort Level:

⚹ = Competency level (all students)

⚹ ⚹ = Intermediate level

⚹ ⚹ ⚹ = Advanced Level

Using the time/effort criteria should help to determine the mix needed for authentic assessment. The following section overviews the basic types of tasks presented in the text.

Explanation of the *Assessment Framework Chart* follows the chart on page 14.

Assessments Framework Chart

This chart is an overview of In-depth Projects which, coupled with End-of-Issue Review and Application Questions, provide a flexible system for course and graduation Portfolio Assessment.

Issue	Learning Standards	Prerequisite Reading	Household Tasks	Diversified Tasks	Long-Range Project Options
Introduction: HOW ARE NOTES TAKEN IN AN ECONOMICS CLASS?	4,6,7,8,9	PREFACE & INTRO TO FRAMEWORKS		SETTING UP A COURSE NOTE-BOOK	
1. WHAT IS HAPPENING TO THE AMERICAN DREAM? *(recent historic perspective)*	1,5,6,7,8	ISSUE 1	FINANCIAL PLAN FOR HYPOTHETICAL HOUSEHOLD ⏱⏱ 🚶➔🏃		
2. WHY MUST WE MAKE CHOICES? *(scarcity, downsizing, opportunity cost, production possibilities)*	1,5,6,7,8,9	ISSUES 1,2	BUDGET PLAN FOR HYPOTHETICAL HOUSEHOLD ⏱⏱ 🚶➔🏃		
3 WHY ARE THERE DIFFERENT ECONOMIC SYSTEMS? *(tradition, command, market – systems depend on economic values)*	1,5,6,7,8,9	ISSUES 1,2,3		DEBATE ON TYPES OF SYSTEMS EMERGING FROM FORMER COMMUNIST STATES ⏱⏱⏱ 🚶➔🏃	
4 HOW DOES THE PRICE SYSTEM OPERATE? *(supply, demand, equilibrium, elasticity)*	1,5,6,7,8,9	ISSUES 2,3,4	MAKING A MAJOR HOUSEHOLD PURCHASE ⏱⏱⏱ 🚶➔🏃	MAKING A MAJOR HOUSEHOLD PURCHASE ⏱⏱⏱ 🚶➔🏃	
5 HOW DO PEOPLE ORGANIZE AND COMPETE IN A MARKET? *(types of business organizations and competitive markets)*	1,5,6,7,8,9	ISSUES 2,3,4,5		CREATING A PLAN FOR A NEW BUSINESS ⏱⏱⏱ 🚶➔🏃	RESEARCH PAPER ON A *FORTUNE 500* COMPANY ⏱⏱⏱⏱ 🚶🏃🏃
6 CAN WORKERS SURVIVE? *(supply and demand for labor, unemployment, unions, economic equity)*	5,6,7,8	ISSUES 1,2,3,4,5,6	INVESTIGATE CAREER PLANNED IN ISSUE 1 HOUSEHOLD FINANCIAL STRUCTURE ⏱⏱⏱ 🚶➔🏃	RESEARCH A CAREER ⏱⏱⏱ 🚶➔🏃	STAGE A SCHOOL COMMUNITY JOB FAIR ⏱⏱⏱⏱ 🚶🏃🏃
7 HOW DO PEOPLE USE MONEY, CREDIT, AND BANKING? *(supply and demand for money, market exchange, inflation, FED – monetary policy, using credit)*	1,5,6,7,8,9	ISSUES 1,2,3,4,5,6,7	CREDIT CARD ROLE v. ISSUE 1 HOUSEHOLD FINANCIAL STRUCTURE ⏱⏱⏱ 🚶➔🏃	CHOOSING CREDIT AND CHECKING ACCOUNTS ⏱⏱⏱ 🚶➔🏃	
8 WHAT ARE THE ECONOMIC ROLES OF GOVERNMENT? *(government influence on market, taxation, deficits, fiscal policy, supply-side v. demand management)*	1,4,5,6,7,8,9	ISSUES 3,4,5,6,7,8	ANALYZE IMPACT OF TAXES ON ISSUE 1 HOUSEHOLD FINANCIAL STRUCTURE ⏱⏱⏱ 🚶➔🏃	ORAL PRESENTATION ON ROLE AND FUNCTION OF A GOV'T. AGENCY ⏱⏱⏱ 🚶➔🏃	RESEARCH REPORT ON ECONOMIC ROLE OF A GOV'T. AGENCY ⏱⏱⏱⏱ 🚶🏃🏃

Assessments Framework Chart continued

Issue	Learning Standards	Prerequisite Reading	Household Tasks	Diversified Tasks	Long-Range Project Options
9 CAN ECONOMIC PERFORMANCE BE MEASURED? *(business cycles, GNP/GDP, aggregate supply and demand)*	1,5,6,7,8,9	ISSUES 4,5,6,7,8,9		SOCIAL HISTORY SURVEY ON SUCCESS	
10 WHAT WILL SHAPE THE NEW GLOBAL ECONOMY? *(new trade alliances, multinationals, balance of payments, barriers)*	1,5,6,7	ISSUES 7,8,9,10	PLAN AN INTERNATIONAL VACATION WITHIN ISSUE 1 HOUSEHOLD FINANCIAL STRUCTURE	PLAN AN INTERNATIONAL VACATION	
11 HOW WILL ENVIRONMENTAL ISSUES AFFECT THE AMERICAN DREAM? *(economic sovereignty v. global commons)*	1,2,4,5,6,7, 8,9,	ISSUES 5,8,9,10,11	ANALYZE EFFECT OF CREATING A "GREEN HOUSEHOLD" FOR ISSUE 1 HOUSEHOLD FINANCIAL STRUCTURE	PLAN AND ESTIMATE THE COST OF AN ENVIRONMENTALLY SAFE HOUSEHOLD	CREATE OR REVITALIZE A SCHOOL-WIDE RECYCLING PROGRAM
12 CAN THE DREAM BE DEFENDED THROUGH ECONOMIC RIGHTS? *(consumer redress, protection, warranties, credit rights, business regulation, antitrust policies)*	2,3,4,5,6,7, 8,9	ISSUES 3,4,5,8,11, 12		PRODUCE A CONSUMER SERVICE VIDEO PROGRAM FOR USE BY CIVIC GROUPS	
13 DO NEW REALITIES THREATEN THE AMERICAN DREAM? *(power of corporations, employee ownership, lobbies, parties, political action)*	1,3,4,5,6,7, 8,9	ISSUES 4,5,6,7,8,12, 13		LETTER WRITING AND RESEARCH ON PACS	ORGANIZE AN INTERSCHOLASTIC AND COMMUNITY SUMMIT MEETING ON ECONOMIC ISSUES
14 CAN THE AMERICAN DREAM SURVIVE IN THE 21ST CENTURY? *(individual training, growing career fields, personal finance decisions)*	1,5,6,7,8,9	ISSUES 5,6,7,8,9,10, 12,13,14	SUMMATION OF PROGRESSIVE CHANGES FOR ISSUE 1 HOUSEHOLD FINANCIAL PORTFOLIO	SELECT AND SET UP PERSONAL FINANCIAL TOOL FOR USE AFTER GRADUATION	

A. REVIEW OF ISSUE QUESTIONS

End-of-Issue, short-response items are for reading guidance, reinforcement of concepts, and re-teaching vocabulary for individuals or small groups. (**Time** = ⏱ ; **Effort** = 👤)

B. APPLICATION ACTIVITIES

Practical, intermediate-range exercises are to deepen understanding of the Issue's reading and concepts. They are designed for individual and small group work in two to three sessions involving succinct research and planning. (**Time** = ⏱⏱ to ⏱⏱⏱); **Effort** = varies; *Teacher's Supplement* has additional information.)

C. IN-DEPTH ASSESSMENT PROJECTS

The in-depth authentic assessments are classified for quick reference on the **Assessment Framework Chart** (pages 12 and 13). Note that there are two major *strands* of in-depth assessments (Household and Diversified), but teachers and students can construct eclectic portfolios by combining any of the 14 assessments at the ends of the Issues, in the Long-Range Alternatives (pages 19–27), or in the auxiliary assessments in the *Teacher's Supplement*.

1. Household Financial Assessment Strand: Progressive series of nine tasks that evolve from a base created in the Issue 1 assessment wherein the student(s) set up a hypothetical financial statement. The objective of the Household Financial Portfolio is to provide a series of authentic tasks for a pragmatic learning experience. Students are free to design the household financial structure in any way they wish, but they must realize that its parameters have to be followed for a series of ensuing tasks. Those parameters may be changed, but only after the instructor approves a thorough documentation and rationale for the change. Additions, deletions, and revisions are natural and essential to the learning process. The final task is to review the experience, documenting and analyzing the changes made throughout the process. (**Time** = ⏱⏱) (**Effort** = 👤➡️👤)

2. Diversified Assessment Strand: An alternative to the Household Assessment Portfolio can be a custom-designed combination of any of the twelve Diversified Assessment Tasks. Taken randomly, they offer a diversified approach that can be custom designed to suit the individual instructor's and learner's needs (see Issues 3, 4, 5, 6, 7, 8, 9, 10, 11, 12, 13, 14 – **Time** and **Effort** vary; see chart for per item classification).

(Of course, with minor alterations, any of the progression tasks earmarked for the Household Portfolio can be adapted as a singular, free standing activity for inclusion in an eclectic student portfolio.)

3. Single, Full Term Activity Options: Four long-range tasks engage students in a focused activity for several months: two college level term papers, Job Fair Committee, and Interscholastic Summit (see pages 19–27). The latter two may help to meet new state community-participation requirements. (**Time** = ⏱⏱⏱⏱) (**Effort** = 👤👤👤)

CAUTIONS AND CONSIDERATIONS

Performance-based assessment is not new. Still, its principles and perspectives require deliberation and experimentation. *ECONOMICS – Assessment of the American Dream* offers the assessment instruments as models and guides. Of course, they must be adapted to individual learning environments. Educational authorities recommend performance assessments be developed, appraised, and refined among colleagues, staff, and the community. And, because each school environment is different, instructors (perhaps with student input) should decide the number, nature, and weighting of tasks.

Many details on evaluation should be decided before undertaking the assessments. How will peer evaluation be combined with instructor evaluation? How will each standard in an evaluation grid be weighted? On interdisciplinary assessments, how will observations of colleagues, parents, or outside experts be used?

FLEXIBILITY IN ASSESSMENT CRITERIA

Performance assessment tasks in *ECONOMICS – Assessment of the American Dream* include evaluation standards so that students know the learning expectations from the outset. However, it must be recognized that matching individual student performances to achievement standards has to be developed within the specific learning environment.

On each assessment, the evaluation items reflect the specific learning standards being applied. The scoring grid accompanying the evaluation items was left blank intentionally. The appropriate choice of scoring descriptor terms is a matter left for instructor, collegial, or administrative decision. Selection of appropriate terms ("minimal," "satisfactory," "distinguished," etc.) can also vary with the nature of a particular assessment. The table below offers suggestions for scoring descriptors that might be inserted in the blank grids.

Sample Scoring Descriptors for Evaluation Grids
Numerical scores or letter scores can be used as well as the descriptor words.

Category 1	Category 2	Category 3	Category 4	Category 5
Poor	Fair	Good	Very good	Excellent
Unacceptable	Minimal	Satisfactory	Mastery	Superior
Unsupported	Competent	Elaborated	Proficient	Distinguished

INTRODUCTORY ASSESSMENT PROJECT:
ECONOMIC NOTE KEEPING

Note: Numbers used to identify *Learning Standards* (on the clipboards throughout the text) correspond with complete listing of *Learning Standards* on page 10.

LEARNING SKILLS

Cooperative Organization. This assessment task involves small group and class discussion work to set up a notebook for the course. Notebooks serve many purposes. The instructor will discuss the major uses of the notebook in the class. The following is an alphabetized starter list of suggested notebook functions:

- Annotated list of library sources
- Answers to questions at the end of issues
- Assessment instructions and records
- Assignment sheets
- Bibliographies
- Biographical profiles
- Book reports
- Career profiles
- Collection of articles on a topic
- Correspondence with economic agencies, groups, and organizations
- End-of-Issue activity preparation notes, demonstrations, and reports
- Field trip reports
- Homework assignments
- Interviews
- Items for final assessment portfolio
- Minutes of cooperative group activities
- Notes and worksheets on daily lessons
- Notes on films or TV programs assigned
- Outlines for oral presentations
- Peer and instructor evaluation reports
- Questions for test and quiz reviews
- Reading assignment questions, notes, and reports
- Simulation reports
- Small group discussion notes
- Study guides

LEARNING STANDARDS

Learners should be able to:

(4) understand that civic values and socially responsible behavior are required of members of school groups, local, state, national, and global communities.

(6) present their ideas both in writing and orally in clear, concise, and properly accepted fashion.

(7) employ a variety of information from written, graphic, and multimedia sources.

(8) monitor, reflect upon, and improve their own and others' work.

(9) work cooperatively and show respect for the rights of others to think, act, and speak differently from themselves within the context of democratic principles and social justice.

STUDENT TASK

Participate in a preparation group and subsequent class discussion to decide on an organized system for taking notes for this economics course.

PROCEDURE

A   According to instructor's specifications, obtain a three-ring binder, a set of loose-leaf index dividers, and a packet of lined, loose-leaf paper.

B   Take notes on instructor's discussion on the range of class activities planned for the course.

C   Participate in a group that generates a plan for continuously evaluating the organization and content of the course notebook. Select a spokesperson to present your group's plan to the class.

D   Participate in a class discussion and vote to decide the best plan for assembling and monitoring the notebook.

EVALUATION

The criteria for the evaluation of this project are itemized in the grid (rubric) that follows. Choice of appropriate category terms (values) is the decision of the instructor. Selection of terms such as "minimal," "satisfactory," and "distinguished" can vary with each assessment.

Rating Of Group Plans – Evaluation Rubric – Task Part C

(Refer to introductory section for suggestions of scoring descriptors for the evaluation categories.)

Evaluation Item	Category 1	Category 2	Category 3	Category 4	Category 5
Item a) (7) Does plan identify and organize a variety of notebook categories?					
Item b) (8) Does plan provide for improvement of note taking for various activities outlined by the instructor?					
Item c) (6) Is the plan presented clearly and effectively?					

Class Discussion Rating – Evaluation Rubric – Task Part D

(Refer to introductory section for suggestions of scoring descriptors for the evaluation categories.)

Evaluation Item	Category 1	Category 2	Category 3	Category 4	Category 5
Item a) (4) Does class demonstrate socially responsible behavior?					
Item b) (9) Does class proposal combine a variety of elements from group presentations?					
Item c) Is class proposal realistic and comprehensive, yet practical?					

ECONOMICS – *Assessment of the American Dream* N&N©

ASSESSMENTS

How do I catch the American Dream?
LONG-RANGE PROJECTS

Project #1 – *Fortune 500 Corporation*   – Research paper
Project #2 – *School / Community Job Fair*   – Community Participation
Project #3 – *Operation of Government Agency*   – Research paper
Project #4 – *Community / Interscholastic Economic Summit*
                         – Community Participation

For a well-rounded perspective in economics, activities should include homework and class work based on the short-term questions and activities found at the end of each issue in *Economics – Assessment of the American Dream.* In addition, the following long-range projects represent life preparatory work and should be an option for performance evaluation portfolios. They are models for activities that engage students in focused activity for several months (Time = ☉☉☉☉ Complexity Level = ♦→♦).

LONG-RANGE ASSESSMENT PROJECT #1:
A FORTUNE 500 CORPORATION

STUDENT TASK

Research Paper on a *Fortune* 500 Corporation. Conduct necessary research and produce a 10-20 page term paper on why a particular firm is listed in the *Fortune* 500 annual listing. (⊕⊕⊕⊘ 🚶 👣 🏃)

PROCEDURE

Phase I

With instructor's guidance, select a corporation from the current *Fortune* 500 annual listing. Set up a research journal as follows:

1 Accumulate library resources (recent articles about the corporation).

2 Write to the corporation describing your project and requesting useful information.

3 Skill Demonstration: According to the time table set by your instructor, your research journal must contain:

   a a temporary source list having a minimum of six (6) references (none from encyclopedias).

   b an adequate amount of information in note section to support a ten to twenty (10-20) page paper.

   c a temporary outline which organizes the topic in logical fashion.

   d a brainstorming section of rough ideas connecting source notes and stating the hypothesis and demonstrating logical organization, transition, and some editing.

   e a series of weekly progress reports demonstrating a dialogue between student and teacher.

Phase II

Produce a ten to twenty (10-20) page term paper on the key reasons why the firm you researched is listed in the *Fortune* 500.

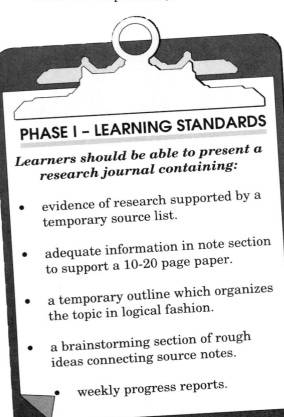

PHASE I – LEARNING STANDARDS

Learners should be able to present a research journal containing:

- evidence of research supported by a temporary source list.

- adequate information in note section to support a 10-20 page paper.

- a temporary outline which organizes the topic in logical fashion.

- a brainstorming section of rough ideas connecting source notes.

- weekly progress reports.

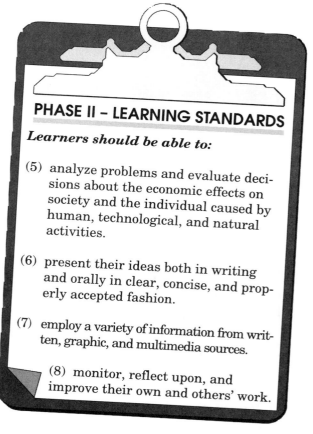

PHASE II – LEARNING STANDARDS

Learners should be able to:

(5) analyze problems and evaluate decisions about the economic effects on society and the individual caused by human, technological, and natural activities.

(6) present their ideas both in writing and orally in clear, concise, and properly accepted fashion.

(7) employ a variety of information from written, graphic, and multimedia sources.

(8) monitor, reflect upon, and improve their own and others' work.

EVALUATION

The criteria for the evaluation of this project are itemized in the grid (rubric) that follows. Choice of appropriate category terms (values) is the decision of the instructor. Selection of terms such as "minimal," "satisfactory," and "distinguished" can vary with each assessment.

Phase I – Research Journal Evaluation Rubric

(Refer to introductory section for suggestions of scoring descriptors for the evaluation categories.)

Evaluation Item	Category 1	Category 2	Category 3	Category 4	Category 5
Item a: Is there evidence of research supported by a preliminary bibliography having a minimum of 6 references (none from encyclopedias)?					
Item b: Is there evidence of research supported by information on note cards to support a 10-20 page paper?					
Item c: Is there evidence of a temporary outline which organizes the topic in logical fashion?					
Item d: Is there evidence of a brainstorming section of rough ideas connecting source notes which states the hypothesis and demonstrates logical organization, transition, and some editing?					
Item e: Is there evidence of a series of weekly progress reports demonstrating a dialogue between student and teacher?					

Phase II – Final Report Evaluation Rubric

(Refer to introductory section for suggestions of scoring descriptors for the evaluation categories.)

Evaluation Item	Category 1	Category 2	Category 3	Category 4	Category 5
Item a: (5) Does the report analyze problems and evaluate decisions about the economic effects on societies and individuals caused by human, technological, and natural activities?					
Item b: (6) Does the report present ideas in writing in clear, concise, and properly accepted fashion?					
Item c: (7) Does the report employ a variety of information from written, graphic, and multimedia sources?					
Item d: (8) Does the report show monitoring of, reflection upon, and improvement of work?					

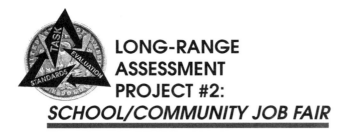

LONG-RANGE ASSESSMENT PROJECT #2:
SCHOOL/COMMUNITY JOB FAIR

STUDENT TASK (COMMUNITY PARTICIPATION)

School/Community Job Fair. The task is to have the economics class(es) organize and conduct a job fair that includes workshops to teach the proper techniques required when applying for a job. (⊙ ⊙ ⊘ ⊙ 🚶 🚶 🏃)

PROCEDURE

1 The program should have two components operating on the day of presentation:

   a   a series of workshops that deal with such subjects as job interview skills, the proper way to complete a job application, how to dress for success, how to construct a résumé, and how to maintain a network of contacts.

   b   a "bazaar" of employers' booths that are actually looking to hire employees.

2 Since the school will be the location, approvals must be obtained to use classrooms, the gym, lecture halls, the cafeteria, etc. With the cooperation of the Administration and the Guidance Department, it may be possible to have the entire school day dedicated to this event or just the senior class.

3 A major task is to get good presenters to accept your invitation to participate. Another is getting employers who are in need of employees to use this event as a recruitment opportunity. Canvassing, letter writing, phone calls, door-to-door investigation are all necessary tasks for the project to be a positive experience for everyone.

4 Help may be obtained from organizations such as the local Chamber of Commerce, the state unemployment office, the local Better Business Bureau, the commerce (commercial) department in your school, local college business administration departments, and local newspaper business editors, all of whom have the resources, contacts, and knowledge that can get your job done.

LEARNING STANDARDS

Learners should be able to:

(1)   understand that while different socioeconomic (as well as national, ethnic, religious, racial, and gender) groups have varied perspectives, values, and diverse practices and traditions, they face the same global economic challenges.

(4)   understand that civic values and socially responsible behavior are required of members of school groups, local, state, national, and global communities.

(5)   analyze problems and evaluate decisions about the economic effects on society and the individual caused by human, technological, and natural activities.

(7)   employ a variety of information from written, graphic, and multimedia sources.

(8)   monitor, reflect upon, and improve their own and others' work.

(9)   work cooperatively and show respect for the rights of others to think, act, and speak differently from themselves within the context of democratic principles and social justice.

EVALUATION

The criteria for the evaluation of this project are itemized in the grid (rubric) that follows. Choice of appropriate category terms (values) is the decision of the instructor. Selection of terms such as "minimal," "satisfactory," and "distinguished" can vary with each assessment.

School / Community Job Fair Evaluation Rubric
(Refer to introductory section for suggestions of scoring descriptors for the evaluation categories.)

Evaluation Item	Category 1	Category 2	Category 3	Category 4	Category 5
Item a: (1) Does the work show understanding that while different socioeconomic (as well as national, ethnic, religious, racial, and gender) groups have varied perspectives, values, and diverse practices and traditions, they face the same global economic challenges?					
Item b: (4) Does the work show understanding that civic values and socially responsible behavior are required of members of school groups, local, state, national, and global communities?					
Item c: (5) Does the report analyze problems and evaluate decisions about the economic effects on societies and individuals caused by human, technological, and natural activities?					
Item d: (7) Does the work employ a variety of information from written, graphic, and multimedia sources?					
Item e: (8) Does the work (report, presentation) show monitoring of, reflection upon, and improvement of work?					
Item f: (9) Does the work show cooperative work and respect for the rights of others to think, act, and speak differently?					

LONG-RANGE ASSESSMENT PROJECT #3:
GOVERNMENT AGENCIES

STUDENT TASK

Research Paper on Government Agencies. Conduct necessary research and produce a 10-20 page term paper describing and judging the operation of a government agency in relation to the economy. (⏲ ⏱ ⏲ ⏱ 🚶💃🏃)

PROCEDURE

Phase I

With instructor's guidance, select a federal or state governmental agency or a private organization from the Appendices. Set up a research journal as follows:

1　Accumulate library resources (recent articles about the corporation).

2　Write to the agency or organization describing your project and requesting useful information.

3　Skill Demonstration: According to the time table set by instructor, your research journal must contain:

a　A temporary source list having a minimum of six (6) references (none from encyclopedias).

b　An adequate amount of information in note section to support a 10-20 page paper.

c　A temporary outline which organizes the topic in logical fashion.

d　A brainstorming section of rough ideas connecting source notes and stating the hypothesis and demonstrating logical organization, transition, and some editing.

e　A series of weekly progress reports demonstrating a dialogue between student and teacher.

Phase II

Produce a 10-20 page term paper on the key reasons why the agency you researched is (or is not) influential in economic affairs.

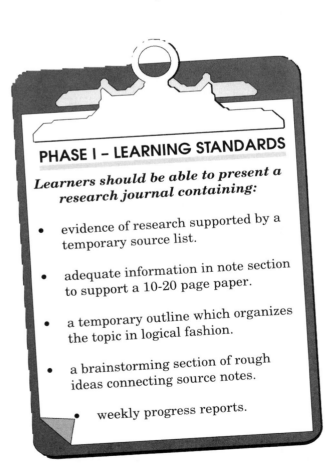

PHASE I – LEARNING STANDARDS

Learners should be able to present a research journal containing:

- evidence of research supported by a temporary source list.

- adequate information in note section to support a 10-20 page paper.

- a temporary outline which organizes the topic in logical fashion.

- a brainstorming section of rough ideas connecting source notes.

- weekly progress reports.

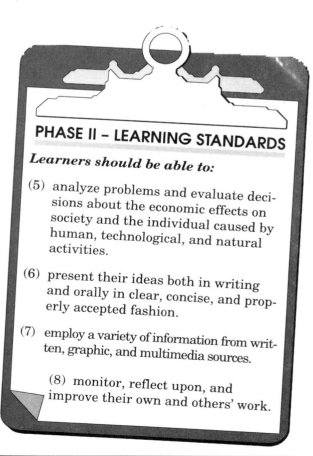

PHASE II – LEARNING STANDARDS

Learners should be able to:

(5)　analyze problems and evaluate decisions about the economic effects on society and the individual caused by human, technological, and natural activities.

(6)　present their ideas both in writing and orally in clear, concise, and properly accepted fashion.

(7)　employ a variety of information from written, graphic, and multimedia sources.

(8)　monitor, reflect upon, and improve their own and others' work.

EVALUATION

The criteria for the evaluation of this project are itemized in the grid (rubric) that follows. Choice of appropriate category terms (values) is the decision of the instructor. Selection of terms such as "minimal," "satisfactory," and "distinguished" can vary with each assessment.

Phase I – Research Journal Evaluation Rubric

(Refer to introductory section for suggestions of scoring descriptors for the evaluation categories.)

Evaluation Item	Category 1	Category 2	Category 3	Category 4	Category 5
Item a: Is there evidence of research supported by a preliminary bibliography having a minimum of 6 references (none from encyclopedias)?					
Item b: Is there evidence of research supported by information on note cards to support a 10-20 page paper?					
Item c: Is there evidence of a temporary outline which organizes the topic in logical fashion?					
Item d: Is there evidence of a brainstorming section of rough ideas connecting source notes which states the hypothesis and demonstrates logical organization, transition, and some editing?					
Item e: Is there evidence of series of weekly progress reports demonstrating a dialogue between student and teacher?					

Phase II – Final Report Evaluation Rubric

(Refer to introductory section for suggestions of scoring descriptors for the evaluation categories.)

Evaluation Item	Category 1	Category 2	Category 3	Category 4	Category 5
Item a: (5) Does the report analyze problems and evaluate decisions about the economic effects on societies and individuals caused by human, technological, and natural activities?					
Item b: (6) Does the report present ideas in writing in clear, concise, and properly accepted fashion?					
Item c: (7) Does the report employ a variety of information from written, graphic, and multimedia sources?					
Item d: (8) Does the report show monitoring of, reflection upon, and improvement of work?					

LONG-RANGE ASSESSMENT PROJECT #4:
COMMUNITY / INTERSCHOLASTIC ECONOMIC SUMMIT

STUDENT TASK (COMMUNITY PARTICIPATION)

Community/Interscholastic Economic Summit. Organize and stage an interscholastic economic summit on an important (local, regional, national, or global) topic, inviting other schools and guests from the community. (☉ ☽ ♪ ☺ 🧍 🚶 🏃)

PROCEDURE

A summit is a high level meeting designed to reach a consensus. While such official hearings are held at all levels of government, most people never get the chance to have their points of view expressed and heard by others in an open and public forum.

Step One

A topic for the summit meeting must be selected. Brainstorm a list of economic issues that may be of interest to your group – chances are what you find intriguing other students will as well. Evaluate and analyze each of the proposed issues, eliminating those that cannot be supported by a consensus of the class. Those concepts that "survive the cut" should be placed into survey form and sent with a letter describing the summit project to several neighboring schools in order to get some reaction to which topic generates the highest level of interest.

Step Two

Use the returned surveys to select a topic for the summit. Set a time and place where the meeting will be held. (Note: Because of the intricacies of scheduling, the teacher or department head may have to set the date and reserve the school auditorium and make chaperoning arrangements quite far in advance.)

Step Three

Create an Executive / Steering Committee which will then divide participants into the subcommittees. Suggestions:

- *Site* (reservations, seating, furniture, insurance, parking)
- *Refreshment / Luncheon*
- *Communications / Publicity*
- *Finance* (budget, accounting, fees, fund-raising)
- *Materials / Equipment* (A-V, program, handouts, end-of-conference evaluation forms, etc.)
- *Speakers* (invitations, accommodations, honorarium, thank you notes)
- *Rules* (important publication and notification to all participants well before the summit. Parliamentary rules may be used or construct your own rules and regulations for exchanges at the summit.)
- *Awards* (e.g., most effective resolution, best presentation, best speaker, etc.; consider adult moderators as well as students to function as judges).

The Steering Committee determines the responsibilities and tasks of these subcommittees and coordinates their efforts.

LEARNING STANDARDS

Learners should be able to:

(1) understand that while different socioeconomic (as well as national, ethnic, religious, racial, and gender) groups have varied perspectives, values, and diverse practices and traditions, they face the same global economic challenges.

(2) understand that interdependence requires personal and collective responsibility for the local and global environment.

(4) understand that civic values and socially responsible behavior are required of members of school groups, local, state, national, and global communities.

(5) analyze problems and evaluate decisions about the economic effects on society and the individual caused by human, technological, and natural activities.

(6) present their ideas both in writing and orally in clear, concise, and properly accepted fashion.

(9) work cooperatively and show respect for the rights of others to think, act, and speak differently from themselves within the context of democratic principles and social justice.

Step Four

An agenda must be set and publicized to all participating groups. The agenda can follow any format decided by the committee members, but the following model is offered as a suggestion:

Summit Meeting on the Crisis in Welfare
I. General Session
   A. Welcoming and General Directions
   B. Keynote Speakers (e.g., County Commissioner, Family Court Judge, State Legislator)
II Breakout Groups (Discuss sub-issues, and formulate resolutions and action plans; e.g., reform of aid to dependent children, food stamps, school lunches, aid to disabled, subsidized housing, eliminating fraud).
III. Luncheon
IV. General Session
   A. Reports of Breakout Groups
   B. Presentation of Resolutions with Debate and Voting
   C. Debate on Follow-up Action Plans
V. Presentation of Awards
VI. Evaluation: Filling-in Forms* and Discussion

Note: Success in this task depends on all committee and general participants knowing about the problem and communicating ideas to others. Students must be able to deliver clear messages to other people who have learned to be active listeners.

In order to accomplish this in both small group and general sessions, the ability to speak and be heard is imperative. Respect for one another and the exchange of ideas among the participants is critical.

*All participants should fill out some form of evaluation to be compiled, analyzed, and summarized by the Steering Committee. This will give guidance for the next group who stage this project. It should be kept simple, using a scale of 1 to 5 to rate items such as organization, food, keynote addresses, opportunity to voice opinion, physical arrangements, resolutions, quality of learning experience, etc. Also, leave space for written comments.

EVALUATION

The suggested focus of the evaluation is the overall work of committees, but instructors and students may wish to broaden the criteria.

Community / Interscholastic Economic Summit Evaluation Rubric

(Refer to introductory section for suggestions of scoring descriptors for the evaluation categories.)

Evaluation Item	Category 1	Category 2	Category 3	Category 4	Category 5
Item a: (1) Does the work show understanding that while different socioeconomic (as well as national, ethnic, religious, racial, and gender) groups have varied perspectives, values, and diverse practices and traditions, they face the same global economic challenges?					
Item b: (2) Does the work show understanding that interdependence requires personal and collective responsibility for the local and global environment?					
Item c: (4) Does the work show understanding that civic values and socially responsible behavior are required of members of school groups, local, state, national, and global communities?					
Item d: (5) Does the report analyze problems and evaluate decisions about the economic effects caused by human, technological, and natural activities?					
Item d: (6) Does the work present ideas in writing (and orally) in clear, concise, and properly accepted fashion?					
Item d: (9) Does the work show cooperative work and respect for the rights of others to think, act, and speak differently?					

ISSUE 1

What is happening to the American Dream?

HISTORICAL ECONOMIC FORCES

"... most of them (today's youth) are striving to carve out lives for themselves and, in some cases, their families, even though they face some daunting obstacles – apparently diminishing economic opportunities and increasingly fierce international economic competition, a spiraling national debt, environmental degradation, a faltering public education system, AIDS."

—Michael Lee Cohen. *The Twenty-something American Dream: A Cross-Country Quest for a Generation.* 3

What Is Happening To

1970s

8 workers pay 1 retiree's SOCIAL SECURITY

expert workers valued by EMPLOYERS

U.S. tops world in PRODUCTIVITY

life easier with CREDIT CARDS

cities have most POLLUTION

car insurance at low PRICES

banks offer monetary SAFETY

little concern over federal DEFICIT

kids will be better-off than PARENTS

general acceptance of moderate TAXES

one expected career for average WORKER

most everyone can afford health INSURANCE

1990s

SOCIAL SECURITY for 1 retiree paid by 3 workers

EMPLOYERS excess their veteran workers

PRODUCTIVITY rivaled by other nations

CREDIT CARD debt can make life miserable

POLLUTION has spread everywhere

PRICES for car insurance out of control

SAFETY of banked money is questionable

DEFICIT major public worry and concern

PARENTS better-off than kids will be

TAXES considered unfair and a burden

WORKER changes jobs throughout career

INSURANCE for health costs is too expensive

The American Dream?

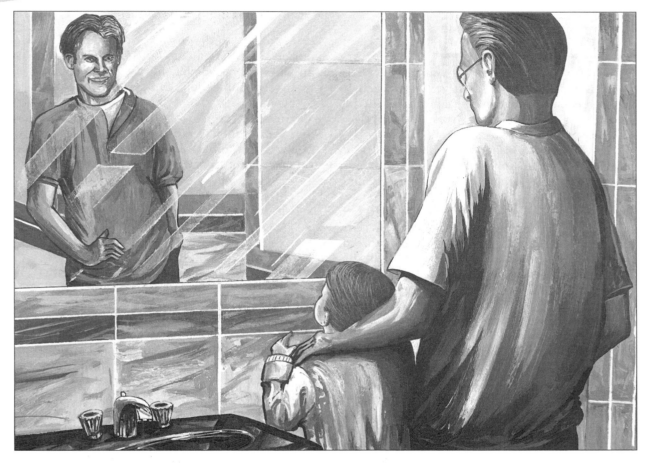

Father and son look in the mirror. The father imagines himself as a young man starting to build his life twenty years ago, but his son is not reflected in the mirror.

Why? Has the chance for freedom to choose and freedom from want disappeared? Is the American Dream gone for the new generation? Recent pieces in the news media label the "Twenty-something Generation," a "dis-" generation: "disgruntled, dissatisfied, disenfranchised, disenchanted, disillusioned, discomfited, disconnected." *(TIME* 15 August 1992, 61)

What is happening to the American Dream?

HISTORICAL ECONOMIC FORCES

IT ISN'T 1974 ANYMORE

Father and son look in the mirror. The father imagines himself as a young man starting to build his life twenty years ago, but his son is not reflected in the mirror.

Why? Has the freedom to choose and freedom from want disappeared? Is the **American Dream** (equality of opportunity, comfort, and success) gone for the new generation? Recent pieces in the news media label this "Generation X," or the "Twenty-something Generation." They call it a "dis-" generation: "disgruntled, dissatisfied, disenfranchised, disenchanted, disillusioned, discomfited, disconnected." (TIME 15 August 1992, 61)

Not everyone agrees. The problems facing the generation of the 1990s are daunting, but this is a better educated generation than that of 1974. Slightly more than 23% of this Twenty-something Generation completed 4 years of college (Michael Lee Cohen. *The Twenty-something American Dream: A Cross-Country Quest for a Generation.* 3). They have enormous knowledge and power they have not yet begun to use. The American Dream is as real for them as it has been for previous generations. It

is a potent and long-standing part of our nation's secular faith. Chasing "the Dream" is an act of devotion that all people, regardless of their sectarian beliefs, can perform (Cohen. 6-8).

In the "The Glass is Half Full," *U.S. News and World Report* editor-in-chief Mortimer B. Zuckerman points to some facts that indicate things are not as bad as they seem.

> "Quality and productivity do not show up in the statistics. New homes are about a third larger than they were a generation ago; they have bigger kitchens and central air conditioning, fireplaces and garages, VCRs and cable-ready TVs. There are other benefits in quality and safety – from air travel to consumer products – that do not show up in the standard measurements. Many more Americans are finishing high school and college. People are joining the workforce later in life and retiring earlier. They work fewer hours and take more paid vacations. Workers, according to one study, have added five years of leisure to their lifetime – three years because of earlier retirement and longer life expectancy."
> – *U.S. News.* 27 February 1995. 80

"The problems facing the generation of the 1990s are daunting, but this is a better educated generation ..."

THE DREAM REQUIRES ECONOMIC LITERACY

What is wrong then? Why does the upcoming generation have such a disconnected sense about the promise of the future? Studying economics can provide answers – a degree of economic literacy is necessary to really grasp what the American Dream is. Of course, studying economics as a subject by itself is a new experience for most students. Yet, as consumers, workers in part-time jobs, and students of history and society in general, most young adults have more economic knowledge than they realize.

Economics is a part of life. There are economic causes behind nearly everything that happens. Of course, political and social events also change the economic pattern of life. It is all integrated. Taking economics out of that integrated pattern of life and studying it all by itself is a little unnatural. However, to see how important it is to the whole society, it has to be separated and analyzed.

THE DREAM REQUIRES HISTORIC PERSPECTIVE

Most students beginning to study economics do not realize it, but they already have a fair knowledge of economic history. If they start from what they know, they can see the pattern of modern economic history evolve.

Students are aware that the United States was just emerging as an industrial power when their great grandparents were children. Before World War I, Britain, France, and Germany were far ahead of the United States in production and industrial development. The Great War's devastation in Europe took a heavy toll on the more advanced nations. Limited participation in the War gave U.S. industry a great boost. Production technology developed before the War (e.g., Ford's refinement of the assembly line) and accelerated during the War.

However, in those days before the electronics revolution, even the advanced technology took a decade or more to affect everyday life. For example, by 1916 Ford's factories could churn out inexpensive cars, but the public did not really get on the road until 1925. Electricity

Occupations and businesses related to the automobile grew in the 1920s and 1930s despite the roller coaster nature of the business cycle. ©PhotoDisc

could be generated on a very large scale in 1900, but U.S. businesses and homes did not use it extensively until the 1920s.

When World War I ended, there was a year-long depression (normal while society readjusts from being at war). Then the economy boomed. During the war, consumers could not (or would not) purchase much. In addition, the government siphoned money away from consumers with the sale of war bonds. In the 1920s boom, consumers bought cars, real estate, electric appliances, indoor bathrooms, and radios. Investors (about 10% of the population) bought stock in the companies that produced the raw materials and finished goods consumers were buying. Many investors made fortunes. It was the "Roaring Twenties." It was a time of very fast and very furious living. Then in 1929, to the shock of millions, it fell apart.

The economic collapse led to great hardship. It showed that the economy is reflective of human existence. Economics is an aspect of human behavior, it is not even-tempered. It is neither steady nor perfectly predictable. (This is

Key Reasons for the Great Crash of 1929

• Wealth was flowing into the hands of only 5–10% of the population.

• American manufacturers were **overproducing** massive amounts of goods. As the years went by, the number of people who could afford to buy goods actually declined. The number of those who could consider themselves **middle class** stagnated.

• Wages had not kept pace with the **GDP (Gross Domestic Product)**. Farmers', miners', and textile workers' incomes were declining from the mid–1920s. The number of poor Americans grew rapidly after 1925. Consumer purchasing began to level off.

• Government saw some of the signs, but the Harding-Coolidge-Hoover Administrations were locked into a laissez–faire philosophy and refused to "tamper" with income taxes, interest rates, or make use of the federal government's regulating powers.

• Congress had raised tariffs, sealing American markets off from other nations. Without U.S. dollars circulating, buying American goods and paying debts to U.S. bankers became impossible. World trade dried up. In the Fall of 1929, business declines caused public confidence to falter. Edgy stockholders began to sell shares rapidly. The wave of selling turned into a panic. The unstable economy collapsed.

a good point to remember when economists get carried away with numerical formulas for quantifying human behavior.)

Immediately after the 1929 collapse, people accepted official explanations by economists and politicians that this was a normal "correction phase" (reorganization) for an overheated economy. Americans had long accepted the idea that their economy needed no socialistic tampering by government. This is what classical economists called **laissez-faire**. In 1929, the people expected no government moves (now called **fiscal policy**) to aid the ailing economy.

At first, there was no sense that the Dream was in jeopardy, but as the Great Depression deepened, and the years went by, the American public became disgruntled, dissatisfied, disenfranchised, disenchanted, disillusioned, discomfited, and disconnected.

THE DREAM REQUIRES A PROACTIVE GOVERNMENT

By 1933, nearly one-fourth of all workers were unemployed. Many more were **underemployed** (working, but for lower wages and fewer hours). After four years, the people's mood changed. They sensed this was no ordinary correction phase. They were desperate for some action – government action to "prime-the-pump" or "jump-start" the economy. The American public took a leap of faith. In 1932, they voted for a political change which promised government action to revitalize the economy – and the Dream. They voted for FDR's New Deal.

Franklin Delano Roosevelt experimented with the new economic role for government. The government borrowed money for programs to stimulate the demand to create new programs (see Figure 1.1). The country grudgingly accepted **deficit spending** (financing expenses by borrowing because of limited revenues). New Deal programs put the unemployed to work on civil projects and created new civil service jobs. These jobs preserved peoples' self-respect and gave them money to demand goods and services, thus "priming the economic pump." Among the nation's priorities, survival replaced the sacred principle of laissez-faire. From that point, the people came to expect government would deal with broad economic problems such as poverty, unemployment, and all other economic problems.

Besides this change in public philosophy, the New Deal also made some permanent economic changes which placed government squarely in the lives of all Americans. Social Security and watchdog agencies were created to avoid the problems of the 1920s. The Securities and Exchange Commission watched the stock markets on Wall Street. The Federal Deposit Insurance Corporation watched the banks.

While the New Deal kept faith in the American Dream alive, the fact remains that it did not cure the Great Depression. It was the massive World War II military spending that began in 1940 that made the economy boom

The New Deal's 3 Rs
"Priming the Pump"

President and Advisors Suggest Fiscal Policy Legislation.

Congress Enacts Recommended Fiscal Legislation.

RELIEF	RECOVERY	REFORM
Immediate Action To Halt The Economy's Deterioration	"Pump – Priming" Temporary Programs To Restart the Flow Of Consumer Demand	Permanent Programs To Avoid Situations Causing Contractions and Insurance for Citizens Against Economic Disasters
Bank Holiday	Agricultural Adjustment	Securities and Exchange Commission
Emergency Banking Act	National Industrial Recovery Act	Federal Deposit Insurance Corporation
Federal Emergency Relief Act	Home Owners Loan Corporation	Social Security Administration
Civil Works Administration	Works Progress Administration	National Labor Relations Board

Figure 1.1

The GI Bill stimulated the economy after WW II. ©PhotoDisc

again. When the war ended, government continued to play a critical role in the economy. (Today, government is responsible for roughly 23% of all spending in the United States.)

Acceptance of the New Deal did not mean that everyone agreed with this new role for government. Traditionally, the heartbeat of a free market economy is the interaction of consumers and producers. Any government economic role alters the market and is always controversial.

As most wars end, economic activity slows. After World War II, as the nation converted to peacetime production, the government moved again to shore up the Dream. Under Truman's "Fair Deal," the federal government continued spending to help the returning veterans go to school and buy homes under the "G.I. Bill." This legislation stimulated the economy through the normal post-war sag. This policy also accelerated the movement of the population out of the cities to where land was available – the suburbs. Life in the suburbs demanded autos. This stimulated another major industry in the late 1940s. More cars on the roads led to demand for more expressways, beltways, and freeways. The

The move to the suburbs following WW II increased demand for cars, homes, expressways, shopping centers, schools, and recreation facilities. ©PhotoDisc

the limit. At the same time, **aggregate demand** (total consumption) grew rapidly because high employment gave more consumers more to spend. The imbalance in aggregate supply and aggregate demand made prices rise. **Inflation** (too many dollars chasing too few goods) became a chronic problem.

Throughout the 1960s, President Kennedy's "New Frontier" and President Johnson's "Great Society" kept the expansion (and inflation) rolling with tax cuts and higher government spending. Medicare, urban renewal, and the "War on Poverty" made high levels of deficit spending fashionable. The added expense of the war in Vietnam sent government spending sky high. The pace of inflation increased. The Dream seemed jeopardized again, and this time big government was the problem instead of the solution.

suburban life also gave rise to demand for more shopping centers, government offices, schools, and recreation facilities. As a result, the construction industry boomed in the 1950s.

There was foreign stimulation, too. World War II destroyed most of the productive facilities in Europe and Asia. Orders for American goods flooded world markets. The Marshall Plan and other U.S. government decisions to keep occupation troops and send aid to Europe and Japan intensified the flood of demand. The defense industry continued high production during the Korean War and with American allies throughout the Cold War.

THE DREAM REQUIRES THE CONTROL OF AN OVERACTIVE GOVERNMENT

As in all human endeavors, there can be too much of a good thing. The government had moved to preserve the Dream in the 1930s and 1940s. In the 1950s, all this government generated demand over-stimulated the economy. Business could not meet all the government demand and simultaneously provide for consumer demand. **Aggregate supply** (total production) of goods and services was stretched to

President Nixon fought with Congress to slow down spending for government programs in the 1970s. Withdrawal from Vietnam also cut military spending. As the economy slowed, unemployment rose, and a recession hit. The economic picture worsened in the middle of the 1970s when OPEC (Organization of Petroleum Exporting Countries) began restricting oil supplies. Prices shot up, and many workers lost their jobs and income. Economists called the problem **stagflation** (inflation and recession hitting at the same time). Under Presidents Ford and Carter, the economy weakened even more. In the late 1970s, the Iranian Revolution and the Iran-Iraq War cut oil supplies and generally inflated prices again.

By 1980, most Americans had a powerless feeling the Dream was about to die. Their way of life was being destroyed by **hyperinflation** (prices rising by more than 10% annually). It was fueled by out-of-control government expenses and soaring oil prices.

With promises to control inflation by cutting deficit spending and taxes, Ronald Reagan won office and the Republicans captured the Senate in 1980. President Reagan's advisors tried a **supply-side** stimulation approach (government policies aimed at giving business and investors more incentive). They proposed to cut federal government spending and shift public programs to private business. This policy was dubbed "Reaganomics" by the media.

Supply-siders claimed that cutting taxes for industry would renew the desire of the wealthy class to invest. They theorized that capital development would surge. Supply-siders declared that investment of untaxed surplus capital in industry would spur growth, which would lead to new jobs. Those working in these new jobs would reduce unemployment claimants and create new taxpayers.

With these aims in mind, Reagan supporters pushed a series of broad tax cuts through Congress. One problem was that they also wanted to increase government spending to strengthen national defense. Of course, the defense companies and their stockholders did very well, but the goods produced did not help nonmilitary consumers. However, the rise in defense spending cancelled the effect of other government spending cuts the supply-siders managed to get from Congress.

In the early 1980s, another recession hit the country before supply-side policies took hold. The Federal Reserve launched its own campaign against inflation by forcing bank interest rates up. However, the high interest rates cut investment and lending so much that businesses cut production and workers. The recession worsened, and unemployment soared above 10 percent.

The supply-siders' tax cuts did lead to some new investment in industrial technology, but failed to contribute to significant growth. Much of the extra money went to foreign investment. Diminishing federal funding for state programs led states to cut expenditures for education, health, cultural, and other social programs, which diminished the quality of life.

The supply-siders also led a drive to cut down government regulation of industry.

Supply-siders deregulated cable TV, telephone, and utilities which cut business costs and opened the market to new technological advances, but raised consumer prices in the long run. ©PhotoDisc

Deregulation helped to cut business costs and increased profits, but it also led to higher consumer prices for telephone, cable TV, and utilities. Banking deregulation led to more services, but to cover new costs, banks raised interest rates for consumer loans, eventually slowing down consumption.

THE DREAM REQUIRES EVEN-HANDED GOVERNMENT POLICIES

As a result of the supply-siders campaign, only one group actually began to enjoy the American Dream again – "the rich." With generous tax breaks, the rich had more money to lend and invest. They profited from the Federal Reserve's policies of keeping interest rates high. However, the lavish media coverage of their conspicuous life-style created an impression on the general public. Even TV dramas such as *Dallas, Dynasty,* and *Falcon Crest* glorified the rich. There was a misperception the Dream was easily attainable for everyone. However, the rich were a small group. *U.S.A. Today* reported that less than 2% of the population had incomes over $100,000 in 1987 (Moore. 1). In *The Politics of Rich and Poor,* a 1990 analysis of what went wrong with the Reagan Era, author Kevin

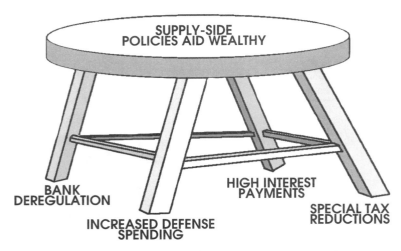

Figure 1.2 The "2nd Gilded Age" supported the wealthiest U.S. taxpayers through President Regan's policy of Supply-side Economics.

Phillips says the 1980s was "a second Gilded Age" (see Figure 1.2). Phillips showed that middle and lower income groups could not really share the Dream (Phillips. 9). They could not afford to borrow at such high interest rates. Amid what appeared to be a general growth in prosperity, their standard of living declined. The gap between rich and poor grew larger. In the 1980s, Americans maintained their standard of living by going deeper in debt and putting more family members to work. In a special 1991 edition of *Fortune*, Thomas Stewart said that the proportion of debt to after-tax income rose 84% for the average American family ("The New American Century," 17). The Dream was elusive for the majority.

Supply-side deregulation allowed large businesses to engage in complicated mergers and buy outs of competitors. There was a great deal of short-term gain. These moves enhanced corporations' market power and stock dividends. **CEO** (corporate Chief Executive Officer) salaries and benefits ran into the millions. In 1987, *Forbes* stated that the average annual corporate CEO salary was $762,253 (Phillips. 176). The corporate takeovers and investor trading made a few speculators very wealthy. However, some trade practices led to Wall Street scandals and banking collapses. In some cases, the short-term gains led to long-term structural damage that carried into

the 1990s. In the long run, none of them led to **real growth** (net increase in jobs, higher productivity, or lower prices). Wealth did not "trickle down" to the American people as the supply-siders hoped.

Amid all the supply-side reforms, Reagan and Congress lost their appetite for cutting government spending. The combination of less tax revenue and massive government spending sent the national debt soaring beyond $4 trillion in the early 1990s (see Figure 1.3). The government's voracious need to borrow, coupled with the Federal Reserve Bank's "tight monetary policy" to hold down inflation, made money scarce and expensive. Interest rates (the price of loans) soared, too. Average Americans could not manage the credit cards, mortgages, and auto loans. Only the rich had large amounts of disposable income to spend or to lend the government (in the form of bonds). They got richer, but the general lack of consumer demand meant a slowdown of production, and layoffs began.

For all the government action, the Dream once more seemed beyond the reach of average Americans. On top of the national debt problem, came a persistent international trade imbalance. Phillips points out reduced taxes for the rich increased their disposable income (*Forbes*. 4). While they did invest, they also began spending lavishly, especially on personal imported goods. A good deal of their money left the country for BMWs, Mercedes, Volvos, and Porsches. This upsurge of competition from Western Europeans, Japanese, and new Pacific Rim industrial countries slowed domestic job growth.

These problems continued into the 1990s under President Bush and threw the economy into another recession. Bill Clinton and the Democrats won election in 1992 on basis of cutting government debt and revitalizing the economy, but the economic problems persisted.

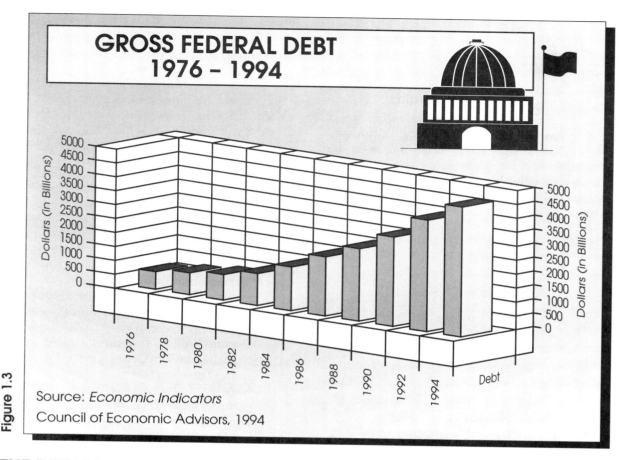

GROSS FEDERAL DEBT 1976 – 1994

Dollars (in Billions): 0, 500, 1000, 1500, 2000, 2500, 3000, 3500, 4000, 4500, 5000

1976, 1978, 1980, 1982, 1984, 1986, 1988, 1990, 1992, 1994

Debt

Figure 1.3

Source: *Economic Indicators*
Council of Economic Advisors, 1994

THE DREAM REQUIRES AN ACTIVE, ECONOMICALLY LITERATE PUBLIC

This is the economic situation in which the upcoming generation must function. A 1992 *Business Week* article said members of the new generation feel "paralyzed by social problems they see as their inheritance" and that they "…[desire to] avoid risk, pain, and rapid change…." (Zinn. "Move Over Boomers…" 14 December 1992, 192)

In *The Twenty-something American Dream*, Michael Lee Cohen debates this negative image of his generation presented by the media. He claims many young people are confused, because the old ways of resolving the problems have broken down. The upcoming generation feels political parties, labor unions, and large corporations are no longer useful mechanisms for channeling their social concerns (Cohen, 300). These young people see political parties as historical artifacts that provide some members with money and some privileges, but they do not see parties as agents of change. They feel labor unions are corrupt and do not work for a service economy as they did for a manufacturing economy. Large corporations are "stateless, self-preserving institutions" treating employee loyalty as peasant foolishness (Cohen, 301). Cohen repeats the famous quote of a recent G.E. Chairman, "Loyalty to a company, it's nonsense." (Cohen, 301)

Does this mean there is no American Dream for the upcoming generation? Hardly. There are plenty of "end-of-the-civilization" doomsayers out there, but the fact remains that the United States is the dominant global economic power. Japan is an important economic power, but the quality of life in Japan still falls behind that in the United States. *Fortune's* Thomas A. Stewart showed Japan's 1991 per capita **Gross Domestic Product** (GDP: total value of all goods and services produced inside the country) was $15,000. He indicated the figure for the United States was $21,000 (*Fortune* 1991. "The New American Century." 15). Still, the pessimists who say the Dream is dead or gone make Americans take stock in themselves. Cohen says, "Dissenters and doubters force us to constantly reconsider and redefine the Dream and revitalize it in the process" (Cohen. 307).

SUMMARY

What students must recognize from recent economic history is that there is still a horizon of opportunity that a new generation can seek. Studying economic decision making is the way to begin that quest. Studs Terkel has been listening and writing what Americans say and think about themselves for decades. In his 1980 book, *American Dreams: Lost and Found*, he mentions a housewife who didn't like the word "dream." She said, "It's not a dream, it's possible. It's everyday stuff." (Terkel xxv)

ASSESSMENT
QUESTIONS • APPLICATIONS

1   This chapter begins with a list of perceptions about the differences between the 1970s and 1990s. Review opposing lists. Discuss it with your parents.
   a   Do you agree with all the items? Explain why or why not.
   b   Can you add any items to the 1990s? Can your parents add to the 1970s?
   c   What do the items have to do with beginning a study of economics?

2   The subheadings of this chapter show that preserving the American Dream involves certain requirements. Explain why the Dream requires each of the following:
   a   an awareness of recent history
   b   a degree of government involvement
   c   control of an overactive government
   d   an economically literate public

3   Consider this quote:
   "There never has been one American Dream on which we must all agree. The belief there ever was a single, clearly defined American Dream is just a sentimental longing for a time of perfect consensus that has never existed in this nation. The dream of creating a shining city on a hill and the settling of the West came at the expense of those who had been here for centuries. The post-war dream of a suburban paradise excluded racial minorities and consigned women to very restrictive roles." – Michael Lee Cohen.
   The Twentysomething American Dream: pages 306-307
   a   Is the American Dream only for the rich? Why, or why not?
   b   Is the Dream only good for one sex, race, or ethnic group? Why, or why not?
   c   Why is it so hard to define the American Dream?

4   For this question, think globally. Economics is universal in nature. Everyone has a struggle for survival. In a group, discuss how similar economic expectations are in other places.
   a   Do you think a Mexican or Canadian (or Nigerian, or Thai, etc.) "Dream" exists? Using facts, explain your position.
   b   Choose a country. Look in a world cultures text, an encyclopedia, an almanac, or the Internet. Find out how the Dream in other countries might be the similar to or different from the American Dream.

5   The American economy is basically a market economy where consumer and producer choices determine its direction. Following the Great Depression, the entry of government as a major force in the American economy altered the system.
   a   How did government become a major economic force, and what were some of the programs initiated?
   b   Why was it necessary for government to play a major role in the economy?
   c   Explain why you are for or against the government role in American economic life.
   d   Do you see government as preserving the Dream or jeopardizing it?

6   Supply-side stimulation of the economy in the 1980s was a departure from economic policies the government had followed since the 1930s.
   a   Why did supply-side advocates feel there was a need for a change?
   b   List and explain the basic ideas behind supply-side strategies.
   c   Evaluate the success of supply-side policies of the 1980s.

ASSESSMENT PROJECT:
HOUSEHOLD FINANCIAL PROFILE

STUDENT TASK

Write a brief sketch of the financial status of a household that you create. Your "adopted" household must be realistic but should be completely fictional. For example, you could choose a "statistically typical" American family of four: head of household, spouse, and two children. Or, choose a single parent household, two–salaried, or one–income family.

This project can be completed by yourself or jointly with a classmate. As a guide, you may use computer software for home budgeting such as Home Office's *M.Y.O.B. Accounting*, Kiplinger's *Simply Money*, Intuit's *Quicken*, Andrew Tobias' *Managing Your Money*, or one of the other personal financial management computer programs. However, you must submit a Household Financial Profile in hard copy. Keep in mind that the household you create will become the basis for several other assessment activities throughout this book (e.g., budgeting, major purchases, paying taxes). Whenever you see the house icon depicted at the beginning of this project, you should refer back to this *Household Financial Profile* for basic data.

PROCEDURE

After creating your "adopted family" for this assessment, complete the following:

1   Fill-in completely the data requested on the *Household Financial Profile* chart (sample on page 43). You may need parental, teacher, or other professional help. Again, this data will be used for this and other "household" projects that follow in other Issues.

2   Write a descriptive essay of the household. In other words, put your *Household Economic Profile* into sentence form. As you write, keep in mind these questions: (1) Do you have a economic basis for a functional family? (2) Does an overview of your profile identify the household as "lower, middle, or upper" income? (3) What are the feasible prospects (goals) for this family and the American Dream? In "real life," a financial profile can be used to determine net worth, which is needed for things such as a new home purchase, college financial assistance, or starting an entrepreneurial enterprise.

3   Identify and list your informational sources for this assignment. Include library and interview sources.

LEARNING STANDARDS
Learners should be able to:

(1) understand that while different socioeconomic (as well as national, ethnic, religious, racial, and gender) groups have varied perspectives, values, and diverse practices and traditions, they face the same global economic challenges.

(5) analyze problems and evaluate decisions about the economic effects on society and the individual caused by human, technological, and natural activities.

(6) present their ideas both in writing and orally in clear, concise, and properly accepted fashion.

(7) employ a variety of information from written, graphic, and multimedia sources.

(8) monitor, reflect upon, and improve their own and others' work.

Household Financial Profile

Personal Information:
Head of Household _____
Address _____
_____
Home Phone _____
Employer _____
Address _____
_____
Work Phone _____
Net Salary (*monthly) _____ (*annual) _____
Other Income (annual) _____
Source _____

*after taxes

Residence of household:
Own _____
Monthly Mortgage (inc. taxes, insurance) _____
Rent _____
Monthly Tenant Rent _____

Personal Information:
Spouse _____
Address _____
_____
Home Phone _____
Employer _____
Address _____
_____
Work Phone _____
Net Salary (*monthly) _____ (*annual) _____
Other Income (annual) _____
Source _____

*after taxes

Dependents in household:
Name _____ Age _____
Name _____ Age _____
Name _____ Age _____
Name _____ Age _____

ASSETS (for all members of household):
Cash on hand _____
Checking account (bank / balance) _____
Savings account (bank / balance) _____
Certificates of deposit (banks / amts/ maturity) _____
_____
Money market account (bank / balance) _____
Mutual funds (companies / amts) _____
_____
Bonds (institutions / amts / maturity) _____
Stocks (companies / amts) _____
_____
Individual Retirement Accounts (companies / amts) ____
_____
Employer pension plan (eligible age / anticipated amt) ____
_____
Business Interests / Rental Properties _____
_____
Annuities (institutions / amts / maturity) _____
Life Insurance (current cash value) _____
_____
Value of 1st home (give location, description) _____
_____
Value of 1st home (contents & personal posessions) _____
Value of 2nd home (give location, description) _____
_____
Value of 2nd home (contents & personal posessions) _____
Value of automobile(s) (make, model, year) _____
Value of RVs, boats, trailers _____
Value of artwork, antiques _____
Value of other items (itemize) _____
_____

TOTAL ASSESTS (for all members of household) _____

LIABILITIES (for all members of household):
Credit Card Balances (list separately & total) _____
_____
_____
Collateral Loans
(Autos, education, boats, etc.; list separately & total) _____
_____
_____
Personal Loans
(To individuals, to institutions.; list separately & total) _____
_____
_____
Co-maker Loans
(List separately & total) _____
_____
Business Loans (institutions / amts / balance) _____
_____
_____
Mortgages (institutions / amts / balance) _____
_____
Charitable Contributions (institutions / amts) _____
_____
_____

TOTAL LIABILITIES (for all members of household) _____

HOUSEHOLD NET WORTH:
TOTAL ASSETS $ _____
Less TOTAL LIABILITIES – $ _____
HOUSEHOLD NET WORTH $ _____

The pain of preparing financial statements and taxes.
©PhotoDisc

EVALUATION

The criteria for the evaluation of this project are itemized in the grid (rubric) that follows. Choice of appropriate category terms (values) is the decision of the instructor. Selection of terms such as "minimal," "satisfactory," and "distinguished" can vary with each assessment.

Household Financial Profile Evaluation Rubric

(Refer to introductory section for suggestions of scoring descriptors for the evaluation categories.)

Evaluation Item	Category 1	Category 2	Category 3	Category 4	Category 5
Item a: (1) Does the report show understanding that while different socioeconomic (as well as national, ethnic, religious, racial, and gender) groups have varied perspectives, values, and diverse practices and traditions, they face the same global economic challenges?					
Item b: (5) Does the report analyze problems and evaluate decisions about the economic effects caused by human, technological, and natural activities on societies and individuals?					
Item c: (6) Does the report present ideas in writing (and orally) in clear, concise, and properly accepted fashion?					
Item d: (7) Does the report employ a variety of information from written, graphic, and multimedia sources?					
Item e: (8) Does the report show monitoring of reflection upon, and improvement of work?					

ISSUE 2

Why must economic choices be made?

SCARCITY AND BASIC CHOICES

Since all productive resources are finite,
And human needs are rather infinite,
The human situation seems none too bright –
No matter what we do, someone loses in the fight.

SCARCITY...BASIC CHOICES DOWNSIZING THE DREAM

Back in April, it all looked very sweet. Kelly Fagan received a thick envelope from Springfield College in Massachusetts. (Seniors know that thin envelopes from colleges often mean rejection.) Springfield accepted her for a five-year program in physical therapy. Kelly was in seventh heaven for a week. And yet, it got better! Kelly's boyfriend Matt received a thick envelope from the University of Hartford. He was accepted as a marketing major in the School of Business. The two schools were separated by only an hour on Interstate-91. They would be able to see each other on weekends. For Kelly, the hard work was paying off, and the dreams of the past few years were coming to fruition.

Of course, Kelly knew the real work was just beginning. She had always been a good student. That would be no problem. It was the financial side that concerned her the most. Kelly's mom and dad were in their forties and both worked. Dad was a production supervisor at "Big Blue" – IBM. He had worked there for nearly twenty-five years. Mom was a dental hygienist now. She had gone back to school for training when Kelly's younger brother and sister were old enough for grade school. At first, Mom worked for Dr. Hartman part-time, then a year ago she went full-time. The Fagans' lived in southern Dutchess County. While it was not exactly an upscale community, it was not a cheap place to raise a family, either. Kelly knew Dad's salary allowed them to get by, but saving for the three kids' education required Mom's income.

When Kelly talked to her parents about her dreams, they said they would manage. Together, they had checked the colleges and had many discussions on the finances involved. Springfield was not the least expensive, but it was a good school. With an education loan and a small scholarship, it was within their means. For Kelly, everything was working out. Life was indeed sweet.

It has been said that "the only thing certain about life is its very uncertainty." Kelly was about to find out the solemn truth of that statement. The bitterness broke through a few days after Kelly acknowledged her acceptance at Springfield. She had stayed late to watch some friends on the girls' softball team at practice. The house was quiet. She assumed the family was out shopping as she headed toward the kitchen. The light over the sink was the only illumination. Out of the corner of her eye, she saw a shadow move, and she froze.

"Hello, Kel," her dad said. She relaxed a bit, but knew his tone had an edge to it.

"Why are you sitting alone in the dark, Dad?"

"Mom took the kids down for a burger. I needed some time alone." He motioned for her to sit down. Kelly had an eerie feeling the news was not going to be good.

"You know the company has been making cuts in operations because of slow sales in mainframes and PCs?"

"I heard you and Mom talking about it." Kelly's voice was quiet and quivering. "Some kids at school have been concerned about their parents' jobs in the past couple of months. Is something wrong with your job? Why didn't you tell me?"

"With all my seniority, I was pretty sure nothing would happen. There were rumors; we didn't want you to worry." He paused. "Kel, they let me go. I have almost a year's salary coming, and my other benefits will continue for a while. We will survive, but we will have to adjust."

"Adjust how, Dad?"

"It may be rough for a little while. We will cut down on household expenses and cancel the cabin at the lake this summer. There may be an opening for me in a company that some of the executives are trying to organize. There is one thing, however." Again Kelly's dad paused. "Your college."

This was it. Kelly had a sick feeling in the pit of her stomach. Her father reached for her hand. "Mom and I hate to do this to you, but we think it may be better for us all if you gave Dutchess Community College a try for a year. If all goes well, we may have the resources for Springfield. I know it hurts, Kel, but we need your help on this one."

Before he finished his sentence, tears welled in Kelly's eyes. She felt so helpless. She heard him yell her name as she dashed upstairs, but things were just a blur at that point. She wasn't mad at him, but the bitterness was there and growing.

ISSUE 2

Why must economic choices be made?

SCARCITY AND BASIC CHOICES

BASIC CHOICES

Graduation is always a bittersweet tradeoff. On the sweet side, the general education is over, and an adult world beckons. A young person is ready to move on to work or more intensive preparation for a career. Now, the quest for the American Dream really heats up.

Graduation also has a bitter side. It is the last time to shout and laugh and embrace many friends in the comfort of protected halls and classrooms. The place and the good times pass on to others, and going back is impossible.

For Kelly Fagan, the balance was not there. The bitterness outweighed the sweet. The quest for the Dream was turning sour before it began.

A deep recession, tougher competition, and some serious management misjudgments in the past five years left IBM with nearly $5 billion in losses in 1992. The company cut twenty-five thousand positions from its 300,000 work force worldwide. In 1993, it cut another 75,000, and our fictitious Mr. Fagan's job as a production supervisor would have been one of them (*Poughkeepsie Journal.* March 28, 1993, 2E). In middle life, his quest for the Dream was also turning sour.

The situation is disturbing, but in a market economy, it is not unusual. The U.S. economy has more than 250 million consumers and 180,000 businesses interacting every day. It is not a perfect system that provides for every need and want of every person. Mistakes and misjudgments are always possible in economic situations. In reality, someone is always getting hurt. When you consider it – linking the United States in with 180 other nations' economic systems, each different in some way – it is astonishing that more people are not disillusioned about the Dream.

EVERYTHING BEGINS WITH SCARCITY

Asking people to define economics reveals quite a few mumbling something about money. Money is certainly an economic concern, but by now, it is apparent there is a little more to the subject. Economics is really about people mak-

These young Americans are ready to move on to work or more intensive preparation for a career. The quest begins for the American Dream. ©PhotoDisc

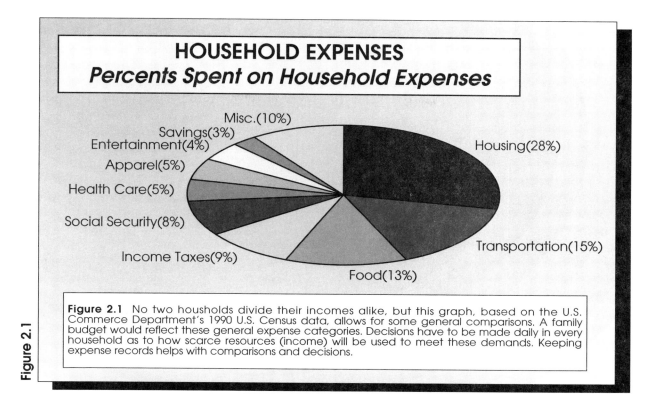

HOUSEHOLD EXPENSES
Percents Spent on Household Expenses

Misc.(10%)
Savings(3%)
Entertainment(4%)
Apparel(5%)
Health Care(5%)
Social Security(8%)
Income Taxes(9%)
Food(13%)
Housing(28%)
Transportation(15%)

Figure 2.1 No two housholds divide their incomes alike, but this graph, based on the U.S. Commerce Department's 1990 U.S. Census data, allows for some general comparisons. A family budget would reflect these general expense categories. Decisions have to be made daily in every household as to how scarce resources (income) will be used to meet these demands. Keeping expense records helps with comparisons and decisions.

Figure 2.1

ing decisions which affect each others' lives. It is really about **scarcity**. There are limits on every resource humans use to meet their needs. Productive resources include:

- Natural resources (land, water, trees, minerals...)
- Human resources (labor, talent, organizational skills...)
- Capital resources (tools, computers, machinery, financial investment...)
- Information resources (research, Internet, "information highway")

By combining these basic resources, people produce the goods and services that sustain them and make living comfortable and even pleasurable.

However, this presents a problem. It is the most basic, timeless, and universal problem that exists. Looking back at the list, it seems simple enough. In fact, most people would not see any problem at all, but they have not studied economics. There is a very large, persistent problem – *all of these resources are limited in some way*. **Scarcity** means there is simply not enough of any of these resources to supply all humankind's demands. There never has been

enough, and there probably never will be. Scarcity is the most basic fact of life.

Growing up in a developed industrial country, students rarely bump into scarcity. Or do they? Kelly Fagan did – there was not enough money to go to Springfield College. Her father did also – there were too many workers and not enough work. The company laid him off. Unusual? Take a good look around. Read the newspapers. Watch TV. Listen to conversations at the lunch counters. There have been famines, recessions, and even the Great Depression. These are major events, but ordinary people face scarcity every day. "Making ends meet" means dividing household income to cover basic expenses (see Figure 2.1). There are difficult situations and personal tragedies. Confidence in the American Dream gets shaken every day.

On community levels, schools, roads, or police sometimes cannot be funded. Nationally, adequate defense is desirable but costly. At the same time, people want government to take care of the unemployed, the homeless, the poor, the elderly, and the terminally ill. It all cannot be done at once. Scarcity forces decisions on priorities, and tradeoffs occur. Viewing things on a global scale, scarcity becomes more and more evident. Consider all the starvation in places where water and arable land are scarce.

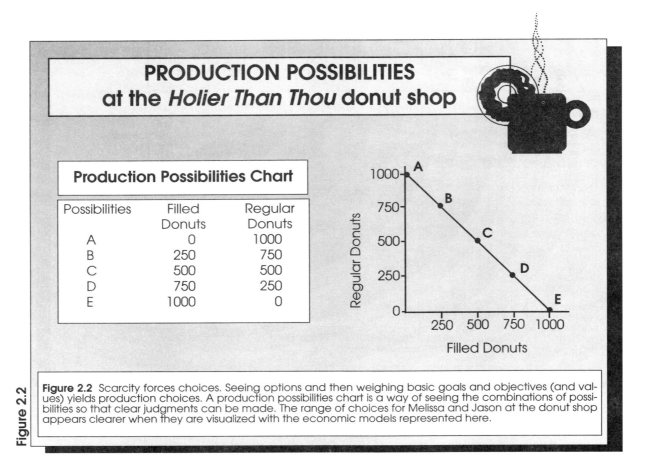

Figure 2.2 Scarcity forces choices. Seeing options and then weighing basic goals and objectives (and values) yields production choices. A production possibilities chart is a way of seeing the combinations of possibilities so that clear judgments can be made. The range of choices for Melissa and Jason at the donut shop appears clearer when they are visualized with the economic models represented here.

Figure 2.2

Essentially, scarcity affects everyone in a variety of ways. It forces humankind to make the most of limited resources.

COPING WITH SCARCITY

How can scarce resources be allocated (used) properly? That is not an easy question. Actually, it is three questions in one:

- What to produce?
- How to produce?
- Who gets what is produced?

Put two or three people together sharing some limited resources – an argument ensues. Put a few thousand people together with limited resources – a war ensues. (Haven't societies warred over land, water, oil, gold?) As old and ever-present as the condition of scarcity is, coping with it is never simple.

Economics is about the search for ways to deal with scarcity. **Economics** is the study of how people cope with scarcity. If there are not enough resources to fulfill everyone's needs and wants, people have to make choices that flow from compromise and sacrifice. Satisfaction, happiness, and even survival hinge on how well people make choices about scarcity.

All choices cost something. Economists call this **opportunity cost**. Deciding to use a resource in one way costs the opportunity to use it for something else. Sometimes the opportunity is only temporarily lost – until more money, other resources, or technological alternatives become available. Sometimes the opportunity is permanently lost. Using irreplaceable minerals, nonrenewable energy, labor, time, and money to develop the Stealth Bomber may cost the society the opportunity to have a new medical research facility – perhaps forever.

Money is spent, but economics is about more than money. This choice involved lost opportunities for better health care that might have saved lives in the future. These are the trade-offs that scarcity demands.

Simple scarcity forces a choice. Consider having only $10.00 and being in the mood for a

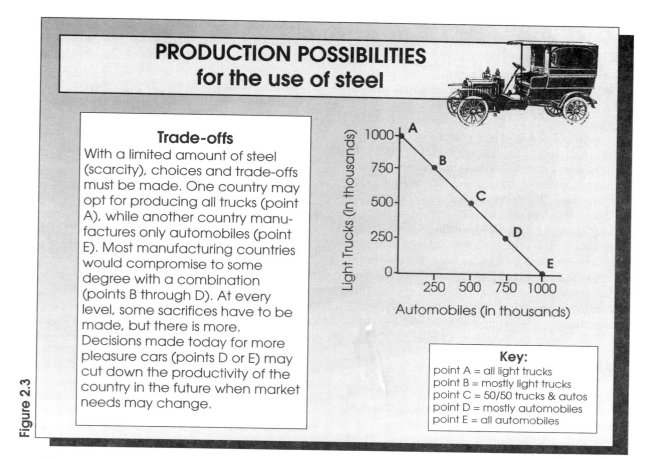

Figure 2.3

PRODUCTION POSSIBILITIES for the use of steel

Trade-offs

With a limited amount of steel (scarcity), choices and trade-offs must be made. One country may opt for producing all trucks (point A), while another country manufactures only automobiles (point E). Most manufacturing countries would compromise to some degree with a combination (points B through D). At every level, some sacrifices have to be made, but there is more. Decisions made today for more pleasure cars (points D or E) may cut down the productivity of the country in the future when market needs may change.

Key:
point A = all light trucks
point B = mostly light trucks
point C = 50/50 trucks & autos
point D = mostly automobiles
point E = all automobiles

---

movie and a pizza. Choosing the movie is fine, but it costs $6.25, and the opportunity to get a pizza is also sacrificed. There are dozens of such routine tradeoff situations in life. Consumers, businesses, and governments constantly face the dilemma of opportunity cost. Sometimes, those costs are minimal. Sometimes, they are awesome. Do the benefits outweigh the burdens?

An **economic model** can clarify what opportunity cost might mean to business. Economic models allow analysis of complex situations and make decisions clearer. With models, the elements of a choice can be systematically analyzed, and opportunity cost illustrated.

ECONOMIC MODEL: GETTING THE "HOLE" PICTURE

The idea of an economic model is to clarify a situation. Melissa and Jason are going to start a donut shop, "Holier Than Thou." They have limited resources – two bakers, butter, flour, sugar, ovens, etc. With all the resources, they know they can produce 1,000 donuts a day. They also

know that producing only one kind of donut will soon bore customers. (Their competitor down the block offers 10 varieties.) They see that they can divide their resources and produce two basic kinds – regular and filled. By changing the toppings and fillings of the two types, they can offer a wide range of donuts.

The question is, how to divide the scarce resources. They make up a simple chart (see Figure 2.2 on left page) which helps them see the possibilities.

The chart numbers can be plotted to a production possibilities graph. Both the chart and the graph illustrate the choices, the sacrifices, and the results of the various levels of production. Jason and Melissa must decide on production combinations that will please their customers and make the best use of their resources. For instance, at point B, they will produce three times more regular donuts (750) than the filled variety (250). This simple plotting of numbers in a model helps them see their options in a clearer way. They can use their limited resources more efficiently.

The model can be changed a little to see about the production possibilities for a nation (see Figure 2.3 on previous page). On a national level, the economic choices might be between producing **consumer goods** or **capital goods** (productive resources such as (1) raw or recycled steel or aluminum, (2) tools, machines, and factories used to make other goods, or (3) transportation). If heavy machinery and/or military hardware are overproduced (such as in the former Soviet Union), basic consumer goods are underproduced. People may become dissatisfied even to the point of the country's collapse. Splitting things down the middle is not always the answer, either. In wartime, nations sacrifice (tradeoff) consumer goods and throw most resources into weapons production. When a new technology emerges (e.g., computers), there could be a shortage of consumer goods while building the new electronics industry.

A SURPLUS IS THE KEY

Of course, the main idea behind learning economic analysis is understanding choices and making better use of resources. When a society makes the most from its resources, it is using them efficiently. Life gets better because there is abundance. When a society produces more of something than it needs, a **surplus** results. Surpluses can be stored for future use or traded for other goods needed. In *The Wealth of Nations* (1776), classical economist Adam Smith stated that the capability to produce surpluses was the key to happiness and prosperity. Therefore, individuals, families, communities, and nations seek ways to become more productive. Productivity is the key to growth.

In primitive times, producing more might have meant simple steps such as specialization, division of labor, and simple machine use.

- **Specialization** means a person develops a talent and becomes skilled at a specific job. The village tanners focused their energies and became adept at producing leather goods. The more proficient they were, the more they could produce. Surpluses resulted. Farmers who broke harnesses did not have to halt their own work waiting for a new one. The tanner (leather specialist) had a surplus stock. The whole community worked more efficiently.

- **Division of labor** means breaking a job into sub-tasks. Assigning different persons to do different tasks allows them to become adept. Producing a harness by oneself might take a month. When each tanner slaughtered the animal, cured the hide, tanned it, then cut, assembled, sewed, and polished, a great deal of time was consumed. Dividing the different jobs among the workers in the shop and letting them each do only one or two of these steps made them more productive. Subdividing the process was more efficient. A surplus of harnesses resulted. In fact, so much more was produced and so much time saved that shoes, boots, and belts could be made. The capacity of the tanner grew and so did the wealth of the community.

- **Using simple machines** (e.g., wheels, levers, inclined planes) at the tanner's meant moving, lifting, and strapping hides could be done quickly with less effort with pulleys, wheelbarrows, and ramps. The time and energy saved meant more could be produced. Once again, the capacity of the tanner grew and so did the wealth of the community.

These simple steps led to economic growth. On a larger scale, some communities specialized and efficiently produced enough surplus that they became dominant in a field. For example, people from entire regions and other countries came to Toledo in Spain for steel. It is still known today for the finest in cutlery.

In modern times, young people choose a profession or trade early so they can be educated with the specialized skills needed. Simple machines have given way to complex high-tech robotics and electronics. The object is still the same. Better use of human, capital, informational, and natural resources produces a surplus – the key to wealth.

SUMMARY

Economic choices are part of everyday life for everyone. Some are routine, and some can change your life completely. In Kelly's story, IBM made choices and changed the Fagans' lives. Using analysis helps to focus on key ideas about resources. Choices are never easy, but making them with open eyes (and minds) eases the pain of choosing. Open eyes and minds are exactly what is needed to focus on the possibilities of the American Dream.

ASSESSMENT
QUESTIONS • APPLICATIONS

1 Use the chart and graph below to analyze and compare household resources familiar to you.

   a Look at the U.S. Median (statistical middle amount) Household Income (March 1990) chart. If you made up a hypothetical household profile for the Issue 1 assessment task, use it to analyze where your household fits in the national and regional comparisons. If not, find out your own actual household income. Is your household above or below medians? Which ones? Where would you do best or poorest?

   b Look at the average household expense graph. Using your actual household figures (or your hypothetical household profile for the Issue 1 task) and the graph percentages, estimate how much money your household spends in each category on the graph.

   c Survey your parents, teachers, or other adults to see if they think the numbers you have arrived at in parts a and b are realistic. How would some of the people you interview rearrange the budget? Find out why. Write a brief essay relating your estimates and survey findings. Discuss what this tells you about scarcity and economic decision-making.

Questions continued on next page.

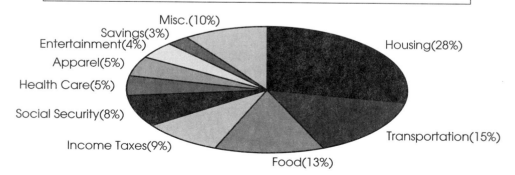

U.S. Median Household Income (March 1990)

Source: Population Reference Bureau, 1875 Connecticut Avenue, NW Suite 520, Washington, DC 20009, (202) 483-1100

Region	Household Income
U.S.	**$28,906.00**
NORTHEAST	**32,643.00**
New England (ME, NH, VT, MA, RI, CT)	35,780. 00
Middle Atlantic (NY, NJ, PA)	31,730. 00
MIDWEST	**28,750. 00**
East North Central (OH, IN, IL, MI, WI)	29,410. 00
West North Central (MN, IA, MO,ND, SD, NE, KA)	27,035. 00
SOUTH	**25,870.00**
South Atlantic (DE, MD, DC, DA, WV, NC, SC, GA, FL)	27,900. 00
East South Central (KY, TN, AL, MS)	21,900. 00
West South Central (AR, LA, OK, TX)	24,666. 00
WEST	**31,086.00**
Mountain (MT, ID, WY, CO, NM, AZ, UT, NV)	27,225. 00
Pacific (WA, OR, CA, AK, HI)	32,482. 00

Misc.(10%)
Savings(3%)
Entertainment(4%)
Apparel(5%)
Health Care(5%)
Social Security(8%)
Income Taxes(9%)
Food(13%)
Housing(28%)
Transportation(15%)

2   A number of factors make the American Dream difficult to achieve. In later chapters, many of the following factors will be studied in detail. However, in thinking about success in life, it may be good to begin considering their impact now. Income levels vary considerably, sometimes through personal choice, sometimes through market forces, and sometimes through social and political conditions.

    a   How do education and type of occupation affect income?
    b   How do age, sex, and location affect income?
    c   How do taxes and inflation affect income?
    d   How does personal financial management affect living conditions?

3   The American Dream is neither singular nor static. Goals change at different stages in life. How would success and happiness be viewed at each of the following periods in life? Identify a specific goal a person might have at each stage:

    a   Young adult stage (age: early twenties)
    b   Early married stage (late twenties through early thirties)
    c   Parenthood (thirties through fifties)
    d   Retirement (sixties plus)

4   Tradeoffs are a part of life. Some are routine, and we make them quickly (for example, buying a concert ticket for a favorite group instead of getting an oil change for the car).

    a   Consider the opportunity cost situation at the Holier Than Thou Donut Shop. Is it more complicated than it looks? What tradeoffs have to be made?
    b   Consider the tradeoff Kelly Fagan's dad is asking her to make in the opening story. What will it really cost? What could the results be?
    c   Brainstorm some of the more serious economic choices ahead of you at different stages of your life (career, relocation, a home, family needs, retirement).

5   Brainstorm some everyday personal choices.

    a   Think about tradeoffs on car repairs, entertainment, clothing, personal care, and savings. Discuss their tradeoffs, advantages and disadvantages, benefits and burdens, and long-term and short-term consequences.
    b   Make a production possibility graph for any two of these items using the amount of money you might have available to spend on them in a week or a month.

6   Recall an event in your past when you were disappointed because you were unable to get what you wanted. Describe the experience in a brief essay. Then complete the following:

    a   In a small group, each member should read their own essay to the group.
    b   By consensus, the group should select one essay to use as a skit with roles and a narrative.
    c   As a group, rewrite the chosen essay as a playwright would. Rewrite passages into dialogue to be spoken by the actors, and do not forget to add stage directions.
    d   Perform the skit for the class. A narrator should ask the class to identify the scarcity, the tradeoffs, and opportunity costs involved.
    e   The entire class should rate the best skits based on the portrayal an understanding of the concept of scarcity.

ASSESSMENT PROJECT:
THE HOUSEHOLD BUDGET

STUDENT TASK

Set up a budget for the household created in Issue 1 – the American Dream chapter. Use the sample Monthly Budget Information Form (see next page). As a guide, you may use computer software for home budgeting, such as Home Office's *M.Y.O.B. Accounting*, Kiplinger's *Simply Money*, Intuit's *Quicken*, Andrew Tobias' *Managing Your Money*, or one of the other personal financial management computer programs. However, you must submit a Monthly Budget Information report in hard copy.

PROCEDURE

1 Transfer the starred (*) items from your "Household Financial Profile" chart used in the Issue 1 project. (Remember, they are annual figures, so in this project you will have to divide by 12 to get monthly figures.)

2 Fill in remaining data by looking in stores, financial newspapers and magazines, using library resources, or interviewing family and friends. Make a list of all your sources.

3 Once your Monthly Budget Information Form is completed, subtract your Total Expenses from your Net Income, and determine if you are in a surplus or deficit situation.

4 Analyze your results. Consider these questions in a written analysis: Am I living "below, within, or above my means"? If there is a surplus, how best can I utilize that surplus to become more efficient? If there is a deficit, why and how can I remedy it?

5 (This step must be audited and approved by your instructor.) Based on your analysis, you may find it necessary to make adjustments to the original Household Financial Profile set up in Issue 1.

Note: You can not just "play around" with the numbers, delete dependents, give yourself a big raise, or hit the lottery. All adjustments must be "real life" possibilities. Consider the consequences carefully. You may have to cut back or drop certain expenses. You could raise your income with a second job. However, you must support in writing why you make these decisions (used in later stages of this ongoing project).

LEARNING STANDARDS

Learners should be able to:

(1) understand that while different socioeconomic (as well as national, ethnic, religious, racial, and gender) groups have varied perspectives, values, and diverse practices and traditions, they face the same global economic challenges.

(5) analyze problems and evaluate decisions about the economic effects on society and the individual caused by human, technological, and natural activities.

(6) present their ideas both in writing and orally in clear, concise, and properly accepted fashion.

(7) employ a variety of information from written, graphic, and multimedia sources.

(8) monitor, reflect upon, and improve their own and others' work.

(9) work cooperatively and show respect for the rights of others to think, act, and speak differently from themselves within the context of democratic principles and social justice.

EXAMPLE OF MONTHLY BUDGET INFORMATION
(* obtain data from Household Financial Profile)

ESTIMATED DISPOSABLE HOUSEHOLD INCOME

Salary / wages
   (include bonuses and tips) $_____ (a)

Total of Federal, State, and local
taxes, FICA, and payroll deductions (e.g. medical, pen-
sion/annuity plans, disability) $_____ (b)

*Net wages (subtract b from a) $_____ (c)

*Other income (e.g. interest,
   dividends, rent, royalties) $_____ (d)

Estimated taxes on other income $_____ (e)

Net other income (subtract e from d) $_____ (f)

Total net income (add c and f) $_____ (g)

ITEMIZED FIXED EXPENSES
(regular monthly expenses – may vary somewhat)

*Mortgage or rent	$_____
Mortgage Insurance	$_____
Homeowners (renters) insurance	$_____
Real property taxes	$_____
Utilities electric	$_____
Utilities heating (gas, oil, electric)	$_____
Water and Sewer	$_____
Garbage and recycling	$_____
Phone	$_____
Cable TV	$_____
Auto loan or lease	$_____
Auto maintenance / repairs	$_____
Auto insurance	$_____
Public transit fares, tokens	$_____
Auto tolls, parking fees	$_____
Auto fuel (gas, diesel)	$_____
*Personal loans (education, etc.)	$_____
*Collateral loans (boat, RV)	$_____
Installment Payments	$_____
*Other loans	$_____
Total Fixed Expenses (add)	$_____ (h)

ITEMIZED VARIABLE EXPENSES
(monthly expenses – may vary significantly)

Grocery (food, beverages)	$_____
Grocery (household items)	$_____
Grocery (pet and personal)	$_____
Restaurants (daily lunches)	$_____
Gifts (family, friends)	$_____
*Credit Card Payments	$_____
Education Expense	$_____

ITEMIZED VARIABLE EXPENSES continued

Personal Care haircuts, salon)	$_____
Medical uninsured	$_____
Medical non-covered expense	$_____
Medical co-payments	$_____
Dental care	$_____
Vision care	$_____
Clothes (inc. work uniforms)	$_____
Clothes cleaning, laundry	$_____
Total Variable Expenses (add)	$_____ (i)

ITEMIZED OPTIONAL EXPENSES
(monthly expenses – not required to survive)

Restaurants (outings)	$_____
Recreation (outings)	$_____
Health, gym, fitness club fees	$_____
*Savings deposits	$_____
*Life Insurance	$_____
Disability insurance	$_____
*Investments (stocks, bonds, etc.)	$_____
*Individual retirement account	$_____
Luxury Items (jewelry, etc.)	$_____
Hobbies (stamps, coins, etc.)	$_____
Vacation expenses	$_____
*Second home expenses (include same items as primary home)	$_____
Boat, RV expenses (dockage, storage, fuel, insurance, etc.)	$_____
Newspapers and Magazines	$_____
Home Entertainment (videos, CDs, system components)	$_____
Lawn, property care	$_____
House maintenance, repair	$_____
House cleaning service	$_____
Total Optional Expenses (add)	$_____ (j)

MONTHLY BALANCE CALCULATION

TOTAL NET INCOME (g)	$_____ (x)
TOTAL FIXED EXPENSES (h)	$_____
TOTAL VARIABLE EXPENSES (i)	$_____
TOTAL OPTIONAL EXPENSES (j)	$_____
TOTAL EXPENSES (h + i + j =)	$_____ (y)
BALANCE (x – y = z)	$_____ (z)
BALANCE = (+)SURPLUS/(–)DEFICIT _____	

EVALUATION

The criteria for the evaluation of this project are itemized in the grid (rubric) that follows. Choice of appropriate category terms (values) is the decision of the instructor. Selection of terms such as "minimal," "satisfactory," and "distinguished" can vary with each assessment.

Household Financial Profile Evaluation Rubric

(Refer to introductory section for suggestions of scoring descriptors for the evaluation categories.)

Evaluation Item	Category 1	Category 2	Category 3	Category 4	Category 5
Item a: (1) Does the work show understanding that while different socioeconomic (as well as national, ethnic, religious, racial, and gender) groups have varied perspectives, values, and diverse practices and traditions, they face the same global economic challenges?					
Item b: (5) Does the work analyze problems and evaluate decisions about the economic effects caused by human, technological, and natural activities on societies and individuals?					
Item c: (6) Does the work present ideas in writing (and orally) in clear, concise, and properly accepted fashion?					
Item d: (7) Does the work employ a variety of information from written, graphic, and multimedia sources?					
Item e: (8) Does the work show monitoring of, reflection upon, and improvement of work?					
Item f: (9) Does the work show cooperative effort and respect for the rights of others to think, act, and speak differently?					

ISSUE 3

Why are there different economic systems?

ECONOMIC SYSTEMS

Can any country or society have its version of the American Dream? There is a universal hope attached to making the quality of life better. Yet Americans do not all agree on the exact meaning of the Dream. It is obvious that different countries will want different things. The drive to achieve a better life takes different forms and that leads to different economic systems.

CAPITALISM ON QUEUE
- A LINE OF OPPORTUNITY

Nedezhda left the apartment near R'azanskij Prospekt early. "Nedda," as her family called her, knew the lines were always there, but they lengthened at dawn. "Queuing up" was what they called it. The British had used it to describe the waiting on the ration lines during World War I. Some people, shut out the day before, simply camped on the street all night. Bread, toilet paper, milk – it did not matter what you needed, the queue was a way of life in Russia ever since Nedda could remember. The waiting took forever. The only things that moved with any speed on a queue were rumors.

The queue began just a block from Pavelec Station. The conversations were always the same. People carped endlessly about the Gorbachev and Yeltsin reformers' failures. They broke down the communist command system. The reformers lack of knowledge of how markets function led to the confusion and supply problems.

Deep down, people knew they had spent most of their lives waiting on lines. The old system had not produced what they needed, either. The government planners were incapable of allocating resources. Under the communists' Gosplan, the government used to regulate raw materials and tell the factory managers what products to make and how much to produce. The central planners rarely brought all the pieces together. Sixteen to twenty percent of all the resources went to military production. Supplies of everyday goods always fell short of demand.

Now, converting state farms and factories to privately owned ones created many problems. Supply shortages kept prices high. Yet, the greatest frustration was not being able to get basic items once you resigned yourself to paying the high prices. Half the population was working, the other half was queuing up.

Of course, Westerners had moved in to assist. The Canadians built a new McDonald's near Smolenskaya Square. It offered hamburgers and created a few new jobs, but who made enough to go there even once a month? Besides, the hour you spent on the Big Mac line was time taken from the potato line.

"What a life!" Nedda grumbled to no one in particular. "You work, you sleep, and queue up the rest of your life. An American can breeze into a supermarket or a mall, choose from thousands of items in an hour or so, and have the rest of her day off for fun."

"I love these lines," said a voice from behind her.

"Spare me the sarcasm," Nedda said over her shoulder. Then she turned to see if she knew the speaker. She was a little surprised. He was a young man, perhaps nineteen, with a leather jacket, expensive high tops, and was wired to a portable CD player clipped to his jeans.

"No, actually I'm making money just standing here," he said. "My name is Aram. I am from Orel in the south. I came here looking for work after I finished school. The jobs we were assigned never materialized after the reforms began."

"If you have no job, then you have no money. What are you doing on line? And by the way, where did you get all those clothes you're wearing?" Nedda asked.

"Oh, I have money, and I made it right here," Aram said. "You just said you'd rather be doing other things than standing in line. It is different for me. I'm getting paid to be here."

"I thought that it was illegal to buy things for others."

"Nope. Not anymore. No one ever enforces that rule anyway. Actually, I am an employer. I have five other people who work for me waiting on lines for others." Aram produced a business card which read, "Right on Queue. Aram Vedev, Purchasing Agent."

"You mean this is what you do for a living?"

"Yes, this is my regular line. I come here with about a dozen orders every day. Many people are willing to pay me and my associates to wait for them and deliver the goods later in the day. That gives them time for second jobs or for recreation. You know, many of my clients have started their own businesses. They could never do it if we didn't queue up for them. Say, you wouldn't want to work for me would you? I have an opening on the produce lines over on Mira Prospekt. You charge customers an additional ten percent of the price of whatever goods you buy. At the end of the day, I take ten percent of your profits."

Nedda considered it. "Everything you do depends on whether people think they can afford your service. Your success also depends on what goods are available. How can you manage not knowing how much you will make from one week to the next? Besides, when would I have time to wait in line for my needs?"

Aram's eyes lit up. "Markets change, you change. As far as your needs, we have something special going. All my comrades … oops, I mean associates, buy a little extra on their lines. We have a small warehouse in the Vychino District. I brought my sister up from Orel to manage it. At the end of the day, we meet there, turn in our money, get paid, and buy what we need. How's that for on-line capitalism?"

Figure 3.1

Why are there different economic systems?

ECONOMIC SYSTEMS

INTRODUCTION

Opportunity and success seem universal. People such as Nedda and Aram in the story lived behind what British Prime Minister Winston Churchill once dubbed "The Iron Curtain," or what became known as the "Communist World." Like Americans – past and present – pursuing the Dream, these people have hopes for a better life.

People everywhere must constantly make very similar choices about scarce human, natural, information, and capital resources. Every society must decide WHAT will be produced, HOW it will be produced, and for WHOM it will be produced. Yet, people see life from different viewpoints, have different experiences, and evolve different values. How they set priorities – and how they order them – can vividly portray those differences.

Economists use economic analysis to make choices about resources seem clear and scientific. Of course, the use of charts and graphs to quantify and clarify resources is helpful and even comforting. It is important to have facts and figures to guide decision-making. Still, it is not unusual for two people to look at the same situation, data, charts, or graphs and come to different conclusions.

ECONOMIC SYSTEMS REFLECT EXPERIENCE AND CULTURE

If individuals differ, then groups of people differ, too. Attitudes and values evolved from diverse cultural characteristics such as tradition, religion, history, conflicts, and prejudices, altering the way people see and do things. If these characteristics alter the way people think and act, they obviously influence the way people make decisions. This includes decisions about using available human, natural, and capital resources (see Figure 3.1).

While scarcity poses the same basic questions (What to produce? How to produce it? For whom will it be produced?), societies approach economic decisions differently. One nation's view of using precious resources may not be satisfactory in the eyes of another. Naturally, disagreements occur within all nations and societies. Still, one political or cultural mindset prevails for a time as to economic priorities. In extreme cases, revolutions and civil wars can erupt if there are enough opponents of the prevalent mindset.

To a person thinking about all this, it may be easy to shrug and say something like, "Well, to each his own ..." or, "Let each society work out its own system. What's the harm?" Often in the distant past, when most societies were primitive and isolated, there was no reason for concern. However, it has been many centuries since the world was like that. Neighbors having strongly different systems run into serious conflicts over resources. There are prominent economic factors in nearly every conflict humankind has ever seen, right down through the "Cold War" of the late 20th century. If people are to achieve a better way of life, how different people answer the same basic economic questions matters very much.

BASIC SYSTEMS: TRADITION, COMMAND, MARKET

Most early societies evolved their economic decision-making approach from past practice, customs, and religion. Economists call this approach a **traditional system**. All economic activities merely followed patterns set earlier.

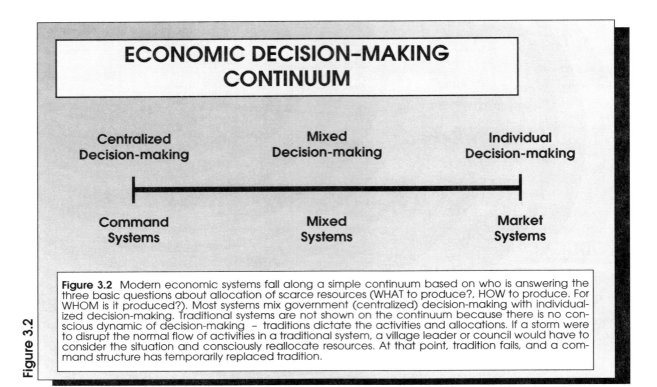

ECONOMIC DECISION–MAKING CONTINUUM

Centralized
Decision-making

Mixed
Decision-making

Individual
Decision-making

Command
Systems

Mixed
Systems

Market
Systems

Figure 3.2 Modern economic systems fall along a simple continuum based on who is answering the three basic questions about allocation of scarce resources (WHAT to produce?, HOW to produce. For WHOM is it produced?). Most systems mix government (centralized) decision-making with individualized decision-making. Traditional systems are not shown on the continuum because there is no conscious dynamic of decision-making – traditions dictate the activities and allocations. If a storm were to disrupt the normal flow of activities in a traditional system, a village leader or council would have to consider the situation and consciously reallocate resources. At that point, tradition fails, and a command structure has temporarily replaced tradition.

Figure 3.2

Traditional systems did not respond well to change. If an emergency occurred such as a typhoon or drought, there were no guidelines for coping. Usually, village or clan elders commanded people to follow new procedures and adjustments. When the crisis faded, people went back to the old ways. Traditional systems did not allow for growth because there was no experimentation. They were unchanging. Traditional systems were labor-intensive, **subsistence level** economies. This meant that all the energy of the society was devoted to producing bare essentials without a surplus.

Labor intensive, subsistence level economies are commonly found in less developed countries (LDCs). Here, Mossi women are cultivating by hand outside of Biba village, the Toma region, Burkina Faso, Africa. ©1994 David Johnson

Not until there was contact with other societies and observations of different ways of doing things did any real change emerge. In Western society, not until the Commercial Revolution in the 14th century did the pace of change accelerate enough to break down the traditional system of feudalism. Tradition could not guide people when they arrived at situations no one had ever experienced. As the pace of change gained momentum, entirely new patterns of decision-making emerged.

Essentially, two new basic patterns emerged: command and market. They still exist as opposite ends of the economic decision-making continuum (see Figure 3.2). At one end are **command systems**. They result when governments attempt to control resources and decision-making. In 14th century Europe, as localized feudal systems disintegrated, national monarchs became strong and tried to control decision-making.

However, the pace of change eventually became too fast for monarchs to systematically control merchants and tradespeople. More and more independent management of economic resources occurred. As Adam Smith showed in his famous tract, *The Wealth of Nations* (1776) (see profile on Adam Smith, page 66), the individual drive to use resources for **profit** (personal gain) is a powerful force. While complete

Characteristics of Basic Economic Systems

Traditional (example: strong in India)

Decision–making:	Problems:
Custom, religion, and tradition determine many economic decisions.	Unable to deal with change; labor-intensive, subsistence level of production; no surpluses to trade and obtain development capital.

Market – "Capitalist" or "free enterprise" (example: United States)

Decision–making:	Problems:
Individual decision-making, consumer demand, and producer supply combine to make basic economic decisions; private property and profit are vital; minimal government involvement (laissez-faire) is desireable.	Inequality between income levels (classes); subject to unpredictable fluctuations of business activities; early capitalists tended to exploit workers to cut costs and maximize profits; some government regulation is usually needed for fairness.

Command (example: Communist China)

Decision–making:	Problems:
Central planning agency makes basic economic decisions of what to make, for whom, and for how much; government controls most of the resources and means of production.	Lack of personal incentive to improve quality of life often leads to inadequate production and poor quality; strong centralization limits flexibility of decision-making.

Mixed (example: Socialism in Great Britain)

Decision–making:	Problems:
Government planning agency makes some of the economic decisions; market and private businesses make other decisions; government owns some of the means of production; extensive social welfare program.	The high cost of extensive government social welfare programs results in high taxes and reduces work incentives, initiative, and creativity.

independence from government was impossible, in isolated places such as the colonies of North America, independence of decision-making flourished, and new economic structures called **market systems** grew.

History indicates that there were powerful political and social forces at work in the 17th and 18th centuries which moved the American settlers toward independence. At the same time, a long neglect by British officials of their system of economic command allowed the American colonists to enjoy a great deal of independent economic decision-making. While many debated his thesis, historian Charles A. Beard made a strong argument in the 1930s in *Rise of American Civilization* that it was this powerful force of economic freedom that moved the Americans to revolt against the British command structure. What emerged in the United States after independence was a modified market economy. It held very dear the concept of

Adam Smith: Defining The Market

Adam Smith had five distinctive characteristics that set him apart. He had a great passion for books, an incredible memory, a weak physical constitution, a warm good nature, and a habit of drifting off into his own world to talk to himself. Yet, none of these indicate the depth of this man, known as the founder of modern economics.

Adam Smith was born in the town of Kircaldy, Scotland, in 1723. For most of his life, Smith was an academic. Beginning as a student at Oxford, Smith spent six years reading independently in what was an excellent library. For two years, after he left Oxford, he remained unemployed. During this time, he wrote *A History of Astronomy*. It was in this work that Smith first used the term "invisible hand," the natural human instinct of self-interest.

Between 1748 and 1751, Dr. Smith gave a series of lectures at Edinburgh University. As a result, he was elected to the academic Chair of Logic at Glasgow University and later to the Chair of Moral Philosophy (which today includes the subjects of theology, ethics, sociology, jurisprudence, politics, psychology, and economics).

In 1759, he published *Theory of Moral Sentiments*, which was so popular that it had six editions printed by 1790. It was concerned with exploring the nature of human actions and their moral merits. Smith wrote that humans have two instincts that serve in creating a natural system of right and wrong – the need to be praised and the ability to feel sympathy. Seeking to satisfy the need to be wanted and cared for, humans act in a manner that benefits society. This idea that individual behavior could benefit the needs of society became a major building block toward Smith's most famous work – *An Inquiry into the Nature and Causes of the Wealth of Nations*.

After twelve years of work, Smith published *The Wealth of Nations* in 1776, the same year the *U.S. Declaration of Independence* was signed. The book was as revolutionary as a colony claiming independence from royal domination. It was an explanation of how a free-market economy operates. Smith's major thesis was that the marketplace is controlled by "an invisible hand" of self-interest and competition. This leads people to individual decision-making that best serves society's interests. Seeking to improve their own standard of living, humans promote the well-being of society.

Smith believed that competition in the marketplace leads producers to provide what consumers want at an acceptable price. If the price was set too high by one producer, another producer would undersell the first and make the profit. The competition was a means of leading everyone "as if by an invisible hand" to a better society.

Smith claimed government should have only limited functions in the society (defense, justice, and public works). He believed government should not attempt to get involved in a society's economic activity. Laissez-faire is the term that has come to describe Smith's idea that government should not interfere with the operation of the economy.

These two themes – the "invisible hand" and "laissez-faire" – strongly connect Smith to today's classical economists. He believed that businesses should be free to seek out the best opportunities for maximizing their gains (which would eventually add to the general welfare of the society, though he was suspicious and distrusting of their motives). He also believed competition, self-interest, and laissez-faire would save the general public from vicious, corrupt profiteers.

Adam Smith was no utopian, just a man who had great faith in the capitalist system. He died in 1790 at the age of 67. The inscription on his tombstone reads, "Adam Smith, Author of *The Wealth of Nations*, Lies Here."

minimizing government interference in individual decision-making, or what will later be discussed as *laissez-faire capitalism*.

MIXED MODERN SYSTEMS

As humankind moved into the modern era, most economic structures became mixtures of the two pure systems. In *every* system, the activities of government alter economic decisions, usually for security and order. So, there is really no such thing as a pure market system.

It is clear that no government can make all the decisions for everyone about everything. Consequently, there is no such thing as a *pure* command system. This does not mean that there have never been attempts at total control. The totalitarian dictatorships of modern times (Hitler's Nazism, Mussolini's fascism, and Stalin's and Mao's communism) were economic command structures that left little decision-making to individuals. Numerous countries still have dictatorial governments in which little

Tradition is still an economic force in the U.S. Evidence for this is that many retail stores depend on the weeks around Thanksgiving, Hanukkah and Christmas for 50% of annual sales. ©PhotoDisc

freedom of individual economic decision-making exists.

It should also be noted that, while tradition-based economies are rare, even in modern times some tradition is blended into mixed economies. Consider how critical Christmas is to the toy and greeting card industries and how many flowers are sold for birthdays, Valentine's Day, and Mother's Day.

VALUES DETERMINE THE MIXTURE

Values play an important role in determining what kind of a mixture of market, command, and tradition emerges in a society's decision-making.

For example, economic **security** means holding some resources for emergencies or future use. People save or buy insurance for protection against conditions and problems that may occur later. Some people worry more about security than freedom. By nature, they are not gamblers or risk takers. Some societies are more prone to worry about security than freedom. Societies that have such a "security focus" are likely to be those in which people have always felt threatened by invasion. People in that society would give up some freedom to use resources to a government promising protection. Perhaps the people of another society in an arid region would contribute some resources to a government which maintains major water projects. In either case, freedom to manage and draw wealth and comfort from some resources is sacrificed, and a command structure dominates the decision-making.

Consider the movements for socialist and communist command systems that emerged in European and Asian nations in the 20th century. Revolutionary leaders often claimed they wanted government control of economic resources to improve the lives of the people in general. *The Communist Manifesto*, written by Karl Marx and Friedrich Engels in 1847, called on workers to overthrow those classes that controlled wealth and create a state that would manage wealth. While the theory attracted many, the states created under Marxist principles became oppressive, mismanaged dictatorships, many of which have disintegrated or are in the process of adopting market reforms.

On the other hand, some societies' highest value is **freedom**. They often develop market systems with the profit motive dominating the mixture of decision-making. Historically, the United States has been such a nation. It was settled by people seeking freedom from oppression. In modern industrial times, the American people's desire for security has led to government provisions for the elderly, unemployment, and medical problems. Still, there is a greater desire to hold and manage personal resources. Americans want the freedom to build their own businesses, change jobs, invest money, and own property. In most cases, these very strong desires for freedom are the predominant values in American culture and tradition. Because individual choice – fired by the profit motive – is so important, a market structure dominates decision-making.

VALUES OFTEN CONFLICT

It seems that nothing about people is as simple as it appears. Americans, like all people, have other basic economic values such as growth, efficiency, justice, and stability. Efficiency and growth are high on any nation's (or person's) priority list.

Economic efficiency means using limited human, natural, and capital resources in such a way as to get the most from them. Research into using resources efficiently usually leads to higher quality and technological breakthroughs. Efficiency can lead to new industries and new products, which bring economic growth into the picture.

Not only do people want to use resources wisely, they want to manage them in such a way that more of everything can be produced. **Economic growth** means increasing output which leads to a better life (standard of living), more jobs, and greater opportunities to expand profits.

Freedom, growth, and efficiency are usually high priority values in a market economy.

Security, stability, and justice are important, too. Still, they can conflict with freedom, growth, and efficiency. They slow down the pace of the economy.

As noted above, security involves holding some resources for future use. **Economic stability** means controlling prices and production so that planning and efficiency can take place. That means the government might take action to slow down the pace of growth.

Economic justice (sometimes called *equity*) means insuring that there is equal opportunity for everyone to achieve the Dream. That means the government might take action to make things fair for people of all sexes, races, religions, ages, and classes. When courts try to adjudicate a fair situation for some people, others suffer.

In America, there is a unique mixture of market and command economics. It is called by different names: mixed free enterprise, capitalism, or a mixed market. The key is to be aware that it is a mixed economy.

How much market and command are present? It is very hard to pinpoint. One way of envisioning it might be to look at the entire pattern of spending. In a *Forbes* article, analyst Peter Brimelow indicated that the government (command) accounted for 34.2% of all the spending in 1992 ("Why the Deficit is the Wrong Number." 15 Mar. 1993, 79).

Another view is to look at Americans' decision-making power regarding their financial resources. One way to measure this is to note the ratio of average Americans' earnings to what they pay to government in taxes. The 1990 census recorded an average per capita annual income of $21,000. Add local, state, and federal taxes together, and their average comes to just below $7,000. This means the average person contributes 33% of their earnings for government goods and services. (Around 1900, the figure was 5%-7%). On that basis, where does the

United States fit on the Figure 3.2 continuum? Two-thirds market, one-third command? It is hard to know exactly.

VALUE CONFLICTS CREATE POLITICAL DIVERSITY

Some people are outraged to see government take so much of their economic resources. Others accept it as the price of security and stability. Naturally, these value conflicts translate into politics. Those that control resources often band together to protect their wealth from those who want a greater share. Political scientists argue about which side the two major political parties in the United States will take in such economic value conflicts.

Although the following views may be over-simplified, they do render some idea of how economic values guide political interaction in modern America.

Today's Republicans tend to identify with the **laissez-faire capitalist** tradition. They try to restrain the growth of government. This position earns them the "conservative" label. Republicans tend to speak as defenders of individual freedom and decry the growth of government as taking too much incentive from people in terms of taxes. They see government regulation as an interference with personal and corporate economic choices. Republicans place priority on growth, efficiency, and freedom.

The Democratic Party nostalgically reflects the New Deal tradition of providing the underclasses with greater economic stability, security, and justice. The actions of the New Deal, New Frontier, and Great Society Eras led to more government programs for housing, job security, old age pensions, medical care, consumer protection, and regulation of business. Political scientists would label this a "liberal" position. Democrats place priority on stability, equality, and security.

Of course, these positions are not "carved in stone." Economic philosophy is often a matter of individual priorities and personal beliefs. Both parties believe in the importance of all the basic economic values. Democrats want to keep the economic atmosphere free and growing, but they want it to occur in a stable and just fashion. Republicans want equal opportunity for all and want people to be secure, but they do not want to see freedom, competition, and initiative diminished by overwhelming government restrictions or regulations.

Because there is a desire to satisfy all the basic values, the two parties are not always clear in their stands on issues. There is usually compromise. Some Americans are confused by the parties. Many citizens choose not to join either major party because the lines are not clear. However, parties hold the power on how much command will be mixed into our basic market structure. Participating in some party activities is a way citizens have of influencing the mix.

SUMMARY

These ideas provide some notion of the nature of the American mixed market structure. Every society evolves its own mixture of market, command, and traditional economic decision-making elements. It is a dynamic process. Mixtures change according to internal and external conditions. There are always conflicts inside societies over economic decisions.

There are also conflicts among societies. No society stands alone. Nations are interdependent. The actions of one nation influence others. The world recently entered a new era without the burden of the Cold War. The collapse of communism in Europe and the demise of the Soviet Union changed the setting of global economic conflict. Former communist nations searched for new systems of making economic decisions. Formerly command-dominant societies sought more personal control of individual and household decision-making. Aram's story at the beginning of this section illustrated this. While this new freedom conflicts with security-oriented traditions in many societies, it has been strengthened by global communications. People have greater knowledge of societies different from their own. They also have greater levels of education. Communication and education cause people to reexamine their systems in a new light and modify them. Expectations rise. In the long run, has the reordering of values brought the world into a period of greater understanding or greater conflict?

ASSESSMENT
QUESTIONS • APPLICATIONS

1 Think about the story of Nedda and Aram.
  a Explain what difference in attitude you see between the two?
  b Which person represents the values needed most for survival in a market economy? Explain why.

2 Think about the basic six economic values: efficiency, freedom, growth, justice, security, and stability.
  a Based on your own judgment, list these six economic values in order from most important to least.
  b Explain why you placed each value where you did as you listed them.
  c Compare your order with that of others.
  d After listening to others' ideas, would you change your priority order? If so, why and how? If not, why not?

3 Go back to the financial role you have set up for yourself in the assessment tasks for Issues 1 and 2. Think about your values and how a person in your position would view public policies.
  a Where do you think your circumstances place you on the political spectrum? (1) Liberal, (2) Conservative, (3) Democrat, (4) Republican, (5) Independent. Why?
  b Make a reason list of the way you feel about key economic issues: (1) education, (2) financial security (minimum wage, unemployment compensation, pensions, medical insurance, etc.), (3) consumer protection, (4) business regu-

lations, (5) environmental regulations, (6) transportation, (7) farm and business subsidies. Why does the order of your list reflect your values?

4 Most economies fall along the decision-making continuum as mixing some market and some command.
  a How would you classify your household on the continuum. Why?
  b How would you classify the United States on the continuum. Why?
  c Some traditions influence economic decision-making even in modern economic structures. Give several examples.

5 Like most modern economies, the United States mixes market and command approaches to decision-making.
  a Give three examples of market decision-making in the United States
  b Give three examples of command decision-making in the United States
  c Research and report on some of the difficulties encountered by Russia in trying to change its economic system in the 1990s.

6 While the United States mixes market and command, basic decision-making rests with buyers and sellers.
  a Explain the importance of self-interest in the United States market.
  b Give an example of decisions formerly made by individuals now made by government.
  c In what way does self interest conflict with a value such as economic justice?

7 Consider the broad economic value structure (at the end of this Issue) used to classify the Republican and Democratic Parties. Analyze your own ranking of the six basic economic values (question 2). Then, based on your analysis, complete the following.
  a Toward which party does your value structure lean? Explain.
  b Where does this leaning put you in relation to others in your household? Your fellow students? Your community?
  c Does your ranking of the six basic economic values influence personal economic decisions? Explain.

ASSESSMENT PROJECT:
FREE MARKET SYSTEM

STUDENT TASK

Research and present a position in a class debate. Resolved: Only a market system will allow the Russian people to survive as a nation.

PROCEDURE

1   In order to have a balanced presentation, a lottery system should be used to assign the prospective debaters to a position (pro or con).

2   Instructor assigns 2 or 3 individuals to each pro team and con team.

3   Each team meets to brainstorm their approach, key arguments, terms and phrases to be used during the debate and determine the library research needed.

4   Members of each team research the items determined by the decision-making session (step 3) and required for support of arguments. It is important that any point of position (argument) have factual backing. Debates are not just opinions.

5   Each team meets after the research to discuss their findings, organize the approach, outline the delivery, and develop team's debate notes and strategy.

6   On the scheduled day of the first debate, a lottery should be used to choose which teams will be opponents in the actual class debate.

7   The debate.
   • 5 minutes for the oral presentation of the pro position.
   • 5 minutes for the oral presentation of the con position.
   • 2 minutes for rebuttal for each position.
   • 5 minutes for peer evaluation.

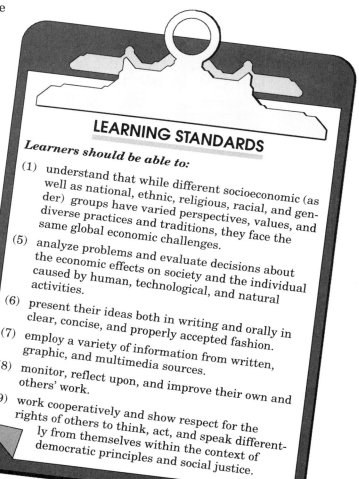

LEARNING STANDARDS

Learners should be able to:

(1)   understand that while different socioeconomic (as well as national, ethnic, religious, racial, and gender) groups have varied perspectives, values, and diverse practices and traditions, they face the same global economic challenges.

(5)   analyze problems and evaluate decisions about the economic effects on society and the individual caused by human, technological, and natural activities.

(6)   present their ideas both in writing and orally in clear, concise, and properly accepted fashion.

(7)   employ a variety of information from written, graphic, and multimedia sources.

(8)   monitor, reflect upon, and improve their own and others' work.

(9)   work cooperatively and show respect for the rights of others to think, act, and speak differently from themselves within the context of democratic principles and social justice.

EVALUATION

The criteria for the evaluation of this project are itemized in the grid (rubric) that follows. Choice of appropriate category terms (values) is the decision of the instructor. Selection of terms such as "minimal," "satisfactory," and "distinguished" can vary with each assessment.

Debate: Russian Economic System – Evaluation Rubric

(Refer to introductory section for suggestions of scoring descriptors for the evaluation categories.)

Evaluation Item	Category 1	Category 2	Category 3	Category 4	Category 5
Item a: (1) Does the presentation show understanding that while different socioeconomic (as well as national, ethnic, religious, racial, and gender) groups have varied perspectives, values, and diverse practices and traditions, they face the same global economic challenges?					
Item b: (5) Does the presentation analyze problems and evaluate decisions about the economic effects caused by human, technological, and natural activities on societies and individuals?					
Item c: (6) Does the presentation present ideas orally in clear, concise, and properly accepted fashion?					
Item d: (7) Does the presentation employ a variety of information from written, graphic, and multimedia sources?					
Item e: (8) Does the presentation show monitoring of reflection upon, and improvement of work?					
Item f: (9) Does the presentation show cooperative work and respect for the rights of others to think, act, and speak differently?					

ISSUE 4

How does the price system operate?

SUPPLY AND DEMAND

Buying a car fits into the American Dream. It is a part of our culture. In youth, the first car signifies a rite of passage. The ability to move away from the home symbolizes a threshold of freedom. It is also the highest priced item bought up to that time in our lives. The purchase involves research and the desire to get the car for the absolute best price. It makes us conscious of the significance of price in our lives.

GLENDA'S USED CAR: PLAYING THE PRICE GAME

After being cut from the state public works department, Glenda Troup's dad was forced to accept a lower paying job with a small plumbing company. Without the higher income, Glenda's dream of going to Penn State seemed to fade away. However, there was the Community College near home, and many of her friends were going there. On the positive side, dad said that she would need a car for the commute and he would help her buy it.

"Of course, it will have to be a used one, girl, but a decent one," he said.

"We can co-sign the loan and help with the money down, but your job will have to cover the payments, your insurance and gas, and whatever maintenance has to be done."

"OK," she said, "I'll start looking around tomorrow. Any recommendations as to where to start?"

"Yes, go down to the library. You have to do a little old fashioned homework first. This is a big purchase, and a long-term one. You have to know what you want, what you can afford, and how to shop."

"Dad, if there is one thing I know how to do, it's shop!"

Mrs. Troup smiled, but Mr. Troup shook his head. "This is not like a trip to the mall, Glen'. Its not just checking the tag and paying the price as marked. Buying cars, new or used, is much more complicated. I know, I've made my share of mistakes. That reminds me, did I ever tell you about that time when ..." "Now Zach, don't bore us with more stories," Mom said. "Get to the point!"

"OK, OK," Zachery Troup sputtered. "I get the message. Now, as I was saying, there are plenty of used cars, but consumers want only the good ones, and those are in short supply. High demand and low supply drives prices up, you know.

"If you start dashing around town looking for something cute, you'll get burned. It's better to do some reading, thinking with pencil and paper, and talking first. Go down to the library and check Edmunds' *Used Car Prices* and *Consumer Reports* annual auto issue. Then we can talk some more. Meantime, I'll call our insurance agent to see what kind of premiums to expect."

A day or so later, Glenda found her parents in the kitchen. She showed them an outline of what she found in the library.

"You were right, Dad. This is complicated. Breaking it down into steps makes it easier. There are four phases: lay the groundwork, figure financing, shop around, and then make the final deal.

"In the first phase, I have to think about my needs. Basically, I need the car to commute, so it has to get real good gas mileage. I'll be traveling back roads in all kinds of weather. It had better be rugged. I don't need much room, so wagons and vans are out. A pickup sounds cute, but they ride hard, handle poorly in snow, and have little secure room without a cap. My best bet seems to be a sedan or a hatchback. It sounds dull, but these sources say used family cars probably have gentler wear than sporty ones.

"I have to know how much I can afford. I have about $1,000 saved, but I can't spend it all. The car will need insurance, and the sources say I should reserve some money for maintenance. I think I can manage $500 for a down payment, if I can get financing. I think I can handle a $100 per month payment for two years."

Used Car Check Sheet

Date _____

Make _____ Model _____ Year _____ Body Type _____

Odometer _____ Dealer _____ Phone _____

Previous Owner _____ Service Record _____ Warranty _____

Item	Problem	Cost to Repair
Fluids	coolant reddish color, transmission oil?	
Leaks	stain on ground (puddle) underneath	
Body	some rust, repainted, new undercoat	
Tires	tread wear, Top play, Shock bounce	
Interior	pedal sloppy, driver seat wear	
Engine	knocking noise on acceleration	
Transmission	smooth shift	
Brak...	45 mph stop (swerve?), pedal resistence	
Align		
Exha...	...oke or vapor	
No...		

"It seems you can afford something in the $3,000 bracket," said Mrs. Troup. "I called Gloria at Bolton Insurance yesterday. She said a single, 18-year-old female can expect to pay between $800 and $1000 a year. She can give us a better idea when she knows the details on the car you choose."

"Thanks, Mom," said Glenda. "The third step is to find out what cars are decent at that price."

Mr. Troup spoke up, "I stopped by the credit union today. Celeste gave me last month's *NADA* book. You know, the National Automobile Dealers Association's listing of average used car prices. Dealers use it to estimate price, but banks also use it to figure loans. We can use it to see what is available in the $3,000 price range. When we have an idea, Celeste said to call for the current *NADA* price. Depreciation changes the prices from month to month. What a market!"

"OK," Glenda continued. "I borrowed *The Consumer Reports 1994 Buying Guide* from the library. It has reliability ratings on models up to six years ago. It helps to see the history of problems certain models have.

"Once I know what cars to look for, the experts say is to see if I can arrange financing at a bank. Dealers have financing, and sometimes it is very good. Still, the books said setting up the loan *before* I start shopping will give me limits. They say if I know exactly how much I can spend, it will help me avoid the temptation of getting in over my head."

"I think that last step is really smart," said Glenda's dad. "Tonight, look at the *NADA* book and the reliability ratings. List some makes and models. Tomorrow we'll go to the credit union and see if we can set up a loan."

Glenda looked in the local classified ads for private sales, then checked used car lots. She asked her friend Midge to go along for moral support. Glenda drew up a check sheet on details for Midge to use while she listened to the salesperson. Her mother said to tell the salesperson what she was looking for, but to emphasize that she was "just looking" and not ready to buy. The library books said to do specific checks before, during, and after the test drive. The checks also help identify the big problems. The sources also said to ask the dealers if they will fix specific minor problems. Glenda's sources also said to check the state's "Lemon Law." It gives you guarantees against a defective auto and recourse against a commercial seller.

After each shopping expedition, Glenda and Midge sorted through the check sheets for the different cars. They discussed all the pros and cons of each. After about two weeks of searching, Glenda found a four-year-old sedan that looked good. She took her mother and father to see it. Mr. Troup arranged with the dealer to take it to his gas station mechanic. It cost $65, but when the mechanic gave his blessing, Glenda knew she had her car at last.

Glenda checks out her "new" used car. ©PhotoDisc

ISSUE 4

How does the price system operate?

SUPPLY AND DEMAND

INTRODUCTION

Shopping makes for an enjoyable outing for most young people. Seeing how prices and quality vary can be an adventure. Some are addicted to it. They wear T-shirts emblazoned with "Born To Shop." Others find shopping a chore and try to avoid it. Prices can get people excited or discouraged, but they can be bewildering, too.

The grocery store is America's number one price comparison, time consuming, competitive marketplace. ©PhotoDisc

Glenda always liked shopping, but she found buying a used car more difficult than any expedition to the mall. Sometimes there were price tags (stickers), and sometimes there were none. If there were tags, she knew the dealers and owners would take less if she asked and bargained. This fluid price game was all new to her. She was glad she had some coaching from her parents.

Acceptable levels of prices keep the whole market functioning; therefore, understanding price is an important step in learning economics. In markets, understanding price is behind all economic decisions. Merchants and manufacturers do not just randomly assign monetary figures to what they sell. They do research, analyze all their costs, and make decisions before they arrive at the price.

MARKET FORCES DECIDE PRICE

Still, the idea of **market price** is not precise. Any item for which a person shops can be found at many price levels, but most buyers and sellers have an idea of the *average* price of an item. Many "shopping" consumers will go miles out of their way – or alter their schedules – to find a store selling an item below the market price.

Yet, the *process* of arriving at the average market price is somewhat mysterious. If pressed, most people would vaguely say, "It has something to do with supply and demand." They would be right. A **market** is where exchanges take place. In a market, consumers and producers try to satisfy their needs and wants from the scarce resources they possess. The mixing of **demand** (what consumers *can* and *will* buy) with **supply** (what goods and services producers are *willing* and *able* to provide) results in an **equilibrium price** (average market price). *Mixing* is the key word. It suggests motion. It is dynamic. Price is not a precise equation. Prices are always in motion. Prices are dynamic because the mix of *desires* and *capacities* of consumers and producers changes. Demand and supply generally meet – but under changing circumstances.

Demand and supply are opposing market forces. The consumer wants to spend as little of her/his hard-earned money as possible. The producer wants to get the most money possible to cover her/his costs and get a good profit. Somewhere, these two opposite lines of thought must meet. That compromise point, where supply and demand meet, is the **equilibrium**, the balance point. It becomes the average market price.

THE ROLE OF DEMAND IN DETERMINING PRICE

Demand is relatively easy to grasp. Most people understand the role of consumer. A look at consumers' needs and abilities gives us an idea of what demand really means. Wishing for something is unimportant here. A person cannot just want or need something. A person must be *able* to buy something. For demand to be real, consumers must have *both*:

- the **desire** to buy – they must be *willing* to use their resources to buy.

- the **capacity** to buy – they must be *able* to buy – possess the financial resources.

For example, in a low income neighborhood, demand for high priced homes is small – perhaps non-existent. While many consumers might desire expensive homes, they are not able to buy. They do not have the financial resources (money) to purchase them. From an economic standpoint, demand is not real in this neighborhood. Economists would say there is no market here.

Price comparison can have its own reward. The same item found at two different stores may have vastly different prices. ©PhotoDisc

CONSUMER GUIDELINES

• **Equate Needs and Wants** – Control your impulses. Take a moment to analyze why you are buying something. Realize you may be sacrificing hard-earned money on items you do not need.

• **Use Personal Budgeting** – Know the limits of what you can afford.

• **Use Advertising** – Get an idea of price in several stores, local and distant. Check availability of substitute goods (features vary among producers). Clip discount coupons.

• **Use Research** – Government and private consumer publications list prices, discuss features, and make recommendations on models, brands, and alternatives.

• **Know Measurements and Standards** – Know the dimensions of what you need. Sizes, grades, weights, and measurement units (sq. feet versus sq. yards) vary among stores and producers.

• **Wait for Sales and Bargains** – Markets change. Watch price cycles. Know when there are sales (e.g., end of season, traditional winter "White Sales," end-of-model year). Use manufacturers' and store coupons. Consider bulk buying in warehouse clubs and factory outlet stores.

THE ROLE OF SUPPLY IN DETERMINING PRICE

Understanding the supply-side of the market is more difficult for the average person. Most people have little experience producing goods and services, yet the requirements for supply to be real are similar to those of demand. For supply to be real, producers must have *both*:

• the **desire** to produce – they must be willing to use their resources to supply something. There must be *incentive* (profit).

• the **capacity** to produce – they must possess adequate production resources.

People often say they would like to go into business, but it is not easy to assemble the right amounts of resources, in the right place, at the right time, to make an acceptable amount of profit. The natural, human, and financial resources themselves may be unavailable or too expensive. Even if they are available and reasonable, if the **margin of profit** (amount after cost of production is subtracted) is too low, a producer will get discouraged and use the resources for something else. So, both the desire and the ability to produce are crucial if a product is to appear on the market. (Notice that while consumer demand is important, the other factors are the key to understanding what drives producers. Someone with the ability, resources, and belief in the product will be able to find consumers and convince them to buy.)

In addition, there is a tremendous amount of risk for producers. Many educated guesses have to be made in any business. According to the U.S. Department of Commerce's Bureau of Economic Analysis, in the 1980s, an average of 643,000 new businesses incorporated per year and an average of 47,300 per year failed (*Business Statistics*: 1963–91, 21–22).

MIXING DEMAND AND SUPPLY IN DETERMINING PRICE

Economists observe that producers and consumers normally follow behaviors they call the "Law of Demand" and the "Law of Supply."

• **The Law of Demand** says that as a product's market price (P) increases, less will be desired – quantity demanded (Q) will decrease. The reason is that consumers will be discouraged by higher prices. Of course, there is an opposite effect, too. If prices decline, consumers will demand more. Lower income groups will be able to afford the products once out of their reach. The relationship between price and quantity demanded is *inverse* [P↑ = Q↓ or P↓ = Q↑] (see Figure 4.1 on next page).

• **The Law of Supply** says that as a product's market price (P) increases, more will be produced – quantity supplied (Q) will increase. The relationship between price and quantity supplied is *direct* (P↓ = Q↓ or P↑ = Q↑). The reason is that producers will be enticed by the chance for greater profits (the profit motive). Of course, there is an opposite effect, too. If prices decline, producers will supply less or even drop out of the market (see Figure 4.2 on next page).

DEMAND SCHEDULE AND CURVE
Price / Demand Comparison

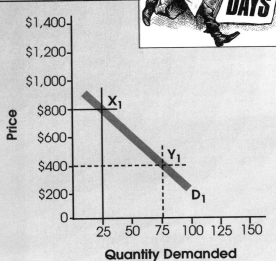

Electronic Notepads at
Carturo's Computer Cave

Price / Demand Schedule

Price per Notebook	Quantity Demanded
$ 200	100
$ 400	75
$ 600	50
$ 800	25
$ 1000	0

████████ **Demand**

Figure 4.1 On the D_1 curve, consumers demand 25 items at $800.00 ($X_1$), but they demand 75 at $400.00 ($Y_1$). As prices drop, consumers demand more items. As prices rise, consumers demand fewer items.

Figure 4.1

SUPPLY SCHEDULE AND CURVE
Price / Supply Comparison

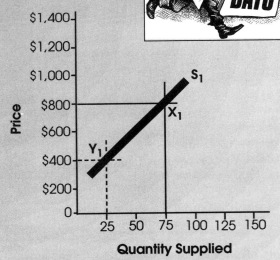

Electronic Notepads at
Carturo's Computer Cave

Price / Supply Schedule

Price per Notebook	Quantity Supplied
$ 200	0
$ 400	25
$ 600	50
$ 800	75
$ 1000	100

████████ **Supply**

Figure 4.2 On the S_1 curve, producers supply only 25 items at $400.00 ($Y_1$), but they supply 75 at $800.00 ($X_1$). As prices rise, producers are encouraged to supply more items. As prices fall, producers supply fewer items.

Figure 4.2

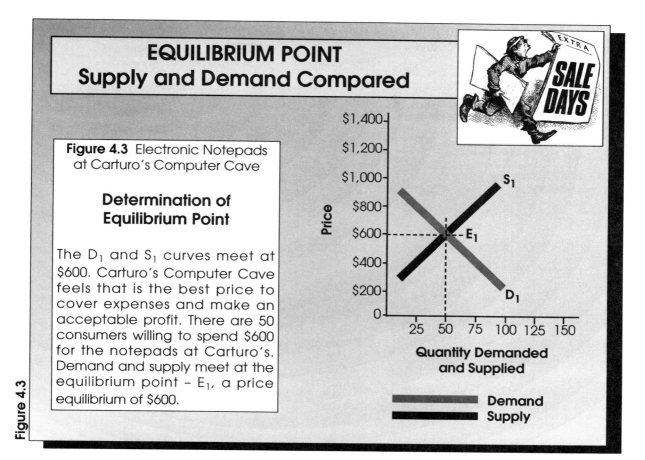

EQUILIBRIUM POINT
Supply and Demand Compared

Figure 4.3 Electronic Notepads at Carturo's Computer Cave

Determination of Equilibrium Point

The D_1 and S_1 curves meet at $600. Carturo's Computer Cave feels that is the best price to cover expenses and make an acceptable profit. There are 50 consumers willing to spend $600 for the notepads at Carturo's. Demand and supply meet at the equilibrium point – E_1, a price equilibrium of $600.

Figure 4.3

Price

Quantity Demanded and Supplied

■■■ Demand
■■■ Supply

The Laws of Demand and Supply suggest consumers and producers operate in opposite directions. This seems simple common sense. Seeing the Laws work is one thing. Seeing *why* they work is another. There are a host of determining forces lurking in the background on both sides of the market.

Determinants of Demand. On the demand side of the market, consumers want and need goods and services, but certain factors determine whether they will act:

• *Income levels* limit buying power (the *ability* to demand).

• *Consumer tastes* vary greatly over time (the *desire* to demand). Demand changes as tastes in clothes, music, and food change.

• *Substitutes* (*if* there are substitutes available) are chosen when prices rise. Think of hot drinks. If the price of coffee shot up, many consumers might lean toward drinking more tea or cocoa. Yet, if the price of gasoline rises, drivers' options are limited. They can cut down on driving to a point, but

for their essential driving, they will still need to buy gas.

• *Size of Market* varies as the population changes, and the potential for demand to expand or contract changes.

Determinants of Supply: On the supply-side of the market, the forces that motivate producers are just as complex as those on the demand side. The existence of consumer demand does not mean producers will jump to meet it. Profits motivate producers, but many factors alter the amount of profit:

• *Resource costs* can rise or fall (e.g., raw material, transportation, wage contracts, materials, rents, loan rates) expanding or reducing income.

• *Technology* changes (e.g., new machinery makes it costly to compete, but it might also make production more efficient, increase productivity, lower labor costs, and increase profit margins).

• *Taxes* rise or fall making it more or less difficult to maintain an acceptable margin of net profit.

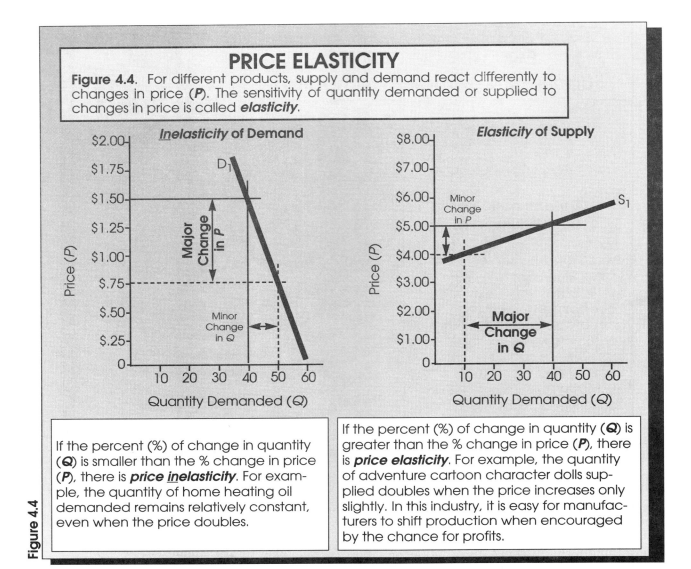

PRICE ELASTICITY

Figure 4.4. For different products, supply and demand react differently to changes in price (*P*). The sensitivity of quantity demanded or supplied to changes in price is called *elasticity*.

_In_elasticity of Demand

Elasticity of Supply

If the percent (%) of change in quantity (*Q*) is smaller than the % change in price (*P*), there is *price inelasticity*. For example, the quantity of home heating oil demanded remains relatively constant, even when the price doubles.

If the percent (%) of change in quantity (*Q*) is greater than the % change in price (*P*), there is *price elasticity*. For example, the quantity of adventure cartoon character dolls supplied doubles when the price increases only slightly. In this industry, it is easy for manufacturers to shift production when encouraged by the chance for profits.

Figure 4.4

If the rising costs of these factors reduce profits, producers (suppliers) become discouraged. Every producer has a personal "cut off point." Some are faster than others to say, "This is not worth my while." When suppliers cut back or drop out of the market, the supply (total amount) of that product drops, and there is less available. Of course, the reverse of these forces also occurs. The right combination of circumstances encourages more producers to create more goods and services.

The Laws of Supply and Demand are universal and are basic to understanding how free markets work. Yet, the nature of a product can vary the relationship of price and quantity. If products are necessities and there are no substitutes, consumers buy about the same amount no matter what the price. With other products, consumers will react dramatically to changes in

price. The same is true for suppliers. They may be limited in what they can produce. Even if some of their other costs decline, the suppliers may not be able to get more land or minerals. Economists refer to the relationship of Q to P as **elasticity**. Elasticity is the sensitivity of changes in quantity demanded (or supplied) to changes in price. See Figure 4.4 above for a discussion of price elasticity.

VISUALIZING HOW DEMAND AND SUPPLY DETERMINE PRICE

Economists create **economic models** to show the result of forces behind supply and demand. First, they create numerical lists, called **schedules**, to visualize the laws of supply and demand. When they plot the numbers from the schedule onto a graph, they produce supply and demand **curves**. For example, in Figure 4.1 on page 80, plotting the demand schedule numbers on a graph produces a demand curve [D_1]. It shows that as price drops, Carturo's customers will buy more.

In Figure 4.2 on page 80, plotting the supply schedule numbers data on a graph produces a supply curve [S_1]. It shows that as price drops, Carturo's owners want to sell fewer computers.

Figure 4.3 on page 81 shows that by combining the two sets of data from the schedules onto one graph, the D_1 and S_1 curves intersect at an **equilibrium price** [E_1]. This $600 point is the average point where most transactions take place.

At this equilibrium point on Figure 4.3, there are enough consumers with $600 willing to buy the 50 electronic note pads Carturo's owners are willing to offer at that price. At $600, the market is in balance. Economists also call it the "market clearing price." It is the point of compromise. There are enough consumers who choose to pay $600 to clear the shelves of what Carturo's chooses to offer.

ABOVE AND BELOW THE EQUILIBRIUM MARKET PRICE

Will there be stores that sell and consumers that buy above and below the equilibrium point? Of course. Above the equilibrium, small local stores with few customers have to sell each item at higher prices to cover operating costs and still make a profit. Many consumers will grudgingly accept higher prices to save time and energy instead of going miles out of their way to a mall. A glimpse at the supply-demand graph Figure 4.3 shows that producers would love to sell twice as many at $1000 (a price $400 above the equilibrium at Carturo's). Yet, no consumers are willing or capable of buying at the high price. Essentially, producers will not sell any (or very few). This means that at $1000, producers would have a **surplus** of 100. Producers have to reduce the price to attract enough buyers to sell all their stock.

Another example would be the difference people pay for items when they run into a local "convenience store" for a few items. To get a lower price, they know they would have to travel farther and wait in line longer at a major supermarket. In a remote area, consumers will usually accept higher prices per item rather than travel long distances to shopping malls or urban stores.

One historic example is Sears, Roebuck Co. It built a major business in the late 1800s by offering the convenience of mail order to the farmers of the Great Plains. To get items they needed, farmers accepted the company's extra charges for shipping. Of course, convenience is still what makes direct mail (e.g., L.L. Bean, Chadwicks, Lands' End) and telemarketing (QVC Network) popular and profitable today.

Below the equilibrium, big discount chains (e.g., Wal★Mart, K-Mart, Service Merchandise) will accept lower profits per item, because they can sell more on a national scale. Making money by selling more for less profit is called **volume selling**. Another look at the Figure 4.3 supply-demand graph shows that there are 75 consumers who would buy at $400 (a price $200 below the equilibrium at Carturo's). These consumers will probably go a distance to shop at discount stores.

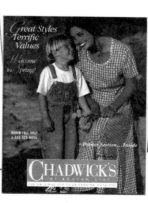

Yet, only a few big-time suppliers are willing to accept a low profit by selling at $400. For smaller stores, it is simply not worth their while. That low a profit margin is a **disincentive**. In general, fewer products are available at that low price in the market. At $400, the Figure 4.3 graph shows 75 consumers but only 25 items available. The gap between demand and supply is 50 units. Low supply in the face of high demand means a **shortage** occurs. A consumer has to search far and wide for a "bargain price" such as $400. That margin of profit discourages the average producer. As a result, supply is low – there is a shortage.

BALANCING SUPPLY AND DEMAND

Equilibrium prices mean the market is in balance. Producers who have a surplus of products at high prices will lower their prices, but they will be discouraged. Many producers may accept lower profits for a short time, but they drop out of that market for the long run. On the other hand, producers who sell below the average price will attract consumers and sell out fast. Eventually, they realize they can raise prices and still sell out.

The market never stands still. The signals people get from the market interaction of supply and demand change their current and future behavior. A consumer who cannot afford something may accept a substitute or save for a future purchase. A producer who has to cut prices to get rid of surplus goods today may plan to cut workers' hours, wages, and benefits – or close a plant altogether.

In either case, the mix of the consumers' and producers' decisions alters the market. Millions of consumers' and producers' decisions intermix daily. The result is a complex, ever-changing market.

CHANGES IN SUPPLY AND DEMAND

Economics is about people making and changing decisions. Since they change often, the market is always changing. An equilibrium price shows the market is in balance – for the moment. Blink for a second, and it all changes.

As mentioned previously, the amount of demand can change because of changes in the forces that determine demand: income levels, consumer tastes, and availability of substitutes. For example, if people in a community have more money due to a recovery or a local factory hiring, disposable income increases. More income would expand the capacity of the people to demand a product at every price level. The left side of Figure 4.5 shows why economists say these forces cause demand to "shift right." (demand generally increases).

On the right side, Figure 4.5 also shows that the amount of supply can change because of changes in the forces that determine supply: resource costs, technology, and taxes. Suppose all coat makers cut workers' wages. With labor costing less, coat makers would be able to produce more coats for the same price as before. They can produce more of every kind of coat at every price level. Economists would say this reduction in wages caused supply to "shift right." (supply generally increases).

With all the interplay of forces shifting the amounts of supply and demand, prices inevitably change. The curve on the left of Figure 4.6 shows what happens when market demand increases (shifts right) and supply remains the same. The equilibrium price increases.

The curve on the right of Figure 4.6 shows what happens when market supply increases (shifts right) and demand remains the same. The equilibrium price drops.

Of course, the forces behind demand and supply can also cause shifts to the left, causing other changes in equilibrium price.

WHEN GOVERNMENTS ENTER MARKETS

The most basic element behind the dynamic interplay of supply and demand is *free choice*. Producers and consumers exercise free choice continually. All this blending and reblending of choices makes equilibrium prices change. Markets for some products change more frequently than others (e.g., toys, clothing styles). What is important to recognize is that the *free interplay* of peoples' choices makes market

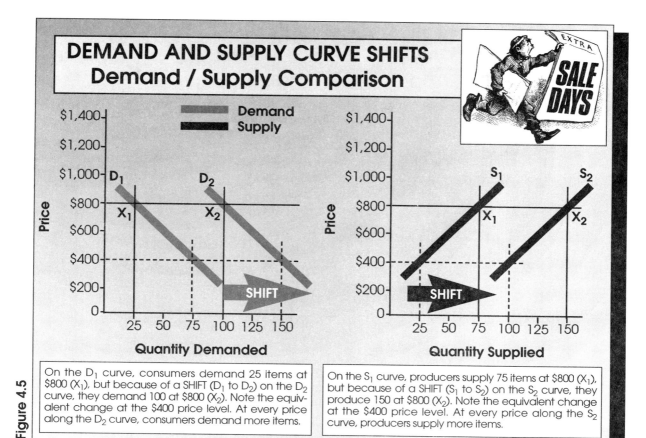

DEMAND AND SUPPLY CURVE SHIFTS
Demand / Supply Comparison

Figure 4.5

On the D_1 curve, consumers demand 25 items at $800 ($X_1$), but because of a SHIFT (D_1 to D_2) on the D_2 curve, they demand 100 at $800 ($X_2$). Note the equivalent change at the $400 price level. At every price along the D_2 curve, consumers demand more items.

On the S_1 curve, producers supply 75 items at $800 ($X_1$), but because of a SHIFT (S_1 to S_2) on the S_2 curve, they produce 150 at $800 ($X_2$). Note the equivalent change at the $400 price level. At every price along the S_2 curve, producers supply more items.

EFFECT OF SHIFTS
On Equilibrium Price

Figure 4.6

When the supply (S_1) remains constant, but the demand shifts right (increase D_1 to D_2), price increases from E_1 (62 items at $500) towards E_2 (100 items at $800). To restate, increased demand with constant supply leads to price increases.

When the demand (D_1) remains constant, but the supply shifts right (increase S_1 to S_2), price decreases from E_1 (75 items at $800) towards E_2 (112 items at $500). To restate, a constant demand with an increase in supply leads to lower prices.

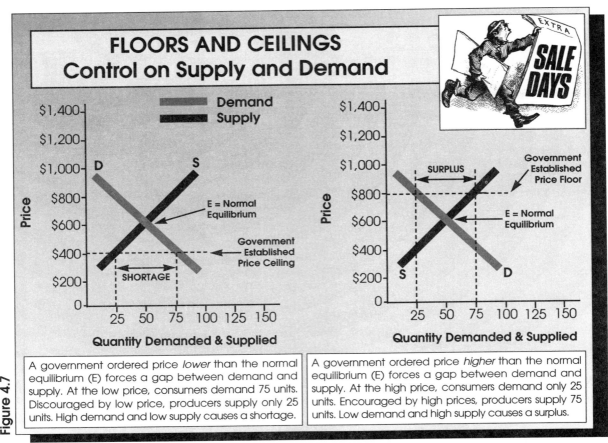

FLOORS AND CEILINGS
Control on Supply and Demand

A government ordered price *lower* than the normal equilibrium (E) forces a gap between demand and supply. At the low price, consumers demand 75 units. Discouraged by low price, producers supply only 25 units. High demand and low supply causes a shortage.

A government ordered price *higher* than the normal equilibrium (E) forces a gap between demand and supply. At the high price, consumers demand only 25 units. Encouraged by high prices, producers supply 75 units. Low demand and high supply causes a surplus.

Figure 4.7

economies work. When government intrudes, it compromises free choice in the market.

Issue 8 discusses the role of government in detail. Still, it is worth noting here that when government becomes a major buyer or seller of goods, it changes supply and demand conditions in the market.

On rare occasions, government imposes price limitations. These laws or actions are sometimes necessary, as in times of national security to alter the behavior of producers and consumers (sometimes intentionally). Of course, such government interference disrupts the natural interplay of supply and demand. Rigid floors and ceilings cause surpluses or shortages.

As Figure 4.7 shows, the market changes when government decrees a **floor** (lower limit) for prices such as farm price supports. Government also alters the market when it decrees a **ceiling** (upper limit) for prices such as urban rent controls.

In wars, these actions are necessary to force reallocations of resources. To fairly distribute artificially scarce goods, governments set up

rationing systems. Government agencies strictly issue ration coupons which act as permission slips for purchases. In World War II, the U.S. Office of Price Administration used an extensive control system for meat, butter, gasoline, and other strategic materials.

Today, all governments are active forces in the market. They alter economic behavior in many ways. Political battles often rage over the effects of government actions. It is important to understand the economic impact of government actions.

SUPPLY, DEMAND, AND THE AMERICAN DREAM

Freedom of choice is part of the American Dream. Freedom of choice drives decision-making about supply and demand. Consumers and producers make endless choices. Those choices synthesize into market prices. Of course, in modern day America, government rules and regulations modify some choices. We all want government to safeguard fairness and to protect consumers, workers, and the environment. Yet, we sacrifice some freedom of choice for such economic security. To achieve the American Dream, each generation has to balance its freedom of choice and its need for security. Issue 8, on the role of government, explores this challenge to freedom in detail.

Finally, there is another element driving producers' choices – competition. Competition raises problems for producers forcing short- and long-range decisions. Yet, it also keeps the market in balance to some extent. Issue 5 deals with competition in more detail.

ASSESSMENT
QUESTIONS • APPLICATIONS

1 Issue 4 begins with a story about buying a used car.
   a How are used car prices figured?
   b Why does the National Association of Automobile Dealers Association (NADA) book use the term "average price"?
   c Have you ever decided not to buy an item you felt you wanted? Give details.

2 Equilibrium price results from a clash of two opposing forces in the marketplace.
   a Explain the forces that determine the demand for luxury automobiles.
   b Explain the forces that determine the supply of luxury automobiles.
   c Explain the messages the price of a luxury automobile communicates to consumers and producers.

3 Toward the end of this issue, there are ideas and graphs discussing what makes total supply and/or total demand increase (shift right) on a graph.
   a List the causes for the increase in supply and the increase in demand.
   b Identify some other causes for increases in supply and increases in demand.
   c Reverse the situation. Think of what causes there might be for both lines to shift left (decrease in aggregate supply and a decrease in aggregate demand).

   d Mix the situation. Suppose supply shifts right, and demand shifts left. Draw a graph to show this. What happens to the equilibrium price? Make a list of what might cause demand to decrease while supply increases.
   e Reverse the situation just discussed in *d*. Suppose demand shifts right, and supply shifts left. Draw a graph to show this. What happens to the equilibrium price? Make a list of what might cause supply to decline while demand increases.

4 Freedom of choice is important in a market, but wars sometimes limit freedom of choice.
   a Why do wars create shortages of goods?
   b In World War II, the U.S. government attempted to do this through a rationing system. Research how the OPA (Office of Price Administration) operated during World War II. Defend your position as to why the WW II rationing system was a success or failure.
   c After World War II, the U.S. government removed economic regulations. Why did it take several years for supply and demand to reach equilibriums in many markets?

5 Government actions alter the market.
   a Explain how taxes change demand in the market.
   b Explain how taxes alter supply in the market.
   c Explain how a local government ceiling on rents for senior citizen apartments could change the supply of apartments.
   d Explain how a local government ceiling on rents for senior citizen apartments could alter the demand for apartments.

6 Government actions affect the market.
   a Research and report on how federal government price supports (floors) on wheat could alter the supply of wheat.
   b Research and report on how federal government price supports (floors) on wheat could alter the demand for wheat.

ASSESSMENT PROJECT:
MAJOR APPLIANCE PURCHASE

STUDENT TASK

Produce a 3-5 page report on making a major household purchase. The task can be done on its own or as part of the Hypothetical Household Portfolio. In the latter form, the purchase must be reconciled with budget and goals set up in assessment for Issues 1 and 2.

PROCEDURE

1   Assume that you wish to buy a major appliance, entertainment equipment, or piece of furniture in the $500-$1000 range.

2   Go to back issues of *Consumer Reports*, *Consumer Reports Annual Buying Guide*, *Consumers' Digest*, and *Consumer Guide*. Find out which makes and models are recommended. Make a list of them. Also, list any other product or buying recommendations of which *Consumer Reports* thinks shoppers should be aware.

3   Visit two different retail stores that sell the item(s) you want, and talk to a salesperson.

4   Tell the store personnel you must obtain the following information on an official dealer invoice (or on their store stationery): a) the delivered price; b) extra charges and taxes that add to the cost of delivering the item; and, c) financial arrangements for purchase, including the down payment, the A.P.R., and the total finance charge for all the years payments will be made.

5   Write a 3-5 page report which: a) summarizes the background information from *Consumer Reports* and other sources; b) discusses the two sets of dealer information

(including prices); c) presents your analysis of the information (including from which dealer you would buy and why); and d) weighs the purchase against household budget and analyzes its consequences.

LEARNING STANDARDS

Learners should be able to:

(1) understand that while different socioeconomic (as well as national, ethnic, religious, racial, and gender) groups have varied perspectives, values, and diverse practices and traditions, they face the same global economic challenges.

(5) analyze problems and evaluate decisions about the economic effects on society and the individual caused by human, technological, and natural activities.

(6) present their ideas both in writing and orally in clear, concise, and properly accepted fashion.

(7) employ a variety of information from written, graphic, and multimedia sources.

(8) monitor, reflect upon, and improve their own and others' work.

(9) work cooperatively and show respect for the rights of others to think, act, and speak differently from themselves within the context of democratic principles and social justice.

EVALUATION

The criteria for the evaluation of this project are itemized in the grid (rubric) that follows. Choice of appropriate category terms (values) is the decision of the instructor. Selection of terms such as "minimal," "satisfactory," and "distinguished" can vary with each assessment.

Major Appliance Purchase Evaluation Rubric

(Refer to introductory section for suggestions of scoring descriptors for the evaluation categories.)

Evaluation Item	Category 1	Category 2	Category 3	Category 4	Category 5
Item a: (1) Does the report show understanding that while different socioeconomic (as well as national, ethnic, religious, racial, and gender) groups have varied perspectives, values, and diverse practices and traditions, they face the same global economic challenges?					
Item b: (5) Does the report analyze problems and evaluate decisions about the economic effects caused by human, technological, and natural activities on societies and individuals?					
Item c: (6) Does the report present ideas in writing (and orally) in clear, concise, and properly accepted fashion?					
Item d: (7) Does the report employ a variety of information from written, graphic, and multimedia sources?					
Item e: (8) Does the report show monitoring of, reflection upon, and improvement of work?					
Item f: (9) Does the work show cooperative effort and respect for the rights of others to think, act, and speak differently?					

ISSUE 5

How do people organize in a market?

ORGANIZATION OF BUSINESS

Growing businesses are the heart of the American market. Henry Ford, Walter P. Chrysler, and Alfred Sloan, Jr., building "The Big Three" of the U.S. auto industry from small beginnings are part of our national lore. Growing a business is not easy, but it is rewarding. If business is the heart of the market, growth and competition are its life blood. Yet, there are times when growth can stifle competition. For instance, in the 1960s "The Big Three" sold 92% of all the passenger cars in the United States. If competition is limited, the whole nature of the market, and perhaps the Dream, changes.

THE ACTION ZONE:
BREAKING INTO THE MARKET

It was a little on the dark side. Just one of those dismal December days that reminds you that winters are mild but very gray around here. Turning off the main highway, I caught a glimpse of a ship's mast. Near a rock outcropping, a pool of gray water reflected the clouds overhead and castle turrets. Castle turrets? A pirate ship? I wondered if I'd driven onto the back lot of a film studio.

This was *The Action Zone*. The new entertainment center was less than a year old, but very popular. Miniature golf, bumper cars, water slide, video arcade – a kids' dream of civilization. It was all there on the edge of beautiful downtown Jacksonville, North Carolina.

My name is Alex Pierce. What brought me there was a research project for my marketing class at Coastal Carolina Community College. Professor Hodges said he wanted us to find out what motivates an entrepreneur. My younger brother said his friends "spent major bucks" at *The Action Zone* this summer. Ahead was a modern white building with neon signs. Behind the building, bulldozers, jackhammers, and back hoes were chomping at layers of shale. I parked and made for the building.

Inside, it was quiet. Yet, the place was ablaze with light and color. There were video games of every size and shape. Beyond the blinking and buzzing was a snack bar. I asked the young woman behind the counter for the owner, Bonnie Wright. After getting my name, she led me through a balloon fringed party room, and we stepped outside. She pointed towards the hard hats and Caterpillar assaulting the rock. So, I walked that direction.

"They make a racket, don't they?" A young woman in slacks and a denim jacket came toward me. "Hi, I'm Bonnie Wright. How can I help you?"

"Hello, Alex Pierce," I said, extending my hand. "I called last week to see if I could interview you for a college paper, remember?"

"Oh sure. You go to Coastal, right? Have you been here before?"

"No, and this is a surprise. My mom said when she and dad were first married, they lived in those garden apartments across the road. There was nothing but a liquor store and a falling rock zone on this side. Now, I take the back roads to school, so I haven't been out on the main highway for a while. This place is amazing, and it looks like you're expanding, too."

"We didn't expect to put in the batting cages so soon, but business is booming!"

"Wait a second," I said. "We're on the same planet, aren't we? The big corporations are downsizing. Unemployment is way up. The economic recovery claims seem a myth around here – and you say business is great?"

"It is! We've nearly paid our initial construction loan. Look, let's back up a bit. I know this will sound strange, but it was the recession that started this business. Let me explain." We sat down on the back of a big green recycled-plastic tortoise bench. "In high school, I worked for a caterer. He did lawn weddings. After high school, my friend Beth and I started our own catering service. We did business lunches, office parties, and company picnics. It went well for about four years. When the recession began, companies started to cut their expenses. As our business dried up, we tried to figure what was happening. What would people spend their money on when they had less?"

"The basics – food, shelter, and clothing," I quipped.

Bonnie looked at me the way Professor Hodges does sometimes. "I believe I once read, 'Man does not live by bread alone.' Alex, no matter how bad it gets, people still want to feel alive. They want entertainment, but not expensive entertainment. We asked ourselves what people did for fun back in the Great Depression. The movies became popular, and amusement parks blossomed, but miniature golf was very hot!

"There are plenty of theaters here, but no small amusement parks. About 300 miles away, there are a few gigantic ones. But, you have to go up to Virginia or way down to Georgia. Still, that makes for half a day's ride.

"Besides, spending the day at the big parks is very expensive. From here, you spend hours traveling and bucking the crowds. You wait on lines for rides, food, and even bathrooms. Then comes the long ride home with cranky kids. It takes the fun out of the whole thing. Actually, these pleasure outings can be a pretty grueling experience for a family."

"Got it," I said. "You can offer excitement without the ride and the lines."

"Now you've really got it, Sherlock," she laughed. "Everyone likes miniature golf. We planned fountains, waterfalls, ships, and haunted houses. It is really fun. The bumper boat ride over there is another winner. Next spring, we will have the batting cages ready. What better place for a kid's birthday party? This room holds almost sixty people. Even in winter, we offer packages in the video arcade. It is very busy. In fact, we have a party this afternoon."

"Wow! How did you ever figure all this out? That is what Professor Hodges really wants us to find out. How does a business person decide to supply a service?"

"Buy me a hot dog?" Bonnie questioned. I nodded as she grabbed my arm and started walking. Without missing a beat, she continued, "Well, once Beth and I had the idea, we hit the library and found some trade organizations. They gave us information on trade shows where we talked to owners and equipment suppliers. We went on trips to the shore and the mountains. We talked to people who ran small entertainment centers. Research is part of the game.

"While we collected facts, I started talking to my dad. He has been in business for himself all his life. I guess that is where I get my independent streak. He had this piece of land, or should I say, rock?" That reminded me that it felt good to get off that tortoise shell.

"How did you know the demand was there?"

"What really sold us on the location was that we contracted for a report from a marketing consultant. A friend of Dad's at the Chamber of Commerce suggested it. It was expensive, but it said there were 40,000 people within a 5-mile radius. It also said the average age of those people was 38. That means teens, young adults, young couples, and little kids. That's an awful lot of young people in their earning years. The market was there. ... Want mustard on yours?"

"Thanks, and heap on the relish." I said, as I handed over a five-dollar bill. "Where did you get the money to get it going?"

"Family. Dad liked the idea from the start. He said he would give us part of the money for a share of the profits. He wanted to be a silent partner. Beth's Aunt Carolyn agreed to a similar arrangement. We run the business itself. ... Napkin? ... Even in the recession, our local bank agreed to take a chance and give us the rest. Of course, we had to sell them on the idea. Dad and Aunt Carolyn co-signed and put up their houses as collateral. Still, we got the money. Four million other little decisions, contracts, leases, and here we are!" She looked at my shirt. "Oops."

I looked down. "I guess I need that napkin. I'd better get this interview back on track. "Professor Hodges says enthusiasm is the entrepreneur's main weapon. You are certainly well armed, but it doesn't sound all that simple."

"It's not simple at all," Bonnie said. "You lose sleep, your stomach churns, and you always wonder if you're making the right moves."

"I know the demand is here, but ..." I said.

Bonnie raised an eyebrow. "But what?" she asked, dabbing mustard from her upper lip.

"Professor Hodges says a business person has to be satisfied with the profit margin to want to keep supplying the demand."

"Like any business, we have to cover our utilities, mortgage, business loans, supplies, and payroll for thirty workers. After all that, we are making a 5% profit."

"That doesn't sound like very much." Although what I was really thinking was they must be getting a much bigger profit on these lousy hot dogs. Of course, I didn't say it out loud.

"Some people might not be happy. Still, we see potential. Next week, we start looking for land down in Holly Ridge for *The Action Zone 2*. We are taking the profits and reinvesting. What does that tell you? Want another dog?"

On my drive home, I began to understand that a good plan is not enough to be a successful entrepreneur. It takes energy, persistence, and stick-to-it-ness. She made a profit on me, didn't she!

ISSUE 5

How do people organize in a market?

ORGANIZATION OF BUSINESS

INTRODUCTION

Owning a business is part of the American Dream. It has the values of independence and self-reliance embedded in it. The "rags-to-riches" stories made famous by 19th century writers such as **Horatio Alger** permeate our culture. Alger made a fortune publishing tales about good, hard-working souls. He elevated the idea that anyone with a dream and determination can succeed to American folklore. Of course, there is a little more to it than that. Yet, the idea has strong allure.

Producers such as Bonnie and Beth form a partnership to go into business. Bonnie and Beth supply entertainment at *The Action Zone*. Consumers respond because the entertainment is offered at a lower price

than distant, big amusement parks. The last chapter showed acceptable prices keep the whole market in equilibrium. Understanding how producers arrive at those prices is important in learning economics. So is understanding how and why people go into business. Organizing and making economic decisions is critical in a market economy. Successful merchants, manufacturers, and service businesses do not emerge randomly. Owners build them very carefully, day by day.

BASIC TYPES OF BUSINESS ORGANIZATIONS

There are three basic ways to organize a business: proprietorships, partnerships, and corporations (see Figure 5.1 on the next page). The key is who

Business Organization
Above: With many large corporations downsizing, laid-off workers are turning in record numbers to "home businesses," often as partnerships among a few former colleagues from the same firm. High tech telephone communications and powerful personal computers have reduced the need for the traditional office.

Left: Although the number of small family farms is decreasing while large corporate farms increase in size and number, there are still 2.4 million American farms. About 86% are proprietorships, 10% partnerships, and 4% corporations.

Right: The corporate structure allows for sizable national and international operations such as this meat packing firm. ©PhotoDisc

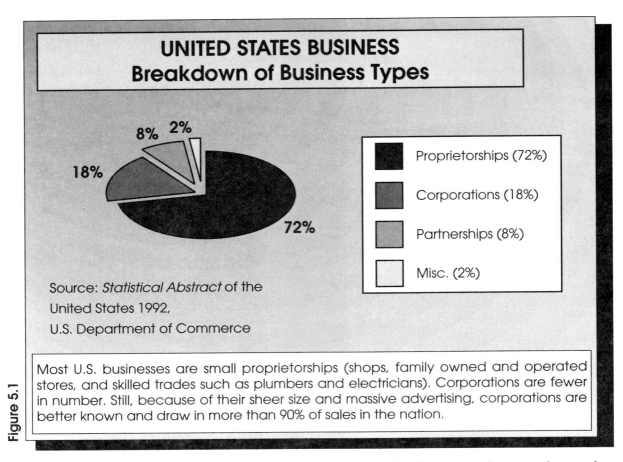

UNITED STATES BUSINESS
Breakdown of Business Types

- Proprietorships (72%)
- Corporations (18%)
- Partnerships (8%)
- Misc. (2%)

8% 2% 18% 72%

Source: *Statistical Abstract* of the United States 1992, U.S. Department of Commerce

Most U.S. businesses are small proprietorships (shops, family owned and operated stores, and skilled trades such as plumbers and electricians). Corporations are fewer in number. Still, because of their sheer size and massive advertising, corporations are better known and draw in more than 90% of sales in the nation.

Figure 5.1

owns them. **Basic business operations** (e.g., production, marketing, finance, personnel) may be delegated to salaried managers (who are employees). Still, an owner makes the life and death decisions. All of the responsibility remains in the hands of the owner(s).

PROPRIETORSHIPS

72% of all businesses. Proprietorships are unincorporated businesses owned by a single person. They are almost always small businesses: shops, groceries, restaurants, farms, gas stations. It should be noted that lawyers today advise some form of incorporation for even the smallest businesses because of the legal protection corporations afford. (Incorporation laws vary from state to state.) These incorporated businesses may still be run by one or two owners. (For purpose of discussion here, we classify businesses by *who* is making the day-to-day decisions and earns the profits.)

PARTNERSHIPS

8% of all businesses. Partnerships are unincorporated businesses owned by two or more people. There is no limit on the number of partners. Usually they are small in size, having only two or three individuals involved. Law firms and accounting offices commonly organize as partnerships. Depending on the size, the day-to-day operation may be divided up among the partners.

Alex Pierce discovered *The Action Zone* is a partnership. Bonnie Wright and friend Beth are **general partners**. They share the operating responsibilities. Bonnie's father and Beth's aunt are **limited partners** since they do not actively run the business but share the profits.

CORPORATIONS

18% of all businesses. A corporation has thousands (or even millions) of owners. In a **closed corporation**, ownership shares (stocks) are limited and privately held. In a large **public corporation**, stocks can be sold to the public through stock markets. A board of directors, acting as the elected representatives of the stockholders, sets general policy. The board hires a **CEO (Chief Executive Officer)** who assembles a management staff and conducts daily operations.

Figure 5.2	Top Fifteen U.S. Corporations	
Source: U.S. Department of Commerce, 1993		
Company	Annual Sales (in billions)	Industry
Prudential of America	$154	insurance
General Motors	$132	automobiles
Metropolitan Life	$118	insurance
Exxon	$103	petroleum
Ford	$100	automobiles
IBM	$ 65	computers
General Electric	$ 62	electronics
Teachers Insurance Annuity	$ 61	insurance
Sears, Roebuck	$ 59	retailing
Mobil	$ 57	petroleum
Wal☆Mart Stores	$ 55	retailing
Philip Morris	$ 50	food and tobacco
E. I. DuPont	$ 37	chemicals
Chevron	$ 37	petroleum
Texaco	$ 37	petroleum

The diminished legal risk makes stock investment attractive to people. Proprietorships and partnerships rest on risking the limited **personal capital** (e.g., savings, loans, gifts) and property that a few people can generate. Corporations offer an investor small risk. They can raise millions by offering thousands of inexpensive shares for sale. Shareholders earn income **dividends** (portions of the profits) for their investment.

The shareholder can sell the stocks on the market. If the company is doing well, the value of the stocks **appreciates** (rises). Selling appreciated stocks returns a profit

There are 3,000,000 corporations in the United States. Most are small with only a few stockholders. Only about 2,000 are large corporations with billion dollar assets such as those that annually make the *Forbes 1000* or *Fortune 500* lists (see Figure 5.2). They make up less than 10% of all business organizations. Yet, these large corporations generate 90% of the sales.

A key element is legal protection for owners. *A corporation exists as an individual in the eyes of the law.* It is responsible for debts and other legal problems. If the business fails, the corporation **liquidates** (sells) its assets. It pays its creditors and bond holders. Stockholders are *not liable* for any other unpaid debts. Stockholders lose only the value of their investment. Unlike proprietors and partners, their personal property is not liable.

The 1994 average composite volume of shares traded on the New York Stock Exchange was 352,288,590. These stock certificates represent public ownership shares in about 10,000 corporations with global operations ©PhotoDisc

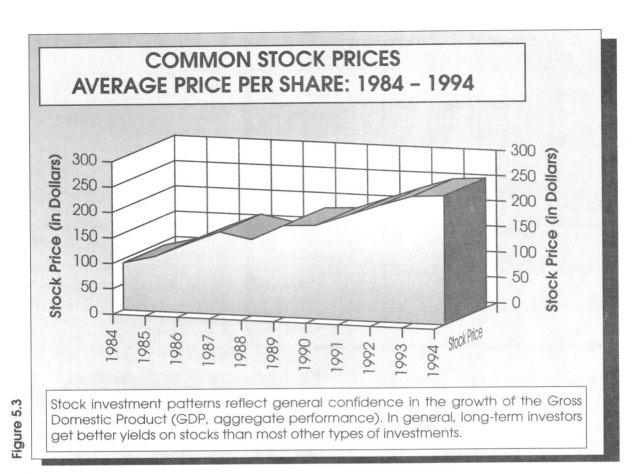

COMMON STOCK PRICES
AVERAGE PRICE PER SHARE: 1984 – 1994

Figure 5.3

Stock investment patterns reflect general confidence in the growth of the Gross Domestic Product (GDP, aggregate performance). In general, long-term investors get better yields on stocks than most other types of investments.

over the original purchase. Of course, corporations do fail, and stocks do **depreciate**. Bankruptcy can make stocks worthless. An investor has to shop carefully, read financial news, and watch stock listings to protect the investment. Figure 5.3 shows that careful investment, over long periods, yields the most impressive gains – a fact that has helped build strong public support for corporate stock investment.

Figure 5.4	Tradeoffs With Different Business Organizations	
	and the Advantages and Disadvantages of Each	
Type	**Advantages**	**Disadvantages**
Proprietorship	• owner close to customers and workers • owner receives all profits • one manager's point of view	• owner assumes all risks • limited operating capital • owner bears total responsibility for management
Partnership	• more capital can be raised • risks are shared • more management ideas	• profits must be shared • unlimited liability for owners • dissolves if one partner leaves
Corporation	• increased capital through sale of stocks • losses limited to investment • increased number of managers • can transfer ownership • larger growth possibilities • research facilities possible • risks shared	• state and federally regulated • subject to corporate taxes • management removed from customers and workers

ADVANTAGES AND DISADVANTAGES OF OWNERSHIP

The table in Figure 5.4 gives an overview of the advantages and disadvantages of the different types of businesses. Owners' goals and dreams move them toward the different types. Ease of getting capital, financial and legal liabilities, and psychic rewards define the choice.

FINANCIAL AND LEGAL LIABILITY

Proprietors usually want to support themselves and their families and be their own boss. If they run into financial or legal trouble, lawsuits could not only destroy the business, but their personal money and property can be lost, too. Partners also stand to lose everything when trouble looms. Partners share the ownership, but the liability for each partner is the same as if they were proprietors. Only in a corporation is the personal wealth and property of owners separated from that of the business.

CAPITAL FORMATION

When it comes to getting money to start or expand a business, there are great differences among the business types. Proprietors and partners stake their personal wealth and property to get capital. A proprietor in need of operating or expansion funds stands alone before the banker. In a partnership, the banks can look at the creditworthiness and collateral of several individuals. Their collective credit and property give them a greater chance for funding. Yet, partners are still limited to their personal ability to raise funds.

Capital formation is one of the big advantages for corporations. They get start-up funds from many stockholders investing small amounts of money. There are regulations on how much stock can be put on the market, but corporations can get capital two other ways: borrowing and bonds. Unlike proprietors, large corporations are not at the mercy of local banks. They can put together loan packages from many sources, perhaps nationwide. Also, corporations can sell bonds on the market. Individuals or institutions (pension funds, insurance companies) buy these **corporate bonds**. Bondholders lend corporations money at interest for a short period. They become creditors of the corporation. If the corporation fails, bondholders must be legally paid just like banks. Stockholders in a bankrupt corporation suffer the loss of the value of their investment, but not the bondholders.

PSYCHOLOGICAL REWARDS

Beyond financial gain, there is a powerful attraction in the emotional compensation an owner-operator receives. For many, owning a business is part of the American Dream. The independence and self-reliance attract them. Some individuals thrive on the constant challenge of "making it" alone. They enjoy being free to make their own decisions. They find satisfaction building a business. They enjoy being in control of their destiny. These are **psychological rewards**.

Psychological rewards (also called psychic rewards) obviously motivate sole proprietors. In partnerships, they are less important. Individuals form partnerships to grow, take advantage of broader capital formation, or to diminish the work load. Yet, partners give up some control and independence in the process.

Individuals who own shares of corporations receive few, if any, psychic rewards. Unless they are on the board of directors, they make no decisions. Stockholders receive financial rewards (dividends), but no noticeable psychic ones.

FRANCHISES

Among the fastest growing businesses in today's market are franchises (see Figure 5.5 on the next page). They are an interesting mix of the three basic types. By definition, a franchise is a license to conduct a business under another person's name. A large franchising corporation

Top 15 U.S. Franchisers (based on number of units in operation, 1993)	
Company	**Product**
Subway	submarine sandwiches
7-Eleven	convenience store
Jani-King	commercial cleaning
Burger King	hamburgers
Dunkin Donuts	doughnuts
McDonald's	hamburgers
Coverall North America, Inc.	commercial cleaning
CleanNet	commercial cleaning
Little Caesar's	pizza
Mail Boxes Etc.	mailing and shipping services
Chem Dry	carpet and upholstery cleaning
Domino's	pizza
O.P.E.N. Cleaning Systems	commercial cleaning
Miracle Ear	health care equipment
Choice Hotels International	hotels and motels

Figure 5.5

(e.g., fast food giants McDonald's, Subway Sandwiches, Burger King) grants a franchisee permission to market its products. A franchisee could be a sole proprietor, a group of partners, or another corporation. Franchise sizes vary. One might be a large undertaking such as a group of Holiday Inns; another might be a small door-to-door operation such as Avon cosmetics.

The franchisee runs the business and gets many of the psychic rewards and most of the profits. Yet, there is a difference. The franchisee is not independent. Psychological rewards are limited. The franchise agreement is a contract to do things the franchisor's way. It sets very definite rules on operations. In many cases, no other products can be offered except the franchisor's. The franchisor requires certain equipment, building designs, uniforms, supplies, operating hours, promotions, and periodic inspections. On the other hand, the franchisee gets nationally known brands, national advertising, mortgages, training, and legal advice. Economists estimate that nearly one half of all business starts are now through national franchises.

GROWTH: MERGERS AND COMBINATIONS

No matter which form of business, growth is a common goal. Proprietors usually wish to increase their profits by offering new products or services. Growth may mean hiring new employ-

ees, moving to a bigger shop, or staying open later. Still, proprietors bump into limits. There is just so much one owner/operator can do. Also, there is a limit on a single owner's ability to raise capital.

People form partnerships to overcome some of these limits. Additional owners mean management tasks can be shared, or additional sites can be opened. Additional owners also means expanded capacity to form capital. Even so, there are limits on the capacities of partners, too.

Corporations have the greatest capacity to grow. Their potential to raise capital is clear. They can grow by merging with other corporations. A **merger** takes place when one company acquires (buys) another or when two join to form a new company. Mergers enable corporations to expand from local, to regional, to state, national, or even international scope. There are several types of mergers or combinations. Economists classify mergers as horizontal, vertical, and conglomerate (see Figure 5.6).

HORIZONTAL MERGERS

The **horizontal merger** is the most logical type: one corporation combines with – or takes over – another in the *same* industry. For example, Chrysler bought American Motors in the early 1980s. The Jeep and Eagle vehicle lines and production facilities were added to the Chrysler line. A historic example is John D. Rockefeller building the Standard Oil Corporation by buying up competing oil refining companies. These were horizontal mergers because the companies were all engaged in similar business activities.

VERTICAL MERGERS

A second type is a **vertical merger**: in which a corporation buys another in a *related phase* of its business. This saves money and adds to productivity. In the 19th century, Andrew Carnegie built the Carnegie Steel

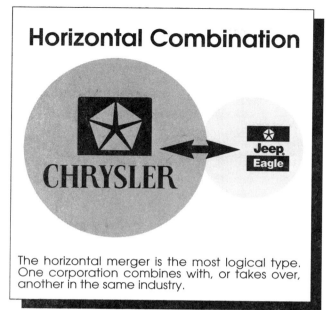

Horizontal Combination

The horizontal merger is the most logical type. One corporation combines with, or takes over, another in the same industry.

Vertical Combination

A second way to combine is through a vertical merger. In this case, a corporation may buy another in a related phase of its business.

Figure 5.6

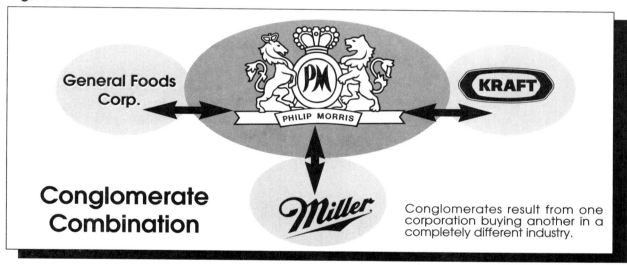

Conglomerate Combination

General Foods Corp.

Conglomerates result from one corporation buying another in a completely different industry.

Corporation by buying mines (ore supplies) and railroads (cut costs of shipping ore to his steel mills). Vertical mergers combine operations that go into making the main product. In 1981, DuPont (petrochemicals) enhanced its production capacities by buying Conoco, then the 13th largest U.S. petroleum refiner for $8 billion.

CONGLOMERATE MERGERS

Traditional horizontal and vertical combinations are easy to see. They are logical building blocks that allow corporations to grow to enormous size. The third type, a **conglomerate merger**, is not as logical. Conglomerates result from one corporation buying another in a *completely different* industry. *Corporation X* buys *Corporation Y* to add to its financial assets and

overall profits. *X* may absorb *Y* completely, or *X* may allow *Y* to operate independently as a **subsidiary** with *X* simply taking *Y's* profits.

Companies do this to broaden profits through **diversification**. In 1989, when *TIME* Inc. saw its growth in publications slowing, it ventured into another field. It diversified by buying motion picture giant Warner Communications for $14 billion. *TIME*-Warner became a new conglomerate.

Diversification helps a corporation insulate itself from the ups and downs of its main market. By the 1980s, U.S. tobacco sales were in serious decline. In 1986, tobacco giant Philip Morris spent $5 billion to acquire General Foods. In 1989, PM spent $13 billion to acquire

Kraft Foods. In between, it bought Miller Brewing Co. Through conglomerate mergers, PM quickly became one of the largest tobacco, food, and beverage corporations in the world.

Critics charge that conglomerate mergers do little to help the economy grow. Borrowing for mergers adds to the purchasing corporation's debt. It uses scarce capital that could have been used to improve its productivity. Conglomerate mergers may add to the profits of a purchasing corporation, but they do not expand production or add jobs. In fact, purchasing companies commonly downsize their new subsidiaries.

COMPETING IN DIFFERENT MARKET STRUCTURES

The mechanics of supply and demand were studied in Issue 4. Supply and demand do make markets run, but market structures vary. The nature of products, ease of entry, and the number of firms in a particular market alter the behavior of competitors. For example, Bonnie's *The Action Zone* offers consumers an alternative amusement to a long ride to big parks. PepsiCo drives to beat Coca-Cola. Ford strives for quality. Big or small, businesses compete with others. There are few exceptions to this fact of economic life. To survive and grow, owner/managers must know their market and be aware of competitor's moves.

Competition takes many forms. Price is the first form that comes to mind. Producers seek ways to offer a product at a lower price to lure customers away from other firms. Still, there are other forms of competition. **Nonprice competition** includes promotions, packaging, sponsorships, quality, and service.

Figure 5.7 illustrates the four basic market structures. Ranging from most competitive to least competitive, they are: perfect competition, imperfect competition, oligopoly, and monopoly.

PERFECT COMPETITION

Perfect Competition is the basic theoretical model studied earlier in Issue 4. The products are identical and easy to produce. Raw agricultural products such as wheat, corn, and oats are examples. There are many sellers and

Although *Perfect Competition* does not really exist in a "non-perfect" economy, the concept of perfect competition can be demonstrated in the farmer's market or the thousands and thousands of small roadside produce stands where competition is high, product is abundant and similar from stand to stand, and where overhead is low, so are the profits. ©PhotoDisc

buyers. The interaction of supply and demand sets the price. Price competition is so intense that there is little nonprice competition (e.g., advertising, location, contests). Sellers cannot afford it.

IMPERFECT COMPETITION

Imperfect Competition is also close to the basic supply and demand model. The products are very similar and relatively easy to produce. Firms are often small operations such as hair cutting, dry cleaning, restaurants, and clothing factories. There are many sellers and buyers in this market structure. For the most part, interaction of supply and demand sets the price. Price competition through sales is intense, but there is some nonprice competition. This

Commonly, *Imperfect Competition* is illustrated in the business practices that exist among small entrepreneurial shops. However, this market structure is easily observed at the thousands of "strips" that guard the entrances and exits of the interstate highway system, in suburban mini-malls, and at the outer limits of cities and towns all over America. ©PhotoDisc

TYPES OF MARKET STRUCTURES

Figure 5.7

Perfect Competition

Many Small Sellers / Many Buyers

Identical products;
little nonprice competition;
market sets prices.

Imperfect Competition

Many Small Sellers / Many Buyers

Slightly different products;
Strong nonprice competition;
sellers have some control of prices.

Oligopoly

Few Large & Some Small Sellers
/ Many Buyers

Slightly different products;
strong nonprice competition;
sellers have some control of prices.

Monopoly

Single Seller / Many Buyers

Unique products;
no substitutes;
no competition;
seller sets prices.

includes advertising, contests, coupons, convenient location and hours, free parking, etc. Competitors spend time and energy making their business distinct from others.

(Note: Economists also refer to this structure as "monopolistic competition." The term is a bit confusing for students. It refers to the fact that there is *one basic product* in this market, but the competition among many suppliers is intense.)

Bonnie and partners' *The Action Zone* mini amusement complex fits into this type of market. She competes not only with other small entertainment facilities, but also with big, far off complexes. In addition, she must position herself as an alternative to other entertainment businesses such as movies.

OLIGOPOLY

Oligopoly is where the basic market model radically changes. In this market structure, the products are similar, but production is complex, large-scale, and expensive. This market includes athletic shoes, autos, beers, breakfast cereals, chemicals, soft drinks, electric appliances, and petroleum refining. These expensive, highly mechanized, high tech industries, are not easy to enter. Therefore, the number of suppliers is very limited. While supply and demand do influence the price, sellers are so few and so big, they have the power to alter supply.

Today's oligopoly markets are like "shared monopolies." Producers are not big enough to dictate prices, but they control a substantial percent of sales. They keep within range of their competitors with products so that price competition is often minimal. No one wants to "break out of the pack" for fear a price war would ruin them. Oligopolists usually solidify their "market share turf" and go along with the other oligopolies.

Yet, oligopolists employ fierce and expensive non-price competition to protect their market shares. Their advertising aims at creating brand name loyalty in consumers' minds to keep long-time customers. Ads do not always mention price, but they tout quality, performance, image, and comparisons.

Does the brand loyalty approach work? Announce loudly in a group of friends that one manufacturer's cola drink is "the best," and the arguments can last for hours. Friends can be lost. Whole families pride themselves on buying Pepsi and never consider any other brand. The products have to be similar for competitors to stay in business. Yet, Pepsi and Coke spend millions on ads and promotions to convince cola drinkers that their product has no equal.

MONOPOLY

Monopoly is the absence of competition. In a pure (unregulated) monopoly, there is just one seller. The lone firm can act as an economic dictator. The product is singular (no substitutes), and many people need it. The monopoly can completely control quantity available (supply). It can charge any price it wishes. Competition is undercut before it can get on its feet.

It should be obvious that a monopoly undermines the basis of a free market. Monopolies eliminate consumer choice. Without competition, they become inefficient. They are not motivated to grow or improve the product. Adam Smith saw them as a great evil capable of destroying a market economy (*Wealth of Nations*, 1776). In the Progressive Era, the U.S. Congress became convinced monopolies were ruinous to economic freedom. It tried to control them with the weak **Sherman Antitrust Act** (1890) and followed up with the stronger **Clayton Antitrust Act** (1914). The Antitrust Division of the United States Justice Department prosecutes violations. In 1914, Congress also set up the Federal Trade Commission. The FTC also investigates unfair competition.

Since their inceptions, public utilities such as electric, telephone, and cable TV have been government regulated *monopolies*. With the breakup of AT&T, regulated competition in the utilities began. ©PhotoDisc

Yet, the government does allow some monopolies. Local phone service, cable TV, and electric companies are examples. Their services are critical. Common sense shows hundreds of utility companies constantly stringing and unstringing wires would be dangerous and chaotic. Therefore, local, state, and Federal agencies license and control these monopolies. They must ask permission from government agencies (public service commissions) to raise rates or alter production. (See Issue 12 for details on antitrust suits.)

SUMMARY

The modern market economy is a complex place. Owning and operating a business is a challenge. A business owner has to set goals and select a type of organization to achieve them. They have to understand what kind of market structure they enter, and how to compete in it. Bonnie Wright and partners launched *The Action Zone* in an imperfect competition market structure. Consumers can choose from many other entertainment facilities, small and large. Bonnie and Beth put ads in the paper, circulated coupons, and ran promotions. They selected a high traffic area. Still, they needed a colorful, lighted sign and the mansions, ships, and castles of their miniature golf course to beckon consumers from the road.

Demand patterns change. Competitors come up with new ways to lure customers away. Organizing a business and competing in an ever changing market is no easy way to make a living. Yet, it is an exciting and essential part of the American Dream. If people did not venture into business as a natural part of the American Dream, from where would products and jobs come?

The high tech industries such as computer hardware and software are dominated by a few companies. For many years IBM "owned" the computer industry. When PCs began replacing the mainframes, Apple and others increased competition. In 1995, 70+% of all PCs worldwide were running on an operating system and software developed by Microsoft. While attempting to contain the growth of this giant through an antitrust suit, *U.S. of America v. Microsoft Corporation*, Judge Sporkin said in reference to the proposed $1.5 billion purchase of financial giant Intuit, makers of *Quicken* (accounting software), "it is a potential threat to the nation's economic well-being." "(If he allowed it) the message will be that Microsoft is so powerful that neither the market nor the Government is capable of dealing with all its monopolistic practices." ©PhotoDisc

ASSESSMENT
QUESTIONS • APPLICATIONS

1   In the opening story, college student Alex Pierce interviewed Bonnie Wright for a report on entrepreneurs.
    a   List some main points you think Alex would include in his report.
    b   What other ideas about entrepreneurs would you advise Alex to add to his report?
    c   Why would Professor Hodges assign a report such as this to someone beginning a study of economics?

2   The opening story's dialogue between Alex Pierce and Bonnie Wright demonstrates that all businesses must engage in several activities. They include production, marketing, finance, and personnel management.
    a   Using the four categories of business activities, list examples of Bonnie performing these functions.
    b   Besides the examples you found in the story, what are some other activities Bonnie would have to perform to start and maintain her business?
    c   Which activities are most important for a new business? Explain your choices.

3   One way to go into business today is to buy a franchise. Suppose you were considering a franchise. Pick one of those listed in this Issue or another one that interests you.
    a   Investigate buying the franchise. Get some facts. Contact the franchisor in writing or by phone.
    b   Make a list of advantages and disadvantages. Would you go into this business? Explain your decision.

4   Corporate combinations allow tremendous growth in some markets.
    a   What are some advantages and disadvantages to producers of having large corporations merge?
    b   What are some advantages and disadvantages to consumers of having large corporations merge?
    c   Mergers often allow corporations to survive in oligopolistic markets. Explain why. Is there any danger in oligopolistic mergers?

5   Think about the meaning of free enterprise. The different market structures studied in this chapter show that not every business operates under the same rules.
    a   Do monopoly market structures violate the idea of free enterprise? Explain your opinion. Is it fair for the government to make a monopoly break up?
    b   Some economists call oligopolies "shared monopolies." Do oligopoly market structures violate the idea of free enterprise? Explain your opinion.
    c   Suppose two camera companies take years to build themselves into giant firms controlling 70% of all sales in the country. Is it fair for the government to sue to break these companies up? Is the government interfering with their freedom, or are they interfering with small entrepreneurs trying to create new camera companies? Explain your opinion.

6   There are four basic market structures.
    a   Identify the four and name a product or service your household purchases from each.
    b   Explain the differences among the four types.

ASSESSMENT PROJECT: "PRE-STARTING" A BUSINESS

This project can be completed in one of the following business types:
- Proprietorship (one student)
- Partnership (two students)
- Corporation (small group of students)

STUDENT TASK

Become an entrepreneur; brainstorm and research your idea for a business. Then, design a plan for starting that business. This is not a formal "Business Plan"; instead, it is an exercise that realistically addresses the questions: What's involved? How much does it cost? Where will I secure the funding? How, when, and where do I get started? Will I need employees? What kind and how many?

PROCEDURE

1   Select a type of small business that interests you. Keep in mind the following: the community needs and resources, local competition, funding possibilities (family assistance, private, commercial, or public), type of business (proprietorship, partnership, or corporation).

2   Write a plan for setting up your business. Include:
- a list of personal goals
- a description of the business (what it does, location, legal status [permits, regulations], equipment needed)
- description of the market, competition, and a marketing plan
- projections of start-up and normal operating costs
- projections of net income and profit

- explanation of how management functions will be done
- description of personnel, try to write the plan so that a potential backer would want to lend you money to reach your goal. Include of list of sources used to guide you in making the plan.

3   Develop an implementation calendar, a month-by-month listing of actions to be taken, while assembling the resources needed for your business.

4   Make a summary analysis of your plan, being a specific as is possible. Answer the questions listed above in the Student Task part of this Project.

LEARNING STANDARDS

Learners should be able to:

(1)   understand that while different socioeconomic (as well as national, ethnic, religious, racial, and gender) groups have varied perspectives, values, and diverse practices and traditions, they face the same global economic challenges.

(5)   analyze problems and evaluate decisions about the economic effects on society and the individual caused by human, technological, and natural activities.

(6)   present their ideas both in writing and orally in clear, concise, and properly accepted fashion.

(7)   employ a variety of information from written, graphic, and multimedia sources.

(8)   monitor, reflect upon, and improve their own and others' work.

(9)   work cooperatively and show respect for the rights of others to think, act, and speak differently from themselves within the context of democratic principles and social justice.

EVALUATION

The criteria for the evaluation of this project are itemized in the grid (rubric on next page) that follows. Choice of appropriate category terms (values) is the decision of the instructor. Selection of terms such as "minimal," "satisfactory," and "distinguished" can vary with each assessment.

One-Year Business Plan Evaluation Rubric

(Refer to introductory section for suggestions of scoring descriptors for the evaluation categories.)

Evaluation Item	Category 1	Category 2	Category 3	Category 4	Category 5
Item a: (1) Does the business plan show understanding that while different socioeconomic (as well as national, ethnic, religious, racial, and gender) groups have varied perspectives, values, and diverse practices and traditions, they face the same global economic challenges?					
Item b: (5) Does the business plan analyze problems and evaluate decisions about the economic effects caused by human, technological, and natural activities on societies and individuals?					
Item c: (6) Does the business plan present ideas in writing (and orally) in clear, concise, and properly accepted fashion?					
Item d: (7) Does the business plan employ a variety of information from written, graphic, and multimedia sources?					
Item e: (8) Does the business plan show monitoring of, reflection upon, and improvement of work?					
Item f: (9) Does the work business plan show cooperative work and respect for the rights of others to think, act, and speak differently?					

ISSUE 6

Can workers survive?

LABOR AND THE CHANGING WORKFORCE

CAUTION

laser light

OPERATION OF LASERS REQUIRES USING COMMON
SENSE. AS WITH OTHER BRIGHT LIGHTS. DO NOT
STARE DIRECTLY INTO BEAM.

INC. GRAND RAPIDS, MICHIGAN 49506

NOT HIRING

CREW ALREADY HIRED

"... From 1980 to 1993, the five hundred largest U.S. manufacturing corporations cut payrolls by 4.7 million jobs – a reduction of more than 25 percent. We are not witnessing a temporary blip caused by the business cycle."

– Mortimer Zuckerman, "The Glass is Half Full"
U.S. News & World Report, 27 Feb. 1995, p. 80

LABOR
AND THE AMERICAN DREAM

"...They never told us what was real..."

The song opens with a blaring whistle, the kind once sounded in industrial towns when a shift ended. It is a sound reminiscent of the booming success of textile mills, car manufacturing plants, and the great steel mills of the past. Billy Joel's *Allentown* first creates an image of people going to work, giving an honest day's labor for an honest wage. Then, it shifts the listener to images of deserted factories and mills.

"Well, we're living here in Allentown, and they're closing all the factories down. Out in Bethlehem, they're killing time, filling out forms, standing in lines."

It is a familiar theme of melancholy – wistful memories of another generation living the American Dream accompanied by anguished disillusion.

"While our fathers fought the Second World War — spent their weekends on the Jersey Shore ... But the restlessness was handed down, and it's getting very hard to stay!"

There is wrenching frustration in the song. It lashes out at those who nurtured the Dream but had no answers when the Dream began to fade.

"All the promises our teachers gave – if we work hard, and we behaved. So the graduations hang on the wall, but they never really helped us at all, because they never told us what was real ... but they've taken all of the coal from the ground, and the union people go away."

The bitter tone builds on the misery of young people caught in an economic debacle which robbed a generation of a future.

"Every child had a pretty good shot to get as far as their old man got, but something happened on the way to that place they threw a ... right in our face."

Amidst the despondency, there seems to be hint of hope that moving away might be the answer – the eternal hope is that there is still a place where the Dream can be recaptured.

"Well, I'm living here in Allentown, and its hard to keep a good man down, but I won't be getting up today. It's getting very hard to stay and live here in Allentown."

Yet, is the American Dream an impossible dream in towns where tens of thousands of people are being "surplused," "downsized," and just plain "let go"? Or could it simply be time is needed to recover, retrain, reeducate, and find different routes to the same goals?

ISSUE 6

Can workers survive?

LABOR AND THE CHANGING WORKFORCE

INTRODUCTION

Is the American Dream an impossible dream in towns where tens of thousands of people are being "surplused," "downsized," and just plain "let go"? Or could it simply be a time to recover, retrain, reeducate, and find different routes to the economic goals?

JOB SECURITY IS ELUSIVE

Hard work has always meant advancement in the workplace. The ethic of doing one's best led to promotions and a better life for one's family. But, something has happened to that belief (see side bar on opposite page on downsizing). As hard as it may be to accept, it is possible that a company struggling to compete in the marketplace must adjust to survive. This often means workers lose their jobs. However, many economists suggest that something is wrong when a company such as Proctor & Gamble, making considerable profits, decides to dismiss 40,000 workers to broaden its profit margins and dividends. Where is the concern for those employees that have helped create the corporate profits?

Lifetime job security was once an accepted tradition in this country. Many companies attached a great value to their workers. Now, after the massive layoffs of the early 1990s, most companies say they see little new hiring in the 1990s. They claim they must make staff reductions and strive for higher efficiency with those who remain. Good or bad, it is a trend in all kinds of companies, big, small, and everywhere between. The industrialized world has producers striving for higher productivity, struggling with cutthroat competition, and adopting technological changes. All this makes jobs the centerpiece of economic, political, and social debate. It does not matter which side one approaches the world's jobless woes – it is getting worse. *Newsweek*'s Scott Sullivan says we are "…squandering our people" as millions of unemployed cannot find work while millions more work on temporary status in jobs that offer no benefits (14 June 1993, 46).

Sullivan proposes that economists and policy makers consider this: "What if there really were no more jobs than we have right now? What if the increasing unemployment of the last 20 years presaged (foreshadowed) a long period in which it would be cheaper for developed countries to keep half or more of their citizens jobless from cradle to grave?" He observes that "… with the most persistent unemployment in modern times, the possibility of a society not based on work as we know it remains a bold and mostly discounted hypothesis." (Sullivan. 47) Yet, what options are there?

The above sign was too often seen during the mid-1990s as major corporations downsized producing a "trickle down" effect of more job layoffs from secondary businesses. ©PhotoDisc

THE CHANGING NATURE OF WORK

The song *Allentown* presents the changing nature of the workplace in the world today. If the workplace changes, so must the worker. As a factor of production, human resources must not only be preserved, they must be helped if future generations are to have their "piece of the pie." Tough global competition inspires rapid technological change. That creates high productivity but fewer jobs. Increasing unemployment and insecurity haunt the world's most prosperous nations. It appears the only salvation for workers is training.

This is not a new situation. By the mid-1800s the nature of work changed markedly. Before the Industrial Revolution, America did not have large-scale unemployment. On farms and in small shops, workers labored hard and did most operations by hand, but they directly provided for their families. With factory work and division of labor, the Industrial Revolution created great urban markets that separated the worker from the customer. An economic and social insecurity arose not much different from that which we face today. The small business, with easily predictable markets, gave way to firms that mass-produced for both domestic and foreign markets with no guaranteed sales.

Of course, mechanization made it easier to produce more, and surpluses meant growth. How bad could that be? As with most major movements in human existence, the Industrial Revolution had positive and negative effects. There were surpluses, and they did improve the standard of living. Still, large-scale producers risked fortunes to outstrip their competition. They overproduced, creating gigantic surpluses that led to periodic price declines and, eventually, unemployment. Small businesses suffered and societies went through wrenching changes. For the first time, societies went through protracted recessions and depressions. Factory workers lacked control over their livelihood. Their entire existence hinged on decisions made in corporate offices by unseen management and owners. The Dream seemed more elusive than when Americans struggled in a less high tech and agrarian society.

DOWNSIZING AND THE FUTURE OF WORK

The recent wave of corporate downsizing has done more than swell the ranks of the retired and the unemployed. The restructuring of America's large corporations has changed the nature of careers and advancement inside their walls. According to *Newsweek* financial columnist Jane Bryant Quinn, people are bumping into barriers and ceilings in their careers much earlier and at much younger ages than in the past. "Almost everyone stalls eventually, but the unrest seems more general today. Able boomers, "thirty-somethings," ready for promotion, see jobs above them being snuffed. With few places to go they are topping out younger and at lower levels than they expected. Older generations weren't stopped until they reached their late 40s." (Quinn. "A Generation Topped Out." *Newsweek.* 20 September 1993, 42)

"Downsized companies need to think about how to encourage talent that can no longer advance," writes Quinn. She says more enlightened corporations are looking at two ways to do this. The first is lateral transfers to broaden employees' experience that can offer challenges and also avoid burn-out. She says, "Some 60 large companies now do without the traditional career ladder completely. Take General Electric. It used to have twenty-nine well defined professional pay grades ... it has replaced them with six occupational bands with varying levels of responsibility (Quinn. 42)."

A second way of encouraging talent is performance pay. This may be the most fundamental change that will affect the future of work in America. Raises will no longer come at regular intervals or by individual effort. Companies will reward teams of workers as they innovate new production techniques. Quinn says, "Twenty-one percent of firms in a recent survey give workers more incentive pay – like $2000 each to a team that launches a new product on time (Quinn. 42)."

In this respect, downsizing places added emphasis on the need for greater job skills. The old rules of career advancement through individual effort have changed. Individuals have to have talent for cooperative problem-solving and decision-making.

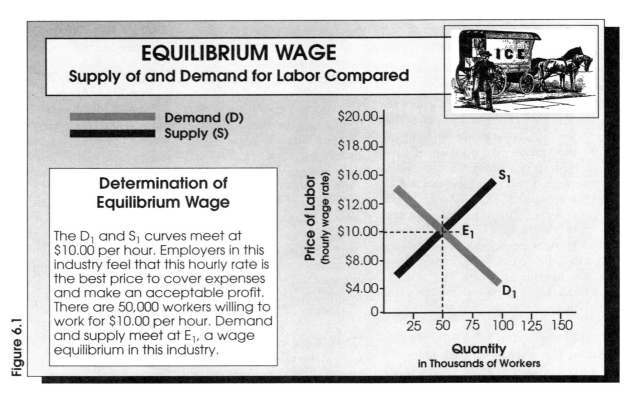

EQUILIBRIUM WAGE
Supply of and Demand for Labor Compared

████████████ **Demand (D)**
████████████ **Supply (S)**

Figure 6.1

Determination of Equilibrium Wage

The D_1 and S_1 curves meet at $10.00 per hour. Employers in this industry feel that this hourly rate is the best price to cover expenses and make an acceptable profit. There are 50,000 workers willing to work for $10.00 per hour. Demand and supply meet at E_1, a wage equilibrium in this industry.

Price of Labor (hourly wage rate)

$20.00 $18.00 $16.00 $14.00 $12.00 $10.00 $8.00 $4.00 0

S_1 E_1 D_1

25 50 75 100 125 150

Quantity
in Thousands of Workers

Although all this seems natural today, it was new a century ago. We are used to workers losing jobs through factors beyond their control. Still, time has not made it any easier on the individual. Workers fear a lack of demand for the products they produce. It always means suffering. With their skills not in demand unless their industry recovers, workers have only one other option – to learn a new set of skills. Imperfect as it is, this is the only survival option. The issue of the changing nature of work has to be confronted.

WHAT IS LABOR?

There comes a time when everyone has to go out and earn a living. In economic terms, when that happens, a person becomes a factor of production – a human resource. He or she places an ability to produce in the market. The worker offers time, education, and skills for wages and benefits.

Like everything in the market, the forces of supply and demand decide how well the sale of a person's labor goes. The **demand for labor** is how many workers companies want to hire at different **wage rates** (amount one gets paid for one's labor), as shown on curve D_1 of Figure 6.1.

As the demand for a product changes, so does the demand for the labor that produces it. Economists call the demand for labor a **derived demand** – demand for labor depends on aggregate consumer demand in a market (see Figure 6.2).

Demand for workers for the cold, remote North Slope pipeline in Alaska led the employer to offer wages at 200 to 300 percent above the national average wage for oil field workers. Figure 6.3 shows demand for labor "shifting to the right." In this situation, the shift from curve D_1 to curve D_2 means more workers are needed by industry at every wage level.

The more consumers buy of what labor makes, the better off workers are. On the other hand, if consumer demand shrinks, workers' jobs and wages are at risk.

The market for labor is also dependent on workers' ability to be productive. **Labor productivity** refers to how much profit a worker creates for an employer. Employers commonly ask:

- Is the amount of money workers are paid going to come back into the company plus a bit more?

- Does the worker's effort enhance the company's income to go beyond the cost of production?

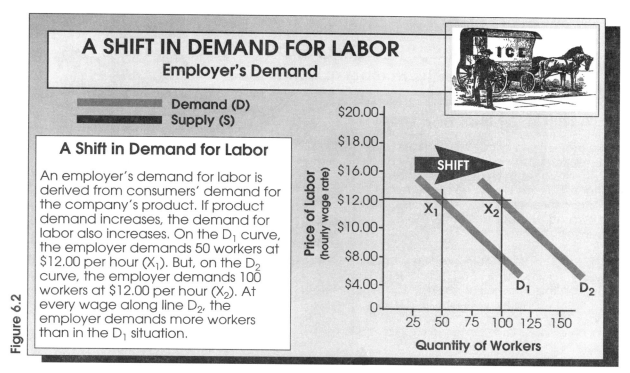

A SHIFT IN DEMAND FOR LABOR
Employer's Demand

■ Demand (D)
■ Supply (S)

A Shift in Demand for Labor

An employer's demand for labor is derived from consumers' demand for the company's product. If product demand increases, the demand for labor also increases. On the D_1 curve, the employer demands 50 workers at $12.00 per hour ($X_1$). But, on the D_2 curve, the employer demands 100 workers at $12.00 per hour ($X_2$). At every wage along line D_2, the employer demands more workers than in the D_1 situation.

Figure 6.2

In order for an employer to succeed, the business must support this formula:

REVENUES minus (–) **COSTS** equals (=) **PROFITS**

Profits lead to expansion of production, which is necessary for job security. Labor productivity, joined with capital, increases the quantity and quality of supply. That generally means growth.

WHAT LABOR FACES TODAY

The **labor force** is made up of people over 16 years of age who have employment or are seeking it. As a member of this labor force, a young person now has to deal with very different situations than past generations. Modern technology replaces human labor at a very rapid pace. Robotics is a prime example. Once placed

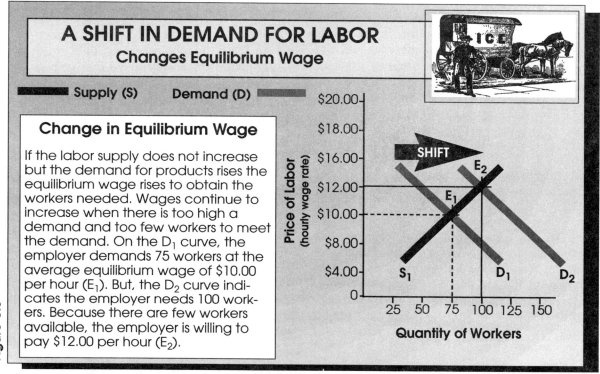

A SHIFT IN DEMAND FOR LABOR
Changes Equilibrium Wage

■ Supply (S)   **Demand (D) ■**

Change in Equilibrium Wage

If the labor supply does not increase but the demand for products rises the equilibrium wage rises to obtain the workers needed. Wages continue to increase when there is too high a demand and too few workers to meet the demand. On the D_1 curve, the employer demands 75 workers at the average equilibrium wage of $10.00 per hour ($E_1$). But, the D_2 curve indicates the employer needs 100 workers. Because there are few workers available, the employer is willing to pay $12.00 per hour ($E_2$).

Figure 6.3

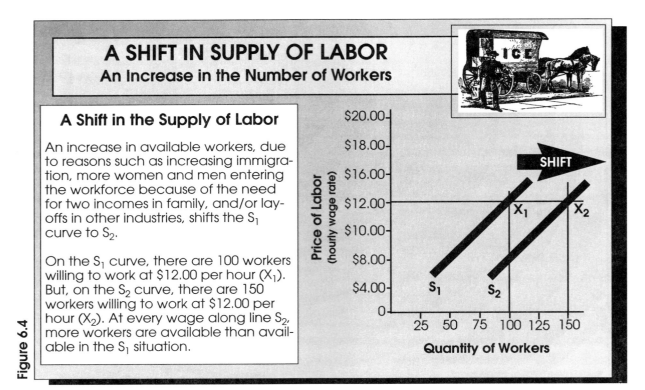

A SHIFT IN SUPPLY OF LABOR
An Increase in the Number of Workers

A Shift in the Supply of Labor

An increase in available workers, due to reasons such as increasing immigration, more women and men entering the workforce because of the need for two incomes in family, and/or lay-offs in other industries, shifts the S_1 curve to S_2.

On the S_1 curve, there are 100 workers willing to work at $12.00 per hour ($X_1$). But, on the S_2 curve, there are 150 workers willing to work at $12.00 per hour ($X_2$). At every wage along line S_2, more workers are available than available in the S_1 situation.

Figure 6.4

on an assembly line, these machines do not have to be relieved for "coffee breaks." They do not call in sick. They do not threaten their employer with strikes or slowdowns. They do not require health insurance, and they never complain about safety and working conditions.

Today's workers need more education than those of a generation ago. As technology and cheaper labor in other countries take manufacturing jobs, more education is critical. Employers do not want to expend large sums of money to train new workers. Today's workers must get the schooling necessary to compete on their own with the others in the labor market.

Career employment will be very different in the coming generation. Twenty years ago, workers retired from life-long jobs. To remain employed or seek advancement, today's worker must switch jobs several times. (Experts predict 10 to 12 switches on the average.)

If regional and global trends such as the European Union and NAFTA continue, political borders may no longer be economic barriers to immigration. People will freely cross national boundaries seeking employment wherever they can find it. It could increase the number of workers in the U.S. labor market. This could shift the supply curve of labor to the right (see Figure 6.4).

If the supply of labor shifts right, but demand for labor remains constant, Figure 6.5 shows the equilibrium wage drops (E_1 to E_2). This increase in the labor force makes competition for the few jobs more intense.

Demand for products triggers employers' demand for more workers. If the number of workers remains the same and the demand for the goods increases, Figure 6.3 (on the previous page) shows that the equilibrium wage will rise (E_1 to E_2). The imbalance of supply of labor and demand for labor may drive the average wage up or down in a certain field.

LABOR UNIONS: WORKERS' SELF–DEFENSE

Unionism simply means workers **organizing** (joining with other workers) to protect their employment and improve their lot in life. Forms of unionism can be traced back to the Middle Ages and the formation of guilds. In this country, various skilled workers came together in trade organizations early in our history.

Yet, it was not until the heavy industrialization of the late 1800s that brought national action to create labor unions. In 1869, a national organization effort began with the **Knights of Labor** seeking to create one big union for all

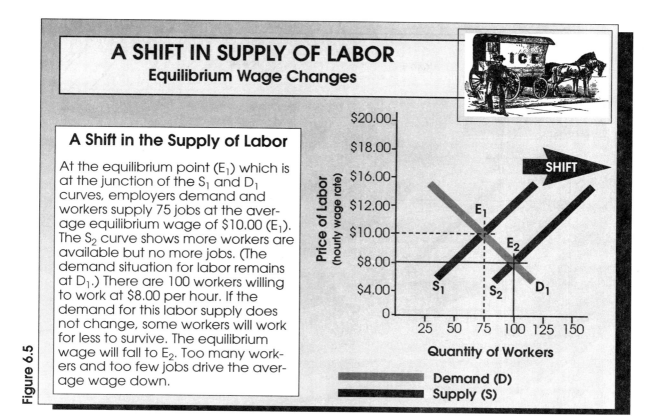

A SHIFT IN SUPPLY OF LABOR
Equilibrium Wage Changes

A Shift in the Supply of Labor

At the equilibrium point (E_1) which is at the junction of the S_1 and D_1 curves, employers demand and workers supply 75 jobs at the average equilibrium wage of $10.00 ($E_1$). The S_2 curve shows more workers are available but no more jobs. (The demand situation for labor remains at D_1.) There are 100 workers willing to work at $8.00 per hour. If the demand for this labor supply does not change, some workers will work for less to survive. The equilibrium wage will fall to E_2. Too many workers and too few jobs drive the average wage down.

Figure 6.5

Price of Labor (hourly wage rate)

Quantity of Workers

Demand (D)
Supply (S)

workers. By 1886, it reached its peak with a membership of 700,000 workers. In that year, the Knights were involved in a series of national strikes that culminated in the bloody **Haymarket Riots** in Chicago. The police accused the Knights of provoking the riots. The Knights' membership declined after losing the confidence of the public and many workers.

In the same year, **Samuel Gompers** began another effort to organize the skilled workers in this country. This immigrant cigar maker began to build the **American Federation of Labor** (**AFL**). The Knights could not draw workers to common political causes. Gompers succeeded by avoiding politics. The AFL pursued those goals most important to the membership: higher wages and better working conditions. By aiming at these basic economic goals and steering clear of political involvement, Gompers built a popular union that had more than four million members by the 1920s.

Yet, even the AFL left a significant void in organizing workers. It unified only small local organizations of skilled tradesmen. It did not accept unskilled industrial workers, women, or African Americans.

In 1935, United Mine Workers President

John L. Lewis began efforts to provide a place for all those groups shut out by the AFL. Passage of the **Wagner Act** (*National Labor Relations Act*) in 1935 aided his efforts. This federal law ensured workers the right to secret ballot referendums to select a bargaining agent. This made the organization of unskilled workers possible, and Lewis formed the **Congress of Industrial Organizations** (**CIO**). In 1955, after a long period of hostility, these two rival national unions joined to create the **AFL–CIO**, the largest affiliation of labor organizations in the country. In 1994, the AFL-CIO had 13.3 million members.

A few of the other AFL-CIO affiliated labor organizations include: the **ILGWU** (International Ladies' Garment Workers' Union – 150,000 members), the **International Brotherhood of Teamsters** (with 1.7 million members), the **UAW** (United Auto Workers – 922,000 members), the **United Steelworkers of America** (650,000 members), and the **NALC** (National Association of Letter Carriers – 315,000 members).

Besides the AFL-CIO, there are more than 100 national unions that function independently. They have no affiliation, are self-governing, and act in their self-interests. These groups rep-

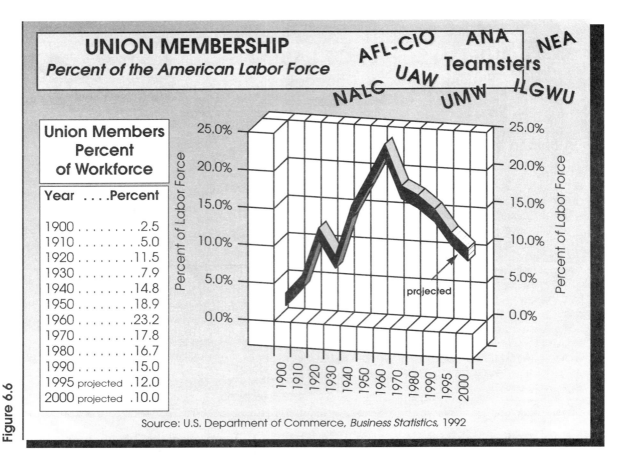

UNION MEMBERSHIP
Percent of the American Labor Force

AFL-CIO ANA NEA Teamsters NALC UAW UMW ILGWU

Union Members Percent of Workforce	
Year	....Percent
1900	........2.5
1910	........5.0
1920	.......11.5
1930	........7.9
1940	.......14.8
1950	.......18.9
1960	.......23.2
1970	.......17.8
1980	.......16.7
1990	.......15.0
1995 projected	.12.0
2000 projected	.10.0

projected

Source: U.S. Department of Commerce, *Business Statistics, 1992*

Figure 6.6

resent approximately 3.3 million workers. A few of the better known independents include: the **ANA** (American Nurses Association – 200,000 members), **NEA** (National Education Association – the largest independent union with 2 million members), **UMW** (United Mine Workers – 240,000 members), and the **International Longshoremen's and Warehousemen's Union** (45,000 members).

RECENT DECLINES IN UNION POWER

Until recently, the objectives of unions were simple. They sought **collective bargaining agreements** (contracts) for better wages, pensions, safe working conditions, job security, better fringe benefits, and grievance procedures to assure contract enforcement. The historical data in Figure 6.6 shows that after World War II, union membership amounted to about 25% of all workers. By 1990, it had dropped to about 16%. Experts suggest that it could decline to 10% by the year 2000.

Why the decline? First, things are very different today. There are changes taking place in the union movement because of changes at work and in the workplace itself. Manufacturing jobs once made up more than 33% of nonagricultural jobs. Today the number has dropped to less than 20% of nonfarm work. It was in factories, mills, and plants that unions found their strength. As these workplaces closed or were converted to modern technology, unions could do little to stop the job losses. Members saw fewer reasons to pay local, state, and national dues to ineffective unions.

Second, unions are partially victims of their success. Laws entitle most workers to what early unions fought to get for their members (e.g., workers' compensation, minimum wage, and safety laws). Unions gained enough power in the mid–20th century to have their contracts become benchmarks for entire industries. To be competitive for labor, employers had to match or improve the contract provisions. Some employers wanted to avoid unions altogether, so they offered workers better wage and benefit packages than those unions received (see Figure 6.7 chart). When the economy boomed and labor was scarce, workers found they could often get better wages and benefits without unions.

Employee Benefits
Percent Having Desired Employee Benefits
Source: U.S. Labor *Occupational Handbook,* 1993

- Health Insurance (30%)
- Cumulative Sick Days (15%)
- Paid Holidays, Vacations (70%)
- Personal leaves (e.g., family, funerals) (28%)
- Pension (29%)
- Income Protection from long–term disability (10%)

Note: Young people seem to think that "everyone gets benefits." These numbers tell a different story. Even among those with benefits, situations vary. For example, health insurance and pension plans vary greatly from employer to employer.

Even when the fast food franchise hires a cashier for $6.50, the cost to the employer of the benefits makes the actual employee cost $10.00. Entry level jobs at $30,000 probably cost the employer $50,000 with benefits and employment taxes that have to be paid.

– Farrell, Christopher, "The Sorry Math of New Hires" *Business Week* 22 Feb 1993

The famous **PATCO Strike** of 1981 may have galvanized the negative attitudes about unions in recent times. The Professional Air Traffic Controllers Organization struck for shorter shifts and more rest between shifts in a very stressful profession. President Ronald Reagan ordered them back to work. Some members did return to the control towers, but approximately 12,000 strikers stayed out. Reagan declared PATCO violated a nonstrike provision of the *Taft-Hartley Act* (1947). He ordered the Department of Transportation to replace the strikers.

This mass firing affected the attitudes of other employers. Before PATCO, they would not have considered using the law to replace an entire segment of their work force because of a strike action. The downsizing in the 1990s showed many employers making wholesale job cuts without consulting unions or employee associations.

Third, beyond collective bargaining, the "heavy weapons" used by unions to get their objectives became less effective. If union leaders call a **strike** (work stoppage), employers now replace union workers with the many nonunion people just waiting to get a job. When a union promotes a **boycott** (refusal to buy product or service of an inflexible employer), people generally ignore it and continue to purchase whatever they want to satisfy themselves. Most consumers and some workers willfully (or ignorantly) cross **picket lines** (lines of striking workers in front of workplaces demonstrating against unfair conditions). Without these weapons, unions have little power.

Fourth, public attitudes toward unions also led to the decline. When surveys ask a crosssection of Americans to say what comes to their mind when they hear the word "union," some common responses include: "corruption," "greed," "incompetence," "selfishness," "ineptitude," "decay," and "lazy." The resulting lists are usually much more negative than positive. Some economists claim that union wages keep prices high and protect incompetence, leading to high cost, low quality goods. True or untrue, once in place, such attitudes are hard to counter.

12,000 PATCO members were fired by President Reagan when the air traffic controllers struck in 1981. ©PhotoDisc

Ignoring unions is common. In 1990, the Pepsi bottling plant owner in Newburgh, NY fired more than 100 striking drivers when they refused to go back to work. Seeking public support, the drivers went to the communities serviced by this bottler and asked the people to boycott the product. Supported by other Teamster locals, the drivers sought to return to their jobs for four years. The Newburgh bottler ignored the strike, then declared it over when nonunion employees replaced the union employees. Despite a union media blitz and store demonstrations, area consumers ignored the boycott. This once strong union local crumbled under the great burden of the 4-year strike.

Another example occurred in October 1993, when members of the Newspaper Guild at the *New York Post* voted to end their strike of six days. They were embittered by the lack of support by the other nine unions at the paper when the other unions decided to cross the picket lines and help the nonunion workers get the paper out. The striking employees could not return to work until they reapplied for the jobs some of them had held for thirty years. Rupert Murdoch, the owner, was known for his "union busting."

NEW DIRECTIONS FOR UNIONS

When a union is without power, can there be true negotiation? In the past, worker and employer saw themselves as adversaries doing battle in collective bargaining negotiations. Traditionally, they believed that what was good for one was harmful to the other. Yet, heavy competition from abroad has caused a new perspective to emerge. Many employers and employees have drawn closer as the market changed due to global competitive pressures. More awareness of the benefits of shared decision–making and profit sharing emerged.

Seeking higher productivity, many companies downsized and reduced the demand for labor. At the same time, they realized an increase in productivity had to come from better communications between labor and management. It could only be done through cooperative, not adversarial bargaining.

An example of the new perspective in labor-

management relations is General Motors' creation of its new Saturn Division. The manufacturer and the United Auto Workers' union decided to create an automobile produced through a new accord. The result was a positive rapport between the employer and employee. Future collective bargaining agreements will focus more on efforts to tie workers wages to producers' profits.

Labor must deal with balancing the labor supply with the producers' demand for it. Different groups handle this balancing act in various ways. Attorneys must be licensed by the state in which they wish to practice their trade. Each state administers a bar examination. Anyone that meets a passing score gets a license to conduct their business. There is no way of calculating how many people will pass or fail this examination. Right now, in this country, there are many more licensed lawyers than there are jobs for them.

Conversely, there is the technique used by Certified Public Accountants. For them, there is no passing score on the licensing test. Only a percentage of the highest scoring candidates are licensed to replace those that are leaving the profession. This way, the supply always remains controlled and limited, keeping the market equilibrium at a higher wage level. Unions must find new and creative ways to defend the worker as employers change their demand for labor.

GOVERNMENT AND LABOR

Unions do not represent everyone. In the 20th century, government has often come to the aid of workers. Affirmative action programs, minimum wage, right-to-work, and comparable worth are significant issues in which government takes the side of workers.

AFFIRMATIVE ACTION PROGRAMS

Government action for workers addresses discrimination. One way is to set up **affirmative action** programs. *Black's Law Dictionary* defines these programs as "employment programs required by federal statutes and regula-

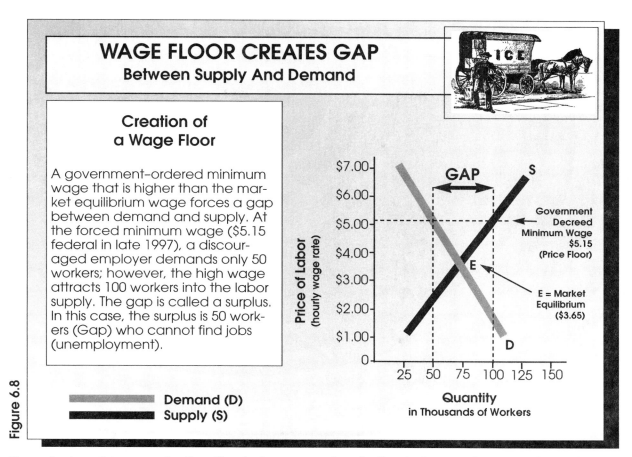

WAGE FLOOR CREATES GAP
Between Supply And Demand

Creation of a Wage Floor

A government–ordered minimum wage that is higher than the market equilibrium wage forces a gap between demand and supply. At the forced minimum wage ($5.15 federal in late 1997), a discouraged employer demands only 50 workers; however, the high wage attracts 100 workers into the labor supply. The gap is called a surplus. In this case, the surplus is 50 workers (Gap) who cannot find jobs (unemployment).

Government Decreed Minimum Wage $5.15 (Price Floor)

E = Market Equilibrium ($3.65)

Price of Labor (hourly wage rate)

Quantity in Thousands of Workers

Demand (D)
Supply (S)

Figure 6.8

---

tions designed to remedy the discriminatory practices in hiring minority group members; designed to eliminate existing and continuing discrimination ...; to create systems and procedures to prevent future discrimination ..."

The original purpose of affirmative action was to insure the equitable recruitment of workers. The idea's backers did not consider the difficulty of being the first "outsider" to be recruited. Imagine being the first female to qualify for employment as a firefighter, or the first African American to take the oath to "serve and protect" in a small town, all-white police department? Many could not or would not put themselves at risk of the psychological and/or physical pressures that were likely to occur.

That is why "recruitment" changed to what critics called **preferential treatment**. Civil rights proponents felt that if enlistment could not increase the number of minority members in the workforce, then partiality might work. What came to be called the "quota system" became the basis of federal and state employment and government contract laws.

Those who support more drastic action to

break discriminatory barriers claim that it is the only way to deal with traditional discrimination. Opponents of such laws believe that they can only lead to **"reverse discrimination."** Lawsuits initiated by individuals and governments have attempted to settle the questions in courts. After years of debate in Congress and the Judiciary, as well as in the private and business sectors, an equitable solution has not yet emerged.

MINIMUM WAGE LAWS

State and federal minimum wage laws create a wage rate that has a floor built under it. This means the hourly rate of pay in most industries cannot go any lower than the law allows. In the 1950s, it was $.75 to $1.00 per hour, and in the late 1960s it had risen to $1.60 per hour. During 1997, planned Congressional increases raised the federal minimum hourly wage to $5.15 per hour.

The original reasoning for such action by the United States Congress was to give low income families more purchasing power. Figure 6.8 presents the situation in graph format. Yet, some problems are evident to those who under-

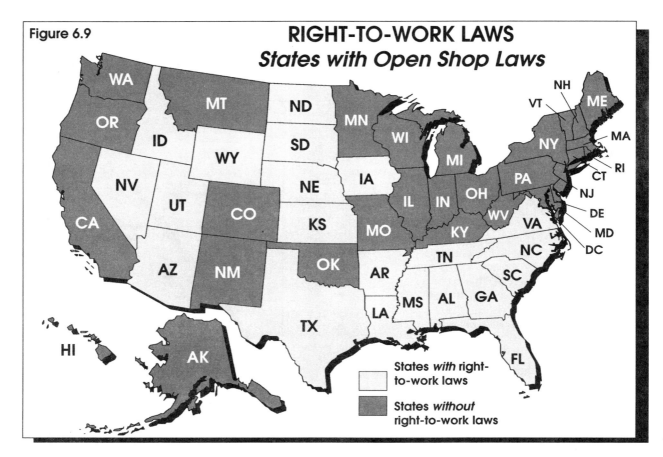

Figure 6.9

RIGHT-TO-WORK LAWS
States with Open Shop Laws

States *with* right-to-work laws

States *without* right-to-work laws

stand how our system works. If government forces employers to raise the wage rate, employers lose profit. If this loss is significant, employers diminish the losses by cutting expenses. One way is to fire employees or cut hours. Another choice is to pass the loss on to the consumer. That means higher prices and inflation. Higher prices may consume any gain in the employees' purchasing power. Minimum wage laws may place the wages for those jobs covered above the equilibrium point of supply and demand for labor. Employers, if pressed, may then be forced to make decisions about laying off workers.

RIGHT-TO-WORK LAWS

Some unions negotiated clauses in their contracts that allow a **closed shop** (all employees must be union members). Other contracts included **union shop** clauses (nonunion employees must pay an agency fee). In 1947, the *Taft-Hartley Act* (*Labor Management Relations Act*) forbade closed shops but allowed union shops to continue. It also allowed states to legislate **open shops** (employment of union and nonunion workers under same contract). Twenty-one states have such **right-to-work laws** (see Figure 6.9 map). While these laws

prohibit union shops, they do allow unions to charge "agency fees" to nonunion employees to cover negotiation of contracts. What these laws establish are open shops that allow employers to hire either union or non-union workers.

COMPARABLE WORTH

Discrimination on the job hurts people in many different ways. Recently, the term "glass ceiling" has gained national attention. It refers to an unspoken bias of many companies. They allow women to rise to a particular place in the company's hierarchy and then stop the promotions, no matter how deserving the female employee is. The *Civil Rights Act of 1964* (amended in 1972), *Equal Pay Act of 1963*, and *United States Code 1963* prohibit gender discrimination. With these as a basis and many other laws passed by the federal and state legislatures, suits for damages from sexual discrimination in the workplace now flood the courts. While there are laws protecting workers from bigotry, firms still pay women only 60-70% of what men collect for doing the "same job." Seeking **pay equity** continues to be a legal battle. Some states, including New York, Connecticut, Iowa, Minnesota, and Wisconsin, have passed laws to combat such chauvinism in the workplace.

Laws that discourage other forms of discrimination in the workplace include:

- The *Rehabilitation Act of 1973* prohibits employers from discriminating on the basis of handicap.

- The *Age Discrimination In Employment Act of 1967* (amended 1978) protects persons between the ages of forty and seventy from arbitrary age discrimination in a workplace of twenty or more people and by all levels of government.

What the future holds for workers is uncertain. Still, the Dream has not changed. Those placing their labor in the marketplace seek honest pay for honest work.

ASSESSMENT
QUESTIONS • APPLICATIONS

1 Hard work has always meant security and advancement in the workplace.
  a Is this statement as true now as it was in the past? Explain.
  b What career do you plan on training for? Analyze the supply and demand aspects of labor in this field.
  c How is your entering the job market going to be different from your parents' experience?

2 For many years, labor unions achieved their goals in the workplace.
  a Is this statement as true now as it was in the past? Explain.
  b In what ways do unions benefit even nonunion workers?
  c Why does the public seem to have a strong anti-union sentiment?
  d How must unions change to meet the changes in global economics?

3 In the United States, workers have basic rights.
  a List the employment rights to which workers are entitled.
  b Assume you thought that you were being denied one of those rights. Explain how you would remedy the situation and what obstacles you think might arise when you seek the remedy.

4 Investigate the Supreme Court decisions in *University of California v. Bakke* (1978) and *United Steel Workers of America, AFL-CIO v. Weber* (1979).
  a Summarize the facts in each case.
  b Identify the issue in each case.
  c Explain the Court's ruling in each case.
  d What impact did each decision have on labor in America?

5 In the 20th century, governments have often helped the worker at the expense of the employer.
  a Explain why you agree or disagree with this statement.
  b Is government involvement in the economy a good or bad thing? Explain your response.

ASSESSMENT PROJECT:
JOINING THE JOB MARKET

Will the job market be ready to accept you when you are ready to join it? This is a major question that many young people do not even consider before they decide to study at a college, attend a trade school, join the military, or just go out looking for a job. The intelligent way to approach your life choices is to research and investigate "the real world."

STUDENT TASK

Write a report analyzing the supply of labor and the demand for labor in a field you wish to work.

PROCEDURE

1   Assume that you are going to college to train for a particular career. Select three schools that specialize in education for that field. Call each of them and get the following information:

   a How many graduates did the school have in the area you are interested in?

   b How many of them got jobs?

   c What was the average starting salary for those who were placed?

   d How many went on for a graduate degree in the field?

   e How many were placed after achieving a graduate level degree and what was their starting salary?

   f How many were not placed in their field of study, and what kind of employment did they find?

2   Locate the current U.S. Dept. of Labor *Occupational Outlook Handbook* in a library. Review the statistics given for your particular interest.

3   Compile all college and government data and make your judgments about the field.

LEARNING STANDARDS

Learners should be able to:

(5)   analyze problems and evaluate decisions about the economic effects on society and the individual caused by human, technological, and natural activities.

(6)   present their ideas both in writing and orally in clear, concise, and properly accepted fashion.

(7)   employ a variety of information from written, graphic, and multimedia sources.

(8)   monitor, reflect upon, and improve their own and others' work.

EVALUATION

The criteria for the evaluation of this project are itemized in the grid (rubric) that follows. Choice of appropriate category terms (values) is the decision of the instructor. Selection of terms such as "minimal," "satisfactory," and "distinguished" can vary with each assessment.

Joining The Job Market Evaluation Rubric

(Refer to introductory section for suggestions of scoring descriptors for the evaluation categories.)

Evaluation Item	Category 1	Category 2	Category 3	Category 4	Category 5
Item a: (5) Does the report analyze problems and evaluate decisions about the economic effects caused by human, technological, and natural activities on societies and individuals?					
Item b: (6) Does the report present ideas in writing (and orally) in clear, concise, and properly accepted fashion?					
Item c: (7) Does the report employ a variety of information from written, graphic, and multimedia sources?					
Item d: (8) Does the report show monitoring of, reflection upon, and improvement of work?					

ECONOMICS – *Assessment of the American Dream*   N&N©

ISSUE 7

How do people use money, credit, and banking?

MONEY, CREDIT, AND BANKING

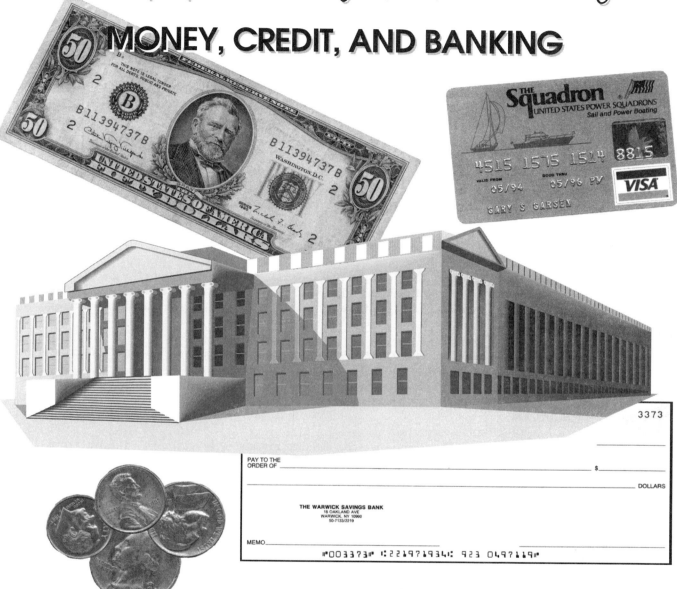

"... We're sorry. It's not us. It's the monster. The bank isn't like a man."

"Yes, but the bank is only made of men."

"No, you're wrong there. The bank is something else than men. It happens that every man in a bank hates what the bank does, and yet the bank does it. The bank is something more than men, I tell you. It's the monster. Men made it but they can't control it."

– John Steinbeck. *The Grapes of Wrath*

THE COLLEGE CRUNCH: GETTING CREDIT FOR MORE THAN COURSES

Jorge Melendez' 1985 CJ-5 kicked up some dust as it turned down the Oroscos' drive. He and Felipe had been friends since grade school in Burnet. Now both were finishing their Associate degrees at Austin Community College.

Felipe shuffled down the steps as the Jeep pulled in front of the house. "Hey, lot of dust, man! Mamma's going to want that porch swept because of you," Felipe said.

Jorge shrugged and smiled, "Dry for this time of year."

They stopped at the mailbox when they got to the road. Felipe jumped back in the seat waving a letter. "This is the third offer for a credit card this week. I must be on a list."

"Me, too," said Jorge. "I really don't want to get one. You know cousin Miguel ... goes to Howard Payne U. up in Brownwood? A credit card burned him. He ran up a balance and had trouble paying it off. His mother made him get rid of it. It's too easy to run up a balance, and the interest you pay is phenomenal."

"Most of the college kids I know at Austin Community have one," Felipe said. "Their parents co–sign. My parents are not very hot on the idea. They are afraid I won't manage it well, and they will wind up bailing me out. These mail offers say I can get one on my own. I don't know. I would like to get some decent clothes to go job hunting. If I move to my own place, I could charge some furniture and stuff."

"Listen, Felipe," Jorge said. "Maybe we can talk to my sister Maria. She's taking Financial Management at Baylor University up in Waco. I want to go there to see the place. I know you are taking those computer skills and going out for a job when we graduate, but I want to transfer credits to a four-year school. What do you say we make a trip to Waco?"

A few weeks later, the CJ pulled in front of a dorm at Baylor. Maria was waiting with a group of friends. After Maria put Jorge and Felipe through the "little brother" and "he's cute" introductions, the group walked around the campus, then headed for the snack bar.

"So, Maria, you're the financial genius. What can you tell me about getting a credit card?" Felipe asked.

Maria smiled at her roommate Liz Colgan. "As one of our professors always says, 'There is good news and bad news. Nothing is easy when it comes to money.'"

"The good news is credit cards can help you manage money, and they are great in emergencies," said Maria, gazing over her glasses as she settled into her accountant mood. "The bad news is, unless you know what you are doing, they get out of control very quickly."

"Maria and I have a test coming up on them next week," Liz said hastily. "It might help us if we went over our notes aloud with you tomorrow. Right now, we have a basketball game to see."

The next afternoon, the four of them were sitting on a couch in the dorm lounge.

"Hey, this is nice. You study here often?" asked Jorge sinking into the cushion.

"No," said Liz. "The place gets too noisy during the week. That is a big problem in college. The dorms are too noisy, even during exam time. When we want quiet, we head for the library.

"Anyway, I looked at my notes about credit cards. There are many ins – and – outs. I have a supplementary American Express charge card on my dad's account, but he told me not to use it unless I am in a bind. I've only used it once when my Toyota needed a battery last winter. I used the card, but Dad paid the bill."

"After Aunt Louisa told Mamma about Miguel's payment problems with his card at Payne, she told me to forget it," said Maria.

Jorge glanced at Felipe. "You two haven't much practical experience, do you?"

"No," said Liz, "but we do have Professor Garnsey's notes. It will help us all to go over them aloud. First, he says to check the cost of revolving credit cards versus charge cards. Different cards charge membership rates, have different APRs, and charge transaction fees."

Felipe blinked. "I thought they were all the same, and what is an APR, anyway?"

Maria held up her hand. "The offers you are getting in the mail may waive the annual fee for a year. That could save you $20 – $30, but the APR, the Annual Percentage Rate, might be high on those offers, sometimes over 20% of any balance you are running."

"There is also a difference in how each card issuer computes the interest. So you really have to do some reading," said Liz. "Hey, between the two of us we sound like we know something!"

Jorge threw his arms in the air. "Wait! You two may know something, but I'm lost. I'm not sure of the difference between a charge card and a credit card."

Liz flipped a couple of pages of her notebook. "Stores issue charge cards, so do gasoline companies, and travel / entertainment services such as Carte Blanche, Diners Club, and American Express. Most have an annual fee, but mostly you have to pay off the entire bill when it comes. So, there is no interest rate on an outstanding balance, because there isn't any balance – OK, but there is an annual fee on most of these cards.

"Almost every bank and credit union issues international credit cards like Master Card, Visa, or Discover. Besides the bankcards, big corporations like AT&T, GM, Shell, and Ford are offering those cards. They allow you to charge purchases, get cash advances, and carry a balance from month to month if you can't pay it all at once."

Felipe blinked and with his exaggerated accentuation said, "Well, if you can stretch out payments, a CREDIT card is better than a CHARGE card."

"Maybe," said the skeptic Maria, "but Miguel got into trouble with his credit card. He ran up bills and just paid the minimum each month. Then, he charged more stuff. For pocket money, he used the card to get cash advances at the college ATM. Miguel forgot they charge a fee for that, too. Miguel wound up carrying a $2000 balance, and Aunt Louisa blew a gut! She made him cut up the card. It took him two years to pay off the balance. At 19% APR, he wound up paying the company $2697."

The boys looked stunned. Then Jorge chuckled,"Wow, almost $700 in interest! No wonder Aunt Louisa went nuts."

"There is a lot more to these things than you think," said Liz, waving her card. "People whip them in and out of their wallets all the time. They are always there. They are too convenient."

"I'll say," said Felipe. "At least with cash, you stop when your wallet's empty. Sounds to me like a wise person would avoid them completely."

Maria smiled. "Actually, Professor Garnsey says they are a good financial tool – if you know your limits. If you control your use and pay off your balance as quickly as possible, they give you a good record of spending. That can help you stay within a budget. If you don't run into problems, they can provide you with a good credit record for later, when you want bigger loans for a car or a house."

Jorge stretched. "I'm hungry! Say, Ms. Colgan, maybe we can use your American Express to get ourselves a nice pizza?"

"Not on your life, buster. Apparently, that is what your cousin Miguel often did. So if you want to eat, climb into the Jeep and we'll enjoy the *inexpensive* but *exotic cuisine* at Baylor's fine college cafeteria."

They roared off to the dining hall, searching their jeans for coins and bills.

How do people use money, credit, and banking?

MONEY, CREDIT, AND BANKING

MONEY, CREDIT, AND BANKING

High school, college, or after – whether learning about credit cards or balancing a checkbook – money situations cause pleasure and pain for everyone. Avoiding the pain takes hard work. There is no easy way around dealing with money. It is a necessity. The better people understand the role money plays in the economy, the more success they will have in dealing with money.

Since money is such an important part of any economic society, keeping the right amount of it in circulation is important. In most market economies, banks circulate money. Throughout U.S. history, crises have arisen because of this arrangement. Today, the government issues the money to banks and regulates them. Following a discussion of some general ideas about money, a look at the U.S. banking system will take a substantial part of this lesson.

MONEY: HISTORY, CHARACTERISTICS, & FUNCTIONS

Money is anything generally accepted for payment in **transactions** (exchanges of goods and services). Early societies used **barter** (exchanging one good for another). Villagers spent much time trading and retrading goods until they could get what they wanted in the first place. Bartering still exists. Kids always trade comic books and baseball cards. People sometimes pay for goods by swapping for something else. Sometimes they perform some acceptable service in exchange for something of similar value. Often, this is called the "gray market" in which some people pay others "in kind" to avoid paying sales and income taxes. For the purpose of avoiding taxes, this is illegal.

As time went by, money began to serve three basic functions. First, universally acceptable **mediums of exchange** began to surface. They simplified transactions and replaced the barter process of endless trades. Salt, shells, jewels, grain, and even cows have served as money over time. The Egyptians used coins as early as 2500 B.C. The use of precious metal coins as money became widespread in early times. They met the criteria for a good medium of exchange: scarce, portable, durable, symbolic, and universal. They were also divisible. They could be minted in different sizes and shapes to denote degrees of value.

Second, as money evolved as a practical medium of exchange, it took on other functions. It became **standard of value**. Today we make purchases based on whether the amount asked by a merchant seems right to us. There is a general awareness of how much money will buy, and people judge what goods and wages are worth in terms of money.

Third, money also functions as a **store of wealth**. This means money is kept for future use. People stockpile it until they have enough

Coins from around the world. ©PhotoDisc

Since medieval times, notes and paper money have been used throughout the world by most governments as legal tender and to represent wealth. ©PhotoDisc

to buy something they cannot buy immediately. People save money and safeguard it to give them security against unseen misfortune.

Paper as a symbol to represent wealth emerged in medieval times. Goldsmiths stored gold and gave out receipts for it. People traded with the receipts (or notes) as **representative money**. Accepting the paper meant one individual had faith the other had gold, silver, or some other wealth to back it. Our paper money of today and our banking system evolved from these practices.

From the days of the goldsmiths to recent times, paper money (notes) represented other tangible wealth. In the 20th century, societies moved away from this to **fiat money**. This is

when a government decrees the notes it issuesare "legal tender" and must be accepted for all "legal transactions." As with most modern nations, U.S. currency is fiat money. It has no metallic backing. (Figure 7.1 shows one of the last dollars the U.S. backed with silver.) Paper money fluctuates in value (inflation/deflation) based on the society's ability to grow and prosper and people's faith in the stability of the government. If that faith is shaken, serious economic problems begin to arise.

MONEY SUPPLY: CURRENCY, CHECKING, AND MORE

Most young people use government currency for transactions. They find it hard to believe that only *one-tenth* of **M-1** (the basic money supply) circulating through the economy is bills and coins.

The other *nine-tenths* of **M-1** is in **demand deposits** (checking accounts) in banks (see Figure 7.2 on opposite page). A satellite view of money changing hands in U.S. businesses and daily life would show most people writing checks and depositing them in banks. Think of how most households pay big bills. The major payments for mortgages, heating, autos, and most goods and services are in the form of checks.

Checks are safe, easy to use, handwritten bank forms. They are the money used for most

Figure 7.1 Silver Certificate

From 1886 to 1968 Silver Certificates were backed and redeemable for silver dollars.

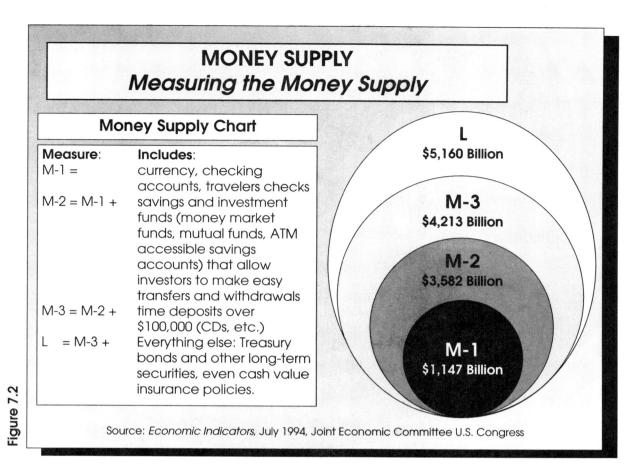

MONEY SUPPLY
Measuring the Money Supply

Money Supply Chart

Measure:	Includes:
M-1 =	currency, checking accounts, travelers checks
M-2 = M-1 +	savings and investment funds (money market funds, mutual funds, ATM accessible savings accounts) that allow investors to make easy transfers and withdrawals
M-3 = M-2 +	time deposits over $100,000 (CDs, etc.)
L = M-3 +	Everything else: Treasury bonds and other long-term securities, even cash value insurance policies.

L
$5,160 Billion

M-3
$4,213 Billion

M-2
$3,582 Billion

M-1
$1,147 Billion

Source: *Economic Indicators*, July 1994, Joint Economic Committee U.S. Congress

Figure 7.2

of the transactions inside and outside America. Banks are private businesses, but through checks, they can radically alter the money supply. To attempt to keep the right amount of money in circulation and to allow the economy to run smoothly and grow, federal and state governments regulate banks (see section on Banks: Gatekeepers of the Money Supply).

Checks represent more than 70% of the money supply and nearly 90% of the transactions for households and businesses. ©PhotoDisc

The actual money supply is broader than **M-1**. There is also a considerable portion of the money supply in **near money**. This includes accounts and securities involving simple formalities to be converted into currency or checks. Therefore, these accounts are very *near* to being money. Economists say they are **liquid** because they flow easily into money. Including near money in the picture gives a much broader measure of the money supply (**M-2**, **M-3**, **L**) as shown in the Figure 7.2 illustration.

MONEY: CREDIT AND CREDIT CARDS

What about those credit cards that are so often used in transactions? Where do they fit in the broad money supply picture? Cards are technically near money. Each time a person charges purchases to a credit account, he/she is borrowing money. In the end, when the card company's bill comes, it has to be paid with a check or currency (**M-1**).

Young people often get frustrated when this whole question of credit arises. Most parents of today's high school and college students did not

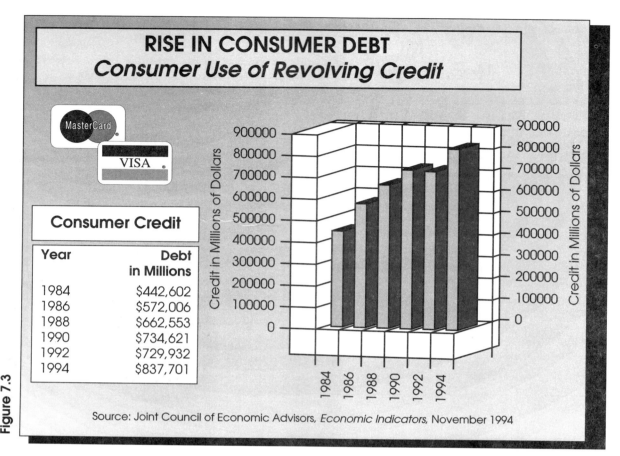

RISE IN CONSUMER DEBT
Consumer Use of Revolving Credit

Consumer Credit	
Year	**Debt in Millions**
1984	$442,602
1986	$572,006
1988	$662,553
1990	$734,621
1992	$729,932
1994	$837,701

Source: Joint Council of Economic Advisors, *Economic Indicators*, November 1994

Figure 7.3

have access to credit cards. The credit cards that are so commonplace today only emerged as financial tools in the 1960s and 1970s. The nation absorbed them into its financial life rapidly. Their advantages and disadvantages were not always well understood.

Figure 7.3 shows that credit card debt grew significantly in the 1980s. According to the Federal Reserve System, in 1992 there was more money outstanding on revolving credit loans than on auto loans: $268 billion v. $260 billion (Council of Economic Advisors, *Economic Indicators*, Nov. '93. 29). Today, credit card debt makes up 33.3% of consumer loans. According to the President's Council of Economic Advisors, the average consumer paid $435 in finance charges in 1992 (*Economic Indicators*, Nov. '93. 29). It is big business, too. Credit card interest is one of the largest income generators for banks. Putting $300 billion in revolving charges on their cards, Americans pay the banks nearly $40 billion in finance charges annually (*Economic Indicators*, Nov. '93. 29).

Usury is the charging of illegally high interest (see page 253). Congress and state governments passed many laws to regulate credit. Yet, twenty states have no interest ceilings, and for those that do, the average is 24%. Even at a 20% rate, carrying a $1,000 balance for 36 months

220 *Million Cardholders*

144 *Million Cardholders*

93 *Million Cardholders*

41 *Million Cardholders*

25 *Million Cardholders*

Worldwide use of credit cards grows annually. In 1992, Silny, Rosenberg reported something like 450 billion dollars changed hands through VISA alone. Also in 1992, VISA averaged 600 transactions every second.

– adapted from an advertisement in *BusinessWeek*, 25 Jan. 1993

Getting Started With Credit
Adapted from American Express Co., *Building a Credit Record*, NY 1993

- Open a savings account and **make regular deposits**. Deposit amounts can be small, but they should show persistence.
- Open a checking account and **do not "bounce" any checks**.

These two simple steps show a bank or other creditor that a person has care and discipline in financial affairs.

- Find a full-time job and establish a steady work record.
- Apply for a small loan from a bank or credit union, ask a relative or friend to co-sign. **Pay it off as quickly as possible without missing any payments.**
- **Pay bills promptly.**
- Apply for a store charge card on your own or as an extension of a relative's account. Pay charges **completely** each month.

How can young persons get credit if they have never had it? The answer is to build a credit history to show *creditworthiness*. From the creditor's point of view, lending money in any amount involves risk. Good credit performance records provide some assurance the money will be repaid. The sidebar "Getting Started" shows steps a young person can take to build a credit history.

Credit bureaus (local credit reporting agencies) are linked to national information networks such as TRW, Equifax, and TransUnion. They keep records and sell them to banks and other creditors. The *Federal Fair Credit Reporting Act* (1971) allows a person to see credit bureau records for a small fee. Errors or omissions can be corrected. A good credit history record is important when it

would cost the card holder an additional $500 in interest. Saving money at 3% or 4% in a bank while carrying a $1,000 credit card loan is foolish. The small gain at the savings bank cannot offset the 20% being paid on the card. It amounts to a 15-17% net loss of money. According to financial columnist Humberto Cruz, a card holder would be better off using the savings deposits to pay off the credit card balance faster ("Credit Cards, Even Unused, Can Cost You." *Poughkeepsie Journal.* 31 January 1994, B1).

Today, society expects young people to come out of high school and college using sophisticated credit devices as a matter of course. In this issue's opening story, Jorge and Maria mentioned their cousin Miguel's problems. This is not uncommon. Choosing and using credit cards properly takes education and discipline.

For young people just starting out in life, qualifying for credit of *any* kind is very frustrating. Their applications for credit may be turned down. The problem is that young people have no credit history. Therefore, convincing a bank or other creditor that they are **credit worthy** becomes a problem. It is exasperating, but a person needs to have used credit to get credit!

Choosing a Credit Card
Adapted from American Express Co., *Building a Credit Record*, NY 1993

Credit can be convenient, but it can easily become a nightmare for an individual who lets it get out of control. A credit advantage is that a monthly bill can help keep track of purchases and control expenses. A disadvantage is that it provides excess purchasing power. Temptations may lead to overspending and carrying a balance. The extra interest payments on that balance may wreck a budget. Choosing the right low cost card can avoid unpleasantness and enhance an individual's creditworthiness.

- Use a budget as a restraint. (Subtract housing expenses from monthly take home pay. Keep credit payments below 15% of this figure.)
- Check the APR. (Call Bankcard Holders of America at 1-800-845-5000. Ask for a free list of banks with low credit card rates.) The *Federal Truth-in-Lending Act* (1968) requires creditors to inform consumers of interest rates applications and bills.
- See if there is an annual fee charged just to carry the card. (Some companies do not charge one and others will waive the fee if asked.)
- See if there is a 25-day grace period before interest is charged.
- See if there are insurance charges.
- Check for special offers. (Shell's Master Card offers gas discounts. GM's offers discounts on the next new GM car.)

Handling a Credit Card

Adapted from American Express Co., *Building a Credit Record*, NY 1993

- Have no more than two or three cards. Too many open accounts scare many bank loan officers. (Just one is plenty for college students.)
- Keep a list of card numbers in a safe place.
- Beware of "Minimum Payment Syndrome." Pay card balance in full when possible to avoid interest charges.
- Grace periods only count when you have no outstanding balance.
- Keep track of charges to avoid exceeding the card's limit.
- Cash advances at banks, ATMs, or by telegraph are very costly.
- Save receipts and compare them to your card statement.
- Be careful in stores. (Get the card back from clerks. Ask for and destroy carbons after the transaction.)
- Inform card company of loss and of change of address.
- Never give card number to an unknown caller.
- Work out a repayment plan if you get in trouble.
- Don't be afraid to switch to cards that offer lower rates or no annual fees. (Remember, this is a consumer service, not a doctor-patient relationship.)

comes time for the bigger loans people need such as mortgages.

BANKS: GATEKEEPERS OF THE MONEY SUPPLY

In the aggregate sense, credit and savings do help the economy grow. Money stored by consumers and businesses provides financial institutions with the funds to lend to others.

Many categories of borrowers spend the money, expanding economic activity. Consumers borrow to buy more goods and services. Businesses borrow to buy capital resources and expand production. Government borrows to provide more services. Therefore, the elements of economic growth depend on money being stored (savings) and made available (credit) to borrowers.

Because the money supply changes with conditions in the economy, it is important to keep watch over it. This is the realm of financial institutions. In particular, regulation of the banking system is the realm of the central bank of the United States, the Federal Reserve System, or "**the FED**."

Financial institutions include commercial banks, savings and loan associations, and credit unions (see Figure 7.4 on opposite page). Although they vary, this discussion refers to them generally as "banks." Banks are private businesses that make profits by lending money. Because loans create new money, banks have enormous power to alter the money supply and economic life in general. Most are habitually careful to make judicious loans.

Yet, 19th and 20th century history shows examples of widespread bank misjudgments, causing the economy to crumble. In 1913, Congress created the independent Federal Reserve System to regulate the supply of money and act as a general supervisor of banks. Before looking at the mechanics of the FED, some groundwork on banking in general is necessary.

Lending rarely takes place in currency. Remember that nearly 90% of the M-1 money supply is in demand deposits or checkbook money. (In 1993, M-1 = $115 trillion.) When a bank gives a loan, it credits the borrower's checking account. The borrower begins writing more checks. Those who receive these new checks deposit them in their banks. Their banks' assets grow, and they can lend more. This scenario takes place in thousands of places, thousands of times in a business day, and it expands the money supply.

"How Banks Expand Money" (Figure 7.5) offers another example. If Jane Olsen, owner of Olsen's Figures & Fitness, arrived at the Sparta National Bank wishing to borrow $14,000 and the bank agreed, this amount would be transferred into Olsen's account. Suppose Jane buys 10 exercycles for the $14,000 from Argonaut Enterprises. Then Argonaut deposits the $14,000 in its accounts at the Athens bank.

The money supply would continue to expand. The Athens Bank would keep 10% of the deposits on reserve and lend the balance of $12,600 to other customers. The loans and

Figure 7.4

Financial Institutions
Types of Financial Institutions and Characteristics

Type	Characteristics
Commercial Bank	• Business banks. • Chartered by state and federal government (latter have "National" in their name). • Cater to large-scale businesses activities with short-term, high risk loans. • Handle approximately 65% of loans in the country. • Offer full range of services (consumer loans, savings and checking accounts).
Savings and Loan Association	• Primarily consumer banks. • Began as consumer mortgage banks. • Still make more than half the country's private home mortgages. • 1980s deregulation allowed S&Ls to enter commercial markets with checking, short-term business loans and other investments.
Mutual Savings Bank	• Primarily small consumer banks (most on east coast). • Make about 10% of nation's mortgages and some installment loans.
Credit Union	• Employee-owned banks within corporations and labor unions that work from payroll deduction deposits. • 1980s deregulation allowed CU's to enter commercial markets with checking, short-term business loans, and other investments plus offer services such as insurance and financial planning. • Through recent growth and collapse of many S&Ls, CU's now exceed all other banks in number.

deposits would keep flowing through the system as new money. Each bank would reduce the deposited amounts by 10% for reserves and make the rest available for loans. Eventually, the flow trickles out. Still, this procedure repeats itself thousands of times a day at banks all over the country – and the globe.

Monetary expansion works, but without limits, it can get out of hand. Like all businesses, banks want to make profits. The more loans, the more profit from borrowers paying back the principal with interest. This all takes place with the stroke of a banker's pen – or actually, a keystroke on the computer. It seems too fragile, too exposed to human error. It is. Some control is needed. In the U.S. economy, the control comes from the FED and other government agencies.

Laws require banks to keep 10-15% of deposits on **reserve** (cannot be lent) as a safety margin. This is to avoid over lending and to have money on hand for depositors' routine withdrawals. The balance is available for loans.

Historically, without some enforceable system of fractional reserve control, banks have been known to lend more than they have in deposits. Banks claim they can manage very well with only 2% on reserve. Isolated cases of reckless lending have local repercussions, but widespread imprudence can wreck the economy. An oversupply of money can cause inflation and confusion. An undersupply of money can slow economic activity to a halt. Both have happened frequently (see "S&L Crisis" at the end of this Issue).

Figure 7.5   **How Banks Expand Money**

See example of Olsen Figures & Fitness, Argonaut enterprises and Athens Bank.

Deposits		Less 10% Reserve		Loan Money Available
A&P Supermarket............$8,000	minus	$800	results in	$7,200
Wendy's Restaurant........$6,000	minus	$600	results in	$5,400
Exxon Service Station......$1,000	minus	$100	results in	$900
Cotillion Hair Salon $750	minus	$75	results in	$675
Total..........................$15,750	minus	$1,575	results in	$14,175

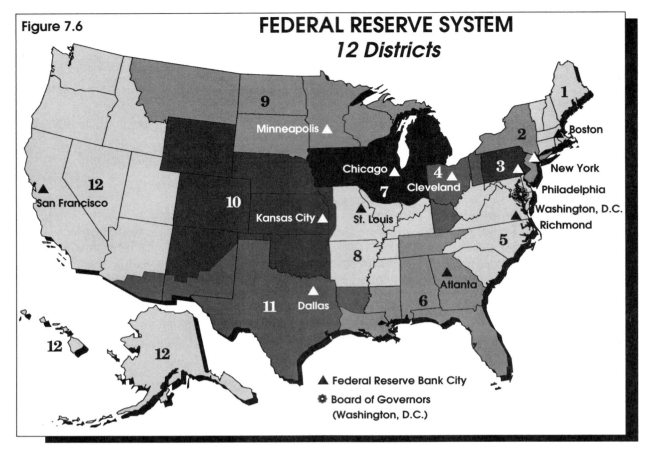

Figure 7.6

FEDERAL RESERVE SYSTEM
12 Districts

9 — Minneapolis ▲

1

2 — Boston

Chicago ▲   4 ▲ Cleveland   3 ▲ — New York

12 — San Francisco   7   Philadelphia

10   Kansas City ▲   St. Louis ▲   Washington, D.C.

Richmond

8   5

Atlanta ▲

11 — Dallas   6

12   12

▲ Federal Reserve Bank City
✿ Board of Governors
(Washington, D.C.)

U.S. BANKING REGULATION:

THE FEDERAL RESERVE

Controlling the amount and flow of money is crucial to economic life. Checkbook money flows rapidly through the country and the world. If the economy falters in a one place and one bank fails, many others are placed in jeopardy. There is much isolated judgment involved, but banks are linked with others in far-off places. Worldwide, they are vulnerable to the unevenness of economic activity, misjudgments, and even the corruption of others.

It is easy to see the important role bank deposits play in the national and global economy. Throughout history, bank failures and financial panics caused the money supply to shrink, hurting thousands of people. After a terrible panic in 1907 that nearly wrecked the national economy, Congress made significant changes in banking law. In 1913, Congress moved to bring some central control to the banking industry. It created the Federal Reserve Bank System, "… to furnish an elastic currency [and] more effective supervision of banking."

The FED, or **Federal Reserve**, is a "central bank." It is where the funds of the government are deposited, and where large commercial banks can borrow and deposit funds. As a major source of funds for member banks, the FED exerts a strong (but not absolute) control over the nation's money supply. It is an independent alliance of nearly one-third (6,000) of the national and state chartered commercial banks in the U.S. Membership is voluntary – except for federally chartered "national banks."

Federal Reserve controls the flow of money in the U.S. banking system through regulations and the adjustment of the interest rate the FED charges to member banks. ©PhotoDisc

Figure 7.7

Organization Of The Federal Reserve

BOARD OF GOVERNORS
Members: 7 appointed by President
(14-year terms)

FEDERAL OPEN MARKET COMMITTEE
Members: Board of Governors
and 5 District Bank Presidents

FEDERAL ADVISORY COMMITTEE
Members: Commercial Banker
from each of FED's 12 Districts

12 DISTRICT RESERVE BANKS (AND 25 BRANCHES)

1	Boston	7	Chicago
2	New York	8	St. Louis
3	Philadelphia	9	Minneapolis
4	Cleveland	10	Kansas City
5	Richmond	11	Dallas
6	Atlanta	12	San Francisco

6,000 MEMBER BANKS AND FINANCIAL INSTITUTIONS

The Board of Governors in Washington consults with the presidents of the FED's 12 district banks and supervises banking operations, regulates the money supply, and establishes credit rules for the nation. The 12 district banks are nonprofit "bankers' banks" owned by the member banks. They perform many services for the banking community:

- Make low interest loans to member banks to keep proper reserves.
- Hold reserves on account for member banks.
- Modify and administer the policies set by FED's Board of Governors to meet the needs of banks in their district.
- Computer process (credit/debit) the 40 billion checks written in the country.
- Transfer funds among the 12 districts.
- Make loans to the government, especially for disaster aid (floods, earthquakes, hurricanes, etc.).
- Disburse new U.S. currency (and destroy old, worn currency).
- Regulate the money supply rules set by the Board of Governors.

The 12 district banks "customize and fine-tune" the basic regulations set down by the Board of Governors to the particular circumstances in their region of the country.

Member banks join by buying stock in one of the 12 district banks of the system (see Figure 7.6).

Every two years the President appoints, and Congress confirms, one of 7 individuals for a 14-year term on the FED's Board of Governors (see Figure 7.7). However, that is the only official connection the Fed has to the government. It is an independent agency that operates out of the realm of politics. In this sense, it is like a "Supreme Court of Banking." The governors are usually very conservative by nature. They see

their primary task as inflation fighters, as opposed to stimulators of the economy. For the most part, they leave the latter task to Congress' fiscal policy.

BANKING AND ECONOMIC PERFORMANCE: MONETARY POLICY

Congress created the FED to monitor banks and keep the money supply in proper balance. In the second half of the 20th century, the FED

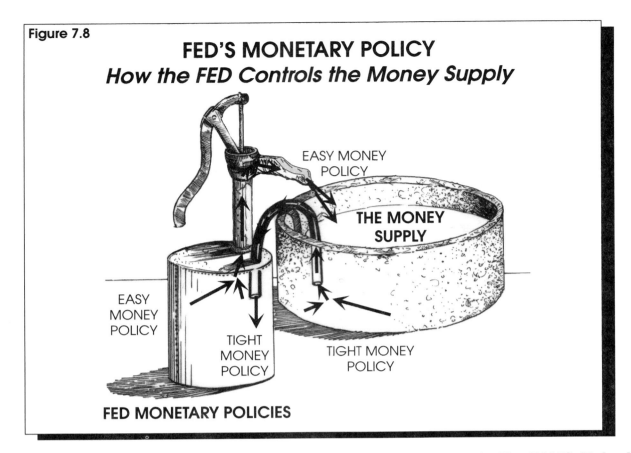

Figure 7.8

FED'S MONETARY POLICY
How the FED Controls the Money Supply

EASY MONEY POLICY

THE MONEY SUPPLY

EASY MONEY POLICY

TIGHT MONEY POLICY

TIGHT MONEY POLICY

FED MONETARY POLICIES

began playing an even more intricate role in the economic life of the United States. It can enact **monetary policies** that *intentionally* alter the money supply to avoid problems such as inflation and unemployment. Therefore, the FED is more than a banking regulator. It can change the whole economy. In truth, its actions are felt around the world.

The FED's Board of Governors can enact **"tight money policy"** to slow down inflation, or the Board can enact **"easy money policy"** to stimulate a sluggish economy. This altering of the flow of money is a broad and controversial power not always popular with the public or politicians. The Board uses its basic tools to regulate banking activities. However, when the Board senses a problem, it can intensify its use of these same tools to change the flow of money through the country – and the world (see Figure 7.8). In order of frequency of use, the three basic tools available to the FED are: open market operations, adjustment of the discount rate, and adjustment of the reserve requirement.

OPEN MARKET OPERATIONS

Open Market Operations is the most fre-

quently used of the tools. The **FOMC** (Federal Open Market Committee) meets often and authorizes the buying and selling of government securities (Treasury bills, notes, and bonds) to registered bond dealers. If the FOMC decides more money is needed in the economy, it puts in an order for the dealers to buy bonds at a price higher than the current market price. Bondholders seize the opportunity to make profits and sell. The FED gets bonds and, in exchange, pumps money to the sellers. The money supply expands, and the economy is stimulated.

If inflation threatens, FOMC sells bonds at high interest. Since they are a solid investment, dealers grab the opportunity. In this way, the FED siphons money out of the economy. FOMC activities allow the FED to make constant adjustments to the money supply over short time periods.

DISCOUNT RATE ADJUSTMENT

Discount Rate Adjustment is a stronger tool but less frequently used. It has a deeper and more longer-lasting effect than FOMC's Open Market Operations. The **discount rate** is

Economic Profile of Economist Alan Greenspan

In 1994 and 1995, Americans were puzzled about the performance of their economy. The U.S. was suffering high rates of unemployment, so it seemed reasonable for "the FED" to loosen the restraints on the money supply. The economic indicators said that the economy was expanding at a snappy pace, but instead of encouraging this growth, the Federal Reserve System decided to tighten the money supply.

The FED's Board of Governors raised short-term interest rates seven times during the 1994-1995 period. Wall Street became concerned about the tightening monetary policies when it seemed the economy would have been better served with an easy monetary policy. Still, the Dow-Jones stock average showed Wall Street making impressive gains.

The Board of Governors' decision to raise the interest rates made money more expensive to borrow. Businesses passed the increased costs on to customers. While this seemed inflationary, the FED claimed that the increases were being instituted to prevent inflation.

Behind the confusion was a man named Alan Greenspan, Chairman of the FED's Board of Governors. One of the most prominent economists in the country, Greenspan was born in New York City on 6 March 1926. He was educated at New York University, where he was awarded three degrees with high honors in economics. Greenspan worked and prospered on Wall Street before being named to President Ford's Council of Economic Advisors (1974-1977). In 1987, he was appointed to head the Federal Reserve System by President Reagan and was reappointed in 1991 by President Bush.

As a conservative economist, Alan Greenspan continued the strong anti-inflationary policies of his predecessor, Paul Volcker. Greenspan's policy is simple: growth is necessary, but it must be a slow, steady, managed growth. If the economy begins to expand too quickly, he feared the "boom" would be followed by a "bust." Greenspan believed that an overactive economy quickly dissolves into serious recession.

Chairman Greenspan testified frequently before Congressional committees. Each time he appeared, his message was clear and concise: the economy must be controlled, avoiding rapid growth, inflation, and recession. William Greider, author of *Secrets of the Temple*, made an analogy of the FED as "...a supervising engineer who has the power to alter the flows inside the plumbing. Its policies could stimulate the flow of lending, choke it off, or nudge it to different channels. The Fed accomplishes this by injecting more fluid into the system or withdrawing it-that is by creating or destroying money." (John Hauchette, "Nation Asks: What Recovery? Fed Hits Brakes," *Poughkeepsie Journal* 19 February 1995, 1)

Greenspan's leadership experienced strong criticism. Many economists believed that there were areas of this country that never really recovered from the 1990-91 recession. They suffered from high unemployment and needed the stimulation that "cheap money" gave to the job market. These people blamed Greenspan's cautious fear of inflation for never having had a "real recovery." Many economic professionals and nonprofessionals alike asked: "Is the FED too preoccupied with inflation? Were people forced into part-time employment without benefits, because the Federal Reserve Board of Governors was unjustifiably afraid of inflation? Could it be that the Fed misread the economy all along? Were the Governors' forecasting antennae out of alignment?"

At the center of the controversy was Greenspan, a man that possessed political power, media access, and control of his colleagues. He was a master of understatement who always appeared frail and slightly bent. Yet, armed with strong conviction and potent ties to Wall Street, this conservative Republican – a strong free trade advocate – continued his fight for what he believed was proper policy. Alan Greenspan survived several presidential administrations and attacks by both Congress and the national press. His vision and strategies have set the economic stage for the 21st century.

Figure 7.9

 CHASE

CHEMICAL

CITIBANK⊕

 Bank of America

Largest Banks in the U.S. in 1993

NationsBank

with combined assets exceeding $1 trillion

Source: U.S. Department of Commerce, 1994

Citicorp (NY)
BankAmerica Corp. (CA)
Chemical Banking Corp. (NY)
Nationsbank Corp. (NC)
J.P. Morgan and Co. (NY)

Chase Manhattan Corp. (NY)
Bankers Trust New York Corp. (NY)
Banc One Corp. (OH)
Wells Fargo Co. (CA)
PNC Bank Corp. (PA)

the rate of interest that the FED district banks charge member banks for loans. Member banks borrow money from the FED's 12 district banks to keep their reserves at the proper level. At different times in the year, such as planting time in agricultural regions, commercial banks have to lend large amounts. Reserves go down and the banks borrow to keep their reserves at legal levels.

- *Lowering* the discount rate encourages banks to borrow more for loans, and money gets pumped into the economy.

- *Raising* the discount rate means banks have to pay more for FED loans. This discourages banks from borrowing, and they will have less to lend customers. Raising the discount rate siphons money out of the economy.

Changing the discount rate has broad implications. The FED's discount rate is a financial benchmark. Banks can only make a profit if they charge customers a higher rate than they themselves are paying for loans. If the FED raises the discount rate, big banks raise the **prime rate**. "The Prime" is the rate the big banks charge big customers on large, short-term business loans (see Figure 7.9). It is usually about 3% higher than the FED's discount rate. Just about all other interest rates in the country are linked to the Prime. For example, banks figure most credit card interest rates at 5-9% over the prime. If the FED alters the discount rate, big banks alter the Prime. The availability of money either increases or decreases.

RESERVE REQUIREMENT ADJUSTMENT

Reserve Requirement Adjustment is rarely used. Altering bank reserves (currently around 12%) is an extremely powerful action. Lowering requirements – even slightly – pumps billions in loan money into bankers' hands. Raising reserve requirements siphons it away. It is so massive and unpredictable a force that using it precisely is very difficult.

LIMITS ON THE FED'S POWER

Judicious use of monetary policy by the FED can do much to keep the economy growing and stable. While this is true, *there are limits to the FED's effectiveness.* It is easier to withdraw money in the face of inflation than to push money through the banks in a recession. This is because in recessions business is very slow. Demand for loans declines. Banks themselves become very cautious about lending in an unstable economy, even to highly rated corporations and individuals.

Monetary policy is also limited because it is **discretionary**. First, members of the Board of Governors and FOMC must use their judgment about what to do, how much to do, and when to do it. While they are experts, they are still human beings, and their judgments can be flawed. Second, time also passes while the banks respond to FED orders. The result may be too little, too late. Lastly, other government actions can offset FED actions. For example, Reagan's tax cuts of the early 1980s pushed money into the economy and worked against FED efforts to stop inflation. It is also worth repeating that the FED Governors are notoriously conservative and see themselves as currency auditors rather than fiscal manipulators. They traditionally prefer to move slowly, in response to events, rather than take preemptive action.

BANKING REFORM:
THE GREAT DEPRESSION

The creation of the Federal Reserve in 1913 was one of the most significant economic actions in U.S. history, but it did not solve all the nation's banking problems. The FED was nearly powerless when banks began collapsing in the Great Depression. People were frightened. "Runs on banks" wiped out reserves quickly. Banks had few alternatives. They foreclosed on bad loans and auctioned repossessed property. This did little to meet the panicking public's demand for money.

When Franklin D. Roosevelt became President in March 1933, he called time out and ordered all banks to close. President Roosevelt went on the radio to calm people's fears. He told the public that after federal examiners gave their approval to reopen a bank, it was solvent. This "Bank Holiday" psychology worked. People went along. Congress then passed an

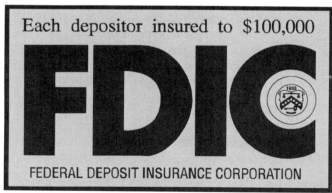

Emergency Banking Act (*Glass-Steagall Act, 1933*). It forbade banks to invest in stocks and began insuring savings accounts through the **FDIC** (Federal Deposit Insurance Corporation). The combination of these unprecedented federal actions stopped the runs on the banks. Later, Congress made the FDIC permanent and created federal deposit insurance programs for savings banks (FSLIC) and other financial institutions.

BANKING DEREGULATION:
S&Ls IN CRISIS

The population explosion and the rapid pace of change in people's lives after World War II led to many changes in banking. In 1980, Congress passed the ***Depository Institutions' Deregulation and Monetary Act***. Its reforms allowed savings banks and credit unions to offer nearly all the services of commercial banks, especially checking accounts. The act also placed many more financial institutions under the FED's reserve regulations. Also, it allowed banks to pay interest on checking accounts. The *Depository Act* broadened banking activities and services for the nation. States changed laws too. Small banks merged with others to become regional banks. The *Depository Act* deregulated consumer interest rates making the whole banking industry a more dynamic market.

However, there were unforeseen repercussions of this deregulation. federal bank examiners could not keep up with inspections and some banks took advantage of the lax atmosphere. The confusion of technological changes, legal changes, and wide-open competition led to mismanagement and even corruption.

A large number of banks failed in the wake of the 1980s deregulation. Bad crop years and dropping oil prices in the middle 1980s put pressure on banks in the Midwest and the Southwest. The recession of 1981-1983 led to failures too. New, inexperienced S&Ls (Savings and Loan Associations) made too many risky loans, particularly in real estate (especially in the South and Southwest).

Some S&L operators were corrupt and manipulated the new laws and depositors' money to finance personal empires. An example was Charles Keating of Lincoln Savings and Loan of California. Keating's fraudulent activities included attempting to bribe U.S. Senators to avoid pressure from federal examiners. Resolving the problems of his bank alone cost taxpayers an estimated $2.6 billion.

Between 1985 and 1993, an average of 175 banks per year closed or were taken over by federal regulators. The Federal Farm Credit System and the FSLIC (Federal Savings and Loan Insurance Corporation) both collapsed try-

ing to pay all the depositors of the failed savings institutions. Congress tried to stop the financial hemorrhaging. It bolstered the FDIC and created the Resolution Trust Corporation to manage failed banks affairs. The cost to taxpayers of bailing out insured depositors and liquidating assets of failed banks exceeded $600 billion.

SUMMARY

Understanding money, credit, and banking are important to everyone. Young people must know how to manage money and credit. As consumers, they must learn to select accounts and credit arrangements that meet their needs and help their earnings grow. The choices are many and often complex. Yet, they are crucial to achieving the American Dream.

ASSESSMENT
QUESTIONS • APPLICATIONS

1   Money's use as a convenient medium of exchange is obvious. However, most people do not even think about the other two important functions of money.
    a   How hard would it be to function without money as a standard of value?
    b   How hard would it be to function without money as a store of wealth?

c   Barter was once a way of life. Could we go back to it? Explain, why or why not.

2   This chapter begins with a story about credit cards. Credit is a critical part of modern American life.
    a   Can a person function without credit? Explain why or why not.
    b   What are the advantages of having credit?
    c   What are the disadvantages of using credit?

3   Suppose banks have to keep 10% of deposits on reserve. Now, suppose you borrow $10,000 for a car loan. Your bank credits your checking account with $10,000 and you write a check for that amount to Mr. Mobilo, the used car dealer. Mr. Mobilo deposits the $10,000 in his bank.
    a   How much of Mr. Mobilo's deposit can his bank lend?
    b   If the original $10,000 loan kept rolling through banks this way, it could create $100,000 in new money. Explain how this happens.

4   The Federal Reserve has great power to control the money supply through banking. Suppose you were a member of the FED's Board of Governors. Explain what policy you would recommend if:
    a   researchers say the economy is going into a period of serious inflation.
    b   researchers say the economy is going into a period of serious recession.
    c   Explain which of these policies has the best chance for success.

5   "The *Depository Institutions' Deregulation and Monetary Act of 1980* caused more problems than it solved." Examine this statement from two points of view:
    a   the *Act* increased competition in the banking industry and benefited consumers with more choices and services.
    b   the *Act* led to instability and the worst rash of bank closings in history.
    c   Explain which point of view you favor.

ASSESSMENT PROJECT:
MANAGING CREDIT CARDS

STUDENT TASK

In this project, research various credit cards, choose one, and write a report on how that credit card fits into your household management program.

PROCEDURE

1　Review the financial status (Household Financial Profile) of the household you created in Issue 1.

2　Research various credit card services. Assume one charge or credit card would be useful to handle financial matters. Decide which type of card is best for your household. In other words, for which one would you apply? Write the Bankcard Holders of America (Box 920, Herndon, VA 22070). Request the "Low Rate List" of card issuers. It costs $1.00.

3　Design a chart comparing at least three credit and/or charge cards (e.g., VISA, MasterCard, Discover, American Express, a department store card). List items such as annual fee, credit limits (cash and purchases), annual and monthly interest rates, number of days of "grace period" (if any), and additional benefits of card (e.g., travel or buying club, insurance, bonuses and premiums, purchase warranty).

4　Write a brief report on which card you have chosen for your household management. Include:

- Which card and card issuer chosen and why.

- Financial data for the card (e.g., APR, annual fee, grace period).

- Why and how you expect the card to help or hinder the look of your Household Financial Profile.

- "Pitfalls" to avoid with use of this card.

- How you intend to use the features of the card.

- How this card will help establish credit for other forms of credit (e.g., mortgage, personal and collateral loans).

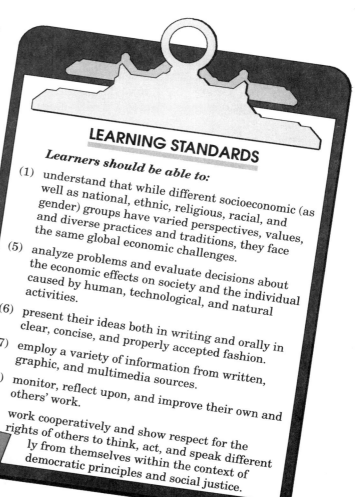

LEARNING STANDARDS

Learners should be able to:

(1)　understand that while different socioeconomic (as well as national, ethnic, religious, racial, and gender) groups have varied perspectives, values, and diverse practices and traditions, they face the same global economic challenges.

(5)　analyze problems and evaluate decisions about the economic effects on society and the individual caused by human, technological, and natural activities.

(6)　present their ideas both in writing and orally in clear, concise, and properly accepted fashion.

(7)　employ a variety of information from written, graphic, and multimedia sources.

(8)　monitor, reflect upon, and improve their own and others' work.

(9)　work cooperatively and show respect for the rights of others to think, act, and speak differently from themselves within the context of democratic principles and social justice.

EVALUATION

The criteria for the evaluation of this project are itemized in the grid (rubric) that follows. Choice of appropriate category terms (values) is the decision of the instructor. Selection of terms such as "minimal," "satisfactory," and "distinguished" can vary with each assessment.

Managing Credit Cards Evaluation Rubric

(Refer to introductory section for suggestions of scoring descriptors for the evaluation categories.)

Evaluation Item	Category 1	Category 2	Category 3	Category 4	Category 5
Item a: (1) Does the report show understanding that while different socioeconomic (as well as national, ethnic, religious, racial, and gender) groups have varied perspectives, values, and diverse practices and traditions, they face the same global economic challenges?					
Item b: (5) Does the report analyze problems and evaluate decisions about the economic effects caused by human, technological, and natural activities on societies and individuals?					
Item c: (6) Does the report present ideas in writing (and orally) in clear, concise, and properly accepted fashion?					
Item d: (7) Does the report employ a variety of information from written, graphic, and multimedia sources?					
Item e: (8) Does the report show monitoring of, reflection upon, and improvement of work?					
Item f: (9) Does the report show cooperative work and respect for the rights of others to think, act, and speak differently?					

ISSUE 8

What are the economic roles of government?

ROLE OF GOVERNMENT

"The citizens of every country ought to help support their government as best they can in proportion to their abilities.

"... Every tax ought to be so managed that it will take out – and keep out – of the pockets of the people as little as possible beyond what it brings in to the public treasury ..."

– Adam Smith. *The Wealth of Nations*

RIDING
THE MERRY-GO-ROUND

The managing editor looked harried; that was normal. "Gene," he said, "I know you're the cartoonist for the Op-Ed page, but I don't have a reporter to cover the school board fracas out at Granville tonight. You live out there; could you do me a favor?"

"Jim, I haven't reported on anything in twenty years!"

"Come on, Gene. You never lose those skills. We have to get coverage out there. And, you know you owe me about 4,000 favors. Besides, the weather is fantastic."

I had to admit, it was a beautiful spring evening as I sat in the Granville H.S. auditorium. The warm breeze was blowing through the windows, and the sunset was coating all the trees outside in a bright yellow-orange haze. I was feeling wonderful and believed that nothing could upset this fantastic feeling of "spring fever." I thought of a balmy spring night years ago at Oceanside Park with Cindy, the woman who became my wife. We strode the boardwalk and rode the carousel ...

A bang of the gavel brought me back to reality. Being at this school board meeting was strange. Both of my children were attending college and I had lost touch with the issues that stirred controversy in the local public school. At a picnic last week, some neighbors voiced concern about the overcrowding of students into elementary classes, but lots of people were moving into the area. Growing pains, I thought.

While I daydreamed, people packed the auditorium. Now they began to yell and scream at one another. When the public comment segment opened, it was easy to see the audience was divided into factions. I was trying to scribble notes on each group's position. Listening to them attack each other for being an "interest group" brought a cynical smile to my face. I was wondering how naive could they be not to realize that everyone seeks out what is best for themselves. Don't we all belong to special interest groups – both, formally and informally, perhaps intentionally or unintentionally?

One group supported smaller class sizes. That meant more teachers and classrooms and more money. Others wanted to increase class size so that teaching positions would be eliminated, and costs brought down.

There was the parent group with banners trying to influence the Granville Board of Education with their presence. There was a taxpayer group waving charts and graphs. Each had perceptions of what was best for them – and everyone else. One group wanted what was best for their children's future. The other group wanted to protect their lifestyle and finances.

Speeches poured forth, some with impressive statistics and figures, others with personal anecdotes. A senior citizen spoke about the possibility of losing her home of 47 years if taxes increased. A group of young parents spoke about the problems their children faced in large classes that would handicap them for life.

There I was, caught in the middle. I was not just a reporter, I was a taxpayer, too. Of course, the final decision had to be made by the elected officials on the school board. They had to read the sense of the community, but they had to weigh all the local, state, and even federal regulations controlling the finances of education.

The gavel banged again. I sat there as the crowd exited. I got the story, but my head was spinning. I thought back to that lovely spring evening at Oceanside. It was like getting off a merry-go-round. ... Hey, maybe there is an editorial cartoon in all this!

ISSUE 8

What are the economic roles of government?

ROLE OF GOVERNMENT

INTRODUCTION

Nothing stirs more controversy than mentioning the role of government in the economy. It is an issue that has existed since the founding of this nation. The American Revolution (1776-1783) was a struggle against the tyranny of unfair taxation and economic restriction. Soon after, a struggle over government's economic power began in President Washington's Cabinet (1790s) between Thomas Jefferson and Alexander Hamilton. Jefferson insisted on a small role for the federal government. Hamilton insisted on a strong, active government as a force for economic development. This sounds somewhat similar to the controversies that flow daily from the national and state capitals in the 1990s.

Alexander Hamilton
First Secretary of the Treasury

CONSTITUTIONAL BATTLES OVER THE ROLES

What does the *United States Constitution* have to say about the role of government in the economy? The authors offered some definition of the role of government in this area, delegating to Congress specific economic powers:

- to impose and collect taxes.

- to provide for the common defense and general welfare of the people.

- to borrow money on the credit of the United States.

- to regulate commerce with foreign nations and among the states.

- to coin money and regulate its value.

- to establish a post office and roads.

- to raise and support military forces.

George Washington
First President of the U.S.

- to make all laws which shall be necessary and proper for carrying into execution the foregoing powers, and all other powers vested by this *Constitution* in the government of the United States.

On the basis of these last words (Art. I, section 8, called the **"Elastic Clause"**), Secretary of the Treasury Hamilton justified his call to create the first Bank of the United States. He argued such a bank was necessary for the government to accomplish its other economic tasks. Hamilton claimed the specific powers to tax, to borrow, and to regulate money and commerce

Thomas Jefferson
First Secretary of State

implied a bank was necessary. This idea of **implied power** justified a loose (elastic), stretching of the meaning of the delegated powers of Congress.

A struggle soon emerged in President Washington's Cabinet. Secretary of State Jefferson rebutted Hamilton. In a paper, he claimed Hamilton was stretching government

The Supreme Court of the United States, Washington, D.C.
©PhotoDisc

authority too far. Jefferson cited the **Tenth Amendment**. It seemed to contradict the Elastic Clause; it reserved for the states all powers not delegated to the federal government. In a strict approach to government power, Jefferson argued that there was no specific banking power delegated to Congress in the *Constitution*. Therefore, under the Tenth Amendment, the power to create such an institution must be reserved for the states, not the federal government.

This early struggle over strict v. loose interpretation of constitutional clauses shaped the two earliest national parties. In the 1790s, Hamilton's view was the conservative political view (Federalist Party) and Jefferson held the liberal position (Democratic – Republican Party). Over the past two centuries, the meanings of liberal and conservative have changed. Today, **liberal** refers to a loose view that calls for a strong government involvement, and the term **conservative** usually reflects a strict view that calls for as little government rule as possible.

In the end, President Washington sided with Hamilton. Congress passed the bill and created the first Bank of the United States in 1791. Later, when the bank's power was challenged in the Supreme Court, Chief Justice **John Marshall** upheld Washington's and Hamilton's view (*McCulloch v. Maryland*, 1819). Marshall legitimized the Hamiltonian view that the federal government did have implied powers (unwritten, but hinted at in the *Constitution*). These powers could be used to strengthen the economic role of the national government. Still, for the first 150 years of our history, the economic role of the federal government grew very slowly.

NEW ROLES IN THE GREAT DEPRESSION

In 1929, everything changed. Prior to the Great Crash, a sense of rugged individualism characterized American thought. The Frontier, or Western Ethic of the 19th century, was a feeling that urged people to "sit tall in the saddle" and "pull yourself up by your bootstraps." The ethic held that individuals could solve their own problems. It implied there was failure, shame, and humiliation in taking charity and welfare. The popular sense was that depressions were part of the normal ups and downs of the economy, and people just had to put up with them. There was an acceptance of **laissez-faire**: government had to remain separated from the business cycle. Left alone, the economy would always heal itself. Meanwhile, people had to make do with what they had. As a result, Congress and Presidents felt no need to get the federal government involved in relieving economic problems.

Franklin D. Roosevelt, 32nd President 1933–1945
FDR helped Americans regain faith in themselves.
(photograph of the Presidential portrait, White House)

Thus, in the early 1930s, there was no established tradition of government intervention. Yet, there had never been a depression affecting the nation so deeply. Understanding of such matters was unrefined. The common feeling was that any interference from government would worsen an economic downturn.

As things deteriorated, President Herbert Hoover managed to follow the worst possible plan. He and Congress raised taxes. *The Federal Revenue Act of 1932* nearly doubled the tax rates. A depression is characterized by a very high rate of unemployment and little consumer spending in society. Taking additional taxes curtails spending even more.

What should Hoover have done? One liberal economist had some ideas. English scholar **John Maynard Keynes** believed that demand (spending) had to be increased. Keynes said increased demand triggers an increase in supply. As people spent more, more goods and services were needed. Factories would rehire people to produce the goods that consumers were demanding. Once the workers were back in the factories earning wages, they would add to the demand. In turn, factories would have to hire more people, and so on (see sidebar on Keynes opposite page).

How would people get more money in their pockets to start this demand chain reaction? The answer came with the **New Deal**. When the Democrats won the 1932 Presidential and congressional elections led by New York Governor **Franklin D. Roosevelt**, the nation prepared for a significant change in economic policy. The Democrats campaigned on a platform that promised a "New Deal" for the victims of the Depression, or for that matter, for all Americans.

When Roosevelt took office in 1933, more than a quarter of all workers were jobless, and he was ready to act immediately. In his inaugural address, Roosevelt said, "The nation asks for action, and action now ... We must act, and act quickly." The words were not empty. A series of extraordinary measures followed. They began the slow and painful recovery out of this horrible economic depression.

President Roosevelt's New Deal program is an example of government's use of **fiscal policy** (see Figure 8.1). This is when the government attempts to use two of its powers, taxation and

Profile of English Economist John Maynard Keynes

The basis for demand-management or demand–side economics originated in the writings of John Maynard Keynes. The British economist was born in Cambridge, England in 1883. His father, John Neville Keynes, made sure his son was well educated at both Eaton College and Cambridge University, where the elder Keynes taught economics and logic. John Maynard Keynes' first love was mathematics. But influenced by many of his instructors, he finally chose to complete his studies in economics. Keynes distinguished himself as a businessman, as well as a scholar in his field. Right up to his death in 1946, he spent his life mixing and blending many different careers – teacher, editor, civil service, college bursar, scholar, author, and patron of the arts – while amassing a fortune by investing in the stock market.

After World War I, Keynes served his government as an advisor to the British delegation at the peace talks in Versailles. From this experience, he wrote *The Economic Consequences of the Peace*. This book was inspired by the harsh treatment of the German people by the Allies. In it, Keynes predicted the collapse of the European economy because of the severity of the conditions imposed on Germany. His analysis of the circumstances proved prophetic and precise.

Keynes writings covered a wide range of topics, but his most important and influential work was presented in *The General Theory of Employment, Interest, and Money* (1936). This book was written during the Great Depression when millions of American and European workers were unemployed. Traditional economists were unable to present a reason for such a long and painful period in which so many desperate people could not find any work. What had happened to Adam Smith's "invisible hand"? Classical economists considered unemployment an irregular and deviant condition that was only a temporary circumstance. They cautioned that if government would not interfere, the economy would right itself, making a few price and wage adjustments that would put full employment back into place.

Keynes' *General Theory* presented a different view of how the market economy operates and a new prescription for curing the terribly high unemployment rates. Left on its own, the economy may get back into balance, but Keynes demonstrated that it would not necessarily return to full employment. At the center of his theory was the message that government had to become involved and could no longer trust any invisible force to right the economy. He said there was no natural method of correction that would easily and quickly force the economy back into full employment. Keynes claimed the level of employment depended on the total demand for goods and services in the market place. In a depression, this aggregate demand diminishes, and so producers cut back on production and lay off employees. This causes a decline in demand and a downward spiral begins.

In order to increase the aggregate demand for goods and services in the marketplace, Keynes proposed that the government must provide the means to stimulate consumer spending. The increased government spending would ignite a need for increased production, and people would have to be rehired.

Since the Great Depression, capitalist governments all over the world have responded to periods of high unemployment with Keynes prescription. Governments engaged in two major activities designed to stimulate aggregate demand: lowering taxes to give people more spending money and providing jobs by increasing government contracts for public works. Eventually, this government money, spent in the marketplace, would prod private business to begin increased production and put people back to work. When this happens, taxes can be collected to pay back the government for the money it had to spend. From Roosevelt's New Deal through the Carter Administration, John Maynard Keynes' ideas were part of our government's economic activities.

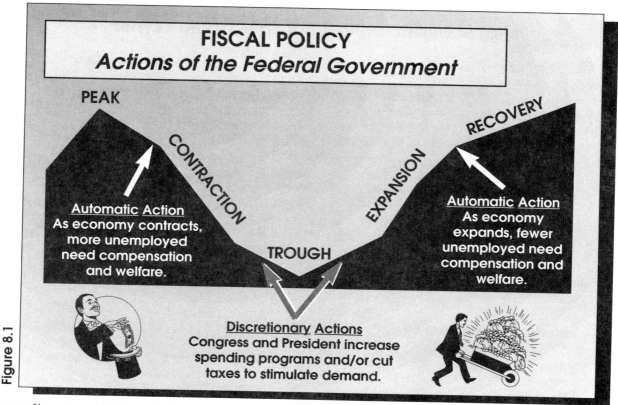

Figure 8.1

FISCAL POLICY
Actions of the Federal Government

PEAK

CONTRACTION

RECOVERY

EXPANSION

TROUGH

Automatic Action
As economy contracts,
more unemployed
need compensation
and welfare.

Automatic Action
As economy
expands, fewer
unemployed need
compensation and
welfare.

Discretionary Actions
Congress and President increase
spending programs and/or cut
taxes to stimulate demand.

spending, to **stabilize the economy** (maintain the level of growth).

Is this role of stabilization Constitutional? It fired up the perpetual loose v. strict battle over implied powers. The New Dealers claimed the role was implied as an evolution of the function of taxation. The Elastic Clause allowed it, just as it did a Bank of the United States to stabilize finances. Hamilton would probably approve, whereas Jefferson and today's conservatives would oppose this new role.

When the economy suffers from recession or depression, Congress can adopt **discretionary** (intentional) **fiscal policies** that reduce taxes and increase spending. The objective is to pump more money into the society to stimulate aggregate demand. When people get a tax break, they take that "extra money" and spend it, increasing demand for goods and services.

In the Great Depression, New Deal leaders avoided fiscal policies related to taxes (increasing or decreasing). Taxes were already low, and raising them for revenue would take away purchasing power. Instead, New Deal programs centered on spending actions such as the **Civilian Conservation Corps** (**CCC**) which put young men to work on environmental projects, and the **Works Projects Administration** (**WPA**) which created public street cleaning and construction jobs for the unemployed (see Figure 8.2 on the next page). To do this, it had to borrow and run a deficit.

ROLE OF STABILIZER: SUCCESS OR FAILURE?

Employment rises when the government increases spending. Sometimes, government spending is massive, and employment in certain industries soars. Examples include defense spending during the Cold War or increased spending in the construction industry when Congress spends for interstate highways and urban renewal. With more people employed, consumer spending (aggregate demand) rises. When used appropriately, discretionary fiscal policy can be an effective means of stabilizing the economy. During the twenty years between the end of World War II and the mid-1960s, the government's taxation and spending grew, and the economy flourished. This convinced many authorities of Keynes' wisdom. It was clear to them that fiscal policy could be used to keep the economy growing.

Besides discretionary action, government has also put into place **automatic fiscal stabilizers** (see Figure 8.1). These are fiscal policies

Figure 8.2

Fiscal Policy: The New Deal's 3 Rs

President and Advisors Suggest Legislation.

Congress Legislates Recommended Programs.

RELIEF	RECOVERY	REFORM
Immediate Action To Halt The Economy's Deterioration	"Pump – Priming" Temporary Programs To Restart the Flow Of Consumer Demand	Permanent Programs To Avoid Situations Causing Contractions and to Provide Insurance for Citizens Against Economic Disasters
Bank Holiday	Agricultural Adjustment	Securities and Exchange Commission
Emergency Banking Act	*National Industrial Recovery Act*	Federal Deposit Insurance Corporation
Federal Emergency Relief Act	Home Owners Loan Corporation	Social Security Administration
Civil Works Administration	Works Progress Administration	National Labor Relations Board

built into the system, and no one in Congress or the White House has to use discretion to trigger them. They provide money to needy people when the economy declines. They maintain a level of demand, softening the downward trend and easing personal loss. An example of an automatic fiscal stabilizer is the unemployment compensation system. It rises as the rate of unemployment rises. As times get better, the amount of unemployment compensation paid declines because the number unemployed declines.

On a national scale, these automatic benefit payments to unemployed workers help to maintain aggregate demand. Other automatic stabilizers include social services and some Social Security payments. They help to smooth out the ups and downs of the business cycle. Automatic stabilizers help the unfortunate survive, but *they are not strong enough to cure the economy.* To really alter the economy, Congress must use discretionary fiscal policies (see Figure 8.1).

Today, Americans are more aware of the limitations of this policy. In order for the government to "prime the pump" (stimulate), it must

have the financial resources to use. To spend more while keeping taxes low, government goes into financial markets to borrow money on a very large scale. In truth, the government begins spending what it does not have. This is called **deficit spending**. This borrowing increases the national debt, and just as in a personal credit situation, the debt can become burdensome.

When any debt is too large, prudence dictates that spending stop. It seems governments should be restricted by this same common sense rule. They are not. Uncontrolled spending created a huge **national debt** (the total amount the federal government owes to creditors). The debt is the accumulated unpaid balance of many past years' deficits (see Figure 8.3). The 1995 debt was approximately 4.5 trillion dollars (see Issue 1, Figure 1.3). The United States federal government is running out of credit. Since the value of the dollar rests on peoples' confidence in the government, there is a great deal at stake in bringing the debt under control. Unfortunately, many state and local governments follow the same pattern and also have massive debts.

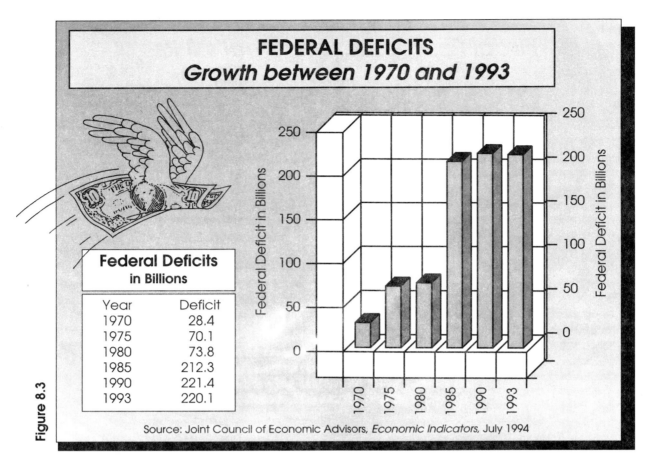

FEDERAL DEFICITS
Growth between 1970 and 1993

Federal Deficits in Billions

Year	Deficit
1970	28.4
1975	70.1
1980	73.8
1985	212.3
1990	221.4
1993	220.1

Figure 8.3

Source: Joint Council of Economic Advisors, *Economic Indicators*, July 1994

ROLE OF STABILIZER: DEMAND-SIDE OR SUPPLY-SIDE?

Since the New Deal, most Presidents and Congresses have followed the liberal Keynesian style of fiscal policy. The ***Employment Act of 1946*** institutionalized the Keynesian approach. By this act, Congress required the President to make an annual report on the condition of the economy. To help, Congress authorized a three-person Council of Economic Advisors for the President, and its own Joint Economic Committee.

The *Employment Act* acknowledged a permanent role for government to use tax policies and spending programs to stabilize the economy. It now had a legal obligation to use discretionary fiscal policy to influence aggregate demand and make other adjustments to the economy. This Keynesian approach of government intervention to change aggregate demand is called **demand management policy**, or **demand-side economics**. By the 1980s, this policy seemed to be out of control. Deficits were mounting, and public reaction also rose (see Figure 8.4 on opposite page).

In 1980, with the election of **Ronald Reagan** to the presidency, the approach to fiscal policy changed. The liberal (loose) v. conservative (strict) battle raged once again. Reagan's conservative supporters denounced most liberal demand-side policy as inefficient, short-term manipulation of demand. Conservative programs sought to generate a balanced budget and end deficit spending. They cut taxes. But, unfortunately they never managed to reduce spending. To replace (Keynesian) demand-side economics, President Reagan's advisors saw a solution in the writings of **Jean-Baptiste Say**, a 19th century French economist (see sidebar).

Say believed that most government intervention with the economy was harmful. He claimed that economic stability can be assured not by stimulating aggregate demand but by increasing aggregate supply. Say's supply-side ideas became the basis for Reagan's conservative economic programs, popularly known as "**Reaganomics**." Conservatives wanted reduction of the economic roles of government. Their program included income tax cuts for citizens and corporations, government spending cuts on social programs (but not military defense), and cuts in government regulation of the economy (deregulation).

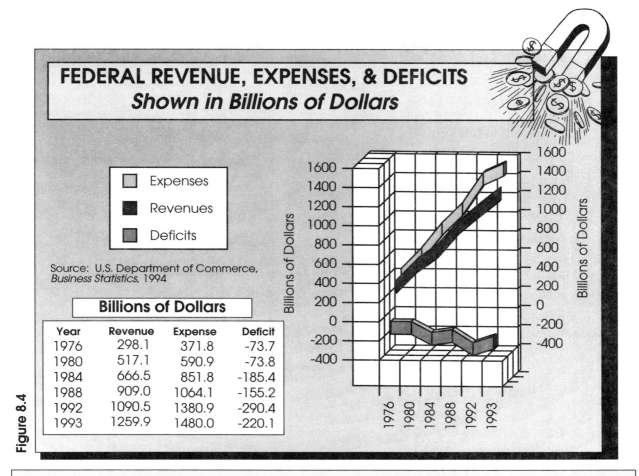

FEDERAL REVENUE, EXPENSES, & DEFICITS
Shown in Billions of Dollars

- ☐ Expenses
- ■ Revenues
- ☐ Deficits

Source: U.S. Department of Commerce,
Business Statistics, 1994

Billions of Dollars

Year	Revenue	Expense	Deficit
1976	298.1	371.8	-73.7
1980	517.1	590.9	-73.8
1984	666.5	851.8	-185.4
1988	909.0	1064.1	-155.2
1992	1090.5	1380.9	-290.4
1993	1259.9	1480.0	-220.1

Figure 8.4

Profile of French Economist Jean Baptist Say

The basis for today's Supply-Side Economics originated in the writings of the French economist Jean Baptiste Say (1767-1832). In his *Treatise on Political Economy* (1803), Say reorganized and popularized Smith's market theories in Europe. Say expounded the theory of entrepreneurship in the six volume *Cours Complet d' economie Politique Practique*, a massive discourse on political economy. In Say's interpretation of Smith's ideas, he argued that supply creates its own demand. Producers, not encumbered by government rules (laissez-faire) act in their own self-interest to realize profits, and in doing so, they stimulate growth. This became the basis for what is now known as Say's Law: Producers create demand by paying for all of the factors of production necessary to put a good or service on the market. That means every payment made by a producer is income for someone else. Once that income is obtained, it is spent, essentially becoming new demand. Thus, Say maintains the production of one good stimulates the creation and consumption of others. To supply-side economists, this means that growth is defined by an economy's ability to produce, not consume. The more the economy produces, the wealthier it is.

Jean Baptiste Say's economic theory also embraced and endorsed Smith's doctrine of laissez-faire. According to Say, any economic depression that existed was caused by trade barriers (tariffs) that government put up to prevent the free exchange of goods and services with other nations. Output must have markets in which to be sold. When government prevents producers from accessing these markets, it causes the depressions. Say claimed overproduction cannot harm the economy if trade is free. Only government interference with trade keeps goods and services from reaching world markets.

FEDERAL DOLLAR
How a Dollar is Budgeted

$.14 State & local grants

$.15 Interest on National Debt

$.05 other operations

$.48 Benefit payments to Individuals

$.18 National Defense

Figure 8.5   Source: Gregg, Scott. "The Budget Dollar: Where It Goes." *Poughkeepsie Journal*, 8 February 1994. A-1

Conservative "supply-siders" claimed these changes would provide producers with incentives to increase investment and production. They reasoned that more production would mean more jobs, and more jobs would mean more income, and more income would mean more spending, and more spending would mean growth and prosperity. Thus, supply-siders believed that stimulating supply would trigger a growth of aggregate demand. Supply-side economic policy has the same objective as demand stimulation. It is a different route for getting to the same place but with a diminished government role.

Still, there is a problem. The supply-side approach assumes business tax cuts will wisely go into investment. But what if this increased investment never occurs? Keynes claimed that putting money in consumers' hands will lead to spending. Say claimed putting money in producers' hands will lead to investing.

Congress cut business taxes with Reagan's *Economic Recovery Act of 1981*. There was a flurry of intense investment that stimulated the economy out of the recession by 1984, but it faded quickly.

In the long run, not enough money went into product research and development or plant expansion as many supply-siders had hoped. Businesses used the extra money to increase corporate executive's salaries, raise dividends for their stockholders, invest overseas, and/or buy out competitors (mergers and acquisitions). In fact, the lower bank interest rates in the early 1990s led to more investment than did the 1980s supply-side tax incentives.

Each Congress and Presidential administration has its own perception of the proper relationship between the government and the economy. That relationship changes as time and power changes. The final response of any Congress and administration is partly made according to public opinion and the political priorities of elected representatives.

ROLE OF GOVERNMENT: THE GREAT SAFETY NET

Increasingly, the American people have become dependent on the government for economic help. The public's desire to create a smaller, less costly government has always been hindered by its dependence on government services. Consider that amid their cries for lower taxes and budget deficit reduction in the 1990s, many Americans still wanted a national government health care program in spite of the cost.

Since the Great Crash of 1929, local, state, and federal bureaucracies have been growing continually. In the 1930s Depression, the situation was desperate enough to alter the sacred doctrine of laissez-faire. In the New Deal, Congress frequently stretched the Elastic Clause to give the federal government more and more economic power, and the public accepted all the help it could get.

From the Great Depression's desperate experience, people came to expect help anytime they needed it. Floods in the Mid-West, earthquakes in the Far West, hurricanes on the East Coast, unemployment in the cities, bad weather freezing crops in the South – it makes no difference. People now *expect* government grants, subsidies, low interest loans, and emergency finances to rebuild, restore, replace, replenish, resurrect, repair, and recover. Today, people demand more from government, and its economic roles have grown (see government agency listings below and in the Appendices). More people, with more problems, means more spending and bigger government.

Think of all the economic roles people expect government to play. Government is expected to:

• provide public goods and services.

• protect consumers and workers from harm in the marketplace.

• furnish the needy with assistance through transfer payments.

• keep jobs safe while keeping the prices stable.

A look at the federal budget dollar (see Figure 8.5 on opposite page) shows the expense of government providing these things. While they often denounce the cost, leaders feel people want a "great safety net" to protect them from life's problems. When the government is unable to meet people's expectations, they blame its activity (or lack of action) for everything that is wrong.

SELECTED U.S. GOVERNMENT AGENCIES INVOLVED WITH ECONOMICS
(see Appendices for listing of Federal and state agencies and of private organizations)

CONGRESSIONAL COMMITTEES

Copyright Office (Library of Congress)
H.R Agriculture Committee
H.R Committee on Interior & Insular Affairs
H.R Energy & Commerce Committe
H.R Interior Committee
H.R Public Works & Transportation Committee
S. Agriculture, Nutrition, & Forestry Committee
Sen. Commerce, Science & Transportation Committee
Sen. Energy & Natural Resources Committee
Sen, Environment & Public Works Committee

PRESIDENTIAL OFFICES

Council of Economic Advisors
Office of Management & the Budget (OMB)

CABINET DEPARTMENTS

U.S. Department of Agriculture
U.S. Department of Commerce
U.S. Department of Energy
U.S. Department of the Health & Human Services (HHS)
U.S. Department of Housing & Urban Development (HUD)
U.S. Department of the Interior
U.S. Department of Justice
U.S. Department of Labor
U.S. Department of Transportation
U.S. Department of the Treasury
U.S. Department of Veterans Affairs

DEPARTMENTAL AGENCIES

Administration for Children & Families (HHS)
Antitrust Division (Justice)
Bureau of Alcohol, Tobacco & Firearms (Treasury)
Bureau of Economic Analysis (Commerce)
Bureau of Indian Affairs (Interior)
Bureau of Labor Statistics (Labor)
Bureau of Land Management (Interior)
Bureau of Mines (Interior)
Comptroller of the Currency (Treasury)
Drug Enforcement Administration (Justice)
Employment Standards Administration (Labor)
Employment & Training Administration (Labor)
Federal Aviation Administration (Transportation)
Federal Crop Insurance Corporation (Agriculture)
Federal Energy Regulatory Commission (Energy)
Federal Housing & Equal Opportunity Office (HUD)
Federal Housing Commissioner (HUD)
Fish & Wildlife Service (Interior)
Food & Drug Administration (HHS)
Food & Nutrition Service (Agriculture)
Food Safety & Inspection Service (Agriculture)
Internal Revenue Service (Treasury)
Labor Management Standards Administration (Labor)
Minority Business Development Agency (Commerce)
National Highway Traffic Safety Administration (Trans.)
National Marine Fisheries Service (Commerce)
National Institute for Occupational Safety & Health (Labor)
Occupational Safety & Health Administration (Labor)
Occupational Safety & Health Review Commission (Labor)
Office of Consumer Affairs (HHS)
Office of Economics (Agriculture)
Office of Surface Mining Reclamation & Enforcement (Int.)
Patent & Trademark Office (Commerce)
Social Security Administration (HHS)
Soil Conservation Services (Agriculture.)
U.S. Coast Guard (Transportation)
U.S. Customs Service (Treasury)
U.S. Forest Service (Agriculture)

INDEPENDENT AGENCIES

AMTRAK (National Railroad Passenger Corporation)
Commodity Futures Trading Commission
Consumer Affairs Council
Consumer Information Center
Consumer Product Safety Commission
Energy Regulatory Commission
Environmental Protection Agency
Equal Employment Opportunity Commission
Export-Import Bank of the United States
Federal Communications Commission (FCC)
Federal Council on Aging
Federal Deposit Insurance Corporation (FDIC)
Federal Highway Administration
Federal Home Loan Mortgage Corporation
Federal Labor Relations Authority
Federal Maritime Commission
Federal Mediation & Conciliation Service
Federal Mine Safety & Health Review Commission
Federal Reserve System
Federal Trade Commission
General Accounting Office
General Services Administration
Government Printing Office
Interstate Commerce Commission
National Bureau of Standards
National Credit Union Administration
National Economic Council
National Labor Relations Board
National Mediation Board
National Transportation Safety Board
Office of Conservation & Renewable Energy
Postal Rate Commission
Resolution Trust Corporation
Regulatory Information Service Center
Securities & Exchange Commission
Small Business Administration
Tennessee Valley Authority (Independent)
U.S. Postal Service
U.S. International Trade Commission

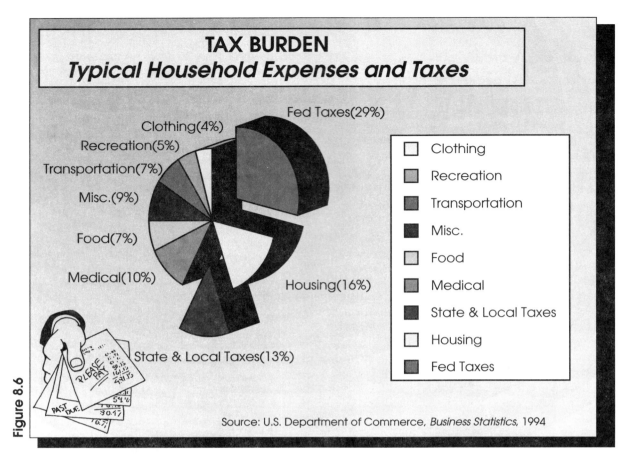

TAX BURDEN
Typical Household Expenses and Taxes

Fed Taxes(29%)

Clothing(4%)
Recreation(5%)
Transportation(7%)
Misc.(9%)
Food(7%)
Medical(10%)
State & Local Taxes(13%)
Housing(16%)

- ☐ Clothing
- ☐ Recreation
- ☐ Transportation
- ☐ Misc.
- ☐ Food
- ☐ Medical
- ☐ State & Local Taxes
- ☐ Housing
- ☐ Fed Taxes

Source: U.S. Department of Commerce, *Business Statistics*, 1994

Figure 8.6

The 1990s brought some rethinking of the massive scope and cost of government. Americans began to question how much government should be expected to do. Conservative criticism led to Republican victories in the mid-1990s elections, causing legislatures to make serious attempts at budget control, cuts in spending, and deficit reduction.

ROLES OF GOVERNMENT: WHO PAYS FOR IT?

Some people feel *entitled* to all the services and protections of this great safety net as if it were a birthright. Yet, when government turns to taxpayers for **revenue** (income), they balk. **Taxes** are the obligatory fees citizens pay for government. Yet, nothing causes more reaction to government than the mere mention of taxes.

Historically, citizens rage against government collection of these revenues. Revolutions start over them. Whatever decreases personal income is viewed as evil. As purchasing power declines, anger escalates. It seems to be a great conspiracy – government changes tax laws and gets a greater portion of the hard-earned money

of people and business, reducing aggregate demand (see Figure 8.6 above).

Today, the array of taxes is bewildering. Some taxes are highly visible, and some nearly invisible. Governments impose taxes on consumers, producers, wage earners, and property owners. The federal, state, and local governments levy taxes. Governments tax people on what they earn, on what they spend, on what they save, and on what they own. Industries are taxed as well as individuals. It all takes a "big chunk" out of individual wealth.

Throughout the United States, the average **"Tax Independence Day"** comes sometime in May. That means that the average taxes paid per year is an amount equalling that earned between January and May. The thought of spending five months a year working to pay your share of government bills has an agonizing effect on most people. The distress hits home every April 15th (federal/state income tax filing deadlines) or when the school or county property tax bills arrive in the mail (see Figure 8.7 on opposite page). Questions begin to whiz through citizens' minds as to why such vast amounts of money are being spent. Government has become

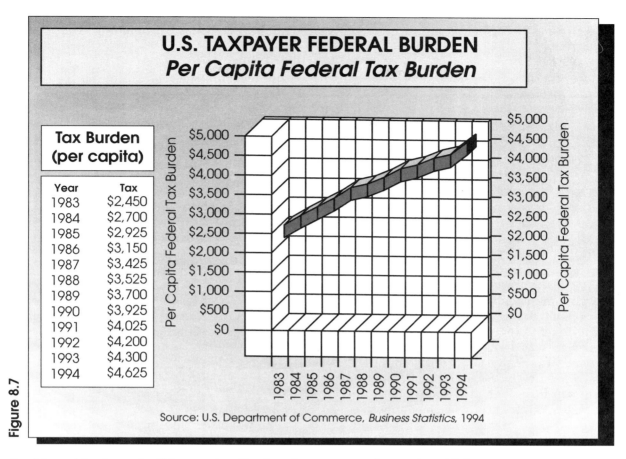

Figure 8.7

U.S. TAXPAYER FEDERAL BURDEN
Per Capita Federal Tax Burden

Tax Burden (per capita)

Year	Tax
1983	$2,450
1984	$2,700
1985	$2,925
1986	$3,150
1987	$3,425
1988	$3,525
1989	$3,700
1990	$3,925
1991	$4,025
1992	$4,200
1993	$4,300
1994	$4,625

Source: U.S. Department of Commerce, *Business Statistics,* 1994

the biggest business in this country. During the last half century, government has grown bigger and bigger trying to respond to more demands and responsibilities. As it grows, it spends greater sums of tax money.

Examining our history provides some idea of why such rapid growth took place:

- As population grew, all levels of government expanded: more teachers, police officers, fire fighters, accountants, judges, public defenders, district attorneys, public health personnel, etc. (According to the 1990 Census, there are over 7 million federal, state, local, and city employees [*Statistical Abstract of the United States 1992*. pgs. 304, 331].)

- With more people, the numbers of disadvantaged or poor citizens grew. Unfortunately, the number of people that need government aid has grown at a much faster pace than the general population.

- In addition, the United States plays a significant role in global affairs. Being a world leader requires responsible reaction toward global emergencies. There are wars, relief efforts, police actions, natural catastrophes,

and terrorism. If the government responds to these events, it costs the taxpayers money.

ROLES OF GOVERNMENT: REDISTRIBUTING WEALTH

Government now assumes a considerable amount of responsibility for the economic well-being of people. Federal, state, and county governments engage in redistributing wealth through **transfer payments** (taxing people that have resources and transferring money to those in need). The system of transfer payments includes public assistance, social insurance, subsidies, and grants-in-aid.

Many individuals and groups devote themselves to influencing the system. There are lobbyists, **PAC**'s (Political Action Committees), factions, coalitions, confederations, unions, blocs, and leagues. All try to influence lawmakers' decisions on public economic policy (see Issue 13). Each struggles to have government act in its best interests. It seems like a nightmare. The system is flawed and perhaps out of control. Yet, people expect government to provide a "safety net" to protect citizens.

Federal and State Tax Revenues

Source: U.S. Department of Commerce, *Statistical Abstract*, 1994

Average Federal Tax Sources (% of total revenue)	Average State Tax Sources (% of total revenue)
Social Security / Medicare Taxes (36.1%) Federal Individual Income Tax (45.6%) Federal Corporate Income Tax (8.5%) Federal Excise Taxes (Alcohol, Tobacco, Jewelry, Furs, Leather, Telephone) (4.4%) Estate and Gift Taxes (0.9%) Other (4.5%)	Property Taxes (2%) Sales Taxes (49.5%) State Excise Taxes (Alcohol, Tobacco – 2.8%) Energy Taxes (6.7%) State Individual Income Tax (31%) State Corporate Income Tax (6.5%) Other (1.5%)

Figure 8.8

At first glance, most people see taxation as a major roadblock to the American Dream. Yet, the government provides a wide range of protective services to help everyone achieve the American Dream. By monitoring the marketplace, agencies keep citizens from harm. Government inspects and examines food, water, air, cars, banks, etc. to protect the public.

A very important aspect of our mixed economy is the maintenance and encouragement of competition. Competition is the life blood of the economy. By promoting competition, the government protects the people from negative side effects of business operation. It maintains the protection of the consumer from the price-fixing practices of oligopolies and monopolies. Antitrust laws that flow from the *Sherman Antitrust Act* (1890) outlawed any contract or combination that worked toward a monopoly or any conspiracy that would restrain trade or commerce. Under the *Sherman Act*, the federal government brought a number of legal actions in the early 1900s that resulted in the breaking up of several large corporations, or "trusts" as they were then called, including Standard Oil of New Jersey (today's Exxon), American Tobacco, and DuPont.

Despite this and other laws created to maintain the element of competition in the economy, combinations kept growing because of weaknesses in the laws. Huge corporations are a fact of modern economic life. They offer economic benefits and technical efficiencies, but ordinary people fear the abuse of corporate power. However, for the American economy to remain viable, competition must be maintained. This takes a "watchdog effort" against those corporate moves that can destroy a competitive market (see Issue 12 for case studies on antitrust).

GOVERNMENT REVENUE: TYPES OF TAXES

The programs and protections people want cost money, and taxes have to pay for them, but taxes also can be used to modify consumer behavior. Placing an excise tax on specific goods may make prices too high for an individual to purchase. **Excise taxes** are commonly known as "sin" or "luxury" taxes. To deter the use of a product, governments add an excise tax. For example, the states of Massachusetts and New York have very high excise taxes on cigarettes in addition to that of the federal government. Economists categorize taxes by the way they affect people – progressive, proportional, and regressive.

PROGRESSIVE TAX

A **progressive tax** is designed to make those most able to pay contribute more than those less able. When thinking of this type of levy, a staircase comes to mind. For example, Family *X* has a yearly income of $25,000 and four people. Family *X* may pay income tax at a rate of 15%. Family *Y*, on the other hand, has four people but an income of $100,000. Family *Y* faces a 31% rate. Family *Z*, with a $250,000 income, will pay their tax income tax at a 36% rate (Omnibus Budget Reconciliation Act of 1993). The higher up you go, the more you pay. Congressional policies often change these rates and steps.

The *U.S. Constitution* and Taxation

The original *Constitution* (effective 1789)
Article I. Section 9, Clause 4
"**Apportionment of Direct Taxes**. No capitation or other direct tax shall be laid, unless in proportion to the census or enumeration herein before directed to be taken."

The 16th Amendment (ratified 1913)
nullifies Article 1, Section 9, Clause 4.
"**the Income Tax**. The Congress shall have power to lay and collect taxes on incomes, from whatever source derived, without apportionment among the several states, and without regard to any census or enumeration."

Note: The original *Constitution* allowed for the taxation of the individual, but only in proportion to each state's population. This provision was included to keep Congress from abolishing slavery by taxing slaves.

PROPORTIONAL TAX

A **proportional tax** creates the same tax rate for everyone. All people are on the same plane, paying the exact same percent. For example, with proportional taxation, all three families above would pay the same percentage. If government set the rate at 10%, Family A would pay $2,500, Family B, $10,000, and Family C, $25,000. Each would pay more not because of what the government charged but because of the difference in their earnings.

REGRESSIVE TAX

A **regressive tax** is the kind that hurts one group more then another. For example, two families live in a state with a sales tax rate of 8%. One family earns $50,000 per year, the other $100,000 per year. Both have similar needs and purchase approximately the same amount of taxable items. For this example, suppose the sales tax amounts to $5,000. For the family with an income of $50,000, this tax is equal to 10% of what it "grosses." For the other family, the tax will take only 5% of its total income. The family that makes less income ends up paying a greater percent of their total income to the government.

GOVERNMENT REVENUE: VARIETIES OF FEDERAL TAXES

Government uses a combination of progressive, proportional, and regressive taxes to raise revenue for operations. It assesses taxes on citizens at each level of government (federal, state, and local). The most common and widely used taxes are: individual income tax, corporate income tax, sales tax, property tax, Social Security tax, Medicare tax, excise tax, estate tax, gift tax, utility tax, custom duties (tariffs), and capital gains tax. Figure 8.8 (see opposite page) gives a view of the proportions of these taxes in the revenues of state and federal governments.

For individuals, government sets an **income tax rate** by law. It is based on **gross income** (total earned and unearned) with certain deductions such as medical expense, mortgage interest, charity, etc. Similarly, the government places an income tax on gross corporate profits but allows certain deductions, too.

In legal terms, reporting and paying income tax is by "voluntary compliance." In most cases, wage earners really have no choice. Wages and

Figure 8.9

salaries are subject to an **employer withholding system**. Employers must deduct a specified amount from an employee's gross wages. Employers decide the amount based on a form filed by the employee (W-4 form – Figure 8.10 on opposite page). At the end of each year, employers provide employees with a statement of how much they have deducted and paid to the government for the worker (W-2 form – Figure 8.9 above). With this information, the worker must file a report with the government by the April 15th deadline – using 1040 forms. The calculations determine if the employer has sent the government enough, too much, or too little from the worker's wages. Adjustments are then made: too little deducted by an employer means the employee has to pay the difference; too much means a refund must be requested. Businesses operate in a similar manner, making payments according to estimates of quarterly revenue.

Tax liability may be adjusted by deductions and exemptions that are continually being changed by law. The government constantly redefines deductions and exemptions ("tax breaks") in new tax laws. These incessant changes force most businesses to utilize special accountants and tax attorneys to keep up with changes in the codes, to keep them in legal compliance, and perhaps to take advantages of "loopholes."

The federal government also collects Social Security and Medicare taxes from both the employee and employer by order of the *Federal Insurance Contribution Act* (**FICA**). This was a New Deal law that established a mandatory three-part insurance policy for contributors (retirement assistance, death benefit insurance, and disability coverage). Medicare, added in the 1960s, provides free or subsidized health insurance for senior citizens. The government computes these Social Security taxes as a percentage of income. In the 1930s, the total contribution was 2% of wages. By 1995, the FICA rate for employee and employers alike had risen to 6.2% on wages earned up to the Wage Base of $61,200. In addition, the federal government added a Medicare Tax of 1.45% on all wages earned with no Wage Base. The largest percentage of federal revenues come directly from income taxes; however, Social Security taxes are the second largest source (see Figure 8.8).

A customs duty is better known as a **tariff** (tax on an import). When a foreign product comes into the United States, the government levies a tariff on it. It is a payment that will eventually be figured into the sale price and passed on to the final buyer. Low revenue tariffs are simple income enhancements for the federal government. Yet, protective tariffs can be set

ECONOMICS – *Assessment of the American Dream*   N&N©

Figure 8.10

Form W-4 (1995)

Want More Money In Your Paycheck? If you expect to be able to take the earned income credit for 1995 and a child lives with you, you may be able to have part of the credit added to your take-home pay. For details, get Form W-5 from your employer.

Purpose. Complete Form W-4 so that your employer can withhold the correct amount of Federal income tax from your pay.

Exemption From Withholding. Read line 7 of the certificate below to see if you can claim exempt status. If exempt, complete line 7; but do not complete lines 5 and 6. No Federal income tax will be withheld from your pay. Your exemption is good for 1 year only. It expires February 15, 1996.

Note: You cannot claim exemption from withholding if (1) your income exceeds $650 and includes unearned income (e.g., interest and dividends) and (2) another person can claim you as a dependent on their tax return.

Basic Instructions. Employees who are not exempt should complete the Personal Allowances Worksheet. Additional worksheets are provided on page 2 for employees to adjust their withholding allowances based on itemized deductions, adjustments to income, or two-earner/two-job situations. Complete all worksheets that apply to your situation. The worksheets will help you figure the number of withholding allowances you are entitled to claim. However, you may claim fewer allowances than this.

Head of Household. Generally, you may claim head of household filing status on your tax return only if you are unmarried and pay more than 50% of the costs of keeping up a home for yourself and your dependent(s) or other qualifying individuals.

Nonwage Income. If you have a large amount of nonwage income, such as interest or dividends, you should consider making estimated tax payments using Form 1040-ES. Otherwise, you may find that you owe additional tax at the end of the year.

Two Earners/Two Jobs. If you have a working spouse or more than one job, figure the total number of allowances you are entitled to claim on all jobs using worksheets from only one Form W-4. This total should be divided among all jobs. Your withholding will usually be most accurate when all allowances are claimed on the W-4 filed for the highest paying job and zero allowances are claimed for the others.

Check Your Withholding. After your W-4 takes effect, you can use Pub. 919, Is My Withholding Correct for 1995?, to see how the dollar amount you are having withheld compares to your estimated total annual tax. We recommend you get Pub. 919 especially if you used the Two Earner/Two Job Worksheet and your earnings exceed $150,000 (Single) or $200,000 (Married). Call 1-800-829-3676 to order Pub. 919. Check your telephone directory for the IRS assistance number for further help.

Personal Allowances Worksheet

A Enter "1" for **yourself** if no one else can claim you as a dependent . . . . **A** _____

B Enter "1" if:
- You are single and have only one job; or
- You are married, have only one job, and your spouse does not work; or
- Your wages from a second job or your spouse's wages (or the total of both) are $1,000 or less. } . . **B** _____

C Enter "1" for your **spouse**. But, you may choose to enter -0- if you are married and have either a working spouse or more than one job (this may help you avoid having too little tax withheld) . . . . **C** _____

D Enter number of **dependents** (other than your spouse or yourself) you will claim on your tax return . . . . . . **D** _____

E Enter "1" if you will file as **head of household** on your tax return (see conditions under **Head of Household** above) . **E** _____

F Enter "1" if you have at least $1,500 of child or dependent care expenses for which you plan to claim a credit . . **F** _____

G Add lines A through F and enter total here. Note: This amount may be different from the number of exemptions you claim on your return ▶ **G** _____

For accuracy, do all worksheets that apply.
- If you plan to **itemize** or **claim adjustments to income** and want to reduce your withholding, see the Deductions and Adjustments Worksheet on page 2.
- If you are **single** and have more than one job and your combined earnings from all jobs exceed $30,000 OR if you are **married** and have a working spouse or more than one job, and the combined earnings from all jobs exceed $50,000, see the Two-Earner/Two-Job Worksheet on page 2 if you want to avoid having too little tax withheld.
- If **neither** of the above situations applies, stop here and enter the number from line G on line 5 of Form W-4 below.

· · · · · Cut here and give the certificate to your employer. Keep the top portion for your records. · · · · ·

Form W-4
Department of the Treasury
Internal Revenue Service

Employee's Withholding Allowance Certificate

▶ For Privacy Act and Paperwork Reduction Act Notice, see reverse.

OMB No. 1545-0010

1995

1 Type or print your first name and middle initial   Last name

2 Your social security number

Home address (number and street or rural route)

3 ☐ Single ☐ Married ☐ Married, but withhold at higher Single rate.
Note: If married, but legally separated, or spouse is a nonresident alien, check the Single box.

City or town, state, and ZIP code

4 If your last name differs from that on your social security card, check here and call 1-800-772-1213 for a new card . . . ▶ ☐

5 Total number of allowances you are claiming (from line G above or from the worksheets on page 2 if they apply) . **5** _____

6 Additional amount, if any, you want withheld from each paycheck . . . . **6** $ _____

7 I claim exemption from withholding for 1995 and I certify that I meet BOTH of the following conditions for exemption:
- Last year I had a right to a refund of ALL Federal income tax withheld because I had NO tax liability; AND
- This year I expect a refund of ALL Federal income tax withheld because I expect to have NO tax liability.
If you meet both conditions, enter "EXEMPT" here . . . . ▶ **7** _____

Under penalties of perjury, I certify that I am entitled to the number of withholding allowances claimed on this certificate or entitled to claim exempt status.

Employee's signature ▶

8 Employer's name and address (Employer: Complete 8 and 10 only if sending to the IRS)

Date ▶ , 19___

9 Office code (optional)

10 Employer identification number

Cat. No. 10220Q

12/14/94 657

high to protect domestic industries from low priced foreign competition (see Issue 10 for more detail on tariffs).

A Capital Gains Tax is levied on profits generated by individuals and businesses. It is applied when a home, stock, or piece of art is bought and later sold for a profit. The profit is subject to the capital gains tax. Many people believe the high rate of this tax discourages individual incentive and corporate motivation to do well and make profit since so much will be taken by the federal government. Of course, it is also possible to suffer a *capital loss*. If an asset is sold for lower price than originally paid, a capital loss can be used as a tax deduction.

Another important element of the New Deal program of President Roosevelt was the **Federal Unemployment (FUTA) Taxes** introduced in 1935 as part of the Social Security Act. FUTA is paid only by the employer. The employer's contribution is 0.8% of the amount of wages per employee on a federal wage base of $7,000.

Federal excise taxes were mentioned previously as "sin taxes" or "luxury taxes." Besides raising revenue on nonessentials such as jewelry, leather, and furs, they are sometimes used to alter behavior. To some extent, excises on cigarettes, alcohol, and gambling are meant to discourage their use.

GOVERNMENT REVENUE: STATE – LOCAL TAXES

When discussing taxes, people immediately think of federal income taxes. Yet many states, counties, towns, and cities levy their own income taxes. States, counties, and municipalities have property taxes and sales taxes. Combined, they take a hefty 12 to 15% out of gross earnings (see Figure 8.6).

PROPERTY TAXES

Property taxes are levied in most states. They are based on assets, but the assessments themselves vary. For example, in most states property tax means **real property** – land and buildings (see Figure 8.11 – a school tax bill, based on real property). In other states, it may mean **chattel** (personal possessions such as autos, boats, stocks, jewelry, etc.). Real property is evaluated by officials called *assessors*. They determine the value of a home or business property in the town or county and try to equalize the values. The towns and counties then set a *tax rate*. If a home and land are assessed at $40,000 and the tax rate is 8% per $1,000 of assessment, the tax is $3,200. If government expenses rise, it may change the rate to 10%. The owner of the $40,000 then pays $4,000.

In some cases, fear of increasing property taxes has led owners to neglect their real estate

Figure 8.11

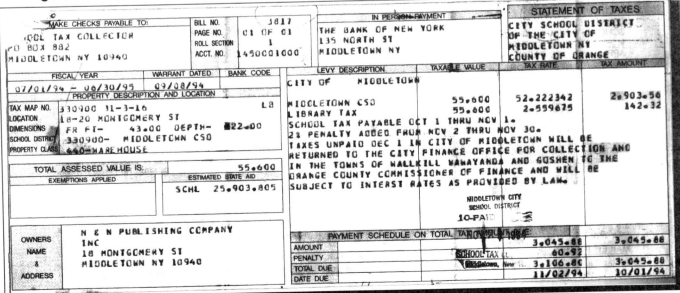

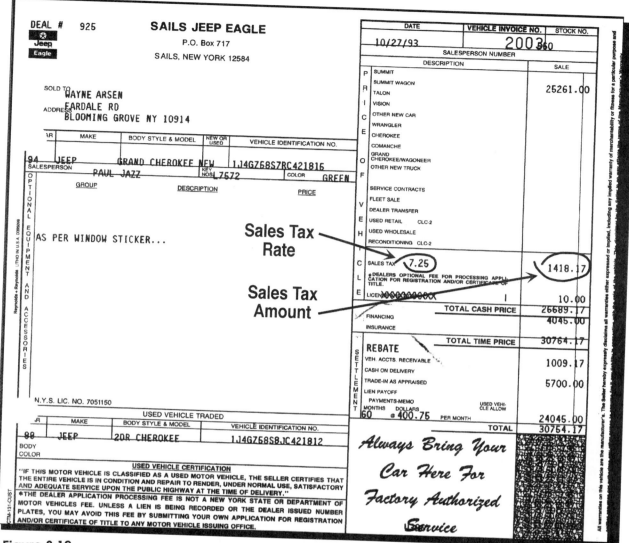

Figure 8.12

or hesitate to improve it because changes may raise its assessed value. Another problem is that this tax does not consider the *ability-to-pay principle* (see following pages). It ignores the income of the owner. As property taxes increase, owners (especially senior citizens) may be unable to pay the increases. That may lead to the loss of the home.

SALES TAXES

Sales tax is collected by the seller of goods and services at the time of the purchase. A percentage of the total sale is added at the cash register for an item or service as a payment to city, county, and state governments (see Figure 8.12). Not every state imposes sales tax. States also have many different methods of determining what is subject to taxation. Often, what is deter-

mined as a "need" is not taxed, but that list is very small and limited (e.g., basic food, medicine and, in some states, "nonluxury" clothes.

ESTATE AND GIFT TAXES

Estate and gift taxes deal with the transfer of property and money from one person to another. An **estate tax** is a payment made to the government when an inheritance is collected. If someone dies and leaves wealth with a specific value, the person that receives it may have to pay a tax on the total amount. Each state has its own regulations. A **gift tax** is placed on the transfer of property or money from one person to another. If someone is given $10,000 or more, the federal government requires that a form be filed acknowledging that the gift is taxable. Many states have similar requirements.

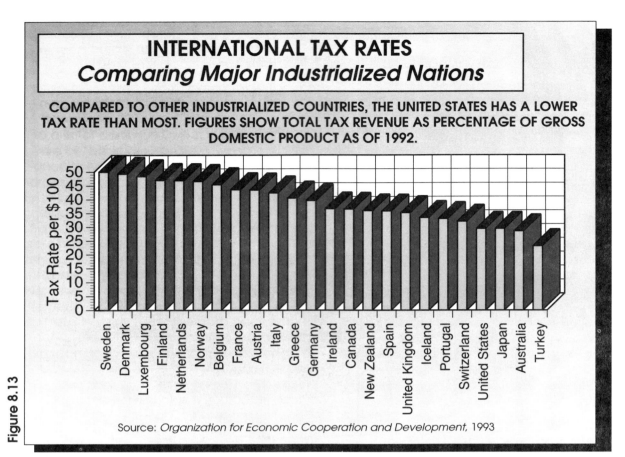

INTERNATIONAL TAX RATES
Comparing Major Industrialized Nations

COMPARED TO OTHER INDUSTRIALIZED COUNTRIES, THE UNITED STATES HAS A LOWER TAX RATE THAN MOST. FIGURES SHOW TOTAL TAX REVENUE AS PERCENTAGE OF GROSS DOMESTIC PRODUCT AS OF 1992.

Tax Rate per $100

Sweden, Denmark, Luxembourg, Finland, Netherlands, Norway, Belgium, France, Austria, Italy, Greece, Germany, Ireland, Canada, New Zealand, Spain, United Kingdom, Iceland, Portugal, Switzerland, United States, Japan, Australia, Turkey

Source: *Organization for Economic Cooperation and Development, 1993*

Figure 8.13

UTILITY TAXES

Utility taxes are paid on electricity, telephone, cable TV, sewer, and water services. This amounts to a user tax (sometimes called a *surcharge*) collected according to consumption. The more you use, the more you pay. Road and bridge tolls also fit into this category.

GOVERNMENT REVENUE: THE FAIRNESS ISSUE

What is fair when it comes to taxes? Some people insist that there is no such thing as a fair tax. Others defend a particular type of tax as being the only kind that is fair. Fairness is a difficult term to use in economics. Many variables affect the definition of the term. Differing values and perceptions cause some people to recognize aspects that others cannot see. Economists have two ideas on fairness of taxes:

- The **ability-to-pay principle** is on one side of the debate. This means tax fairness is based on a progressive idea: those who have the most have a social obligation to pay more than those that have less.

- The **benefits-received principle**, on the other hand, establishes the simple rule that if you use or benefit from a particular government good or service, you pay the tax on it. Tolls on roads and gasoline taxes are used to build and maintain roadways. Those that use the roads are responsible for paying for them. A town may borrow money to construct a sewer and water system for a section of the town that needs it. The benefits-received principle says that those residents not able to "hook-up" to the system should not be expected to pay off the loan by having taxes increased. Instead, users of the system pay off the loan and pay for the maintenance of the system through fees.

SUMMARY

Although paying taxes is not enjoyable, most taxpayers agree that life would be more difficult without the government services paid for through taxation. Compared to other industrialized nations, Americans pay less in taxes (review Figure 8.13 above). However, it is important to not only compare the taxes, but also the services provided.

ASSESSMENT
QUESTIONS • APPLICATIONS

1 The Granville story at the beginning of this chapter is about local government. The reporter / cartoonist observed, "Of course, the final decision had to be made by the elected officials on the school board. They had to read the sense of the community, but they had to weigh all the local, state, and even federal regulations controlling the finances of education."
   a What does the reporter mean when he says that the school board must "read the sense of the community?"
   b List the sources of revenue for schools.
   c When you look at the sources of revenue, does "read the sense of the community" take on a different meaning?
   d If the financial role of a school board is so complex, what does this mean about the roles of other local, state, and federal governments?

2 The *U.S. Constitution* defines several economic functions for government.
   a Which functions presented in the *Constitution* affect your life now?
   b Which functions presented in the *Constitution* will affect your life in the future?
   c Explain which roles of government are most critical to the country's survival and security.

3 Government attempts to stabilize the economy by using fiscal policy.
   a In your own words, explain how discretionary and automatic policies stabilize the economy.
   b How do political issues affect the use of discretionary fiscal policy?
   c Explain the difference between demand-side and supply-side economic theories?

4 The Great Depression created a major change in American economic thought.
   a Describe this change in detail.
   b Make a personal judgement whether this change has benefited or harmed the economic life of this country. Give facts to defend your judgement.

5 Opinions on taxation vary greatly.
   a Interview 5 taxpayers (at different stages of their lives – e.g., in school, working, unemployed, on public assistance, retired). Ask their opinion on the fairness of income, sales, and property taxes.
   b In a small group, discuss your findings which you have outlined in writing.
   c Choose the strongest arguments both pro and con for one of the taxes. Elect two persons from your group to present the arguments to the class.

6 With the class divided into 3 or 4 small groups, complete the following chart of Taxes identifying Categories and Principles. After reaching a consensus on all of the taxes, put the group's results on the board. The class should debate the similarities and differences among the group charts.

TAX	Category	Principle
Income Tax	_____	_____
Social Security	_____	_____
Medicare	_____	_____
Tariff	_____	_____
Capital Gains	_____	_____
Federal Excise	_____	_____
Real Property	_____	_____
Chattel Property	_____	_____
Sales Tax	_____	_____
Estate/Gift Tax	_____	_____
Utility Tax	_____	_____

7 Review the International Tax Rates chart (Figure 8.13, page 168). Additional research will be needed to support your conclusions.
   a Classify the countries listed into economic systems according to the Economic Systems Continuum discussed in Issue 3, Fig. 3.2 (page 64).
   b Analyze your answer to part *a* above. Is there a relationship between a country's economic system and its rate of taxation? Give examples and support your conclusion.
   c Compare the benefits and burdens of the taxpayers in the countries you used in part *b* with those of the American taxpayer.

ASSESSMENT PROJECT: 8A GOVERNMENT AGENCIES

STUDENT TASK

Participate in a group presentation on the operation of a government agency and its economic impact on society. The task develops an understanding and insight into the operation of government's economic responsibilities.

PROCEDURE

The class should be divided into cooperative learning groups of no more than 4 students. Each group should:

1 Examine the directories of state and federal government agencies in the appendix at the end of this book and determine which ones apply to an assigned area of government intervention. Examples: EPA – environment, FED – money supply, Federal Trade Commission – marketplace competition.

2 Choose one agency from the research. No two groups should choose the same agency.

3 Using the research, compose a thorough presentation that explains what the agencies do and how they do it. For example,
   • protect a competitive market
   • protect consumers
   • redistribute wealth
   • provide public goods and services
   • stabilize the economy
   • act in the best interest of the United States

4 Make an oral presentation to the class. Include visual support materials.

5 Contact a local village, town, city, or county government agency which mirrors the work of the federal or state agency in the best presentation and request a guest speaker from that local agency to speak to the class, explaining what his/her agency does on the local level.

LEARNING STANDARDS

Learners should be able to:

(1) understand that while different socioeconomic (as well as national, ethnic, religious, racial, and gender) groups have varied perspectives, values, and diverse practices and traditions, they face the same global economic challenges.

(4) understand that civic values and socially responsible behavior are required of members of school groups, local, state, national, and global communities.

(5) analyze problems and evaluate decisions about the economic effects on society and the individual caused by human, technological, and natural activities.

(6) present their ideas both in writing and orally in clear, concise, and properly accepted fashion.

(7) employ a variety of information from written, graphic, and multimedia sources.

(8) monitor, reflect upon, and improve their own and others' work.

(9) work cooperatively and show respect for the rights of others to think, act, and speak differently from themselves within the context of democratic principles and social justice.

EVALUATION

The criteria for the evaluation of this project are itemized in the grid (rubric) that follows. Choice of appropriate category terms (values) is the decision of the instructor. Selection of terms such as "minimal," "satisfactory," and "distinguished" can vary with each assessment.

Government Agency Presentation Evaluation Rubric

(Refer to introductory section for suggestions of scoring descriptors for the evaluation categories.)

Evaluation Item	Category 1	Category 2	Category 3	Category 4	Category 5
Item a: (1) Does the report show understanding that while different socioeconomic (as well as national, ethnic, religious, racial, and gender) groups have varied perspectives, values, and diverse practices and traditions, they face the same global economic challenges?					
Item b: (4) Does the report show understanding that civic values and socially responsible behavior are required of members of school groups, local, state, national, and global communities?					
Item c: (5) Does the report analyze problems and evaluate decisions about the economic effects caused by human, technological, and natural activities on societies and individuals?					
Item d: (6) Does the report present ideas in writing (and orally) in clear, concise, and properly accepted fashion?					
Item e: (7) Does the report employ a variety of information from written, graphic, and multimedia sources?					
Item f: (8) Does the report show monitoring of, reflection upon, and improvement of work?					
Item g: (9) Does the report show cooperative work and respect for the rights of others to think, act, and speak differently?					

ASSESSMENT PROJECT: 8B
ANALYZING THE IMPACT OF TAXES ON A HYPOTHETICAL HOUSEHOLD

STUDENT TASK

Compute the federal and state income taxes for all income earners in Hypothetical Household developed in Issue 1. Then, submit a report (accompanied by an IRS 1040 tax form) analyzing the fairness of these taxes and weighing their impact on your household and lifestyle.

PROCEDURE

1   Obtain federal IRS income tax form 1040 and a state income tax form, if your state has one. (If your state doesn't, you should try to compute household tax liability for operative state property or other major taxes.)

     (Note: individuals within the household may each file a 1040 or may file jointly on one 1040 as a couple.)

2   Fill in forms and use tax tables to figure taxes. Include dependents, itemize the household deductions, and add estimated interest income from savings or investments mentioned in the Issue 1 Household Financial Profile.

     (Note: if you use a computer tax calculation program, be sure to fill in the actual 1040 forms with the figures the computer produces.)

3   After determining taxes to be paid, note percentages of taxes in relation to your household income and add a statement comparing your taxes to the Figure 8.6 graph on page 160.

4   Conclude your report with a discussion analyzing the fairness of these taxes and weighing their impact on your household and lifestyle.

LEARNING STANDARDS
Learners should be able to:

(1)   understand that while different socioeconomic (as well as national, ethnic, religious, racial, and gender) groups have varied perspectives, values, and diverse practices and traditions, they face the same global economic challenges.

(4)   understand that civic values and socially responsible behavior are required of members of school groups, local, state, national, and global communities.

(5)   analyze problems and evaluate decisions about the economic effects on society and the individual caused by human, technological, and natural activities.

(6)   present their ideas both in writing and orally in clear, concise, and properly accepted fashion.

(7)   employ a variety of information from written, graphic, and multimedia sources.

(8)   monitor, reflect upon, and improve their own and others' work.

(9)   work cooperatively and show respect for the rights of others to think, act, and speak differently from themselves within the context of democratic principles and social justice.

EVALUATION

The criteria for the evaluation of this project are itemized in the grid (rubric) that follows. Choice of appropriate category terms (values) is the decision of the instructor. Selection of terms such as "minimal," "satisfactory," and "distinguished" can vary with each assessment.

Impact of Taxes on Household Evaluation Rubric

(Refer to introductory section for suggestions of scoring descriptors for the evaluation categories.)

Evaluation Item	Category 1	Category 2	Category 3	Category 4	Category 5
Item a: (1) Does the report show understanding that while different socioeconomic (as well as national, ethnic, religious, racial, and gender) groups have varied perspectives, values, and diverse practices and traditions, they face the same global economic challenges?					
Item b: (4) Does the report show understanding that civic values and socially responsible behavior are required of members of school groups, local, state, national, and global communities?					
Item c: (5) Does the report analyze problems and evaluate decisions about the economic effects caused by human, technological, and natural activities on societies and individuals?					
Item d: (6) Does the report present ideas in writing (and orally) in clear, concise, and properly accepted fashion?					
Item e: (7) Does the report employ a variety of information from written, graphic, and multimedia sources?					
Item f: (8) Does the report monitoring of, reflection upon, and improvement of work?					
Item g: (9) Does the report show cooperative work and respect for the rights of others to think, act, and speak differently?					

ISSUE 9

Can economic performance be measured?

INDICATORS AND BUSINESS CYCLES

RIDING THE CYCLONE
IS ANY YOUNGSTER'S GLORY
BUT, THE WAY TO THE FUTURE
THAT'S ANOTHER STORY

WHIP

"THE RISING OF THE DOUGH"
– A DOUBLE MEANING!

Curtis was nervous that day. He had not been himself in class. As the buzzer sounded, he very slowly rose to leave. Mrs. Cortes signaled to him. They had a good relationship, and she was concerned about his unusual lack of enthusiasm.

Reluctantly, he began to admit he was pensive about his job at the bakery in town. He had been working there for nearly three years, and each year Mr. Krug had given him a raise, praising him as a valued and productive worker. Curtis loved the job because he liked working with his hands. The 3 to 8 AM hours three days a week didn't bother him either. He arranged his college schedule around his work, making his evenings free for study.

Curtis explained he was counting on the annual raise for some badly needed repairs on his car, but Mr. Krug had not said a word about it. Curtis told Mrs. Cortes he had good work habits, was always on time, and responded to all the requests his boss made. It was a small bakery, and Mr. Krug and the staff were all very friendly. Curtis never minded going in early or staying late, and he always worked the counter weekends so that the full-time people could have time with their families. Mr. Krug had even congratulated Curtis on the compliments customers often gave him. Curtis just couldn't figure out why he had not received the raise.

Mrs. Cortes had to get back to her office in the Faculty Tower for an appointment with the Dean of Students and asked Curtis if he would walk with her. Curtis had an hour break and was heading in the same direction.

Mrs. Cortes asked Curtis if he had begun his economics term paper yet. He chuckled, and said he was waiting for her third lecture on procrastination. She said as long as he was heading for the Thorne Library, he should check out some of the recent material on growth she had put on reserve. She said he could discover that his job performance might be the last thing to worry about. He was about to ask why, but by that time, they were at the Tower. Mrs. Cortes realized the Dean would be waiting and ducked inside.

At Thorne, Curtis checked out two articles on growth. One was from the *Wall Street Journal* on weak recovery shown by Gross Domestic Product figures and leading economic indicators. The other was from *Business Week*. It was on the slow recovery in Pennsylvania's Lehigh Valley after IBM's massive downsizing layoffs. The quiet of the library always made it a great place to think. He took a few notes and still wondered why Mrs. Cortes saw some connection between the article and his problem at Krug's. At any rate, Curtis decided to talk to his boss the next morning.

At Krug's Bakery, the 4:30 AM break came after the hard rolls and Danish were in the ovens. Curtis saw Mr. Krug doing some paper work on the counter in the back. He was still pretty discouraged. He went to the office door and hesitated.

"Hi, Curtis, dough ready on the rye?"

"Yes, sir. George is starting on it now." Curtis was not sure if this was the right time, but the frustration with his boss boiled up. "Mr. Krug, are you unhappy with me?"

"Not at all. Why?"

"Well, last month marked three years that I've been working for you, and I thought I would be getting a raise. I think I am a pretty hard worker and ..."

"Hey, hold on, Curtis. Sit down, you are getting a little worked up. First of all, you are the best part-timer I have, no question about it. You are important to me and the way things work around here. Second, you are a very smart kid, but you live in an academic world. Do you ever listen to a radio newscast or read the daily paper? Take a look around. Have you noticed there are fewer customers on the weekends? Well, it is like that out at the counter all week. Things are slow because of the recession and all the cutbacks at the big firms around here. You know about those, don't you?"

"Well, yes ... but people still need bread. I thought a business like this was protected from those things "

"Don't they discuss this at your college? This is real, Curtis. My customers are upscale people. They are the ones willing to pay for quality, but some of them are losing their jobs because of the corporate downsizing and leaving this area. The others are buying cheaper stuff in the supermarkets. This store's gross income in the last six months has taken a nose dive!"

"I had no idea. Then it's not my work ... it's the economy?"

"Definitely, but I guess I should have talked to you sooner. I saw you were a little down, but I thought it was a personal problem, and I didn't want to pry. Listen, I'm not sure you young people have a good grasp of how we are all linked to economic performance. Let me show you something."

Krug pulled two pies from the line in front of his work table, one large and one small.

"Look at the difference between these two. Suppose the large one represented the economic performance last year when I gave you a nice raise, and the smaller one represented this year."

"You mean what Mrs. Cortes called the GDP – Gross Domestic Product?"

"Exactly. Last year, when my slice of the pie was this big, I could share it with you. Now, look at my slice this year. What do you think?"

"Not much there to share."

"You know it! Being a good worker or a good manager can help, and the rewards are there if the total economic pie is getting bigger, but if things are shrinking, your piece shrinks. No way around it."

"OK. I guess there is not much you can do right now. I understand, Mr. Krug."

"I'll take care of you when things get better. But there is still something we can do right now, kid. Get a fork and have some of this pie I ruined – you deserve a break."

Can economic performance be measured?

INDICATORS AND BUSINESS CYCLES

MEASURING ECONOMIC PERFORMANCE

When asked to define the term success, people come up with varied responses. For some, it means accumulating a great deal of wealth. Others would say it means having enough to support a family. For many, it might mean the ability to help those less fortunate than themselves. For others, being a success would be nothing less than earning the recognition of being the best at what they do. Some dream of finding a new discovery or intellectual insight that adds to the encyclopedia of human knowledge. Still others want to be able to live in peace

What is success?

or travel when they want. For the homeless family, success may be the ability to get off of the streets into a clean, private, and warm bed every night and "three square meals" every day. No matter what the individual interpretation may be – no matter how unique or common the response – there is one necessary aspect of every reply: having enough money to do what one wants.

Whatever is identified as the American Dream, obtaining it depends not only on the individual and his/her abilities but also on the right economic conditions. Those conditions affect all people, everywhere, no matter whether they live in technologically advanced nations or underdeveloped, agricultural "Third World" countries. People everywhere gain or lose the ability to be successful because of conditions within their economic systems. The ability to make an individual choice is often determined by what happens far from one's personal world.

Knowing what these ever-present conditions are and understanding what they mean to particular situations in life helps people to act and react in their own self-interest. No matter how puzzling some data may seem, using that information gives everyone a better chance at riding the roller coaster of the "bad times" and the "good times."

At the center of any prosperous economic system is its ability to produce up to its potential. That potential must grow year after year if the scarcity problem is to be minimized and the promise of a better standard of living is to be fulfilled. This means that production of goods and services must increase. Measurement of this growth is critically important to determine an economy's success or to see if it needs stimulation.

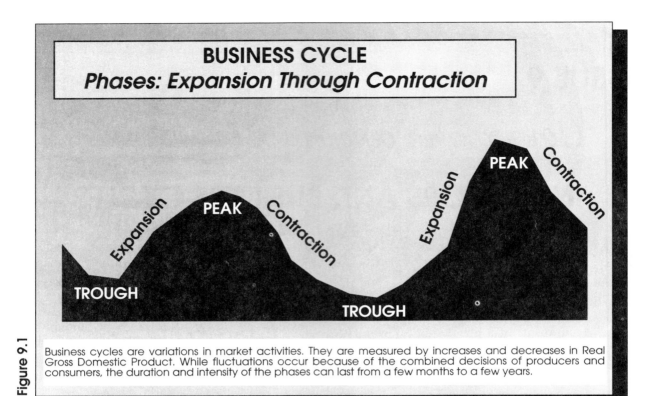

Figure 9.1

Business cycles are variations in market activities. They are measured by increases and decreases in Real Gross Domestic Product. While fluctuations occur because of the combined decisions of producers and consumers, the duration and intensity of the phases can last from a few months to a few years.

THE BUSINESS CYCLE

The economy's roller coaster ride is generally referred to as the **business cycle**. It has four key phases: **Prosperity** (the peak), **Recession** (the contraction), **Depression** (the trough) and **Recovery** (the expansion) (see Figure 9.1). These roller coaster ups and downs are measured according to many technical indexes. However, simply put: the "ups" are defined by high employment and high spending, while the "downs" are defined as low employment and low spending. Employment and spending are variables that are determined by **aggregate demand** (total spending). When the aggregate demand is up, and people are working and spending, the response will be a high total output of goods and services. When aggregate supply is up, the response will be more goods and services available in the marketplace.

Some economists prefer to call the business cycle the "demand cycle." As long as people have money to spend and actually use that purchasing power in the marketplace, then producers have the incentive to provide the goods and services the consumers want. Seeking increased profits, the producers will hire more people to provide what is selling. This gives more people income and greater purchasing power. As a result, economic growth moves upward.

Yet, all good things do end, and the cycle can also move downward. Judgments to not buy, to cut production, or to keep it level influence the decisions of others. Spending slows, and **aggregate economic activity** can begin to decline. Such negative signals cause producers to cut hours and eliminate jobs, causing unemployment to rise. The corporate downsizing of the early 1990s is an example. The underemployed and unemployed workers then have less purchasing power. If aggregate demand diminishes further, nervous producers' decrease aggregate supply. This means that more employees will be "laid-off," and the downward phase of the cycle gains momentum.

In the recent history of tracking this cyclical activity, the good times seem to last much longer than the bad times. At best, the peaks seem to last five years, and except for the Great Depression, the troughs last a little more than one year (see Figure 9.2).

There is no set rhythm or time frame to the cycle. Periods of expansion or contraction are never equal in length or intensity. While in the past, periods of growth have usually been longer than periods of decline, this may be changing.

In the past half century, government fiscal policies aimed at intervening if production or

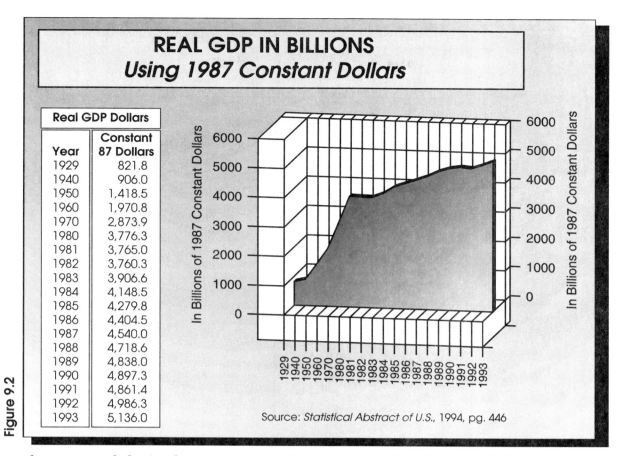

REAL GDP IN BILLIONS
Using 1987 Constant Dollars

Real GDP Dollars	
Year	Constant 87 Dollars
1929	821.8
1940	906.0
1950	1,418.5
1960	1,970.8
1970	2,873.9
1980	3,776.3
1981	3,765.0
1982	3,760.3
1983	3,906.6
1984	4,148.5
1985	4,279.8
1986	4,404.5
1987	4,540.0
1988	4,718.6
1989	4,838.0
1990	4,897.3
1991	4,861.4
1992	4,986.3
1993	5,136.0

Source: *Statistical Abstract of U.S.*, 1994, pg. 446

Figure 9.2

employment needed stimulation (see Issue 8). The actions were discretionary, but there are no hard and fast rules for predicting how long or strong phases of the cycle will be. Still, the public has an expectation that government can protect the society from "bad times."

VARIABLES IN THE CYCLE TODAY

Conditions today are different. The old tools of fiscal policy are less effective. The already high debt levels make new deficit spending less acceptable, and the need for revenue makes tax cutting difficult. There is less leeway to stimulate aggregate demand than during the past two generations. Without this intervention, some economists predict the contractions of the business cycle will become more painful. The recession of the early 1990s is a case in point. It lasted for considerably longer than any other recent decline, and the recovery was very uneven, with the Northeast and California experiencing prolonged suffering. With government impotence, the "bad times" may last longer than in previous history.

In addition to government impotence, another variable affecting the cycle is **business** **consumption** (how much businesses spend). The amounts that businesses spend affect aggregate demand (and the business cycle) just as much as consumer choices do. Businesses purchase new machinery, build more facilities (factories, offices, warehouses), and put capital into research and the development of new products. Business spending stimulates technology and competitive development for better products at lower costs. When these things happen, there is expansion. When they do not, there is contraction.

The **money supply** is another variable altering the cycle. The greater the amount of money available, usually the cheaper it is to borrow. The more scarce money is, the higher the cost of borrowing it. When money is cheap (interest rates are low), consumers and businesses borrow more and spend it. When interest rates are high, discouraged consumers and businesses borrow less and spend less. As the cost of credit changes, so do the conditions affecting supply and demand.

Expectations are variables altering the cycle, too. What people believe and predict about economic activity has a great deal to do

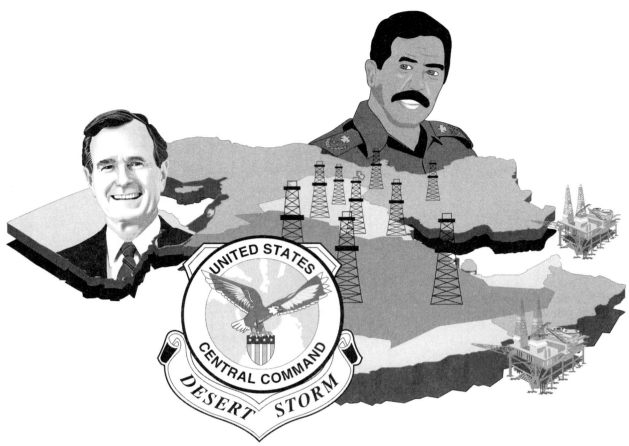

In 1991, U.S. President Bush led an international coalition's military operation in the Persian Gulf to free oil–rich Kuwait from Iraqi leader Saddam Hussein's invasion and annexation. Iraq's aggression, the Western retaliation, and resulting dislocations illustrate the economic, political, and social realities of such global actions. The initial Iraqi aggression may have been triggered by Iraq's inability to repay tens of billions of dollars of debt from its earlier war with Iran. The Western coalition spent an estimated $50 billion to push the Iraqis out of Kuwait. The cost to rebuild Kuwait exceeded $40 billion. The cost to Iraq in dollars was more than 100 billion. Six hundred of Kuwait's oil wells were destroyed, and 11 million gallons of oil were released into the Persian Gulf, causing severe damage to the environment as well as great economic loss. The long-term effects on the G-7 industrialized nations included a decline in the GDP, deepened the economic recession, and increased unemployment (note: "G-7" became "G-8" in 1997 with the admission of Russia).

with their behavior in the marketplace. If people expect they may be laid-off, they will spend less and save more in anticipation of being unemployed. If such negative expectations are widespread – as they were during the early 1990s – then spending diminishes everywhere, demand decreases, and the economy can go into a contraction phase.

Negative expectations have an enormous influence on consumption. They generally cause less spending on goods and services, and sometimes more saving. Businesses also have even finer tuned perspectives on what is happening in the economy, and they react dramatically to those perceptions. In the early 1990s, as a few big companies began a trend in "downsizing," medium companies laid-off workers, as many of the firms were vendors and subcontractors of big businesses. When industries believe that

there are good times ahead, they invest in new growth programs. Yet, the opposite also holds true. If the view of the economic future is gloomy, then the pessimism will lead to a decrease in investment, product development, and employment.

Domestically, both consumers and producers can spur an expansion or contraction based on their expectations or visions about economic activity. Yet, economic activity does not occur in a vacuum. What happens in the world also has a profound effect on the domestic U.S. economy, and ultimately, what goes on in our personal lives.

In the modern world, the linkage is astounding. Economic, political, and social events all over the globe are reflected quickly in the economic realities of other nations. For

Figure 9.3 — Components of Gross Domestic Product 1994

Source: Bureau of Economic Analysis - U.S. Dept. Commerce

Where:

C = $4,535.0 billion – **personal consumption** expenditures

I = $996.6 billion – gross private **investment** by business

G = $1,159.8 billion – **Government** consumption

X = –$86.7 billion – net **exports**

Then:

$$C + I + G + X = \$6,574.7 \text{ billion (current dollars)} = GDP$$

Not long ago, economists believed that their quandry was ended when an economist working for the National Bureau of Economic Research developed a system that would accomplish the task of measuring the economy. The Nobel Prize in Economics (1971) was awarded to **Simon Kuznets** for his improved methods of determining Gross National Product and National Income.

example, if **OPEC** (Organization of Petroleum Exporting Countries) could consistently enforce loyalty to the agreements made at its annual conferences, the price of oil would certainly rise, increasing OPEC profits. OPEC's political decisions to restrict oil production and exports to the Western nations in 1973 and 1980 caused inflation and hardship in the everyday lives of Americans and Europeans.

Another example is the cost of being involved in any military action. Although not beneficial to human existence, wars temporarily stimulate economic prosperity as governments spend great amounts of money on national defense contracts. However, wars also cause downturns after they end. When the massive government demand stimulating the whole economy declines, the economy declines. (Note the Desert Storm illustration on opposite page.)

Panic and irrational moves can cause negative reactions and harm to the economy, too. Understanding the cycle allows knowledgeable predictions that encourage prudent activities. Being able to read economic measurements helps individuals predict direction of the cycle and act accordingly.

PERFORMANCE MEASUREMENT: GNP AND GDP

Measuring the performance of an economic system is not an easy task. The aim is to measure the economy as a whole, but what does this mean? What must be examined in order to measure how well or poorly the economy is doing? What data must be collected? What is included and excluded?

While Kuznets' is not the only method used by economists to analyze the direction in which the economy is headed, it is a popular measure of growth. The Kuznets' method depends on the production of goods and services as a benchmark of economic advancement. **Gross National Product** is the calculation of all new and finished goods produced in a one year period by American companies (domestically and everywhere in the world).

More recently, another measure has gained popularity with economists – the **Gross Domestic Product**. GDP is defined as the total output produced *within* the country (no matter what the nationality of the producer). The preferred U.S. government and U.N. measurements now use GDP figures for comparisons and general economic reporting.

GNP and GDP are calculated similarly, by adding four chief components of economic expenditure: **C** = all of the consumer goods (personal consumption of goods and services), **+I** = capital goods (investment by business into new factories, machinery, or houses), **+G** = government consumption of goods and services, **+X = net exports** (exports minus imports) (see Figure 9.3).

Annual GNP and GDP figures are both gauges of economic performance. With adjustment, they also allow comparisons to other time periods. Growth is a very good thing for any economy. If the economy is like the pies at Mr. Krug's bakery, he, Curtis, and everyone else gets a piece. With growth, the pie gets bigger, and the bigger the pie, the bigger the individual's piece. Perhaps the analogy is oversimplified, but the richer the country is, the higher an individual's standard of living. Working at a job

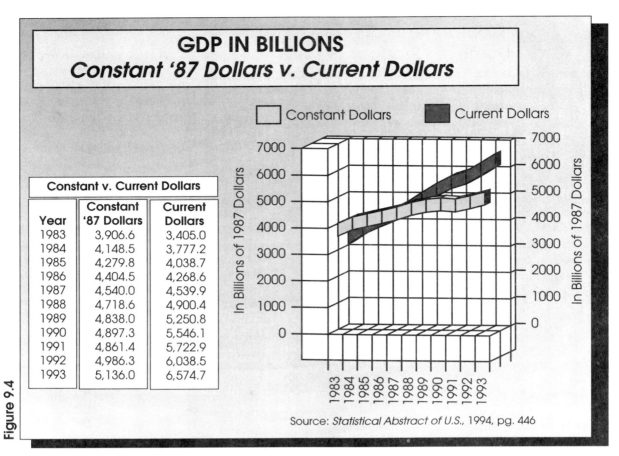

GDP IN BILLIONS
Constant '87 Dollars v. Current Dollars

Figure 9.4

Constant v. Current Dollars		
Year	Constant '87 Dollars	Current Dollars
1983	3,906.6	3,405.0
1984	4,148.5	3,777.2
1985	4,279.8	4,038.7
1986	4,404.5	4,268.6
1987	4,540.0	4,539.9
1988	4,718.6	4,900.4
1989	4,838.0	5,250.8
1990	4,897.3	5,546.1
1991	4,861.4	5,722.9
1992	4,986.3	6,038.5
1993	5,136.0	6,574.7

Source: *Statistical Abstract of U.S.*, 1994, pg. 446

and being a cooperative employee for a productive company leads a worker like Curtis to expect to be rewarded. The reward can be a raise in salary or wages or in benefits and bonuses. If the company that employs the worker is growing and making a substantial profit, it is likely that the worker will get an increased share.

Conversely, if the company does not have a growth in profit, how can an employee expect more? The same is true for the entire economy. Growth leads to more demand and the need for more supply. Understanding this aspect of measuring the economy allows a worker to know if a raise or "pink slip" will be on the horizon.

GDP is computed either on an income base or an expenditure base. The income base adds up all the money earned by households and business firms in a given year. The expenditure base adds up the value of all the money spent for final goods and services by four sectors of the economy (**C+I+G+X**).

How the GDP (or GNP) is expressed gives a true or distorted image of the economic horizon. Growth is expressed by these two measures in

dollar values, but some expressions are more accurate to use than others. Growth can be expressed as a simple **Money GDP** or a **Real GDP**. The difference is important.

Suppose a company produces luxurious yachts at a rate of four per year. These products are sold at $200,000 each. In 1993, the company produced and sold four brand new yachts for a total of $800,000 (which is added to the GDP for that year). In 1994, the company produces another four, but because of an increase in the cost of stainless steel (a component used to make yachts), the price rises to $225,000. The income from the four yachts is now $900,000. When this amount is added to the raw GDP, it increases by one hundred thousand dollars. This gives the impression that there was growth.

Yet, in 1993 there were only four products built and again in 1994, only four were produced. There was no change in output – no *real* growth – only an increase in price (an indication of inflation). So the raw or **Money GDP**, reported in **current dollars**, does not always indicate if the economy actually grew in terms of production or profit.

Rapid advances in high-tech electronics make equipment such as computers obsolete in just a few years. Depreciation is a costly part of modern industry. ©PhotoDisc

To get a more realistic image of growth, **Real GDP** is used. This figure uses a "price deflator" formula to eliminate the inflationary value added to the total of the goods and services produced. Real GDP uses a benchmark value of the dollar called **constant dollars** to compare how much more is produced in the country this year than last (see Figure 9.4).

Real GDP establishes a rate of growth so one can see "how much bigger the pie is" and possibly be able to estimate what would be a reasonable increase in the size of "one's slice." In the opening story, if Curtis had understood this, he would not have been disturbed about his job at Krug's.

PERFORMANCE MEASUREMENT: NNP (NET NATIONAL PRODUCT)

There are other statistical measurements that indicate if the economy is growing. The amount of new machinery that businesses purchase every year is a significant indicator of where the economy is going. This is measured in the **Net National Product** (**NNP**).

For businesses to respond to increased demand by increasing the production of goods and services that people want to purchase, they must buy more capital goods. Purchasing new facilities, machines, and tools used to put more products into the marketplace ordinarily means growth. To achieve a precise calculation of how much growth, the sale of all of this new machinery must be figured out carefully.

However, if the new capital purchases only represent expenditures for **depreciation** (replacing existing worn out, nonoperating capital goods), there is no growth. For example, if a car manufacturer orders twenty new machines that stamp sheet metal into fenders for new cars, the manufacturer's capital goods expenditures might be said to increase by the cost of the twenty machines. However, eleven of the machines were purchased to replace capital that no longer works. Only nine actually show growth in the NNP figure. Not bad, but not as good as originally thought. If each machine cost $20,000 and twenty were purchased, the total added to the NNP appears to be $400,000, but $220,000 is merely replacement value and cannot be counted into the figure showing growth. In this case, the NNP is increased by $180,000, not $400,000.

PERFORMANCE MEASUREMENT: INCOME LEVELS

Income is another way of examining how much growth the economy is experiencing. Certainly the more we earn, the more we have; the more we have, the more we spend; the more we spend, the more should be produced; and the more we produce, the more we grow. The pie should be bigger.

What people earn is commonly known as **Gross Income**. This is the amount of money paid to people for their labor. When all sources of income are added together (**earned income** – for labor and **unearned income** – received from investments, rents, and all other sources), another major economic indicator is created: Personal Income.

Department	Emp. No.	Name		Soc. Sec. No.	Clock No.	Filing Status	Period Ending		Pay Statement	This Pay	Year To Date
100	44	HABIB, CURTIS		103-88-8778		S 1	011495		Total Earnings	53.63	407.89
Hours	Rate	Earnings Type	Deductions Type	Year To Date	Other Pay Information				Fica Tax	4.10	31.20
8.25	6.500	53.63 REG							Federal Income Tax		23.71

3659 P&T LOST AUTO PARTS, INC   Check Date 01/18/95 Check Number 1048

Net Pay 49.53

Figure 9.5 The part-time employee's paycheck stub (above) shows an hourly rate of $6.50 for a gross income of $53.63. Because the gross income is small as compared to the full-time employee's pay (below), the part-time employee has no withholding (income tax withheld) and only $4.10 deducted for FICA (Social Security) taxes – giving the employee a net pay of $49.53 (92.3% take-home). For the full-time employee with benefits, the gross income for the 2 week work period is much higher than the part-time employee at $1,314.96. However, after federal and state income taxes, FICA, and the medical insurance premiums are deducted, the full-time employee nets $967.24 (73.6% take-home).

The Hospital of North Orange — 18 Montgomery St. Middletown, NY 10940 — EMPLOYEE EARNINGS STATEMENT — NO. 088703

EMPLOYEE NAME	EMPLOYEE NUMBER	DEPARTMENT EXPENSE NO.	REGULAR RATE	SOCIAL SECURITY NUMBER	PERIOD END DATE	CHECK DATE	CHECK NUMBER
GARSEY, JAN	37357	6166 033	21.356	114464778	03/19/95	03/26/95	088703

DESC - SHIFT	HOURS	EARNINGS	DESC	AMOUNT	YTD AMOUNT	FEDERAL	STATE	FICA	GROSS PAY
REG 1	40.00	854.24	INS	1.26	7.56	139.14	63.37	97.00	1314.96
REG 2	20.00	457.72	SIBPUP	42.05	252.30	956.84	640.87	640.91	8652.58
CHARG 1	4.00	3.00	DNTPOP	4.90	29.40				

BENEFIT HOURS AVAILABLE AND TAKEN

VAC	SICK	HOLIDY	PERS
295.60	196.61	7.50	.00
.00	24.00	.00	.00

CURRENT AND YEAR TO DATE ADDITIONAL TAXES

NET PAY 967.24

DETACH AND RETAIN FOR YOUR PERSONAL RECORDS NOT NEGOTIABLE

Personal Income is the income a person has *before taxes are collected by the government*. After the taxes are taken from Personal Income, economists call what is left **Disposable Personal Income** (see Figure 9.5). Disposable Income is also known as purchasing power. Disposable Income is what people have to spend, save, and invest to achieve the Dream. Of course it differs throughout the country (see Figure 9.6 on opposite page). Many economists consider Disposable Income the best measurement to determine if growth has been large enough to increase "one's piece of the pie."

Aggregate income, or the amount of money earned by everyone in the country (less business taxes), is known as **National Income**. Economists arrive at this total figure by adding everything paid out to people in salary, wages, and commissions, plus all of the profits earned by people that are self-employed as owners or partners in their own businesses. To this is added corporate profits, investment dividends, rental income, and interest paid to people. As National Income gets larger or smaller, it is a measure of how well or poorly the entire economy of the country is doing.

PERFORMANCE MEASUREMENT: SAVINGS LEVELS

Income has only two practical uses: spending and saving. Most of what the Americans earn, they spend. Still, the amount that the nation saves, called the **savings rate**, is important as an economic indicator (measurement). It shows how much we have put aside from our Disposable Personal Income into savings accounts.

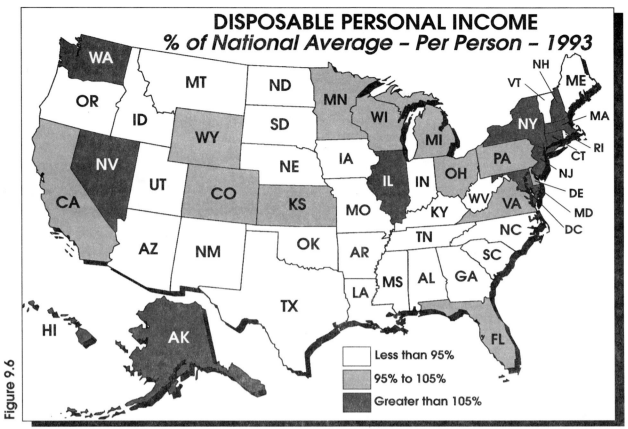

DISPOSABLE PERSONAL INCOME
% of National Average – Per Person – 1993

Less than 95%

95% to 105%

Greater than 105%

Figure 9.6

The savings rate changes as income and employment change. When the income is high and people are working, the savings rate goes up. When income declines during downswings of the business cycle, people have less and use what they earn to survive. Saving becomes a luxury, and the savings rate drops. As the cycle goes into recovery or expansion, people go back to work and are able to earn more and save more. Figure 9.7 (on the next page) shows this relationship. Note the rate changes in recession of mid-1980s and early 1990s.

As an economic measurement, the savings rate gives mixed signals. It can indicate the danger of inflationary trends – sometimes. Rising prices mean people must spend more of their Disposable Personal Income just to maintain their standard of living. This leaves less to put into savings, and the savings rate declines. Inflation not only causes people to save less, it usually causes more withdrawals, too. Some people decide to make major purchases with their savings, fearing loss of purchasing power as their dollars decline in value.

However, there is another side to inflationary pressure on the savings rate. As inflation causes the price of limited supplies to rise, and

Disposable Personal Income has less purchasing power, some consumers may actually decide not to buy, and save *more* – at least temporarily.

Because of these mixed signals, using the savings rate as an indicator on its own is vexing. However, used with other indicators, a rising savings rate can confirm expansion.

Americans seem to save less than the citizens of other industrialized nations. Part of the reason for this is cultural, stemming from our desire to achieve the American Dream. Owning a home, car, and possessions of all kinds means a great deal. Americans seem to "want it all." Traditionally, they spend much and save little. Note the chart in Figure 9.7: The savings rate in the 1980s and early 1990s is about 4%. Japanese and German rates in this period were 8%-12%. Examining how much Disposable Personal Income goes into saving helps indicate how the economy is performing.

PERFORMANCE MEASUREMENT: UNEMPLOYMENT LEVELS

Ever since the Great Crash of 1929, no other economic measure carries the weight of

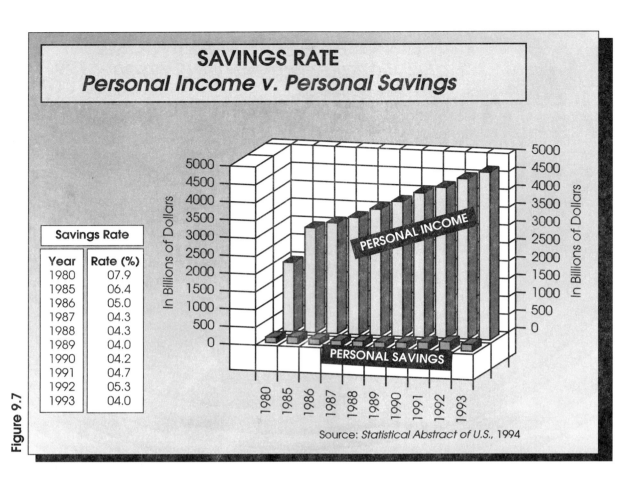

SAVINGS RATE
Personal Income v. Personal Savings

Figure 9.7

Savings Rate	
Year	**Rate (%)**
1980	07.9
1985	06.4
1986	05.0
1987	04.3
1988	04.3
1989	04.0
1990	04.2
1991	04.7
1992	05.3
1993	04.0

Source: *Statistical Abstract of U.S., 1994*

Figure 9.7

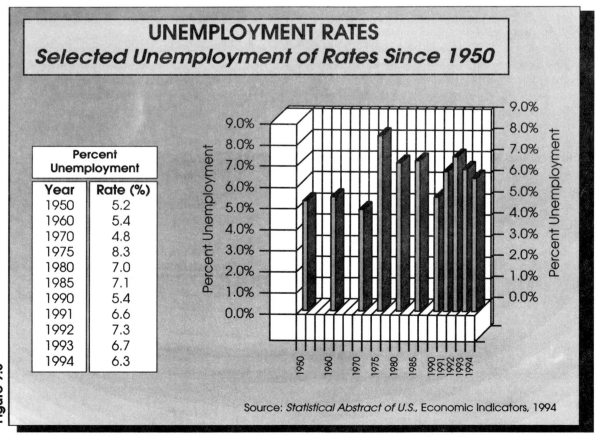

UNEMPLOYMENT RATES
Selected Unemployment of Rates Since 1950

Percent Unemployment	
Year	**Rate (%)**
1950	5.2
1960	5.4
1970	4.8
1975	8.3
1980	7.0
1985	7.1
1990	5.4
1991	6.6
1992	7.3
1993	6.7
1994	6.3

Source: *Statistical Abstract of U.S., Economic Indicators, 1994*

Figure 9.8

the unemployment rate. The **unemployment rate** measures the people not working but seeking employment. If after a while, an unemployed person gives up and stops seeking work, he/she is no longer considered to be part of the workforce. These people are now given another label. They are considered to be **discouraged workers** and do not show up in labor statistics.

Some unemployment is acceptable in a free economy. Modern economists are not disturbed by a 4 or even 5 percent unemployment rate. In fact, economists would classify such a level as near to **full employment** (the ideal that everyone wanting a job can find one) as possible. People change jobs frequently, and employers fire employees who do not meet their expectations. People take time for raising families or for travel and projects. All this is considered normal, **frictional unemployment**.

Cyclical unemployment is more serious, it results from contractions of the business cycle itself. **Structural unemployment** is also serious and may be prolonged because it results from jobs being eliminated because of technology. Structurally unemployed workers cannot easily rejoin the work force as the economy recovers, they must retrain themselves for new, more sophisticated jobs.

Whatever the cause, high unemployment is a serious problem not only for individuals and their families, but in a broader sense, for the economy on the whole. In the worst years of the Great Depression, some unemployment estimates went as high as 25%. The *Selected Unemployment Rates Since 1950* chart (Figure 9.8) gives averages, but in recessions in the 1970s, and 1980s, and 1990s, there were months that the numbers exceeded 10%.

When unemployment figures climb, businesses lose sales because the unemployed do not have

The Consumer Price Index (CPI) indicates that food shopping takes a larger part of the family budget. ©PhotoDisc

purchasing power. The economy loses the goods and services that would have been produced by laid-off workers. The workers and businesses that are still productive are often subject to higher taxes for **public assistance** (unemployment compensation, medical subsidies, and welfare) to help support the unemployed.

A high number of unemployed workers is an indication of even further economic grief for the society. Significant unemployment also means that there are many nonproductive resources such as buildings and machinery (capital). Significant unemployment means that the entire nation will have less productivity and less income. The GDP pie gets smaller and so does each person's piece.

PERFORMANCE MEASUREMENT: INFLATION LEVELS

Statistics showing prices paid for goods and services are another important measure of the economy. An examination of how prices change in the economy can indicate how healthy and stable the system is. The tool used to calculate the average price level is the **Consumer Price Index** (CPI). It is a key measurement of **inflation** – an increase in the average level of prices. CPI measures the difference in prices paid for goods and services purchased by consumers over time.

CPI was first used in 1919 and is now generated by the United States Bureau of Labor Statistics every month. Its data is given to business, government, and labor. The information leads to price changes and adjustment of wage demands. Congress alters food stamp allocations, social security payments, and even school lunch programs on CPI. The FED uses it to help in determining its monetary policies.

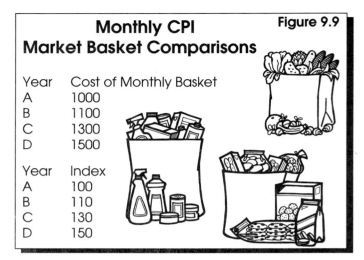

Monthly CPI
Market Basket Comparisons

Figure 9.9

Year	Cost of Monthly Basket
A	1000
B	1100
C	1300
D	1500

Year	Index
A	100
B	110
C	130
D	150

Each month, this agency prices 400 commonly purchased goods and services (known as the "market basket," see Figure 9.9) in 85 different locations throughout the country. These prices are compared to what the costs were in a "base year" which the Bureau arbitrarily chooses and assigns a reference point of 100. All other yearly prices are compared as percentages of this base year.

Assume that in Year A, the base year, the cost of the 400 goods and services in the "market basket" is $1,000. During the next year, the cost goes up to $1,100, then $1,300 in year C, and finally in Year D, $1,500. In Year A, the $1,000 is converted to 100(%) on the price index. During Year B, the cost went up by $100, (or 10%) of the Year A (base year) figure. In Year C, a $300 increase translates to a price index change of 30%, and so on.

What this means to the consumer is that it will cost 10%, then 20%, and then 30%, more to buy the same things purchased in the base year. Figure 9.10 illustrates what happens over time. As prices continually go up, a person must spend more in order to simply maintain his/her standard of living. If a person's income does not keep pace with the increased costs, purchasing power is lost, and the piece of the pie gets smaller.

PRODUCER PRICE INDEX

Consumers are not the only part of the economy that is affected by inflation. The **Producer Price Index** (**PPI**) indicates the changes in what producers pay to assemble their products. Just like the CPI, the Producer Price Index is calculated by the government and published monthly.

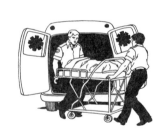

Figure 9.10   Consumer Price Index

Selected Monthly CPI Items for Urban Areas, 1980-1993, (1983 constant dollars = 100). Figures show expense for item as percent above or below the 1983 base year. For example, to buy the same food items you bought in 1983 for $100, you would need $141.60 in 1993.

Source: Statistical Abstract of U.S., 1994

Expense	1980	1985	1990	1993
All Items	82.4	107.6	130.7	144.5
Food and beverages	86.7	105.6	132.1	141.6
Housing	81.1	107.7	128.5	141.2
Apparel	90.9	105.0	124.1	133.7
Transportation	83.1	106.4	120.5	130.4
Medical Care	74.9	113.5	162.8	201.4
Entertainment	83.6	107.9	132.4	145.8
Fuel and utilities	86.0	101.6	102.1	104.2

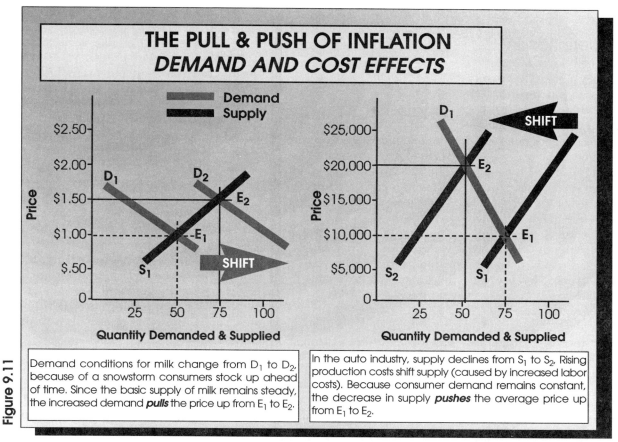

THE PULL & PUSH OF INFLATION
DEMAND AND COST EFFECTS

Figure 9.11

Demand conditions for milk change from D_1 to D_2, because of a snowstorm consumers stock up ahead of time. Since the basic supply of milk remains steady, the increased demand **pulls** the price up from E_1 to E_2.

In the auto industry, supply declines from S_1 to S_2. Rising production costs shift supply (caused by increased labor costs). Because consumer demand remains constant, the decrease in supply **pushes** the average price up from E_1 to E_2.

There is an important connection between the CPI and the PPI. When businesses pay more to produce their products today, consumers will pay more for them tomorrow. It seems that it is important to maintain a perspective on both of these indicators since a change in the Producer Price Index will lead to a future change in the Consumer Price Index.

WHEN PRICES RISE

Economists have a rather simple definition for a very complex economic problem: **inflation**. They call it "a period of rapidly rising prices." Of course, if prices are rising and income is not, the economy is in trouble. It means it takes more money to buy goods and services.

What causes prices to rise? The technical explanation sounds simple enough: demand exceeds supply. Since a market works by people making educated guesses about what, when, and how to produce, it is natural for there to be miscalculations.

Local misjudgments about supply are frequent, but they are not often too serious. Perhaps an impending snowstorm sends many more customers into the stores to buy bread and milk, rent video tapes, or buy rock salt. Normal supplies vaporize, and stores have to send out quickly for more. Perhaps stores have to pay more to get delivery from distant sources. Stores pass the added cost on to slightly panicky customers. Without much choice, the larger number of customers begin paying a little more for things they need. It is almost like an auction scenario. High demand "pulls prices up." This is **demand-pull inflation**. As the left graph in Figure 9.11 shows, when the supply is fixed and the demand for a product increases (shifts right on graph), the equilibrium price rises.

In the 1970s, U.S. auto manufacturers stopped producing convertibles. Rising thefts, poor gas mileage, air conditioning, and discomfort experienced with high speed turnpike driving in open cars made demand for convertibles decline. In the 1980s, Mazda Motors' market research showed the growing youth market

Hyperinflation

The best known example of **hyperinflation** (extreme, rapid inflationary spiral) took place in Europe in the early 1920s. The devastation of World War I caused great economic disorder. In Germany, the Weimar Republic experienced the worst fate of any government – the repudiation of its money. The value of the German mark was totally destroyed. As the currency value plummeted, the prices of goods and services rose so quickly people could not believe what was happening. A loaf of bread went up in price from one mark to a million. People carted money in wheelbarrows rather than wallets. Money was used to wallpaper rooms instead of being spent in stores. People were seen running to stores to spend whatever they had to avoid increases in price in the time it normally took to walk.

More recently, Brazil and Argentina suffered through horrible double digit rises in the weekly cost of living. In 1990, these two countries risked political and social collapse because of hyperinflation. Prices increased at an alarming 70% to 195% a month.

– *New York Times* 11 March 1990

might support a sporty little convertible for around town. When the Miata hit dealerships, demand exceeded supply by such a great amount that astonished dealers began letting customers bid against each other. The manufacturer's suggested price was around $12,000. Miata dealers were selling them for over $15,000. Eventually, the price came down as supply increased and the market came back into equilibrium. Similar inflationary episodes surrounded Power Ranger products, Cabbage Patch Dolls, and Water Soaker Guns.

When people are willing to spend more and more money, the result may be demand-pull inflation. If there is an increase in the money supply or credit is too readily available, consumers compete intensely for supplies and prices escalate. To prevent this, the Federal Reserve will act to "tighten the money supply" (see material on FED in Issue 7).

On the supply side of price inflation is the influence of production costs on producer decisions. **Profits** (revenues – costs) drive producers' decisions. When, for example, nature causes crop failures or wars make oil hard to get or union contracts raise labor costs, production costs rise, and producers see their profits shrink. To avoid profit loss, producers pass along the added costs by raising their prices, fueling inflation.

If the situation continues, it prompts decisions which shift supply even more. Producers may convert some of their facilities to making something more profitable, or they may drop out of the market completely. Either way, the supply shrinks. With fewer goods available but demand remaining normal, prices rise. This is called **cost-push inflation**. As the graph on the right side of Figure 9.11 shows, when the demand is fixed and the supply of a product decreases (shifts left on graph), the market equilibrium price rises.

Whatever the cause, inflation can be an inconvenience for some people and devastating for others. Some employment contracts contain **Cost of Living Adjustments** (**COLAs**) that raise income according to some inflation index such as the Consumer Price Index. Contract COLAs are rare, however. Upper income groups find budget and expense shifts irksome, but middle and lowe_ income groups may have to make considerable sacrifices when faced with inflation. Retirees on fixed income, unable to go out and earn more, have to juggle expenses frantically when their heating bills rise due to inflation. Often, they make up the added heating oil expense from food allocations, and malnutrition can result. Middle income groups often have to give up small luxuries and then shop for cheaper brands of food and clothing.

Everyone has to juggle finances during inflation. Yet, inflation does benefit a few individuals. Suppose a student has to borrow money for four years of college. During the four years, inflation hits. After graduation, the student begins to pay back the loan. The purchasing power of the current dollars used to pay back the loan is perhaps 3 to 10 percent less than the dollars borrowed four years before. In this case, the borrower is at an advantage and the bank loses. Banks now protect themselves with "adjustable rates" on mortgages and even short-term loans. They can raise the interest rate if necessary to make up for the losses inflicted by inflation. For the most part, however, everyone is hurt by inflation.

WHEN PRICES FALL

Two additional terms associated with inflation need to be examined: deflation and disinflation. **Deflation** is a general and steady decrease in prices. In the United States, prices have generally been increasing since the 1930s, and so there has not been a significant deflation.

While it seems that deflation would be a good thing for consumers, lower prices do not always help stimulate the economy as a whole. An examination of the recession of 1990 may help. Prices dropped because consumers were not buying. Supply exceeded demand, and surpluses accumulated. Businesses cut prices as a natural response. But these softened prices created personnel and production problems.

Suppose a worker needed to move in order to get a job. The family home had to be put on the market. With the prices down, the selling price of the house may at best be a very small increase above what the family paid for the home originally. The family could get less than it paid for the house, too. For businesses, the selling prices of their goods could be less than the production costs. This may cause, at best, a loss to the company. At worst, it may cause the end of the business, and its employees could face unemployment.

Disinflation is any reduction of the inflation rate. It does not refer to prices but to a slowdown in the rate of growth of inflation. For example, the rate of inflation dropped from approximately 13% in 1980 to 4% in 1985. Prices were still increasing, but their *rate* of increase was considerably slower. Disinflation is

usually associated with actions by the Federal Reserve Board's manipulation of its monetary policy (see Issue 7).

WHEN GROWTH STAGNATES

When the two negative conditions of high unemployment and high inflation occur at the same time, economists call it **stagflation**. If there is an attempt to work on curing one condition, that cure seems to make the opposite condition worsen. If the government uses tight fiscal and monetary policies to lower inflation, unemployment usually rises. If the government uses expansionary fiscal and monetary policies to lower the unemployment rate, then the action makes inflation worse.

To illustrate, suppose the economy is stagnant, but there is inflation. In the late 1960s, government spending for social programs (the Great Society) and the Vietnam War inflated the money supply, but fear of recession led firms to cut back production. Fear caused production to slow down, and jobs were cut. Yet, the government continued its rampant spending. Congress put a surcharge on taxes to sop up some of the excess money, but that slowed growth even more, and a recession began.

The most frequent approach to controlling inflation has been for the Federal Reserve (the FED) to "tighten" the money supply. Tightening the money supply means raising FED interest rates, eventually making it more expensive to borrow money. This additional expense discourages producers and consumers and slows aggregate demand. This decrease in spending creates a surplus. To get rid of the excess supply, producers cut prices, and inflation slows.

Such FED actions alter inflation, but they also slow down demand. This means there will

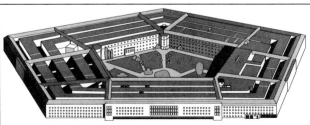

Pentagon, Arlington, VA

Difficult Tradeoffs
In order to get control of spending and reduce the rate of increase in the deficit in the 1990s, Congress reduced the Federal Budget. This required major cuts in defense funds. To meet these reductions, the Pentagon closed military bases. These closures helped improve the budget but produced ripple effects in the economies of the communities where the base closings were made. Due to the loss of income, unemployment increased, local businesses closed reducing the tax base for schools and services, and people moved to find jobs.

be layoffs and job cuts by businesses. The only way to combat unemployment is to increase aggregate demand. In the past, Congress tried to do this with spending programs or tax reductions to flush more money into the economy. Theoretically an increase in demand would inspire producers to put more workers back to work to meet the higher demand.

The result is often what novelist Joseph Heller called "Catch-22" – an unending loop wherein solving one problem worsens the other. If unemployment is to be dealt with, more spending is required. Yet, if inflation is to be reduced, less spending is required. One treatment cancels out the other.

Treating one condition at the expense of the other is just not acceptable. Government must adopt a new, coordinated outlook and attitude toward the problem, but individuals and unions must also restrain the desire for increased wages. Acting for the greater good is often a very difficult process.

GLOBAL PERFORMANCE MEASUREMENT: FOREIGN EXCHANGE

There are also global dimensions to measuring economic life. The United States is the world's foremost economic power. How its image is perceived by other countries has a great effect on the operation of our economy. An indicator of how the world perceives our economic wellbeing is how well our currency is doing in relation to the money of other countries.

If a country's economic outlook is perceived as bad in the eyes of other countries, there is reaction to the perception. In late 1994 and early 1995, the Mexican peso took a horrific drop in value on world markets. This global loss of confidence in Mexico's economy kept investors and business expansion at bay. Intervention from friends sometimes helps. U.S. government backing for loans to Mexico helped stem the peso's decline.

Everyday, billions of dollars are traded in markets where national currencies are bought and sold. The currencies of all nations are exchanged. The reasons for this swapping are: international trade, international investment, and international aid (loans and grants).

Each nation has its own money. So, what happens when an American wants to buy a Japanese – made Nikkon camera or a Japanese firm wants to buy a piece of heavy equipment from the Caterpillar Corporation of America? The Japanese manufacturer wants to be paid in yen, and the American producer wants to be paid in U.S. dollars. The practice of replacement of one currency for another at equal value is known as the **foreign exchange rate**. The price of the camera and the heavy equipment is set by each manufacturer in the amount of the country where it was produced. How the yen and dollar get to the right place and in the proper amount is established by a rate of exchange.

Banks all over the world keep currencies of all countries to finance the global exchanges of goods and services. The American corporation deposits dollars and withdraws yen and vice versa. The amount of yen received by these banks is compared to the amount of dollars they receive, and this creates a rate of exchange. What dollars are worth in comparison to all other world monies is an important measure of how well or poorly our country is doing. It is a means of measuring the financial relationship of our country to all others.

When the foreign exchange rate goes up (meaning the value of other countries' money in relation to ours goes up), our dollar is **depreciated** (loses value). It costs more to purchase the money of other nations with American dollars. When the foreign exchange goes down (meaning the value of other countries' money in relation

to ours goes down), the U.S. dollar is **appreciated** (gains value). It costs less to purchase the money of other nations. Figure 9.12 gives an idea of the variations in international currency exchange rates in relation to the United States dollar.

This value change of our money compared to other currencies affects the business we do with those countries. This means that a nation's international economic position depends upon what payments are made for imports and what receipts are obtained from exports. The record of these transactions is known as the **balance of payment accounts**, and it is another indicator of the economic health of a country. (See Issue 10 for additional discussion on this subject.) Nations want to have a *favorable* balance of payments. This means the country has a greater flow of money *into* it than *out of* it.

The balance of payments is primarily affected by the **balance of trade**. This is the difference between the value of what a country imports and exports. A **trade deficit** means that the value of goods a country has imported is more than the value of goods it has exported (an *unfavorable* balance of trade). When the value of exports exceeds the value of imports, a **trade surplus** exists which is also known as a *favorable* balance of trade. Since the late 1970s, the United States has had a large and costly trade deficit. It has caused the depreciation of the U.S. dollar, and it has created a situation which lowers the purchasing power of our currency throughout the world. (Issue 10 explores this topic further.)

All this means that other countries are getting more of our wealth. The more they get, the less we have for ourselves. The story at the beginning of this issue noted that growth meant all of us want a bigger piece of the GDP pie. We may be producing more, but when our net exports show a deficit, our share of the pie is smaller. A trade deficit means the raises we expect from our hard work and increased efficiency trickle out to workers in other countries. It also means some loss of confidence in the U.S. economy. That can decrease the value of our currency. The way others view our strength affects our ability to get a bigger share of world markets, and that can have a negative effect on the American Dream.

Figure 9.12 Currency Exchange Rate		
Source: Harold Reuter & Company, Inc , 7 May 1995		
Currency	Exchange Rate per U.S. Dollar	Value in U.S. Dollars
Argentinian pesos	1.00	$1.0000
Austrian schilling	9.50	0.1053
Australian dollar	1.30	0.7675
British pound	0.60	1.6650
Canadian dollar	1.33	0.7519
China renminbi	10.00	0.1000
German mark	1.35	0.7407
Egyptian pound	2.94	0.3400
French franc	4.80	0.2083
Israeli shekel	2.75	0.3636
Indian rupee	32.00	0.0313
Japanese yen	81.50	0.0123
Mexican new peso	5.50	0.1818
Russian ruble	4900.00	0.0003
Swiss franc	1.11	0.9009

Figure 9.13	Classifying Economic Indicators	
	Source: Statistical Abstract of the U.S., 1994, pg. 556	
Leading Indicators	**Coincidental Indicators**	**Lagging Indicators**
Building Permits (new private dwellings) Common Stock Price Index Initial Unemployment Insurance Claims Producer Raw Material Prices (PPI) Average Work Week (manufacturing industries) Plant and Equipment Contracts and Orders Manufacturers' Orders for Consumer Goods Money Supply (M2) Change in Manufacturers' Unfilled Orders	Industrial Production Index Employee Payrolls –nonagricultural Personal Income less government transfer payments Sales	Change in Labor Costs (manufacturing) Ratio: Consumer Installment Credit to Personal Income Average Prime Rate of Banks Average Duration of Unemployment Ratio: Manufacturing Inventories to Sales Commercial Loans Outstanding Change in CPI for Services

PERFORMANCE MEASUREMENT: ECONOMIC INDICATORS

When examining data about how well the economy is doing, it is customary to compare the information according to a time frame. **Economic indicators** are based on the U.S. Department of Commerce's statistics on 300 aspects of the economy (see Figure 9.13). In a particular period, **key indicators** are reported monthly and tracked by economists to gauge the general performance of the economy. **Leading Indicators** are statistics that show a general change may occur in the future. **Coincidental Indicators** are statistics that show changes are in progress. **Lagging Indicators** are statistics that confirm changes have already happened.

SUMMARY

A word of caution about economic measurement is necessary. **Econometrics** (the application of mathematical and statistical methods to study economic and financial data) is still only a method of analyzing and predicting human activity in the short run. No matter which measurement is examined and analyzed, forecasts are still educated guesses as to how the economy will behave. Predicting the direction of the economy is like predicting the weather. It is an inexact science that often turns out differently than conditions indicate.

Yet, knowing that this data exists and what it means is still a great deal better than ignoring it. Changes in all of the indicators discussed are not just studies in the academics of economics. These indicators have an important impact on decision-makers' actions which help decide the stability and growth of the economy. They also guide personal financial decisions such as how to save and invest, when to borrow, or when to buy a house. Achieving the American Dream is very difficult without a working knowledge of economic measurement.

ASSESSMENT
QUESTIONS • APPLICATIONS

1 What, in your life, determines if you are a success?
   a Why is income such a dramatic indicator of the economy in this country?
   b Explain in detail what you will be doing to achieve a sense of accomplishment in life.
   c Describe the work environment you will seek to accomplish your career goals.

2 It is normal for the the economy to go through phases of the business (demand) cycle.
   a Describe each of the four phases of the cycle.
   b What causes each of these phases?
   c What really determines prosperity?

3 Understanding measurements are critical to making business and career decisions and achieving the American Dream.
   a Explain the difference between GNP and GDP.
   b Why is the distinction important?
   c Which of the following is a better measure of the health of the economy: Real GDP or Money GDP? Why?
   d For the average person, the CPI has more meaning than the GDP or GNP. Explain why you agree or disagree with the above statement.

4 Examine the CPI numbers on the chart (Figure 9.10, page 190).
   a Which category of expense increased the most from 1980 to 1993? Which showed the least increase?
   b Describe how the CPI figures for "All Items" you see for 1980 to 1993 would affect a household making the median income of $17,710 in 1980. For example, what would the family income have to be in 1993 just to stay even with their 1980 purchasing power?

5 World opinion affects our economy far more than the average person perceives.
   a How is the American economy affected when one of your neighbors buys her dream car – a new – Lexus at a local dealer?
   b How may the foreign exchange rates affect your dream of a vacation in a foreign country?
   c How is international trade affected by foreign exchange rates?

6 Wars produce enormous effects on economic performance.
   a How does government demand during wars affect economic performance?
   b What happens to economic performance at the end of a war when government demand declines?
   c What kind of long-range effects do wars have on the countries involved (e.g., productive capacities, population)?

ASSESSMENT PROJECT:
FIELD RESEARCH INTERVIEW

STUDENT TASK

Write an individual report on field research interviews and participate in a group presentation on perceptions of success.

PROCEDURE

Part One: (Individual Summary)

1 Based on the statement – "The meaning of the American Dream has changed during the last two generations." – prepare a list of questions to be asked during a social history survey to determine how three individuals (senior citizen, a middle-aged person, and a young adult) view the term "success."

2 Organize your interview as follows:

   a Develop a short statement of purpose to share with the interviewee.

   b Design your questions to elicit a simple "yes" or "no" – but provide the interviewee the opportunity to make a brief explanation or qualification.

   c After the last question has been asked, give the interviewee the opportunity (in light of the entire interview) to elaborate on the causes of the change.

   d When the interview is finished, thank the interviewee.

3 Compare, contrast, and analyze the three interviews. This can be done in chart or outline form.

4 Write an essay summarizing your findings.

Part Two: (Group Activity and Report)

1 Using the Part One summary, participate in a small group discussing the interview findings.

2 Produce a summary of the group's discussion of the interviews – citing differences and commonalities.

3 Present the group's findings orally for discussion by the whole class.

LEARNING STANDARDS

Learners should be able to:

(1) understand that while different socioeconomic (as well as national, ethnic, religious, racial, and gender) groups have varied perspectives, values, and diverse practices and traditions, they face the same global economic challenges.

(5) analyze problems and evaluate decisions about the economic effects on society and the individual caused by human, technological, and natural activities.

(6) present their ideas both in writing and orally in clear, concise, and properly accepted fashion.

(7) employ a variety of information from written, graphic, and multimedia sources.

(8) monitor, reflect upon, and improve their own and others' work.

(9) work cooperatively and show respect for the rights of others to think, act, and speak differently from themselves within the context of democratic principles and social justice.

EVALUATION

The criteria for the evaluation of this project are itemized in the grid (rubric) that follows. Choice of appropriate category terms (values) is the decision of the instructor. Selection of terms such as "minimal," "satisfactory," and "distinguished" can vary with each assessment.

Part One: Individual Field Interview Evaluation Rubric

(Refer to introductory section for suggestions of scoring descriptors for the evaluation categories.)

Evaluation Item	Category 1	Category 2	Category 3	Category 4	Category 5
Item a: (5) Does the essay show how three individuals view the term "success"?					
Item b: (1) Does the essay show an understanding that peoples' values, practices, and traditions are diverse?					
Item c: (6) Does the essay present ideas in clear, concise, and properly accepted fashion?					

Part Two: Group Field Interview Evaluation Rubric

(Refer to introductory section for suggestions of scoring descriptors for the evaluation categories.)

Evaluation Item	Category 1	Category 2	Category 3	Category 4	Category 5
Item a: (9) To what extent does the group work cooperatively and show respect for the rights of others to think, act, and speak?					
Item b: (7) Does the group use a variety of good sources?					
Item c: (8) To what extent does the group monitor, reflect upon, and improve their members' work?					
Item d: (6) Does the group's summary present ideas in clear, concise, and properly accepted fashion?					
Item e: (9) How well does the group's discussion engage the whole class?					

ISSUE 10

What will shape the new global economy?

GLOBAL ECONOMIC INTERDEPENDENCE

"How much are the major industrial countries
willing to subordinate near-term nationalistic
interests, which are often politically quite
popular, to longer term benefits?"

– Economist Henry Kaufman

BEYOND
THE CHAIN WALL:
A NEW TRADE IS BORN

Maya pointed far across the desert floor. "There, by the rift at the edge of the cliff," she said.

Tok could barely see it – a small black dot. It must be two klicks away, but the old binoculars caught the movement. The Unsa village council had assigned the young couple to the village's outpost for two years. Their time was nearly up, and Maya and Tok had not seen anything but animals and sunrise on the east horizon. This had to be a person, judging from the slow, steady motion. Maya had taken the early morning scan along the edge of the vast, arid plateau. There were only two breaks in the far precipice. The moving dot appeared in the Arkai Pass, the one that twisted down to the TRIAD Chain Wall.

Maya and Tok were just in their twenties. In all their lives, they had not seen anyone from beyond the desert's edge. They were Inlanders. They were born in 2030, long after the Eco War. In the village school, they learned that a decade before, the old industrial nations had fallen apart trying to deal with population migrations from LDCs (less developed countries). The "Have-nots" of the Southern Hemisphere were collapsing from the HIV epidemic, starvation, and government corruption. Millions of refugees set out for the "Have" countries of the Northern Hemisphere. The northern peoples feared the waves of refugees would overburden them. They taxed their populations and raised large armies and navies to repel the refugees. After six years of trying to stop the flow, the overtaxed military economies collapsed. Nuclear weapons were useless. How could you use missiles against the small crafts of these desperate souls? The United Nations was no help. It disintegrated because no one had the money to contribute to its peacekeeping forces. Negotiations and world conferences were useless when half the nations were socially and economically bankrupt.

Only two forces remained: the three trade alliances (the TRIAD) and the MNCs (MultiNational Corporations). Amid the chaos of the mass migrations, the MNCs closed down their facilities in the LDCs. They withdrew to their headquarters in Northern Hemisphere. When it appeared the overstrained northern nations were collapsing, the MNCs threw their resources behind the trade alliances. The "TRIAD" (Europa [the European Union], AFTA [the Americas' alliance – all Western Hemisphere], and APEC [the Asia Pacific alliance driven by Japan and China]) became the great trade empires. The TRIAD merged military forces and built elaborate secure cities to protect the MNCs.

After almost a decade of negotiation, the TRIAD Empires strengthened ties among themselves and forced the refugees into the interiors of the continents. The coastal areas grew to look like overgrown medieval manors. The TRIAD Empires built successive rings of tall electrified fences for miles around the cities and their agricultural fields. Strict birth control measures kept the populations small. All supplies came by ship. Air travel ceased. There was no room for airports and no need to move people. Everyone stayed put. Hydroponic factories provided food. Desalinization plants provided water, and only armed garbage convoys ventured out beyond the Chain Walls.

Excluded, the refugees became "Inlanders." They turned to subsistence farming and herding in small, isolated communities. Fear and poverty kept Inlander communities from contact with each other.

Now, on a cool, sunlit morning in 2050, Tok and Maya watched the man trudge along the desert floor. Finally, when they were sure there were no others, they went forth to meet him. He was elderly and had a small shoulder bag and a walking staff. He halted when he saw them approach, and the old man raised his palm in friendship.

"I am Lon Gehr of Pacifica, the TRIAD city 90 klicks east. I come in peace. What is this place?"

"We are Maya and Tok of Unsa. This is our village's outpost. Come, share our fire."

Later, Lon Gher told them the Pacifica Board sent him to negotiate trade with Inlander villages for fresh meat. For fear of disease and for lack of room, no animals were allowed inside the Chain Walls of Pacifica. The herds of closer villages were already being bought. Those villagers told Lon that Unsa had larger herds.

The next day, they escorted Lon to Unsa. Lon sat with the village's council. On the way back to the outpost, Tok told Maya this man had been a dot on the horizon at yesterday's sunrise. He might be the new dawn for the Inlanders.

ISSUE 10

What will shape the new global economy?

GLOBAL ECONOMIC INTERDEPENDENCE

SHAPING A GLOBAL ECONOMY: THE RICH AND POOR NATIONS

The Chain Wall story presents a grim prospect for generations to come. Society degenerating into a new feudal era is possible. Yet, the world may be able to weather the problems that confront it and not dissolve into an "Eco War." History teaches that there are always options. Preserving the American Dream requires people to look beyond their local needs. People must realize that global economic performance links everyone's lives and determines if they can achieve their dreams.

It is certain that today's challenges will bring sweeping change. Understanding the issues and devising new answers will shape the future. In *Preparing for the Twenty-First Century*, historian Paul Kennedy says:

"*Economic change and technological development, like wars or sporting tournaments, are usually not beneficial to all. Progress, welcomed by optimistic voices since the Enlightenment to our present age, benefits those groups or nations that can take advantage of the newer methods and science, just as it damages others that are less prepared technologically, culturally, and politically to respond to change.*" (Kennedy 15)

The developed nations already manage technological progress. This will enable them to deal with the challenges of the 21st century. Less developed countries (LDCs) may be the ones that suffer. A look at conditions may help in predicting the future for various nations.

THE RICH NATIONS IN THE 1990s

The developed nations struggled out of a recession in the first half of the 1990s. The U.S. economy stalled in the 1980s. The blistering pace of over borrowing, corporate buyouts, and mergers could not offset the lack of productivity. There were political obstacles as well. Western Europe faltered trying to reorganize after the downfall of communism in Eastern Europe and the former Soviet Union. Germany was strained trying to absorb East Germany's aged, failing industries and poorly trained workforce. Even the strong, export-driven economy of Japan felt recession when its U.S. and European customers stopped buying.

Flags of NAFTA: Mexico, United States, and Canada ©PhotoDisc

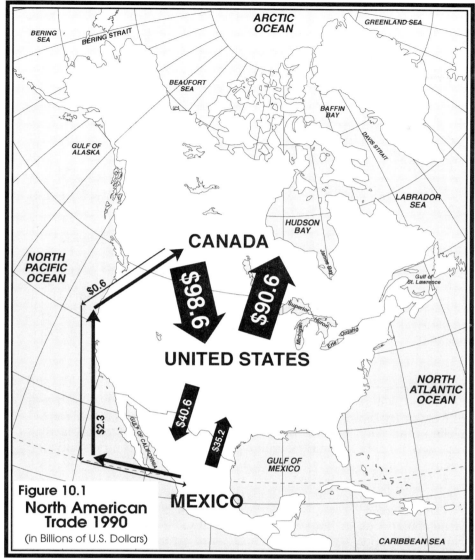

Figure 10.1
North American Trade 1990
(in Billions of U.S. Dollars)

In January 1994, Canada, Mexico, and the United States created NAFTA – the world's largest "low-tariff" trading zone. It encompasses 370 million people with a combined GDP of 6.7 trillion dollars. In 1994, total trade exceeded 242 billion U.S. dollars.

Market) and **APEC** (Asian Pacific Economic Conference), a loose-knit, East Asia / Pacific Rim group. The United States also explored a free trade agreement for all of the Western Hemisphere by 2005.

On the other side of the Atlantic, European diplomats refashioned the "Common Market" into the European Union. In the 1980s and early 1990s, American and Japanese firms accelerated their investments and facilities in Europe. They wanted to beat a proposed European economic unification date in 1993 (which passed unfulfilled). Unfortunately, recession, disintegration of the U.S.S.R. and its communist satellites, plus the brutal civil war in the Balkans slowed Europe's integration plan.

One global bright spot was the 1993 version of the **GATT** (General Agreement on Trade and Tariffs). This on-going, U.N.-sponsored treaty system tries to standardize international rules for commerce among nations recommends general tariff rates and mediates trade disagreements between members. In GATT's 1993 Uruguay Round, European nations gained some protection for agriculture and light industry. That bought some time for recovery from the recession and for building the European Union.

During the global recession, the larger U.S. companies downsized and regrouped. They cut personnel and reduced debt. Some big businesses failed, but most strengthened themselves. They cut costs, especially labor costs, and they refocused on efficiency. As the United States slowly worked out of the recession, the FED became obsessed with keeping inflation in check. This slowed the pace of recovery, but revitalization drew more foreign investment – a sign of renewed world confidence. Joining with Canada and Mexico in **NAFTA** (the North American Free Trade Association) also boosted investment (see Figure 10.1). NAFTA prepared the North American nations for a global economy revolving around trade alliances such as the **European Union** (formerly called the Common

The export economy of Japan also slowed with the softening of the American and European markets. Yet, its business with China and other rising economies of East and Southeast Asia allowed it to stay out of the recession longer. Still, the large amounts of capital it invested abroad drew Japan into the global recession. When it did start to decline, Japan's economy went into a kind of shock.

The Economic Tug-of-war

With the signing of economic treaties, the developed nations of the world
created massive trade alliances. Japan, Australia, Taiwan, and other nations of
the Pacific Rim tentatively formed the Asian Pacific Economic Conference (APEC).
The former Common Market countries of Western Europe evolved through the European Community (EC)
to the newly enlarged European Union. Feeling the international pressure, the United States, Canada, and
Mexico formed the North American Free Trade Association (NAFTA), the largest trade association.

Japan's long-term growth after World War II ultimately created a strong middle class. By the 1980s, Japan was more consumer-oriented than a generation earlier. The average saving rate (nearly 20% of the average Japanese family's income) dropped to 14% in the 1980s. The Japanese were spending more of their income. In the recession, this thinner "savings cushion" meant Japan's industries could not borrow as much to maintain normal production. Like American and European companies, Japan's corporations began downsizing, cutting operations, and laying off workers. The cuts by Japan's paternal **keiretsu** (mega corporations, formerly called zaibatsu) shook the nation's tradition of job security and steady pay raises. By 1995, only 35% of Japanese workers had job security. Irate voters unseated the long powerful Liberal Democratic Party.

While painful, the "streamlining" of companies in the United States and Japan increased competitiveness. To cut the costs of overseas trade, both countries deepened their commitments to regional trade alliances (NAFTA, APEC) and the GATT. Also, multinationals based in both countries strengthened their presence in Europe anticipating new trade barriers there.

The Europeans did not act as decisively, and the European Union struggled to admit Austria,

Sweden, and Norway in the mid-1990s and prepare Eastern European states for partial membership. Still, as *Fortune* reporters Tom Martin and Deborah Greenwood showed the rich nations advanced as a whole. Japan, Europe, and the United States showed GDP growth of over 4% in the mid-1990s ("The World Economy in Charts." 26 July 1993, 89). With inflation around 2%, growth was slow, but strength appeared to be returning. Except in Russia, the less tense situation after the Cold War helped developed nations meet the challenges presented by the 21st century.

THE "FOUR DRAGONS"

In Asian nations other than Japan, the 1990s recession hardly slowed growth. China, Thailand, Indonesia, Philippines, and Vietnam expanded with a deluge of foreign investment capital. *Fortune*'s Martin and Greenwood showed that China's real growth was over 10%, even with 12% inflation. But, its growth was geographically uneven. It was concentrated in only the south coast cities. Yet, China's future depends on the expansion of economic freedom. Economist Kari-yiu Wong stated that if the new wealth can get to people inland, the China could remain stable (Martin and Greenwood, 94).

Asia's "Four Dragons," the **NIEs** (newly industrializing economies) of Hong Kong,

Asia's "Four Dragons"
Symbol of the newly industrializing economies of Hong Kong, Singapore, South Korea, and Taiwan.

competing with cheaper Asian-made toys, electronics, and clothing. Many **low-end manufacturers** (cheaper, lesser quality goods) in older, developed nations converted to higher quality, upscale products.

Once the Four Dragons gained economic momentum, new capital from foreign investors poured into these countries. They developed more sophisticated exports. South Korea's Hyundai autos and Goldstar appliances are examples.

HYUNDAI

When the 1990s recession hit the U.S. and European markets, the Four Dragons' business accelerated. In the rich nations, consumption of expensive high-end domestic and imported goods suffered. Yet, consumers continued buying the cheaper products of the Four Dragons (see Figure 10.2). In addition, rising income from exports increased the spending power of Asians. The Four Dragons' domestic markets grew as their own workers bought more of their products. Trade within the Pacific region grew also. Regional consumption of goods made in the Pacific Rim rose from 31% to 43% between 1986 and 1993. The new GATT agreement insured lower global tariffs for the Dragons' major exports. Also, **APEC (Asian Pacific Economic Conference)** became more organized and laid the groundwork for new trade relations.

Singapore, South Korea, and Taiwan exhibited even more exceptional growth. They earned the "Dragons" nickname because of their astounding commercial growth in the late 1980s. This growth flowed from access to unrestricted Western markets and, in Taiwan and Korea, U.S. political and military aid. Low tariffs allowed these nations to compete in the developed countries. They marketed inexpensive goods carried in discount chains (e.g., Wal★Mart and K-Mart). After World War II, grants from America helped to build new, state-of-the-art factories. Some of this industrial technology placed NIEs ahead of the older industrial bases in the United States and Europe. In the high-spending 1980s, some manufacturers in older developed nations stopped

WAL★MART

Kmart

THE LDCs: POOR NATIONS AND THE GLOBAL ECONOMY

Historian Paul Kennedy's quotation at the opening of this chapter says growth is uneven, and some nations suffer when others prosper. Gloomier forecasters point to a 21st century where they say there will be a greater gap between rich nations and poor ones. According to the World Bank, rich nations are those with an average annual per capita GDP of more than

Figure 10.2	Growth of the Four Dragons (1992 figures)	
Source: U.S. Department of Commerce, 1993		
Country	**Annual U.S. Purchases** (in U.S. dollars)	**Direct Foreign Investment** (in U.S. dollars)
Singapore	$9 billion	$3.6 billion
Hong Kong	$9 billion	$2.1 billion
Taiwan	$21 billion	$2.3 billion
South Korea	$18 billion	$3.8 billion

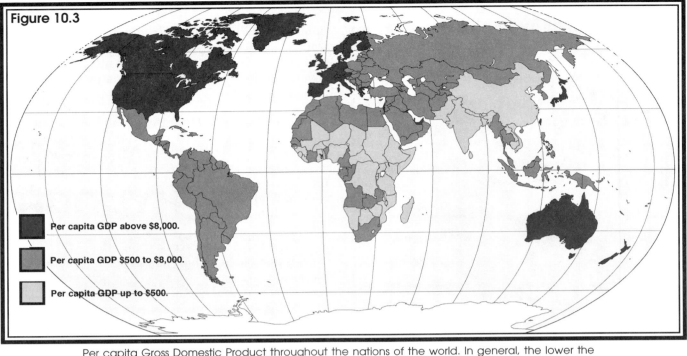

Figure 10.3

Per capita GDP above $8,000.

Per capita GDP $500 to $8,000.

Per capita GDP up to $500.

Per capita Gross Domestic Product throughout the nations of the world. In general, the lower the per capita GDP, the lower the standard of living and the poorer the country. In most cases, the low GDP countries are the "have not"nations – the Less Developed Countries or Third World nations.

eight thousand dollars. The Bureau of Economic Analysis says the 1992 U.S. figure was $22,183 (*Statistical Abstract.* 675). Yet, LDCs such as India, Ghana, and Egypt have annual per capita figures of less than $500. It is obvious that the LDCs are where long-term global concerns lay (see map, Figure 10.3).

Population growth is the LDCs' foremost problem. More than any other factor, it exhausts scarce economic resources. From the Amazon to the Ganges, growing populations and ignorance of conservation cause overgrazing, erosion, desertification, and deforestation. The food supply in these countries is not enough to feed the expanding population. They remain impoverished because they must sell low value **primary resources** (raw materials). Instead of using their capital for development, they must import food from developed countries.

Even when LDCs can buy new technology from the developed world, it causes problems. Corrupt bureaucracies pilfer funds or ineptly misallocate them. Their education systems are weak, and training people to use high tech methods is nearly impossible. Even when LDCs apply new technology, it destroys traditional occupations and raises unemployment. Simultaneously, global communications inform the people in LDCs that life should be better,

and frustration grows. Many seek to migrate to other more prosperous nations, but immigration restrictions block them.

This TIME cover illustrates the concern for the problems of overpopulation and resulting world hunger in many LDCs such as Somalia in Africa where thousands of babies, children, and adults die from starvation annually.

Figure 10.4	**Protectionist Trade Barriers & Sanctions**
	Source: U.S. Department of Commerce, 1993
Tariffs	High taxes on imports make imported products more expensive, give home industries temporary competitive advantages, and discourage foreign trade. (They also lead to reciprocation in which outside nations fight back with their own high tariffs.)
Quotas	Limits on import quantities also give home industries competitive advantages.
Red Tape	Complicated import applications, procedures, and paperwork.
Export Control (licenses)	Government restricts what producers send abroad. Cuts trade opportunities and prevents others from obtaining strategic resources.
Legal Currency Limits	Government restricts overseas investment and import firms' spending to keep currency stable.
Boycotts	Civilian organizations (unions, trade groups) rally public support for not buying goods of certain foreign firms or whole nations.
Embargoes	Government order banning importation of the goods of a particular country.

LDC governments are also part of the problem. In "Cheer Up, Troubled World," Henry S. Rowen says governments account for nations remaining poor for several reasons:

• First, command government policies in LDCs limit trade, control prices, and ruin incentives.

• Second, unstable and corrupt governments create unstable growth. Dictatorships put money into unnecessary military programs and ignore health and education. Reaction leads to coups that overthrow the dictators. Instability results, and nations again slide backward. This usually paves the way for new dictators to restore order. The political cycle generates economic tragedy.

• Third, autocratic governments actually make war on their own people. Power groups deny ethnic or religious groups political and economic freedom. Fear of risk prevents growth. (*Wall St. Journal.* 31 August 1993, 5)

Not all LDCs are weak. For security reasons, nations such as Iran, Bolivia, India, and even China spend large portions of their resources on weaponry. These are funds that could be devoted to education and research on productive technology. But, these priorities keep them as impoverished as Mali or Guyana.

Understanding the gap between rich and poor nations can help in seeing how life may change and how people can adjust to those changes. That kind of knowledge could help Americans be more open to altering policies and trade patterns. Also, it can help them perceive other nations' policies in a less hostile way.

SHAPING A GLOBAL ECONOMY: BREAKING TRADE BARRIERS

Too often, nations frustrated with internal problems overreact to the trade policies of others. They don the ancient armor of **protectionism**. This often leads to raising **trade barriers** or even "trade war" sanctions (punishments) (see Figure 10.4).

United States tariff history (shown in Figure 10.5 on the next page) indicates that American protectionist policies have varied considerably over the years. The isolationist sentiment is especially clear in the high tariffs between the two world wars. The graph also shows the powerful effect of the GATT negotiations in the past half-century. When the economy is not performing well (as during the 1930s Great Depression), advocates of protectionism press for government action. They rely on several traditional arguments for higher tariffs and other trade barriers:

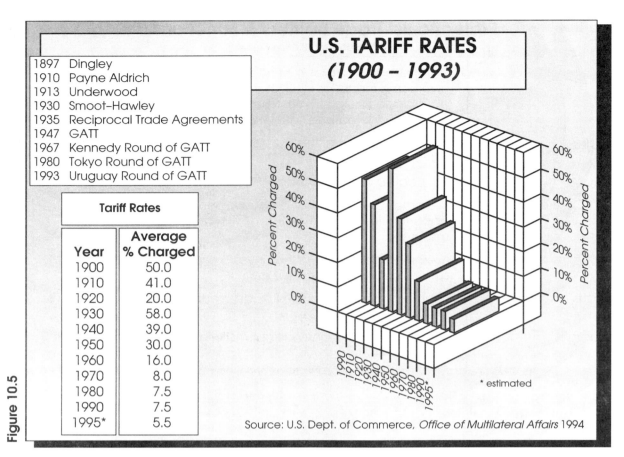

U.S. TARIFF RATES (1900 – 1993)

1897	Dingley
1910	Payne Aldrich
1913	Underwood
1930	Smoot-Hawley
1935	Reciprocal Trade Agreements
1947	GATT
1967	Kennedy Round of GATT
1980	Tokyo Round of GATT
1993	Uruguay Round of GATT

Tariff Rates

Year	Average % Charged
1900	50.0
1910	41.0
1920	20.0
1930	58.0
1940	39.0
1950	30.0
1960	16.0
1970	8.0
1980	7.5
1990	7.5
1995*	5.5

Source: U.S. Dept. of Commerce, *Office of Multilateral Affairs* 1994

* estimated

Figure 10.5

- New industries need protection from foreign competition while they get on their feet.

- Protection from foreign competition gives domestic workers job security.

- Domestic wage rates must be preserved from low wage foreign industries to keep domestic living standards high.

- Most nations use higher protections than the U.S., putting the U.S. at a disadvantage.

Normally, a free flow of trade benefits all parties. Yet, in economic contractions, when everyone is suffering, protectionists lobby for barriers. The barriers often backfire. Other nations **reciprocate** (fight back) with their own high tariffs. The high tariffs of the 1930s killed international trade when nations needed it most. The mid-1990s saw bitter negotiations with threats and counter-threats of sanctions and higher tariffs between the United States and Japan.

Avoiding overreaction and protectionism is hard when people see foreign competition robbing them of jobs. "Buy American" media campaigns sponsored by unions and trade councils are evidence of this. Yet, if nations keep trade open and flowing, it can revitalize ailing economies. Open trade points nations in the direction of recovery and growth, and that usually means new jobs. Increased trade enables rich and poor nations to raise standards of living and address internal problems. So, aligning international trade to a new world situation can help solve some global problems and avoid "Eco Wars."

SHAPING A GLOBAL ECONOMY: INTERDEPENDENCE

Scarcity forces people to trade for their needs and wants. The fact is, every nation (and every person in every nation) is part of a global economy. People routinely shrug and ignore civil wars, floods, or famines on the other side of the world. Yet, people can no longer isolate themselves without cutting themselves off from needed resources. Americans often romanticize about self-sufficiency. Yet, they are no longer pioneers isolated on a remote frontier. Very few of them could feed, clothe, warm, shelter, or transport themselves without the products of others. They need others to survive. They must trade their knowledge and skills to others for these things. Trade means one thing: **interdependence**.

More than ever, global relations revolve around trade. Involvement in world issues comes with trade. The list of issues is long. It entwines environmental and socioeconomic issues. Among them are: population growth, depletion of natural resources, global warming, the growing gap between rich nations and LDCs, political power after the fall of the U.S.S.R., the rise of Islamic fundamentalism, automation, biotechnology, and international trade associations. Regardless of what nations want, if there is to be a viable future, people and nations must work cooperatively to address the issues.

Adam Smith pointed out that self-interest drives economic interchange. Mutual profit from trade has always been a base for international relationships. If parties see advantages, they will make the effort. Of course, if a party feels cheated from an exchange, the future of the relationship is in jeopardy.

In most cases, specialization makes international trade worthwhile. The firms of one nation often specialize in trading commodities that they can produce efficiently. Colombia, Brazil,

and equatorial Africa focus on coffee they can produce because of their climate. They depend on products that are **exclusive** (hard to get elsewhere). South Africa is one of the world's few sources of diamonds. It is not hard to see why Venezuela trades its petroleum on the global markets and does not compete with high tech cybernetics suppliers such as Japan. Venezuela has vast amounts of petroleum and takes aid from international firms (e.g., Exxon, Mobil, Shell, Texaco) to build technology to extract it. Venezuela has an **absolute advantage** over Japan, which has no oil. Specializing in oil production makes sense for Venezuela.

Even when a nation may have resources, it may choose not to use them fully. For example, the United States has considerable oil supplies, and it does produce approximately 48% of its own oil. Yet, it buys from Venezuela (see Figure 10.6 below). Why pay Venezuela for oil? The answer lies in an idea economists call **comparative advantage**. The cost of U.S. labor, compared to Venezuelan labor, makes Venezuelan crude oil cheaper per barrel. U.S. refining companies import Venezuelan crude because it costs less. They can use their capital more efficiently in other pursuits. Economists would say Venezuela has a comparative advantage in this trade relationship. Again, the relationship illustrates interdependence.

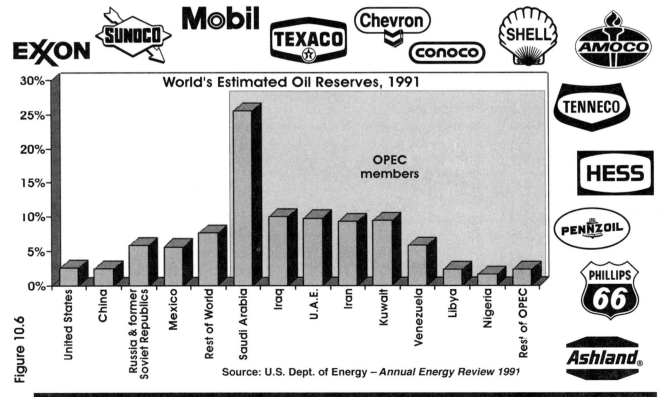

Figure 10.6

World's Estimated Oil Reserves, 1991

OPEC members

Source: U.S. Dept. of Energy – *Annual Energy Review 1991*

SHAPING A GLOBAL ECONOMY: MULTINATIONALS

Whatever the economic advantages in a particular place, to speak in terms of fully self-sufficient and independent nations is not as realistic as it once was. Governments do not trade much, firms do. Yet, quite often governments make rules that get in the way of firms engaged in international trade. (It might be well to remember protests against British trade restrictions sparked the American Revolution.)

International businesses are certainly not new. From ancient times, traders set up caravans to exchange products among empires and kingdoms. That is what brought Marco Polo to the Khan's court in the 13th century. Most European colonies in the "New World" in the 16th and 17th centuries were commercial ventures.

In the 20th century, a new form of international commercial agency emerged – the **MNC** (multinational corporation – a firm with business operations in more than one country). At first, they were just large corporations wishing to branch out for overseas markets. Yet, in the last generation, they expanded beyond looking for customers. In the process of seeking broader markets, they found advantages in **direct investments** (outright ownership of facilities in other countries). By setting up shop in other countries, MNCs lower production and resource costs, reduce patent royalty fees, and avoid tariffs and other trade barriers.

Figures on direct investment in production facilities all over the world illustrate the globalization of MNCs. In 1950, U.S. firms had $12 billion directly invested in other countries. In 1992, the U.S. Bureau of Economic Analysis says that figure stood at $486 billion. Of that, MNCs invested the largest amounts in Britain, Canada, Germany, Switzerland, and Japan (BEA. *Business Statistics*. A-106). Coca Cola and Chrysler operate bustling plants in China, too.

The amount foreign MNCs invest in the United States often brings home the economic globalization idea to Americans. The 1992 BEA figure for foreign direct investment in U.S. firms and property was $419 billion. Of that, Europe had $249 billion, and Japan had $96 billion (BEA. *Business Statistics*. A-107). For example, Japanese and German auto firms operate major assembly plants in Kentucky (Toyota), Ohio (Honda and Mazda), Tennessee (Nissan), Alabama (Mercedes), and South Carolina (BMW).

Today's MNCs have such widespread presence that economists see them as the foundations of a "borderless world economy." MNCs advanced the reduction of trade barriers in the European Union and NAFTA. MNCs also influence updates of the GATT. While it is a general guide for nations, it is not an ironclad set of rules. Yet, constant pressure from MNCs has caused nations to renegotiate the GATT ten times since 1947. The most recent Uruguay Round concluded in 1993.

The GATT provides only weak guidelines. National governments still negotiate **bilateral trade agreements** (two-nation mutual arrangements). The United States still designates some countries as "Most Favored Nations" (receiving lowest tariff rates and least restrictions). Still, for banking, service, and manufacturing MNCs, the GATT guidelines are vital. They want minimum standards for global stability. They also want national barriers minimized so that goods and payments flow easily in the globalized economy.

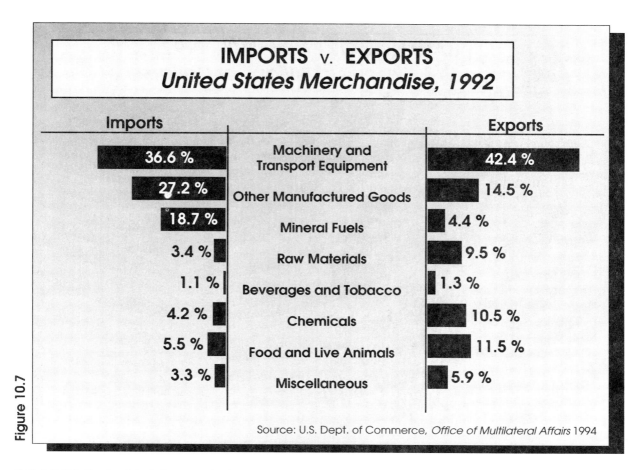

IMPORTS v. EXPORTS
United States Merchandise, 1992

Imports		Exports
36.6 %	Machinery and Transport Equipment	42.4 %
27.2 %	Other Manufactured Goods	14.5 %
18.7 %	Mineral Fuels	4.4 %
3.4 %	Raw Materials	9.5 %
1.1 %	Beverages and Tobacco	1.3 %
4.2 %	Chemicals	10.5 %
5.5 %	Food and Live Animals	11.5 %
3.3 %	Miscellaneous	5.9 %

Source: U.S. Dept. of Commerce, *Office of Multilateral Affairs* 1994

Figure 10.7

SHAPING A GLOBAL ECONOMY: BALANCING TRADE

FINANCIAL EXCHANGE

People trade to get needed goods and services and to make profits. This is just as true globally as in a neighborhood shop or a suburban mall. Some businesses specialize in international trade. Their specialization and comparative advantage makes it profitable to deal with mazes of rules and regulations in many countries. Just as people in a town, international traders expect mutual satisfaction. Theoretically, the financial exchanges for imports and exports should be equal. Economists refer to this as the **balance of payments**. It measures the flow of goods and money and gives some indication of the health of an economy (see Figure 10.7).

The government calculates balance of payments in complex statements. The two major parts are the current account and the capital account. The **current account** shows the balance of imports and exports. It includes goods and services, shipping, insurance, short-term loans, and expenditures by tourists. The **capital account** includes long-term financial transactions such as direct and indirect overseas investments (franchise investments are among the fastest growing segments), private loans, and government foreign aid.

Seaport and airport cargo manifests, customs records, and corporate investment statements provide data for these accounts. Yet, in many cases, measuring the balance of payments is not easy. In "Exporting the Truth on Trade," Susan Dentzer said services such as lawyers fees, tourist hotel rooms, and rental car fees are hard to record (*U.S. News & World Report.* 4 April 1992, 47). Dentzer noted the government can only use surveys to estimate these "soft numbers" (*USNWR.* 47).

THE TRADE DEFICIT

The annual balance of payment statement tells a country how well it fares in trading with others. Before 1950, U.S. exports exceeded imports, and there was usually a **trade surplus**. Since 1950, the statements show the United States paying out more money to residents of other countries than it receives from

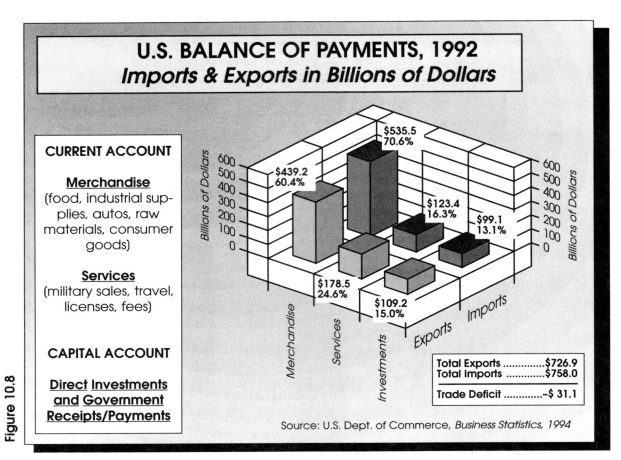

Figure 10.8

U.S. BALANCE OF PAYMENTS, 1992
Imports & Exports in Billions of Dollars

CURRENT ACCOUNT

Merchandise
(food, industrial supplies, autos, raw materials, consumer goods)

Services
(military sales, travel, licenses, fees)

CAPITAL ACCOUNT

Direct Investments and Government Receipts/Payments

$439.2 60.4%
$535.5 70.6%
$178.5 24.6%
$123.4 16.3%
$99.1 13.1%
$109.2 15.0%

Total Exports	$726.9
Total Imports	$758.0
Trade Deficit	–$ 31.1

Source: U.S. Dept. of Commerce, *Business Statistics, 1994*

them – a **trade deficit**. Causes for the U.S. trade deficit include: high amounts of foreign aid, overseas military operations, inflation devaluing the U.S. dollar, a high degree of investing abroad, and Americans buying large quantities of foreign products (see Figure 10.8). The end of the Cold War allowed reduction of overseas military expenses and foreign aid. Still, Americans' taste for imported clothes and autos kept the trade deficit high.

EXCHANGE RATES

One of the things that complicates world trade is that each nation has its own currency. Economists measure currency conversions with the **foreign exchange rate**. A network of specialized import/export banks in major foreign exchange markets (Hong Kong, Tokyo, London, Paris, New York) set the rate. These banks act as financial intermediaries with other banks of other nations. They hold supplies of various national currencies for transactions.

Just as national economies vary, currencies of different nations vary in value against others. (Review Issue 7's outline of the rise of gold as an international exchange standard in the hands of medieval goldsmiths.) National governments backed their currencies in gold until the 20th century. This system of gold flowing among nations kept prices stable.

Yet, two world wars and the Great Depression strained national currencies and gold resources to the point of collapse. Tying money to gold was too rigid. Governments could not use monetary policy (altering their money supply) when needed. At the end of World War II, the industrial nations created the **Bretton Woods System**. It used the U.S. dollar as the basis for exchange. The dollar could be converted at $35 per ounce of gold. The **IMF** (**International Monetary Fund**) took charge of this new system. It made temporary loans to countries needing dollars for exchange. The Bretton Woods System worked until U.S. trade deficits and the inflation of the Vietnam War Era reduced the base U.S. gold supply. In 1971, President Nixon halted gold conversion of the dollar (see Figure 10.9 on opposite page).

In 1973, the major industrial nations agreed to a **Floating Exchange System**. In this system, supply and demand govern the rates of

Figure 10.9	International Exchange Systems		
	Source: U.S. Department of Commerce, 1993		
The Gold Standard	(1850s-1930s)		Trade agreements between nations specified the amount of gold a particular nation's currency was worth.
Gold Exchange Standard	(1940s-1970s)		(Bretton Woods System) International Monetary Fund created fixed exchange rates pegged to the U.S. dollar's gold conversion price of $35 per ounce.
Floating Exchange Rates	(1971-)		Supply and demand of currencies decide their exchange rates on the world's major foreign exchange markets.

exchange in the major world finance markets. The dollar is still the leading world currency, but values of currencies change frequently. Strong governments, supporting strong economies, have strong currencies.

The international money market is volatile. Frequently, political events or fluctuations in interest rates in one country alter exchange rates. When money investors buy dollars (and other currencies) in which they have confidence, values appreciate. Buying up dollars makes them scarce and drives up their value. More expensive dollars makes U.S. goods sold abroad more expensive. It also makes weaker currencies (and their countries' products) cheaper. The strong dollar of the late 1980s and early 1990s made other countries' exports look good to

Americans. However, in the mid-1990s, the U.S. dollar fell to an all time low in value on the world currency markets. This drove the value of the German mark and Japanese yen up, resulting in higher prices for foreign products sold in the United States The weakened U.S. dollar coupled with high imports and low exports deepened the trade deficit and further weakened the U.S. economic position in the global economy.

The Floating Exchange Rate created an intricate international money market system. Government moves make it even more complex. Sometimes, governments have their central banks move to alter the supply of their money on the international market. When appreciating too fast, central banks sell their currencies at lower rates to the exchange markets. This increases supplies and lowers their exchange rate. They also buy their own currencies at higher rates to slow depreciation (see Figure 10.10).

Figure 10.10   Currency Exchange Rate

Source: Harold Reuter & Company, Inc , 7 May 1995

Currency	Exchange Rate per U.S. Dollar	Value in U.S. Dollars
Argentinian pesos	1.00	$1.0000
Austrian schilling	9.50	0.1053
Australian dollar	1.30	0.7675
British pound	0.60	1.6650
Canadian dollar	1.33	0.7519
China renminbi	10.00	0.1000
German mark	1.35	0.7407
Egyptian pound	2.94	0.3400
French franc	4.80	0.2083
Israeli shekel	2.75	0.3636
Indian rupee	32.00	0.0313
Japanese yen	81.50	0.0123
Mexican new peso	5.50	0.1818
Russian ruble	4900.00	0.0003
Swiss franc	1.11	0.9009

SUMMARY

International trade is complex. There are no simple rules. Sometimes, it is a matter of governments negotiating with other countries to smooth out problems. More often, trade is companies struggling with the language barriers, currency differences, and elaborate regulations that complicate international commerce. The host of bilateral and multilateral agreements, the behavior of MNCs, the fate of LDCs and NIEs – they are all entwined in shaping the new global economy. On that new world structure rests the aspirations of all people in general and the American Dream in particular.

ASSESSMENT
QUESTIONS • APPLICATIONS

1 This chapter begins with a story about the results of an Eco War in the future. The story is based on some of the facts about LDCs, trade alliances, and MNCs in this chapter.
   a Do you agree with such a scenario? Explain why or why not.
   b Make a list of elements you think would make the story more realistic.

2 Historian Paul Kennedy says: "Economic change and technological development, like wars or sporting tournaments, are usually not beneficial to all. Progress, welcomed by optimistic voices since the Enlightenment to our present age, benefits those groups or nations that can take advantage of the newer methods and science, just as it damages others that are less prepared technologically, culturally, and politically to respond to change."
   — Preparing for the Twenty-First Century, 15

   a Does this quote suggest there is no future for LDCs (Less Developed Countries) that have difficulty breaking away from tradition?
   b What steps can LDCs take to enhance economic growth?
   c How will regional trade alliances such as APEC, NAFTA, and the EU affect LDCs and NIEs (Newly Industrialized Countries)?

3 Global interdependence makes the U.S. economy vulnerable to events and actions throughout the world.
   a Should the United States try to become self-sufficient? Why or why not?
   b Should the United States adopt economic isolation and stop buying from other nations? Why or why not?
   c What is the real cost of buying cheaper products from other nations?

4 This chapter begins with this quotation from economist Henry Kaufman: "How much are the major industrial countries willing to subordinate near-term nationalistic interests, which are often politically quite popular, to longer term benefits?"
   a What does he mean by "near-term nationalistic interests which are often quite politically popular"?
   b What does he mean by "longer-term benefits"?
   c Is choosing the long-term benefits critical to shaping the new global economy? Explain.

5 "Regional trade alliances must shape the future."
   a Take a position on this statement – agree or disagree.
   b Use library resources to validate your position on this statement.
   c Defend your position in a class debate, a learning group discussion, or a written report.

6 The dynamic nature of world trade sometimes displaces workers and companies.
   a List and explain three types of barriers to free trade.
   b Why do labor unions generally favor protective trade barriers?
   c Assume the role of a member of the United States Senate faced with voting on the North American Free Trade Agreement (NAFTA). What would be the key influences on how you would vote – in favor or opposed to the trade agreement?

ASSESSMENT PROJECT: PLANNING A VACATION

STUDENT TASK

Write a detailed plan for an overseas vacation.

PROCEDURES

1   Decide the total amount of money you can afford to spend on the vacation using your ongoing family budget structure set up in the assessment activities in Issue 1 and Issue 2.

2   Design a Daily Expense Vacation Work Sheet that shows in easy-to-compare form what you will spend on your vacation (e.g., transportation, meals, accommodations, entertainment, gifts).

3   Contact a travel agent about the project, and see if the agent will work with you and design a hypothetical foreign vacation. Stay within your budget. Add to your Vacation Work Sheet the transportation, accommodation, and meal options that various "travel plans" offerer.

4   Prepare a final summary report of the vacation plan. Include

- itinerary and spending plan.

- explanation of the choices (tradeoffs) made in relation to your household budget.

- calculate the amount of foreign currency needed (based on Figure 10.10).

LEARNING STANDARDS

Learners should be able to

(1) understand that while different socioeconomic (as well as national, ethnic, religious, racial, and gender) groups have varied perspectives, values, and diverse practices and traditions, they face the same global economic challenges.

(5) analyze problems and evaluate decisions about the economic effects on society and the individual caused by human, technological, and natural activities.

(6) present their ideas both in writing and orally in clear, concise, and properly accepted fashion.

(7) employ a variety of information from written, graphic, and multimedia sources.

EVALUATION

The criteria for the evaluation of this project are itemized in the grid (rubric) that follows. Choice of appropriate category terms (values) is the decision of the instructor. Selection of terms such as "minimal," "satisfactory," and "distinguished" can vary with each assessment.

Overseas Vacation Planning Evaluation Rubric

(Refer to introductory section for suggestions of scoring descriptors for the evaluation categories.)

Evaluation Item	Category 1	Category 2	Category 3	Category 4	Category 5
Item a: (1) Do the choices examined in the report show differing views of economic, social, and cultural ideas and issues have been considered?					
Item b: (5) Does the report use realistic data and give a complete profile reflective of socioeconomic limits of the household?					
Item c: (5) Do the choices examined in the report take into account the effect of the household's decisions on societies?					
Item d: (6) Is the report presented in a clear, concise fashion?					
Item e: (7) Does the report show the use of a variety of good sources?					

ISSUE 11

How will the environment affect the Dream?

ENVIRONMENTAL ECONOMIC IMPACT

There is a linkage between nature and economic life. The natural environment always limits or enhances economic potential. Location, topography, climate, soil compositions, water supplies, natural disasters and many other factors circumscribe economic activity. In every country or region, the physical environment creates a special set of economic circumstances that underscore the interdependence of modern life. Environmental issues affect the present and the future. Therefore, they also affect the American Dream. Environmental factors were usually "outside the loop" of daily exchanges and transactions. When governments try to repair or preserve the natural environment, economic conflicts erupt.

LUCIA'S SONG – FROM RIO WITH HOPE

In June 1992, one hundred and seventy-two nations sent representatives to Rio de Janeiro, Brazil. They came for the "Earth Summit" – the United Nations Conference on Environment and Development. Their purpose was to strengthen environmentally-sound paths to economic development, especially for LDCs (less developed countries). Thousands of observers from private organizations and the media also came.

Among the observers were young people from organizations such as the Rainforest Alliance, the Nature Conservancy, and the Sierra Club. A little group of them sat about a flickering fire on the beach near Niteroi. From behind the Costa e Silva Bridge, the setting Autumn Sun cast long shadows on the sands of Guanabara Bay. Lucia strummed her guitar softly. They chatted quietly in Portuguese and English. There was a touch of sadness in their voices. The Americans would go tomorrow.

The last week had been a frenzy. Jorge, Lucia, Maria, and Palo brought Erin, Michael, Shelley, and Ed here to escape the choking Summit throngs and souvenir hawkers in Rio's downtown. A jet roared off from Galeao Airport. The diplomats and reporters were leaving. For weeks, the media relentlessly covered the Earth Summit. It was all so hectic, so intense, but so vital.

Shelley lowered her eyes from the plane's wake and stared into the fire, looking sad for a moment. Then she glanced up, smiled, and started to hum. "Let's sing your song, Lucia."

Dimming Sun touches Guanabara Bay.
Darkening rings turn its beaches gray.
Filtering clouds blur Corcovado's crown,
Obscuring the Redeemer – statue of renown.

Some come to rescue forests from harm,
Some to make a more productive farm.
Some come to reclaim the desert land,
Some to merely lend a helping hand.

Dipping planes break the yellow haze,
Descending summit-goers somberly gaze –
Spotting Cariocas on Niemeyer's promenade,
Languishing favelas down the hills cascade.

Some come to help birds fly,
Some to purge the festering sky.
Some come to mourn the day,
Some to find a better way.

Sitting down in the Earth Summit halls,
Listening to colleagues' despairing calls –
Hoping the hour is not too late,
Decrying Earth's despondent fate.

Some come to preserve and protect,
Some to halt the greenhouse effect.
Some come to deal and buy,
Some only to ask, "Why?"

Writing contracts grimly in the sand,
Preening powers once rich and grand,
Blaming others in endless debate,
Shrugging at their powerless state.

Some come of sheer remorse,
Some to steer a brighter course.
Some come to find a way to cope,
Some to mold a future hope.

Their voices and the soft chords of Lucia's guitar trailed off. None of them knew what this Earth Summit would do. No one really did. Maria stood – a signal that it was time. The young Brazilians took the hands of the Americans – and prayed silently for the Earth.

ISSUE 11

How will the environment affect the Dream?

ENVIRONMENTAL ECONOMIC IMPACT

INTRODUCTION

The 172 national delegates to the "Earth Summit" along with 1,300 representatives of private organizations and 9,000 members of the world press descended on Rio to preserve and renew the environment while seeking paths to economic development for **LDCs** (less developed countries – see map Figure 11.1). The Conference Secretary, Canada's Maurice Strong, said world development must continue, but, "the mode of development that has produced unprecedented wealth and prosperity is not viable either for developing countries to replicate (imitate) or for [industrial countries] to con-

tinue." (Dermont O'Sullivan. *Chemical & Engineering News.* 15 June 1992, 17-18) His statement shows that methods of development employed over the last century were environmentally destructive. Strong's hope lies in the fusion of economic development and environmental vigilance. Judicious use of natural resources to meet basic human needs must be considered with a dual vision – for now and for the future.

The Earth Summit brought the term "sustainable development" into global focus. As the Earth's population moves toward 10 billion in the 21st century, its limited resources must meet current needs and be preserved to meet

© U.N. Photo, 1992. Used By Permission

United Nations Conference on Environment and Development (UNCED), Earth Summit, Rio de Janeiro, Brazil, 3rd - 14th June 1992. A small portion of the delegates from 172 nations at a discussion of *Agenda 21.* In the foreground are Norway's Prime Minister Brundtland and Sweden's King Karl XVI Gustaf.

Figure 11.1

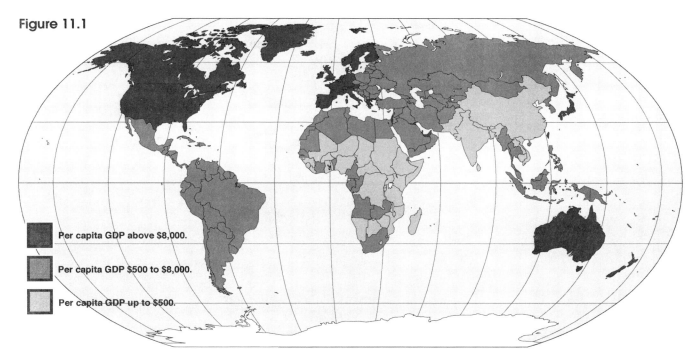

The per capita Gross Domestic Product in world nations. In general, the lower the per capita GDP, the lower the standard of living and the poorer the country. In most cases, the low GDP countries are the "have nots" or LDCs.

the demands of the future. To support the ideal of sustainable development, five major international agreements emerged from the Earth Summit (see chart Figure 11.2).

ECONOMIC SOVEREIGNTY

Not every nation attending the Earth Summit signed every agreement. The reasons were mainly economic in nature. Not only was there a U.N. estimate of a $125 billion cost for the industrialized nations, but there was the issue of **economic sovereignty** – both developed nations and LDCs want to control their resources and realize income from them as well. To some, signing international agreements seemed to be forfeiting sovereignty over those vital resources (Heilman, Bette. *Chemical and Engineering News*. 22 June 1992. 4-5).

The Conference stressed the protection of "Global Commons." This concept holds that certain resources are so vital to the world that they do not belong to any nation. The oceans and

Figure 11.2	**Earth Summit Agreements** United Nations Conference on Environment and Development (UNCED) Earth Summit, Rio de Janeiro, Brazil, 3rd – 14th June 1992
Agreements	**Goals**
Rio Declaration	Promotes twenty-seven principles on rights and obligations concerning the environment; cites international responsibility for "Global Commons."
Agenda 21	Sets social goals (elimination of poverty and ecological management of human settlements).
Climate Convention	Aspires to reduce or hold greenhouse gas emissions to 1990 levels.
Biodiversity Convention	Proposes funding for protection of all plant, animal, and marine species; international sharing of biotechnology.
Statement of Agreement on Forest Principles	Seeks protection of forests – resisted by rain forest countries especially those in South Asia.

Figure 11.3

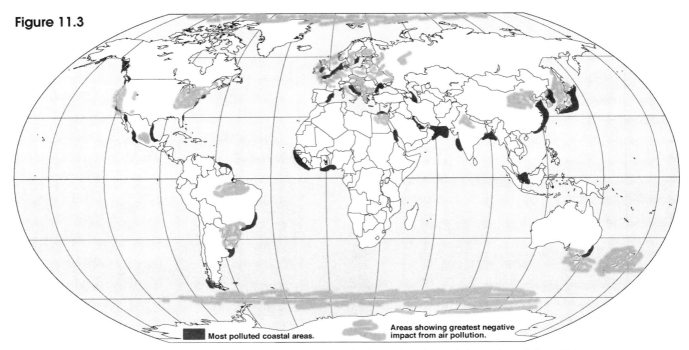

Most polluted coastal areas.

Areas showing greatest negative impact from air pollution.

Areas of major pollution and areas with the greatest negative impact from air pollution. Note that it is not just the areas near the industrial nations that have major pollution but also areas around some of the less developed areas of the world.

atmosphere are obvious global commons. Yet, the rain forests exist within nations, and those nations depend on the revenues the rain forests generate. At the same time, destruction of the rain forests contributes to global warming – which has potentially harmful effects for all nations. It becomes necessary to make **trade-offs** (sacrifices) of income for the good of the global environment.

Not all nations are willing to make those sacrifices. LDCs balked at outside pressures to limit the use of their resources. Industrial nations balked at higher prices and the lower supplies of raw materials from LDCs. Industrial nations also predicted that providing massive aid to LDCs would increase prices and reduce production incentives for developed countries. For example, *Agenda 21* calls for each developed nation to give 0.7% of its GDP for development assistance. Industrialized nations claim recessions and internal economic problems prevent committing some $6-7 billion in annual development assistance (Heilman, 22 June 1992. 4-5).

ENVIRONMENT: THE GLOBAL DILEMMA

The Rio Earth Summit attempted to address the great problems of modern times:

- *Should humankind use scarce resources to provide a decent quality of life for its rapidly growing population?*

- *Should it place priority on preserving the natural environment for the future?*

- *Can sustainable development provide a compromise between these two questions?*

Sustainable development demands global peace and freedom. Yet, all the diplomatic efforts and political arrangements to achieve peace and freedom will be wasted – unless there is environmental security on which to build.

Prior to the Industrial Revolution, human-made pollution occurred in very limited instances in confined places. (Natural environmental disasters have always upset life and economic activity – and still do. Consider the cost of Hurricane Andrew in Florida or the impact of Mt. St. Helens' eruption on the Pacific Northwest.)

In the 19th century, mass production necessitated large-scale activity that had widespread environmental consequences. Extensive mining operations, massive mills, and immense factories were unregulated. Their operations ravaged and contaminated the air, water, and land on a large scale (see map, Figure 11.3).

Figure 11.4

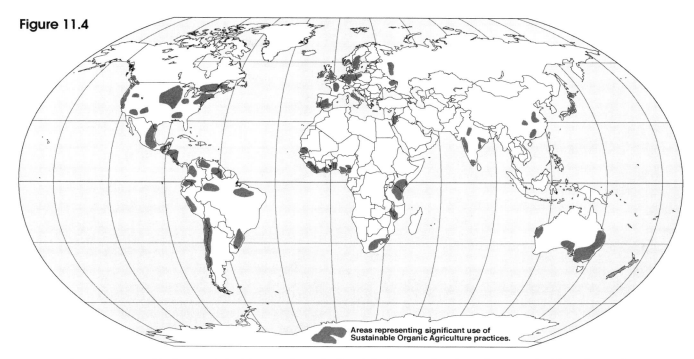

Areas representing significant use of Sustainable Organic Agriculture practices.

Areas of the world where sustainable organic agriculture is being practiced on a large-scale. Many "green" scientists and environmentalists are encouraged by widespread cooperation among many nations.

Conservation efforts of the Progressive Reform Era (c. 1900) had only a small effect. Not until the 1960s did such works as Rachel Carson's *The Silent Spring* rally a broad-based environmental movement. It seemed that everywhere people looked, human activity put the environment at risk. The new movement slowed wanton resource waste. It forced humans to look at the delicacy of the global ecosystem and recognize the danger inherent in traditional patterns of development. Today, traditional resource-intensive, pollution-prone production methods strain and degrade the environment. Sustainable development must employ new technology that is cleaner and more sparing of natural resources (see map Figure 11.4).

The United Nations Environmental Programme estimates that the world economy will have to increase its production to five times its current level to support the global population in the next 50 years. Yet, the U.N. agency also points out that loss of arable land to desertification and alteration of climate by greenhouse gases from commercial use of fossil fuel will reduce future crop yields (*World Resources 1992-93*, 1). This raises a question: *Does environmental collapse threaten economic growth and development?*

In addition to the Earth Summit's main concerns (see Figure 11.5 chart on next page), environmental issues encompass chemical disasters, groundwater contamination, industrial waste disposal, loss of wetlands, lead poisoning, oil spills, pesticide poisoning, anoxia, sewerage disposal, and toxic waste dumping. The list grows annually.

Because the cost of preserving the environment both enhances and limits the quality of human life, solutions for environmental problems often clash with how people make their liv-

Desertification with little or no green vegetation and water is evident in the emaciated cattle in Senegal. ©David Johnson

Top Ten Environmental Concerns

Source: *Earth Council*, San José, Costa Rica, 1992

- Pollution: Air, Water, and Land
- Nuclear Accidents
- Loss of Natural Resources
  (Deforestation, Desertification, ...)
- Pollution: Air and Smog (Acid Rain,...)
- Health in Home, School, or Work
- Depletion of the Earth's Ozone
- Global Warming and Greenhouse Effect
- Renewable and Nonrenewable Resources
- Endangered Wildlife Species
- Human Health Crisis

Figure 11.5

ings or with the great economic aspirations of nations. Many people, especially in LDCs, would still opt for accelerated growth knowing full well that unchecked growth often leaves devastation in its wake. For more than a generation, the focus on environmental issues has shown the suicidal nature of ruining the Earth in the name of economic growth.

Of course, not every environmental issue involves irreparable damage. For example, an oil spill can be prevented with better procedures and safer ships (see Figure 11.6). Even when a serious oil spill does occur, nature can come back if cleanup is properly conducted. It takes time, and cleanup is an expensive process, but most of the effects of oil spills can be overcome or prevented with technology. However, there are other events that can have permanent, irre-

versible outcomes. Ozone loss and desertification are far more difficult to restrain and have more catastrophic consequences than oil spills.

ENVIRONMENT: REAL COST OF SOLUTIONS

At the core of the clash between economic growth and environmental preservation is a basic question: *Can governments, businesses, and ordinary people make the compromises and decisions to achieve environmental security?* Saving the Earth is not a job for ivory tower scientists in research labs and corporate engineers in "think tanks." The burden of the struggle must be borne largely by ordinary people at every level of human existence.

People must come to grips with the economic concept of **externalities**. These are the costs outside the measurable cost of economic activity. External costs such as pollution are often paid by persons involved in neither the production nor the consumption of a product or service. The market system has no apparatus for dealing with such externalities. They are "outside the loop" of exchange and transactions. The price is high, and it is not just borne by the manufacturer or the customer buying a particular product – the real cost of environmental stabilization is a universal burden.

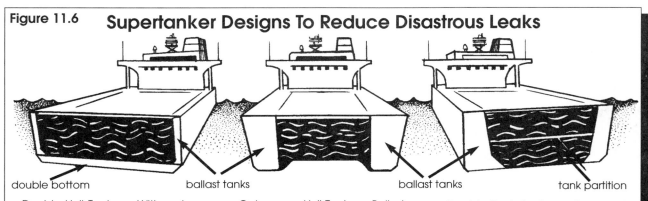

Figure 11.6 Supertanker Designs To Reduce Disastrous Leaks

double bottom   ballast tanks   ballast tanks   tank partition

Double Hull Tanker – With a double-hull design, the Exxon Valdez may have spilled up to 60% less oil; however, some experts express concern that the space between the hulls could result in corrosion problems, weakening the hull structure, or increase the chance for explosion by trapping gases between the two hulls.

Catamaran Hull Tanker – Ballast tanks provide added lateral stability, but increase the overall tanker size or reduce the load capacity. In the event of a grounding, the recessed bottom design reduces the chances of tank rupture and may make it easier to "re-float" the grounded tanker.

Double Tank Tanker -- Pressure leaks and the speed of spillage during a grounding and tank rupture could be reduced through the double tank design. "Above waterline" oil pressure is virtually eliminated, oil volume is cut in half, and less internal pressure slows the release of oil from a ruptured tank.

Hazardous Waste And Expenditure Statistics In The United States

Source: Chart compiled from Environmental Protection Agency Reports, 1988-1992; *Statistical Abstract of the U.S.,* 1992; U.S. Bureau of Census, 1990; Council of State Governments, 1988; World Resources Institute, 1993

Figure 11.7 State	State Population	Avg. Per Capita Income (U.S. dollars)	Avg. Per Capita Solid Waste (in tons)	Per Capita Toxic Pollutant Releases (in pounds)	State Budget Per Capita For All Environmental Activity (in U.S. dollars)
Alabama	4,041,000	$9,615	1.11	27.86	$15.82
Alaska	550,000	$13,263	0.91	37.41	$251.31
Arizona	3,665,000	$11,521	.79	19.65	$13.36
Arkansas	2,351,000	$9,061	.85	24.60	$18.45
California	29,760,000	$13,197	1.51	3.26	$52.49
Colorado	3,294,000	$12,271	.73	2.25	$23.07
Connecticut	3,287,000	$16,094	.88	6.49	$19.18
Delaware	666,000	$12,785	1.13	9.88	$50.26
Florida	12,938,000	$12,456	1.45	8.24	$37.75
Georgia	6,478,000	$11,406	.68	12.02	$14.72
Hawaii	1,108,000	$12,290	1.17	0.77	$25.35
Idaho	1,007,000	$9,159	.84	11.51	$61.26
Illinois	11,431,000	$12,437	1.28	10.41	$33.83
Indiana	5,544,000	$11,070	1.03	30.45	$9.50
Iowa	2,777,000	$11,198	.83	14.65	$31.07
Kansas	2,478,000	$11,520	.97	36.28	$19.17
Kentucky	3,685,000	$9,380	.95	11.51	$32.28
Louisiana	4,222,000	$8,961	.83	101.28	$43.97
Maine	1,228,000	$10,478	.77	12.07	$32.64
Maryland	4,781,000	$14,697	1.07	3.36	$32.47
Massachusetts	6,016,000	$14,389	1.13	3.46	$40.40
Michigan	9,295,000	$11,973	1.26	12.89	$23.96
Minnesota	4,375,000	$12,281	1.01	11.90	$29.31
Mississippi	2,573,000	$8,088	.54	40.28	$20.67
Missouri	5,117,000	$11,203	1.47	13.43	$23.32
Montana	799,000	$9,322	.75	53.41	$86.41
Nebraska	1,578,000	$11,139	.82	11.02	$17.47
Nevada	1,202,000	$12,603	.83	2.72	$34.62
New Hampshire	1,109,000	$13,529	.99	7.48	$30.96
New Jersey	7,730,000	$15,028	.92	3.36	$67.85
New Mexico	1,515,000	$9,434	.99	21.55	$29.72
New York	17,990,000	$13,167	1.22	3.36	$13.20
North Carolina	6,629,000	$10,856	.91	18.70	$14.94
North Dakota	639,000	$9,641	.63	3.30	$48.76
Ohio	10,847,000	$11,323	1.45	15.52	$11.58
Oklahoma	3,146,000	$9,927	.95	10.53	$12.61
Oregon	2,842,000	$11,045	1.16	7.99	$67.38
Pennsylvania	11,882,000	$11,544	.80	7.52	$24.06
Rhode Island	1,003,000	$12,351	1.20	5.25	$36.13
South Carolina	3,487,000	$9,967	1.15	19.28	$20.50
South Dakota	696,000	$8,910	1.15	4.22	$29.82
Tennessee	4,877,000	$10,448	1.03	42.45	$16.58
Texas	16,987,000	$10,645	1.06	24.65	$6.76
Utah	1,723,000	$9,288	.70	72.8	$30.43
Vermont	563,000	$11,234	.69	1.81	$36.31
Virginia	6,187,000	$13,658	1.45	12.87	$25.29
Washington	4,867,000	$12,184	1.05	8.51	$53.11
West Virginia	1,793,000	$8,980	.95	21.30	$29.95
Wisconsin	4,892,000	$11,417	.70	9.20	$34.56
Wyoming	454,000	$9,826	.70	2.51	$267.33

Changing environmentally threatening activities will be costly in numerous ways, but delay can be even more costly (see chart 11.7). U.S. government's 1993 Environmental Protection Agency expenses exceeded $6 billion. Writing in the *New Scientist*, author Michael Allen gave an example. He says that according to the U.N. Environment Programme (Paris) and the International Institute for Sustainable Development (Winnipeg), industrial waste doubled in the 1980s in **NIEs** (Newly Industrializing Economies) such as Singapore and Shanghai ("Eco Systems for Industry," 5 Feb 1994, 22). Such a situation means NIEs' expanding economies face collapse from environmental catastrophe unless they change course.

Yet, it is not impossible to change national and corporate behavior. In the same *New Scientist* article, Michael Allen notes a recent Canadian study showed that economic motivation can be a key. When managers at an industrial park in Nova Scotia were provided information on recycling waste into needed raw

By 1991, the U.S. EPA had identified almost 9,000 hazardous waste sites – 1,177 were classified "Superfund" sites. ©PhotoDisc

materials at substantial savings, they responded positively (Allen, 22). Allen says cost-cutting can be great motivation for creating the kind of sustainable development the Earth Summit promoted. For example, he says General Motors operates four foundries in Ohio that use only scrap iron from its other plants (Eco-Systems, 21). Allen also notes that Kalundborg, Denmark has created an ecologically linked power station, chemical company, plasterboard manufacturer, greenhouse, and fish hatchery that use each others' waste (Allen, 21).

Still, there is a perception in business that doing good things for the environment hurts the economy. An example may help to see why many people believe this. Congress designed the array of U.S. environmental regulations to solve many problems (see Figure 11.8 on opposite page). Yet some critics believe we are overregulated. They say regulations make it difficult to do business with nations with fewer restrictions. Trade officials working under **NAFTA** (North American Free Trade Agreement) are trying to deal with the differences between U.S. and Mexican environmental laws. The *1993 Earth Journal* reports that Mexico protests the California ban on imports which do not specify carcinogenic and toxic chemicals on packaging (Kotin. *Ear. Journal*, 169). Environmentalists fear many such U.S. laws will be weakened by NAFTA.

Legal environmental restrictions also have significant impact on domestic economic activities. From a business standpoint, government regulations to deter pollution usually add to the cost of production. Managers complain that filling out forms as well as buying, installing, and maintaining smoke scrubbers and discharge filters involves expensive training and time. federal and state rules require costly and expensive environmental impact studies and declarations

Toxic waste testing at an industrial storage facility.
©John Cancalosi, Tom Stack Assoc.

Figure 11.8
United States Environmental Laws
Some key environmental Acts legislated between the years 1948 and 1990

Year	Law	Federal Regulation of ...
1948	Water Pollution Control Act	problems of pollution concerning coastal and interstate waterways.
1955	Air Pollution Control Act	air pollution at its source.
1956	Fed. Water Pollution Control Act	federally funded sewerage treatment plants
1965	Motor Vehicle Air Pollution Act	maximum auto emissions.
1965	Air Quality Act	standards for ambient air and to specify air pollution reduction technologies.
1968	Pipeline and Safety Act	standards for all pipelines carrying hazardous and flammable fluids.
1970	National Environmental Policy Act	Environmental Impact Statements for all federal construction projects.
1970	Reorganization Order N. 38	environmental activities by the Environmental Protection Agency.
1970	Fed. Hazardous Substance Act	transport of hazardous substances in interstate commerce.
1972	Federal Water Pollution Act	discharge of substances into any body of water especially point sources of pollution.
1972	Marine Protection Research and Sanctuaries (Ocean Dumping) Act	dumping of sewerage and municipal garbage into coastal waters (total ban in 1990).
1976	Resource Conservation and Recovery Act	"cradle-to-grave" control of hazardous waste generated by manufacturers and transporters.
1976	Toxic Substances Control Act	manufacturers to establish the toxicity of new and existing chemicals in their products.
1976	Comprehensive Environmental Response, Compensation, and Liability Act	manufacturers to provide release notification of hazardous substances beyond their production and storage facilities.
1980	Acid Precipitation Act	emission of acid rain contributors.
1980	Superfund Amendment to Comprehensive Environmental Response, Compensation, and Liability Act of 1976	cleanup of abandoned toxic waste sites.
1986	Emergency Planning and Community Right to Know Act	hazardous substance-producing companies to plan emergency responses to accidents (spills) with public officials.
1990	Clean Air and Acid Precipitation Acts	amounts of industrial and municipal sulfur dioxide and nitrogen oxide emitted into air.
1990	Oil Prevention Act	crew training for oil tankers and responsible parties to pay for spills.

before commercial construction projects of any size can begin. In two recent federal Environmental Protection Agency (EPA) lawsuits, Louisiana Pacific Corporation agreed to $11 million in settlements and agreed to spend $70 million for pollution control equipment, and CSX Transportation paid a $3 million penalty and agreed to fund a $4.1 million environmental audit in 80 of its facilities (Himelstein & Regan. "Legal Affairs." *Business Week.* 29 November 1993, 138). Many economists claim environmental regulations not only discourage business expansion but trans-

late into higher prices for consumers and thus slow down aggregate economic growth.

Environmentalists do not accept this argument. The World Resources Institute believes governments can design effective use taxes – (such as energy taxes) to spread out the cost of cleaning the environment among the general population. Taxes with environmental objectives do not have to add to the corporate and consumer tax burden and slow economic growth. The Institute says that an enlightened

Environment And The Market

Sources: Compiled from *Science* 25 June 1993, *Business Week* 29 Nov. 1993, and *Fortune* 19 Oct. 1992

Up to now, the greatest drawback of saner environmental policy has been its cost. Governments have passed laws imposing expensive procedures that discourage businesses. It has been a command situation that has led to fraud and deceit rather than cooperative effort. Science writer Tim Appenzeller questions the argument of Vice-President Gore and other leaders that environmental protection and economic growth are complimentary ("Environment and the Economy." *Science* 25 June 1993, 1883). He says there are bold claims and some progress, especially in changing the dangerous harvest of the rain forests, but the union of economic advancement and environmentalism still falls short of being "an article of faith" (Appenzeller, 1883).

Yet, there is a desire to blend the two seemingly opposing forces. Another science writer, Joe Alper, says the late 1980s saw leaders discovering "a common ground that sound economics and sound environmental practice could go hand-in-hand" ("Protecting the Environment With the Power of the Market" *Science*. 25 June 1993, 1884). Alper quotes World Resources Institute's economic director Robert Repetto, "We can enact policies that adjust prices so that they more accurately reflect all the costs associated with producing a particular pollutant or using a particular resource" (Alper, 1884).

The problem is that most of the environmental legislation passed in the last 20 years are "command-and-control" laws. Because the laws have specified the technology an industry must use, or set a limit on emissions, the costs have been too high and offered no incentives to develop cost-effective alternatives.

Newer, market-based thinking was reflected in the *Clean Air Act* of 1990. For example, it allows companies to choose the most efficient way of meeting standards by investing in newer technology or switching to cleaner fuel and allows the EPA to award saleable credits when targets are met (Faye Rice, "Next Steps for the Environment" *Fortune*. 19 October 1992, 99). Rice notes chemical giants Monsanto and DuPont each filed plans with the EPA to use cleanup technology of their choice. So far, each has expended over $100 million on the project, but each is also marketing the technology to other companies (Rice. 99). Experts feel this kind of market incentive approach will reduce all emissions faster and in more profitable ways.

On the other hand, Alper points out that politics can skew the true economic cost of environmental preservation. Business pressures keep government subsidies alive in industries such as logging and cattle ranching. The cost of repairing forests and replanting range grasses are never factored into these business ventures from the planning stage. However, the government could award the subsidies to plans that offset environmental damage through competitive bidding. Such competition could launch a quest for cost-effective, environmentally protective alternatives (Alper. 1885).

There is no easy way that all the environmental costs of production can be estimated and built into a system of repricing resources. Consumers would probably revolt against any system that imposed realistic prices for an industry's direct and indirect damage to the environment, but employing more market incentives to address the direct impact is a start.

tax policy should use energy use taxes to replace or reduce income and social security taxes (*World Resources, 1992-93*, 23).

Energy tax revenues can fund subsidies and abatements to help companies prevent pollution or clean up harmful production situations. For example, the *Comprehensive Environmental Response, Compensation, and Liability Act* (1980) amended the *Superfund and Reauthorization Act* to help clean up abandoned toxic waste sites. In the November 1989 issue of *Chemtech*, Charles H. Conner, Jr. estimated the cost of such cleanups to be between $23 billion and $39 billion ("Mergers and Acquisitions in the Environmental Age." 662). Not all of this money (but a substantial amount) comes from taxes and borrowing.

The real cost of environmental solutions is staggering. At present, the increased taxes slow economic growth, and borrowing to fund programs and enforce laws contributes in a large way to a growing national debt that has to be paid by future generations.

ENVIRONMENT: SANITY, ECONOMIC GROWTH, AND OPPORTUNITY

A century and a half of industrial development endowed many humans with a better life, but now that same development threatens to destroy the good life. Ignoring environmental problems is perilous. In his forward for the *1993 Earth Journal*, Vice-President Al Gore notes:

"The Earth Summit was also a very powerful learning process, moving us to a better understanding of how future progress in inextricably linked to environmental protection and sound stewardship of natural resources. No economy can flourish if the natural resource base that supports it has been ruined." *(Earth Journal, xiii)*

Today, there is greater awareness of the danger of continuing the destructive patterns of past economic development. The Earth Summit agreements, although difficult and costly to implement, were at least an acknowledgment that change must occur. There is also another sign that environmental action is stirring. It is a sign that is perhaps more impressive than lofty international proclamations because it involves market activity.

For more than two decades, all levels of American government have responded to environmental crises. Michael Silverstein is president of a research firm called Environmental Economics. In a news article, he noted laws forcing polluters to clean up the environment do not drain the incentive from the economy, but help it grow. He notes the results that former polluters are less wasteful and more competitive today *(Wall Street Journal* 10 Oct. 1992, B-1).

The effort to clean up, maintain, and improve the environment has spawned new companies such as Waste Management, Inc., Safety-Kleen, Isco, and Seventh Generation. There are nearly 100,000 such companies, employing close to two million people. *U.S. News & World Report* indicates environmentally related jobs are one of the top 20 strongest career tracks (31 Oct. 1994, 116). Companies will need thousands of attorneys, managers, engineers, consultants, and field technicians for domestic and foreign projects. This translates into monumental opportunity and expansion. In the *Earth Journal* piece previously cited, Vice-President Gore also stated:

> "The global market for environmental technologies is currently at $270 billion a year and is growing at 7 percent a year ... One sector of our economy that has shown impressive growth over the last four years is the environmental products and service industries. Environmental businesses grew six times during this period. And in 1991, America's 40 largest environmental firms reported payroll increases of nearly 9 percent." (*Earth Journal*, xiii)

SUMMARY

For nearly a generation, there has been a broad-based, slowly-building commitment to clean up the pollution, preserve forests, find renewable energy sources. Much of the hope for the American Dream and a world setting conducive to it depends on a new world economic order in the 21st century. That new order must seek sustainable development. It must reconcile development needs for both the "have" and "have not" nations with environmental preservation and repair. National environmental regulation must dovetail with international regulation to save the Earth. Still, such an integration of rules must aim at promoting efficiency and competition toward "greener" products and services.

ASSESSMENT
QUESTIONS • APPLICATIONS

1 This chapter begins with a group of young people singing about the Earth Summit.
  a What is the reference in Lucia's Song to "preening powers"? Are they the key to the success of the Earth Summit?
  b Do you think anything was accomplished in Rio? Explain why or why not.

c Do environmental problems make you optimistic or pessimistic about achieving the American Dream? Defend your opinion.

2 Review the chart, Top Ten Environmental Concerns At the Earth Summit (Figure 11.5).
  a Is it an accurate list of the main environmental problems? How would you rearrange it? What would you add?
  b Complicated as they are, most of the problems have solutions. Pretend you are an entrepreneur. Select one of the items for study as to how a business person would assess the possibilities.

3 Externalities are the key problem in any modern economic activity.
  a Why must externalties (external costs) be borne by nearly everyone?
  b When must external costs be acceptable to all and when must they be turned back on those involved in the production and use of a product?
  c Do external costs mean sustainable development is impossible?

4 Review the Chart, Selected U.S. Environmental Laws (Figure 11.8).
  a This partial selection portrays considerable government involvement in environmental regulation. Considering the cost of just one law, the Superfund, which exceeds $14 billion annually, is all this regulation productive?
  b The U.S. Department of Labor's Bureau of Labor Statistics estimates that by 1998, government and industry will be spending $162 billion annually on cleanup and compliance with environmental laws. Jobs in environmental engineering start at above $30,000. Environmental technicians start at $21,000. What meaning do these statistics have for a generation seeking the American Dream?
  c The United States has more environmental regulation than Mexico. Explain why this presents a problem for NAFTA officials.

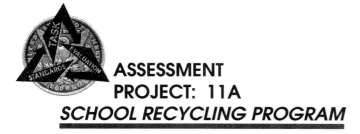

ASSESSMENT PROJECT: 11A
SCHOOL RECYCLING PROGRAM

STUDENT TASK

Form a group to create a recycling program for your school (or reform and revitalize the existing program). The project can be designed as a one-time effort or a permanent program that functions continuously.

PROCEDURES

1   Investigate the school's disposal of waste. What happens to objects that are recyclable? Are they disposed of properly, or are they merely put in the dumpsters as garbage?
2   Investigate what the law (local, county, state and federal) says about recycling. Is it mandatory? What is included? Is the school obeying the laws on what should be done with all recyclable materials? If there are problems, your group must bring them before school authorities.
3   If the school community is obeying the law on recycling, plan a course of action that may cut back on waste and garbage, or make an existing program more efficient (e.g., perhaps only classroom and office paper is recycled, or the school might need a plan for metals [aluminum soda cans] or plastics.)
4   Coordinate your efforts with the local recycling programs and garbage collectors.
5   Create a workable collection and storage plan.
6   Use the program to educate the school and community about the importance of protecting the environment.
7   Advertise your efforts and possibly combine them with those of students in other schools throughout the area.
8   Present an oral summation of the group's activities and experiences to the class.

OTHER SUGGESTIONS

•   Adopt-a-Highway section and recycle the materials.

•   Have fund-raisers in order to purchase recycling bins for classrooms.

•   Create and publish guides to such things as disposal of used motor oil, pesticide spraying, car pooling to school, indoor air pollution audits, etc.

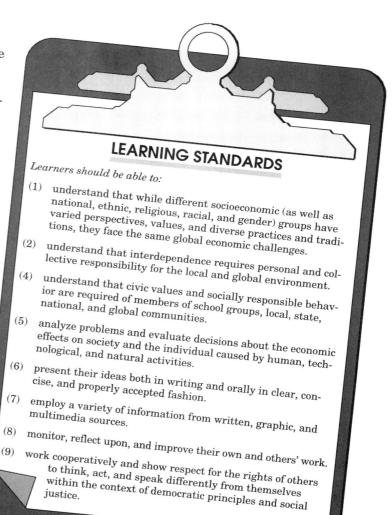

LEARNING STANDARDS

Learners should be able to:

(1)   understand that while different socioeconomic (as well as national, ethnic, religious, racial, and gender) groups have varied perspectives, values, and diverse practices and traditions, they face the same global economic challenges.

(2)   understand that interdependence requires personal and collective responsibility for the local and global environment.

(4)   understand that civic values and socially responsible behavior are required of members of school groups, local, state, national, and global communities.

(5)   analyze problems and evaluate decisions about the economic effects on society and the individual caused by human, technological, and natural activities.

(6)   present their ideas both in writing and orally in clear, concise, and properly accepted fashion.

(7)   employ a variety of information from written, graphic, and multimedia sources.

(8)   monitor, reflect upon, and improve their own and others' work.

(9)   work cooperatively and show respect for the rights of others to think, act, and speak differently from themselves within the context of democratic principles and social justice.

EVALUATION

The criteria for the evaluation of this project are itemized in the grid (rubric) that follows. Choice of appropriate category terms (values) is the decision of the instructor. Selection of terms such as "minimal," "satisfactory," and "distinguished" can vary with each assessment.

School Recycling Program Evaluation Rubric

(Refer to introductory section for suggestions of scoring descriptors for the evaluation categories.)

Evaluation Item	Category 1	Category 2	Category 3	Category 4	Category 5
Item a: (1) Does the summation show understanding that while different socioeconomic (as well as national, ethnic, religious, racial, and gender) groups have varied perspectives, values, and diverse practices and traditions, they face the same global economic challenges?					
Item b: (2) Does the summation show understanding that interdependence requires personal and collective responsibility for the local and global environment?					
Item c: (4) Does the summation show understanding that civic values and socially responsible behavior are required of members of school groups, local, state, national, and global communities?					
Item d: (5) Does the presentation analyze problems and evaluate decisions about the economic effects on society and the individual caused by human, technological, and natural activities?					
Item e: (6) Does the summation present ideas in writing (and orally) in clear, concise, and properly accepted fashion?					
Item f: (7) Does the summation employ a variety of information from written, graphic, and multimedia sources?					
Item g: (8) Does the summation show monitoring of, reflection upon, and improvement of work?					
Item h: (9) Does the summation show cooperative work and respect for the rights of others to think, act, and speak differently?					

ASSESSMENT PROJECT: 11B
COST OF A GREEN HOUSEHOLD

STUDENT TASK

Write a report explaining how to make your household environmentally correct – a "green household." This assessment offers library and field research and application to basic course portfolio program.

PROCEDURE

1   Work in the "household team" set up in earlier assessments in Issue 1 and Issue 2. Review the budget and goals set in these earlier stages.

2   Use interviews with parents, library resources, and information from "green" catalogs to identify and compile a list of items within the budget that would be environmentally friendly.

3   Make a comparison price list of "green items" v. ordinary products (paper towels, diapers, cleaning products, etc.) and determine the difference in cost for your household.

4   Write a three to five (3–5) page report on making your household "greener." Include your reasons for doing this, "green" product cost comparison, and a conclusion as to what tradeoffs will be made to "go green."

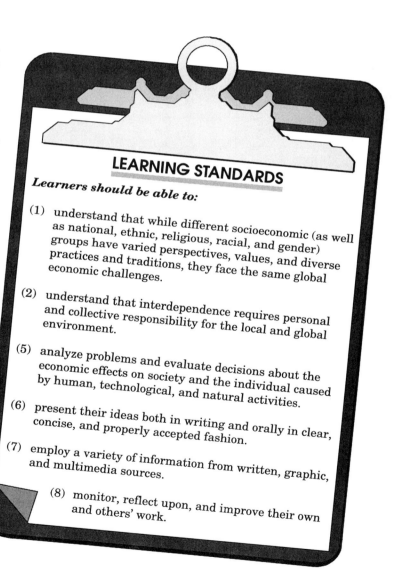

LEARNING STANDARDS

Learners should be able to:

(1) understand that while different socioeconomic (as well as national, ethnic, religious, racial, and gender) groups have varied perspectives, values, and diverse practices and traditions, they face the same global economic challenges.

(2) understand that interdependence requires personal and collective responsibility for the local and global environment.

(5) analyze problems and evaluate decisions about the economic effects on society and the individual caused by human, technological, and natural activities.

(6) present their ideas both in writing and orally in clear, concise, and properly accepted fashion.

(7) employ a variety of information from written, graphic, and multimedia sources.

(8) monitor, reflect upon, and improve their own and others' work.

EVALUATION

The criteria for the evaluation of this project are itemized in the grid (rubric) that follows. Choice of appropriate category terms (values) is the decision of the instructor. Selection of terms such as "minimal," "satisfactory," and "distinguished" can vary with each assessment.

Green Household Evaluation Rubric

(Refer to introductory section for suggestions of scoring descriptors for the evaluation categories.)

Evaluation Item	Category 1	Category 2	Category 3	Category 4	Category 5
Item a: (1) Do the choices examined in the report show differing views of economic, social, and cultural ideas and issues have been considered?					
Item b: (2) Does the report show understanding that interdependence requires personal and collective responsibility for the local and global environment?					
Item b: (5) Do the choices examined in the report take into account the effect of the household's decisions on societies?					
Item c: (6) Does the written (and oral) report present ideas in clear, concise, and properly accepted fashion?					
Item d: (7) Does the report use realistic data and give a complete profile reflective of socioeconomic limits of the household?					
Item g: (8) Does the report show monitoring of, reflection upon, and improvement of work?					

ISSUE 12

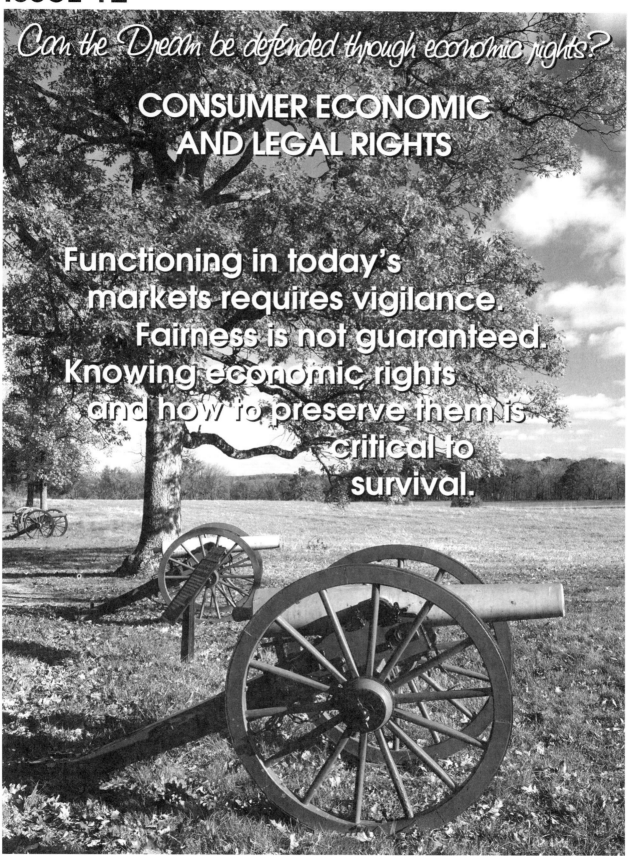

Can the Dream be defended through economic rights?

CONSUMER ECONOMIC AND LEGAL RIGHTS

Functioning in today's markets requires vigilance. Fairness is not guaranteed. Knowing economic rights and how to preserve them is critical to survival.

The Express to Danger

A special day was coming up for Peter and Sandra. They wanted to do something unique to celebrate the first anniversary of their marriage. Looking through the paper, Peter saw an advertisement for *The Express to Danger*. It was a 4-hour train ride that included dinner and a special "roaring 20s" murder mystery with rider participation. "All that for $60.00 a person," he figured, "Not bad." Certainly, it would be a good way to enjoy the special evening. After calling several of his friends, reservations for twenty were arranged, and the idea turned into an anniversary party.

Who would have believed it? The night was perfect – an autumn evening with a chill in the air. Perhaps it was the anticipated excitement. Or perhaps, it was the mist and fog rolling in that gave a real degree of mystery to the night's planned events.

With umbrellas and in trench coats, everyone arrived at the station ahead of the scheduled departure time, 1800 hours (railroad time), ready to celebrate the anniversary of good friends and excited about the simulated mystery murder. Dressed in their 1920s best, the ladies in their flapper short skirts and long beads and the debonair gentlemen in tails and top hats, they boarded the train filled with the sounds of American jazz. Their four-hour adventure was about to roll.

While dancing to the Charleston and snacking on decadent hors d'oeuvres, somehow things got derailed – figuratively at least. Thirty minutes out of the station, glasses spilled, and plates slid off tables. The sudden darkness triggered vocal exclamations and a few screams as the train jerked to an unexpected stop. The emergency brakes had activated when the main generator blew. The train was at a standstill for the entire evening.

Once the emergency lighting came on and the disarray was cleaned up, dinner was served, although a little cold. Following the somewhat subdued dinner, the murder mystery was performed, but without the dramatics of lighting and sound effects, since the electrical system was running on low power.

Although the evening was memorable, Peter, Sandra, and just about everyone in their party were disappointed with the dinner and the "somewhat less than perfect" performance of the mystery murder. They made their discontent known to the manager and owner of *The Express to Danger*. Still, they were given no satisfaction – not even an apology for Sandra's stained and ruined special dinner dress. In a seemingly curt manner, the owner, through his secretary, stated that he was the one who lost out that evening, "Seven thousand bucks to replace that burned out generator. What do they have to complain about! They got dinner and a murder, didn't they?" He continued sarcastically, "The only thing that was spoiled that evening was the attitude of the group who in my opinion acted like a bunch of spoiled brats, crying over spilled milk!"

It would be an understatement to suggest that Peter and and his friends were not satisfied with the company's response to their complaints. As consumers, they felt that the goods and services promised and paid for had not been properly provided. They felt a contract – a promise to perform – between themselves and *The Express to Danger* had been violated.

Peter decided to take legal action. The next day, Peter and several of his friends went to the Wallkill Town Hall in the town where *The Express to Danger* had its office and filed a lawsuit against the owner of the amusement. This sounds more complicated than it was. Peter and his friends simply went to the justice department at the Town Hall and filled out and paid a small fee for filing the papers. In the law suit papers, they claimed that, as consumers, they had entered a contract with the seller to provide a particular good and service (dinner and a mystery) in a particular way and format. What they received was not what had been promised.

Since they were unable to get a settlement for what was believed to be a problem between consumer and supplier, a third neutral party was needed to decide who was right. Lawsuits in the amount of $120.00 for each couple were filed as a "small claims complaint."

The "Express to Danger" had switched to a "Railway to Rights."

Can the Dream be defended through economic rights?

CONSUMER ECONOMIC & LEGAL RIGHTS

INTRODUCTION

Money does not define economics, but it represents wealth and is an important variable in the operation of economics. Accumulation of wealth is a central motivation in a capitalistic system. Money is often at the center of conflict within the system. In the introductory story, the issue was the quality of the product delivered in

The local small claims court is an informal court where individuals can sue for money up to a limit without a lawyer. ©PhotoDisc

relationship to the price. Since the amount for each complaint was relatively small, the court of jurisdiction was the civil inferior (lower) court, better known as **small claims court**. This inferior court operates on a local level. The term "local" refers to village, city, or town in our legal system. There are other higher courts, but considering the amount of money involved in Peter's case, it was within the local jurisdiction.

For many years, consumers had little legal recourse. The Latin phrase "caveat emptor" prevailed. This meant that consumers were responsible for their own behavior in the marketplace. They had to fend for themselves against unfair and misleading activities of sales people. Usually, consumers were "stuck with the product" once something was purchased. They had to be prepared to suffer with the consequences of what the system viewed as their "careless purchases."

THE MARCH TOWARD ECONOMIC JUSTICE

Today, things have changed dramatically. Consumers have many protections against unscrupulous practices in the marketplace. Local, state, and federal statutes and court decisions have created a shield of protection for consumers.

Through acts by the United States Congress and state, county, and/or municipal legislatures, consumers have many protections against unfair or misleading advertising, pricing, labeling, safety, quality, reliability, and substance (see Figure 12.1).

Today, people are much more familiar with terms such as "cease and desist," "restitution," "injunction," and "class action." TV news pro-

Figure 12.1 — Federal Help For Consumers
U.S. Agency's and their Functions

Agency (date established)	Purpose
Consumer Products Safety Commission (1972)	CPSC tests products and creates safety standards for toys, appliances, and sports equipment.
Food And Drug Administration (1906)	FDA tests and approves drugs, cosmetics, and food additives, plus methods of preparing, handling, and selling food.
Federal Communications Commission (1934)	FCC licences radio and television broadcasters and sets standards for station operation.
Federal Trade Commission (1914)	FTC regulates advertising, selling activities, and business procedures.

grams, magazines and newspapers, and classrooms (from elementary to graduate schools) all use such legal terms frequently. Issue 12 surveys some of the many rights that have emerged from the long process of seeking economic justice for the consumer.

EXERCISING CONSUMER RIGHTS: PRE-LEGAL ACTIONS

Before turning to the legal system for assistance, there are some common sense protections consumers must use. All purchases (but especially large ones) require several actions.

- **Understanding the terms of the sale or contract**. Consumers must know the terms of payment, total costs, fees charged, the kind of guarantee, and how long the guarantee remains in effect.

- **Investigating the seller**. Consumers must know the business firm's reputation. They should check to see if there are any complaints recorded against the firm, store, or dealer. Consumers should find other people that have bought from this concern. There are local groups that can be contacted in your area that keep information on local merchants. Examples include the Better Business Bureau, branches of a state's Attorney General's Office on Consumer Fraud, the local Chamber of Commerce, and Small Claims Court records.

- **Becoming informed about the product**. Consumers must gather information. They can consult periodicals such as *Consumer*

Reports, *Money* magazine, *Kiplinger's Personal Finance Magazine* (formerly *Changing Times*), *Consumer Digest*, advertisements, consumer columns of local papers, and TV consumer reports.

If a consumer has problems, he/she must be sure to control his/her temper and act with rational calm. Persistence is a virtue in any consumer conflict. A consumer must be ready to deal with aggravation, lost time, and possibly some financial loss. A consumer should always start with direct contact with the source of discontent (see Figure 12.2 below). Most businesses are reputable and want satisfied consumers. Calling and speaking with a store manager will usually get the problem resolved. So will calling a company's "800" number (usually printed on the product or packaging). Still, it is a good idea for the consumer to maintain very accurate records – a log or journal – of what the problem is, what the warranty includes, and what the consumer and the business have done to solve the problem.

If help is not forthcoming from the business, a consumer should warn the seller that he/she intends to pursue the issue. The next step is

Figure 12.2 — Handling Complaints

1. Contact the seller.
2. If no resolution, contact company.
3. Still no resolution, contact organizations and government agencies.
4. Last resort, take legal action.

Figure 12.3

SAMPLE COMPLAINT LETTER

(Your Street Address, Apt. #)
(Your City, State, Zip)
(Date)

(Name of Contact Person)
(Person's Title)
(Company Name)
(Company Street Address and P.O. Box #)
(Company City, State, and Zip)
(Dear Contact Person):

Last week I purchased (or had repaired) a (name of product with serial number or model number or service performed). I made this purchase at (location, date, and other important details of the transaction).

Unfortunately, your product (or service) has not performed satisfactorily (or the service was inadequate) because (state the problem).

Therefore, to solve the problem, I would appreciate your (state the specific action you want). Enclosed are copies (copies – NOT originals) of my records (receipts, guarantees, warranties, canceled checks, contracts, model and serial numbers, and any other documents).

I am looking forward to your reply and resolution of my problem and will wait (set time limit) before seeking third-party assistance. Contact me at the above address or by phone (home and office numbers – with area codes).

Yours truly,

Sign Your Name
Print your name
Account number (if appropriate)

Paragraph 1 Note:
- describe purchase
- name of product and serial numbers
- date and location of purchase

Paragraph 2 Note:
- state problem

Paragraph 3 Note:
- ask for specific action
- enclose copies of documents

Paragraph 4 Note:
- allow time for action or response
- include how you can be reached

writing a clear, straightforward letter of complaint (no sarcasm or threats) to a store owner, regional manager, company consumer affairs division, or the company president (see Figure 12.3 above). References and addresses can be obtained through a local library. Sources include: *Standard and Poor's Register of Corporations, Directors and Executives, Trade Names Directory, Standard Directory of Advertisers, Thomas Register of American Manufacturers.*

The consumer should send correspondence so that a receipt is signed and returned to the consumer (e.g., registered mail). Copies of all correspondence and related documents should be put in a folder. Also, it is wise to keep a record of everything done (letters, visits, interviews, phone calls — with names positions, dates, etc. — and the responses received). If it is necessary to involve third parties (e.g., Better Business Bureau, trade associations, licensing boards, government agencies, lawyers, etc.) the

ECONOMICS – *Assessment of the American Dream* N&N©

record clarifies the history of the consumer's actions.

EXERCISING CONSUMER RIGHTS: USING LEGAL MEANS

What if nothing happens after the consumer goes to the business associations mentioned above, contacts the government agencies in the phone book's "Blue Pages," and even calls the media? The next step is seeking a third, neutral party to help mediate the problem. If the consumer decides to use the court system, there are three general things that must be considered: some financial burden, lots of aggravation, and lost time. If the consumer is not willing to put up with these aspects of obtaining satisfaction, the quest has probably ended.

The legal system divides the law into civil and criminal litigation. Consumers can seek remedies (satisfaction) to their problems in either or both areas. In **civil** cases, consumer **plaintiffs** (accusers) believe that business **defendants** (accused) harmed them. Because of this, consumer plaintiffs seek **damages** (money). Also, consumers may ask the court for **rescission** (cancel the contract and get back any money already paid). On the other hand, a consumer may not be able to find another "deal" like the one originally contracted and may petition for **specific performance** (a court order to fulfill the contract). Any of these are possible remedies issued from civil law.

Sometimes, the seller's actions violate criminal law. Here, the consumer may want to bring both civil *and* criminal action against the person or firm. **Criminal fraud** is the most commonly charged crime. For example, assume the consumer gives a builder several thousand dollars as a down payment for the construction of a home. Suppose the contractor has no intention of building the home. Instead, he/she collects several down payments from other unsuspecting people and plans to leave the area with the money. Or, perhaps a salesperson goes to a senior citizen's home and uses threats to get a frightened elderly person to sign a contract for some good or service they do not want.

Both scenarios represent **criminal acts** which victimize consumers and take their money. Cases like these can be brought to a criminal court. Injured consumers do not need lawyers since county prosecutors represent them. They file a **criminal complaint** that police investigate. If the police see **probable cause** (enough evidence to support the consumer's complaint), prosecutors can bring criminal charges against the accused.

USING CIVIL COURTS (SMALL CLAIMS COURTS)

Most of the time, people will seek civil satisfaction in the Small Claims Court or a "People's Court." Here, the consumer/plaintiff may represent her/himself against the business/defendant. The amount of money that may be collected for damages differs from state to state. This means that if a consumer/plaintiff has lost $7,000 and small claims action has a maximum limit of $3,000, the plaintiff may have to seek a remedy in a higher court (and probably engage an attorney).

The procedure for using small claims court is simple. The consumer/plaintiff must file claim in the town where the business/defendant lives or does business. The plaintiff calls the court clerk (see the "Blue Pages" of phone directory)

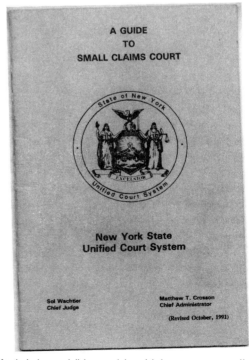

Most states publish a guide which answers questions that plaintiffs and defendants need to know to pursue or defend against a small claim.

Figure 12.4a

NOTICE TO DEFENDANT
SMALL CLAIMS COURT

Form No. SC-1

State of New York _____ COUNTY

_____ COURT

_____ SMALL CLAIMS PART No. _____

_____ OF _____

NOTICE TO DEFENDANT:

To: _____

_____

_____

_____ PLAINTIFF,

_____ TAKE NOTICE THAT _____ together with costs,

asks judgment in this Court against you for $ _____

upon the following claim:

In agreement with which the Plaintiff hereby signs and demands Judgment.

_____ and Address

_____
Plaintiff Signature

_____ There will be a hearing before the Court upon this claim on _____

_____ o'clock, _____ .M., in the Small Claims Part of this Court, held at

at _____. YOU MUST APPEAR to present your defense, or to present any

claim that you may have against the other party at the hearing described above. IF YOU DO NOT APPEAR IN PERSON OR BY AN ATTORNEY, JUDGMENT WILL BE ENTERED AGAINST YOU, EVEN THOUGH YOU MAY HAVE A DEFENSE. If your defense or counter claim is supported by witnesses, account books, receipts or other documents, you must bring them to the hearing. A counter claim cannot exceed $3,000.00 and must be for money damages ONLY. A notice must be sent to the Court Clerk prior to your hearing.

_____ If you admit the claim but desire time to pay, you must appear personally on the day set for the hearing, state to the Court that you require time to pay and show your reason for same.

Dated: _____ 19 _____

_____
Justice - Court Clerk

_____ NOTE: If you desire a jury trial, you must, before the day set for the hearing, file with the Justice or Clerk of the Court a written demand for a trial by jury. You must also pay to the Justice or Clerk a jury fee of $10.00 and file an undertaking in the sum of $50.00 or deposit such sum in cash to secure the payment of costs that may be awarded against you. You will also be required to make an affidavit specifying the issues of fact which you desire to have tried by jury stating that such trial is desired and demanded in good faith.

_____ Under the law, the Court may award $25.00 additional costs to the plaintiff if a jury trial is demanded by you and a decision is rendered against you.

Adjourn to _____ , 19 _____ , 19 _____ , 19

BRING THIS NOTICE WITH YOU.

to see if this is the proper place to file and to check the court calendar. The clerk may mail the forms directly to the plaintiff, or he/she may have to go to the Town Hall to get them (see Figure 12.4a and 12.4b – two sides of same Small Claims Court Notice).

☐ AFFIDAVIT OF SERVICE ON INDIVIDUAL(S)
State of New York, County of

SS:

being duly sworn, deposes and says, that he resides at

at No.

and that on the ________ day of ________________, 19____,

he served the within Notice on the defendant(s) therein named, by delivering to and leaving a true copy of each thereof with said defendant(s) personally; deponent knew the said person(s) so served as aforesaid to be the same person(s) mentioned and described in said notice as the defendant(s) therein; deponent is over eighteen years of age and not a party to this action.

☐ AFFIDAVIT OF SERVICE ON A CORPORATION
State of New York, County of

SS:

being duly sworn, deposes and says, that he resides at

at No.

and that on the ________ day of ________________, 19____,

a

, he served the within Notice on

Corporation, the defendant therein named by delivering to and leaving a true copy of each thereof personally with

an officer of

said corporation, to wit, its deponent knew said corporation so served as aforesaid to be the same corporation mentioned and described in said notice as the defendant therein, and knew said to be an officer thereof at that time; deponent is over eighteen years of age and not a party to this action.

☐ I asked the defendant whether defendant was in active military service of the United States or the State of New York in any capacity whatever. Defendant told me defendant was not. Defendant wore ordinary civilian clothes and no military uniform. The source of my information and the grounds of my belief are the conversations and observations as narrated.

Upon information and belief I aver that the defendant is not in the military service of New York State or of the United States as that term is defined in either the State or in the Federal statutes.

☐ The person so served was male / female

Color of skin____________

Hair color ____________

Approximate age____________

Approximate weight ____________ Pounds

Approximate height ________ ft. ________ in.

Sworn to me this____________ day of ____________ 19____

____

Notary Public - Justice

____

____

Figure 12.4b

After filling out the papers, the plaintiff files them with the court clerk and pays a small fee. (The fee will be recovered as part of the judgment if the plaintiff wins the case). These papers are "served" to the defendant, and the court sets a date to hear the case. If either side does not appear at the court at the appointed time without giving notice of their inability to be there, a **forfeit judgment** could very well be granted to the party that does appear.

Before a consumer appears as a plaintiff, he/she must prepare a case. (It may be worth watching a couple of episodes of the *People's Court* on TV.) The consumer/plaintiff should gather all the evidence needed. The consumer should have any persons that he/she wants to testify and ready to tell their story. If a witness does not want to give evidence, the plaintiff may have the court issue a **subpoena** (an order to appear and give testimony). The consumer/plaintiff should practice her/his presentation before the actual appearance. Taping the presentation with a video camera can help. Playing it back can help decide what is effective and what is not.

If the consumer/plaintiff wins the civil case in Small Claims Court, the judgment is only financial (see Figure 12.5 on next page). The plaintiff will receive money, but there will be neither an order to perform a contract nor incarceration for the defendant. The court gives the judgment to the county sheriff's civil law office which collects the judgment from the defendant after adding a collection service fee.

NOTICE OF SMALL CLAIMS JUDGMENT   Form SC-5   WHITE · JUDGMENT DEBTOR
                                                            CANARY · JUDGMENT CREDITOR
                                                            PINK · COURT COPY

STATE OF NEW YORK

_____of _____Small Claims Part   No. _____

     Honorable_____ , Presiding

Claimant: _____ vs. Defendant:_____

     PLEASE TAKE NOTICE THAT after hearing the proof and facts between the parties and deliberating thereon, the Court's decision is:

_____   A.   Award in favor of   _____
                                                    (NAME)

              for a TOTAL JUDGMENT of $ _____
                                         (SEE INFORMATION BELOW FOR FURTHER PROCEDURES)

_____   B.   Claim Dismissed

_____   C.   No monetary award

_____   D.   Judgment in favor of Defendant, dismissing claim

Date:_____   By: _____
                                                         JUDGE / JUSTICE

INFORMATION FOR THE JUDGMENT DEBTOR

     An Appeal to this judgment can be made. Refer to the Small Claims Guide for proper procedure. This is to advise you that failure to pay the judgment may subject you to any one / or combination of the following actions:

1.   Garnishment of wage;
2.   Garnishment of bank account(s);
3.   A lien on personal property;
4.   A lien / seizure and / or sale of real property;
5.   Seizure and sale of personal property, including automobiles;
6.   Suspension of motor vehicle license and registration, if claim is based on defendant's ownership or operation of motor vehicle;
7.   Revocation, suspension or denial of renewal of any applicable business license or permit;
8.   Investigation and prosecution by the Attorney General for fraudulent or illegal business practice;
9.   A penalty equal to three times the amount of the unsatisfied judgment plus attorney's fees, if there are other unpaid claims.

INFORMATION FOR THE JUDGMENT CREDITOR

This is to advise you of your recourse in the event the judgment you have been awarded is not satisfied:

1.   Contact the judgment debtor and request payment within thirty days;
2.   If the debtor fails to pay within thirty days, contact the Court Clerk and request an income execution and transcript of judgment;
3.   In addition to these rights a judgment creditor may utilize:
     a.   the issuance by the Small Claims Clerk of an information subpoena where a judgment remains unsatisfied for thirty days;
     b.   an action against the debtor where that debtor is a business, for three times the amount of the judgment and attorney's fees where there are two other unsatisfied small claim judgments against the debtor;
     c.   an action to recover an unpaid judgment through the sale of the judgment debtor's real or personal property;
     d.   an action to recover judgment through suspension of the debtor's motor vehicle license and registration if the claim is based on ownership or operation of a motor vehicle;
     e.   notification of the appropriate licensing authority of an unsatisfied judgment as a basis for possible revocation, suspension or denial of renewal of a business license;
     f.   notification of the Attorney General if the judgment debtor is a business and appears to be engaged in fraudulent or illegal business practices.

Figure 12.5

     Other civil courts are available when other needs must be met. Generally speaking, the more money a plaintiff seeks, the higher the court that hears the case. For example, in New York, a plaintiff would go from Small Claims Court (a maximum amount to be awarded set at $3,000) to County Civil Court (can award damages up to the amount of $15,000) to the New

York State Supreme Court (no limit to what it may grant to a plaintiff that wins).

KNOWING CONSUMER RIGHTS: DECEPTIVE SALES PLANS

Most people are honest, but there are those who are not. Consumers ought to be informed about whatever product or service they wish to purchase. Most people depend on word-of-mouth and seek the advice of friends and experts. Consumers should "ask around" about a merchant, product, or service before they buy anything.

KNOWING CONSUMER RIGHTS: DOOR-TO-DOOR SELLING

When someone comes to the door to sell something (**direct sale**), most people do not have a second thought about saying yes or no to a purchase. Most consumers are familiar with door-to-door techniques because of the many reputable companies that use this sales method. By avoiding the cost of maintaining a sales room or store, these companies can usually pass on savings to consumers. Well-known examples include Avon Cosmetics, Mary Kay Cosmetics, Electrolux (vacuum cleaners), Fuller Brush, and of course – Girl Scout Cookies.

Still, consumers are often victimized by fraudulent door-to-door sales of home improvement services and other expensive items. Many states have a law allowing the consumer a three-business-day "cooling-off period" to cancel any door-to-door sales contract and "back out" of the contract for no reason at all. However, consumers should be aware that the three days include the day they sign the contract to purchase. More often than not, the salesperson will come to a person's door in the evening or nighttime. If the consumer signs right then, he/she has already lost one of the three days given to change his/her mind.

KNOWING CONSUMER RIGHTS: CONTEST FRAUD

Consumers should always be aware of any mailing that comes to their homes announcing that they have won a contest, but to collect their prize they must pay a fee, handling charge, or other cost. A legitimate contest will not ask for a payment from consumers to collect their prizes. However, be aware that if you win a contest, you are responsible for the taxes on the prize(s). For example, if you win $15,000 on a TV show, you must claim that as income and pay the appropriate tax bill – local, state, and federal. The same is true of merchandise won.

KNOWING CONSUMER RIGHTS: UNSOLICITED MAILINGS

Whenever consumers receive merchandise in the mail and a donation is requested, they may or may not contribute to the cause sending the product. If the merchandise (generally greeting cards, calendars, or return address labels) is unsolicited (not asked for) by the consumer, he/she has no responsibility to pay anything and may keep whatever was sent.

When consumers do decide to buy something, they should be careful that they understand every aspect of the sale. If they are buying something on credit,

Consumers are often victimized by fraudulent door-to-door sales. The relaxing safety of one's own home and gentle persuasion by a friendly salesperson may cause consumers to forget their contract rights. That is the reason for the three-day "cooling off period" during which the consumer may cancel the contract. ©PhotoDisc

they should:

- Make certain that they understand all the terms of the agreement.
- Make certain that there are no empty spaces on any paper that they sign.
- Always check under and behind any document that they sign to be sure that they understand everything that may be attached.
- Know what the rate of interest is and for how long they will be paying.
- Be aware of any hidden charges not discussed (e.g., delivery or contract fees).
- Always shop around and look for genuine sales, specials, or promotions. Comparison shopping saves money.

(See more detailed discussion on credit in Issue 7.)

KNOWING CONSUMER RIGHTS: WARRANTIES

If consumers have trouble with products after purchase, they should examine the warranty that came with the product. A **warranty** is a promise made by the seller that guarantees the quality and performance of the purchased product for a specific time. Within this promise is a declaration to remedy any problem that prevents the product from functioning as it should.

Almost everything purchased has some type of warranty attached to it, and it provides consumers with legal rights. The two most widely used types are expressed warranties and implied warranties.

LIMITED WARRANTY INFORMATION
MANTIS TILLER

Mantis Manufacturing Co. (referred to hereinafter as MANTIS) extends only to the original consumer purchaser a limited warranty against defects in material and workmanship for a period of two years when used exclusively for personal, family or household purposes; or a period of ninety days when used for commercial purposes. This warranty covers all portions of the MANTIS Tiller product except the engine, which is guaranteed separately by the engine manufacturer.

MANTIS will repair or, at its option, replace any defective part or parts of the product free of charge. In the event of a defect or malfunction, the purchaser must send the product postage prepaid, to Warranty Department, Mantis Manufacturing Co., 1458 County Line Road, Huntingdon Valley, Pennsylvania 19006.

MANTIS assumes no responsibility in the event that the product was assembled or used in contravention of any assembly, care, safety or operating instructions contained in the consumer brochure; was not used with reasonable care; or was used for other than normal and intended purposes.

MANTIS MAKES NO EXPRESS WARRANTIES OR REPRESENTATION EXCEPT THOSE CONTAINED HEREIN, THE DURATION OF ANY IMPLIED WARRANTY, IN-CLUDING MERCHANTABILITY AND FITNESS FOR A PARTICULAR PURPOSE, IS LIMITED TO THE DURATION OF THE EXPRESS WARRANTY. MANTIS DISCLAIMS ALL LIABILITY FOR INDIRECT AND/OR CONSEQUENTIAL DAMAGES. SOME STATES DO NOT ALLOW LIMITATIONS ON HOW LONG AN IMPLIED WARRANTY LASTS AND/OR DO NOT ALLOW THE EXCLUSION OR LIMITATION OF INCIDENTAL OR CONSEQUENTIAL DAMAGES, SO THAT ABOVE LIMITATIONS AND EXCLUSIONS MAY NOT APPLY TO YOU. THIS WARRANTY GIVES YOU SPECIFIC LEGAL RIGHTS, AND YOU MAY HAVE OTHER RIGHTS WHICH VARY FROM STATE TO STATE.

MANTIS MANUFACTURING CO.
1458 COUNTY LINE ROAD
HUNTINGDON VALLEY, PA 19006
TELEPHONE 215-355-9700

RASTEROPS®
Limited Warranty

RasterOps Corporation ("RasterOps") warrants this product against defects in materials and workmanship for a period of THREE (3) YEARS from the date of original retail purchase.

If you discover a defect, RasterOps will, at its sole option, repair or exchange the product at no charge to you, provided you contact RasterOps Technical Support to obtain a Return Material Authorization (RMA) Number and instructions on where and how to obtain repair. Note that a copy of the bill of sale bearing the RasterOps' serial numbers as proof of date of original purchase is required for each product returned for warranty service. Before returning product, remove all non-RasterOps accessories and options. RasterOps cannot be liable for the return or care of any non-RasterOps products, nor accept responsibility for loss or damage of product in transit.

This warranty does not apply if the product has been damaged by accident, installation or removal of product, abuse, misuse, misapplication, accident, neglect, fire, water, lightning, or other acts of nature, failure to follow supplied instructions; has been modified, repaired or undergone attempted repair by unauthorized personnel without the written consent of RasterOps; has a serial number that has been removed, modified, or defaced. RasterOps reserves the right to use remanufactured, refurbished, or used parts and components in making warranty repairs.

This warranty specifically excludes the normal aging of the CRT, which reduces the luminance and focus characteristics of the video display, and phosphor burns on the face of the CRT. RasterOps suggests that users of its video displays use a "screen saver" program at all times in order to minimize CRT aging and phosphor burns.

RasterOps products are designed to work with the Macintosh, Sun and IBM computers. Certain features of third-party software or hardware designed for the host system may not be available when used with this product. Accordingly, RasterOps does not warrant or represent that all software or hardware will function error-free when used in conjunction with this RasterOps product.

An **expressed warranty** is a written or spoken statement of what the seller will do if the product does not perform as advertised. Consumers should always be aware that something *said* to them may be hard to prove later. They should always ask the salesperson to *write* anything they promise. Consumers should read the warranty for conditions, terms, and time limits *before* purchasing.

Beyond the standard, expressed warranty, is the **extended warranty** – often a benefit of buying on credit. A credit card company may give it to consumers using their card to buy products. If the item comes with a full year warranty, a credit card company gives an additional year of coverage beyond the normal warranty's time limit (see Figure 12.6 on opposite page).

The other type of warranty is an **implied warranty**. The law holds this is an *unwritten promise* to make sure that when something is sold, it will do what it is supposed to do. It establishes a minimum standard of performance. These warranties are only applicable to new products sold by a dealer. New cars have

LOSE IT.   DROP IT.   BREAK IT.   IT QUITS.

But pay for it in full with a credit card and you're protected.

TEG Federal Credit Union

EXTENDED WARRANTY
Program Description

For new retail purchases paid with an eligible account from your sponsoring financial institution, the Extended Warranty Program doubles the manufacturer's original written U.S. warranty period up to one additional year for warranties of five years or less. See Program Exclusions section for a full list of items not covered.

Product Registration Procedure

No product registration is required.

Claims Procedure

Any defect discovered during the period of the manufacturer's original warranty will be covered by the manufacturer. Should repair be necessary after the original warranty has expired, but while the Extended Warranty is still in effect, simply call our toll-free number 1-800-937-4639 anytime day or night to request a claim form. While your claim is being prepared, send copies of the following to customer service:

* Copy of itemized store receipt
* Copy of cancelled check, share draft or other negotiable instrument
* Copy of manufacturer's warranty, warranty card and the product serial number (or other reasonable identifier)
* Other reasonable additional information if necessary
* Your full name, address and day and evening phone numbers.

You will be referred to the nearest authorized service center. An unauthorized service center may be selected only if the administrator has given prior approval. If proper documentation is received in time, the service centers will be reimbursed directly by the program administrator. In certain cases, you may have to pay for the repairs and be reimbursed by the administrator. If in-home service is included with your manufacturer's warranty, you may request service in your home.

Covered Purchases

Most new consumer retail products paid with an eligible account from your sponsoring institution are covered. Products must come with a manufacturer's written warranty of five years or less to qualify which is valid in the U.S.

Please see Program Exclusions for a full list of what is not covered under the program.

Figure 12.6

an implied warranty, so do bicycles or new lawnmowers sold by firms such as Sears or Service Merchandise. However, there is no such guarantee when buying a used car (unless a state has a specific law), a bicycle from a friend, or a lawnmower at a flea market.

Implied **warranties of merchantability** exist as protection that a product will meet the reasonable criteria of most people to be, at the very least, a good that is of average quality. Suppose a consumer pays $79.00 for a pair of cross-training athletic shoes. The sole of one shoe separates from the upper after only three weeks of regular use at the gym. It must be assumed that this is an unreasonably short amount of time for the shoe to wear out. This product should last considerably longer under normal use conditions. Friends and acquaintances at the gym agree it is ridiculous that the cross-trainers were no longer any good after only three weeks. The shoes should be repaired or replaced because they did not meet the implied warranty of merchantability. The con-

sumer has the right to return them to the store and expect **redress** (right of compensation under law).

Implied **warranties of fitness for purpose** exist as protection that a product does what it is designed to do. Suppose a consumer needs a particular tool to complete a plumbing job at home. The consumer goes to a hardware store to explain what the job is and to find out what kind of tool is needed. The salesperson indicates exactly what tool is needed. However, the recommended tool does not accomplish the purpose the consumer explained at the store. The consumer returns the tool. The salesperson says the consumer bought the tool and now owns it. The consumer claims the "implied warranty of fitness for purpose" was not met and asks for a refund. If the store still refuses, the consumer has the right to seek redress from the company's regional management, reporting the incident to the state Attorney General's Office, and filing for a review in the local small claims court.

A final type of implied warranty is the **warranty of title**. This means that a sale is legal because the person selling something owned it and is legally able to sell it if desired. This means that the title or ownership of an item may be transferred between the seller and the buyer. Many states have "Titles of Ownership" for items such as cars, boats, and RVs. When you buy a car, a title transfer must take place. In California, the title is commonly known as the "pink slip." No matter what it is known as, the transfer of property must be legally made. Reading and understanding any expressed warranty and having all oral promises put in writing lays the groundwork for redress.

In New York State, a used car is covered by a **limited warranty**. This "Lemon Law" is based on what the state legislature decides to be a fair amount of time for the car to operate properly (90 days). Any known defect must be declared at the time of the sale. This law only applies when a licensed used car seller offers a vehicle for sale. When individuals sell to other individuals there is no protection and caveat emptor is the rule. Other states have similar laws, but some have no protection when a consumer purchases a used item.

removes after-sale responsibility, a seller should say that the product is sold "as is" or "with all faults" or without any warranty of merchantability.

Like warranties, contracts are based on promises, but these promises have the power of enforcement behind them – if made in a particular and proper manner. When a car is in need of repair and it is taken to a shop to be fixed, a mechanic (seller of service) will offer the owner (buyer of service) a written estimate describing what must be repaired and approximately what it will cost to make the repairs. When the owner of the car tells the mechanic to do the repair work, it is legal **acceptance**. There is **consideration** when the mechanic begins to do the work or the car owner signs the agreement on the estimate sheet or when an amount of money is exchanged to get parts. The signature establishes a legal contract. One person promises to make proper repairs to the automobile, and the other promises to make payment for the work. This contract is known as a **mechanic's lien**. It is a legally binding agreement that is routine in modern life. The sample in Figure 12.7 shows that consumers risk a great deal to have their cars repaired.

KNOWING CONSUMER RIGHTS: DISCLAIMERS AND CONTRACTS

At times, consumers become sellers. Suppose a young woman named Jean wants to sell her car. She tells a prospective buyer that she is offering it "as is." Jean is attempting to limit her liability if something goes wrong after the sale. The law calls such a statement a **disclaimer**. Most sellers try to protect themselves with such a statement. Disclaimers must be clearly written in reasonable size print and be easy to understand. Sometimes, a consumer buys something, and the sales receipt disclaimer says that the sale is final – there will be no returns or exchanges. Suppose a consumer buys a musical instrument at a school auction. The school may attach a tag to the trumpet or tuba simply stating that there are no warranties, expressed or implied, made by the seller. To be absolutely sure that the disclaimer

Auto Service Contract

I hereby authorize the repair work hereinafter set forth to be done along with the necessary material and agree that you are not responsible for loss or damage to the vehicle or articles left in vehicle in case of fire, theft or any other cause beyond your control or for any delay caused by unavailability of parts or delays in parts shipments by the supplier or transporter. I hereby grant you and/or your employees permission to operate the vehicle herein described on streets, highways or elsewhere for the purpose of testing and/or inspection. In addition to all liens granted by law, an express lien is hereby acknowledged on the above vehicle to secure the amount of repairs and parts thereto.

ABC Autobody Shop, INC.,
PO BOX 333
NEW HAMPTON, N.Y. 10958

Figure 12.7

The mechanic's lien is a contract that also allows the repair shop's employees permission to drive the car. The owner's – not the shop's – insurance is responsible if an accident occurs. If the car is lost due to fire or theft, the repair shop is not responsible. (Frequently, this allows repair shops to claim any damage to be "beyond the shop's control.") The vehicle may be at the shop for a long period, depending on many variables. Under this arrangement, if a dispute arises over the bill and the car owner does not pay in a timely fashion, the shop can legally sell the car to collect their costs.

To have an enforceable contract three things must be apparent: **offer**, **acceptance**, and **consideration**. Suppose someone *offers* to marry another person and the person *accepts* the offer. There is no contract until the physical *consideration* is exchanged (something of value is given for something else of value). The engagement ring is consideration for the vow to marry. The contract is that each promises to marry the other at some future time. If the person with the ring decides not to "go through" with the marriage – the contract is broken. The ring should legally be returned (since it represented the intention of getting married).

If a consumer wants to buy a piece of land, the consumer makes an offer, and the seller accepts. Once there is agreement on the terms of the sale, the consumer gives the owner a down payment of $500.00 as a *consideration*. The consumer now has a contract. If the seller decides not to sell the land, the contract is **breached** (broken). If this breach is acceptable, the down payment is returned. If the breach (violation of the promise) is not acceptable, the buyer may go to civil court. The court may reward the consumer **compensatory damages** (redress for losses). The court may punish the seller by imposing **punitive damages** (additional payments beyond ordering the return of the down payment). Also, the court may order the contract to be **performed** (fulfilled).

CREDIT TRANSACTIONS

Earlier, the importance of establishing and managing credit was discussed (Issue 7). Since credit is also a contracted transaction, there is another important dimension of credit to be learned – **consumer credit rights**.

The word credit means a great deal in the American economy today. More often than not, the American public makes purchases using credit rather than cash. **Credit** is the purchase of goods and services based on the *promise to pay* for them at some time in the future. It is also a term that is used to describe the practice of borrowing money. The person that provides the merchandise or money is legally known as the **creditor**, and the person that makes a purchase without the use of his/her own money or borrows money is known as the **debtor**. The amount of money lent out to someone is called **principal**, the charge for the loan is called **interest**, and the combination is called **debt** (total liability or obligation).

LEGAL DIMENSIONS OF CREDIT

Credit comes in many forms and has a number of different costs for its use. When borrowing money, the first place to go is a bank. An application is made by the consumer and evaluated by a bank loan officer. The **credit history** of the applicant is evaluated and an analysis of four important aspects of who the debtor is are considered:

- the applicant's **ability to pay back the loan** (usually considered by examining the applicant's total yearly income).

- the **total assets** an applicant possesses (what is the total value of all of the property – real and personal – that the applicant owns).

- the **character** the applicant has shown through past actions (this generally refers the applicant's attitude and honesty).

- the **performance** on other loan arrangements (as well as handling of checking and savings and paying routine bills).

The safer the bank feels about getting its money back, the better the deal a loan applicant gets. If the bank can give a borrower a **secured loan**, the rate of interest is lower than an unsecured loan. The difference is that **collateral** (something of value) is part of the agreement. This collateral may be taken by the bank if a debtor **defaults** (does not pay). This collateral is "security" that can be sold to repay the amount owed. If the bank can get more from the

Another costly situation that is often part of a credit arrangement is the use of a **balloon payment**. When a contract is signed that includes such a clause, the borrower accepts large payments in the future in order to keep the current monthly payments low and affordable. The last payments are "the balloon" that must be paid or the loan is in default. Younger people are attracted to such an arrangement because they believe that later pay raises will enable them to pay the larger, final installments.

An **acceleration clause** should be avoided. It allows the creditor to ask for full payment of the loan in case the debtor misses a *single* payment. If, for some reason, such a clause is part of a credit contract, a creditor must be absolutely sure that all payments are made on time. If the acceleration clause is invoked, most people would be unable to muster the resources required to pay the balance of a loan on demand. The property would be forfeited (lost).

CREDIT CARDS

Unlike a closed-end loan for a specific amount, a credit card is an *open-ended borrowing arrangement*. Credit cards are offered in two categories: regular and revolving. The regular type, sometimes called a **charge card**, never has an interest charge attached to its use. Many store and gasoline cards, as well as the standard versions of the *American Express* and *Diners Club* cards, fit this category. A consumer must pay the entire amount charged during the billing period. With no balance due, there is no interest charged. For cards such as *American Express* and *Diners Club*, a consumer pays a considerable annual fee for use privileges.

With the second type, a **revolving card**, the consumer must only pay a portion of the amount due. *MasterCard, VISA, Discover,* American Express' *Optima*, and many store and gasoline cards are set up as revolving credit arrangements. Whatever is not paid is carried over to the next billing. A fee for postponing the payment is added at a rate of interest that changes periodically. The rate of interest is usually tied to a percentage above the Prime Rate (see Issue 7), but it still differs from one lender to another. Some lenders also charge an annual fee. A consumer must shop around for the best

sale of the collateral than is owed to it, the difference is given to the defaulted borrower. However, if the sale produces less than the amount still outstanding on the loan, the borrower is still responsible for the difference. Mortgages (house loans), boat loans, car loans, and business loans are all forms of secured loans. If payments are not made, the bank can repossess the property that the loan was used to obtain.

An **unsecured loan** is the type that has no collateral that may be repossessed. It involves a higher risk element for the bank. Because the bank lacks this security, it must charge a higher rate of interest to protect itself against a borrower's default.

THE COST OF CREDIT

When a percentage rate is charged that is above the legal rate, the word **usury** applies. Individual states set the legal limits on loan rates. Nationally, no state allows rates to exceed 36% (see sidebar on usury on the next page).

Usury

When someone or some firm charges a rate of interest on a loan that is more than the legal limit allowed, a crime called usury is committed. In street slang, usury is called "loansharking" – a type of extortion where someone borrows money at a rate of interest that makes it impossible for most people to ever pay off the principal. Their payments to the lender are so high that they merely pay the interest month after month, year after year. What happens is that once money is taken from a "loanshark," the borrower never escapes but is continually caught in the grasp of the lender as the debt is never paid in full.

Sometimes, even legitimate businesses try to charge more than the law authorizes.

For example, suppose a consumer goes into a store to purchase a printer for a computer. The sign reads, "$500, Easy Installment Plan Available." The consumer decides to purchase the printer by paying for it over a period of time. The salesperson explains the terms as $50 down and $50 per month for a year. That means that you are paying $50 on the spot plus $50 x 12 for a grand total of $650. The finance charge for the $500 purchase was an additional $150. It doesn't sound too bad until you figure out the interest paid on such a purchase is equal to approximately 33% of the amount borrowed.

Such instances of usury are not as uncommon as many consumers think. In 1975, the case of *Haas v. Pittsburg National Bank* reached the United States Court of Appeals. The case was about the interest charges placed on accounts of people who had obtained Master Charge cards and BankAmericards (now VISA) from three banks in Pittsburg (Pittsburg National Bank, Mellon Bank, and Equibank). The basis of the suit was that the charges assessed on accounts that were outstanding (past the due date) were illegally high. At issue was the fact that the banks were charging compounded interest not only on the unpaid balance, but also on service charges. The court ruled the banks' action was illegal under the conditions of the contracts and state law. (James R. McCall. *Consumer Protection: Cases, Notes and Materials.* St. Paul, MN: West Publishing Company, 1977, 478-486)

In another instance in 1977, William Sylvester of Tennessee borrowed some money from the Merit Finance Company. He never expected to be in court fighting to keep his home. When borrowing a small amount from the finance company, Sylvester used his home as collateral. On an open line of credit, Merit Finance continued to lend Mr. Sylvester money. Each time they did, they "flipped," or refinanced his original loan and consolidated it into the new one. The judge that heard the case decided, "It is my conclusion that Merit 'flipped' the loans so that it could again collect interest on old balances even though interest had already been imposed. Does such a practice constitute usury under the Tennessee statute and decisions? ... It is my conclusion that the 'flipping' of loans in the transactions under consideration was a plan or scheme to enable Merit to obtain an excess over the legal rate of interest." (John A. Spanogle and Ralph J. Rohner. *Consumer Law: Cases and Materials.* Paul, MN: West Publishing Company, 1978. 191-195)

Experts advise that when consumers sign contracts for buying on credit or borrowing money they should be sure that all papers are in order. If there is any doubt, they should have the numbers checked by someone that they trust – perhaps an attorney. They should never sign simply because the salesperson tells them that everything is "standard and legal." Consumers must be sure that when they need to borrow that they go to a reputable bank or loan agency, but they should never take any terms or conditions for granted. Consumers must learn to question whatever seems out of the ordinary.

Figure 12.8 — Federal Consumer Credit Protections

Source: *Consumer Protection*. U.S. Government Prining Office, 1992

Act	Protection
Fair Credit Billing Act (1971)	Protects all card holders from mistakes made on their account; establishes a required written response by the creditor to any complaint made by a customer within 90 days; card holder may withhold payment for the alleged credit error (without interest being charged) until an investigation determines an outcome; card holder is still responsible for all other items on the bill; inquiry must be made in writing and sent to the address noted on the statement for such problems, but a phone call to the number on bill may get an immediate answer. Questions must be postmarked no later than 60 days of the dated statement being contested. If the bill does turn out to be correct, the card holder may have to pay a finance charge for the delayed payment.
Fair Debt Collection Act (1977)	Deals with the proper and legal means for a debt to be collected from a debtor; prohibits any harassment by a collection agency and clearly states what is not proper behavior (generally any form of intimidation) in their efforts to collect on an outstanding debt.
Fair Credit Reporting Act (1971)	Protects consumers from unfair and inaccurate credit reports; allows a person the right to see a summary of the information collected by a credit bureau and challenge any part of the report that is untrue or misrepresented; maintains the right to submit a statement explaining their own version of disputed information; if a report contains negative information but no new incident has arisen in the last seven years, the unfavorable information must be erased (bankruptcy can remain for a period of 14 years).
Truth in Lending Act (1968)	Protects credit applicants against misunderstanding the total cost of getting credit; provides that the entire cost of borrowing money is clearly stated in a document presented to the borrower before the loan is given.
The Civil Rights Act (1968)	Prevents the rejection of credit applications simply on the basis of race, sex, religion, marital status, national origin, or public assistance.
The Equal Credit Opportunity Act (1977)	Clarifies *Civil Rights Act's* protections against prejudicial rejection of a credit application.

deal they can find (the lowest interest rates and no annual fees).

Because credit cards are now such a central part of financial management, consumers must know their basic rights regarding them. If a credit card is lost or stolen, the owner should contact the company that issued the card immediately. A list of the cards, their numbers, and the "800 numbers" to call in case of loss should be kept in a safe place. Under the **Truth in Lending Act** (1968), a consumer may be responsible for any unauthorized charges made with the card up to fifty dollars. After the notification is made, the consumer has no liability for unauthorized use. The Figure 12.8 chart summarizes this and other credit protection laws.

KNOWING CONSUMER RIGHTS: LOAN DEFAULT

There was a time when persons unable to meet their obligations were thrown into debtors' prison. Today, while it is still not unusual for consumers to have difficulty paying their bills, debtors are not sentenced to jail. Many times, the cause is beyond the control of the individual. An injury may prevent someone from working or may cause an increase in costs to the household and creates a money shortage.

Whatever the reason for the indebtedness, there are certain legal protections. The debtor should notify each and every creditor that he/she is having problems. He/she should explain the nature of the problem and ask for help. The creditor may allow a late payment or arrange refinancing so that installments are smaller. (A debtor should be aware that smaller payments are the result of paying for a longer period of time and thus paying more in interest over that time.) A troubled debtor may want to get help from a **credit counseling service**. Often, this can be accomplished for little or no cost at a volunteer service.

Debt reorganization is available under the law using Chapter XIII of the *Federal Bankruptcy Law*. This allows a debtor to meet with the creditors and a court-appointed referee to work out a plan for debt repayment. The referee's plan must be approved by a federal court and is placed under that court's supervision.

The last resort action is to declare **bankruptcy**. State laws vary, but usually this action places all of a debtor's assets at risk (except for her/his home and necessary clothes – mink coats and luxury items are not protected). All other assets can be sold by the court in order to pay back what is owed. The bankruptcy law is divided according to **chapters** that determine many different courses of action as to how a debtor will be treated. Bankruptcy is a very complicated procedure that demands the representation of an attorney. A debtor does not have to have counsel, but experts say it is in a debtor's best interest to contact a legal specialist for a consultation before proceeding with bankruptcy action.

A debtor may be completely excused from repayment, be given a longer amount of time to repay, or have the interest charges reduced. It all depends on individual circumstances. Besides having property **repossessed** (taken back by the creditor), a person's salary may be **garnisheed**. This means that the court will order the troubled debtor's employer to take part of her/his income and send it directly to creditors.

Another type of court order may allow the **attachment** of property or money. In this action, the court awards a **lien** on a debtor's property and allows the collection and sale of it

in order to satisfy the debt. A lien may be placed on a bank account which would force the bank to release funds to satisfy the lien obligation. If a lien is placed on property, such as an automobile or tractor, it can be taken and sold by the lien holder. All of these actions are traumatic, but they are common in an economic system that depends so heavily on credit consumption.

INSURING ECONOMIC RIGHTS: AN AMERICAN DILEMMA

Not all consumer rights are as immediate and personal as those presented thus far. In fact, a great deal of consumer protection is maintained by statute and common law about which the average person knows very little. This protection is rooted in the philosophy of maintaining competition in a free market. The political conservative wants less government involvement in the operation of the market, while the political liberal claims that there is a need for government to become more and more involved in the economic system's function.

In *The Wealth of Nations* (1776), Adam Smith first presented a warning to government that the marketplace must be allowed to take care of itself. He believed imbalances that arise will be brought back into line by the natural forces of the marketplace's operation. Smith's principle, **laissez-faire**, simply declares the market is self-correcting. Applying artificial forces to keep it balanced only makes things worse. Smith's warning has been repeated by a great number of conservative economists ever since his book appeared.

Yet, the course of U.S. history has presented a case for a more liberal interpretation which promotes government intervention in a free market economy. Liberal economists see a marketplace that must be protected by law and regulation in order to establish equity, fairness, justice, and security to maintain the well-being of both consumer and producer.

Both the liberal and conservative views hold competition to be at the center of solid, strong, and healthy economic activity. The difference between them is *how* to maintain a healthy competitive rivalry in the economy. These two views are at opposite ends of a wide spectrum of opinions about the **economic role of government** (appropriate type and amount of intervention). To understand why economists debate how much government protection versus how much freedom there should be, a student must analyze how the laws of the land act upon the market to control and manipulate it.

Most Americans would not want to give up the security that government intervention provides. In the past, most welcomed New Deal pump-priming, stock market regulation (SEC), G.I. Bill stimulus, the actions of the Federal Reserve Bank, and auto lemon laws, to cite a few examples.

Today however, Americans perceive that government is excessive, wasteful, and very costly. This, of course, creates a dilemma. In the conservative approach, government does threaten the free interplay of market forces, but liberals feel those forces must be held in check.

In the November 1994 elections for local, state, and federal political offices, the voting citizens decided that they would support the conservative point of view. With overwhelming regularity, the voters decided that the actions of government for the past forty years had been unsatisfactory. Conservative politicans, promising less government intervention and less regulation, were voted into office. They promised lower taxes by eliminating the need for revenue to support business regulation. To do this, they promised less government bureacracy. The Republicans even published their "Contract with America."

Pediment of U.S. Supreme Court Building, Washington, D.C.. ©PhotoDisc

LEGISLATING FAIR BEHAVIOR: CORPORATE POWER V. PUBLIC INTEREST

In the 1790s, Alexander Hamilton and the Federalists (see Issue 8) tried to establish a strong role for the federal government in the early years of the republic. However, this liberal view did not gain strength until the Progressive Era in the late 19th and early 20th centuries. Laws were passed in order to influence market forces in two ways: antitrust legislation and agency (state and federal) regulations on business decision-making.

Antitrust means regulating and monitoring big business to prevent monopolistic practices that prevent competition (review competition in Issue 5). The first federal antitrust law was the ***Sherman Antitrust Act*** (1890). Almost everyone thinks of this legislative wonder as the "Grand Daddy" of all federal laws aimed at prohibiting the creation of monopoly power within the economy. The Sherman law also attempted to prevent the use of contracts, combinations (mergers), and conspiracies which could restrain trade in any manner or form. For example, during the strike that ended the 1994 baseball season, players cited the *Sherman Act* while attempting to prevent their contracts from including terms that imposed **salary caps** (ceilings) and free agency. There are many other antitrust laws to prohibit other commercial practices that limit or prevent competition (see Figure 12.9 on opposite page).

Still, compromising the doctrine of laissez-faire in favor of government checking the power of big business did not start with the *Sherman Act*. In 1837, the U.S. Supreme Court dealt with limiting corporate rights in *Charles River Bridge v. Warren Bridge*. Chief Justice Roger B. Taney ruled that a corporation's right to protection of its private property and freedom to do business was not and could not be absolute in nature. The Court voiced its concern about the excessive use of corporate power to harm public interests.

In the "Bridge Case," a corporation that owned the single bridge over the Charles River (between the cities of

Figure 12.9 — Federal Antitrust Laws

Act	Concept
Sherman Antitrust Act (1890)	Created broad foundations for government antitrust action by prohibiting all agreements and contracts "in restraint of trade" that caused monopolies.
Clayton Antitrust Act (1914)	Strengthened the Sherman Act by outlawing price-discrimination (charging customers different prices for the same thing if it led to monopoly or lessened competition).
Federal Trade Commission Act (1914)	Established the Federal Trade Commission to enforce the Clayton Act to regulate unfair methods of competition in interstate commerce by issuing cease and desist orders.
Robinson-Patman Act (1936)	Strengthened Clayton Act by forbidding large-scale discounts on sale of goods to large buyers unless rebate and discounts were available to all.
Celler-Kefauver Act (1950)	Bolstered Clayton Act by preventing mergers and buyouts to reduce competition in a market.

Boston and Cambridge) attempted to prevent the state from chartering other corporations to build other bridges. In the decision, the Court declared that a corporation had no more political power or character than any other individual in the Commonwealth of Massachusetts.

The Charles River decision recognized that corporations had rights of freedom of enterprise and the protection of private property just as any American citizen had. This allowed the corporation to operate without a continuous threat of interference from the government. Yet, the Court also announced that it would prevent any corporation from becoming a government itself. Exercising monopoly power at the expense of the state or of private individuals would not be tolerated.

What this all meant was that a business could be privately owned, could be conducted for profit, and could have the freedom of choice to seek its own economic self-interest. However, in order for this to happen, competition had to be maintained. It is the basic force that directs, coordinates, and regulates the efforts of individuals and businesses.

ECONOMICS AND PUBLIC INTEREST: REACTING TO MONOPOLY

By the late 1800s a reaction grew against the great industrialists' attempt to restrict competition. Their price-fixing drove up market prices and increased profits at the expense of the consumer. Support for antitrust legislation grew, resulting in the passage of the Sherman Antitrust Act in 1890. As dramatic as that sounds, the Sherman Act did not prevent much illegal activity in the 1890s. Yet, it would be a mistake to believe that the Sherman Act was completely ineffective. The federal government did use it – sometimes succeeding in breaking up combinations that were found to be in obvious restraint of trade. However, the Sherman Act's real power was felt later when it was used by the U.S. Justice Department under many Presidents to protect the economy from abuse by trusts.

CASE STUDY:
BIG BLUE AND
FAIRNESS IN THE COMPUTER MARKET

In 1936, "Big Blue" (IBM – International Business Machines) was in court to appeal a decision that ruled against their restraint of competition (*International Business Machines Corp. v. United States*, 1936):

"This is an appeal of a decree of a District Court preventing IBM from leasing its tabulating and other machines upon the condition that the leases shall use with such machines only tabulating cards manufactured by IBM as a violation of the Clayton Act ...

"IBM's machines and those of Remington Rand, Inc., are now the only ones on the market that perform certain mechanical tabulations and computations. ... by the use in them of cards upon which are recorded data ...

"To insure satisfactory performance by IBM machines, it is necessary that the cards used in them conform to precise specifications as to size and thickness, and that they be free from defects which cause unintended electric contacts and consequent inaccurate results. The cards manufactured by IBM are electrically tested for such defects ...

"IBM leases its machines for a specified rental and period (with a provision that calls for the termination of the lease if any cards not manufactured by IBM are used in the leased machine...

"IBM's contentions are that its leases are lawful (partly because their) purpose and effect are only to preserve to IBM the good will of its patrons by preventing the use of unsuitable cards which would interfere with the successful performance of its machines ...

"(It appears) that others are capable of manufacturing cards suitable for use in IBM's machines ..."

The ruling in the case basically said that IBM certainly had the right to proclaim the virtues of the use of its cards and warn of the possible defect of other cards that did not meet the specifications that IBM had established. But, IBM could not make the lease of its machines dependent on the purchase and exclusive use of IBM cards. The case was decided against IBM.

In 1952, the Justice Department again charged International Business Machines, Inc. with antitrust violations. In 1953, lawyers from IBM and the federal government were in a heated legal battle at the Southern Federal District Court in Manhattan. At issue was, if International Business Machines, Inc. was such a monopolistic colossus astride the computer industry, then, was IBM "... so potent that special court rules are needed to protect competitors?" (Peter Passell, *New York Times*. 6/9/94, D21)

By 1956, the government and IBM agreed to a **consent decree** (basically an out-of-court settlement that establishes a contract in which the company agrees to stop behaving in a particular manner), and the government dropped its lawsuit. This consent decree was a tool that was used quite a bit by the Justice Department in the 1950s. Such a decision is like a promise where both sides agree to act in a particular way, but it is not binding on the court. That means that the court can pick up and reinstitute the action at anytime (*Black's Law Dictionary*, 5th ed. West Publishing, St. Paul Minn. 1979).

(Note: a consent decree forced the restructuring of Metro-Goldwyn-Mayer, a major motion picture studio. The Culver City, CA studio was accused of being a monopoly. To avoid the legal battle that was sure to follow the accusation, the studio accepted a consent decree. It forced the MGM Studios to sell all of its theaters throughout the country. Some critics of the action by the Justice Department held this consent decree to be a major cause of the failure of the film producer.)

It was 1969 when the Justice Department brought proceedings against IBM again, and the case dragged on for years. In 1982, the government decided to drop its prosecution for antitrust. "...IBM dominated the mainframe computer market, its shares of other computer markets were relatively small..." (Gregory and Ruffin, Basic Microeconomics. 267). It took the Justice Department thirteen years to decide this.

In June of 1994, attorneys for IBM began work to eliminate the 1956 consent decree. "International Business Machines Corp. counsel filed a 50-page motion, supported by three boxes of documents..." not only to end the long-standing restrictions, but also to stop U.S. District Court Judge David Edelstein from being the presiding officer. (He was judge in both of the other IBM cases.) (Bart Ziegler. *Wall Street Journal*. 14 June 1994. B5)

For more than 38 years, the Federal District Court for the Southern District of New York upheld the (consent decree) agreement. The "Big Blue" attorneys claimed that the judge that heard the case was originally (and remained) biased and prejudiced against the company. Some experts saw the judge as simply being tough with corporate defendants and playing his role strictly "by the book." The claim made by legal experts is that the judge was tough on IBM "...because he apparently believed that the Government had a strong case against the company." (Passell, 21)

It seems impossible to determine how much was spent by both sides in the litigation of this one aspect of antitrust legislation. It also seems impossible to determine if it was all worth the cost. For some, antitrust legislation and enforcement means security and safety. For others, it means a waste of limited resources that can be put to better use helping to build strong industries to compete with other industrialized nations in the world. For the liberal, it is about protecting the common man and the marketplace within which we must all do business. For the conservative, it is about a meddling and intrusive government that should keep its "hands off" business.

MA BELL AND FAIRNESS IN THE COMMUNICATIONS MARKET

In 1984, the biggest antitrust suit in history resulted in the breakup of "Ma Bell" (American Telephone and Telegraph Corporation). AT&T had been an exception to the antitrust legislation for a long time. Telephone communication was considered a **natural monopoly** (market in which a single firm supplies a product or service such as electricity or water for which there are no substitutes and no other sources). AT&T did not exploit the consumer, but it did provide a reasonably priced and efficient communication system for its customers.

The utilities that consumers use daily (electric, natural gas, local telephone, and water) are all natural monopolies. They are situated in a market that reasonably allows for only one supplier. There are no substitutes and there are no other sources for what these companies provide. The government allows natural monopolies when it is much more efficient (cheaper) and safer to provide the public with the good or service when there is only one supplier.

Still, such companies cannot change the service provided or the cost of that service without approval of a state government agency – usually called the **Public Service Commission**. If a regulated natural monopoly wants to quit service or another wants to enter the market, or even make a modification to service (raise rates), this regulatory agency must grant permission. The justification for such control is "to protect the public interest." The public has a right to be sure that such a critical service will be provided through proper and fair operation.

The problem that the Justice Department had with AT&T pertained to the **ease of market entry**. The inability of any other company to provide alternative long distance service stemmed from AT&T's technological monopoly. It prevented the offering of alternative equipment to the consumer.

The federal court found that the situation "blocked the public access to new technologies." Other manufacturers could produce microwave transmissions and an array of other telephone equipment, but AT&T would not allow any other equipment to be "hooked-up" to its lines or make use of its transmission services.

The result of the 1984 court decision can be seen every day. The AT&T company split the telephone service from Western Electric, its equipment manufacturing division. It separated the telephone service division into eleven separate and distinct corporations.

In the mid-1990s, radio, television, and print media bombarded consumers with competitive and spirited ads for several long distance providers (Sprint, MCI, and AT&T). According to industry analyst Robert Crandall, this competition has lowered prices on equipment and service. A wide variety of styles and designs flooded the market (Robert Crandall. "Has the AT&T Breakup Raised Telephone Rates?" *The Brookings Review*. No. 5, Winter 1987). The result of this government regulation on the communication industry was mixed. Although the marketplace grew more competitive, consumers – faced with more and more plans, options, and carriers – became more confused than ever.

ECONOMIC RIGHTS AND REGULATING BUSINESS

Government regulation influences business decision-making. Critics say it is costly to business and taxpayers, interferes with freedom, and impedes economic growth.

The sheer number of regulatory agencies is staggering. On the federal level, key regulatory agencies include:

- **ICC** (Interstate Commerce Commission – 1887)

- **FDA** (Food and Drug Administration – 1906)

- **FTC** (Federal Trade Commission – 1914)

- **SEC** (Securities and Exchange Commission – 1934)

- **FCC** (Federal Communications Commission – 1934)

- **EPA** (Environmental Protection Agency – 1970)

- **NHTSA** (National Highway and Traffic Safety Administration – 1970)

- **OSHA** (Occupational and Safety Health Administration – 1970)

- **CPSA** (Consumer Product Safety Administration – 1972)

There are parallel agencies on the state and even local levels, and the number of such bodies (more than fifty on the federal level) seems to grow steadily.

Regulation differs from antitrust action. Antitrust laws are concerned with the relationship between business and the level of competition in a specific market. Regulation, on the other hand, is designed to watch over specific businesses or interests in the economy. For example, the Federal Trade Commission is concerned with consumer safety, and the National Highway Traffic Safety Administration watches out for the safety of people who drive and use the interstate highway system. The Occupational Safety and Health Administration protects workers from hazardous or unhealthy workplaces.

The regulatory agencies, commissions, and administrations are created by the United States Congress or state legislatures to enforce a law's specific purpose (see *U.S. Gov't. Agencies* chart, page 159 and Appendices). Each agency imposes its own interpretations of rules and regulations on business. Often, the government agency negotiates with the business in question in order to reach a settlement to the "mutual" benefit of the public and the business. Should a serious violation of regulations be determined, the penalty for the violation of these rules is generally in the form of a fine. Occasionally, incarceration of the corporation officials results when a violation of a criminal nature is found or there is continued disregard of the rules. If a decision is disputed, an appeal may settle the issue of proper or improper treatment by the regulator.

Protecting the public interest is the most common justification for regulation of businesses. Some businesses (e.g., interstate commerce, television and radio broadcasting, public transportation) are so important to the well-being of the public that the government believes that it must make sure that such businesses "operate properly."

Government sometimes uses regulation to correct a situation that generates problems for a particular group. The 1980s was a decade of financial manipulation. There was glory in mergers and big stock deals – at least for a few. There was also a growing danger to the entire American securities industry. Behind the names of superstar Wall Street deal makers, Ivan Boesky and Michael Milkin, was a story of power, greed, and corruption. It shocked even the most seasoned and cynical brokers. These men with clever plans and fraudulent operations made earlier financial deceptions look like children's games.

Most of the fortunes accumulated by these men were from illegal activities known as **insider trading**. The term refers to anyone who has knowledge of information not available to the general public and who uses it to buy or sell corporate shares for profit. It is information that is illegally obtained and allows individuals or groups to have an unfair advantage in a market that depends on everyone having the same opportunity to make a profit. Obtaining insider information illegally and using it for insider trading earned huge sums of money for many unscrupulous men during the 1970s and 1980s. (Milkin made $550 million in one year from "junk bonds"). With the help of the Justice Department and the Federal Attorney General's Office, the Securities and Exchange Commission conducted investigations and found informants. Layer by complicated layer, the SEC uncovered the activities of these men and others. The probe shook the very foundation of the stock market, and it severely damaged the financial industry in this country.

SUMMARY

Some critics would say that all this government protection is unnecessary, while others point to the corruption and magnitude of crime that exists in the economy as justification for government intervention. Antitrust prosecution and regulation are negative activities in an economy grounded in a free market philosophy. Government intervention contradicts the concept of a truly free market. Yet, the society accepts the contradiction for several reasons: the concern over the level of competition in the marketplace, the need to protect the public interest, and the achievement of a level of security that cannot be provided in any other way.

ASSESSMENT
QUESTIONS • APPLICATIONS

1 This chapter begins with a story about an evening's entertainment going awry. Review the story. Discuss it with others.
   a Do you agree Peter and friends have a legitimate lawsuit?
   b Prepare a presentation Peter might give in small claims court.
   c Prepare a presentation for the owner of the "Express To Danger."
   d Explain how and why the judge might rule.

2 Considering that the study of economics deals with how societies deal with the problem of scarcity, does it seem reasonable to you that the government spends so much money on the legal action against those businesses that they consider to be a trust or may become a trust? Explain your reaction.

3 In New York State, the Long Island Lighting Company (LILCO) charges the highest electricity rate of any power utility in the country, while Con Edison of New York City is second.
   a Call or write your state power authority. Find out the highest and lowest rate charges for the power companies in your state.
   b How does your home rate compare to the highest and lowest rates in your state?
   c Research why there is a difference among companies.

4 Why are such men as Ivan Boesky, Michael Milkin, Solomon Brothers, and Charles Keating considered dangerous to the economic well-being of this country? Research who they are and analyze their criminal activity.

5 Can you remember ever being disappointed because you were unable to get what you wanted? Take a minute and think back into the memories of your life and discover if such an experience existed.

   a Describe the memory as if it were a journal entry.
   b Your instructor will divide the class into cooperative groups in which each student will read their journal entry to the other group members.
   c After all of the compositions have been read, the group should select one on which to write a script. The story that is created should describe where the problem of scarcity exists, what tradeoff had to be made, and what opportunity cost was paid.
   d The group should role-play the story and the class should be able to identify the three events that define the economic terms of scarcity, tradeoff, and opportunity cost.

6 In 1994, professional baseball players went to court to prevent team owners from placing salary caps into their contracts. They cited the *Sherman Antitrust Act* as a reason for preventing salary caps.
   a What is in this antitrust law that can be related to the baseball players situation?
   b Why isn't baseball franchising overruled by the *Sherman Antitrust Act*'s "restraint of trade" clauses?
   c Would you consider yourself an economic Liberal or Conservative in regard to government antitrust policies? Explain your answer.

7 Every year thousands of Americans lose millions of dollars – sometimes their entire savings – to "con-artists" through clever but illegal scams. Find an article in the newspaper or summarize information you heard on the radio, saw on TV, learned from friends or neighbors, or experienced yourself.
   a Write outline notes to be shared with your class. Include a brief summary of what the scam was, how the victims were "taken-in" by the "con," how the scam was discovered, who it was reported to, and what the outcome was for the victims and for the criminals.
   b Develop some general guidelines to help prevent scams.

ASSESSMENT PROJECT:
CREATING AV PROGRAMS FOR CONSUMER ASSISTANCE

STUDENT TASK

Form a production group and create a video (or other multimedia format) to assist consumers as part of community education outreach programs (organization meetings, cable TV public service campaigns, public library distribution, etc.).

PROCEDURE

1 Group must choose a topic. Examples include:
   - How to Buy a Used Car
   - Rights and Responsibilities When signing Contracts
   - How to File a Small Claims Court Complaint
   - When You Need an Attorney
   - When You Need Help From the Police
   - Common Frauds
   - Getting Consumer Assistance from the Attorney General's Office

   Also, the topic may come from those discussed in this chapter, personal experience, news stories, etc.

2 Decide on a format (video documentary, docudrama, animation, computer graphic, slide-tape program; serious or comedic approach).

3 Enlist production assistance from faculty (e.g., drama coach, English teacher for scripting, technology teacher for graphics, art teacher for sets, etc.).

4 Secure equipment and physical resources (location, tape, film, cameras, lights, etc.).

5 Divide among the group the production responsibilities (e.g., script writing, prop and set design and procurement, audio visual technician, director, graphic design, etc.

6 Research information in library and contact and interview agencies and individuals that work in the field (for both on and off camera material).

7 Create a workable plan for advertising and circulating the program (public library, community service group, etc.).

8 Use the program to educate the school (start with your class) and community.

9 Present an summation of the group's activities and experiences to the class.

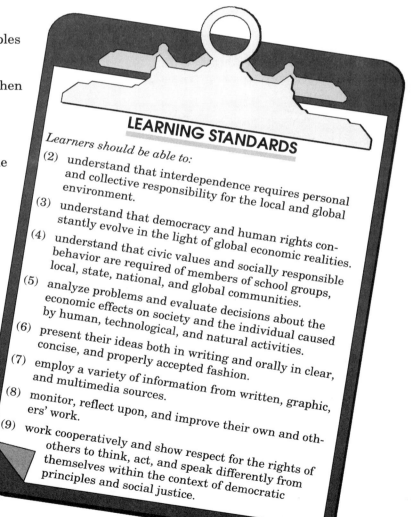

LEARNING STANDARDS

Learners should be able to:

(2) understand that interdependence requires personal and collective responsibility for the local and global environment.

(3) understand that democracy and human rights constantly evolve in the light of global economic realities.

(4) understand that civic values and socially responsible behavior are required of members of school groups, local, state, national, and global communities.

(5) analyze problems and evaluate decisions about the economic effects on society and the individual caused by human, technological, and natural activities.

(6) present their ideas both in writing and orally in clear, concise, and properly accepted fashion.

(7) employ a variety of information from written, graphic, and multimedia sources.

(8) monitor, reflect upon, and improve their own and others' work.

(9) work cooperatively and show respect for the rights of others to think, act, and speak differently from themselves within the context of democratic principles and social justice.

EVALUATION

The criteria for the evaluation of this project are itemized in the grid (rubric) that follows. Choice of appropriate category terms (values) is the decision of the instructor. Selection of terms such as "minimal," "satisfactory," and "distinguished" can vary with each assessment.

Consumer Assistance Program Evaluation Rubric

(Refer to introductory section for suggestions of scoring descriptors for the evaluation categories.)

Evaluation Item	Category 1	Category 2	Category 3	Category 4	Category 5
Item a: (2) Does the presentation show understanding that interdependence requires personal and collective responsibility for the local and global environment?					
Item b: (3) Does the presentation show understanding that democracy and human rights constantly evolve in the light of global economic realities?					
Item c: (4) Does the presentation show understanding that civic values and socially responsible behavior are required of members of school groups, local, state, national, and global communities?					
Item d: (5) Does the presentation analyze problems and evaluate decisions about the economic effects on society and the individual caused by human, technological, and natural activities?					
Item e: (6) Does the presentation present ideas in writing (and orally) in clear, concise, and properly accepted fashion?					
Item f: (7) Does the presentation employ a variety of information from written, graphic, and multimedia sources?					
Item g: (8) Does the presentation show monitoring of, reflection upon, and improvement of work?					
Item h: (9) Does the presentation show cooperative work and respect for the rights of others to think, act, and speak differently?					

ISSUE 13

Can Political Participation Save the Dream?

NEW REALITIES AND THE AMERICAN DREAM

"... that this nation, under God, shall have a new birth of freedom – and that government of the people, by the people, and for the people, shall not perish from the earth."

– Abraham Lincoln
The Gettysburg Address, 1863

EIGHT DOLLARS WORTH OF REALITY

It was a sunny fall day, and Jack Neyland was heading home with a paycheck from his new job at Deep's IGA Market. Jack slid his '85 Grand Prix into his grandfather's driveway. He had been dropping by Gramps' house almost every day since he started grade school. Jack's mom and dad both worked and his grandparents looked after him in the afternoons. Now that he was in high school and had a job, Jack was pretty independent, but he found it difficult not to say hello everyday on his way home from the market. Besides, Gramps was pretty proud of Jack now that he had a job and was supporting the Grand Prix, which they had both worked on last summer.

Gramps was at his shop table at the back of the garage working on one of the decorative plaques he made and sold at outdoor flea markets. He worked on carving and painting a supply of them in the cold months for when the nice weather would come.

"Hi, Gramps!"

"Hey, Jack. What's the big grin all about?"

"Got my first paycheck from Deep's IGA."

"Well, let's celebrate. Grandma left some iced tea for me. She's at her crafts class this afternoon. Knowing you, I'd have thought you'd have cashed that check already and headed for an auto parts store."

"Well, that's still on the agenda, but I wanted to ask you about something first." Then seriously, Jack went on, "You told me not to be surprised about the FICA and federal and state tax deductions on this check, but I didn't think the union dues for a part-timer would be this much."

"Let's see. Well, I'd check with the union rep to see if that's the right amount. What did you say his name was?"

"Sonny. He said it wouldn't be too much, but $8.00 is a chunk for what I take home. I don't know why I joined anyway. What can they do for a part–timer?"

"You said they help you if there are any problems on the job, and all the other part-timers were members," reminded Gramps.

"Right. Besides, I didn't want to offend anyone. The folks down at the IGA seem pretty strong on this union thing."

"You know, Jack, I never took much stock in unions. When I had the furniture store, I was always butting heads with unions. Every time they pressed the government there in Washington to get new labor laws, it made my life miserable. Those factory workers' contracts sent the wholesale cost sky high for the furniture I bought for the store. It cut into my profits in a big way. I still think they were a big part of the inflation in the late 1970s."

Gramps continued, "But over the years, I realized how things got done in a country this size. I joined the National Federation of Independent Businesses. It fought for my interests in Washington, just like the unions fought for their members. When I retired, I joined AARP, the American Association of Retired Persons, because they fight for folks like me.

"The AARP is one of the most powerful lobbies in the country right now. They argue for Medicare benefits and to keep the politicians hands off Social Security. The dues are really low, and everyone my age that I know is a member. I get insurance from them, too. They're so strongly united, they can get rates that are reasonable, even though older folks are risky to insure."

"So, you think that being in this retail clerks' union is worth my money?"

"Jack, I've seen the way things have changed in this country. Believe me, the lone, rugged individual has a very hard time surviving, to say nothing of prospering. Yes, I'd stick with that clerks' outfit down at the IGA. It is probably worth the money. Just talk to people, especially Sonny. Get a better handle on it. Make sure they are working for you.

"This is your first job, but you have to realize that these groups, if they work for you, can be very effective. Remember, though, the leadership can drift away from their members. You need them to survive, but you have to make sure they are doing the job for you. You can't let them float free."

"Thanks, Gramps. I'll talk to Sonny. Right now, I'm going to cash this check and buy some oil for the Neyland chariot."

ISSUE 13

Can political participation save the Dream?

NEW REALITIES AND THE AMERICAN DREAM

"WHAT HAPPENS TO A DREAM DEFERRED? DOES IT DRY UP, LIKE A RAISIN IN THE SUN?"
– Langston Hughes

NEW REALITIES: WORK IS DIFFERENT

Today, it seems that many dreams have dried up and have been blown away by winds of despair. The American Dream itself is still alive, though those who seek it must struggle for it. This chapter presents some the tools and methods necessary to achieve it in a new and difficult world.

Signs of despair are commonplace today. Not since the Great Depression of 1929 have there been so many homeless. The old cliche, "the rich get richer and the poor get poorer," seems to have new meaning. During the 1980s, the nation's richest one percent of the population captured more than half of the nation's increase in wealth. During the last twenty years, the real income (purchasing power) of American workers has declined. With the 21st century upon us, Americans must realize that the apathetic attitudes of the past will not solve problems. Civic involvement must become the new norm if problems such as these are to be solved.

The economy that this generation faces has good news for only a few people in the system. For most, the news is simple: become actively involved or suffer. The decisions of most major corporations are based on the interests of the stockholder. In the 1980s and 1990s however, these decisions led to losses of jobs, benefits, security, and dignity for workers. As in the Industrial Revolution of the late 19th century, employees seem to be little more than cogs in the wheels of production. In *The Quickening of*

America, Frances Lappé and Paul DuBois note that to reduce costs and "remain competitive," American companies cut and slashed their costs of production. For those workers that held their jobs, new "get tough" policies have meant more work, longer hours with lower wages, and fewer benefits (Lappé, 77-78).

THE DIFFERENCE OF A GLOBALIZED ECONOMY

As discussed in Issue 10, part of the new situation is attributable to global change. As the countries of the world opened up free trade, more and more companies became international or multinational in scope. Today, many so-called "American cars" are made in other countries. American consumers can be reasonably sure that even if a car is actually manufactured in the United States, a very high percentage of its parts are manufactured in other countries. On the other hand, purchasing a Japanese or German brand car may mean you are buying an automobile that has been assembled in the United States. Ford has an agreement with Mazda for its Probe and Explorer models. General Motors' Geo brands are made jointly with Toyota and Suzuki. Honda and BMW automobiles are assembled in this country. The Dodge Stealth, made for Chrysler by the Japanese, and the Mitsubishi 3000 GT, made in Japan, are basically the same car (see opposite page). Many Jeeps and all Eagles are made in Canada and sold in the United States. Most major corporations are international in scope.

In 1993, the Green Giant Division of Pillsbury announced that 270 Watsonville, CA employees would be out of work. The reason was simple: it was cheaper to process vegetables in Mexico. After 20 years of service, California workers averaged $64.80 per 8-hour day with benefits. Green Giant executives announced workers at its new plant in Irapuato, Mexico would earn $7.58 per day with no benefits. According to one excessed American, "Pillsbury left here to exploit the workers in Mexico." (Jaclyn Fierman. "What Happened to the Jobs?" *Fortune* 12 July 1993, 41)

The Reebok trademark is well known to the American consumer. The footwear giant's U.S. advertising budget is in the hundreds of millions annually. Yet, its athletic shoes are made in foreign countries by men, women, and children who collect poverty wages. Since 1986, the company has deserted shoe assembly operations in the United States and gone to Taiwan, China, Korea, Thailand, and Indonesia leapfrogging across Asia to lower its labor costs.

But shoe manufacturers are not alone. As companies received more and more freedom to move from one country to another, they have often left hardship and disillusion behind. As trade barriers have fallen, and multilateral trade agreements have spread throughout the world, it appears that the "good corporation" has died. The global spread of the major corporations was supposed to provide stable jobs and generous fringe benefits ... "[but] for more and more, the process is sliding into reverse ... The resulting psychic void explains much of today's sense of economic insecurity." (Samuelson, Robert J. "R.I.P.: The Good Corporation." *Newsweek.* 5 July 1993, 41)

In 1994 and 1995, workers at a number of General Motors plants went on strike to get relief from sixty-hour (or more) per week shifts. The complaint was not the money that they were making, but the quality of life they were forced to live because the company wanted to save money by not hiring any more workers. General Motors was willing to work these men and women as hard as possible to save the cost of benefits and taxes involved in hiring more workers for additional shifts.

For years, the image and power of labor unions have been deteriorating. "Labor didn't do much to help itself, to say the least. It grew fat, stupid, corrupt, bureaucratic; it never had been very democratic." In his column, commentator Joe Klein said, "the unions lost touch, and became dinosaurs ..." ("Labor's Leverage Lost." *Newsweek.* 6 December 1993, 25). He offers the opinion that organized labor is no longer a counterweight force in a world that needs it ... "to make sure that entrepreneurs pay their workers enough to buy the products other companies are producing." (Klein, 25) The loss of organized labor's power has led wages to fall far behind the pace of productivity. Labor has lost its leverage (Klein, 25).

THE DIFFERENCE OF DOWNSIZED CORPORATIONS

Middle class Americans fear for their future as real wages (purchasing power) drop. Young Americans know entry level salaries are smaller than in the two previous decades and job security appears to be evaporating (see Figures 13.1 and 13.2 on next pages). In the mid-1990s, many workers at IBM stated that working hard, caring about the company, and believing that what is good for the company is good for the employee is a self-defeating ideology which

Figure 13.1

"There, that ought to relieve the pressure from the stockholders."

leads to the impoverishment of this country's middle class.

Many employees have been "excessed" or "let go" in order for corporations to reorganize and downsize. Often, these were the very people who helped the company grow and become profitable. In 1993-1994, Proctor and Gamble let thousands of employees go. Yet, the company was not losing money. In fact, they were very profitable. Proctor and Gamble downsized – cutting labor costs – so that it could show even more profit. As a result of such moves throughout American industry, the demand curve for workers is shifting to the left, while the excess supply of workers shifts the supply curve to the right (see Figure 13.2). This creates a situation that drops standard wages and creates downward pressure on entry level wages and salaries.

The search for wider profit margins and higher stock dividends seems to have blinded many corporations to the reality that their most important assets are their employees. In the past generation, those industries that 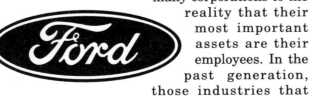 empowered their workers found it led to a higher level of quality in production. In the 1980s and 1990s, Ford's "Quality is Job 1" ad campaign touted its workers as its most important asset. In the long run, corporations discovered that they grew more productive not because of some sense of humanism or kindness, but because of the positive incentive workers experienced when drawn into the corporate decision-making process.

In this new and complicated world, labor's performance will make or break the economy. During the late 1990s, business decisions will determine how well people will be able to achieve the American Dream. The crucial factor will be how effectively workers respond to the changing workplace, technology, education, and labor market.

No company can operate as a closed system, unaffected by the climate surrounding it. In the 1990s, as companies began to downsize and eliminate jobs, nearby communities were also affected. There is a destructive "domino effect" as more and more people are forced out of work. Where do they go? In addition to the corporate giants, other companies began to downsize, too. These companies placed their employees in precarious situations. Pressures mounted as workers wondered if the company was going to place them on part-time hours, take away their benefits, change their shift, and give them tougher working conditions.

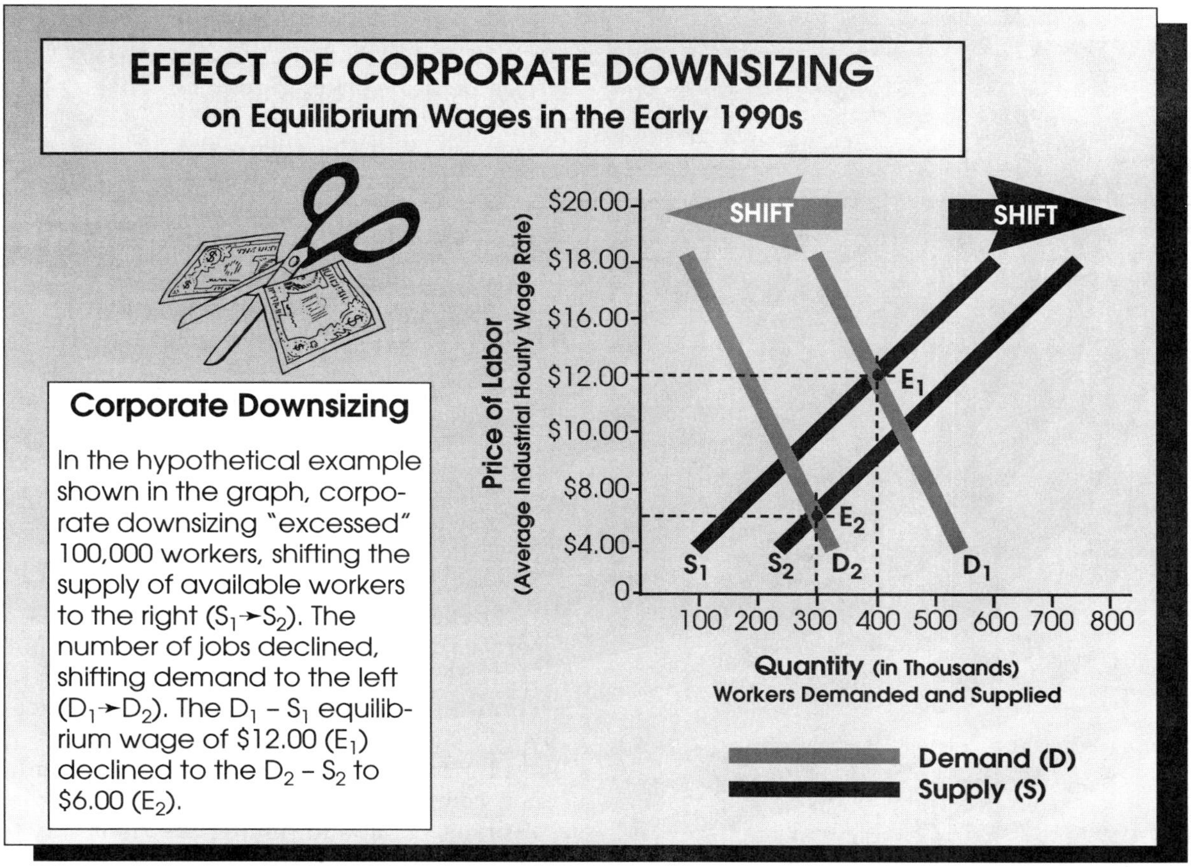

EFFECT OF CORPORATE DOWNSIZING
on Equilibrium Wages in the Early 1990s
Corporate Downsizing
In the hypothetical example shown in the graph, corporate downsizing "excessed" 100,000 workers, shifting the supply of available workers to the right ($S_1 \rightarrow S_2$). The number of jobs declined, shifting demand to the left ($D_1 \rightarrow D_2$). The $D_1 - S_1$ equilibrium wage of $12.00 ($E_1$) declined to the $D_2 - S_2$ to $6.00 ($E_2$).
SHIFT
SHIFT
Price of Labor
(Average Industrial Hourly Wage Rate)
$20.00
$18.00
$16.00
$12.00
$10.00
$8.00
$4.00
0
E_1
E_2
S_1
S_2
D_2
D_1
100 200 300 400 500 600 700 800
Quantity (in Thousands)
Workers Demanded and Supplied
Demand (D)
Supply (S)

Figure 13.2

THE DIFFERENCE OF EMPLOYEE OWNERSHIP

Productive workers cannot be living in fear that they will go to work only to be escorted from the premises by a guard after they have been told that they no longer have a job. There are alternatives.

UNITED AIRLINES

As more and more people faced uncertainty and fear, they began looking for alternatives. Many people joined with others to create their own companies. They have created new corporations, cooperatives, and nonprofit businesses. Incorporations in the 1990s were up nearly twenty-three percent over the figures of the early 1980s. Faced with downsizing, the employees of the nation's third largest carrier, United Airlines, pooled their assets and used creative financing to buy the company and began operating it themselves.

Other experienced people faced with layoffs from the major airlines founded their own company in 1994 – Kiwi Airlines. They were willing and able to challenge the established airlines and compete with a pride and strength that came from ownership.

At Kiwi, workers made decisions everyday that most people would be afraid to make. Yet, this was a true expression of faith in a free market economy. They no longer depended on corporate executives "upstairs" to call the shots.

The employee-owners at Kiwi made new rules because they faced the challenges of a new game. In this new economy, Americans everywhere are discovering that they can have power and control over a great many economic situations that they used to believe were controlling them. It may be a new idea, but it is catching on throughout this country – ordinary people can become powerful enough to control their own economic destinies. It may not be easy, but people do not have to sit by and wait to be manipulated and discarded as just some worn-out piece of machinery. The future depends on whether people are passive or active in determining their success or collapse.

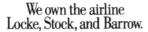

Employee ownership is the new catch phrase for workers' survival and prosperity, but new skills for finding help and aid are required. New alliances, new financial planning, new lending procedures, new production, sales, management, advertising, and allocation techniques have helped people maintain an income and dignity that drive the American Dream.

THE DIFFERENCE OF EMPLOYEE EMPOWERMENT

Changing old habits and taking risks is difficult. But adapting to new realities flows from a sense of self-interest, national pride, caring for and about other people, and the courage and energy to act as never before. A change in corporate attitude can give workers a real voice in the decision-making process throughout the economy.

The Saturn Division of General Motors ran a television commercial in the first couple of

months of 1995 that showed that it understood the importance of the worker in determining quality. Like the Ford commercials of the 1980s, the Saturn ad had a line worker speaking to the viewer explaining how he has the power to stop the entire assembly line if he thinks something is wrong. No retaliation, fear, or loss – just a faith in the worker that he/she could spot a problem and can take care of it. According to the ads, GM spent $3.5 billion dollars developing a different kind of company. Saturn became a place where the worker felt appreciated and where there was no need to track through a management hierarchy in order to do the job.

There are not too many companies that operate this way. Still, many discovered that old strategies no longer fit the new realities. Actions and strategies designed and carried out by colleagues, friends, and communities have saved many jobs in recent years. More enlightened companies turned workers into problem solvers, seeking and finding the right way to be innovative and proactive.

Things will not change overnight. In a market economy, companies naturally seek lower production costs. Many corporate managers think the best policy for making profits is to get tough with workers. Others are convinced that smaller is better. For both reasons, the 1990s witnessed a flurry of managerial decisions that cut pay, hours, and jobs. This downsizing forced people to stop taking job security for granted. The rest of this issue will show why people must change the way they think.

REDESIGNING LARGE CORPORATIONS

The cost-effective activities that corporate America engaged in during the 1990s led to some important changes in the way companies operated. Many, like some of General Motors automobile divisions, decided to impose longer work weeks on the employees that survived the cuts. Others turned to employee empowerment. Many of the people that were eliminated from the workplace were middle managers – people who oversaw the work of those below them. Without this group of overseers, new thinking began to infiltrate top management. The new ideas were concerned with the abilities of workers. Many corporate hierarchies came to the realization that the success of the individual and the success of the organization are linked.

According to Frances Lappé and Paul DuBois in *The Quickening of America*, a great deal of research and the insights of thousands of managers all testify to the belief that "... the closer workers feel to the company, the more their frontline experience ... creates business success." (Lappé, 82). Having a voice in what goes on is an incentive to do well because it joins the interest of all levels of work together, helping the company as a whole. Finding a company that believes in this philosophy may be something to consider when a young person goes out in the workplace seeking employment. It is not easy to find such companies, but a few strategic questions during a job interview can help determine if an employer wants planners and problem solvers. Chances are that such a company will have a greater success in the marketplace and will offer their employees a more secure position, and a more exciting place to be.

In *The Quickening of America*, Lappé and DuBois make a series of recommendations to employers seeking to create a more productive atmosphere of employee empowerment:

- Help employees earn a voice in decision-making.

- Find ways to share information in a democratic fashion.

- Reward employees for learning (formal course work at colleges, trade schools, or inservice) and innovating (bonuses for ideas that lead to better products and efficiency).

- Set up programs that teach workers team work and mutual respect for one another.

In other words, Lappé and DuBois counsel making the workplace democratic in process and function (Lappé, 85-89).

RETHINKING SMALL COMPANIES AND ENTREPRENEURSHIP

In the 1990s, mergers creating big companies slowed. It was downsizing that became a more dominant trend in corporate America. What were once huge industries divided themselves into smaller and smaller divisions. There were greater opportunities for "the little guys." An example is the fantastic rise in popularity of the microbrewery companies all over the country. Pete's of St. Paul, MN, Boston's Samuel Adams™ Brewery, and Colorado's Black Dog™ take pride in their roots as midgets among giants such as Anheuser-Busch, Coor's, and Miller. Through its ads and commercials, Samuel Adams constantly reminded the public that the big breweries spilled more than Adams bottled.

As always, there existed the requirement to be better if new products were going to succeed

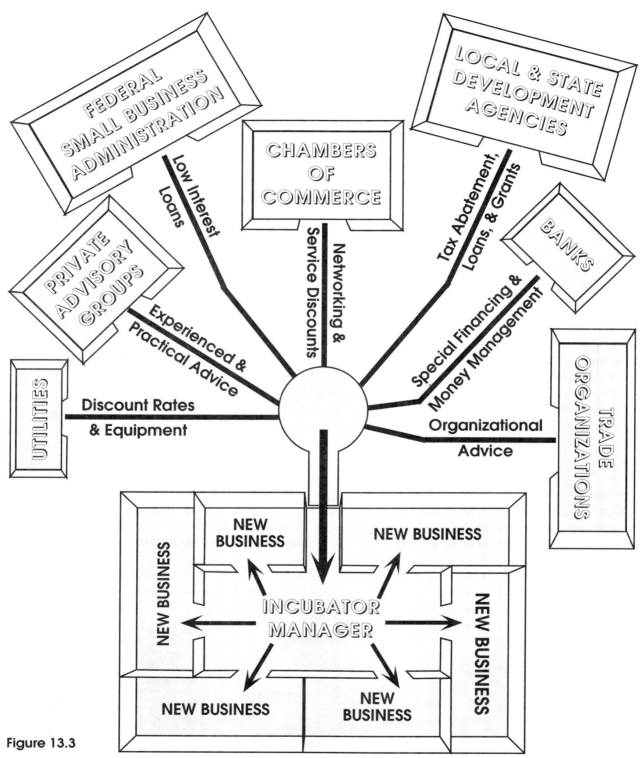

Figure 13.3

in a marketplace dominated by the established name brands of giant companies. In 1995, a small chocolate company opened in the Bronx, New York, with eight local employees. The owner took advantage of tax incentives and special loan conditions to finance his first business, but he made sure workers received profit-sharing incentives. The profit-sharing business prof-

its will grow based on product quality, regional market domination, and employee enthusiasm.

In some cases, new businesses emerged from mutual aid between local business organizations and local and state governments – the **business incubator** (see Figure 13.3 above). It is both a process and a place where people with

"According to the Washington bureaucrats, fecundation of these entrepreneurial enterprises will increase the GDP and the Congressional incumbents' chances for reelection."

entrepreneurial ideas can get help making the idea become a reality. Incubators offer entrepreneurs education in how to get started, and some modest help such as space, phone service, and "seed" money which can get them started on the road to productive businesses and a life that they control. As more and more regions experienced changes caused by corporate downsizing, the small businesses offered hope for future growth.

Many people find that starting a home-based business is a way to keep start-up costs to a minimum. Many home-based business are services and require minimum initial capital investment. Because this is a significant trend in the modern American economy, an illustration may be useful.

In 1993, after being "excessed" from positions with two major television networks, Peter Habib decided to start his own business.

Preparing for a career in broadcasting, Peter earned a Bachelor's degree from Syracuse University's Newhouse School of Communications, a nationally known institution. Over several years, Peter went through several appointments, moving from New York City to Washington. With each change, he advanced up the corporate ladder: from Katz Broadcasting, to NBC, to ABC. Then the recession of 1990-91 hit. As the head of a department, Peter watched as layoffs progressed. Finally, he was told he was being let go since the company was eliminating the job his department was doing. Peter was given a month's severance pay and began seeking other jobs, but with a recession going on, there was not much available.

Madison Media Inc.

Media, Marketing & Design

Peter Habib

7823 Vanity Fair Drive ◆ Greenbelt ◆ Maryland 20770
Phone: 301/982-1142 ◆ FAX: 301/982-1143

That was when Peter decided to start his own advertising business. Using a spare room in his home, he bought some basic equipment: computer, Fax machine, and printer/copier, and had a separate business phone line installed. He printed up some cards, used some of his contacts, and now enjoyed running his own advertising and promotional agency. He helped many of his clients get a better quality service for less money than they were formerly paying. He is now expanding by renting commercial property. It was not easy, but it was rewarding. Peter offered this list of some prerequisites for becoming an entrepreneur:

- a sense of optimism and confidence
- willingness to work long hours
- education, experience, and expertise
- sufficient capital
- something to sell in a market that needs it
- support of your family
- a business plan

The last item, the business plan, must include an objective assessment of the probability of success. This is where the staff at a business incubator can help. There are also agencies such as SCORE (Service Corps of Retired Executives) or government agencies such as the Small Business Administration (see Figure 13.3). More than 600,000 businesses start up every year, but nearly one fourth fail within two years. Seeking the necessary help and doing the proper research can reduce the risk of failure.

REVITALIZING CIVIC PARTICIPATION

On *Donahue* one afternoon, an audience member got to his feet and shouted that it was time that the government start paying for man-

dated programs it requires and take the cost "off the back" of the taxpayer (Lappé and DuBois 167). This man actually thought that the government was a separate entity with its own source of revenues and not an organ of the people. The government *is* the people – on the local, state, and federal levels. Because American government belongs to the people, citizens must know how to direct it, use it, and have it function on their behalf. Citizens must learn to participate and solve problems instead of just sitting there and blaming others for what is wrong.

Every day, more and more people come to the realization that they will not accept the despair that the "new economy" may place upon them. They revitalize their spirits and enter a renaissance of ability and attitude. People make a difference. They make a difference not because they are unique, but because they have personal problems to solve.

Through the examples of what others do, Americans can best identify what can be done. This idea is not new. At one time or another, it has been called by many different names: direct democracy, living democracy, grassroots democracy, participatory democracy, etc. Yet, what it comes down to is what Abraham Lincoln described as "... government of, by, and for the people."

In the years since the New Deal, Americans developed a dependency on the government. Most Americans believed it could get them out of any problem that developed. Americans' attitudes and expectations shifted from strong independence to dependence. With increased government benefits, came higher taxes, more deficit spending, more debt, more intervention, more protection, and more public assistance.

In the 1990s, reality finally hit Americans like avant-garde comedian Gallagher's sledge hammer coming down on a watermelon. It became clear government could no longer afford to "bail out" everyone and every com-

Production teams facilitate dialogue among colleagues to review, analyze, and revitalize all levels of a successful corporation. ©PhotoDisc

pany. Local, state, and federal budgets are unable to continue to support everything that every special interest group needs and wants. Drastic cuts in budgets add to the economic woes of a great number of people as government cut employment, spending, and public assistance. As scarcity impacts government operations, citizen involvement become a vital issue.

How can Americans create an environment where every citizen becomes a decision-maker and problem solver? There is a perception that American society has been dominated by powerful and wealthy institutions at the expense of the common good. This perception provides some elements of the society with an excuse for civic apathy and alienation that prevents taking action. Yet, in the past thirty years, many individuals accomplished many wonderful things. People have made a difference.

BECOMING A PROACTIVE CITIZEN

The first step to becoming a proactive citizen is to recognize that government has to be accountable and responsible to the people. Involvement must become a social norm – not something extraordinary. Next, people must recognize that they are shareholders in their future. They must come together and translate issues into small, attainable goals with suggested solutions.

When faced with a problem, citizens have to be sure that it is defined in such a way that everyone can understand its effects on them. Those that are harmed by the procedure, rule, regulation, or condition must be identified and invited to discuss solutions.

With such an audience established, a forum must facilitate a dialogue. This should occur in stages, with each meeting including more and more people. Information must be in order, verified, and disseminated so that participants have an honest and complete image of the issue. The forum must allow for questions and interaction of all points of view. Organizers should be sure that the space for the meeting is comfortable and convenient and that all participants can be heard when they speak.

The process must be repeated, each time inviting people with another perception of the issue. Before each meeting, it must be made clear that a *dialogue*, not an argument, is being solicited. The forum provides citizens an opportunity to listen, learn, and formulate a position.

In February of 1995, the new governor of New York, George Pataki, found that a five billion dollar state deficit necessitated deep cuts in state programs and state benefits. Pataki's first announcement was that 11,400 state employees would lose their jobs as he began to keep his promise to reduce the size of government and lower taxes. Cuts were made in school aid to local districts throughout the state, the State University system, the Department of Transportation, State Police programs, welfare grants, Medicaid, and aid to local municipalities.

Reaction to Pataki's program echoed from every corner of the state. Groups of all kinds tried to change the governor's direction. The chairman of the Ways and Means Committee of the NY State Assembly asked Pataki if a citizen

who might save a couple of hundred dollars in state taxes, but had to pay an additional thousand dollars to send his/her child to the State University, "would be happy with the governor's cuts?" The reply was, "No, but his 15 neighbors who do not have children will be." (Jay Gallagher. "Pataki May Pay Price For Spending Reductions" *Poughkeepsie Journal* 6 March 1995, 2b) How much better off will the state be if competent students are kept from going to college so that a general decrease in taxes may be achieved? It may be a long time before there will be any answer to that. The real problem was that there was not much discussion with the public as to where the cuts ought to be made.

Participatory democracy allows a broader exchange of perceptions, solutions, and supports. An answer might be to use the Town Meeting concept. In such a localized, participatory setting, Americans can find solutions for themselves. When making tradeoffs on government budget issues whether paving the streets in a neighborhood or hiring a police officer to patrol an area – the community should have a sense of shared decision-making to create a sense of common ownership.

Learning by doing is the most important aspect of revitalizing good government programs. There must be a place where citizens can speak out, listen to other points of view, confront problems, negotiate, evaluate, make public presentations, reflect, assess, and learn to be well prepared. Just as on the job, there is a need to have a sense of *empowerment* in a community.

On the local level, citizens can start by selecting the target. For instance, it may be the local budget (village, town, city, or school). Participants must decide what can be done to get more people to attend committee and neighborhood meetings to discuss issues. Another avenue is to join political party committees to understand the power structure that exists and evaluate its operations. Who is in power? Who is sympathetic to what cause? Who will help? Who will be an obstacle?

Such questions must be answered if any change is to occur. There is symbolic power and real power that operates in any system. Identifying the real power sources is very important. The hierarchy of command can be traced to the ultimate rung on the ladder.

REVITALIZING VOTING POWER

Only half the people eligible in this country vote in Presidential elections (see Figure 13.4). In state and local elections, the percentages are usually worse. Voting is an important tool to change their lives, but most people do not participate in even this minimal way. Decisions about health care, the economy, jobs, wages, the environment, public safety, and housing are determined by representatives for whom voters cast their ballots. Still, the majority of citizens choose not to use their influence. Among the many reasons cited for not voting are: a sense of apathy, alienation, cynicism, the inability to register, the difficulty of registering process, or just plain loss of faith in "the system."

A great number of people are statistically categorized as "underrepresented" in the electoral process. The groups least likely to vote include women, African Americans, Hispanic Americans, Native Americans, the poor and near poor, the illiterate, and the poorly educated. These are all groups that could make a difference in elections.

Whether they know it or not, nonvoters could have played significant roles in past elections. For example, polls in 1980 showed that

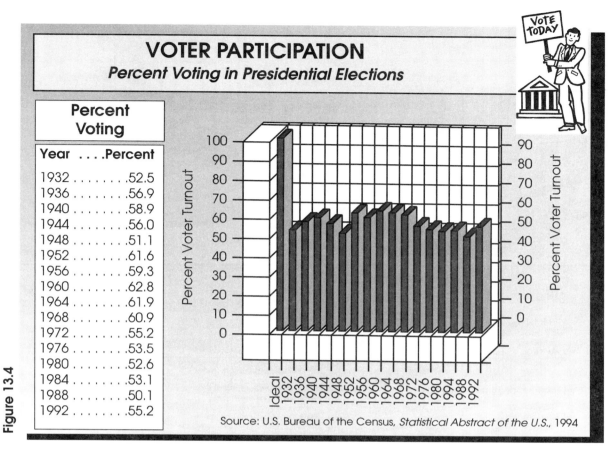

VOTER PARTICIPATION
Percent Voting in Presidential Elections

Percent Voting	
Year	**....Percent**
1932	.52.5
1936	.56.9
1940	.58.9
1944	.56.0
1948	.51.1
1952	.61.6
1956	.59.3
1960	.62.8
1964	.61.9
1968	.60.9
1972	.55.2
1976	.53.5
1980	.52.6
1984	.53.1
1988	.50.1
1992	.55.2

Figure 13.4

Source: U.S. Bureau of the Census, *Statistical Abstract of the U.S.,* 1994

voters favored Ronald Reagan 52 to 38 percent over Jimmy Carter, while nonvoters favored Carter 51 to 37 percent over Reagan. (Frances Fox Priven and Richard A. Cloward. *Why Americans Don't Vote.* New York: Pantheon Books. 1988, 5)

Getting people to participate is not easy, but it may be in everyone's best interest to get more people registered to vote. Nothing influences public office holders more than being held accountable to the voter. No matter what they say, their end objective, before all others, is to be reelected. To be heard, the voter must find a place at the table of public opinion that reminds the politicians, clearly and definitely, who "butters their bread."

Historically, there have been numerous barriers to voter participation. In 1965, the *Voting Rights Act* eliminated a great many obstacles, but a number still exist. One myth which acts as a barrier is that people believe registration results in being called to jury duty. Many people believe that voter rolls are the only source of names for jury duty. That is not true. Driver license lists, telephone books, subscription lists, and other sources are used in addition to voter registration lists.

There are some reasonable reforms that can be made in order to enhance the democratic process of voter participation:

• Allow people to register to vote on election day. Three states currently allow their citizens to register at the polls on election day (Maine, Minnesota, and Wisconsin). North Dakota does not require registration at all. All of these states claim a higher percentage of voter participation than the rest of the country. To avoid any attempt at fraud, the voters that register on election day can use a special ballot known as a "challenged ballot" which requires verification of information before it is counted.

• About half of the states allow mail-in voter registration which certainly makes the process a great deal easier to accomplish. The printing and distribution costs of the forms can be paid by state budget funds or could be sponsored by a partnership with private organizations, service organizations, and volunteers.

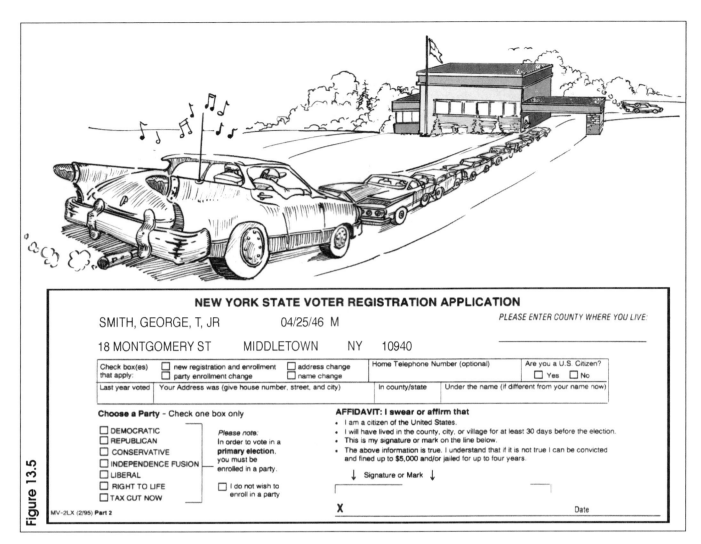

NEW YORK STATE VOTER REGISTRATION APPLICATION

SMITH, GEORGE, T, JR   04/25/46 M   PLEASE ENTER COUNTY WHERE YOU LIVE:

18 MONTGOMERY ST   MIDDLETOWN   NY   10940

Check box(es) that apply:	☐ new registration and enrollment ☐ party enrollment change	☐ address change ☐ name change	Home Telephone Number (optional)	Are you a U.S. Citizen? ☐ Yes ☐ No
Last year voted	Your Address was (give house number, street, and city)		In county/state	Under the name (if different from your name now)

Choose a Party - Check one box only

☐ DEMOCRATIC
☐ REPUBLICAN
☐ CONSERVATIVE
☐ INDEPENDENCE FUSION
☐ LIBERAL
☐ RIGHT TO LIFE
☐ TAX CUT NOW

Please note:
In order to vote in a **primary election**, you must be enrolled in a party.

☐ I do not wish to enroll in a party

AFFIDAVIT: I swear or affirm that
- I am a citizen of the United States.
- I will have lived in the county, city, or village for at least 30 days before the election.
- This is my signature or mark on the line below.
- The above information is true. I understand that if it is not true I can be convicted and fined up to $5,000 and/or jailed for up to four years.

↓ Signature or Mark ↓

X _____   Date _____

MV-2LX (2/95) **Part 2**

Figure 13.5

- Congress passed a "motor-voter law" in 1994 so that registration can take place when drivers' licenses are applied for or renewed, but not all states have implemented the system. There are 20 states that make voter registration forms available at the Department of Motor Vehicles. It allows easy access and collection. It has been shown that people respond much more positively when they are asked directly, "Would you like to register to vote today?" (Katherine Isaac. *Civics For Democracy*. Washington, D.C.: Essential Books. 1992, 229-230) (See Figures 13.5 and 13.6.)

Throughout U.S. history, citizens have created new parties to introduce new perspectives. In 1828, workers rebelling against the inequalities of industrialization began to form political parties outside of the two major parties. Their platform was a wide variety of reforms that would give the workers greater access to public life, including the vote for all adults, free public education, civil service reform, more equitable taxation, better working conditions, a shorter workday, and an end to child labor. These were people that were basically against the tyranny of the machine and rallied around the cry for free land. The Workingman's Party spread throughout the Northeast and ran their own candidates in many elections, with some success. They published newspapers, books, and pamphlets. During the 1830s, the major parties incorporated some of their positions. Though the Workingman's Party could not compete with the Democratic and Whig Parties, it did have an influence on political philosophy and did help the development of organized labor in this country (Isaac, 56).

In U.S. history, the formation of new political parties produced some effects on government. Between World Wars I and II, the Farmer Labor Party began in North Dakota. The Non Partisan League (begun by Socialists) also was

New York State Department of Motor Vehicles
DRIVER LICENSE RENEWAL APPLICATION

IT'S TIME TO RENEW YOUR DRIVER LICENSE. YOUR CURRENT LICENSE WILL EXPIRE   APRIL 25, 1995

You can renew your license at any Motor Vehicles office. Please read the instructions on the back of Part 1 before you complete the Driver License Renewal Application (Part 3).

For your convenience, you can also register to vote with the Board of Elections by completing the Voter Registration Application (Part 2). Please read the information below before you complete the Voter Registration Section.

RENEWAL

SMITH, GEORGE, T, JR
18 MONTGOMERY ST
MIDDLETOWN   NY   10940

If you decline to register, your decision will remain confidential. If you register to vote, all information you provide on the Voter Registration Application will also remain confidential and be sent directly to the Board of Elections for voter registration purposes only. You will be notified by your County Board of Elections when your voter registration application has been accepted.

MV-2LX (2/95) Part 1

NEW YORK STATE VOTER REGISTRATION APPLICATION INFORMATION
(Please read before you complete application on back)

You Can Use This Form To:

- . register to vote in New York State
- change your name and/or address, if there is a change since you voted
- enroll in a political party or change your enrollment

Información en español: si le interesa obtener este formulario en español, llame 1-800-367-8683

中文資料：如果你有興趣索取本中文資料
表格 請電 1 - 800 - 367-8683

To Register You Must:

- be a U.S. Citizen
- be 18 years old by December 31 of the year in which you file this form *(note: you must be 18 years old by the date of the general, primary or other election in which you want to vote.)*
- live at your present address at least 30 days before an election
- not be in jail or on parole for a felony conviction
- not claim the right to vote elsewhere

If you need help in filling out the voter registration application form, you should call your County Board of Elections or call 1-800-FOR-VOTE.

If you believe that someone has interfered with your right to register or decline to register to vote, your right to privacy in deciding whether to register or in applying to register to vote, or your right to choose your own political party or other political preference, you may file a complaint with the NYS Board of Elections, 6 Empire State Plaza, Suite 201, Albany NY 12223-1650, Phone 1-800-469-6872.

If you have any questions about registering to vote, you should call your County Board of Elections or call 1-800-FOR-VOTE. Hearing impaired people with TDD may call 1-800-533-8683. If you live in New York City, you should call 1-800-VOTE-NYC.

MV-2LX (2/95) Part 2

DRIVER LICENSE RENEWAL APPLICATION

If you are not registered to vote where you live now, would you like to apply to register?
NOTE: IF YOU DO NOT CHECK EITHER BOX, YOU WILL BE CONSIDERED TO HAVE DECIDED NOT TO REGISTER TO VOTE AT THIS TIME.

☐ YES - Complete Voter Application on Other Side
☐ NO Decline to Register/Already Registered

EYE TEST REQUIRED

CHANGE OF ADDRESS

_____
(ADDRESS WHERE YOU GET YOUR MAIL)   (COUNTY)

_____
(ADDRESS WHERE YOU LIVE-IF DIFFERENT FROM MAILING ADDRESS)   (COUNTY)

CLIENT ID:

138746627 0105040471777

NEED IMAGE

SMITH, GEORGE, T, JR
18 MONTGOMERY ST
MIDDLETOWN   NY   10940

Figure 13.6

MV-2LX (2/95) Part 3

PAY THIS FEE: $22.25

---

begun in North Dakota. Both spread to other states. Not many third parties have gained national attention, but they have made a difference in the lives of many people on local and even state levels. They serve an important function in a democracy by bringing vital issues to the attention of voters. It takes some people that care and some good organizational skills to get a third party started and a candidate on the ballot (Isaac, 67).

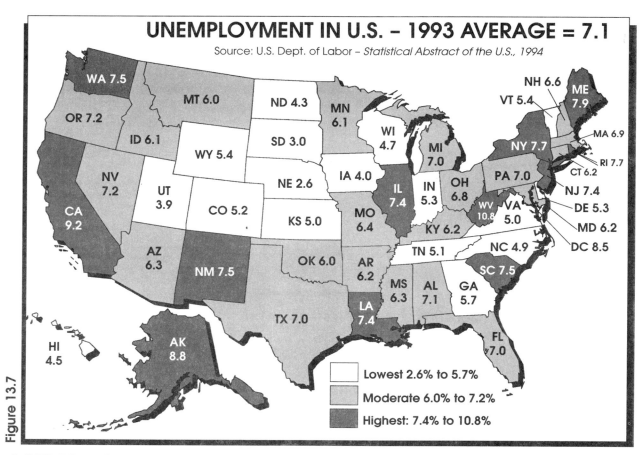

UNEMPLOYMENT IN U.S. – 1993 AVERAGE = 7.1

Source: U.S. Dept. of Labor – *Statistical Abstract of the U.S., 1994*

Figure 13.7

WA 7.5, OR 7.2, MT 6.0, ND 4.3, MN 6.1, NH 6.6, VT 5.4, ME 7.9, ID 6.1, SD 3.0, WI 4.7, MI 7.0, NY 7.7, MA 6.9, WY 5.4, IA 4.0, RI 7.7, NV 7.2, UT 3.9, NE 2.6, IN 5.3, OH 6.8, PA 7.0, CT 6.2, IL 7.4, NJ 7.4, CA 9.2, CO 5.2, KS 5.0, MO 6.4, WV 10.8, VA 5.0, DE 5.3, AZ 6.3, KY 6.2, MD 6.2, NM 7.5, OK 6.0, AR 6.2, TN 5.1, NC 4.9, DC 8.5, MS 6.3, AL 7.1, GA 5.7, SC 7.5, LA 7.4, TX 7.0, FL 7.0, HI 4.5, AK 8.8

Lowest 2.6% to 5.7%
Moderate 6.0% to 7.2%
Highest: 7.4% to 10.8%

ACTIVISM ON THE LOCAL LEVEL

Beyond political parties, people can organize for economic causes in other ways. Large sections of the nation were already struggling with unemployment when IBM downsized its worldwide workforce in 1993-1995 (see Figure 13.7 map). There was a possibility that the large corporation would completely close its many facilities in New York's Hudson Valley Region. That loss of jobs and residents would impact local communities in a serious way. An exodus of ex-IBM employees from the region would damage local businesses and could mean the loss of thousands of non-IBM jobs along with reduced tax revenues in local communities.

Realizing the importance of the issue, remaining employees worked with county legislatures and state officials to do what they could to keep "Big Blue" right where it was. It worked. Due to the efforts of local businesses and residents, chambers of commerce, town and county Economic Development Committees, town boards, as well as the governor and the state legislature, a deal was worked out.

In addition, these efforts drew new opera-

tions into portions of plants vacated by the computer giant. The state also negotiated a deal to consolidate (and downsize) its dispersed data operations in some of the sites. On the morning of 17 February 1995, headlines in the daily papers of the Hudson Valley read, "4,500 Jobs to Region: State Taking IBM Kingston, East Fishkill Space. Deal Adds $175M to Economy." (Jacqueline Sergeant and Michelle Leder *Poughkeepsie Journal* 17 February 1995, 1)

In *The Quickening of America*, Lappé and Dubois note an even larger effort was launched in Connecticut during the 1980s. As industries began to close and leave the Naugatuck Valley, the people that lived in the communities began to ask the key question that led them to action, "What can we do?" Ken Galdston, a citizen organizer, was able to get diverse groups throughout the community to organize. The result was the Naugatuck Valley Project. This civic coalition drew a membership from 68 different groups (churches, businesses, unions, different community groups, etc.).

"What we are all about is developing leaders who take control of their lives," said Project Director Susan Wefald (Lappé and Dubois 102). By

Figure 13.8 Special interest groups such as the National Rifle Association exercise great lobbying power because they have large memberships with strong convictions and the motivation to work hard for their goals.

leaders, Wefald meant "regular people who were encouraged to discover their power" (Lappé and Dubois, 103). The project responded to its members' concerns – medical care, affordable housing, or it helped with the maintenance of their own health care facility. These people made things happen. They didn't just talk – they saved jobs, provided housing, food, and health care. They helped each other take care of what other people just talk about (Lappé and Dubois 103).

ORGANIZING TO INFLUENCE POLICIES

People often join organizations that can represent their concerns on the national level. Examples include groups such as the AARP (American Association of Retired Persons), MADD (Mothers Against Drunk Driving), NOW (National Organization of Women), and the NRA (National Rifle Association) (see Figure 13.8). Two organizations have gained significant notoriety in recent times through their influence on economic policies. One is "Common Cause," a national citizen lobby devoted to making government at the national and state levels more open and accountable to citizens. The other is the "Concord Coalition," an organization committed to the reduction of government spending and the national debt. Both have national, state, and regional branches.

Such organizations work for their membership's interests and are receptive to member input. The stronger the "grassroots" organization created "at home," the more the decision-makers above will listen. Local vigor leads to leverage at every level, all the way to the national offices. National politicians are often more open to listen to representatives of groups they know have large, active memberships in their home states and districts.

Once citizens understand that taking an active stand on public issues can affect their lives, the phone calls, letters, meetings, public addresses, use of the media, research, lobbying, legal action, and fundraising can get results. While those tasks are often onerous, they become easier when done with a number of other like-minded people.

Pamphlets, newsletters, leaflets, flyers, and bulletin boards are all important resources to spread a group's ideas and positions on public issues (see Figure 13.9 on the next page). Computers and desktop publication processes have enhanced the production of such items, making them easier to produce and distribute. The computer also provides the reformer with on-line bulletin boards that are read by many people without the cost and handling of printed materials. The "information highway" also offers an unlimited source of information and research that aids in the efforts of any participatory group.

Once information is gathered, organized, and prioritized, organizations sometimes act as clearing houses. They become a link between individuals and groups with common interests and concerns. They require a dedicated staff of volunteers perpetually updating and disseminating information.

Figure 13.9

Another aspect of participatory organizations' activities is the creation of speakers bureaus. This calls for assembling people willing and able to give presentations on specific topics. These individuals must be flexible to create different presentations for the varied audiences that they will be asked to address. While the speakers themselves must have special public speaking talents, volunteer staffs must support them through research, surveys, and reports. The American Bar Association has a program that provides attorneys to go into classrooms. The project is known as "Lawyer in the Classroom." This is a speakers bureau that helps students understand legal matters and problems. Most local bar associations conduct public service talks at local sites on many topics – consumer law is a frequent topic.

ORGANIZING
FOR DIRECT ACTION

Beyond phone calls, disseminating informa-

tion, and letter writing, groups also engage in direct action. **Direct action** occurs when people use a method of confrontation against a target. It depends on large numbers of people acting in unison to place pressure on opponents. The most commonly known direct action technique is a boycott. A **boycott** is a refusal by consumers to purchase a good or service in order to apply economic pressure to achieve change. The 1956 Montgomery, Alabama Boycott of public transportation is one of the more famous instances of direct action. Rosa Parks refused to give up her seat and move to the back of the bus according to segregation laws. Parks' arrest triggered a movement by church leaders that led to a year-long boycott of the city's bus system. It ended in the abolition of segregated seating on the transportation system.

Such actions may be as simple as individuals joining refusals to purchase products or as encompassing as a worldwide effort of protest. In the 1970s and 1980s, international human rights groups opposing Apartheid pressured shareholders of multinational corporations to get the businesses to drop investments in the Republic of South Africa. Such economic pressures eventually contributed to the release from prison of Nelson Mandela, the new constitution, all-race elections, and an end to Apartheid.

An event that showed how a boycott can raise public concern was the Exxon oil spill in Alaska. In 1989, the tanker *Exxon Valdez* spilled eleven million gallons of crude oil in pristine Prince William Sound. The result was televised all over the world. Within hours, people were reacting. Attention was sharply focused on this corporation. Executives at Exxon got busy organizing a public opinion campaign. They knew that there was very little that they could do to correct the tragedy, but they knew that they had to begin to rebuild a positive image for the company.

Their efforts did not dissuade thousands of people who spontaneously began to boycott Exxon products to protest the company's actions surrounding the spill. Tens of thousands of past customers sent their credit cards back to Exxon. Such a reaction by so many customers undoubtedly made a lasting impression at company headquarters.

The efforts by people to stop the use of animal experimentation in the cosmetic industry was also an example of direct action. The attention brought to the inhumane treatment of test animals caused a public uproar that cost many companies millions of dollars in business and millions more in advertising costs in an attempt to "clear their name." Many people still maintain their refusal to purchase the cosmetic products of certain manufacturers because they want to stop a brutal practice.

Though sometimes controversial, the direct actions of animal activists brought about a decline in the popularity of animal fur coats. Many people have had their awareness heightened to the point where they have boycotted fur clothing and become activists themselves attempting to get other people to find garment alternatives to animal pelt attire.

THE INFLUENCE OF LOBBIES

Most major organizations engage in **lobbying** – formal attempts to influence the votes of public officials on issues of concern. Group members are usually well aware of their organization's lobbying efforts. The group's methods of lobbying a decision-maker are basically the same. At the center of any lobby effort is the number of potential voters. The public officeholder responsible for policy is usually concerned with what their constituency sees as the right way to go because they want to be reelected. Board of Education members, local village, town, or city council members, or state or federal legislators can be influenced by the opinions of large numbers of voters. The more organized the voters are, the more powerful their voices.

Most major groups employ professional lobbyists who maintain direct links with influential people – committee chairs, long-time

Political Action Committees (PACs) 1991-1992

Figure 13.10 Source: *Statistical Abstract of the U.S., 1994*

Type	Number of Organizations	Disbursements (in millions)
Corporate	1,715	$68.4
Labor Unions	338	$41.4
Professional	767	$53.9
Independent Associations	1,011	$18.3
Cooperatives	55	$ 3.0
Small Business	139	$ 4.0

incumbents, or office candidates. Through organizations' PACs (Political Action Committees), lobbyists funnel money to help candidates friendly to the group's interest get elected and reelected (see Figure 13.10).

Lobbyists engage such individuals in dialogue because they routinely make public statements and promises that can be used. Some public office holders are particularly sympathetic (or antagonistic) toward a certain interest. Professional lobbyists are paid to know who the most influential people are and go after them.

Professional lobbyists sometimes write bills themselves and supply them to legislators for sponsorship. Professional lobbyists in Washington, DC and state capitals are usually lawyers. Their assistants are often law school students because they are in positions to research and observe examples of model legislation. On the local level, most states require counties to maintain a law library (usually at the site of the county court house) where researchers can get help and easily gain access to law books for research.

Professional lobbyists and the organization's officers and directors monitor the bills from the offices of legislative sponsors through committee and legislative hearings. They continuously apply pressure and support. They recruit experts and make arrangements for experts to testify at every hearing level. Lobbyists also provide committee staffers with written copies of testimonies supporting the group's position on the bill.

Persuasion is continuous and unrelenting. Lobbyists use the local news channels to involve the media. Often, they turn to the group's members to write letters to newspapers to get reporters to examine what is being done.

Professional lobbyists contact government representatives and gain knowledge of any legislation, proposed legislation, committee reports, and lists of agencies and personnel that pertain to a particular issue they want addressed. ©PhotoDisc

fully planned and supervised. Such a public tactic must have maximum participation to be effective. Legal permits must be obtained and details worked out before any announcement is made of the march, picketing, or demonstration. Such tactics are often only effective on a local basis, while marches on Washington and state capitals are usually used only for momentous causes.

Lobbyists must work on the executive branch, too. If proposed legislation is passed, an executive veto may end it all. Even after full passage, a number of things may go wrong. Lobbyists must monitor the implementation of the law. Monies may be cut, or the agency chosen to enforce the new law may be ineffective. Lobbyists have to continually monitor the laws and the programs that operate under them.

USING LEGAL AND CONSTITUTIONAL ROUTES

Besides the legislative path, citizen groups may have to use the courts to win a victory, have a law enforced, or obtain damages for an action that has caused harm. Except for small claims courts, an attorney is always necessary when using the court system to obtain the enforcement of the law, to get a restraining order, or to win financial rewards for harm done.

Members are mobilized to write supportive letters to editors, call in to talk radio shows, send petitions and letters directly to legislators, and make financial contributions to the lobbying efforts (see Figure 13.8).

Often, lobbyists ask the organization's leaders to have members conduct "grassroots campaigns." Members are asked to act locally to marshal support for the legislation they want. Through the organization's newsletter or a special mailing, members are asked to contact other groups throughout the neighborhood, region, and state to create a constant bombardment from all over.

A less frequently used tactic is sponsorship of some kind of demonstration or protest. These mass movements are difficult and expensive to arrange and stage. Such activities must be care-

In large "class action" suits, the plaintiffs must have "established standing." That is, to sue, attorneys must establish a "sufficient interest" and show that there is a "direct effect on the plaintiff" caused by the problem. A time limit is also established in which a case must be brought. If action is not taken in a specified amount of time, a suit may not be brought against the person, group, agency, or government. In bringing a lawsuit, there are three important considerations. It will

- take a great deal of time.

- cost a great deal of money.

- cause more aggravation than most people can take.

Most lobbies and interest groups retain attorneys, but if a group has a good case (a winnable one), a lawyer will usually take on such an action for a contingency fee – accepting payment based on a percentage of a victorious award. The lawyer's fee is generally one third of the judgment or settlement plus whatever expenses have been incurred (which may amount to as much as 50% of the award). If the attorney is willing to work on the case for the contingency fee, a group can be pretty sure that they can win at trial.

Some states allow citizen action groups to bypass the state legislature in order to get a law passed using **initiative** and **referendum** procedures. Of particular renown is California where every so often a proposition is placed on the ballot for the people to approve or disapprove a specific new law. Individuals or groups convinced that their representatives will not generate a law initiate such processes. They work to place a specific law on the ballot for the people to decide. A majority of the states allow a public vote on laws placed on the ballot. Information on types of petition, format of petition, number of required signatures, proper registration of the documents, etc. must be given to citizens. Once this massive effort is concluded, it will be up to the state voters to make decisions through the ballot box.

THE NEW REALITIES: A MATTER OF COURAGE AND CHANGE

Young Americans must keep in mind that a great many of the benefits that they enjoy today were not available in the past. People who cared about reform fought for them and won. Women were not always able to vote, there was not always a forty-hour work week with overtime, or a minimum wage. Eighteen-year-olds were not always able to vote, and a workmen's compensation law or civil rights legislation did not always exist. The world is filled with people launching initiatives and rethinking traditions to make it a better place for everyone. To achieve the Dream, young people must get involved, care, and work hard for what they believe. It is their world, and their children's and grandchildren's world, that they must make into a better place.

SUMMARY

The American Dream remains a viable achievement for the American people. By understanding that there are new and different methods of succeeding in the quest, we accept the challenge of a new economy that has changed from what it once was.

Citizen participation is the key that will allow the Dream to endure. There is no easy way to achieve a place in the economy without accepting the role of a knowledgeable, proactive citizen. It is a necessary part of taking control of economic life. An understanding that all citizens are shareholders in the maintenance and well being of this country's economy will enable them to organize themselves as problem solvers. As individuals and members of groups citizens must learn and understand the new rules of life in order to succeed and fulfill dreams.

Through future expectations may be different than they were in the past, and financial security may be a bit more fleeting than it was for the last generation, adaptation, change, courage, and education will allow for the attainment of the American Dream.

ASSESSMENT
QUESTIONS • APPLICATIONS

1   This chapter begins with a dialogue between Jack Neyland and his grandfather about joining groups.
   a   Do you agree with Gramps' advice? Explain why or why not.
   b   Find out if any student you know is in a union at work. See if she/he thinks the dues are worthwhile. Why or why not?
   c   Find out if any adults you know are in a union or group that does lobbying. See if they think the dues are worthwhile. Why or why not?

2   In the 1990s, corporate reorganization and downsizing caused a rethinking of ownership and business organization in America.
   a   Explain the effect that downsizing has had on equilibrium wages.
   b   What is employee empowerment? How is it changing America's workplaces?
   c   Use library sources to write a brief report on how employee ownership of a corporation works (e.g., Kiwi, Avis).

3   Participatory democracy revolves around proactive citizenship.
   a   What steps can individuals take to make government more accountable?
   b   How have states sought to broaden voter participation?
   c   How can active participation in special interest groups influence the economic life of the society?

4   Corporate reorganization and downsizing caused many communities to revitalize participatory democracy.
   a   Why is the downsizing of a major corporation a cause for community or regional concern?
   b   How have communities sought to deal with corporate downsizing?
   c   What is a business incubator? How does it work? Find out if there is such a facility in your region, see if you can get any information on it and share it in a brief oral report.

5   From local newspapers, select an economic issue and observe the behavior of interest groups on both sides. In a brief report:
   a   Define the issue and give its backgrounds.
   b   Outline the positions of key groups on both sides of the issue.
   c   Describe the tactics used by interest grou   to make their position known. (This may involve contacting and interviewing leaders of groups.)
   d   Based on your experience or observations, identify which groups you feel are most effective in influencing the situation. For each group, explain your reason for selecting that group and give two or three examples to support the groups effectiveness.

ASSESSMENT
PROJECT:
ECONOMIC INTEREST GROUPS

STUDENT TASK

Research, plan, and execute a group presentation on the activities and influence of PACs and special interest groups on economic policies.

PROCEDURES

1 Research Special Interest Groups.

 a With your instructor's guidance, construct a letter and send it to three or more private economic interest groups or PACs of your choice, asking about their activities to influence public policies. (You could write to some of the groups in the Appendices.) Realize that it may take 4-6 weeks for a reply. Making both phone and Fax follow-ups may be useful.

 b Go to the library and research the roles of special interest groups in books, periodicals, or the Internet (if your library has computer access). Obtain background information on special interest groups for your report.

 c Interview a local person who is a member of a special interest group (someone you know or obtain a name through a local newspaper or politician's office). Ask the person for general information about her/his special interest group, how it functions, what its main goals are, and in their opinion, what successes or failures has her/his special interest group experienced.

2 In a cooperative study group, summarize your notes from the library research and replies from the groups contacted.

3 Within your group, try to reach a consensus* about the behavior of interest groups and PACs. Then formulate and deliver a class presentation of your cooperative study group's ideas. (*If your class group cannot reach a consensus, the class presentation could be framed as a debate – majority and minority positions.)

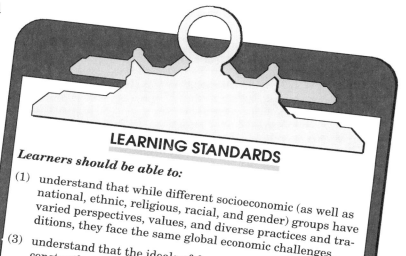

LEARNING STANDARDS

Learners should be able to:

(1) understand that while different socioeconomic (as well as national, ethnic, religious, racial, and gender) groups have varied perspectives, values, and diverse practices and traditions, they face the same global economic challenges.

(3) understand that the ideals of democracy and human rights constantly evolve in the light of global economic realities.

(4) understand that civic values and socially responsible behavior are required of members of school groups, local, state, national, and global communities.

(5) analyze problems and evaluate decisions about the economic effects on society and the individual caused by human, technological, and natural activities.

(6) present their ideas both in writing and orally in clear, concise, and properly accepted fashion.

(7) employ a variety of information from written, graphic, and multimedia sources.

(8) monitor, reflect upon, and improve their own and others' work.

(9) work cooperatively and show respect for the rights of others to think, act, and speak differently from themselves within the context of democratic principles and social justice.

EVALUATION

The criteria for the evaluation of this project are itemized in the grid (rubric) that follows. Choice of appropriate category terms (values) is the decision of the instructor. Selection of terms such as "minimal," "satisfactory," and "distinguished" can vary with each assessment.

Economic Interest Groups Evaluation Rubric

(Refer to introductory section for suggestions of scoring descriptors for the evaluation categories.)

Evaluation Item	Category 1	Category 2	Category 3	Category 4	Category 5
Item a: (1) Does the work show understanding that while different socioeconomic (as well as national, ethnic, religious, racial, and gender) groups have varied perspectives, values, and diverse practices and traditions, they face the same global economic challenges?					
Item b: (3) Does the work show understanding that the ideals of democracy and human rights constantly evolve in the light of global economic realities?					
Item c: (4) Does the work show understanding that civic values and socially responsible behavior are required of members of school groups, local, state, national, and global communities?					
Item d: (5) Does the work analyze problems and evaluate decisions about the economic effects caused by human, technological, and natural activities?					
Item e: (6) Does the work present ideas in writing (and orally) in clear, concise, and properly accepted fashion?					
Item f: (7) Does the work employ a variety of information from written, graphic, and multimedia sources?					
Item g: (8) Does the work show monitoring of, reflection upon, and improvement of work?					
Item h: (9) Does the work show cooperative work and respect for the rights of others to think, act, and speak differently?					

ISSUE 14

Can the Dream survive?
21ST CENTURY CAREER DECISIONS

The viability of the American Dream lies in this generation's ability to assess and manage global competition, high technology, crippling government deficits, and a threatened environment. Understanding these realities and acting on that knowledge will determine the quality of the American Dream.

Aye, ...for the Dream

For The Dream... aye, the Dream
Set the rudder for the Dream
Things will be better than they seem
Pull your oars – Pull your oars for the Dream

Waves crashing on craggy shores
Hands grasping slippery oars
The powers of humankind arrayed
Impeding their journey toward the Dream

Boat launching from shifting sands
Gunwales sliding in unsure hands
The force of unknown seas arrayed
Hindering their journey toward the Dream

Darkness dimming compass blind
Parental light fading far behind
The weight of self-doubt arrayed
Obstructing their journey toward the Dream

Dead reckoning now invoked
Presenting an illusory hope
Invisible hand of Smith arrayed
Steering their journey toward the Dream

Vessel plunging toward a rainbow
Currents roaring as they row
Knowledge of the system arrayed
Guiding their course toward the Dream

ISSUE 14

Can the Dream survive?

21ST CENTURY CAREER DECISIONS

INTRODUCTION

The viability of the American Dream rests on this generation's ability to define the new economic context and adapt to it. Japan's industry, aided by its government and cooperation of unions, has led the world into an age of automation and robotic manufacturing. Firms in newly industrialized economies in Asia reinvest their profits in technological advancement. Their efficiency and output grow remarkably. Newly Emerging Economies (NIEs) believe in sacrificing some immediate return to accelerate future growth. Their governments also reshape their traditional education systems to a post-industrial climate. The spirit of this adaptability once moved America to the forefront of the global economy. That spirit must be recaptured.

DEFINING THE ECONOMIC CONTEXT

In a 1994 *U.S. News & World Report*, editor Mortimer Zuckerman said a new economic context has redefined life in America ("Who Does Feel Your Pain?" 26 Dec. 1994, 126). Zuckerman notes that recent surveys showed 57% of Americans are no longer optimistic about the future. He also states that blue collar jobs (base industry, assembly line, and factory jobs) are down from 40% of the labor force in the World War II days to 25%. Jobs today involve higher skills and greater education.

To some extent, Zuckerman feels that the current situation echoes what happened in the 19th century. At that time, the Industrial Revolution destroyed the careers of skilled craftsmen and shifted jobs from domestic service or farm to the factory floor. Although this shift was a change of workplace and life environment, the new jobs were not highly skilled ones.

However, Zuckerman points out that today's transition is more difficult. This skill shift is to "knowledge work" in 80% of the new jobs. School drop out rates and other social ills mean 40% of young men cannot earn enough to support a family of four. Zuckerman notes the inflation of the past generation also caused **real wages** (actual purchasing power) to fall 20% since 1973 for the bottom 60% of America's income levels (Zuckerman, 126).

Stability escapes today's workers, too. Today, most people can expect to change jobs or career tracks seven times. All this change, says

Graduation is an end and a beginning – a step to a successful career. ©PhotoDisc

Zuckerman, leaves Americans frustrated and yearning for leadership that provides a vision for a better life (Zuckerman, 126).

The Zuckerman scenario describes an economic context that shakes belief in the American Dream. Looking to political leadership to restore confidence is frustrating. American politicians do not talk of a new industrial policy, they pin their expectations on tax cuts and entrepreneurship. Some American companies resist investment in high technology by transferring their older, labor-intensive operations to less developed countries where labor is cheap. Some critics of NAFTA-style trade agreements point to this transfer as an "avoidance tactic." They say American companies use such tactics to sidestep reducing dividends and profits. Too often, they say, American companies neglect capital investment in research and development. Given such ingrained corporate behavior, reform will not come easily. Young Americans' best hope rests in astute planning of careers and learning how the economic climate can enhance or restrain opportunities.

CAREER PATHS

Thinking seriously about careers is probably more important in today's economy than it was a generation ago. Among young adults in high school, the traditional perception of the world of work is usually limited to part-time jobs to get spending money.

Health Care Workers – About one fourth of all RN's work part-time. Jobs are not expanding but demand to fill existing jobs is high. Therefore, employment of RN's is will grow faster than the national average (21%). In the 1990's, full-time RN's earned an average of $32,000. Shortages in cities pushed that average to over $37,000 annually. ©PhotoDisc

Woodworkers / Carpenters – New housing and commercial building demand should keep employment for carpenters at national average (21%) from the mid 1990's through 2005. Median salary (non-self-employed) is $412 weekly. ©PhotoDisc

When the term "career" arises, an entirely new mindset is needed. The new mental approach must begin with specific focus on career goals. **Career** means a whole-life work environment and may include many jobs and levels of responsibility. In American society, career means more than income-producing activity. It is a way of getting social equality, economic fulfillment, recognition, respect, and self-realization (success and happiness).

A first step in career planning involves asking what a young person wants from her/his work life. The answer is never simple. A number of career variables must be decided and prioritized. These variables include the importance to the individual of salary, challenge, responsibility, power, comradeship, security, opportunity, prestige, geographic location, helping others, fringe benefits, job title, hours, and

Engineer / Architects – Employment will improve through 2005, but number of college degrees will not keep pace. Demand for architects is dependent on local level of construction since the industry is very sensitive to business cycle. Median earnings are $36,000, but firm owners earnings often exceed $100,000 in good times. ©PhotoDisc

surveys usually suggest several suitable fields, or what the Labor Department calls "career clusters" – groups of related jobs in broad fields such as services, retail trade, finance, wholesale, transportation, government, construction, and others. Occupational counselors say it is better for an individual to see her/his strengths as useful in this cluster sense (broad fields) rather than a single, specific job. If a particular job does not work out, an awareness of related ones is important.

Career variables – values, interests, or specific desires – form in our minds in certain ways. The combination of variables is what causes people we know and love to walk down different paths in life that we may find unusual. People look at the variables differently and come to different conclusions. That is, if they ever consciously look at them at all. Many people drift through this process in a semiconscious state, never trying to focus on their goals.

Consciously sorting out the variables gives job seekers a better awareness of their priorities in life. This sorting process also makes job seekers more conscious of the tradeoffs they have to make. Seeking a career with challenges may mean years of costly education and financial sacrifice.

While it is important to understand personal ambitions and capabilities in deciding career choices, understanding the current and future

travel. Accurately assessing personal values, talents, abilities, and interests is crucial.

School Guidance Departments usually have survey tools to help with this analysis and prioritizing. According to Kenneth Tonkinson, a veteran counselor in the Wappingers Central Schools in upstate New York, "There are paper-and-pencil surveys such as *VIESA*, and computerized surveys that can help students focus on their interests. Surveys help in selecting students' critical next steps in education. Some schools administer these to all seniors, but most counselors have large student loads, and it is best for the individual student to request such surveys and then request a session with the counselor to analyze the results."

Such surveys at least identify strengths and get a person to look at her/his talents and values. The

Elementary Teachers – Employment of kindergarten and elementary school teachers is expected to grow about as fast as the average for all occupations from the mid-1990s to 2005. Average salary is $33,000. ©PhotoDisc

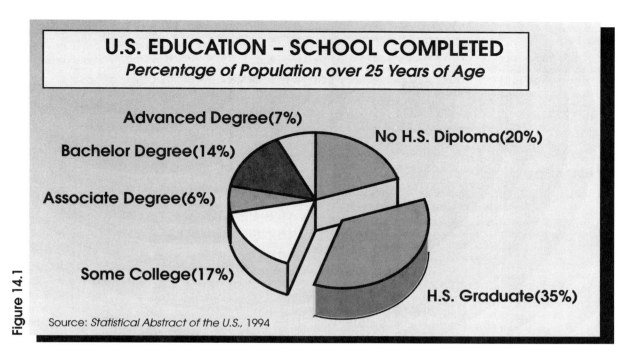

U.S. EDUCATION – SCHOOL COMPLETED
Percentage of Population over 25 Years of Age

Advanced Degree(7%)

Bachelor Degree(14%)

Associate Degree(6%)

No H.S. Diploma(20%)

Some College(17%)

H.S. Graduate(35%)

Source: *Statistical Abstract of the U.S.,* 1994

Figure 14.1

job market is also a key factor. Knowing where the economy is heading, what the growth fields are, along with what qualifications are needed in those fields can help a person make sound career choices.

Education is crucial in the quest for success and earning power. While it may seem that everyone goes to college these days, the Figure 14.1 pie graph (*Years of School Completed*) and the Figure 14.2 chart (*1990 Mean Annual Income By Highest Degree Earned*) indicate the percentage of individuals with higher degrees is still relatively low. This scarcity of higher degrees usually means the more highly educated can hope for higher wages.

Of course, there is wide discrepancy among holders of Bachelor's degrees. For example, the 1990 census indicated that the mean monthly salary for BA degrees in economics, engineering, math, and statistics was $2,300-$2,800, while for degrees in education, liberal arts, nursing, and English, was $1,100-$1,400. Still, the U.S. Department of Commerce indicates careers of the future will demand a much greater educational background. (On the next two pages, see Figure 14.3, *21st Century Fastest Growing Occupational Fields* chart and Figure 14.4, *Fastest Growing Occupations* 1992-2005 graph.)

Most of the growth fields of the future demand specific, formal education and special certifications. Yet, as the new career paths come

into view, job certification has added meaning. According to Columnist Dave L'Heureux, the U.S. Department of Labor funds studies by trade groups such as the American Electronics Association and the National Retail Federation ("Forging the Skills for the Future: New Standards Being Demanded for the Workplace." *Poughkeepsie Journal*, 27 March 1994, 1E). The article says these groups codify job skills, establish standard certificates for job entry, and set standards for performance evaluation and promotion (L'Heureux. 1-2E). These groups are upgrading the work environment in America to make the country more competitive with the rising economies of Asia and Europe. Their new performance standards transcend the traditional meaning of the term "job skills." This familiar term now includes more than just the physical handling of tools or the awareness of production processes (L'Heureux. 1E). The breadth of such skills includes abstract abilities to communicate, han-

Mean Annual Income – 1990
Highest Degree Earned Age 18 and Over
Source: U.S. Department of Commerce
Bureau of Census - *Current Population Reports,* 1993

Level of Degree	Mean Income
Not High School Graduate	$10,272
High School Graduate	$16,284
Some College, No Degree	$18,540
Vocational Degree	$18,816
Associate's Degree	$22,548
Bachelor's Degree	$29,868
Advanced Degree	$53,204

Figure 14.2

Field	Salary Range (rank)	Qualifications
Accounting	$27,000-$80,000 (09)	B.A. + certification
Architecture	$24,700-$60,000 (11)	B.A. + certification
Change Management Consulting	$46,000-$300,000 (04)	B.A. + experience
Computer-Operations Research Analyst	$30,000-$90,000 (07)	M.A.
Corporate Finance Attorney	$50,000-$130,000 (03)	J.D. (Dr. of Jurisprudence)
Corrections Officer	$16,000-$51,000 (18)	civil service
Early Childhood Education	$16,000-$32,000 (20)	license or B.A. + certification
Electrical Engineering	$33,000-$78,000 (06)	B.A. + field experience
Environmental Management	$30,000- $120,000 (08)	B.A. + M.B.A.
Financial Planner	$50,000-$80,000 (02)	B.A. + certification
Home Health Social Worker	$18,000-$59,000 (17)	M.S.W. + experience
Human Resources Technical Trainer	$37,000-$70,000 (05)	college + certification + experience
Information Services Developer	$20,000-$75,000 (15)	technical training + experience
Manufacturing Logistics and Supply Manager	$24,000-$200,000 (12)	college + experience
Medical Assistant	$16,000-$30,000 (19)	certification
Medical Scientist	$20,000-$77,000 (16)	Ph.D. + experience
Merchandise Planner-Distributor	$21,500-$75,000 (13)	field experience
Primary Care Physician	$75,000-$115,000 (01)	M.D.
Print Media Reporting Specialist (Computer-Assisted)	$21,000-$60,000 (14)	college + experience
Telecommunication Integration Specialist	$27,500-$150,000 (10)	B.A. + experience

dle conflict, set and meet quotas, work cooperatively, and interact creatively for company and product improvement (L'Heureux. 2E). The new standards and **trade proficiency certificates** that these groups generate will become an integral part of work life in the years to come.

CAREER PASSAGES

All careers advance through several key stages or passages. The initial stage involves part-time, seasonal, or occasional jobs. These work experiences can furnish more than expense money. They can provide some awareness of what employers seek in terms of attitude, motivation, and responsible behavior.

A second stage is experimental work. Usually, young people pursue full-time jobs in fields in which they think they have an interest. There is quite a bit of frustration, disillusion, and shifting employers before a certain degree of satisfaction and direction emerge.

A third stage is a steady work period within a field or with a particular firm that enables the worker to feel satisfied and productive.

Finally, there is retirement. It comes earlier for some than others, but to be tranquil and comfortable, it must be carefully planned and built throughout the steady work period with attention to pension plans, savings, individual retirement accounts, and long-term investment.

THE AMERICAN WORK ETHIC

As a career begins, some time should be spent thinking about a set of attitudes called the "American Work Ethic." It underlies both the entrepreneurial spirit and the relationship of employer and employee. The work ethic entails dedication to a job and a desire to perform required tasks to the best of one's ability. It is a view that every job is a contract between employer and employee.

Yet, the work ethic goes beyond mere competent service. The traditions of the American work ethic imply that a covenant exists between employer and employee. "Get a *real* job," people sometimes say. What they mean is a job that has a bond transcending the simple market transaction of payment for services rendered. The employer expects a certain loyalty and intensity from the employee to "do their duty." The employer feels employees should be on time, show effort, efficiency, initiative, and in word and deed act in a way that enhances the

Scientists / Chemists – Difficulty of achieving proper degrees will keep demand for chemists high and jobs growing at the average 21% through the year 2005. The American Chemical Society claims the median salary for members with a bachelor's degree is $39,000. ©PhotoDisc

business. In return for this effort and consistency, the employer provides a supportive environment in every way possible. In other words, an employee who merely "does the job and collects

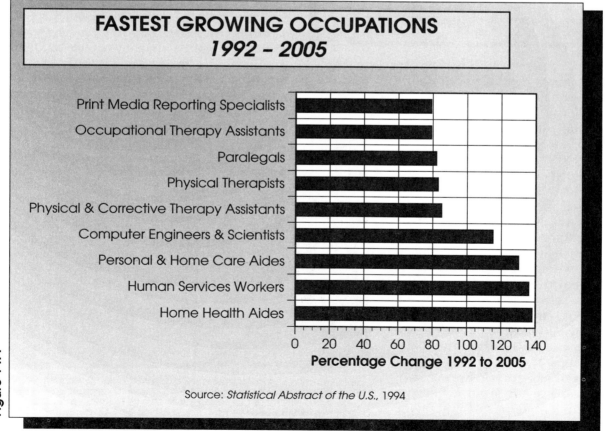

Figure 14.4

FASTEST GROWING OCCUPATIONS
1992 – 2005

- Print Media Reporting Specialists
- Occupational Therapy Assistants
- Paralegals
- Physical Therapists
- Physical & Corrective Therapy Assistants
- Computer Engineers & Scientists
- Personal & Home Care Aides
- Human Services Workers
- Home Health Aides

Percentage Change 1992 to 2005
(0 20 40 60 80 100 120 140)

Source: *Statistical Abstract of the U.S.*, 1994

Food Service / Chef – Employment in food services will grow at the national average (21%) through 2005, since this field usually reflects the general economic growth pattern. Chef salaries vary depending on the establishment and region of the country. Executive chefs in elegant restaurants and hotels earn over $40,000, but cooks average $25,000. ©PhotoDisc

"Each team of twelve to sixteen people is set up as a business, with their own purchasing, budgeting, and maintenance. The team leader is elected, not as a boss, but as a resource to give direction." (Lappé, 85)

The workplace is changing rapidly, and yet, "getting ahead" usually means immersing oneself in the work ethic. Of course, it does not mean employees should subject themselves to exploitation or harassment by an unscrupulous employer. Yet, showing enthusiasm and seeking opportunities for advancement are important qualities that should guide a worker during initial job search campaigns and throughout a career.

JOB SEARCH CAMPAIGN

The elements of a job search campaign include application letters, résumés, recommendations, and handling interviews.

RÉSUMÉS

In most cases, the job searcher's first contact with a prospective employer is most often through the mail. Experts agree that the résumé sent with a company application form or application letter is undoubtedly the most important career search document. Without it paving the way, a searcher rarely gets granted

a check" without much enthusiasm, lacks "professionalism" – and usually will not advance and earn the good paying promotions.

Some of the more successful employers realize that workers' job skills have to be actively developed to keep their companies competitive. In *The Quickening of America*, Frances Moore Lappé and Paul Martin Du Bois interviewed some of those employers (San Francisco, CA: Josey-Bass, 1994). Among them were Tandem Computers, Chapparal Steel, Xerox, and the 1990s great success story, GM's Saturn automobiles. These employers talked about a "change in the culture of work life" (Lappé, 85). Lappé and Du Bois quote Joe Caldwell of Saturn's Spring Hill, Tennessee plant about employees working in teams to put more brain power to work:

Cashiers – Employment of cashiers is expected to increase faster than average for all occupations through 2005, because of demand from population growth. Most openings come from transfers to higher paying jobs. Earnings range from minimum wage upward, $8,500 to $19,000 annually. ©PhotoDisc

an interview. New York State's *Guide to Preparing A Résumé* says a **résumé** is a catalog of what you have to offer a particular employer for a particular job" (*Guide*, 1). This forces the searcher to do what is taught in English class: consider the *task* and the *audience*.

- First, the searcher must ask what her/his résumé's task is. At base, the objective is to get the job, but the résumé is supposed to show *why* the searcher should get the job. The searcher must decide what "up-front things" he/she wants a particular employer to see. That is the task: *to say the most strategic things first*. This will alter the format, clarifying which basic parts come first.

- Second, the searcher must consider the audience. To *whom* is this message about the searcher being addressed? The small firm president may be a vastly different audience than the personnel manager of a national corporation. Background sheets on companies are available in school placement offices, business departments, and libraries. They can help a searcher see skills and qualities desired. If the résumé is done with a computer/word processor, it is easy to reshuffle the order of presentation for different audiences.

Firefighters / Police Officers – These "to serve and protect" jobs will increase at the average for occupational growth in the nation due to population increases. Competition for jobs is expected to be more intense due to municipal budget constraints. Non-supervisory firefighters earn an average of $25,000 annually and police officers slightly more, but city firefighters and police officers generally earn considerably more. ©PhotoDisc

Computer Systems Analyst – The job growth outlook for almost any computer technical speciality is far faster than the national occupational average growth and is projected past the year 2005. Demand will rise as firms seek electronic solutions to efficiency and cutting labor costs. The American Mathematical Society estimates computer analysts in private businesses average $49,000 annually with many more making greater consulting fees. ©PhotoDisc

Once on a disk, the résumé to can be taken to specialty shops to have it laser printed with distinctive fonts and other design features on impressive paper stock. Considering that the future is at stake, these steps are worth the time and small cost. Statistics say the average searcher will go through this process a number of times in a career. Having a résumé on a computer disk means the frequent rewriting, updating, and reforming will be easier.

New York State's *Guide to Preparing A Résumé* says résumés have four basic parts: Work History, Education, Personal Characteristics, and Resources (*Guide*, 1). However, Peggy Schmidt,

CHRONOLOGICAL RÉSUMÉ (PRESENTS WORK EXPERIENCE)

Maureen E. Stich
5 Macintosh Way
Appleton, New York 14566
(305) 118-3209

RETAIL EXPERIENCE:

Assistant Manager
The Disney Store, Poughkeepsie, New York 1993
*

Sales Associate
Filene's (formerly G. Fox Co.), Poughkeepsie, New York 1992
* merchandised and created place setting displays
* trained new sales associates
* opened and closed registers in the department

Sales Associate
The Concord Depot, Concord, Massachusetts 1992
* planned, designed, and created displays
* often top sales associate in department

Senior Associate
Hold Everything (Williams-Sonoma Inc.), Buffalo, New York 1990
* designed product display and grouping
* calculated and reported daily and monthly sales figures
* tracked product success/failure rate

OTHER EXPERIENCE:
Customer Service Clerk, *Poughkeepsie Journal*, Poughkeepsie, NY 1992
* solved customer delivery problems
* recorded and adjusted subscriber accounts
* merged records with U.S. Post Office for a geo-coding program
* trained in geo-coding for routing and target marketing

EDUCATION:
* Master of Science, Learning and Instruction, S.U.N.Y. at Buffalo, 1991
* Bachelor of Science, Elementary Education, S.U.N.Y. at Oneonta, 1987
* Associate in Applied Science, Retail Business Management, Dutchess Community College
  (in progress 1994)

REFERENCES:
Available upon request

Figure 14.5

author of *The 90 Minute Résumé*, points out the *way* you arrange the material can make big differences (Schmidt, 26). Schmidt says there are three basic résumé formats: Chronological, Analytical, and Functional. She notes that the traditional chronological résumé (Figure 14.5) – the most common kind – is a straightforward listing of jobs from the most recent to earliest, with other credits tacked on afterwards (Schmidt, 25).

Schmidt feels chronological résumés are often "lackluster and unclear about job descriptions" (Schmidt, 77). She prefers analytical and functional résumé. An analytical résumé (Figure

FUNCTIONAL RÉSUMÉ

(CALLS ATTENTION TO JOB SKILLS)

Andrew Glover
22 Carton Road
Barton, Iowa 41775
(481) 246-8246

Property Claims Examiner, Security Insurance Co., Des Plains, Iowa, 1990-Present

Awarded P.A.C.E. (Public Acknowledgment of Contributions to Excellence) Card for thoroughness in reviewing appraisals.

SKILLS:

Investigative: Liability investigation and application of surcharges according to state standards. Investigate automobile collision claims by gathering information from a variety of sources.

Evaluative: Apply standards of liability and comparative negligence. Respond to arbitration applications.

Informational: Explain difficult insurance laws, standards, etc. in simplified way to claimants and insureds. Maintain files and company subrogation interests.

Interpersonal: Negotiate settlements with insureds, claimants, attorneys, and other parties. Resolve problems with claimants, attorneys, and others. Pleasant phone personality, empathetic yet firm manner in negotiating settlements, able to maintain composure under pressure, enjoy the challenge of special assignments.

VARIED EXPERIENCE:

Associate Editor *The Enterprise*, Bristol, New Hampshire, 1988-1990
- Managed news coverage of 14-town region in Central New Hampshire for weekly newspaper.
- Promoted from reporter (hired 1988) to Area Editor for eight towns (1989) to Associate Editor (1990).
- Supervised staff of 6 freelance writers.

Census Enumerator U.S. Census Bureau, Lakes Region, New Hampshire, 1990
- Canvassed assigned region to interview residents and gather census information.

EDUCATION:

Bachelor of Arts, English (Emphasis in Writing, Minor in History)
- Hartwick College, Oneonta, New York
- John Christopher Hartwick Award — highest academic recognition given by college.

REFERENCES / RECOMMENDATIONS:
Available upon request

Figure 14.6

14.6) emphasizes what significant achievements you have had in your career (Schmidt, 30). A functional format (Figure 14.7) allows you to call attention to particular job skills (Schmidt, 28).

The simple fact about résumés for job searches is that there is no single format that satisfies all job search requirements. A résumé has to be tailored to the job being sought (*audience*). There are employment agencies and résumé specialists in most communities that will interview and listen to what a job searcher

feels is special in her/his background and help to custom design an effective job search and résumé. After all the time and effort a person puts into preparing for a career in a field, paying a fee for this critical service should not be considered a luxury.

A thoughtfully constructed résumé is the critical first element to presenting qualifications to a prospective employer. A good cover application letter is the second element (see Figure 14.8). It personalizes and paves the way for the

ANALYTICAL RÉSUMÉ (STRESSES KNOWLEDGE & ACCOMPLISHMENTS)

Andrew Glover
22 Carton Road
Barton, Iowa 41775
(481) 246-8246

ACHIEVEMENTS:
Awarded P.A.C.E. (Public Acknowledgment of Contributions to Excellence) Card for thoroughness in
    reviewing appraisals.
Achieved four Presidential Performance Citations for investigative and evaluative excellence.

CAPABILITIES:
Investigation of liability and automobile collision claims and application of surcharges according to
    state standards.
Evaluation of arbitration applications using standards of liability and comparative negligence.
Utilization of technical underwriting and editing process experience.
Interpretation of difficult insurance laws, standards, for claimants and insureds.
Negotiation of settlements with insureds, claimants, attorneys, and other parties.
Resolution of problems with claimants, attorneys, and others.

SKILLS:
Working knowledge of interrelational computer systems (Lotus 1-2-3, Filemaker, Quark, Microsoft
    Works).
Extensive proofreading skills.
Internet and Database research experience.
Maintain files and company subrogation interests.
Pleasant phone personality, empathetic yet firm manner in negotiating settlements, able to maintain
    composure under pressure, enjoy the challenge of special assignments.

EXPERIENCE:
Property Claims Examiner, Security Insurance Co., Des Plains, Iowa, 1990-Present

Associate Editor *The Enterprise*, Bristol, New Hampshire, 1988-1990
• Managed news coverage of 14-town region in Central New Hampshire for weekly newspaper.
• Promoted from reporter (hired 1988) to Area Editor for eight towns (1989) to Associate Editor
    (1990).
• Supervised staff of 6 freelance writers.

Census Enumerator U.S. Census Bureau, Lakes Region, New Hampshire, 1990
• Canvassed assigned region to interview residents and gather census information.

EDUCATION:
Bachelor of Arts, English (Emphasis in Writing, Minor in History)
• Hartwick College, Oneonta, New York
• Received John Christopher Hartwick Award — highest academic recognition given by college.

REFERENCES / RECOMMENDATIONS:
Available on request

Figure 14.7

résumé. It allows the job seeker to express her/himself beyond the concise, hard facts listed in a résumé. A well crafted letter, personalized to the prospective employer, can be the "edge" that gets the seeker an interview. This makes a separate letter of application a very strategic ingredient in the job search package.

The same rules apply as above: analyze the task and the audience. The task here is creating

Figure 14.8

SAMPLE COVER LETTER

22 Carton Road
Barton, IA 41775
27 February 1995

Michael Clemson
Personnel Director
Trend-Mark Productions, Inc.
1835 Alamo Concourse
San Antonio, TX 78265

Dear Mr. Clemson:

Dr. Philip Bronson of Hartwick College Placement Office drew my attention to your company brochure and an article about Trend-Mark in the January 13th issue of The *Wall Street Journal*. I was impressed by your stress on imagination and creativity. I believe I can be of use in such a dynamic environment.

My interest in the advertising field stems from my summer work in Bristol, NH on *The Enterprise* and marketing projects undertaken in my computer graphics course work here at Hartwick. The *WSJ* article indicated your staff's electronic inventiveness has been a key element in the company's success. My technical skills in this area are solid and should benefit Trend-Mark.

My résumé shows strong academic preparation, but my work experience in publication and market analysis points out skills and initiatives that give me a broad knowledge of media production.

I will be visiting San Antonio the week of April 10th and would like to arrange for an opportunity to meet with you. My phone number is (481) 246-8246. I look forward to hearing from you.

Yours truly,

Sign Your Name

Andrew Glover

Opening Paragraph:

Arouse interest but avoid being "theatrical" or overbearing.

2nd Paragraph:

State why you are interested in working there.

3rd Paragraph:

Point out your skills and special qualities in your résumé.

Last Paragraph:

Ask for an interview and include how to contact you.

---

an enticement. It should seize the employer's interest, saying why this particular application and résumé is worth considering. The audience changes with each company, so the letter has to be customized. Again, the advantage of customizing a base letter on a word processor is obvious. As with the résumé, common sense requires tailoring the letter to the specific job. A "blanket letter," with only the address and salutation changed, is simply not enough.

A job searcher should also take care with recommendations offered in the résumé or in follow-up inquiries from prospective employers. The searcher should choose people who are gen-

uinely interested in helping her/him and who have a good knowledge of her/his work and character. Employers and teachers are natural choices. Still, some searchers do not take the time to *ask* the people they use as references in their résumé. It is best to sit down with them, not just as a proper courtesy, but to discuss aspirations and objectives. The better they know the searcher, the more effectively they can write recommendations.

If the résumé, application letter, and recommendations garner the searcher an interview, careful thought and preparation are once again needed. Preparation involves several key steps.

Preparation for Interview

1 Assemble a portfolio of papers – a copy of the résumé, cover letter, and letters of recommendation (with phone numbers), an article, design, or some other example of work, licenses, military records, and a list of questions to ask – if given the opportunity.

2 Mentally prepare for the questions an interviewer will ask:
   - What are your strengths?
   - What are your career objectives?
   - Why do you want to work for that particular company?
   - What salary do you expect?
   - Are you willing to relocate?

3 Take some care about appearance at the interview.
   The searcher should:
   - make sure of the interview site and arrive a little early.
   - not take any friends or relatives for company.
   - dress conservatively – especially avoid appearing too casual.
   - act in a friendly, but businesslike manner.

GETTING AHEAD ON A CAREER TRACK

Once in a good job situation, a career takes active managing. A career worker has to be aware of what is going on beyond her/his workstation. Sensing movements within the company's management can present new opportunities for advancement. This is true of knowing industry-wide trends, too. Reading business magazines and trade journals is useful.

Understanding management styles is useful also. Some managers control all phases of production, while others create a team atmosphere, delegating authority and minimizing supervision. Working under the latter allows a person to show abilities and exhibit potential. Working with managers who themselves are seeking advancement has advantages – they often take on challenges which, when successfully met, reflect well on subordinates' evaluation/performance records. Working with a team-oriented manager not only means an exciting dynamic environment, but increases opportunities for cross-training. This is an excellent way to acquire and broaden skills by learning from others. It allows the individual to exhibit initiative. It also increases a worker's exposure to other executives as well as personnel from other related firms in an industry. All this may present alternative career options.

Career moves to other firms may beckon. When this occurs, it is best to control the situation. Sometimes circumstances merit quitting, but career counselors caution workers not to leave for emotional reasons. A job may be hard to bear for many reasons, but it is always better to take time and look for alternatives before quitting. Jobs within companies change, companies themselves change, as do industries, and of course, personal lives change. A career is often complicated by both on-the-job forces and external forces. Taking care of dependents often tempers decisions about career moves. Those obligations make workers consider

Team-oriented management, think-tanks, committee brainstorming, circles of quality, and shared problem solving represent the progressive new management-style. ©PhotoDisc

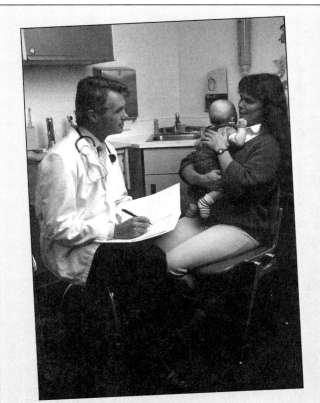

Physicians – An aging population will cause demand for physicians along with all health care professionals to grow at a faster rate than average. Annual salaries average about $155,000. ©PhotoDisc

edge given randomly to high school students. They answered only 42% of the questions correctly. There were particularly poor showings on questions on credit, checking and savings accounts, auto insurance, types of lenders, and contract obligations. While some of the findings can be attributed to inexperience in the market place, weak reading and math skills and lack of adequate consumer education also played a disturbing role in the results.

Improving personal financial literacy is to every individual's advantage. It seems unavoidable that everyone encounters a variety of misperceptions about finances. For instance, older people sometimes refer to financial "rules of thumb" such as "never trust a bank" that they followed when they were younger. Yet the old rules have a way of losing validity over time. New financial circumstances, trends, and tools can quickly make older ideas obsolete.

This is why basic consumer knowledge must be reevaluated as times change. Senior citizens who heard of relatives' banks collapsing and savings disappearing in the Great Depression may be very wary of banks all their lives. Yet, trying to manage without banking services is much more difficult than in the past. Paying bills in person, in cash, is very difficult in two-breadwinner commuter households. While making all purchases locally and in person is nostalgic, it is nearly impossible in a computer-

the broader ramifications of moving on, out, or up. As careers progress, it is normal for many factors to complicate decisions: relocations, benefits, lifestyle, cost-of-living, friendships, second jobs, security. Dealing with them is part of the career environment. Such factors can cause stress, disappointment, and make life unstable, but among them are also the challenges and rewards of working in the modern world.

PERSONAL FINANCIAL LITERACY

While pursuing a satisfying career is a component of the American Dream, achieving success also involves capable financial management to make life comfortable and enjoyable. In 1991, the Consumer Federation of America sponsored a nationwide test of consumer knowl-

Precision Assemblers (Production Occupations) – Assembly jobs will decline through the year 2005 due to automation and the relocation of assembly operations to countries where labor is less costly. With notable exceptions in the auto and brewing industries, most line-assemblers earn from $12,000 to $18,000 annually. ©PhotoDisc

Line Installers and Cable Splicers – Employment in this field will decline through the year 2005 due to technological efficiencies. For example, low maintenance fibre optic lines carry many more transmissions thus reducing the number of lines needed. Median weekly salary is $600. ©PhotoDisc

ized, broad-based, internationalized economic structure. Writing checks and sending them through the mail has become necessary for most households today.

GAINING FINANCIAL EXPERIENCE

Lack of experience also narrows young adults' perspectives on financial matters. While working part-time and getting spending money in high school, most students use cash (government currency) for their transactions. Because of this, students often find it hard to fully understand that most business and household transactions employ checkbook money. Issue 7 on money and banking made this point and examined its impact on the aggregate economy. Still, it is worth some attention here to see how students can approach the more complex levels of financial management needed after high school. Taking some steps now can make the transition to those levels easier. This groundwork provides the tools for successful, independent, financial management in the future.

The first step is opening joint checking and savings accounts at a bank or credit union with a parent. (At a point where young people are trying to break away from parental influence, this idea may seem confining, but it helps when the young person is away [at college or the armed forces] and needs money.) With joint accounts, a parent can conveniently transfer funds and make quick deposits for the young person. The parent does not have to write a check or mail or wire money, and the young person does not have to wait a long period to use the money. Within a day of the parent's deposit back home, the young person can write a check to pay for a purchase, cash a check, or withdraw from an ATM machine for spending money. Most college campuses have an office or facility where students can cash personal checks within certain limits. Most now have ATM machines, too.

Later, when the young person is striking out on her/his own, being aware of the costs of checking accounts (minimum balance and various fees) is important, but not at this initial stage in a joint situation with parents. In later situations, the young person must be aware that different banks have different rules on accounts, and the interest rates and methods of compounding and calculating interest differ. At that point, shopping around becomes wise.

The second step is not as critical as learning to use checking and savings accounts. This is getting an extension card on a parent's bank or travel credit card account. Although it can be very useful in emergencies, the use of a parent's credit can be a tender subject. In fact, many parents may not want to entertain this step (see the opening story in Issue 7). Most parents do not want to see the card used for routine purchases or impulse buying. Rules have to be set for its use. For example, a parent may only wish it to be used with pre-approval or in emergencies.

If a young person will be commuting or using a car on campus, another step is to arrange for an extension card on a parent's oil company charge card. (Depending on company rules the young person may even qualify for a separate card in her/his own name.) These cards can help keep track of gasoline expenses for budgeting. They can also be used for emergency service.

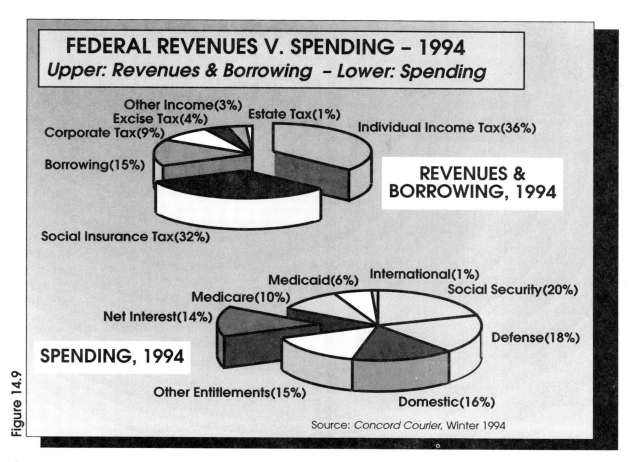

FEDERAL REVENUES V. SPENDING – 1994
Upper: Revenues & Borrowing – Lower: Spending

Other Income(3%)
Excise Tax(4%)
Corporate Tax(9%)
Estate Tax(1%)
Individual Income Tax(36%)
Borrowing(15%)

REVENUES & BORROWING, 1994

Social Insurance Tax(32%)

Medicaid(6%)
International(1%)
Medicare(10%)
Social Security(20%)
Net Interest(14%)
Defense(18%)

SPENDING, 1994

Other Entitlements(15%)
Domestic(16%)

Source: *Concord Courier,* Winter 1994

Figure 14.9

SUMMARY: RESURGENCE OF THE AMERICAN DREAM

Understanding career management and acquiring personal financial literacy are critical steps to achieving the American Dream. Yet the basic question remains: *Will this generation be able to achieve the Dream?* This book has presented the opinion that the answer lies inside the individual.

Each person plays many economic roles: worker, employer, consumer, saver-investor, interest group member, taxpayer, voter, civic participant. Knowing, probing, and redefining those roles not only shapes one's personal economic life but also contributes to entire social patterns. As Frances Moore Lappé and Paul Martin DuBois say in *The Quickening of America,* individual growth and learning can energize people and help overcome dread, alienation, and despair (Lappé, 26). Learning about economic roles is certainly a pathway to success in life.

Yet, there is no set pattern for success – America's pragmatism and diversity do not allow for it. Success stories are as diverse as are the American people. Even trying to prescribe an ideal model suppresses creativity. Diversity and flexibility are the life blood of America's advancement.

Still, Lappé and DuBois say it is easy to be discouraged. There are all too familiar barriers to advancement: racism, sexism, low wages, corporate dominated media, and ineffective institutions among them (Lappé, 298-299). Yet, the history of this country is the story of generation after generation overcoming barriers.

Should this generation see themselves any differently? Today's barriers to the Dream seem daunting. America's world status as the only superpower presents difficulties. Even with the Cold War over, defense spending saps some of its productivity (see Figure 14.9). In *Preparing for the Twenty-First Century,* Yale historian Paul Kennedy notes America is a "hard power" (military based) with global reach beyond anything the world has seen. He notes the sophistication of U.S. missiles and Stealth bombers plus the rapid deployment of U.S. and multinational troops in the Persian Gulf War are clear evidence of this power (Kennedy, 291).

Financial Manager/Executive – Employment for financial managers is expected to increase faster than the 21% national occupation average through the year 2005. Demand for managers has been spurred by need for efficiency in industry and expansion of international markets. Median annual salary is more than $36,000 plus bonuses in private industry. ©PhotoDisc

The post-Cold War period saw at least some reductions in military spending, but the U.S. defense industry remains a large and powerful **monopsony** (market with one customer, many suppliers). That industry absorbed many resources and created many jobs in the half century after World War II. As such, it is the only industry whereby the government has actually fashioned some sort of industrial policy (if one discounts the frequent and massive cost overruns the Department of Defense tolerates). Some economists propose the government could adapt the policies it established with defense to aid industry in general and press for high tech development.

Beyond defense spending, the gargantuan national debt may be the most important factor in deciding the economic future of the American Dream. Decades of Cold War military spending is only a portion of what created the national debt. In the past three decades, the government borrowed billions to fund the numerous **entitle-ment programs** (e.g., Medicaid, Social Security, Aid to Families with Dependent Children, veterans' programs, welfare). These entitlement programs made up 51% of federal spending in 1994 (see Figure 14.9).

There are groups dedicated to educating the people about the danger of the mounting debt and its implications for the future. According to one group, the Concord Coalition, Congress' current approach to the national debt will sap the wealth of coming generations. The Coalition's newsletter, *The Concord Courier*, projects that accumulated borrowing to offset annual deficits will push the national debt to $6 trillion before the year 2000 (Winter 1994, 2). In the same issue, *The Courier* says that the average family share of the debt equalled $71,496 (*The Courier*, 3).

The problem of paying off the debt is not just a matter of scarce resources. It is a political tug-of-war. Politicians know it is popular to keep taxes low. Yet, reducing taxes not only cuts the revenues needed to pay off the old debt, it also results in new borrowing and increasing annual deficits. Politicians continue to spend while trying to cut tax revenues. This is fiscal insanity. No individual or household could cut income so blatantly, while simultaneously borrowing to cover burgeoning expenses. Yet, that is what Congress and the Presidents have been doing for decades. Also, state and local governments follow a similar pattern of overspending. Incurring debt and not accumulating savings seems to be a contagious national malady.

One remedy during the 1990s was the **Balanced Budget Amendment** (BBA). This proposed Constitutional Amendment requires that the budget expenditures equal revenues to avoid new deficits and new borrowing. (An exception in the BBA allows borrowing and imbalances in wartime or other national emergency if approved by a full majority of the Congress.) Narrowly defeated in the U.S. Senate in early 1995, its proponents vowed to continue bringing the Balanced Budget Amendment to a vote until passage.

Yet, the BBA can only control future debt. The problem of reducing the current debt remains. Today, fourteen cents of every tax dollar goes to paying just the interest on the accumulated debt (see Figure 14.9). As any

Bye, bye Miss American pie,
Took my Chevy to the levy, but the levy was dry,
Got a gen-er-ation thinkin, "It can't be a lie,"
Singing, "We'll never let the Dream die."

seen in recent times.

Some courageous political leaders and economists who believe that reducing the debt and the scope of government will free millions of individuals and firms to follow their instincts for self-improvement and preservation. They believe this can restore vigor to the America economy.

Freeing people from the stifling nature of big government can certainly help. It sounds wonderful – so wonderful that Presidential candidates through all of U.S. history have advocated the reduction of big government. Each has found that the huge government bureaucracy is very difficult to reduce. The danger is believing it will work without reformulating government, schools, corporations, environmental responsibility, and even the family in America. Taking responsibility for helping to redefine and reformulate society's institutions is essential to the process of rebuilding the Dream, but it is also the hardest task facing the next generation of Americans.

One of most heartening things about all this is that there is no stronger tradition in U.S. history than the country's ability to adapt and change. The viability of the American Dream partially rests in whether society can make the right changes to its institutions at the right time. These changes will set the parameters of economic life. For the individual, the challenge is understanding, interpreting, and deciding what the changes mean.

householder knows, paying only the interest on a debt makes the debt perpetual. To relieve the problem, the principal has to be reduced. If we began to pay off the principal, the debt service figure would rise to more than fifty cents of every tax dollar. That would leave less than half the tax revenues to support federal government operations. Without substantial cuts in programs, the only way to support the government would be to double taxes. The country could not stand such a tax increase. Keeping taxes high while radically cutting government spending and applying the surplus to principal reduction seems to be the only answer. It is a painful solution and it would involve far more courageous political leadership than this country has

ASSESSMENT
QUESTIONS • APPLICATIONS

1   This chapter begins with a poem about the American Dream.
   a   Explain how and why you would classify it as optimistic or pessimistic.
   b   Explain how you would change certain lines to make it fit your view.
   c   What facts would you cite to justify your view of the viability of the Dream?

2   Understanding the American work ethic is critical to achieving the American Dream.
   a   What is the work ethic?
   b   Why is it so critical for someone launching a career to understand its significance?
   c   Why is the answer to relieving the national debt so difficult for political leaders to accept?
   d   How would devoting half the federal tax revenues to true reduction of the national debt affect the average American?

3   Attempts to rein in the debts of big government can help, but achieving the American Dream without redefining and reformulating society's institutions may be impossible.
   a   Explain how cutting the size and scope of government can help.
   b   Why is reformulating government, schools, corporations, environmental responsibility, and even the family also necessary?
   c   Research and explain how any one of the institutions mentioned in part b can be reformed to help the next generation reach the American Dream.

4   Handling interviews is an important career skill. In a small group, create a business firm. Identify its size and the work it does to the group. The firm is conducting a search for new workers.
   a   Decide the job designation and basic qualifications for the position.
   b   Pick one person to play the role of the firm's personnel manager conducting a job search. That person should prepare the questions to be used in the job interview.
   c   The remaining members of the group are job candidates. They should prepare application letters, résumés, and an interview portfolio.
   d   Stage the job interviews, one at a time, in front of the class. (Other candidates should not be present during a person's interview.) With the manager and candidates out of the room, the teacher should have the class vote on most acceptable applicant.
   e   Have the personnel manager and candidates return. They ask the manager explain his/her choice.
   f   Class discussion should be conducted afterwards with criticisms of the questions and answers including "incorrect" behavior by both the interviewer and searcher (e.g., bias of age, gender, race, religion), suggests for improvments, and recommendations for application of the lessons learned to the real-life job interview.

5   The proposed Balanced Budget Amendment (BBA) requires that federal budget expenditures equal revenues to avoid deficits. Yet, the BBA can only control future debt. The problem of reducing the current debt remains an obstacle to the American Dream.
   a   Why is the BBA only a partial answer to the problem of the national debt?
   b   What is the key to relieving the national debt problem?

ASSESSMENT
PROJECT: 14A
FINANCIAL MANAGEMENT

LEARNING STANDARDS

Learners should be able to:

(1) understand that while different socioeconomic (as well as national, ethnic, religious, racial, and gender) groups have varied perspectives, values, and diverse practices and traditions, they face the same global economic challenges.

(5) analyze problems and evaluate decisions about the economic effects on society and the individual caused by human, technological, and natural activities.

(6) present their ideas both in writing and orally in clear, concise, and properly accepted fashion.

(7) employ a variety of information from written, graphic, and multimedia sources.

(8) monitor, reflect upon, and improve their own and others' work.

(9) work cooperatively and show respect for the rights of others to think, act, and speak differently from themselves within the context of democratic principles and social justice.

STUDENT TASK

Write a report which unitizes, summarizes, and analyzes all of the projects completed under the Hypothetical Household Plan.

PROCEDURE

1   Make a list of the projects completed under the Hypothetical Household Plan and review their relationship to each other.

2   Develop an outline that takes the budget, financial statements, and related studies developed in your original hypothetical household plan (Issue 1) and traces its evolution over the course. Show where the original plan was modified and why.

3   Write a final documented report. In your conclusion, summarize the differences between the original and current material and state what you have learned about financial management.

EVALUATION

The criteria for the evaluation of this project are itemized in the grid (rubric) that follows. Choice of appropriate category terms (values) is the decision of the instructor. Selection of terms such as "minimal," "satisfactory," and "distinguished" can vary with each assessment.

Financial Management Evaluation Rubric
(Refer to introductory section for suggestions of scoring descriptors for the evaluation categories.)

Evaluation Item	Category 1	Category 2	Category 3	Category 4	Category 5
Item a: (1) Does the report show understanding that while different socioeconomic (as well as national, ethnic, religious, racial, and gender) groups have varied perspectives, values, and diverse practices and traditions, they face the same global economic challenges?					
Item b: (5) Does the report analyze problems and evaluate decisions about the economic effects caused by human, technological, and natural activities?					

Financial Management Evaluation Rubric continued

(Refer to introductory section for suggestions of scoring descriptors for the evaluation categories.)

Evaluation Item	Category 1	Category 2	Category 3	Category 4	Category 5
Item c: (6) Does the report present ideas in writing (and orally) in clear, concise, and properly accepted fashion?					
Item d: (7) Does the report employ a variety of information from written, graphic, and multimedia sources?					
Item e: (8) Does the report show monitoring of, reflection upon, and improvement of work?					
Item f: (9) Does the report show cooperative work and respect for the rights of others to think, act, and speak differently?					

ASSESSMENT PROJECT: 14B
PERSONAL FINANCIAL TOOL

STUDENT TASK

After consultation with parents, conduct field research at financial institutions to select and set up an account (checking, share draft, etc.) for personal financial management. Write a 3-5 page report on needs, goals, surveying the financial institutions, and rationale for decisions on type of account and financial institution chosen.

PROCEDURE

1   Review the advisory material on post-graduation personal financial management needs on the previous pages. Decide (with parental guidance) on type of account needed and location needs.

2   Choose 3 to 5 financial institutions in your area. Arrange interviews with the new

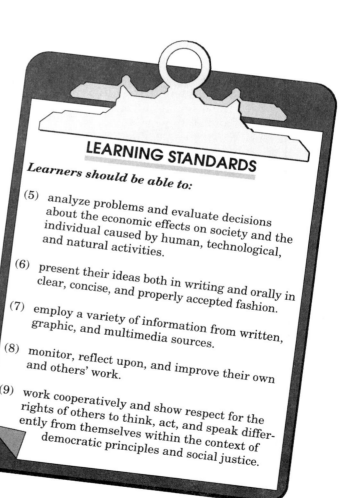

LEARNING STANDARDS

Learners should be able to:

(5) analyze problems and evaluate decisions about the economic effects on society and the individual caused by human, technological, and natural activities.

(6) present their ideas both in writing and orally in clear, concise, and properly accepted fashion.

(7) employ a variety of information from written, graphic, and multimedia sources.

(8) monitor, reflect upon, and improve their own and others' work.

(9) work cooperatively and show respect for the rights of others to think, act, and speak differently from themselves within the context of democratic principles and social justice.

account officer at each. (It is best to inform those individuals of your school project in advance and set up a convenient appointment.)

3 After meeting with the new account officers and reviewing notes and literature collected, decide on an account and institution. A comparison chart would be most useful in facilitating your decision–making process.

4 Write a 3-5 page report summarizing your goals, shopping experience, and the rationale for your decision to pick a particular type of account and a specific institution.

5 As a courtesy, thank the new account officers for their assistance with the project and perhaps share your summary report with them.

EVALUATION

The criteria for the evaluation of this project are itemized in the grid (rubric) that follows. Choice of appropriate category terms (values) is the decision of the instructor. Selection of terms such as "minimal," "satisfactory," and "distinguished" can vary with each assessment.

Personal Financial Tool Evaluation Rubric

(Refer to introductory section for suggestions of scoring descriptors for the evaluation categories.)

Evaluation Item	Category 1	Category 2	Category 3	Category 4	Category 5
Item a: (5) Does the report analyze problems and evaluate decisions about the economic effects on society and the individual caused by human, technological, and natural activities?					
Item b: (6) Does the report illustrate ideas in writing (and orally) in clear, concise, and properly accepted fashion?					
Item c: (7) Does the report employ a variety of information from written, graphic, and multimedia sources?					
Item d: (8) Does the report show monitoring of, reflection upon, and improvement of work?					
Item e: (9) Does the report show cooperative work and respect for the rights of others to think, act, and speak differently?					

ECONOMICS – *Assessment of the American Dream*   N&N©

APPENDICES

Where do I find the American Dream?
RESOURCE MATERIALS

Federal Agencies
State Agencies
Private Organizations
Sources and References
Glossary and Index

ECONOMICS – *Assessment of the American Dream*   N&N©

APPENDIX 1

Where do I go for information?

U.S. GOVERNMENT AGENCIES

There are a bewildering number U.S. government organizations (agencies, bureaus, commissions, corporations, councils, departments, offices) involved in the regulation of the economy. Besides administering and enforcing congressional laws, their activities include investigation and assessment of problems and economic controversies and developing and implementing social, political, and economic solutions, both short-term and long-range. Agencies and organizations are listed alphabetically by common names and as either independent or with their departmental affiliation.

The authors have made every reasonable attempt to insure that the addresses and phone numbers for the listed agencies are accurate. However, as laws, and economic problems change, so do departments, bureaus, and agencies. The authors would appreciate being informed about all changes. Help us to ensure our readers have the most accurate and current addresses. Please write. Any comments or suggestions are always gratefully received.

Address Sources:
• *New York Public Library Desk Reference.* NY: Stonesong Press, 1989
• *1994 National Directory of addresses and Phone Numbers.* Detroit: Omnigraphics Inc., 1994
World Almanac and Book of Facts. Mawah, NJ: Funk and Wagnalls Corp., 1995
• *The United States Government Manual.* Washington, DC: Office of The Federal Register, National Archives and Records Administration, 1994

U.S. GOVERNMENT HOTLINE NUMBERS

This is a list of federal government "Hot Lines" that can be called to register complaints of waste, abuse, fraud, or neglect.

Agriculture 1-800-424-9121
Commerce 1-800-424-5197
Commission on Civil Rights. . . 1-800-552-6843
Defense 1-800-424-9098
Drug Abuse Treatment
    Info Referral 1-800-662-HELP
Energy. 1-800-541-1625
Environmental Protection
    Agency (EPA). 1-800-424-4000

Federal Deposit Insurance
    Corporation (FDIC). 1-800-964-3342
General Services
    Administration 1-202-501-1780
Health & Human Services 1-800-368-5779
Housing & Urban Develop. . . . 1-800-347-3735
Interior 1-800-424-5081
Justice. 1-800-869-4499
Labor. 1-800-347-3756
National AIDS Hotline 1-800-342-AIDS
Resolution Trust Corp. 1-800-833-3310
Transportation 1-800-424-9071
Treasury 1-800-359-3898
Veterans Affairs 1-800-488-8244

EXECUTIVE AND INDEPENDENT AGENCIES

Alcohol, Tobacco and Firearms, Bureau of
U.S. Department of the Treasury
650 Massachusetts Avenue NW – Rm 8000
Washington DC 20226
Phone (202) 927-7777 / Fax (202) 927-7862

Agriculture, U.S. Department of
Office of Economics
U.S.D.A. Administration Building
14th Street at Independence Avenue SW
Washington DC 20250
Phone (202) 720-4614 / Fax (202) 690-4915

AMTRAK (National Railroad Passenger
  Corporation – Independent)
60 Massachusetts Avenue NE
Washington DC 20002
Phone (202) 906-3000 / Fax (202) 906-3865

Antitrust Division
U.S. Department of Justice
10th Street and Pennsylvania Avenue SW
Washington DC 20530
Phone (202) 5410-2410 / Fax (202) 541-8123

Children and Families, Administration for
U.S. Department of Health and Human Services
370 L'Enfant Promenade SW – 6th Floor
Washington DC 20447
Phone (202) 401-9200 / Fax (202)252-4683

Coast Guard, United States
Department of Transportation
2100 2nd Street SW
Washington DC 20593
Phone (202) 267-2229 / No Fax Listing

Commerce, U.S. Department of
Economic Affairs – Rm 4855
14th Street and Constitution Avenue NW
Washington DC 20230
Phone (202) 482-2235 / Fax (202) 482-0432

Commodity Futures Trading Commission
  (Independent)
2033 K Street NW
Washington DC 20581
Phone (202) 254-8630 / Fax (202) 254-6265

Comptroller of the Currency
U.S. Department of the Treasury
250 E Street NW
Washington DC 20219
Phone (202) 874-4900 / Fax (202) 874-4950

Consumer Affairs, Office of
U.S. Department of Health and Human Services
1620 L Street NW – Suite 700
Washington DC 20036
Phone (202) 634-9610 / Fax (202) 634-4135

Consumer Information Center
(U.S. Government Publications Clearing House)
Pueblo CO 81009
No Phone Listing / No Fax Listing

Consumer Product Safety Commission
  (Independent)
Office of the Commissioner
5401 Westbard Avenue – Westwood Towers
Bethesda MD 20816
Phone (301) 504-0500 / Fax (301) 504-0124

Copyright Office
Library of Congress
101 Independence Avenue SE – Rm 401
Washington DC 20559
Phone (202) 707-3000 / Fax (202) 707-8366

Customs Service, U.S.
U.S. Department of the Treasury
1301 Constitution Avenue NW – Rm 3422
Washington DC 20229
Phone (202) 622-2000 / Fax (202) 633-7645

Drug Enforcement Administration
U.S. Department of Justice
700 Army Navy Drive – Rm 12060
Arlington VA 22202
Phone (202) 307-8000 / Fax (202) 307-8320

Economic Advisors, Council of
(Executive Offices)
Old Executive Office Building – Rm 314
Washington DC 20500
Phone (202) 395-5107 / Fax (202) 395-6947

Economic Analysis, Bureau of
U.S. Department of Commerce
Tower Building – Rm 705 1401 K Street NW
Washington DC 20230
Phone (202) 523-0707 / Fax (202) 523-7538

Employment Standards Administration
U.S. Department of Labor
200 Constitution Avenue NW – Rm S-2321
Washington DC 20210
Phone (202) 219-6191 / Fax (202) 219-8457

Employment and Training Administration
U.S. Department of Labor
200 Constitution Avenue NW – Rm S-2307
Washington DC 20210
Phone (202) 219-6050 / Fax (202) 219-6827

Energy Regulatory Commission
  (Independent)
825 North Capitol Street NE – 3rd Floor
Washington DC 20002
Phone (202) 208-0200 / Fax (202) 208-0147

Energy, U.S. Department of
1000 Independence Avenue SW
Washington DC 20585
Phone (202) 586-5000 / Fax (202) 586-4073

Environmental Protection Agency
(Independent)
401 M Street SW Washington DC 20460
Phone (202) 260-2090 / Fax (202) 260-9232

Equal Employment Opportunity Commission (Independent)
1801 L Street NW Washington DC 20507
Phone (202) 663 - 4900 / Fax (202) 663-4912

Export-Import Bank of the United States
(Independent)
811 Vermont Avenue NW
Washington DC 20571
Phone (202) 566-8990 / Fax (202) 566-7524

Federal Aviation Administration (FAA)
U.S. Department of Transportation
800 Independence Avenue SW – Rm 1010
Washington DC 20591
Phone (202) 267-3484 / Fax (202) 267-3505

Federal Communications Commission
(FCC – Independent)
1919 M Street NW Washington DC 20554
Phone (202) 632-7000/ Fax (202) 653-5402

Federal Council on Aging (Independent)
330 Independence Avenue SW – Rm 4547
Washington DC 20201
Phone (202) 619-2451 / Fax (202) 619-3759

Federal Crop Insurance Corporation
U.S. Department of Agriculture
2101 L Street NW – Suite 500
Washington DC 20037
Phone (202) 254-4581 / Fax (202) 254-8356

Federal Deposit Insurance Corporation
(FDIC – Independent)
Consumer Programs
550 17th Street NW Washington DC 20429
Phone (202) 393-8400 / Fax (202) 347-2775

Federal Highway Administration
U.S. Department of Transportation
400 7th Avenue SW
Washington DC 20590
Phone (202) 366-0660 / Fax (202) 366-3235

Federal Home Loan Mortgage Corporation
("Freddie Mac" – Independent)
8200 Jones Branch Drive
McLean VA 22102
Phone (202) 903-2000 / Fax (202) 903-2447

Federal Housing and Equal Opportunity Office
U.S. Department of Housing and Urban Development
451 7th Street SW – Rm 5100
Washington DC 20410
Phone (202) 708-4252 / Fax (202) 708-4483

Federal Housing Commissioner
U.S. Department of Housing and Urban Development
451 7th Street SW – Rm 9100
Washington DC 20410
Phone (202) 708-3600 / Fax (202) 755-2580

Federal Labor Relations Authority
(Independent)
607 14th Street NW
Washington DC 20424
Phone (202) 482-6550 / Fax (202) 482-6608

Federal Maritime Commission
(Independent)
800 N Capitol Street NW
Washington DC 20573
Phone (202) 523-5725 / Fax (202) 523-3782

Federal Mediation and Conciliation Service (Independent)
2100 K Street NW
Washington DC 20006
Phone (202) 653-5300 / Fax (202) 653-2002

Federal Mine Safety and Health Review Commission (Independent)
1730 K Street NW
Washington DC 20006
Phone (202) 653-5633 / Fax (202) 653-5030

• • • • • • • • •

FEDERAL RESERVE SYSTEM (INDEPENDENT)

Board of Governors
20th & Constitution Avenue NW
Washington DC 20551
Phone (202) 452-3204 / Fax (202) 452-3819

District 1
Federal Reserve Bank of Boston
Public Affairs Department
600 Atlantic Boston MA 02106
Phone (617) 973-3000 / Fax (617) 973-5819

District 2
Federal Reserve Bank of New York
Public Information Department
33 Liberty Street New York NY 10045
Phone (212) 720-6134 / No Fax Listed

District 3
Federal Reserve Bank of Philadelphia
Public Affairs Department
10 Independence Mall Philadelphia PA 19106
Phone (215) 574-6000 / Fax (215) 574-3980

District 4
Federal Reserve Bank of Cleveland
Public Affairs Department
1455 E. 6th Street Cleveland OH 44114
Phone (216) 579-2000 / Fax (216) 579-2813

District 5
Federal Reserve Bank of Richmond
Public Affairs Department
701 E. Byrd Street Richmond VA 23219
Phone (804) 697-8000 / Fax (804) 697-8044

District 6
Federal Reserve Bank of Atlanta
Public Affairs Department
104 Marietta Street SW Atlanta GA 30303
Phone (404) 521-8500 / No Fax Listed

District 7
Federal Reserve Bank of Chicago
Public Affairs Department
230 LaSalle Street Chicago IL 60604
Phone (312) 322-5322 / Fax (312) 322-5959

District 8
Federal Reserve Bank of St. Louis
Public Affairs Department
411 Locust Street St. Louis MO 63102
Phone (314) 444-8444 / Fax (314) 444-8452

District 9
Federal Reserve Bank of Minneapolis
Public Affairs Department
250 Marquette Avenue
Minneapolis MN 55401
Phone (612) 340-2345 / Fax (612) 340-2545

District 10
Federal Reserve Bank of Kansas City
Public Affairs Department
925 Grand Avenue Kansas City MO 64198
Phone (816) 881-2000 / No Fax listed

District 11
Federal Reserve Bank of Dallas
Public Affairs Department
2200 N. Pearl Street – Station K
Dallas TX 75222
Phone (214) 922-6000 / No Fax Listed

District 12
Federal Reserve Bank of San Francisco
Public Affairs Department
101 Market Street San Francisco CA 94105
Phone (415) 974-2000 / Fax (415) 974-2318

• • • • • • • • •

EXECUTIVE AND INDEPENDENT AGENCIES CONTINUED

Federal Trade Commission (Independent)
6th Street and Pennsylvania Avenue NW
Washington DC 20580
Phone (202) 326-2000 / Fax (202) 326-2050

Fish and Wildlife Service
U.S. Department of the Interior
1849 C Street NW – Rm 3256
Washington DC 20240
Phone (202) 208-4717 / Fax (202) 208-4473

Food and Drug Administration
U.S. Department of Health and Human Services
Consumer Affairs
5600 Fisher's Lane – Rm 14–71
Rockville MD 20857
Phone (301) 443-2410 / Fax (301) 443-0755

Food and Nutrition Service
U.S. Department of Agriculture
3101 Park Center Drive – Rm 803
Alexandria VA 22302
Phone (703) 305-2062 / Fax (703) 305-2908

Food Safety and Inspection Service
U.S. Department of Agriculture
14th Street and Independence Avenue SW – Rm 331–A
Washington DC 20250
Phone (202) 720-7025 / Fax (202) 720-9063

Forest Service, U.S.
U.S. Department of Agriculture
14th Street and Independence Avenue SW – Rm 5071
Washington DC 20250
Phone (202) 720-3935 / Fax (202) 720-7729

General Accounting Office (Independent)
441 G Street NW Washington DC 20548
Phone (202) 512-3000 / Fax (202) 512-9899

General Services Administration
(Independent)
18th and F Streets NW – Rm 6137
Washington DC 20405
Phone (202) 501-1231 / Fax (202) 501-1489

Government Printing Office (Independent)
732 North Capitol and H Streets NW
Washington DC 20401
Phone (202) 512-0000 / Fax (202) 512-2232

Health and Human Services, U.S. Department of
200 Independence Avenue SW
Washington DC 20201
Phone (202) 690-7000 / Fax (202) 690-7203

Housing and Urban Development, U.S. Department of
451 7th Street SW Washington DC 20410
Phone (202) 708-0980 / Fax (202) 708-0299

Indian Affairs, Bureau of
U.S. Department of the Interior
1849 C Street NW – Rm 4160
Washington DC 20245
Phone (202) 208-7163 / Fax (202) 208-6334

Interior, U.S. Department of the
Public Affairs – Main Interior Building
1849 C Street NW Washington DC 20240
Phone (202) 208-3171 / Fax (202) 208-5048

Internal Revenue Service
U.S. Department of the Treasury
111 Constitution Avenue NW
Washington DC 20224
Phone (202) 622-5164 / Fax (202) 622-8653

International Trade Commission, U.S.
(Independent)
500 E Street SW Washington DC 20436
Phone (202) 205-2000 / Fax (202) 205-2798

Interstate Commerce Commission
(Independent)
Compliance and Consumer Assistance
12th Street and Constitution Avenue NW
Washington DC 20423
Phone (202) 927-7597 / Fax (202) 927-5984

Labor Management Standards Administration
U.S. Department of Labor
200 Constitution Avenue NW
Washington DC 20210
Phone (202) 219-9674 / No Fax Listed

Labor Statistics, Bureau of
U.S. Department of Labor
441 G Street NW
Washington DC 20212
Phone (202) 606-7800 / Fax (202) 606-7797

Labor, U.S. Department of
200 Constitution Avenue NW
Washington DC 20210
Phone (202) 219-7316 / Fax (202) 219-7312

Land Management, Bureau of
U.S. Department of the Interior
1849 C Street NW – Rm 5660
Washington DC 20240
Phone (202) 208-3801 / Fax (202) 208-5902

Management and the Budget, Office of
(OMB — Executive Office)
Old Executive Office Building
Washington DC 20503
Phone (202) 395-3000 / Fax (202) 395-3746

Mines, Bureau of
U.S. Department of the Interior
1849 C Street NW – Rm 604
Washington DC 20241
Phone (202) 501-9300 / No Fax Listed

Minority Business Development Agency
U.S. Department of Commerce
14th St. and Constitution Ave. NW – Rm 5063
Washington DC 20230
Phone (202) 482-1015 / Fax (202) 482-1441

National Credit Union Administration
(Independent)
1776 G Street NW – 6th Fl.
Washington DC 20456
Phone (202) 682-9600 / Fax (202) 682-9620

National Economic Council
(Executive Offices)
17th Street and Pennsylvania Avenue NW
Washington DC 20500
Phone (202) 456-1414 / No Fax Listed

National Highway Traffic Safety Admin.
U.S. Department of Transportation
400 7th Street SW – Rm 5220
Washington DC 20590
Phone (202) 366-9550 / Fax (202) 366-2106

National Institute for Occupational Safety and Health (NIOSH)
U.S. Department of Labor
200 Constitution Ave., NW
Washington DC 20240
Phone (202) 343-4953 / No Fax Listed

National Institute of Standards and Technology
U.S. Department of Commerce
Route I–270 and Quince Orchard Road
Gaithersburg MD 20899
Phone (301) 975-2000/ Fax (301) 948-3716

National Labor Relations Board
(Independent)
1717 Pennsylvania Avenue NW – Rm 701
Washington DC 20570
Phone (202) 632-4950 / Fax (202) 634-4832

National Marine Fisheries Service
Department of Commerce (U.S.)
1335 East–West Highway
Silver Springs MD 20910
Phone (301) 427-2370 / No Fax Listed

National Mediation Board (Independent)
1425 K Street NW – Suite 910
Washington DC 20572
Phone (202) 523-5920 / Fax (202) 523-1494

National Transportation Safety Board
490 L'Enfant Plaza East SW
Washington DC 20594
Phone (202) 382-6600 / Fax (202) 382-6808

Occupational Safety and Health Administration
U.S. Department of Labor
200 Constitution Avenue NW – Rm S-2315
Washington DC 20210
Phone (202) 219-8151 / Fax (202) 219-5986

Occupational Safety and Health Review Commission
U.S. Department of Labor
1825 K Street NW – Rm 409A
Washington DC 20006
Phone (202) 634-7943 / Fax (202) 634-4008

Office of Conservation & Renewable Energy
1000 Independence Avenue SW
Washington DC 20585
Phone (202) 586-9220 / No Fax Listed

Patent and Trademark Office
U.S. Department of Commerce
211 Crystal Drive – Suite 700
Arlington VA 20002
Phone (703) 305-4537 / Fax (703) 305-6369

Postal Rate Commission (Independent)
Consumer Advocate
1333 H Street NW
Washington DC 20268
Phone (202) 798 - 6800 / Fax (202) 798-6861

Postal Service, U.S. (Independent)
475 L'Enfant Plaza SW
Washington DC 20260
Phone (202) 268-2284 / Fax (202) 268-6980

Regulatory Information Service Center
(Executive Offices)
750 17th Street NW – Suite 500
Washington DC 20006
Phone (202) 643-6220 / Fax (202) 643-6224

Resolution Trust Corp.
801 17th Street NW
Washington DC 20434
Phone (202) 416 - 6900 / Fax (202) 416-7557

Securities and Exchange Commission
(Independent)
450 5th Street NW Washington DC 20549
Phone (202) 272-2650 / Fax (202) 272-7050

Small Business Administration
(Independent)
409 3rd Street SW Washington DC 20416
Phone (202) 205-6600 / Fax (202) 205-6802

Social Security Administration
U.S. Department of Health and Human Services
6401 Security Blvd. Baltimore MD 21235
Phone (410) 965-8822 / Fax (410) 966-1463

Soil Conservation Services
U.S. Department of Agriculture
14th St. & Independence Avenue SW
PO Box 2890 Washington DC 20013
Phone (202)447-4543 / No Fax Listed

Surface Mining Reclamation and
Enforcement, Office of
U.S. Department of the Interior
1951 Constitution Avenue NW – Rm 262
Washington DC 20240
Phone (202) 208-2807 / Fax (202) 219-3106

Tennessee Valley Authority (Independent)
400 West Summit Hill Drive
Knoxville TN 37902
Phone (615) 632-8063 / Fax (615) 632-6634

Transportation, U.S. Department of
400 7th Street SW
Washington DC 20590
Phone (202) 366-4000 / No Fax Listing

Treasury, U.S. Department of the
1500 Pennsylvania Avenue NW
Washington DC 20220
Phone (202) 622-2960 / Fax (202) 622-0073

Budget Committee
U.S. House of Representatives
214 O'Neill Building
Washington DC 20515
Phone (202) 226-7200 / No Fax Listing

Energy & Commerce Committee
U.S. House of Representatives
2125 Rayburn Building
Washington DC 20515
Phone (202) 255-2927 / Fax (202) 225-2525

Interior Committee
U.S. House of Representatives
Washington DC 20515
Phone (202) 255-2761

Public Works & Transportation Committee
U.S. House of Representatives
Washington DC 20515
Phone (202) 255-4472/ No Fax Listing

Small Business Committee
U.S. House of Representatives
2361 Rayburn Building
Washington DC 20515
Phone (202) 225-5821 / Fax (202) 225-7209

Ways and Means Committee
U.S. House of Representatives
1102 Rayburn Building
Washington DC 20515
Phone (202) 225-3625 / No Fax Listing

U.S. HOUSE OF REPRESENTATIVES

Agriculture Committee
U.S. House of Representatives
1301 Longworth Building
Washington DC 20515
Phone (202) 225-2171 /Fax (202) 225-8510

Appropriations Committee
U.S. House of Representatives
Capitol Building – Suite H-218
Washington DC 20515
Phone (202) 255-2771 / No Fax Listing

Banking and Finance Committee
U.S. House of Representatives
2129 Rayburn Building
Washington DC 20515
Phone (202) 225-4247 / Fax (202) 225-6580

U.S. SENATE

Agriculture, Nutrition, & Forestry
Committee
U.S. Senate
328-A Russell Building
Washington DC 20510
Phone (202) 224-2035 / Fax (202) 224-2001

Appropriations Committee
U.S. Senate
Capitol Building – Rm S128
Washington DC 20510
Phone (202) 224-3471 / Fax (202) 224-8553

Banking and Urban Affairs Committee
U.S. Senate
534 Dirksen Building
Washington DC 20510
Phone (202) 224-7391 / Fax (202) 224-5137

Budget Committee
U.S. Senate
621 Dirksen Building
Washington DC 20510
Phone (202) 224-0642 / Fax (202) 224-4835

Commerce, Science & Transportation Committee
U.S. Senate
508 Dirksen Building
Washington DC 20510
Phone (202) 224-5115 / No Fax Listing

Energy & Natural Resources Committee
U.S. Senate
304 Dirksen Building
Washington DC 20510
Phone (202) 224-4917 / No Fax Listing

Environment & Public Works Committee
U.S. Senate
456 Dirksen Building
Washington DC 20510
Phone (202) 224-6176 / Fax (202) 224-1273

Finance Committee
U.S. Senate
205 Dirksen Building
Washington DC 20510
Phone (202) 224-4515 / Fax (202) 224-3014

Labor and Human Resources Committee
U.S. Senate
428 Dirksen Building
Washington DC 20510
Phone (202) 224-5375 / Fax (202) 224-5128

Small Business Committee
U.S. Senate
428-A Russell Building
Washington DC 20510
Phone (202) 224-5175 / Fax (202) 224-5619

U.S. HOUSE/SENATE JOINT COMMITTEES

Joint Committee on Taxation
G-01 Dirksen Building
Washington DC 20510
Phone (202) 224-3621 / Fax (202) 224-0832

Joint Economic Committee
G-01 Dirksen Building
Washington DC 20510
Phone (202) 224-5171 / Fax (202) 224-0240

Veterans Affairs, U.S. Department of
Public and Consumer Affairs
810 Vermont Avenue NW
Washington DC 20420
Phone (202) 535-8300 / Fax (202) 233-2807

INTERNATIONAL

International Monetary Fund (U.N. agency)
1 U.N. Plaza – Rm DC1-1140
New York NY 10017
Phone (212) 963-6900 / Fax (212) 319-9040

World Bank (U.N. agency – International Bank for Reconstruction and Development)
809 U.N. Plaza – Suite 900
New York NY 10017
Phone (212) 963-6008 / Fax (212) 697-7020

APPENDIX 2

Where do I go for information?

STATE GOVERNMENT AGENCIES

There are many governmental organizations – bureaus, departments, offices, and agencies – whose activities involve them in the management of their state economies. Their activities include the investigation and assessment of problems and economic controversies. Their responses involve the development and implementation of social, political, and economical policies, both short-term and long-range. Entries marked with a * signify agencies being reorganized as of 1995. State organizations and agencies are listed according to their areas of responsibility, including:

The authors have made every reasonable attempt to insure that the addresses and phone numbers for the listed agencies are accurate. However, as government, laws, and environmental problems change, so do divisions, departments, bureaus, and agencies. The authors would appreciate being informed about all changes. Help us to ensure our readers have the most accurate and current addresses. Please write. Any comments or suggestions are always gratefully received.

•••••••••

AGRICULTURE	FINANCE
ATTORNEY GENERAL	GOVERNOR
BANKING	HUMAN RIGHTS/CIVIL RIGHTS
BUDGET	LABOR
COMMERCE	OCCUPATIONAL SAFETY / HEALTH
COMMUNITY AFFAIRS	SECURITIES
CONSUMER AFFAIRS	TAXATION & REVENUE
CORPORATE RECORDS	TREASURER
ECONOMIC OPPORTUNITY	UNEMPLOYMENT
EMPLOYMENT SECURITY	WORKERS' COMPENSATION
ENVIRONMENTAL AFFAIRS	

AGRICULTURE

ALABAMA
Agriculture & Indust. Dept.....205-242-2650
PO 3336, Montgomery AL 36109-0336
ALASKA
Agriculture Div........................907-745-7200
PO 949, Palmer AK 99645-0949
ARIZONA
Agriculture Dept......................602-542-0998
1688 Adams, Rm 421, Phoenix AZ 85007
ARKANSAS
Development Finance Auth......501-682-5900
PO 8023, Little Rock AR 72203
CALIFORNIA
Food & Agriculture Dept.........916-654-0433
1220 N St, Sacramento CA 95814

COLORADO
Agriculture Dept......................303-239-4100
700 Kipling St Ste 4000, Lakewood CO 80215
CONNECTICUT
Agriculture Dept......................203-566-4667
165 Capitol Ave, Hartford CT 06106
DELAWARE
Agriculture Dept......................302-739-4811
2320 S Dupont Hwy, Dover DE 19901..........
FLORIDA
Agri & Consumer Ser Dept.....904-488-3022
Plaza Level 10, The Capitol
Tallahassee FL 32399-0001
GEORGIA
Agriculture Dept......................404-656-3600
Agriculture Bldg Capitol Sq.
Atlanta GA 30334

HAWAII
    Agriculture Dept......................808-973-9551
    PO 22159, Honolulu HI 96822-0159

IDAHO
    Agriculture Dept......................208-334-3240
    PO 790, Boise ID 83701

ILLINOIS
    Agriculture Dept......................217-782-2172
    PO 19281, Springfield IL 62794-9281

INDIANA
    Office of the Commissioner of Agriculture ...
   317-232-8770
    ISTA Ctr – 150 W Market St – Ste 414.
    Indianapolis IN 46204

IOWA
    Agriculture & Land Stewardship Dept.........
   515-281-5322
    Wallace State Ofc Bldg
    Des Moines IA 50319

KANSAS
    Agricultural Board 913-296-3556
    901 S Kansas Ave., Topeka KS 66612-1280

KENTUCKY
    Agriculture Dept......................502-564-4696
    Capitol Plaza Tower, 7th Fl – 500 Mero St
    Frankfort KY 40602

LOUISIANA
    Agriculture & Forestry Dept...504-922-1234
    PO 631 Baton Rouge LA 70821-0631

MAINE
    Agriculture, Food & Rural Resources Dept..
   207-287-3871
    State House Station 28, Augusta ME 04333

MARYLAND
    Agriculture Dept......................410-841-5880
    50 Harry S Truman Pkwy
    Annapolis MD 21401

MASSACHUSETTS
    Food & Agriculture Dept.........617-727-3003
    100 Cambridge St – Rm 2103
    Boston MA 02202

MICHIGAN
    Agriculture Dept......................517-373-1050
    PO 30017, Lansing MI 48909

MINNESOTA
    Agriculture Dept......................612-297-3219
    90 W Plato Blvd, St Paul MN 55107

MISSISSIPPI
    Agriculture & Commerce Dept
   601-354-7050
    PO 1609, Jackson MS 39215-1609

MISSOURI
    Agriculture Dept......................314-751-3359
    PO 630, Jefferson City MO 65102

MONTANA
    Agriculture Dept......................406-444-3144
    PO 20029, 301 N Roberts St, Rm 220, ...
    Capitol Station, Helena MT 59620-0201

NEBRASKA
    Agriculture Dept......................402-471-2341
    PO 94947, Lincoln NE 68509

NEVADA
    Agriculture Div.......................702-688-1180
    PO 11100, 350 Capitol Hill
    Reno NV 89510

NEW HAMPSHIRE
    Agriculture Dept......................603-271-3551
    PO 2042, Concord NH 03302-2042

NEW JERSEY
    Agriculture Dept......................609-292-3976
    John Fitch Plaza, CN 330
    Trenton NJ 08625-0330

NEW MEXICO
    Agriculture Dept......................505-646-3007
    PO 30005, Dept 3189
    Las Cruces NM 88003-0005

NEW YORK
    Agriculture & Markets Dept...518-457-8876
    1 Winners Circle, Albany NY 12235

NORTH CAROLINA
    Agriculture Dept......................919-733-7125
    2 W Edenton St., Raleigh NC 27611

NORTH DAKOTA
    Agriculture Dept......................701-224-2231
    600 E Boulevard, Bismarck ND 58505

OHIO
    Agriculture Dept......................614-466-2732
    65 S Front St, 6th Fl, Columbus OH 43215

OKLAHOMA
    Agriculture Dept......................405-521-3868
    2800 N. Lincoln Blvd.,
    Oklahoma City OK 73105

OREGON
    Agriculture Dept......................503-378-4152
    635 Capitol St NE, Salem OR 97312

PENNSYLVANIA
    Agriculture Dept......................717-772-2853
    2301 N Cameron St, Harrisburg PA 17110

RHODE ISLAND
    *Agriculture Div 401-277-2781
    22 Hayes St, Providence RI 02908

SOUTH CAROLINA
    Agriculture Dept......................803-734-2210
    PO 11280, Columbia SC 29211-1280

SOUTH DAKOTA
    Agriculture Dept......................605-773-3375
    445 E Capitol, Anderson Bldg
    Pierre SD 57501

TENNESSEE
Agriculture Dept......................615-360-0100
PO 40627, Nashville TN 37204
TEXAS
Agriculture Dept......................512-463-7435
PO 12847, Austin TX 78711
UTAH
Agriculture Dept......................801-538-7100
350 N Redwood Rd
Salt Lake City UT 84116
VERMONT
Agriculture Dept......................802-828-2430
116 State St, Montpelier VT 05620-2901
VIRGINIA
Agriculture & Consumer Services Dept ....
....804-786-2373
1100 Bank St – Rm 210
Richmond Va 23219
WASHINGTON
Agriculture Dept......................206-902-1801
PO 42560, Olympia WA 98504-2560
WEST VIRGINIA
Agriculture Dept......................304-558-3550
Agriculture Ctr – Capitol Bldg,
Charleston, WV 25305-0170
WISCONSIN
*Agri Resource Mgt Div 608-266-7130
PO 8911, Madison WI 53708
WYOMING
Agriculture Dept......................307-777-6569
2219 Carey Ave, Cheyenne WY 82002-0100

ATTORNEY GENERAL

ALABAMA
Attorney General......................205-242-7300
11 S Union St, Montgomery AL 36130
ALASKA
Law Dept.................................907-465-3600
PO 110300, Juneau AK 99811-0300
ARIZONA
Attorney General......................602-542-4266
1275 W Washington, Phoenix AZ 85007
ARKANSAS
Attorney General......................501-682-2007
200 Tower Bldg, 323 Center St
Little Rock AR 72201
CALIFORNIA
Administrative Law Office......916-323-6221
555 Capitol Mall, Ste 1290
Sacramento CA 95814

COLORADO
*Policy & Initiatives Div
Chief Legal Advisor.................303-866-2471
State Capitol Bldg, Rm 136
Denver CO 80203
CONNECTICUT
Attorney General......................203-566-2026
55 Elm St, Hartford CT 06106
DELAWARE
Attorney General......................302-577-3838
820 N French St, Wilmington DE 19801
DISTRICT OF COLUMBIA
Attorney Advisor 202-727-1179
441 4th St NW, Washington DC 20001
FLORIDA
Attorney General......................904-487-1963
The Capitol, Tallahassee FL 32399-1050
GEORGIA
Attorney General......................404-656-4585
40 Capitol Sq SW, Atlanta GA 30334-1300
HAWAII
Attorney General......................808-586-1500
415 Queen St, Honolulu HI 96813
IDAHO
Attorney General......................208-334-2400
Rm 210 Statehouse, Boise ID 83720
ILLINOIS
Attorney General......................217-782-1090
500 S. Second, Springfield IL 62706
INDIANA
Attorney General......................317-232-6201
402 W Washington St, Rm C553, ...
Indianapolis IN 46204
IOWA
Attorney General......................515-281-8373
Hoover State Ofc Bldg, 2nd Fl, Des Moines
IA 50319
KANSAS
Attorney General......................913-296-2215
2nd Fl, Kansas Judicial Center, Topeka KS
66612
KENTUCKY
Attorney General......................502-564-7600
116 Capitol Bldg, 700 Capital Ave ....
Frankfort KY 40601
LOUISIANA
Attorney General......................504-342-7013
PO 94005, Baton Rouge LA 70804
MAINE
Attorney General......................207-626-8800
State House Station 6, Augusta ME 04333
MARYLAND
Attorney General......................410-576-6300
200 St Paul Pl, Baltimore MD 21202-2020

MASSACHUSETTS
Attorney General.....................617-767-2200
1 Ashburton Pl, Rm 2010
Boston MA 02108
MICHIGAN
Attorney General.....................517-373-1110
PO 30212, Lansing MI 48909
MINNESOTA
Attorney General.....................612-296-6196
State Capitol, St Paul MN 55155
MISSISSIPPI
Attorney General.....................601-359-3680
PO 220, Jackson MS 39205
MISSOURI
Attorney General.....................314-751-3321
PO 899. Jefferson City MO 65102
MONTANA
Attorney General.....................406-444-2026
Justice Bldg, 215 N Sanders
Helena MT 59620
NEBRASKA
Attorney General.....................402-471-2682
2115 State Capitol Bldg, Lincoln NE 68509
NEVADA
Attorney General.....................702-687-4170
Heroes Memorial Bldg, 198 S Carson St, ...
Carson City NV 89710
NEW HAMPSHIRE
Attorney General.....................603-271-3655
208 State House Annex, Concord NH 03301-6397
NEW JERSEY
Attorney General.....................609-292-4925
Justice Complex, CN 080, Trenton NJ ....
08625-0080
NEW MEXICO
Attorney General.....................505-827-6000
PO Drawer 1508, Santa Fe NM 87504-1508
NEW YORK
Attorney General.....................518-474-7330
State Capitol, Rm 221 Albany NY 12224
NORTH CAROLINA
Attorney General.....................919-733-3377
PO 629, Raleigh NC 27602
NORTH DAKOTA
Attorney General.....................701-224-2210
600 E Boulevard Ave, Bismarck ND 58505
OHIO
Attorney General.....................614-466-3376
30 E Broad St, Columbus OH 43215
OKLAHOMA
Attorney General.....................405-521-3921
112 State Capitol Bldg
Oklahoma City OK 73105

OREGON
Attorney General.....................503-378-6002
100 Justice Bldg, Salem OR 97310
PENNSYLVANIA
Attorney General.....................717-787-3391
16th Fl, Strawberry Sq
Harrisburg PA 17120
RHODE ISLAND
Attorney General.....................401-274-4400
72 Pine St, Providence RI 02903
SOUTH CAROLINA
Attorney General.....................803-734-3970
PO 11549, Columbia SC 29211
SOUTH DAKOTA
Attorney General.....................605-773-3215
500 E Capitol, Pierre SD 57501-5090
TENNESSEE
Attorney General.....................615-741-6474
450 James Robertson Pkwy
Nashville TN 37243-0485
TEXAS
Attorney General.....................512-463-2191
PO 12548, Austin TX 78711-2548
UTAH
Attorney General.....................801-538-1015
236 State Capitol, Salt Lake City UT 84114
VERMONT
Attorney General.....................802-828-3171
109 State St, Montpelier VT 05609-1001
VIRGINIA
Attorney General.....................804-786-2071
101 N 8th St, Richmond VA 23219
WASHINGTON
Attorney General.....................206-753-6200
PO 40100, Olympia WA 98504-0100
WEST VIRGINIA
Attorney General.....................304-558-2021
State Capitol 26 E, Charleston WV 25305
WISCONSIN
Attorney General.....................608-266-1221
PO 7857, Madison WI 53707-7857
WYOMING
Attorney General.....................307-777-7841
123 Capitol Bldg, Cheyenne WY 82002

BANKING

ALABAMA
Banking Dept..........................205-242-3452
101 S Union St, Montgomery AL 36130
ALASKA
Banking, Securities & Corp Div
....907-465-2521
PO 110808, Juneau AK 99811-0208

ARIZONA
Banking Dept...........................602-255-4421
2910 N 44th St, Ste 310, Phoenix AZ 85018
ARKANSAS
Bank Dept..............................501-324-9019
323 Center St, Ste 500
Little Rock AR 72201
CALIFORNIA
Banking Dept...........................415-557-3535
111 Pine St, 11th Fl San Francisco CA 94111
COLORADO
Banking Div............................303-894-7575
1560 Broadway, Ste 1550, Denver CO 80202
CONNECTICUT
Banking Dept...........................203-566-4560
44 Capitol Ave, Hartford CT 06106
DELAWARE
State Bank Commissioner......302-739-4235
540 S DuPont Hwy, PO 1401, Dover DE .....
19903-1401
DISTRICT OF COLUMBIA
Banking & Financial Institutions Office......
....202-727-1563
1250 I St NW, Ste 1003, Washington DC ....
20005
FLORIDA
Banking & Finance Dept........904-488-0370
Plaza Level, PL-09, Capitol Bldg, ...
Tallahassee FL 32399-0350
GEORGIA
Banking & Finance Dept........404-986-1633
2990 Brandywine Rd, Ste 200
Atlanta GA 30341-5565
HAWAII
Financial Institutions Div.......808-586-2820
PO 2054, Honolulu HI 98605
IDAHO
Banking Bur 208-334-3678
700 W State St, Boise ID 83720-2700
ILLINOIS
Banks & Trust Companies......217-782-7966
117 S 5th St, Rm 100, Springfield IL 62701
INDIANA
Financial Institutions Dept 317-232-3955
402 W Washington St, Rm W066, ...
Indianapolis IN 46204-2294
IOWA
Banking Div............................515-281-4014
200 E Grand Ave, Ste 300
Des Moines IA 50309
KANSAS
Office of the State Bank Commissioner........
....913-296-2266
700 Jackson St, Ste 300, Topeka KS 66603

KENTUCKY
Banking Div............................502-564-3390
477 Versailles Rd, Frankfort KY 40601
LOUISIANA
Financial Institutions Ofc.......504-925-4660
PO 94095, Baton Rouge LA 70804-9095
MAINE
Banking Bureau 207-624-8570
State House Station 35
Augusta ME 04333
MARYLAND
Financial Regulation Div........410-333-6330
501 St Paul Pl, Baltimore MD 21202
MASSACHUSETTS
Banks Div...............................617-727-3120
100 Cambridge St, Rm 2004
Boston MA 02202
MICHIGAN
Financial Institutions Bur......517-373-3460
PO 30224, Lansing MI 48909
MINNESOTA
Financial Examinations Banks Div
....612-296-2715
133 E 7th St, St Paul MN 55101
MISSISSIPPI
Banking & Consumer Finance Dept.............
....601-359-1031
PO Drawer 23729
Jackson MS 39225-3729
MISSOURI
Savings & Loan Div.................314-751-4243
PO 836, Jefferson City MO 65102-0836
MONTANA
Financial Institutions Div.......406-444-2091
1424 9th Ave, Helena MT 59620-0501
NEBRASKA
Banking & Finance Dept 4023-471-2171
PO 95006, Lincoln NE 68509
NEVADA
Financial Institutions Div.......702-687-4259
406 East 2nd St, Carson City NV 89710
NEW HAMPSHIRE
Banking Dept...........................603-271-3561
169 Manchester St, Concord NH 03301
NEW JERSEY
Banking Dept...........................609-292-3420
CN 040, 20 West State St
Trenton NJ 08625-0067
NEW MEXICO
Financial Institutions Div.......505-827-7102
PO 25101, Santa Fe NM 87504
NEW YORK
Banking Dept..........................212-618-6557
2 Rector St, New York NY 10006

NORTH CAROLINA
    Banking Commission 919-733-3016
    430 N Salisbury St, Raleigh NC 27611
NORTH DAKOTA
    Banking & Financial Institutions Dept........
   701-224-2253
    600 E Boulevard, Bismarck ND 58505-0080
OHIO
    Banks Div................................614-466-2932
    77 S High St, 23rd Fl
    Columbus OH 43266-0544
OKLAHOMA
    Banking Dept..........................405-521-2782
    4100 N Lincoln Blvd
    Oklahoma City OK 73105
OREGON
    Finance & Corp Securities 503-378-4140
    Busick Bldg, 280 Court St, NE
    Salem OR 97310
PENNSYLVANIA
    Banking Dept..........................717-787-3094
    PO 569, Harrisburg PA 17108-0569
RHODE ISLAND
    Banking Div.............................401-277-2246
    233 Richmond St, Providence RI 02903-4237
SOUTH CAROLINA
    Financial Institutions Board ..803-734-2688
    PO 11194, Columbia SC 29211
SOUTH DAKOTA
    Banking Div.............................605-773-3421
    500 E Capitol, Pierre SD 57501
TENNESSEE
    Financial Institutions Dept 615-741-2236
    500 Charlotte Ave, 4th Fl
    Nashville TN 37243-0705
TEXAS
    Banking Dept..........................512-475-1300
    2601 N Lamar Blvd, Austin TX 78705
UTAH
    Financial Institutions Dept 801-538-8830
    PO 89, Salt lake City UT 84110-0089
VERMONT
    Banking Dept Cmr. 802-828-3301
    1 West State St, Montpelier VT 05620-3101
VIRGINIA
    Financial Institutions Bur. 804-371-9657
    1300 E Main St, Richmond VA 23219
WASHINGTON
    Banking Div.............................206-753-6520
    PO 41000, Olympia WA 98504-1000
WEST VIRGINIA
    Banking Div.............................304-558-2294
    State Capitol, Bldg 3, Rm 311, Charleston .
    WV 25305-0240

WISCONSIN
    Banking Commission 608-266-1621
    PO 7876, Madison WI 53707-7876
WYOMING
    Banking Div............................307-777-7797
    Herschler Bldg, 3rd Fl E
    Cheyenne WY 82002

BUDGET

ALABAMA
    Budget Ofc 205-242-7230
    600 Dexter Ave, Ste 105
    Montgomery AL 36130
ALASKA
    Management & Budget Ofce...907-465-3568
    PO 110001, Juneau AK 99811-0020
ARIZONA
    Strategic Planning & Budgeting...................
   602-542-5381
    1700 W Washington St, W Wing
    Phoenix AZ 85007
ARKANSAS
    Budget Ofc 501-682-1941
    PO Box 3278, Little Rock AR 72201
COLORADO
    Planning & Budgeting Ofc......303-866-3317
    State Capitol Bldg, Rm 111
    Denver CO 80203
DELAWARE
    Budget Ofc 302-739-4204
    Thomas Collins Bldg, Dover DE 19901
DISTRICT OF COLUMBIA
    Budget Ofc 202-727-6343
    441 4th St NW, Washington DC 20001
FLORIDA
    Budget Mgmt. Ofc 904-487-1880
    The Capitol, Tallahassee FL 32399-0001
GEORGIA
    Planning & Budget Ofc 404-656-3820
    254 Washington St SW, Rm 614
    Atlanta GA 30334
HAWAII
    Budget & Finance Dept...........808-586-1518
    250 S Hotel St, Honolulu, HI 96810
IDAHO
    Budget & Policy Analysis Unit208-334-3903
    Statehouse, Rm 122, Boise ID 83720
ILLINOIS
    Budget Bureau........................217-782-4520
    State House, Rm 108, Springfield IL 62706
INDIANA
    State Budget Agency. 317-232-5612
    212 State House, Indianapolis IN 46204

IOWA
    Management Dept 515-281-3322
    Capitol Bldg, Rm12, Des Moines IA 50319
KANSAS
    Budget Div 913-296-2436
    152 E State House, Topeka KS 66612
KENTUCKY
    Management & Budget 502-564-4240
    383 Capitol Annex, Frankfort KY 40601
LOUISIANA
    State Budget & Planning Ofc .504-342-7410
    PO 94095, Baton Rouge LA 70804-9095
MAINE
    Budget Bureau.........................207-624-7810
    State House Station 78, Augusta ME 04333
MARYLAND
    Budget & Fiscal Planning Dept ....
   410-974-2114
    45 Clavert St., Annapolis MD 21404
MASSACHUSETTS
    Budget Bureau.........................617-727-2081
    State House, Rm 272, Boston MA 02133
MICHIGAN
    Budget & Accounting Div........517-373-3165
    430 W Allegan, Lansing MI 48922
MINNESOTA
    Budget Svcs Div.......................612-297-7881
    400 Centenniel Bldg, 658 Cedar St
    St Paul MN 55155
MISSISSIPPI
    Budget & Fund Mgt Div..........601-359-3402
    PO 267, Jackson MS 39205
MISSOURI
    Budget & Planning Dept Dir. .314-751-2345
    PO 809, Jefferson City MO 65102
MONTANA
    Budget & Prog Planning Ofc...406-444-3616
    Capitol Station, Helena MT 59620-0801
NEBRASKA
    Budget Div 402-471-2526
    Rm 1315, State Capitol Bldg
    Lincoln NE 68509
NEVADA
    Budget Div 702-687-4065
    209 E Musser St, Rm 204, Carson City NV .
    89710
NEW HAMPSHIRE
    Budget Ofcr.............................603-271-3202
    State House Annex, Concord, NH 03301
NEW JERSEY
    Capitol Budgeting & Planning Commission
   609-292-9022
    CN 004 33 W State St
    Trenton NJ 08625-0004

NEW MEXICO
    Budget Div 505-827-3642
    180 Bataan Memorial Bldg
    Santa Fe NM 87503
NEW YORK
    Budget Div 518-474-2300
    State Capitol, Rm 113, Albany NY 12224
NORTH CAROLINA
    Budget Ofc 919-733-4240
    116 W Jones St, Raleigh NC 27603-8001
NORTH DAKOTA
    Management & Budget Office 701-224-2680
    600 E Boulevard, Bismarck ND 58505
OHIO
    Budget & Management Dept ..614-466-4034
    30 E Broad St, 34th Fl
    Columbus OH 43266-0411
OKLAHOMA
    Budget Sec'y.............................405-521-2141
    122 State Capitol Bldg
    Oklahoma City OK 73105
OREGON
    Budget & Management Div 503-378-3103
    155 Cottage St NE, Salem OR 97310
PENNSYLVANIA
    Budget Office 717-787-4472
    7th Fl, Strawberry Sq
    Harrisburg PA 17120
RHODE ISLAND
    Budget Office 401-277-6300
    1 Capitol Hill, Providence RI 02908-5886
SOUTH CAROLINA
    Budget & Control Board 803-734-2320
    Box 12444, Columbia SC 29211
SOUTH DAKOTA
    Finance & Management Bur ..605-776-3411
    500 E Capitol Ave, Pierre SD 57501
TENNESSEE
    Budget Div 615-741-0320
    304 John Sevier Bldg, Nashville TN 37219
TEXAS
    Budget Div 512-463-6000
    PO 12608, Austin TX 78711-2608
UTAH
    Planning & Budget Ofc 801-538-1027
    116 State Capitol Bldg
    Salt Lake City UT 84114
VIRGINIA
    Planning & Budget Dept.........804-786-5375
    9th & Grace St, PO 1422
    Richmond VA 23211
WASHINGTON
    Budget Div 206-753-4757
    PO 43113, Olympia WA 98504-3113

WEST VIRGINIA
    Budget Sec'y..............................304-558-2344
    208 7th Ave SW,
    S Charleston WV 25303-1510
WISCONSIN
    Exec Budget & Planning Div ..608-266-1035
    101 S Webster, PO 7864
    Madison WI 53707
WYOMING
    Budget Div 307-777-7203
    2001 Capitol Ave, Cheyenne WY 82002

COMMERCE

ALABAMA
    Development Office 205-242-0400
    401 Adams Ave, Ste 600
    Montgomery AL 36130
ALASKA
    Commerce & Economic Development Dept
   907-465-2500
    PO 110800, Juneau AK 99811-0208
ARIZONA
    Commerce Dept 602-280-1300
    3800 N Central Ave, Ste 1500
    Phoenix AZ 85012
ARKANSAS
    Development Finance V-P.......501-682-5900
    PO 8023, Little Rock AR 72203
CALIFORNIA
    Trade & Commerce Agency.....916-322-3962
    801 K Street, Sacramento CA 95814
COLORADO
    Business Development Office .303-892-3840
    1625 Broadway, World Trade Ctr, Ste 1710
    Denver CO 80202
CONNECTICUT
    *Economic Development Dept 203-258-4296
    865 Brook St., Rocky Hill CT 06067
DELAWARE
    *Business Dev..........................302-739-4271
    99 Kings Hwy, PO 1401, Dover DE 19903
DISTRICT OF COLUMBIA
    Business & Economic Dev.......202-727-6600
    717 14th St, NW, 10th Fl
    Washington DC 20005
FLORIDA
    Commerce Dept 904-488-3104
    Collins Bldg, Ste 536
    Tallahassee FL 32399-2000
GEORGIA
    Industry, Trade & Tourism Dept
   404-656-3556
    PO 1776, Atlanta GA 30301

HAWAII
    Commerce & Consumer Affairs Dept
   808-586-2850
    1010 Richards St, Honolulu, HI 96809
IDAHO
    Commerce Dept 208-334-2470
    700 W State St, Boise ID 83720-2700
ILLINOIS
    Commerce Commission 217-782-2024
    PO 19280, Springfield IL 62794-9280
INDIANA
    Commerce Dept 317-232-8800
    1 North Capitol Ste 700
    Indianapolis IN 46204-2248
IOWA
    Commerce Dept 515-281-7401
    1918 Se Hulsizer Ave, Ankney IA 50021
KANSAS
    Commerce & Housing Dept 913-296-3480
    700 SW Harrison St, Ste 1300
    Topeka KS 66603-3712
KENTUCKY
    Economic Devel. Cabinet 502-564-7670
    Capitol Plaza Tower, 24th Fl., 500 Metro St
    Frankfort, KY 40601
LOUISIANA
    Commerce & Industry Ofc 504-342-5361
    box 94185, Baton Rouge LA 70804-9185
MAINE
    Economic & Community Development Dept
   207-287-2656
    State House Station 59
    Augusta ME 04333
MARYLAND
    Economic & Employment Development ......
    Dept...410-333-6901
    217 E Redwood St, Baltimore MD 21202
MASSACHUSETTS
    Business Development Div 617-727-3206
    1 Ashburton Pl, Rm 2101, Boston MA 02114
MICHIGAN
    Commerce Dept 517-373-7230
    4th Fl Law Bldg, Box 30004
    Lansing MI 48909
MINNESOTA
    Commerce Dept 612-296-6848
    133 E 7th St, St Paul MN 55101
MISSISSIPPI
    Economic & Community Development Dept
   601-359-3449
    PO 849, Jackson MS 39205
MISSOURI
    Economic Development Dept ..314-751-3946
    PO 1157, Jefferson City MO 65102

MONTANA
    Commerce Dept 406-444-3494
    1424 9th Ave, Helena MT 59620-0501
NEBRASKA
    Economic Development Dept ..402-471-3747
    PO 94666, Lincoln NE 68509
NEVADA
    Business & Industry................702-486-5150
    2500 W Washington Ave, Ste 100, Las ....
    Vegas NV 89109
NEW HAMPSHIRE
    Resources & Economic Development Dept
   603-271-2411
    PO Box 856, Concord NH 03302-0856
NEW JERSEY
    Commerce & Economic Development Dept
   609-292-2444
    CN 820, 20 West State St
    Trenton NJ 08625-0820
NEW MEXICO
    Economic Development Dept ..505-827-0305
    1100 St Francis Dr, Santa Fe NM 87503
NEW YORK
    Economic Development Dept ..518-474-4100
    Twin Towers, 1 Commerce Plaza
    Albany NY 12245
NORTH CAROLINA
    Commerce Dept 919-733-4962
    430 N Salisbury St, Raleigh NC 27611
NORTH DAKOTA
    Economic Development & Finance ....
    Commission............................701-221-5300
    1833 E Bismarck Expressway
    Bismarck ND 58504
OHIO
    Commerce Dept 614-466-3636
    77 S High St, 23rd Fl
    Columbus OH 43266-0544
OKLAHOMA
    Commerce Dept 405-843-9770
    PO 26980, Oklahoma City OK 73126-0980
OREGON
    Consumer & Bus Serv Dept 503-378-4100
    21 Labor & Industries Bldg
    Salem OR 97310
PENNSYLVANIA
    Commerce Dept 717-787-3003
    433 Forum Bldg, Harrisburg PA 17120
RHODE ISLAND
    *Business Development Div ...401-277-2601
    7 Jackson Walkway, Providence RI 02903
SOUTH CAROLINA
    Commerce Dept 803-737-0400
    PO 927, Columbia SC 29202

SOUTH DAKOTA
    Commerce & Regulations Dept
   605-773-3177
    500 E Capitol, Pierre SD 57501
TENNESSEE
    Commerce & Ins Dept.............615-741-2241
    500 James Robertson Pkwy
    Nashville TN 37243-0565
TEXAS
    Commerce Dept 512-472-5059
    Box 12728, Austin, TX 78711
UTAH
    Commerce Dept 801-530-6701
    PO 45802, Salt Lake City UT 84145-0801
VERMONT
    Development & Community Affairs Agency
   802-828-3211
    Pavilion Ofc Bldg
    Montpelier VT 05609-0501
VIRGINIA
    Commerce & Trade..................804-786-7831
    9th St Ofc Bldg, Rm 723
    Richmond VA 23219
WASHINGTON
    Trade & Economic Development Dept
   206-753-7426
    PO 42500 Olympia WA 98504-2500
WEST VIRGINIA
    Commerce, Labor & Environmental ....
    Resources Dept 304-558-0400
    State Capitol Bldg, Rm M146
    Charleston WV 25305-0310
WISCONSIN
    Development Dept 608-266-8976
    PO 7970, Madison WI 53707
WYOMING
    Commerce Dept 307-777-6303
    Barrett Bldg, 2301 Central Ave
    Cheyenne WY 82002

COMMUNITY AFFAIRS

ALABAMA
    Economic & Community Affairs Dept ....
   205-242-5369
    401 Adams Ave, Montgomery AL 36130
ALASKA
    Community & Regional Affairs Dept
   907-465-4700
    PO Box B, Juneau AK 99811
ARIZONA
    Community Development Div.602-280-1300
    3800 N Central Ave, Ste 1500
    Phoenix AZ 85012

ARKANSAS
  Community Assistance Div.....501-682-5193
  1 Capitol Mall, Little Rock AR 72201
CALIFORNIA
  Community Affairs Div...........916-322-1560
  PO 952050, Sacramento CA 94252-2050
COLORADO
  Local Affairs Dept....................303-866-2771
  1313 Sherman St, Rm 518
  Denver CO 80203
CONNECTICUT
  Community & Business Financing
 203-258-4218
  865 Brook St, Rocky Hill CT 06067-3405
DELAWARE
  Community Services Office.....302-577-3491
  820 N French St, Wilmington DE 19801
DISTRICT OF COLUMBIA
  Community Development Office
 202-727-6240
  441 4th St NW, 6th Fl
  Washington DC 20001
FLORIDA
  Community Affairs Dept.........904-488-8466
  2740 Centerview Dr,
  Tallahassee FL 32399-2100
GEORGIA
  Community Affairs Dept.........404-656-3836
  100 Peachtree St, 1200 Equitable Bldg........
  Atlanta GA 30303
HAWAII
  Human Services Dept..............808-848-3230
  1002 N School St, Honolulu HI 96817
IDAHO
  Community Development Div.208-334-2470
  700 W State St, Boise ID 83720-2700
ILLINOIS
  Commerce & Community Affairs Dept
 217-782-7500
  620 E Adams, Springfield IL 62701
INDIANA
  Community Development Div.317-232-8911
  1 North Capitol Ste 700
  Indianapolis IN 46204-2248
IOWA
  Community Progress Div........515-242-4807
  200 E Grand Ave, Des Moines IA 50309
KANSAS
  Community Development Div
 913-296-3485
  700 SW Harrison St, Ste 1300
  Topeka KS 66603-3712

KENTUCKY
  Community Development Dept
 502-564-7140
  Capital Plaza Tower, 500 Mero St...............
  Frankfort KY 40601
LOUISIANA
  Human Services Office............504-342-2570
  PO 4049, Baton Rouge LA 70821
MAINE
  Human Services Office............207-287-2736
  State House Station 11, Augusta ME 04333
MARYLAND
  Community Development Administration ..
  Div...410-514-7500
  100 Community Pl
  Crownsville MD 21032-2023
MASSACHUSETTS
  Communities & Development Executive .....
  Office.......................................617-737-7765
  100 Cambridge St, Rm 1404
  Boston MA 02202
MINNESOTA
  Community Development Dept
 612-297-2515
  121 7th Pl East, Rm 500, St Paul MN 55101
MISSISSIPPI
  Community Svcs Div...............601-949-2040
  PO Box 352, Jackson MS 39201-1205
NEBRASKA
  Community & Rural Development Div
 402-471-4388
  PO 94666, Lincoln NE 68509
NEVADA
  Community Services Ofc.........702-687-4990
  Capitol Complex, Carson City NV 89710
NEW HAMPSHIRE
  Energy & Community Services
 603-271-2611
  57 Regional Dr, Concord NH 03301-8506
NEW JERSEY
  Community Affairs Dept.........609-292-6420
  CN 800, 101 S Broad St
  Trenton NJ 08625-0800
NEW MEXICO
  Public Affairs Div....................505-827-3000
  State Capitol, Santa Fe, NM 87503
NEW YORK
  Housing & Community Renewal Div
 518-486-3370
  Hampton Plaza, 38-40 State St
  Albany NY 12207
NORTH CAROLINA
  Public Affairs Div....................919-733-4984
  PO Box 27687, Raleigh NC 27611

OHIO
    Community Development Div.614-466-5863
    77 S High St, Box 1001
    Columbus OH 43266-0101
OKLAHOMA
    Community Affairs & Dev Div
   405-843-9770
    PO 26980, Oklahoma City OK 73126-0980
OREGON
    Community Dev Sec. 503-378-3732
    775 Summer St NE, Salem OR 97310
PENNSYLVANIA
    Community Affairs Dept.........717-787-7160
    Forum Bldg, Rm 317, Harrisburg PA 17120
RHODE ISLAND
    Community Services................401-464-2423
    600 New London Ave, Cranston RI 02920
SOUTH CAROLINA
    Human Affairs Commission....803-253-6336
    PO 4490, Columbia SC 29240
TENNESSEE
    Economic & Community Development Dept
   615-741-1888
    320 6th Ave N, 8th Fl
    Nashville TN 37243-0405
TEXAS
    Housing & Community Affairs Dept
   512-475-3934
    PO 13941, Austin TX 78111-3941
UTAH
    Community Development Div.801-538-8700
    324 S State St, Salt Lake City UT 84111
VERMONT
    Development & Community Affairs Agency
   802-828-3211
    Pavilion Ofc Bldg
    Montpelier VT 05609-0501
VIRGINIA
    Housing & Community Development Dept
   804-371-7000
    Jackson Ctr, 501 N 2nd St
    Richmond VA 23219-1321
WASHINGTON
    Community Dev Dept..............206-753-2200
    PO 48300, Olympia WA 98504-8300
WEST VIRGINIA
    Community Dev Div................304-558-4010
    Big 6, Capitol Complex, Rm 553
    Charleston WV 25305-0311
WISCONSIN
    Community Dev Div................608-266-9944
    PO 7970, Madison WI 53707

CONSUMER AFFAIRS

ALABAMA
    Attorney General.....................205-242-7300
    11 S Union St, Montgomery AL 36130

ALASKA
    Public Advocacy Office 907-274-1684
    900 W. 5th, Anchorage AK 99501

ARIZONA
    Consumer Protection & Fraud Div
   602-542-3702
    1275 W Washington, Phoenix AZ 85007
ARKANSAS
    Consumer Advocacy Div..........501-682-2007
    200 Tower Bldg, 323 Center St
    Little Rock AR 72201
CALIFORNIA
    Consumer Affairs Dept 916-445-4465
    400 R St, Ste 3000, Sacramento CA 95814
COLORADO
    Consumer Protection Sec 303-866-5230
    1525 Sherman St, 5th Fl
    Denver CO 80203
CONNECTICUT
    Consumer Protection Dept......203-566-4999
    165 Capitol Ave, Hartford CT 06106
DELAWARE
    Consumer Affairs Div..............302-577-3250
    820 N French St, Dover DE 19903
DISTRICT OF COLUMBIA
    Consumer Affairs & Trade Div202-727-3500
    441 4th St NW, Rm 1020S
    Washington DC 20001
FLORIDA
    Consumer Services 904-488-3022
    Plaza Level 10, The Capitol
    Tallahassee FL 32399-0810
GEORGIA
    Consumer Affairs Div..............404-656-3383
    40 Capitol Sq SW, Atlanta GA 30334-1300
HAWAII
    Consumer Protection Div........808-586-2636
    828 Fort St Mall, Ste 600B
    Honolulu HI 96813
ILLINOIS
    Consumer Protection Div........217-782-1090
    500 S Second, Springfield IL 62706
INDIANA
    Consumer Protection Chief Counsel
   317-232-6205
    402 W Washington St, Rm C553...................
    Indianapolis IN 46204

IOWA
    Consumer Advocate Ofc 515-281-5984
    Hoover State Ofc Bldg, 2nd Fl
    Des Moines IA 50319
KANSAS
    Consumer Protection Div 913-296-3751
    2nd Fl, Kansas Judicial Center
    Topeka KS 66612
KENTUCKY
    Consumer Protection Div 502-564-2200
    116 Capitol Bldg, 700 Capital Ave, ...
    Frankfort KY 40601
LOUISIANA
    Public Protection Div...............504-342-7900
    PO 94095, Baton Rouge LA 70804-9095
MAINE
    Public Protection Unit.............207-626-8800
    State House Station 6, Augusta ME 04333
MARYLAND
    Consumer Protection Div 410-576-6550
    200 St Paul Pl, Baltimore MD 21202-2020
MASSACHUSETTS
    Consumer Affairs Executive Ofc
   617-727-7755
    1 Ashburton Pl, Rm 1411, Boston MA 02108
MICHIGAN
    Consumer Protection & Charitable Trusts .
    Div 517-335-0855
    PO 30212, Lansing MI 48909
MINNESOTA
    Consumer Div 612-296-1006
    State Capitol, St Paul MN 55155
MISSISSIPPI
    Consumer Protection Div 601-354-7063
    PO 1609, Jackson MS 39215-1609
MISSOURI
    Consumer Services Office 314-340-6830
    111 N 7th St, Rm 229, St Louis MO 63101-.
    2176
MONTANA
    Legal & Consumer Affairs Unit
   406-444-3553
    1424 9th Ave, Helena MT 59620-0501
NEBRASKA
    Consumer Protection Div 402-471-2682
    2115 State Capitol Bldg, Lincoln NE 68509
NEVADA
    Consumer Services Div 702-687-4250
    2500 W Washington Ave, Ste 100
    Las Vegas NV 89109
NEW HAMPSHIRE
    Consumer Protection Div 603-271-3641
    208 State House Annex
    Concord NH 03301-6397

NEW JERSEY
    Consumer Affairs Div..............201-504-6320
    PO 45027, Newark NJ 07101
NEW MEXICO
    Consumer Protection Div 505-827-6060
    PO Drawer 1508, Santa Fe NM 87504-1508
NEW YORK
    Consumer Protection Board....518-474-3514
    99 Washington Ave, Albany NY 12210
NORTH CAROLINA
    Consumer Protection Sec 919-733-7741
    PO 629, Raleigh NC 27602
NORTH DAKOTA
    Consumer Fraud & Antitrust Div
   701-224-3404
    600 E Boulevard Ave, Bismarck ND 58505
OHIO
    Consumer Protection Sec 614-466-3376
    30 E Broad St, Columbus OH 43215
OKLAHOMA
    Consumer Div 405-521-3921
    112 State Capitol Bldg
    Oklahoma City OK 73105
OREGON
    Consumer & Business Services Dept
   503-378-4100
    21 Labor & Industries Bldg
    Salem OR 97310
PENNSYLVANIA
    Public Protection Ofc...............717-787-9716
    16th Fl, Strawberry Sq
    Harrisburg PA 17120
RHODE ISLAND
    Consumer Protection Unit 401-274-4400
    72 Pine St, Providence RI 02903
SOUTH CAROLINA
    Consumer Affairs Dept 803-734-9458
    PO 5757, Columbia SC 29250
SOUTH DAKOTA
    Consumer Protection Div 604-773-4400
    500 E Capitol, Pierre SD 57501-5090
TENNESSEE
    Consumer Affairs Div..............615-741-4737
    500 James Robertson Pkwy
    Nashville TN 37243-0565
TEXAS
    Consumer Protection Div 512-463-2070
    PO 12548, Austin TX 78711-2548
UTAH
    Consumer Protection Div 801-530-6619
    PO 45802, Salt Lake City UT 84145-0801
VERMONT
    Consumer Assurance Div 802-828-2436
    116 State St, Montpelier VT 05620-2901

VIRGINIA
  Consumer Affairs Ofc.............804-786-2042
  1100 Bank St, Rm 210
  Richmond VA 23219
WASHINGTON
  Consumer & Producer Protection
 206-902-1801
  PO 42560, Olympia WA 98504-2560
WEST VIRGINIA
  Consumer Advocate Div..........304-558-0526
  7th Fl, 723 Kanawha Blvd E,
  Charleston WV 25301
WISCONSIN
  Consumer Protection Bur 608-266-8512
  PO 8911, Madison WI 53706
WYOMING
  Consumer Affairs Div.............307-777-7891
  123 Capitol Bldg, Cheyenne WY 82002

CORPORATE RECORDS

ALABAMA
  Secretary Of State 205-242-5324
  PO 5616, Montgomery AL 36130-5616
ALASKA
  Corporate Information 907-465-2570
  PO 110808, Juneau AK 99811-0208
ARIZONA
  Corporation Commission.........602-542-4143
  1200 W Washington St, Phoenix AZ 85007
ARKANSAS
  Corporations 501-682-3409
  State Capitol Bldg, Rm 256, Little Rock AR
  72201
CALIFORNIA
  Corporate Filing Div................916-445-0620
  1230 J St, Sacramento CA 95814
COLORADO
  Corporation Ofc 303-894-2251
  1560 Broadway, Ste 200
  Denver CO 80202
CONNECTICUT
  Records & Legislative Svc.......203-566-5827
  State Capitol, Hartford CT 06106
DELAWARE
  Corporations Administrator....302-739-3073
  Townsend Bldg, Dover DE 19901
DISTRICT OF COLUMBIA
  Archives Public Records Ofc ...202-727-2052
  441 4th St NW, Washington DC 20001
FLORIDA
  Corporations Div 904-487-6000
  PO 6327, Tallahassee FL 32314

GEORGIA
  State Records Center...............404-756-4860
  1050 Murphy Ave, Bldg 15
  Atlanta GA 30310
HAWAII
  Records Management Br.........808-831-6780
  Iolani Palace Grounds
  Honolulu HI 96813
IDAHO
  Corporation Div 208-334-2300
  Statehouse, Rm 203, Boise ID 83720
ILLINOIS
  Archives & Records Div...........217-782-4682
  Capitol Bldg, Rm 213, Springfield IL 62756
INDIANA
  Public Records Commission 317-232-3373
  IGCS, 402 W Washington St, #W472, ...
  Indianapolis IN 46204
IOWA
  Corporations Div 515-281-7550
  1300 Walnut St, Des Moines IA 50319
KANSAS
  Corporation Commission.........913-271-3100
  1500 SW Arrowhead Rd, Topeka KS 66604
  OR
  Corporations Div 913-296-4564
  Statehouse, 2nd Fl, Topeka KS 66612
KENTUCKY
  Corporation Records................502-564-7330
  150 Capitol Bldg, 700 Capital Ave, ...
  Frankfort KY 40601
LOUISIANA
  Archives & Records Div...........504-922-1200
  PO Box 94125
  Baton Rouge LA 70804-9125
MAINE
  Corporate Div 207-287-6308
  State House Station 101
  Augusta ME 04333
MARYLAND
  State Documents Div...............410-974-2486
  11 Bladen St, Old Armory Bldg, Annapolis .
  MD 21401-2249
MASSACHUSETTS
  Corporations 617-727-2853
  State House, Rm 337, Boston MA 02133
MICHIGAN
  Corporation Div 517-334-6327
  PO 30222, Lansing MI 48909
MINNESOTA
  Records, Renewals, Registrations Div
 612-297-4802
  100 Constitution St, Rm 180
  St Paul MN 55155

MISSISSIPPI
Corporations 601-359-1350
PO 136, Jackson MS 39205
MISSOURI
Records Mgt Div 314-751-4502
PO 778, Jefferson City MO 65102
MONTANA
Business Svc Div 406-444-3665
State Capitol, Rm 225, Helena MT 59620
NEBRASKA
Corporation Div 402-471-4079
PO Box 94608, Lincoln NE 68529-4608
NEVADA
Secretary of State 702-687-5203
Capitol Complex, Carson City NV 89710
NEW HAMPSHIRE
Corporations 603-271-3244
State House, Rm 204, Concord NH 03301
NEW JERSEY
Corporations Div 609-984-1900
State Capitol Bldg, CN 300
Trenton NJ 08625-0300
NEW MEXICO
Corporation Commission.........505-827-4529
PO Crawer 1269, Santa Fe NM 87502-5160
NEW YORK
Corp & State Records Div 518-474-6200
162 Washington Ave, Albany NY 12231
NORTH CAROLINA
Corporations Div 919-733-4161
300 N Salisbury St, Raleigh NC 27603-5909
NORTH DAKOTA
Corporation Div 701-224-2900
600 E Boulevard, Bismarck ND 58505-0500
OHIO
Corporations 614-466-1145
30 E Broad St, 14th Floor
Columbus OH 43266-0418
OKLAHOMA
Corporate Records Div 405-521-3048
101 State Capitol Bldg
Oklahoma City OK 73105
OREGON
Corporation Div 503-378-4166
158 12th St NE, Salem OR 97310
PENNSYLVANIA
Corporation Bur......................717-787-1978
North Office Bldg, Harrisburg PA 17120
RHODE ISLAND
Corporation Div 401-277-3040
State House, Rm 218, Providence RI 02903
SOUTH CAROLINA
Corporations Div 803-734-2158
PO Box 11350. Columbia SC 29211

SOUTH DAKOTA
Corporations Div 605-773-4845
500 E Capitol, Ste 204
Pierre SD 57501-5077
TENNESSEE
Corporation Sec 615-741-0529
State Capitol, 1st Fl, Nashville TN 37243-..
0305
TEXAS
Corporation Div 512-463-5586
PO 12887, Austin TX 78711-2887
UTAH
Corporations & Uniform Commercial Code
Div 801-530-6027
PO 45802, Salt Lake City UT 84145-0801
VERMONT
Corporations Div 802-828-2371
26 Terrace St, Montpelier VT 05609-1101
VIRGINIA
State Corporation Commission
....804-371-9608
1300 E Main St, Richmond VA 23219
WASHINGTON
Corporation Div 206-753-2896
PO 40220, Olympia WA 98504-0220
WEST VIRGINIA
Corporations Div 304-558-8000
State Capitol Bldg
Charleston WV 25305-0770
WISCONSIN
Corporations Div 608-266-3590
PO Box 7848, Madison WI 53707
WYOMING
Corporations Div 307-777-7311
State Capitol, Cheyenne WY 82002-0020

ECONOMIC OPPORTUNITY

ALABAMA
Development Office 205-242-0400
401 Adams Ave, Ste 600
Montgomery AL 36130
ALASKA
Economic Dev Div....................907-465-2017
PO 110804, Juneau AK 99811-0804
ARIZONA
Economic Security Dept 602-542-5678
PO 6123, Phoenix AZ 85005
ARKANSAS
Economic Development 501-682-2345
State Capitol, Rm 250
Little Rock AR 72201

CALIFORNIA
Economic Opportunity Ofc......916-322-2940
700 N 10th St, Rm 258, Sacramento CA .....
95814
COLORADO
Economic Development Div 303-866-2771
1313 Sherman St, Rm 518
Denver CO 80203
CONNECTICUT
Economic Dev Dept 203-258-4202
865 Brook St, Rocky Hill CT 06067-3405
DELAWARE
Economic Dev Authority 302-739-4271
99 Kings Hwy, PO 1401, Dover DE 19903
DISTRICT OF COLUMBIA
Economic Dev.........................202-727-6365
441 4th St NW, Ste 1140
Washington DC 20001
FLORIDA
Economic Dev Div...................904-488-6300
Collins Bldg, Ste 536
Tallahassee FL 32399-2000
GEORGIA
Economic Industry Dept 404-656-3573
PO 1776, Atlanta GA 30301
HAWAII
Business & Economic Dev & Tourism Dept
....808-586-2360
220 S King St, Honolulu HI 96804
IDAHO
Economic Dev Div...................208-334-2470
700 W State St, Boise ID 83720-2700
ILLINOIS
Economic & Fiscal Commission
....217-782-5320
703 Stratton Bldg, Springfield IL 62706
INDIANA
Economic Policy Coordinator ..317-232-4581
State Capitol, Rm 206 Indianapolis IN 46204
IOWA
Economic Dev Dept 515-242-4814
200 E Grand Ave, Des Moines IA 50309
KANSAS
Development Finance Authority
....913-296-6747
700 Jackson Jayhawk Twrs, 10th Fl
Topeka KS 66603
KENTUCKY
Economic Dev Cabinet 502-564-7670
Capitol Plaza Tower, 24th Fl, 500 Mero St,
Frankfort KY 40601
LOUISIANA
Economic Dev Dept 504-342-5388
Box 94185, Baton Rouge LA 70804-9185

MAINE
Economic &Community Dev Dept
....207-287-2656
State House Station 59. Augusta ME 04333
MARYLAND
Economic & Employment Dev Dept
....410-333-6901
217 E Redwood St, Baltimore MD 21202
MASSACHUSETTS
Economic Affairs Executive Ofc
....617-727-8380
1 Ashburton Pl, Rm 2101, Boston MA 02108
MICHIGAN
Economic Dev & Governmental Affrs Ofc
....517-373-0870
PO 30026, Lansing MI 48909
MINNESOTA
Economic Dev Unit...................612-296-2394
121 7th Pl East, Rm 500, St Paul MN 55101
MISSISSIPPI
Economic & Community Dev Dept
....601-359-3449
PO Box 849, Jackson MS 39205
MISSOURI
Economic Dev Dept 314-751-3946
PO 1157 Jefferson City MO 65102
MONTANA
Development Div 406-444-3814
1424 9th Ave, Helena MT 59620-0501
NEBRASKA
Economic Dev Dept 402-471-3747
PO 94666, Lincoln NE 68509
NEVADA
Economic Dev Commission 702-687-4325
Capitol Complex, Carson City NV 89710
NEW HAMPSHIRE
Resources & Economic Dev Dept
....603-271-2411
PO 856, Concord NH 03302-0856
NEW JERSEY
Commerce & Economic Dev Dept
....609-292-2444
CN820, 20 West State St
Trenton NJ 08625-0820
NEW MEXICO
Economic Dev Dept 505-827-0305
1100 St Francis Dr, Santa Fe NM 87503
NEW YORK
Economic Dev Dept 518-474-4100
Twin Towers, 1 Commerce Plaza
Albany NY 12245
NORTH CAROLINA
Business Dev Office.................919-733-4151
430 N. Salisbury St., Raleigh, NC 27611

NORTH DAKOTA
  Economic Dev & Finance Commission
 701-221-5300
  1833 E Bismarck Expwy
  Bismarck ND 58504
OHIO
  Development Dept...................614-466-3379
  77 S High St, Box 1001
  Columbus OH 43266-0101
OKLAHOMA
  Development Finance Authority
 405-848-9761
  PO 53424, Oklahoma City OK 73152
OREGON
  Economic Dev Dept 503-373-1205
  775 Summer St NE, Salem OR 97310
PENNSYLVANIA
  Economic Dev & Marketing Dept Secy
 717-787-3418
  2301 N Cameron St, Harrisburg PA 17110
RHODE ISLAND
  Economic Dev...........................401-277-2601
  7 Jackson Walkway, Providence RI 02903
SOUTH CAROLINA
  Economic Dev Sr Exec Asst 803-734-9718
  PO 11369, Columbia SC 29211
SOUTH DAKOTA
  Economic Dev & Tourism Ofc.605-773-5032
  711 Wells Ave, Pierre SD 57501-3369
TENNESSEE
  Economic & Community Dev Dept
 615-741-1888
  320 6th Ave N, 8th Fl
  Nashville TN 37243-0405
TEXAS
  Business Dev. Dep.Dir. 512-472-5059
  PO12728, Austin, TX 78711
UTAH
  Business & Econ Dev Div........801-538-8700
  324 S State St, Salt Lake City UT 84111
VERMONT
  Economic Dev Div....................802-828-3221
  Pavilion Ofc Bldg
  Montpelier VT 05609-0501
VIRGINIA
  Economic Dev Dept 804-371-8106
  PO 798, Richmond VA 23206-0798
WASHINGTON
  Trade & Economic Dev Dept...206-753-7426
  PO 42500, Olympia WA 98504-2500
WEST VIRGINIA
  Economic Dev Authority 304-558-3650
  525 Bldg 6, Capitol Complex
  Charleston WV 25301-0311

WISCONSIN
  Economic Dev Div....................608-266-3203
  PO 7970, Madison WI 53707
WYOMING
  Economic Dev & Stabilization Div
 307-777-7284
  Barrett Building, 2301 Central Ave
  Cheyenne WY 82002

EMPLOYMENT SECURITY

ALABAMA
  Economic & Community Affairs Dept ....
 205-242-5300
  401 Adams Ave, Montgomery AL 36130
ALASKA
  Employment Security Div.......907-465-2711
  PO 25509, Juneau AK 99802-5509
ARIZONA
  Employment & Security Admn
 602-542-3667
  PO 6123, Phoenix AZ 85005
ARKANSAS
  Employment Security Dept.....501-682-2121
  2 Capitol Mall, Little Rock, AR 72201
CALIFORNIA
  Employment Dev. Dept...........916-654-8210
  PO 826880, Sacramento CA 94280-0001
COLORADO
  Labor & Employment Dept.....303-837-3801
  600 Grant St, Ste 900
  Denver CO 80203-3528
CONNECTICUT
  Employment Security Div Exec Dir
 203-566-4280
  200 Folly Brook Blvd
  Wethersfield CT 06109
DELAWARE
  Employment & Training Services Div
 302-368-6810
  University Office Plaza
  Newark DE 19714-9029
DISTRICT OF COLUMBIA
  Employment Security Svc.......202-724-7139
  500 C Street NW, Washington DC 20001
FLORIDA
  Labor & Employment Security Dept
 904-922-7021
  2012 Capitol Circle SE, Hartman Bldg
  Tallahassee FL 32399-2152
GEORGIA
  Labor Dept 404-656-3011
  148 International Blvd, Atlanta Ga 30303

HAWAII
Employment Service Div.........808-586-8610
550 Halekauwila St, Rm 201
Honolulu HI 96813

IDAHO
Employment Dept...................208-334-6112
317 Main St, Boise ID 83735

ILLINOIS
Employment Security Dept.....312-793-5700
401 S State St, Chicago IL 60605

INDIANA
Employment Standards Div....317-232-2683
402 W. Washington St., Rm W195
Indianapolis IN 46204

IOWA
Employment Services Dept.....515-281-5365
1000 E Grand Ave
Des Moines IA 50319-0209

KANSAS
Employment Security Div.......913-296-0821
401 Topeka Ave, Topeka KS 66603

KENTUCKY
Employment Standards & Mediation Div
....502-564-2784
1047 US 127 South, Ste 4
Frankfort KY 40601

LOUISIANA
Employment Security Asst Secy.
....504-342-3013
PO 94094, Baton Rouge LA 70804-9094

MAINE
Employment & Training Programs Bur.
....207-287-3377
PO 309, 20 Union St
Augusta ME 04332-0309

MARYLAND
Employment & Training Div ..410-333-5070
1100 N Eutaw St, Rm 501
Baltimore MD 21201

MASSACHUSETTS
Employment & Training Dept
....617-727-6600
Hurley Bldg, Government Ctr
Boston MA 02108

MICHIGAN
Employment Security Commission
....313-876-5500
7310 Woodward Ave, Detroit MI 48202

MINNESOTA
Jobs & Training Dept..............612-296-3711
390 N Robert St, St Paul MN 55101

MISSISSIPPI
Employment Security Com 601-354-8711
PO 1699, Jackson MS 39203

MISSOURI
Employment Security Div.......314-751-3976
421 E Dunklin St
Jefferson City MO 65101

MONTANA
Employment Relations Div 406-444-6530
PO 1728, Helena MT 59624

NEBRASKA
Labor Dept 402-471-900
PO 94600, Lincoln NE 68509

NEVADA
Employment Security Research Sec
....702-687-4550
500 East 3rd St, Carson City NV 89713

NEW HAMPSHIRE
Employment Security Dept.....603-224-3311
32 S Main St, Concord NH 03301-4857

NEW JERSEY
Employment Security & Job Training Asst
Cmr..609-984-5666
John Fitch Plaza, CN 110
Trenton NJ 08625-0110

NEW MEXICO
Employment Security Div.......505-841-8437
PO 1928, Albuquerque NM 87103

NEW YORK
Employment & Trng Dept Cmr
....518-457-4317
State Campus, Bldg 12, Albany NY 12240

NORTH CAROLINA
Employment Security Commission
....919-733-7546
700 Wade Ave, Box 25903
Raleigh NC 27611

NORTH DAKOTA
Job Service 701-224-2836
PO 5507, Bismarck ND 58502-5507

OHIO
Employment Services Bureau 614-466-2100
145 S Front St, Columbus OH 43216

OKLAHOMA
Employment Security Commission
....405-557-0200
2401 N Lincoln Blvd
Oklahoma City OK 73105

OREGON
Employee Svcs Div 503-378-3200
21 Labor & Industries Bldg
Salem OR 97310

PENNSYLVANIA
Employment Security & Job Training Dept
Secy 717-787-1745
Labor & Industry Bldg
Harrisburg PA 17120

RHODE ISLAND
    Employment & Training Dept 401-277-3732
    101 Friendship St, Providence RI 02903
SOUTH CAROLINA
    Employment Security Commission
   803-737-2655
    PO 995, Columbia SC 29202
SOUTH DAKOTA
    Job Service Div 605-622-2452
    PO 4730, Aberdeen SD 57402-4730
TENNESSEE
    Employment Security Dept.....615-741-2131
    12th Fl, Volunteer Plaza Bldg
    Nashville TN 37245-0001
TEXAS
    Employment Commission 512-463-2800
    101 E 15th St, Austin TX 78778
UTAH
    Employment Security Div.......801-536-7401
    PO 11249, Salt Lake City UT 84147
VERMONT
    Employment & Training Dept
   802-229-0311
    Green Mt Dr, PO 488
    Montpelier VT 05601-0488
VIRGINIA
    Employment Commission 804-786-3001
    703 E Main St, Richmond VA 23219
WASHINGTON
    Employment Security Dept.....206-753-5114
    PO 9046, Olympia WA 98507-9046
WEST VIRGINIA
    Employment Programs Bur 304-558-2630
    112 California Ave
    Charleston WV 25305-0112
WISCONSIN
    Industry, Labor & Human Relations Dept
   608-266-7552
    PO 7946, Madison WI 53707
WYOMING
    Employment Dept....................307-777-7672
    Herschler Bldg, 2nd Fl E
    Cheyenne WY 82002

ENVIRONMENTAL AFFAIRS

ALABAMA
    Environmental Management Dept
   205-271-7706
    1751 Congressman W L Dickinson Dr
    Montgomery AL 36130
ALASKA
    Environ Conserv Dept.............907-465-5050
    410 Willoughby Ave, Juneau AK 99811-1795

ARIZONA
    Environmental Quality Dept ..602-207-2300
    3033 N Central, Phoenix AZ 85012
ARKANSAS
    Pollution Control & Ecology Dept
   501-562-7444
    PO 8913, Little Rock AR 73319-8913
CALIFORNIA
    Environmental Protection Agency
   916-445-3846
    PO 2815, Sacramento CA 95832
COLORADO
    Natural Resources Dept..........303-866-3311
    1313 Sherman St, Rm 718
    Denver CO 80203
CONNECTICUT
    Environmental Protection Dept
   203-566-2110
    79 Elm St, Hartford CT 06106
DELAWARE
    Natural Resources & Environmental ....
    Control Dept 302-739-4403
    89 Kings Hwy, PO 1401
    Dover DE 19903-1401
DISTRICT OF COLUMBIA
    Environmental Regulation Adm
   202-404-1136
    2100 Martin Luther King Ave SE
    Washington DC 20020
FLORIDA
    Environmental Protection Dept
   904-488-1554
    3900 Commonwealth Blvd
    Tallahassee FL 32399-3000
GEORGIA
    Natural Resources Dept..........404-656-3500
    205 Butler St SE, Ste 1252
    Atlanta GA 30334
HAWAII
    Environmental Quality Control Ofc
   808-586-4185
    220 S King St, 4th Fl, Honolulu HI 96813
IDAHO
    Natural Resource Policy Bur ..208-334-3180
    PO 25, 600 S Walnut, Boise ID 83707
ILLINOIS
    Environmental Protection Agency
   217-782-3397
    PO 19276, Springfield IL 62794
INDIANA
    Environmental Management Dept
   317-232-8162
    PO 6015, 100 N Senate Ave, ...
    Indianapolis IN 46206-6015

IOWA
Natural Resources Dept..........515-281-5385
Wallace State Ofc Bldg
Des Moines IA 50319
KANSAS
Environment Div.....................913-296-1535
Landon State Ofc Bldg, Rm 620
Topeka KS 66612
KENTUCKY
Environmental Protection Dept
....502-564-3035
Fort Boone Plaza, 18 Reilly Rd
Frankfort KY 40601
LOUISIANA
Environmental Quality Dept..504-765-0741
PO 44066, Baton Rouge LA 70804
MAINE
Environmental Protection Dept
....207-287-2812
State House Station 17
Augusta ME 04333
MARYLAND
Environment Dept...................410-631-3084
2500 Broening Hwy, Baltimore MD 21224
MASSACHUSETTS
Environmental Affairs Exec Ofc
....617-727-9800
100 Cambridge St, 20th Fl
Boston MA 02202
MICHIGAN
Natural Resources Dept..........517-373-2329
Box 30028, Lansing MI 48909
MINNESOTA
Environmental Protection Division ....
....612-296-7341
State Capitol, St Paul MN 55155
MISSISSIPPI
Environmental Quality Dept..601-961-5000
PO 20305, Jackson MS 39209
MISSOURI
Natural Resources Dept..........314-751-4422
PO 176, Jefferson City MO 65102
MONTANA
Natural Resources & Conservation Dept
....406-444-6699
1520 E 6th Ave, Helena MT 59620
NEBRASKA
Environmental Quality Dept..402-471-2186
PO 98922, Lincoln NE 68509-8922
NEVADA
Conservation & Natural Resources Dept
....702-687-4360
123 W Nye Lane, Rm 230
Carson City NV 89710

NEW HAMPSHIRE
Environmental Protection Div 603-271-3679
208 State House Annex
Concord NY 03301-6397
NEW JERSEY
Environmental Protection & Energy Dept
....609-292-2885
401 E State St, CN 402
Trenton NJ 08625-0402
NEW MEXICO
Environment Dept...................505-827-2850
PO 26110, Santa Fe NM 87502
NEW YORK
Environmental Conservation Dept
....518-457-3446
50 Wolf Rd, Albany NY 12233
NORTH CAROLINA
Environment, Health & Natural Resources
Dept...919-733-4984
PO 27687, Raleigh NC 27611
NORTH DAKOTA
Environmental Health Sec......701-221-5150
PO Box 5520, Bismarck ND 58502-5520
OHIO
Environmental Protection Agency
....614-644-2782
Box 1049, 1800 Watermark
Columbus OH 43266-0149
OKLAHOMA
Environmental Quality Dept..405-271-8050
PO 53504, Oklahoma City OK 73152
OREGON
Environmental Quality Dept..503-229-5395
811 SW 6th Ave, Portland OR 97204
PENNSYLVANIA
Environ Resources Dept..........717-787-2814
PO 2063, Harrisburg PA 17105-2063
RHODE ISLAND
Environmental Mgmt Dept.....401-277-2771
9 Hayes St, Providence RI 02908
SOUTH CAROLINA
Health & Environment Control Dept
....803-734-4880
2600 Bull St, Columbia SC 29201
SOUTH DAKOTA
Environment & Natural Resources Dept
....605-773-3151
Joe Foss Bldg, 523 E Capitol Ave
Pierre SD 57501
TENNESSEE
Environment & Conservation Dept
....615-532-0109
401 Church St, 21st Fl
Nashville TN 37248-0438

TEXAS
    Natural Resource Conservation Commission
   512-462-7901
    PO 13087 Austin TX 78711
UTAH
    Environment Div 801-538-1015
    236 State Capitol, Salt Lake City UT 84114
VERMONT
    Natural Resources Agency 802-341-3600
    103 S Main St, Waterbury VT 05671-0301
VIRGINIA
    Environment Quality Dept 804-786-8750
    629 E Main St, Richmond VA 23219
WASHINGTON
    Natural Resources Dept 206-902-1004
    PO Box 47001, Olympia WA 98504-7001
WEST VIRGINIA
    Environmental Protection Div
   304-759-0515
    10 McJunkin Rd, Nitro WV 25143-2506
WISCONSIN
    Natural Resources Dept 608-266-2121
    PO 7921, Madison WI 53707
WYOMING
    Environmental Quality Dept ..307-777-7938
    Herschler Bldg, 4th Fl W
    Cheyenne WY 82002

FINANCE

ALABAMA
    Finance Dept...........................205-242-7160
    600 Dexter Ave, Ste 105
    Montgomery AL 36130
ALASKA
    Finance Div.............................907-465-3435
    PO 110204, juneau AK 99811-0204
ARIZONA
    Finance Div.............................602-542-1500
    1700 W Washington Rm 210
    Phoenix AZ 85007
ARKANSAS
    Finance & Admn Dept..............501-682-2242
    PO 3278, Little Rock AR 72201
CALIFORNIA
    Finance Dept...........................916-445-4141
    State Capitol, Rm 1145
    Sacramento CA 95814
COLORADO
    Housing & Finance Authority.303-297-2432
    1981 Blake St, Denver CO 80202-1272
CONNECTICUT
    Comptroller Office 203-566-5565
    55 Elm St, Hartford CT 06106

DELAWARE
    Finance Dept...........................302-739-4201
    540 S DuPont Hwy, Dover DE 19901
DISTRICT OF COLUMBIA
    Finance Office.........................202-727-2476
    441 4th St NW, Washington DC 20001
FLORIDA
    Banking & Finance Dept 904-488-0370
    Plaza Level, PL 09, Capitol Bldg
    Tallahassee FL 32399-0350
GEORGIA
    Banking & Finance Dept 404-986-1633
    2990 Brandywine Rd, Ste 200
    Atlanta GA 30341-5565
HAWAII
    Budget & Finance Dept...........808-586-1518
    250 S Hotel St, Honolulu HI 96810
IDAHO
    Finance Dept...........................208-334-3313
    700 W State St, Boise ID 83720-2700
ILLINOIS
    Comptroller.............................217-782-6000
    201 State House, Springfield IL 62706
INDIANA
    Financial Affairs Div..............317-233-3723
    State Capitol, Rm 206
    Indianapolis IN 46204
IOWA
    Revenue & Finance Dept 515-281-3204
    Hoover State Office Bldg
    Des Moines IA 50319
KANSAS
    Fiscal Ofc 913-296-3011
    Rm 263 E, State Capitol
    Topeka KS 66612-1572
KENTUCKY
    Finance & Administration Cabinet
   502-564-4240
    383 Capitol Annex, Frankfort KY 40601
LOUISIANA
    Finance Ofc 504-342-7000
    PO 94095, Baton Rouge LA 70804-9095
MAINE
    Administrative & Financial Services Dept
   207-624-7800
    State House Station 78, Augusta ME 04333
MARYLAND
    Budget & Fiscal Planning Dept ....
   410-974-2114
    45 Calvert St, Annapolis MD 21404
MASSACHUSETTS
    Administration & Finance Exec Ofc
   617-727-2040
    State House, Rm 373, Boston MA 02133

MICHIGAN
Management & Budget Dept ..517-373-1004
PO 30026, Lansing MI 48909
MINNESOTA
Finance Dept............................612-296-9721
400 Centenniel Bldg, 658 Cedar St
St Paul MN 55155
MISSISSIPPI
Finance & Administration Dept
....601-359-3402
PO 267, Jackson MS 39205
MISSOURI
Administration Office..............314-751-1851
PO 809, Jefferson City MO 65102
MONTANA
Administration Dept 406-444-2032
Sam W Mitchell Bldg, Rm 155
Helena MT 59620
NEBRASKA
Finance & Research Div..........402-471-5890
PO Box 94818, Lincoln NE 68509
NEVADA
Administration Dept 702-687-4065
209 E Musser St, Rm 204
Carson City NV 89710
NEW HAMPSHIRE
Administrative Services Dept.603-271-3201
State House Annex
Concord NH 03301
NEW JERSEY
Administration Ofc..................609-292-6000
State House, CN 001
Trenton NJ 08625-0001
NEW MEXICO
Finance & Administration Dept
....505-827-4985
180 Bataan Memorial Bldg
Santa Fe NM 87503
NEW YORK
State Comptroller Office 518-474-4040
Alfred E Smith State Ofc Bldg
Albany NY 12236
NORTH CAROLINA
Administration Dept 919-733-7232
116 W Jones St, Raleigh NC 27603-0003
NORTH DAKOTA
Economic Devel & Finance Commission
....701-221-5300
1833 E Bismarck Expwy
Bismarck ND 58504
OHIO
Administrative Services Dept.614-466-6511
30 E Broad St, Rm 4040
Columbus OH 43266-0401

OKLAHOMA
State Finance Office 405-521-2141
122 State Capitol Bldg
Oklahoma City OK 73105
OREGON
Administrative Services Dept.503-378-3104
155 Cottage St NE, Salem OR 97310
PENNSYLVANIA
Budget Office 717-787-4472
7th Fl, Strawberry Sq, Harrisburg PA 17120
RHODE ISLAND
Accounts & Control Office.......401-277-2271
1 Capitol Hill, Providence RI 02908-5883
SOUTH CAROLINA
Budget & Control Board 803-734-2320
Box 12444, Columbia SC 29211
SOUTH DAKOTA
Finance & Management Bur ..605-776-3411
500 E Capitol Ave, Pierre SD 57501
TENNESSEE
Finance & Admin Dept 615-741-2401
1st Fl State Capitol
Nashville, TN 37243-0285
TEXAS
Comptroller of Public Accts.....512-463-4000
111 E 17th St, Austin TX 78774
UTAH
Finance Div.............................801-538-3020
3120 State Ofc Bldg
Salt Lake City, UT 84114
VERMONT
Finance & Management..........802-828-2376
Pavilion Ofc Bldg, 109 State St
Montpelier VT 05609-0201
VIRGINIA
Finance Office 804-786-1148
9th St Ofc Bldg, PO 1475
Richmond Va 23212
WASHINGTON
Financial Management Ofc.....206-753-5450
PO 43113, Olympia WA 98504-3113
WEST VIRGINIA
Finance Div.............................304-558-1369
208 7th Ave SW
S Charleston WV 25303-1510
WISCONSIN
Finance & Program Mgt Div...608-267-7996
101 S Webster, PO 7864
Madison WI 53707
WYOMING
Administration & Info Dept....307-777-7201
2001 Capitol Ave, Cheyenne WY 82002

GOVERNOR

ALABAMA

....205-242-7100
600 Dexter Ave, Montgomery AL 36104

ALASKA

....907-465-3500
PO 110001, Juneau AK 99811-0001

ARIZONA

....602-542-4331
1700 W Washington St, Phoenix AZ 85007

ARKANSAS

....501-682-2345
State Capitol, Rm 250
Little Rock AR 72201

CALIFORNIA

....916-445-2841
State Capitol, 1st Fl, Sacramento Ca 95814

COLORADO

....303-866-2471
State Capitol Bldg, Rm 136
Denver CO 80203

CONNECTICUT

....203-566-4840
Executive Chambers, State Capitol, ...
Hartford CT 06106

DELAWARE

....302-739-4101
Legislative Hall, Dover DE 19901

DISTRICT OF COLUMBIA

Mayor 202-727-6319
441 4th St NW, Washington DC 20001

FLORIDA

....904-488-4441
The Capitol, Tallahassee, FL 32399-0001

GEORGIA

....404-656-1776
203 State Capitol, Atlanta GA 30334

HAWAII

....808-586-0034
State Capitol, 5th Fl, Honolulu HI 96813

IDAHO

....208-334-2100
State Capitol, 2nd Fl, Boise ID 83720

ILLINOIS

....217-782-6830
Capitol Bldg, Rm 207, Springfield IL 62706

INDIANA

....317-232-1048
State Capitol, Rm 206, Indianapolis IN ......
46204

IOWA

....515-281-5211
State Capitol Bldg, Des Moines IA 50319

KANSAS

....913-296-3232
State Capitol, Topeka KS 66612-1590

KENTUCKY

....502-564-2611
The Capitol, Frankfort KY 40601

LOUISIANA

....504-342-7015
PO Box 94004, Baton Rouge LA 70804-9004

MAINE

....207-287-3531
State House Station 1, Augusta ME 04333

MARYLAND

....410-974-3901
State House, Annapolis MD 21401

MASSACHUSETTS

....617-727-3600
Executive Ofc, State House
Boston MA 02133

MICHIGAN

....517-373-3400
PO 30013, Lansing MI 48909

MINNESOTA

....612-296-3391
State Capitol, Rm 130, St Paul MN 55155

MISSISSIPPI

....601-359-3100
PO 139, Jackson MS 39215

MISSOURI

....314-751-3222
PO 720, Jefferson City MO 65102

MONTANA

....406-444-3111
Capitol Station, Helena MT 59620-0801

NEBRASKA

....402-471-2244
State Capitol Bldg, 2nd Floor
Lincoln NE 68509

NEVADA

....702-687-5670
Capitol Complex, Carson City NV 89710

NEW HAMPSHIRE

....603-271-2121
208-214 State House, Concord NH 03301

NEW JERSEY

....609-292-6000
State House, CN 001
Trenton NJ 08625-0001

NEW MEXICO

....505-827-3000
State Capitol, Santa Fe NM 87503

NEW YORK

....518-474-8390
State Capitol, Albany NY 12224

NORTH CAROLINA
....919-733-5811
116 W Jones St, Raleigh NC 27603-8001
NORTH DAKOTA
....701-224-2200
600 E Boulevard, Bismarck ND 58505-0001
OHIO
....614-644-0813
77 S High St, Columbus OH 43215
OKLAHOMA
....405-521-2342
State Capitol, Rm 212
Oklahoma City OK 73105
OREGON
....503-378-3111
State Capitol Bldg, Rm 254
Salem OR 97310
PENNSYLVANIA
....717-787-2500
Main Capitol Bldg, Rm 225
Harrisburg PA 17120
RHODE ISLAND
....401-277-2080
State House, Providence RI 02903
SOUTH CAROLINA
....803-734-9818
PO 11369, Columbia SC 29211
SOUTH DAKOTA
....605-773-3212
500 E Capitol, Pierre SD 57501
TENNESSEE
....615-741-2001
State Capitol Bldg
Nashville TN 37243-0001
TEXAS
....512-463-2000
PO 12428, State Capitol Austin TX 78711
UTAH
....801-538-1000
210 State Capitol, Salt Lake City UT 84114
VERMONT
....802-828-3333
Pavilion Ofc Bldg, 109 State St
Montpelier VT 05609-0101
VIRGINIA
....804-786-2211
Capitol Bldg, 3rd Fl, Richmond Va 23219
WASHINGTON
....206-753-6780
Legislative Bldg, Olympia WA 98504
WEST VIRGINIA
....304-558-2000
Capitol Bldg, Charleston WV 25305-0370

WISCONSIN
....608-266-1212
PO 7863, Madison WI 53707-7863
WYOMING
....307-777-7434
State Capitol, Cheyenne WY 82002-0010

HUMAN RIGHT/CIVIL RIGHTS

ALABAMA
Attorney General......................205-242-7300
11 S Union St, Montgomery AL 36130
ALASKA
Human Rights Commission 907-276-7474
800 A St, Ste 202
Anchorage AK 99501-3669
ARIZONA
Civil Rights Div 602-542-5263
1275 W Washington, Phoenix AZ 85007
ARKANSAS
Civil Div 501-682-2007
200 Tower Bldg, 323 Center St
Little Rock AR 72201
CALIFORNIA
Human Rights Ofc...................916-654-1888
1600 9th St, 2nd Fl
Sacramento CA 95814
COLORADO
Civil Rights Div 303-894-7505
1560 Broadway, Ste 1550
Denver CO 80202
CONNECTICUT
Human Rights & Opportunities Commission
....203-566-4895
90 Washington St, Hartford CT 06106
DELAWARE
State Solicitor Civil Div 302-577-2520
820 N French St, Wilmington DE 19801
DISTRICT OF COLUMBIA
Human Rights Commission 202-727-0656
441 4th St NW, Washington DC 20001
FLORIDA
Legal Affairs Dept 904-487-1963
The Capitol, Tallahassee FL 32399-1050
GEORGIA
Civil Div 404-656-3336
40 Capitol Sq SW, Atlanta GA 30334-1300
HAWAII
Attorney General......................808-586-1500
415 Queen St, Honolulu HI 96813
IDAHO
Human Rights Commission 208-334-2873
450 W State St, Boise ID 83720

ILLINOIS
Human Rights Dept 312-814-6245
100 W Randolph St, Ste 10-100
Chicago IL 60601
INDIANA
Civil Rights Commission.........317-232-2612
100 N Senate Ave, Rm N103
Indianapolis IN 46204
IOWA
Human Rights Dept 515-281-5960
321 E 12th St, Lucas State Ofc Bldg
Des Moines IA 50319
KANSAS
Human Rights Commission 913-296-3206
Ste 851 S, 900 SW Jackson St,
Topeka KS 66612-1258
KENTUCKY
Human Rights Commission 502-564-3550
832 Capital Plaza Tower
Frankfort KY 40601
LOUISIANA
Civil Rights Div 504-342-1532
PO 3776, Baton Rouge LA 70821
MAINE
Human Rights Commission 207-624-6050
State House Station 51, Augusta ME 04333
MARYLAND
Human Relations Commission410-333-1715
20 E Franklin St, Baltimore MD 21202-2274
MASSACHUSETTS
Public Protection Bureau........617-727-2200
1 Ashburton Pl, Rm 2010
Boston MA 02202
MICHIGAN
Civil Rights Dept.....................517-335-3165
303 W Kalamazoo, 4th Fl
Lansing MI 48913
MINNESOTA
Human Rights Dept 612-296-5665
5010 Bremer Tower, 7th Pl & Minnesota St,
St Paul MN 55101
MISSISSIPPI
Attorney General.....................601-359-3680
PO 220, Jackson MS 39205
MISSOURI
Human Rights Commission 314-751-3325
3315 W Truman Blvd
Jefferson City MO 65102
MONTANA
Human Rights Commission 406-444-2884
PO 1728, Helena MT 59624
NEBRASKA
Attorney General.....................402-471-2682
2115 State Capitol Bldg, Lincoln NE 68509

NEVADA
Equal Rights Commission.......702-486-7161
1515 E Tropicana Ave, Ste 590
Las Vegas NV 89119
NEW HAMPSHIRE
Human Rights Commission 603-271-2767
169 Manchester St, Concord NH 03301
NEW JERSEY
Civil Rights Div 609-984-3101
383 W State St, Trenton NJ 08625-0089
NEW MEXICO
Human Rights Div...................505-827-6838
1596 Pacheco St, Santa Fe NM 87502
NEW YORK
Human Rights Div...................212-870-8790
55 W 125th St, New York NY 10027
NORTH CAROLINA
Justice Dept 919-733-3377
PO 629, Raleigh NC 27602
NORTH DAKOTA
Attorney General.....................701-224-2210
600 E Boulevard Ave, Bismarck ND 58505
OHIO
Civil Rights Commission.........614-466-2785
220 Parsons Ave
Columbus OH 43266-0543
OKLAHOMA
Human Rights Commission 405-521-3441
2101 N Lincoln Blvd, Rm 480
Oklahoma City OK 73105
OREGON
Justice Dept 503-378-6002
100 Justice Bldg, Salem OR 97310
PENNSYLVANIA
Civil Rights Enforcement Div.717-787-0822
16th Fl, Strawberry Sq\
Harrisburg PA 17105
RHODE ISLAND
Human Rights Commission 401-277-2661
10 Abbott Park Pl
Providence RI 02903-3768
SOUTH CAROLINA
Human Affairs Commission....803-253-6336
PO 4490, Columbia SC 29240
SOUTH DAKOTA
Human Rights Div...................605-773-4493
500 E Capitol, Pierre SD 57501
TENNESSEE
Human Rights Commission 615-741-5825
530 Church St, Ste 400
Nashville TN 37243-0745
TEXAS
Attorney General.....................512-463-2191
PO 12548, Austin TX 78711-2548

UTAH
    Attorney General.....................801-538-1015
    236 State Capitol, Salt Lake City UT84114
VERMONT
    Attorney General.....................802-828-3171
    109 State St, Montpelier VT 05609-1001
VIRGINIA
    Human Rights Council............804-225-2292
    Washington Blvd, 12th Fl
    Richmond Va 23219
WASHINGTON
    Human Rights Commission 206-753-6770
    711 S Capitol Way, Olympia WA 98504
WEST VIRGINIA
    Human Rights Commission 304-558-2616
    1321 Plaza E, Rm 104-106
    Charleston WV 25301-1400
WISCONSIN
    Equal Rights Div 608-266-0946
    PO 8928, Madison WI 53707
WYOMING
    Attorney General.....................307-777-7841
    123 Capitol Bldg, Cheyenne WY 82002

LABOR

ALABAMA
    Labor Dept 205-242-3460
    1789 Congressman W L Dickinson Dr
    Montgomery AL 36130
ALASKA
    Labor Dept 907-465-2700
    PO 21149, Juneau AK 99802-1149
ARIZONA
    Labor Div 602-542-4515
    PO 19070, Phoenix AZ 85005-9070
ARKANSAS
    Labor Dept 501-682-4500
    10421 W Markham St
    Little Rock AR 72205
CALIFORNIA
    Industrial Relations Dept 415-703-4590
    455 Golden Gate Ave
    San Francisco CA 94102
COLORADO
    Labor & Employment Dept.....303-837-3801
    600 Grant St, Ste 900
    Denver CO 80203-3528
CONNECTICUT
    Labor Dept 203-566-4384
    200 Folly Brook Blvd Wethersfield CT 06109
DELAWARE
    Labor Dept 302-577-2710
    820 N French St, Wilmington DE 19801

DISTRICT OF COLUMBIA
    Labor Relations Office.............202-724-4953
    441 4th St NW.Ste 200
    Washington DC 20001
FLORIDA
    Labor & Employment Security Dept
   904-922-7021
    2012 Capitol Circle SE, Hartman Bldg
    Tallahassee FL 32399-2152
GEORGIA
    Labor Dept 404-656-3011
    148 International Blvd, Atlanta GA 30303
HAWAII
    Labor & Industrial Relations Dept
   808-586-8844
    830 Punchbowl St, Honolulu HI 96813
IDAHO
    Labor & Industrial Services Dept
   208-334-3950
    State house Mall, Boise ID 83720
ILLINOIS
    Labor Dept 312-793-2800
    310 S Michigan 10th Fl, Chicago IL 60604
INDIANA
    Labor Dept 317-232-2378
    402 W Washington St, Rm W195
    Indianapolis IN 46204
IOWA
    Employment Services Dept.....515-281-5365
    1000 E Grand Ave
    Des Moines IA 50319-0209
KANSAS
    Human Resources Dept...........913-296-7474
    401 Topeka Ave, Topeka KS 66603
KENTUCKY
    Labor Cabinet..........................502-564-3070
    1047 US 127 S, Ste 4, Frankfort KY 40601
LOUISIANA
    Employ & Training Dept` 504-342-3011
    PO 94094, Baton Rough LA 70804-9094
MAINE
    Labor Dept 207-287-3788
    PO 309, 20 Union St
    Augusta ME 04332-0309
MARYLAND
    Labor & Industry Div..............410-333-4180
    501 St Paul Place, Baltimore MD 21202
MASSACHUSETTS
    Labor & Industries Dept.........617-727-3454
    100 Cambridge St, Rm 1100
    Boston MA 02202
MICHIGAN
    Labor Dept 517-373-9600
    PO 30015, Lansing MI 48909

MINNESOTA
Labor & Industry Dept............612-296-2342
443 Lafayette Rd, St Paul MN 55155
MISSISSIPPI
Vocational Rehabilitation Services Dept......
....601-936-0200
PO 1698, Jackson, MS 39215
MISSOURI
Labor & Indust Relations........314-751-4091
3315 W Truman Blvd
Jefferson City MO 65102
MONTANA
Labor & Industry Dept............406-444-3555
PO 1728, Helena MT 59624
NEBRASKA
Labor Dept 402-471-9000
PO 94600, Lincoln NE 68509
NEVADA
Labor Commission...................702-687-4850
1445 Hot Springs Rd, Ste 108
Carson City NV 89710
NEW HAMPSHIRE
Labor Dept 603-271-3171
95 Pleasant St, Concord NH 03301
NEW JERSEY
Labor Dept 609-292-2323
John Fitch Plaza, CN 110
Trenton NJ 08625-0110
NEW MEXICO
Labor Dept 505-841-8406
PO 1928, Albuquerque NM 87103
NEW YORK
Labor Dept 518-457-2741
State Campus, Bldg 12, Albany NY 12240
NORTH CAROLINA
Labor Dept 919-733-7166
4 W Edenton St, Raleigh NC 27601
NORTH DAKOTA
Labor Dept 701-224-2660
600 E Boulevard, Bismarck ND 58505
OHIO
Employment Services Bureau 614-466-2100
145 S Front St, Columbus OH 43216
OKLAHOMA
Labor Dept 405-528-1500
4001 Lincoln Blvd
Oklahoma City OK 73105
OREGON
Labor & Industries Bureau.....503-731-4070
800 NE Oregon St, #32, Portland OR 97232
PENNSYLVANIA
Labor & Industry Dept............717-787-3756
Labor & Industry Bldg
Harrisburg PA 17120

RHODE ISLAND
Labor Dept 401-272-0700
610 Manton Ave, Providence RI 02907
SOUTH CAROLINA
Labor Dept 803-734-9594
PO 11329, Columbia SC 2921191329
SOUTH DAKOTA
Labor Dept 605-773-3101
700 Governors Dr, Pierre SD 57501
TENNESSEE
Labor Dept 615-741-2582
501 Union Bldg, Nashville TN 37243-0655
TEXAS
Employment Commission 512-463-2800
101 E 15th St, Austin TX 78778
UTAH
Industrial Commission............801-530-6880
PO 146600, Salt Lake City UT 84114-6600
VERMONT
Labor & Industry Dept............802-828-2286
National Life Ins. Bldg
Montpelier VT 05620-3401
VIRGINIA
Employment Commission 804-786-3001
703 E Main St, Richmond VA 23219
WASHINGTON
Labor & Industries Dept.........206-956-4203
PO 44000, Olympia WA 98504-4000
WEST VIRGINIA
Labor Div 304-558-7890
Capitol Complex, Bldg 3, Rm 319, ...
Charleston WV 25305
WISCONSIN
Industry, Labor & Human Relations Dept
....608-266-7552
PO 1728, Madison WI 53707
WYOMING
Employment Dept....................307-777-7672
Herschler Bldg, 2nd Fl E
Cheyenne WY 82002

OCCUPATIONAL SAFETY / HEALTH

ALASKA
Occupational Safety & Health 907-465-4855
PO 21149, Juneau AK 99802-1149
ARIZONA
Occupational Safety Div..........602-542-5795
PO 19070, Phoenix AZ 85007
ARKANSAS
OSHA Consultation Sec 501-682-4500
10421 W Markham St
Little Rock AR 72205

CALIFORNIA
Occup Safety & Health Div.....415-703-4590
455 Golden Gate Ave
San Francisco CA 94102
COLORADO
Labor Dept./Risk Mgmt. Div...303-873-3952
600 Grant St., Denver, CO 80203
CONNECTICUT
Occupational Safety & Health Div
....203-566-4550
200 Folly Brook Blvd
Wethersfield CT 06106
DELAWARE
*Employment & Training Services Div
....302-368-6810
University Office Plaza
Wilmington, DE 19801
DISTRICT OF COLUMBIA
*Labor Relations Office..........202-724-4908
441 Fourth St NW, Washington DC 20001
FLORIDA
Safety Div................................904-488-3044
2012 Capitol Circle SE, Hartman Bldg
Tallahassee FL 32399-2152
GEORGIA
*Support Services...................404-656-7392
148 International Blvd, Atlanta, GA 30303
HAWAII
Occupational Safety & Health Research Br
....808-586-9005
830 Punchbowl St, Honolulu HI 96813
IDAHO
*Safety Div..............................208-334-2327
State House Mail, Boise, ID 83720
ILLINOIS
*Employment Security Dept...312-793-5700
401 S. State St., Chicago IL 60605
INDIANA
IOSHA Compliance Dept........317-232-3325
402 W Washington St, Rm W195, ...
Indianapolis IN 46204
IOWA
Occupational Safety& Health Bur...............
....515-281-3606
100 E Grand Ave,
Des Moines IA 50319-0209
KANSAS
Employment Security Div.......913-296-0821
401 Topeka Ave., Topeka, KS 66615
KENTUCKY
Occupational Safety & Health Review
Commission.............................502-564-6892
Airport Bldg, Louisville Rd
Frankfort KY 40601

MAINE
Occupational Information Coordinating ......
Committee...............................207-624-6200
PO 309, 20 Union St
Augusta ME 04332-0309
MARYLAND
Occupational Safety& Health Sec
....410-333-4180
501 St Paul Pl, Baltimore MD 21202
MASSACHUSETTS
OSHA Consultation Div..........617-727-3463
100 Cambridge St, Rm 1100
Boston MA 02202
MICHIGAN
Safety & Regulation Bur.........517-322-1814
PO 30015, Lansing MI 48909
MINNESOTA
OSHA Consultation Unit........612-296-5433
443 Lafayette Rd, St Paul MN 55155
MISSISSIPPI
Occupational Safety & Health 601-987-7518
PO 1700, Jackson MS 39215-1700
MISSOURI
Employment Services Sec. 314-751-3791
421 E. Dunklin St
Jefferson City MO 65101
MONTANA
Occupational Health Bur........406-444-3671
Cogswell Bldg, Rm C108, Helena MT 59620
NEBRASKA
Safety Div................................402-471-2239
PO 94600, Lincoln NE 68509
NEVADA
Enforcement for Industrial Safety & Health
Sec 702-687-5240
1390 S Curry St, Carson City NV 89710
NEW JERSEY
Occupational Health & Safety Ofc
....609-984-3507
John Fitch Plaza, CN 110
Trenton NJ 08625-0110
NEW MEXICO
*Employment Security Div 505-841-8437
PO 1928, Albuquerque, NM 87103
NEW YORK
Occupational Safety & Health Div
....518-457-3518
State Campus, Bldg 12, Albany NY 12240
NORTH CAROLINA
OSHA Div 919-733-4585
4 W Edenton St, Raleigh NC 27601
NORTH DAKOTA
*Labor Standards Div 701-224-2660
600 E. Blvd, Bismarck ND 58505

OHIO
Occupational Health Bur 614-466-4183
246 N High St, Columbus OH43266-0588
OKLAHOMA
OSHA Consultation Div..........405-528-1500
4001 Lincoln Blvd
Oklahoma City OK 73105
OREGON
Occup Safety & Health Div.....503-378-3272
21 Labor & Industries Bldg
Salem OR 97310
PENNSYLVANIA
Occupational & Industrial Safety Bur
....717-787-3323
Labor & Industry Bldg
Harrisburg PA 17120
RHODE ISLAND
Occupational Safety Div..........401-457-1877
610 Manton Ave, Providence RI 02907
SOUTH CAROLINA
OSHA Education, Trng & Consultation Div
....803-734-9599
PO 11329, Columbia SC 29211-1329
TENNESSEE
Occupational Safety Div..........615-741-2793
501 Union Bldg, Nashville TN 37243-0655
TEXAS
Occupational Safety Div..........512-458-7287
1100 W 49th St, Austin TX 78761
UTAH
OSHA Div 801-530-6901
PO 146600, Salt Lake City UT 84114-6600
VERMONT
Occupational Safety& Health Div
....802-828-2765
National Life Ins Bldg
Montpelier VT 05620-3401
VIRGINIA
Occupational Safety & Enforcement Div
....804-786-2391
Occupational Health Div.........804-786-0574
Power Taylor Bldg, 13 S 13th St
Richmond VA 23219
WASHINGTON
Industrial Safety & Health Div
....206-956-5495
PO 44600, Olympia WA 98504-4600
WEST VIRGINIA
Safety & Boiler Div..................304-558-7890
Capitol Complex, Bldg 3, Rm 319
Charleston WV 25305
WISCONSIN
Safety & Buildings Div............608-266-1816
PO 7969, Madison WI 53707

WYOMING
Occupational Health & Safety Dept
....307-777-7786
Herschler Bldg, 2nd Fl E
Cheyenne WY 82002

SECURITIES

ALABAMA
Securities Commission 205-242-2984
770 Washington St, Ste 570
Montgomery AL 36130-4700
ALASKA
Banking, Securities & Corporations Div
....907-465-2521
PO 110808, Juneau AK 99811-0208
ARIZONA
Securities Div...........................602-542-4242
1200 W Washington St, Phoenix AZ 85007
ARKANSAS
Securities Dept 501-324-9260
201 E Markham, Rm 300
Little Rock AR 72201
CALIFORNIA
Securities Regulation Div 213-736-3481
3700 Wilshire Blvd, Ste 600
Los Angeles CA 90010-2901
COLORADO
Securities Div...........................303-894-2320
1580 Lincoln, Ste 420, Denver CO 80203
CONNECTICUT
Securities Div...........................203-566-4560
44 Capitol Ave, Hartford CT 06106
DELAWARE
Securities Commissioner.........302-577-3847
820 N French St, Wilmington DE 19801
DISTRICT OF COLUMBIA
Regulatory Affairs Sec.............202-727-6278
441 4th St NW, Rm 1020S
Washington DC 20001
FLORIDA
Securities Div...........................904-488-9805
Plaza Level, PL-09, Capitol Bldg, ...
Tallahassee FL 32399-0350
GEORGIA
Investment Div 404-656-2174
254 Washington St, Rm 214
Atlanta GA 30334
HAWAII
Business Registration Div.......808-586-2744
PO 40, Honolulu HI 96810
IDAHO
Securities Bur 208-334-3684
700 W State St, Boise ID 83720-2700

ILLINOIS
Securities Div...........................217-782-2256
Capitol Bldg, Rm 213, Springfield IL 62756
INDIANA
Securities Div...........................317-232-6690
State House, Rm 201
Indianapolis IN 46204
IOWA
Secretary of State....................515-281-5104
1300 Walnut St, Des Moines IA 50319
KANSAS
Secretary of State....................913-296-2236
Statehouse, 2nd Fl, Topeka KS 66612
KENTUCKY
Securities Div...........................502-564-2180
477 Versailles Rd, Frankfort KY 40601
LOUISIANA
Securities Commission............504-568-5515
1100 Poydrus St, Ste 2250
New Orleans LA 70163
MAINE
Securities Div...........................207-624-8551
State House Station 35, Augusta ME 04333
MARYLAND
Securities Div...........................410-576-7783
200 St Paul Pl, Baltimore MD 21202-2020
MASSACHUSETTS
Securities 617-727-3548
State House, Rm 337, Boston MA 02133
MICHIGAN
Securities Div...........................517-334-6200
PO 30222, Lansing MI 48909
MINNESOTA
Secretary of State....................612-296-2079
100 Constitution St, Rm 180
St Paul, MN 55155
MISSISSIPPI
Securities Div...........................601-359-1350
PO 136, Jackson MS 39205
MISSOURI
Securities Div...........................314-751-4704
PO 778, Jefferson City MO 65102
MONTANA
Secretary of State 406-444-2034
State Capitol, Rm 225, Helena MT 59620
NEBRASKA
Securities Div...........................402-471-2171
PO 95006, Lincoln NE 68509
NEVADA
Securities Div...........................702-486-6440
Capitol Complex, Carson City NV 89710
NEW HAMPSHIRE
Security Bur............................603-271-1463
State House, Rm 204, Concord NH 03301

NEW JERSEY
Securities Bureau....................201-504-3600
PO 45027, Newark NJ 07101
NEW MEXICO
Securities Div...........................505-827-7140
PO 25101, Santa Fe NM 87504
NEW YORK
State Dept...............................518-474-0050
162 Washington Ave, Albany NY 12231
NORTH CAROLINA
Securities Div...........................919-733-4161
300 N Salisbury St
Raleigh NC 27603-5909
NORTH DAKOTA
Securities Dept 701-224-2651
600 E Boulevard
Bismarck, ND 58505-0709
OHIO
Securities Div...........................614-644-7381
77 S High St, 23rd Fl
Columbus OH 43266-0544
OKLAHOMA
Securities Dept 405-235-0230
621 N Robinson, Ste 400
Oklahoma City OK 73102
OREGON
Securities 503-378-4387
158 12th St NE, Salem OR 97310
PENNSYLVANIA
Securities Commission............717-787-3828
1010 N 7th St, 2nd Fl
Harrisburg PA 17102
RHODE ISLAND
Securities Associate Dir 401-277-3048
233 Richmond St, Providence RI 02903-4237
SOUTH CAROLINA
Securities Div...........................803-734-1089
PO 11350, Columbia SC 29211
SOUTH DAKOTA
Securities Div...........................605-773-4823
500 E Capitol, Pierre SD 57501
TENNESSEE
Securities Div...........................615-741-2947
500 James Robertson Pkwy
Nashville TN 37243-0565
TEXAS
Securities Board 512-474-2233
PO 13167, Austin TX 78711
UTAH
Securities Div...........................801-530-6600
PO 45802, Salt Lake City UT 84145-0801
VERMONT
Securities Dep Cmr 802-828-3301
1 W State St, Montpelier VT 05620-3101

VIRGINIA
Securities & Retail Franchising Bureau
....804-371-9051
1300 E Main St, Richmond VA 23219
WASHINGTON
State Investment Board`.........206-664-8907
PO 40916, Olympia WA 98504-0916
WEST VIRGINIA
Securities Div...........................304-558-2257
1st Fl, 100 State Capitol
Charleston WV 25305-0230
WISCONSIN
Securities Commission............608-266-3431
PO 1768, Madison WI 53707-7910
WYOMING
Securities Div...........................307-777-7370
State Capitol, Cheyenne WY 82002-0020

TAXATION & REVENUE

ALABAMA
Revenue Dept............................205-242-1175
50 N Ripley St, Gordon Persons Bldg
Montgomery AL 36132
ALASKA
Revenue Dept............................907-465-2300
PO 110400, Juneau AK 99811-0400
ARIZONA
Revenue Dept............................602-542-3572
1600 W Monroe, Rm 910, Phoenix AZ 85007
ARKANSAS
Revenue Div..............................501-682-7000
PO 1272, Little Rock AR 72203
CALIFORNIA
Tax Administration Div 916-445-6321
3301 C St, Ste 301
Sacramento CA 95816
COLORADO
Revenue Dept............................303-866-3091
1375 Sherman St, Denver CO 80261
CONNECTICUT
Revenue Services Dept............203-297-5650
92 Farmington Ave, Hartford CT 06105
DELAWARE
Revenue Div..............................302-577-3315
820 French St, Wilmington DE 19801
DISTRICT OF COLUMBIA
Finance & Revenue Dept 202-727-6020
441 4th St NW, Washington DC 20001
FLORIDA
Revenue Dept............................904-488-5050
5050 W Tennessee St
Tallahassee FL 32399-0100

GEORGIA
Revenue Dept............................404-656-4015
270 Washington St SW, Atlanta GA 30334
HAWAII
Taxation Dept...........................808-587-1510
PO 259, Honolulu HI 96809
IDAHO
Revenue & Taxation Dept.......208-334-7500
800 Park Plaza 2, Boise ID 83712
ILLINOIS
Revenue Dept............................217-785-2602
101 W Jefferson, Springfield IL 62708
INDIANA
Revenue Dept............................317-232-2101
248 State Office Bldg
Indianapolis IN 46204
IOWA
Revenue & Finance Dept 515-281-3204
Hoover State Ofc Bldg
Des Moines IA 50319
KANSAS
Revenue Dept............................913-296-3041
915 Harrison St, Topeka KS 66612-1588
KENTUCKY
Revenue Cabinet.......................502-564-3226
Capitol Annex, Frankfort KY 40601
LOUISIANA
Revenue & Taxation Dept.......504-925-7680
PO 201, Baton Rouge LA 70821
MAINE
Taxation Bur............................207-287-2076
State House Station 78
Augusta ME 04333
MARYLAND
Assessments & Taxation Dept410-225-1184
301 W Preston St
Baltimore MD 21201-2395
MASSACHUSETTS
Revenue Dept............................617-727-4201
100 Cambridge St, Rm 806
Boston MA 02204
MICHIGAN
Revenue Bur 517-373-3196
430 W Allegan, Lansing MI 48922
MINNESOTA
Revenue Dept............................612-296-3403
10 River Park Plaza
St Paul MN 55416-7100
MISSISSIPPI
Tax Commission 601-359-1098
PO 22828, Jackson MS 39225
MISSOURI
Revenue Dept............................314-751-4450
PO 311, Jefferson City MO 65105

MONTANA
  Revenue Dept..........................406-444-2460
  205 N Roberts St, Rm 455
  Sam W Mitchell Bldg, Helena MT 59620
NEBRASKA
  Revenue Dept..........................402-471-5604
  PO 94818, Lincoln NE 68509
NEVADA
  Taxation Dept 702-687-4892
  Capitol Complex, Carson City NV 89710
NEW HAMPSHIRE
  Revenue Administration Dept 603-271-2191
  61 S Spring St, Concord NH 03302-0451
NEW JERSEY
  Taxation Div 609-292-5185
  State House, CN 002
  Trenton NJ 08625-0002
NEW MEXICO
  Taxation & Revenue Dept.......505-827-0341
  PO 630, Santa Fe NM 87509
NEW YORK
  Taxation & Finance Dept........518-457-2244
  W A Harriman Campus, Albany NY 12227
NORTH CAROLINA
  Revenue Dept..........................919-733-7211
  501 N Wilmington St, Raleigh NC 27640
NORTH DAKOTA
  Tax Dept................................701-224-2770
  600 E Boulevard, Bismarck ND 58505
OHIO
  Taxation Dept 614-466-2166
  PO 530, Columbus OH 43216-0030
OKLAHOMA
  Tax Commission 405-521-3115
  2501 Lincoln Blvd
  Oklahoma City OK 73194
OREGON
  Revenue Dept..........................503-945-8214
  457 Revenue 955 Ctr St NE
  Salem OR 97310
PENNSYLVANIA
  Revenue Dept..........................717-783-3680
  11th Fl, Strawberry Sq
  Harrisburg PA 17128-1100
RHODE ISLAND
  Taxation Office 401-277-3050
  1 Capitol Hill, Providence RI 02908-5800
SOUTH CAROLINA
  Revenue & Taxation Commission
 803-737-9850
  PO 125, Columbia SC 29214
SOUTH DAKOTA
  Revenue Dept..........................605-773-3311
  700 Governors Dr, Pierre SD 57501-2276

TENNESSEE
  Revenue Dept..........................615-741-2461
  1200 Andrew Jackson Bldg
  Nashville TN 37242
TEXAS
  Tax Administration 512-463-4783
  Revenue Administration 512-463-4041
  111 E 17th St, Austin TX 78774
UTAH
  Tax Commission 801-530-4848
  160 E 300 South
  Salt Lake City UT 84134
VERMONT
  Tax Dept.................................802-828-2505
  109 State St, Montpelier VT 05609-0201
VIRGINIA
  Taxation Dept 804-367-8005
  2200 W Broad St, Box 6L
  Richmond VA 23282
WASHINGTON
  Revenue Dept..........................206-753-5574
  PO 47454, Olympia WA 98504-7454
WEST VIRGINIA
  Tax & Revenue Dept 304-558-2500
  State Capitol Complex
  Charlestown WV 25305
WISCONSIN
  Revenue Dept..........................608-226-1611
  PO 8933, Madison WI 53708
WYOMING
  Revenue Dept..........................307-777-7961
  122 W 125th St, Herschler Bldg
  Cheyenne WY 82002

TREASURER

ALABAMA
  Treasury Dept..........................205-242-7501
  600 Dexter Ave, Montgomery AL 36130
ALASKA.
  Treasury Div 907-465-2300
  PO 110405, Juneau AK 99811-0405
ARIZONA
  Treasurer 602-542-5815
  1700 W. Washington St
  Phoenix AZ 85007
ARKANSAS
  State Treasurer 501-682-5888
  220 State Capitol Bldg
  Little Rock AR 72201
CALIFORNIA
  State Treasurer 916-653-2995
  PO 942809, Sacramento CA 94209-0001

COLORADO
Treasury Dept...........................303-866-2441
140 State Capitol Bldg, Denver CO 80203
CONNECTICUT
Treasurer Dept 203-566-5050
55 Elm St, Hartford CT 06106
DELAWARE
State Treasurer Ofc.................302-739-3382
Thomas Collins Bldg
Dover DE 19903-1401
DISTRICT OF COLUMBIA
Treasurer Dept 202-727-6055
441 4th St NW, Ste 360
Washington DC 20001
FLORIDA
Insurance & Treasurer Dept...904-922-3100
The Capitol, Plaza Level 11
Tallahassee FL 32399-0300
IDAHO
Treasurer 208-334-3200
Rm 102, State Capitol Bldg, Boise ID 83720
ILLINOIS
Treasurer 217-782-2211
219 State House, Springfield IL 62706
INDIANA
Treasurer 317-232-6386
242 State House, Indianapolis IN 46204
IOWA
State Treasurer 515-281-5366
Capitol Bldg, Des Moines IA 50319
KANSAS
State Treasurer 913-296-3171
Landon State Ofc Bldg, Topeka KS 66612
KENTUCKY
Treasury Dept..........................502-564-4722
Capitol Annex, Frankfort KY 40601
LOUISIANA
Treasury Dept..........................504-342-0010
PO 44154, Baton Rouge LA 70804
MAINE
Treasury Dept..........................207-287-2771
State House Station 39, Augusta ME 04333
MARYLAND
State Treasurer Ofc.................410-974-3533
PO 666, Annapolis MD 21404-21401
MASSACHUSETTS
Treasurer & Receiver General617-367-3900
State House, Rm 227, Boston MA 02133
MICHIGAN
Treasury Dept..........................517-373-3223
430 W Allegan, Lansing MI 48922
MINNESOTA
State Treasurer 612-296-7091
303 Admn Bldg, St Paul MN 55155

MISSISSIPPI
Treasury Dept..........................601-359-3531
PO 138, Jackson MS 39205
MISSOURI
State Treasurer 314-751-4123
PO 210, Jefferson City MO 65102
MONTANA
Treasurers Bur 406-444-2625
Sam W Mitchell Bldg, Rm 155
Helena MT 59620
NEBRASKA
State Treasurer Office.............402-471-2455
PO 94788, Lincoln NE 68509
NEVADA
State Treasurer Ofc.................702-687-5200
Capitol Complex, Carson City NV 89710
NEW HAMPSHIRE
Treasury Dept..........................603-271-2621
State House Annex, Rm 121
Concord NH 03301
NEW JERSEY
Treasury Dept..........................609-292-6748
State House, CN 002
Trenton NJ 08625-0002
NEW MEXICO
State Treasurer 505-827-6400
PO 608, Santa Fe NM 87503
NEW YORK
Treasury Ofc 518-474-7918
Alfred E Smith Ofc Bldg, Albany NY 12225
NORTH CAROLINA
Treasury Dept..........................919-733-3951
325 N Salisbury St
Raleigh NC 27603-1388
NORTH DAKOTA
State Treasurer 701-224-2643
600 E Boulevard, Bismarck ND 58505
OHIO
Treasurer 614-466-2160
30 E Broad St, 9th Fl
Columbus OH 43266-0421
OKLAHOMA
Treasurer 405-521-3191
217 Capitol Bldg
Oklahoma City OK 73105
OREGON
Treasury Dept..........................503-378-4329
159 State Capitol, Salem OR 97310-0840
PENNSYLVANIA
Treasury Dept..........................717-787-2465
129 Finance Bldg, Harrisburg PA 17120
RHODE ISLAND
Treasury Dept..........................401-277-2397
102 State House, Providence RI 02903

SOUTH CAROLINA
    Treasurer 803-734-2101
    PO 11778, Columbia SC 29211
SOUTH DAKOTA
    State Treasurer 605-773-3378
    500 E Capitol, 2nd Fl, Pierre SD 57501
TENNESSEE
    Treasury Dept.........................615-741-2956
    State Capitol, 1st Fl
    Nashville TN 37243-0225
TEXAS
    Treasury Dept.........................512-463-6000
    PO 12608, Austin TX 78711-2608
UTAH
    Treasurer 801-538-1042
    215 State Capitol
    Salt Lake City UT 84114
VERMONT
    Treasurer 802-828-2301
    133 State St, 2nd Fl
    Montpelier Vt 05633-6200
VIRGINIA
    Treasury Dept.........................804-225-2142
    101 N 14th St, PO 6H
    Richmond Va 23215
WASHINGTON
    Treasurer 206-753-7130
    PO 40200, Olympia WA 98108
WEST VIRGINIA
    Treasury Ofc 304-343-4000
    145 E Wing, State Capitol Bldg
    Charleston WV 25305
WYOMING
    Treasurer 307-777-7408
    State Capitol, Cheyenne WY 82002

UNEMPLOYMENT

ALABAMA
    Industrial Relations Dept 205-242-8025
    649 Monroe St, Montgomery AL 36131
ALASKA
    Unemployment Insurance.......907-465-2712
    PO 120630, Juneau AK 99802-5509
ARIZONA
    Employment Security Div.......602-542-1645
    1275 W. Washington, Phoenix AZ 85007
ARKANSAS
    Employment Security Dept.....501-682-2121
    2 Capitol Mall, Little Rock AR 72201
CALIFORNIA
    Unemployment Ins Ofc 916-263-6783
    PO 944275, Sacramento CA 94244-3528

COLORADO
    Unemployment Ins Ofc 303-837-3819
    600 Grant St, Ste 900
    Denver CO 80203-3528
CONNECTICUT
    Employment Security Div.......203-566-4280
    200 Folly Brook Blvd
    Wethersfield CT 06109
DELAWARE
    Unemployment Ins Div 302-577-2851
    PO 9029, Newark DE 19714-9029
DISTRICT OF COLUMBIA
    Employment Security Div.......202-724-7139
    500 C St, Washington DC 20032
FLORIDA
    Unemployment Comp Div.......904-488-6093
    Ste 201, Caldwell Bldg
    Tallahassee FL 32399-0204
GEORGIA
    Unemployment Ins Div 404-656-3050
    148 International Blvd
    Atlanta GA 30303
HAWAII
    Unemployment Ins Research Br
   808-586-8899
    830 Punchbowl St, Honolulu HI 96813
IDAHO
    Unemployment Ins Div 208-334-6466
    317 Main St, Boise ID 83735
ILLINOIS
    Unemployment Ins Cmr..........312-793-4240
    401 S State St, Chicago IL 60605
INDIANA
    Unemployment Ins Admn Dep Cmr
   317-232-7681
    IGCS, 10 N Senate Ave, Rm SE 302, ...
    Indianapolis IN 46204-2277
IOWA
    Job Insurance Bur. 515-281-5526
    1000 E. Grand Ave, Des Moines IA 50319
KANSAS
    Employment Security Div.......913-296-0821
    401 Topeka Ave, Topeka KS, 66603
KENTUCKY
    Workers Claims Dept 502-564-5550
    US 127 South Bldg, Frankfort KY 40601
LOUISIANA
    Unemployment Ins Div 504-342-3017
    PO 94094, Baton Rouge LA 70804-9094
MAINE
    Unemployment Ins Comm 207-822-0200
    Unemployment Comp Div.......207-287-2316
    PO 309, 20 Union St
    Augusta ME 04332-0309

MARYLAND
Unemployment Ins Ofc 410-333-5306
1100 N Eutaw St, Rm 501
Baltimore MD 21201
MICHIGAN
Employment Security Commission
....313-876-5500
7310 Woodward Ave, Detroit MI 48202
MINNESOTA
Jobs Svcs & Unemployment Ins OpnsDiv
....612-296-3625
390 N Robert St, St Paul MN 55101
MISSISSIPPI
Employment Security Commission
....601-345-8711
PO 1699, Jackson MS 39203
MISSOURI
Unemployment Ins Sec 314-751-3641
421 E Dunklin St
Jefferson City MO 65101
MONTANA
Unemployment Ins Div 406-444-2749
PO 1728, Helena MT 59624
NEBRASKA
Unemployment Ins Div 402-471-9979
PO 94600, Lincoln NE 68509
NEVADA
Unemployment Ins Div 702-687-4510
500 E 3rd St, Carson City NV 89713
NEW HAMPSHIRE
Unemployment Comp Bur 603-224-3311
32 S Main St
Concord NH 03301-4857
NEW JERSEY
Employment Security Commissioner
....609-984-5666
John Fitch Plaza, Trenton NJ 08625
NEW MEXICO
Unemployment Ins Bur...........505-841-8431
PO 1928, Albuquerque, NM 87103
NEW YORK
Unemployment Ins Div 518-457-2878
State Campus, Bldg 12, Albany NY 12240
NORTH CAROLINA
Employment Security Commission
....919-733-7546
700 Wade Ave, Box 25903
Raleigh NC 27611
NORTH DAKOTA
Job Ins Div 701-224-2833
PO 5507, Bismarck ND 58502-5507
OHIO
Unemployment Comp Div.......614-466-9755
145 S Front St, Columbus OH 43214

OKLAHOMA
Unemployment Ins Div 405-557-0200
2401 N Lincoln Blvd
Oklahoma City OK 73105
OREGON
Employment Relations Board.503-378-3807
528 Cottage St NE, Ste 400
Salem OR 97303
PENNSYLVANIA
Unemployment Comp Benefits & ....
Allowances Bur.......................717-787-3547
Labor & Industry Bldg
Harrisburg PA 17120
RHODE ISLAND
Unemployment Ins 401-277-3651
101 Friendship St, Providence RI 02903
SOUTH CAROLINA
Unemployment Comp Div.......803-737-2787
PO 995, Columbia SC 29202
SOUTH DAKOTA
Unemployment Ins Div 605-622-2452
PO 4730, Aberdeen SD 57402-4730
TENNESSEE
Unemployment Ins Asst Cmr .615-741-3178
12th Fl, Volunteer Plaza Bldg
Nashville TN 37245-0001
TEXAS
Employment Commission 512-463-2829
PO 135207, Austin, TX 78711-3207
UTAH
Reemployment Div 801-530-6837
PO 146600, Salt Lake City UT 84114-6600
VERMONT
Unemployment Comp, Pol & Info
....802-229-0311
Green Mt Dr, PO 488
Montpelier VT 05601-0488
VIRGINIA
Unemployment Ins Div 804-786-4043
703 E Main St, Richmond VA 23219
WASHINGTON
Unemployment Ins Div 206-753-5120
PO 9046, Olympia WA 98507-9046
WEST VIRGINIA
Unemployment Comp Div.......304-558-2624
112 California Ave
Charleston WV 25305-0112
WISCONSIN
Unemployment Comp Div.......608-266-7074
PO 7905, Madison WI 53707
WYOMING
Unemployment Ins 307-777-7675
122 W 25th St, Cheyenne WY 82002-0700

WORKERS' COMPENSATION

ALABAMA
  Industrial Relations Dept 205-242-2868
  649 Monroe St, Montgomery AL 36131
ALASKA
  Workers Compensation Div 907-465-2790
  PO 25512, Juneau AK 99802-5512
ARIZONA
  State Compensation Fund 602-631-2050
  3031 N 2nd St, Phoenix AZ 85012
ARKANSAS
  Workers Comp Commission....501-682-3930
  PO 950, Little Rock AR 72203-0950
CALIFORNIA
  State Compensation Ins Fund 415-565-1456
  1275 Market St, San Francisco CA 94103
COLORADO
  Workers Compensation Sec 303-894-7550
  1120 Lincoln St, 13th Fl
  Denver CO 80203
CONNECTICUT
  Workers Comp Commission....203-789-7783
  1890 Dixwell Ave, Hamden CT 06514
DELAWARE
  *Vocational Rehabilitation Div ....
 302-577-2851
  321 E 11th St., Elwyn Bldg
  Wilmington DE 19801
DISTRICT OF COLUMBIA
  Comp & Benefits Bur 202-727-9625
  441 4th St NW, 3rd Fl
  Washington DC 20001
FLORIDA
  Workers Compensation Div 904-488-2514
  2012 Capitol Circle SE, Hartman Bldg
  Tallahassee FL 32399-2152
GEORGIA
  Workers Comp Board 404-656-2034
  1000 S Tower, 1 CNN Ctr
  Atlanta GA 30303-2788
HAWAII
  Disability Compensation Div ..808-586-9151
  830 Punchbowl St, Honolulu HI 96813
IDAHO
  Compensation Bur....................208-334-3346
  700 W State St, Boise ID 83720-2700
ILLINOIS
  *Employment Security Dept...312-793-5700
  401 S. State St., Chicago IL 60605
INDIANA
  Workers Comp Board 317-232-3809
  IGCS, 402 W Washington St, Rm W196
  Indianapolis IN 46204

IOWA
  Compensation & Benefits Bur 515-281-6770
  Grimes Bldg, Des Moines IA 50319-0150
KANSAS
  Workers Compensation Div 913-296-3441
  401 Topeka Ave, Topeka KS 66603
KENTUCKY
  Workers Compenstion Board..502-564-5550
  1047 US 127 S, Ste 4, Frankfort KY 40601
LOUISIANA
  Workers Comp & Admin Asst Secy
 504-342-7836
  PO 94094, Baton Rouge LA 70804-9094
MAINE
  Workers Comp Board 207-287-3751
  State House Station 27
  Augusta ME 04333
MARYLAND
  Workers Comp Commission....410-333-4775
  6 N Liberty St, Baltimore MD 21201-3735
MASSACHUSETTS
  Industrial Accident Dept.........617-727-4900
  600 Washington St, 7th Fl
  Boston MA 02111
MICHIGAN
  Workers Comp Appellate Commission
 517-335-5828
  PO 30015, Lansing MI 48909
MINNESOTA
  Workers Compensation Div 612-296-6490
  443 Lafayette Rd, St Paul MN 55155
MISSISSIPPI
  Workers Comp Commission....601-987-4200
  PO 5300, Jackson MS 39296-5300
MISSOURI
  Workers Compensation Div 314-751-4231
  3315 W Truman Blvd
  Jefferson City MO 65102
MONTANA
  Workers Comp Regulation 406-444-6530
  PO 1728, Helena MT 59624
NEBRASKA
  *Labor Dept Safety Div...........402-471-2239
  PO 94600, Lincoln NE 68509
NEVADA
  Industrial Ins System..............702-687-5284
  515 E Musser St, Carson City NV 89714
NEW HAMPSHIRE
  Workers Compensation Div 603-271-3172
  95 Pleasant St, Concord NH 03301
NEW JERSEY
  Workers Compensation Div 609-232-2414
  John Fitch Plaza, CN 110
  Trenton NJ 08625-0110

NEW MEXICO
    Workmen's Comp Admin 505-841-6000
    PO 27198, Albuquerque NM 87125
NEW YORK
    Workers' Comp Board 718-802-6666
    180 Livingston St, Brooklyn NY 11248
NORTH CAROLINA
    *Labor Dept Wage 919-733-2152
    4 W. Edenton St., Raleigh NC 27601
NORTH DAKOTA
    Workers Comp Bur..................701-224-3800
    500 E Front Ave, Bismarck ND 58504-5685
OHIO
    Workers Comp Bureau............614-466-8751
    3 W Spring St, 29th Fl, Columbus OH 43266
OKLAHOMA
    *Labor Dept 405-528-1500
    4001 Lincoln Blvd
    Oklahoma City,OK 73136
OREGON
    Workers Comp Board 503-378-3308
    480 Church St SE, Salem OR 97310
PENNSYLVANIA
    Workers Compensation Bur....717-783-5421
    Labor & Industry Bldg
    Harrisburg PA 17120
RHODE ISLAND
    Workers Compensation Unit ..401-272-0700
    610 Mantun Ave, Providence RI 02909
SOUTH CAROLINA
    Workers Comp Commission....803-737-5744
    PO 1715, Columbia SC 29202-1715
SOUTH DAKOTA
    *Labor Dept 605-773-3101
    700 Governors Dr., Pierre, SD 57501
TENNESSEE
    Workers Compensation Div 615-741-2395
    501 Union Bldg, Nashville TN 37243-0655
TEXAS
    Workers Compensation Div 512-322-3486
    PO 149104, Austin TX 78714-9104
UTAH
    *WIC Bur. 801-584-8232
    PO Box 16700, Salt Lake City, UT 84116
VERMONT
    Employment & Training Dept 802-229-0311
    Green Mt. Dr., PO 488
    Montpelier, VT 05401-1219
VIRGINIA
    Compensation Board 804-786-3886
    9th St Ofc Bldg, Box 710
    Richmond VA 23206-0710

WASHINGTON
    Workers Benefits Sec 206-956-4617
    PO 44000, Olympia WA 98504-4000
WEST VIRGINIA
    Workmen's Comp Div..............304-558-0475
    PO 3151, Charleston WV 25332
WISCONSIN
    Workers Compensation Div 608-266-6841
    PO 7901, Madison WI 53707
WYOMING
    Workers Compensation Div 307-777-7441
    122 W 25th St, Cheyenne WY 82002-0700

APPENDIX 3
Where do I go for information?
PRIVATE ECONOMIC ORGANIZATIONS

There are many federal, state, educational, and private and nonprofit organizations that are involved in economic issues and policies. The following is a list of some of the many organizations currently operating in the United States. Consult your local library for additional organizations.

In listing these organizations in *Economics – Assessment of the American Dream*, N&N Publishing makes no endorsement of the particular organization or of that organization's views or legitimacy. In most cases, the "information statement" is directly quoted from received letters of permission to list. N&N Publishing and the authors warn teachers and students that any person considering making a donation to any nonprofit organization should, before sending any money, carefully research that organization, their mission, operations, and economic distributions.

The authors have made every reasonable attempt to insure that the addresses and phone numbers for the listed agencies are accurate. However, organizations move and personnel, names, addresses, and phone and FAX numbers change. The authors would appreciate updated information should you know of a correction. Please write. All comments or suggestions are always gratefully received.

Most all of these organizations have agreed to provide informational materials to teachers and students. In some cases, the area served by the group is limited. Check individual listing. Persons requesting information should consider that most of these organizations are nonprofit, and they have limited economic resources. Most appreciate the requests include a large, self-addressed, stamped envelope or small donation to help pay the mailing costs.

70001 Ltd.
Office of the President
600 Maryland Ave SW – Suite 300 West Wing
Washington DC 20024
(202) 484-0103

Founded: 1969; Area: National
Focus: Youth Education
Objective: To assist disadvantaged high school dropouts in obtaining private sector employment through a program of pre-employment training, educational upgrading, motivational activities, and job placement assistance.

The Academy for Economic Education
Office of the President
1000 Virginia Center Parkway
Richmond VA 23295
(804) 264-5851

Founded: 1982; Area: National
Focus: Economic and Free Enterprise Education
Objective: To strengthen basic understanding of and appreciation for our American economic system, especially among teachers, and to provide teachers with the opportunity to improve their teaching skills.

ACES, Inc.
(Americans for the Competitive Enterprise
   System, Inc.)
Office of the Executive Director
4701 Limestone Road, Wilmington DE 19808
(302) 999-1545

> Founded: 1949; Area: DE, MD, PA
> Focus: Business, Economic, and Free
> Enterprise Education
> Objective: To explain our economic system
> and to correct public misconceptions about
> market capitalism by providing first-hand
> presentations of free market economics for
> students and educators.

The Advertising Council, Inc.
Office of the President
825 Third Avenue
New York NY 10022
(212) 758-0400

> Founded: 1942; Area: National
> Focus: Economic Education
> Objective: To promote voluntary citizen
> action to solve national problems through
> multimedia public service advertising cam-
> paigns in the public interest.

American Council of Life Insurance
Office of the President
Education Relations and Resources Unit
1850 K Street NW
Washington DC 20006-2284
(202) 862-4082

> Founded: 1976; Area: National
> Focus: Consumer Education
> Objective: To develop information about life
> and health insurance for distribution to the
> education community and to improve rela-
> tions between the education community and
> the life and health insurance business.

American Council on Consumer Interests
   (ACCI)
Office of the Executive Director
University of Missouri
240 Stanley Hall
Columbia MO 65211
(314) 882-3817

> Founded: 1953; Area: International
> Focus: Consumer and Economic Education
> Objective: To identify and clarify consumer
> interests with respect to issues, policies, and
> developments in the marketplace and in leg-
> islative and regulatory matters; to stimulate
> research on consumer issues; and to pro-
> mote better consumer education.

American Economic Association (AEA)
Office of the Secretary
1313 21st Avenue South
Nashville TN 37212
(615) 322-2595

> Founded: 1885; Area: International
> Focus: Economic Education
> Objective: To encourage economic research;
> to issue publications on economic subjects;
> and to encourage freedom of economic dis-
> cussion.

American Economic Foundation (AEF)
Office of the Chairman
1215 Terminal Tower
Cleveland OH 44113
(216) 781-1212

> Founded: 1939; Area: National
> Focus: Economic and Free Enterprise Educ.
> Objective: To increase understanding of the
> basic economic facts of the free enterprise
> system through research and to publish
> simplified explanations of economic princi-
> ples for dissemination to general audiences.

American Enterprise Institute for Public
   Policy Research (AEI)
Office of the President
1150 17th Street NW
Washington DC 20036
(202) 862-5800

> Founded: 1943; Area: International
> Focus: Business, Consumer, Economic, and
> Free Enterprise Education
> Objective: To assist policymakers, scholars,
> business leaders, media, and the public by
> providing objective research and analysis of
> national and international issues and to fos-
> ter effective competition of ideas.

American Federation of Small Business (AFSB)
Office of the Executive Vice President
407 South Dearborn Street
Chicago IL 60605
(312) 427-0206

Founded: 1963; Area: National
Focus: Business, Consumer, Economic, and Free Enterprise Education
Objective: To serve as a voice for 25 million small businesses in the U.S. and to act as an advocate for the consumer choice free market.

American Institute for Economic Research (AIER)
Office of the President
Division Street
Great Barrington MA 01230
(413) 528-1216

Founded: 1933; Area: International
Focus: Consumer, Economic, and Free Enterprise Education
Objective: To develop useful solutions to general economic problems; to disseminate information to help individuals understand and cope with financial problems; and to aid the progress of American society.

The American Institute of Cooperation (AIC)
Office of the President
1800 Massachusetts Avenue NW
Washington DC 20036
(202) 296-6825

Founded: 1925; Area: National
Focus: Agricultural Cooperative and Economic Education
Objective: To promote a better understanding of the cooperative method of conducting business.

The American Institute of Fellows in Free Enterprise (FIFE)
Office of the President
PO Box 217, FIFE Hall, Broad Street
Houston DE 19954
(302) 422-5403

Founded: 1972; Area: National
Focus: Economic and Free Enterprise Education
Objective: To give young Americans an understanding and appreciation of our free enterprise system and the nation that makes it work.

American Iron and Steel Institute (AISI)
Office of the Director of Educational Services
1000 16th Street NW
Washington DC 20036
(202) 452-7118

Founded: n/a; Area: National
Focus: Economic Education
Objective: To develop economic education programs that encourage information flow between the academic community and the steel industry and maximize understanding and appreciation of the role and contribution of each in the American socioeconomic system.

American Management Association (AMA)
Office of the Director of Communications
135 West 50th Street
New York NY 10020
(212) 586-8100

Founded: 1923; Area: International
Focus: Business and Management Educ.
Objective: To improve the performance of people and their organizations through developing, marketing, and presenting programs and materials designed to strengthen management skills and practice.

American Petroleum Institute (API)
Office of the President
1220 L Street NW
Washington DC 20005
(202) 682-8118

Founded: 1919; Area: International
Focus: Business, Consumer, and Economic Education
Objective: To provide a forum for cooperative research and establishment of industry-wide technical standards.

Americanism Educational League

Office of the Executive Director
PO Box 5986
Buena Park CA 90622
(714) 828-5040

Founded: 1927; Area: National
Focus: Economic and Free Enterprise Educ.
Objective: To conduct a sustained campaign
of public education to promote
Constitutional principles; to advance the
private enterprise system and increase individual responsibility; and to encourage the
renewal of those moral and spiritual values
that guided our Founding Fathers.

Americanism Foundation

Office of the President
48 North Linwood Avenue
Norwalk OH 44857
(419) 668-8282

Founded: 1979; Area: National
Focus: American Heritage, Business,
Economic, and Free Enterprise Education
Objective: To bring awareness of the essentials of leadership, citizenship, freedom, the
free market private enterprise system, productivity, and our great American heritage
and legacy of freedom to youth and to all
other community members.

Americans for Responsible Government (ARG)

Office of the Vice President
900 17th Street NW – Suite 610
Washington DC 20006
(202) 659-4595

Founded: 1983; Area: National
Focus: Business, Economic, and Free
Enterprise Education, and Voter Programs
Objective: To promote the American system
of representative government and to encourage active participation in government
through research and educational programs.

America's Future, Inc.

Office of the Chairman
514 Main Street
New Rochelle NY 10801

(914) 235-6000

Founded: 1946; Area: National
Focus: Economic, Free Enterprise, and
Political Education
Objective: To educate the people of the U.S.
about the history, character, importance,
and value of our constitutional republic and
institutions and the social, economic, and
political principles upon which they are
founded, with emphasis on the advantages
of the free enterprise system.

Association for Private Enterprise Education (APEE)

Office of the Secretary/Treasurer
Hankamer School of Business
Baylor University – Suite 316
Waco TX 76798
(817) 755-3766

Founded: 1974; Area: International
Focus: Business, Economic, Free Enterprise,
and Entrepreneurship Education
Objective: To promote a better understanding of the operation and benefits of a private
enterprise system by encouraging the formation of chairs and centers for private
enterprise/entrepreneurship education
throughout the U.S. and to serve as a network for individuals holding those chairs
and directing those programs.

Atlas Economic Research Foundation

Office of the President
220 Montgomery Street – Suite 1063
San Francisco CA 94104
(415) 392-2699

Founded: 1981; Area: International
Focus: Consumer Education
Objective: To advise and support existing
and developing independent institutes
throughout the world that publish and promote authoritative studies on important
public policy issues intended to increase
public understanding of economic cause and
effect.

Boy Scouts of America
Office of the Chief Scout Executive
1325 Walnut Hill Lane, Irving TX 75038-3096
(214) 659-2000

Founded: 1910; Area: National
Focus: Consumer and Economic Education
and Youth Development
Objective: To build character; to train in citizenship; and to foster fitness of the mind
and body.

The Brookings Institution
Office of the President
1775 Massachusetts Avenue NW
Washington DC 20036
(202) 797-6000

Founded: 1927; Area: International
Focus: Business, Consumer, Economic, Free
Enterprise, and Foreign Policy Education
Objective: To improve public policy and its
implementation through research and education in economics, government, and foreign policy.

Business Economics Education Foundation (BEEF)
Office of the Executive Director
S-297 Griggs Midway Building
1821 University Avenue
St. Paul MN 55104
(612) 645-5501

Founded: 1976; Area: Minnesota
Focus: Business, Consumer, Economic, and
Free Enterprise Education
Objective: To facilitate the study of marketplace economics by developing academically
sound, custom-made programs to support
teachers and assist high school students in
understanding the private enterprise system.

Business History and Economic Life Program, Inc. (BHELP)
Office of the Chairman
Dept. of Education, One Lake Hall
Northeastern University, Boston MA 02115
(617) 437-5912
Founded: 1967; Area: International
Focus: Business and Economic Education

and American Business History
Objective: To develop student awareness of
the role of economic institutions in the history and life of our country, primarily
through the development of cases which
show the influence of the decision-maker on
the evolving pattern of the American economic system.

Cato Institute
Office of the President
224 Second Street SE, Washington, DC 20003
(202) 546-0200

Founded: 1977; Area: National
Focus: Economic and Free Enterprise
Education and Foreign Policy
Objective: To broaden the parameters of policy debate to allow consideration of more
options that are consistent with the traditional American principles of limited government, individual liberty and peace.

Center for Business and Economics (CBE)
Office of the Director
Lakeland College, PO Box 359
Sheboygan WI 53082-0359
(414) 565-1286

Founded: 1976; Area: Wisconsin
Focus: Business, Economic, and Free
Enterprise Education
Objective: To promote a greater awareness
and understanding of the American free
enterprise system and to serve as a resource
for the business community, teachers, and
students.

Center for Constructive Alternatives
Office of the Executive Director
Hillsdale College
33 East College St, Hillsdale MI 49242
(517) 437-7341

Founded: 1972; Area: International
Focus: Business, Economic, and Free
Enterprise Education
Objective: To examine the principal problems of our time and offer solutions drawn
from traditional values and liberties of
American society.

Center for Economic Education
Office of the Dean
School of Business and Administration
Duquesne University
Pittsburgh PA 15282
(412) 434-6261

Founded: 1971; Area: Western PA
Focus: Economic Education
Objective: To teach economics as a methodology which enables users to improve the prediction and evaluation of the consequences of alternative courses of action for individuals, organizations, and society.

Center for Education and Research in Free Enterprise
Office of the Director
Texas A & M University
College Station TX 77843
(409) 845-7722

Founded: 1977; Area: International
Focus: Economic and Free Enterprise Education
Objective: To safeguard the system of free enterprise and to effectively increase knowledge about free enterprise, its premises and economic consequences.

The Center for Entrepreneurship and Small Business Management (CESBM)
Office of the Director
College of Business Administration
Box 147, Wichita State University
Wichita KS 67208
(316) 689-3000

Founded: 1977; Area: National
Focus: Free Enterprise Education
Objective: To educate people about the role of the entrepreneur in the American enterprise system.

Center for International Business Cycle Research
Office of the Director
323 Uris Hall, Graduate School of Business
Columbia University
New York NY 10027
(212) 280-2916

Founded: 1979; Area: International
Focus: Economic Education
Objective: To measure, analyze, and interpret short-term fluctuations in aggregate economic activity, inflation, employment, and foreign trade flows in major industrial countries and to develop and test new methods of tracking and forecasting the world's economies.

Center for Private Enterprise
Office of the Director
Hankamer School of Business
Baylor University
Waco TX 76798
(817) 755-3766

Founded: 1977; Area: International
Focus: Business, Economic, and Free Enterprise Education
Objective: To provide training and materials in the area of private enterprise and entrepreneurship education for teachers, students, and community groups.

Chamber of Commerce of the United States
Office of the President
1615 H Street NW, Washington DC 20062
(202) 463-5436

Founded: 1912; Area: International
Focus: Business, Economic, and Free Enterprise Education
Objective: To advance human progress by advocating an economic, political, and social system based on individual freedom, incentive, opportunity, and responsibility.

Chicago Board of Trade (CBOT)
Office of the President
141 West Jackson Boulevard
Chicago IL 60604
(312) 435-3500

Founded: 1848; Area: International
Focus: Business, Economic, and Free Enterprise Education
Objective: To provide a commodity exchange, a marketplace for buyers and sellers. The CBOT provides futures markets

in agricultural products, financial instruments, and precious metals, as well as markets for options on futures contracts.

Close Up Foundation
Office of the President
1235 Jefferson Davis Highway
Arlington VA 22207
(703) 892-5400

Founded: 1971; Area: National
Focus: Citizenship Education
Objective: To promote a greater awareness and appreciation of the individual's role in society by providing learning experiences for people of all ages. The Foundation is dedicated to the principle that informed, active citizens are essential to a responsive government and a healthy community.

Conference on Economic Progress
Office of the President
2610 Upton Street NW, Washington DC 20008
(202) 363-6222

Founded: 1954; Area: National
Focus: Business, Consumer, and Economic Education
Objective: To conduct economic research and education and to publish studies on economic issues and related problems and policies in the U.S.

Delta Pi Epsilon
Office of the Executive Director
Gustavus Adolphus College
St. Peter MN 56082
(507) 931-4184

Founded: 1936; Area: National
Focus: Business Education
Objective: To improve business education through encouraging research, recognizing exceptional research achievement and publicizing research in business education.

Distributive Education Clubs of America (DECA)
Office of the Executive Director
1908 Association Drive

Reston VA 22091
(703) 860-5000

Founded: 1946; Area: National
Focus: Business, Economic, and Marketing Education
Objective: To provide an avenue for career identification and development, an understanding of our economic system, an understanding of their responsibilities to society, and self-development opportunities for marketing education students.

Econ-ed Foundation
Office of the Executive Director
PO Box 76, La Mesa CA 92041
(619) 442-4151

Founded: 1976; Area: California
Focus: Economic Education
Objective: To establish economic literacy as a high school graduation requirement so that students will enter the "real world" after graduation prepared to make decisions as producers, consumers, and citizens.

Economic Institute for Research and Educ.
Office of the President
3870 Cloverleaf Drive
Boulder CO 80302
(303) 443-1716

Founded: 1977; Area: National
Focus: Economic and Free Enterprise Educ.
Objective: To support and promote the American free enterprise economic system through research and education.

Economics in Argumentation
Office of the Director
4800 San Felipe – #440
Houston TX 77056
(713) 621-6062

Founded: 1979; Area: National
Focus: Economic Education
Objective: To teach economics to high school speech and debate students.

Edison Electric Institute (EEI)
Office of the President
1111 19th Street NW
Washington DC 20036
(202) 828-7400

Founded: 1933; Area: National
Focus: Business, Consumer, Economic, Free
Enterprise, and Energy Education
Objective: To assist its members at the
national, state, and local levels by providing
information and education regarding ener-
gy-related issues.

The Charles Edison Memorial Youth Fund
Office of the Executive Director
1000 16th Street NW – Suite 401
Washington DC 20036
(202) 293-5092

Founded: 1969; Area: National
Focus: Economic and Free Enterprise
Education, Government and Political
Journalism
Objective: To promote and support the
development of campus leadership for the
assumption of leadership roles in the com-
munity and nation.

Enterprise and Education Foundation
Office of the President
200 Commerce Court Building
Pittsburgh PA 15219
(412) 394-5771

Founded: 1975; Area: DE, MD, NY, PA, and
WV
Focus: Economic Education
Objective: To provide an understanding of
the private enterprise system and to promote economic education for secondary
school social studies and economics students.

Enterprise Square, USA
Office of the Executive Director
Oklahoma Christian College
Route 1, Box 141
Oklahoma City OK 73111
(405) 478-5190

Founded: 1982; Area: National
Focus: Business, Economic, and Free
Enterprise Education
Objective: To use state of the art technology
to teach about the American free enterprise
system.

The Entrepreneurship Institute
Office of the President
3592 Corporate Drive, Suite 100
Columbus OH 43229
(614) 895-1153

Founded: 1976; Area: National
Focus: Business, Free Enterprise, and
Entrepreneurial Education
Objective: To provide programs and services
for entrepreneurs in growing businesses and
firms which support entrepreneurs (e.g.,
banks, law firms, venture capitalists, etc.)
which result in the start up or expansion of
the entrepreneurial firm.

The Fisher Institute
Sherrill E. Edwards, President
6350 LBJ Freeway – Suite 183E
Dallas TX 75240
(214) 233-1041

Founded: 1977; Area: International
Focus: Business, Economic, and Free
Enterprise Education
Objective: To increase knowledge among
government and business leaders and the
public about the usefulness of competitive
markets as the best means to solve
America's long-range economic problems.

The Foundation for Economic Education, Inc. (FEE)
Office of the President
30 South Broadway
Irvington-On-Hudson NY 10533
(914) 591-7230

Founded: 1946; Area: International
Focus: Economic and Free Enterprise Educ.
Objective: To promote the free market, limited government, private philosophy
through publications, lecture, and seminars.

Foundation for Free Enterprise
Office of the President
411 Hackensack Ave, Hackensack NJ 07601
(201) 487-4600

Founded: 1975; Area: NJ
Focus: Economic and Free Enterprise
Education
Objective: To expand the understanding of
economic concepts, theories, and principles
inherent in the free market system and to
disseminate this information to encourage
positive, constructive participation in the
free enterprise system.

Foundation for Research in Economics and Education (FREE)
Office of the Director of Special Projects
1100 Glendon Avenue – Suite 844
Los Angeles CA 90024
(213) 208-7735

Founded: 1970; Area: National
Focus: Economic Education
Objective: To teach secondary school students how the private enterprise economy
works and to support research in economics
and management.

Foundation for Teaching Economics
Office of the President
550 Kearny Street – Suite 1000
San Francisco CA 94108
(415) 981-5671

Founded: 1975; Area: National
Focus: Economic Education
Objective: To improve economic literacy by
establishing the study of economics as a
basic part of middle/junior high school cur-
ricula in schools throughout the U.S.

Free Enterprise Education Center
Office of the President
4800 San Felipe – Suite 440
Houston TX 77056
(713) 621-1156

Founded: 1976; Area: Houston TX
Focus: Economic and Free Enterprise
Education

Objective: To promote the ideals of individual responsibility and constitutional government as prerequisites to the sustenance of
free markets and to increase public understanding of free markets in theory and in
practice.

The Free Enterprise Institute
Office of the Coordinator
7575 East Fulton Road
Ada MI 49355
(616) 676-6986

Founded: 1972; Area: International
Focus: Economic and Free Enterprise
Education
Objective: To explain, communicate and
reinforce the reciprocal relationship
between personal and economic freedom; to
serve as a clearinghouse for information on
free enterprise, bringing together individuals and organizations sharing a common
belief in freedom.

Freedoms Foundation at Valley Forge
(FFVF)   Contact: Michael Moyer
Office of the President
Route 33, Valley Forge PA 19481
(215) 933-8825 / Fax: (215) 935-0522

Founded: 1949; Area: National
Focus: Economic and Free Enterprise
Education
Objective: To create a better understanding
and appreciation of the basic principles of
our American heritage and to contribute to
the development of responsible citizenship.

Fund for Education in Economics (FEE)
Office of the Administrator
1120 Connecticut Avenue NW
Washington DC 20036
(202) 467-4928

Founded: 1925; Area: National
Focus: Business, Consumer, Economic, and
Free Enterprise Education
Objective: To promote increased knowledge
of the economy and increased skill in personal economics as they relate to commercial banking and the financial system.

Future Business Leaders of America – Phi Beta Lambda, Inc. (FBLA-PBL)
Office of the President
PO Box 17417 - Dulles
Washington DC 20041
(703) 860-3334

>Founded: 1942; Area: National
>Focus: Business, Economic, and Free Enterprise Education
>Objective: To bring business and education together in a positive working relationship through programs and services that create a forum in which students, educators, and business people learn about one another.

General Fed. of Women's Clubs (GFWC)
Office of the International President
1734 N Street NW, Washington DC 20036
(202) 347-3168

>Founded: 1890; Area: International
>Focus: Consumer, Economic, and Free Enterprise Education
>Objective: To unite women's clubs in order to enhance community service efforts by volunteers.

The Hudson Institute
Office of the President
620 Union Drive – PO Box 648
Indianapolis IN 46206
(317) 632-1787

>Founded: 1961; Area: International
>Focus: Economic, Free Enterprise, and Employment Policy Education
>Objective: To help policy makers make the best possible decisions, given the constraints of time, money, and information.

Hugh O'Brian Youth Foundation (HOBY)
Office of the Chief Operating Officer
10880 Wilshire Boulevard – Suite 1500
Los Angeles CA 90024
(213) 474-4370

>Founded: 1958; Area: International
>Focus: Business, Economic, and Free Enterprise Education
>Objective: To seek out, recognize, and reward leadership potential in high school

sophomores in America and abroad and to provide a forum for these potential leaders to interface with recognized leaders in business, government, science, education, and the professions through give and take workshops.

Institute for Economic Awareness
Office of the Director
The University of Kansas
202 Bailey Hall
Lawrence KS 66045
(913) 864-3103

>Founded: 1972; Area: KS
>Focus: Economic Education
>Objective: To promote economic education.

Invest-in-America National Council, Inc.
Office of the President
2400 Chestnut Street – Suite 1710
Philadelphia PA 19103
(215) 568-7311

>Founded: 1949; Area: National
>Focus: Business, Consumer, Economic, and Free Enterprise Education
>Objective: To provide teachers with a fundamental and positive understanding of the American market system.

Joint Council on Economic Education (JCEE)
Office of the President
2 Park Avenue, New York NY 10016
(212) 685-5499

>Founded: 1949; Area: National
>Focus: Economic Education
>Objective: To enhance the quality and increase the quantity of economic education provided in the nation's schools and universities.

Junior Achievement, Inc. (JA)
Office of the President
550 Summer Street
Stamford CT 06901
(203) 359-2970

Founded: 1919; Area: International
Focus: Business, Consumer, Economic, and Free Enterprise Education
Objective: To provide young people with practical economic education programs and experiences in the competitive private enterprise system through a partnership with the business and education communities.

Lincoln Filene Center for Citizenship and Public Affairs (LFCCPA)
Office of the Executive Director
Tufts University
Medford MA 02155
(617) 381-3453

Founded: 1948; Area: National
Focus: Economic, Civic, and Global Educ.
Objective: To develop and disseminate a body of knowledge concerning how citizens can most effectively and constructively participate in social and governmental institutions.

National 4–H Council
Office of the Programs Administrator
7100 Connecticut Avenue
Chevy Chase MD 20815
(301) 656-9000

Founded: 1976; Area: National
Focus: Consumer, Economic, and Agricultural Education
Objective: To provide opportunities for young people to develop marketable skills, become aware of career opportunities, and become involved in personal and business economics.

National Association of Investors Corporation (NAIC)
Office of the Chairman
1515 East Eleven Mile Road
Royal Oak MI 48067
(313) 453-0612

Founded: 1961; Area: National
Focus: Economic Education
Objective: To interest people in all aspects of equity investment, create new shareholders and to teach sound investment principles.

The National Association of Life Underwriters (NALU)
Office of the Executive Vice President
1922 F Street NW
Washington DC 20006-4387
(202) 331-6031

Founded: 1890; Area: National
Focus: Business, Consumer, and Economic Education
Objective: To support and maintain the principles of life and health insurance; to promote high ethical standards; to inform the public and render community service.

National Association of Manufacturers (NAM)
Office of the President
1776 F Street NW
Washington DC 20006
(202) 626-3700

Founded: 1895; Area: National
Focus: Economic Education
Objective: To promote America's economic health and productivity, particularly in the manufacturing sector, by developing and advocating sound industrial practices; to make the American business community more aware of and involved in the process of public policy formation; and to reinforce public understanding of the importance of the competitive market system in promoting the national interest at home and abroad.

National Coalition for Consumer Education
Office of the President
4 Apple Lane
New Milford CT 06776
(203) 354-8409

Founded: 1981; Area: National
Focus: Consumer Education
Objective: To promote and expand consumer education.

National Education Program (NEP)

Office of the President
Oklahoma Christian College
Route 1, Box 141
Oklahoma City OK 73111
(405) 478-5190

> Founded: 1936; Area: National
> Focus: Economic and Free Enterprise
> Education
> Objective: To promote an understanding
> among the American people of the impor-
> tance of faith in God, strictly limited consti-
> tutional government, private enterprise and
> private ownership and control of property.

National Federation of Independent Business (NFIB)

Office of the President
600 Maryland Avenue, SW – Suite 700
Washington DC 20024
(202) 554-9000

> Founded: 1943; Area: National
> Focus: Business, Consumer, Economic, and
> Free Enterprise Education
> Objective: To promote and protect our free
> enterprise system.

National Foundation for Consumer Credit (NFCC)

Office of the President
8701 Georgia Avenue – Suite 601
Silver Spring MD 20910
(301) 589-5600

> Founded: 1951; Area: National
> Focus: Consumer Education
> Objective: To foster a better understanding
> of consumer credit through sound educa-
> tional, research, and counseling programs.

National Live Stock and Meat Board

Office of the President
444 North Michigan Avenue
Chicago IL 60611
(312) 467-5520

> Founded: 1922; Area: National
> Focus: Consumer Education
> Objective: To enhance the profit opportuni-
> ties for the livestock and red meat industry
> by protecting and improving consumer
> demand for beef, pork, lamb, veal, and
> processed meats.

National Schools Committee for Economic Education, Inc. (NSCEE)

Office of the President
PO Box 295 – 86 Valley Road
Cos Cob CT 06807-0295
(203) 869-1706

> Founded: 1953; Area: National
> Focus: Consumer, Economic, and Free
> Enterprise Education
> Objective: To research, develop, and dissem-
> inate supplementary classroom teaching
> aids which use nontechnical concepts,
> words, and phrases appropriate for elemen-
> tary through high school students to teach
> simple, functional, enterprise economics.

National Taxpayers Union (NTU)

Office of the Executive Director
325 Pennsylvania Avenue, SE
Washington DC 20003
(202) 543-1300

> Founded: 1969; Area: National
> Focus: Economic and Free Enterprise
> Education
> Objective: To reduce government taxes and
> spending and to promote constitutional limi-
> tations on Federal and state spending and
> taxes.

Office Education Association (OEA)

Office of the Executive Director
5454 Cleveland Avenue
Columbus OH 43229
(614) 895-7277

> Founded: 1966; Area: National
> Focus: Business and Free Enterprise
> Education
> Objective: To provide skill and personal
> leadership programs for students enrolled
> in vocational business and office education
> programs.

Operation Enterprise
Office of the Director
PO Box 88
Hamilton NY 13346
(315) 824-2000

Founded: 1963; Area: International
Focus: Business, Economic, and Free
Enterprise Education
Objective: To offer high school and college
students an opportunity to learn management principles, leadership skills and ways
of improving their personal effectiveness.

Pacific Academy for Advance Studies
(PAAS)
Office of the Director of Special Projects
1100 Glendon Avenue – Suite 844
Los Angeles CA 90024
(213) 208-7735

Founded: 1976; Area: International
Focus: Economic Education
Objective: To provide nonnormative instruction and materials concerning economic
principles and current economic issues.

A Presidential Classroom for Young
Americans
Office of the Executive Director
441 North Lee Street
Alexandria VA 22314
(703) 683-5400

Founded: 1968; Area: National
Focus: Business, Economic, and
Government Education
Objective: To inform high school juniors and
seniors about American government at the
Federal level through seminars and work-
shops given by national leaders in
Washington DC.

Reason Foundation
Office of the President
1018 Garden Street
Santa Barbara CA 93101
(805) 963-5993

Founded: 1978; Area: National
Focus: Economic and Free Enterprise
Education
Objective: To educate the public on the prin-
ciples of a free society: private property,
individual liberty, and free markets.

Securities Industry Foundation for
Economic Education, Inc.
Office of the Secretary
120 Broadway
New York NY 10271
(212) 608-1500

Founded: 1977; Area: National
Focus: Business, Consumer, Economic, and
Free Enterprise Education
Objective: To foster understanding of the
American free enterprise system and the
vital role of the securities industry in the
system.

Students in Free Enterprise (SIFE)
Office of the President
1601 South Springfield
Bolivar MO 65613
(417) 326-3611

Founded: 1975; Area: International
Focus: Economic and Free Enterprise
Education
Objective: To encourage and help young people anticipating business careers to commit
themselves to an individual endeavor that
advocates the American Free Enterprise
System and helps promote its continued
improvement and progress by bringing to
the system new life and new leadership.

Tax Foundation, Inc.
Office of the President
One Thomas Circle NW – Suite 500
Washington DC 20005
(202) 822-9050

Founded: 1937; Area: National
Focus: Business, Economic, and Free
Enterprise Education
Objective: To aid in the development of a
more efficient and economical government
by monitoring, analyzing, and reporting on
fiscal and management aspects of government.

Texas Bureau for Economic Understanding, Inc.
Office of the Executive Director
611 Ryan Plaza Drive – Suite 1119
Arlington TX 76011
(817) 265-0983

Founded: 1954; Area: TX
Focus: Economic and Free Enterprise Educ.
Objective: To help young Americans understand their heritage – what this country has, how it got it, and how it can keep it.

Tomorrow's America Foundation
Office of the President
PO Box 37106
Charlotte NC 28237
(704) 376-9068

Founded: 1979; Area: National
Focus: Economic and Free Enterprise Educ.
Objective: To teach young people the principles of leadership, goal setting, motivation, self-development and Americanism.

W.E. UpJohn Institute for Employment Research
Office of the Director
300 S. Westnedge Ave
Kalamazoo MI 49001
(616) 343-5541

Founded: 1945; Area: National
Focus: Business and Economic Education
Objective: To conduct or financially support research designed to seek solutions to problems of employment and unemployment and to disseminate such findings through publications.

Wisconsin Federation of Cooperatives
Office of the Executive Secretary
30 West Mifflin Street – #401
Madison WI 53703
(608) 258-4400

Founded: 1969; Area: Wisconsin
Focus: Business, Consumer, and Cooperative Education
Objective: To improve, foster, and promote a better understanding of cooperatives' princi-

ples and practice; to promote the interests of its members; and to promote further growth and strengthening of cooperatives.

World Research Incorporated (WRI Films)
Office of the President
11722 Sorrento Valley Road
San Diego CA 92121
(619) 566-3456

Founded: 1969; Area: International
Focus: Economic and Free Enterprise Education and Contemporary Issues
Objective: To produce thought-provoking educational films, videos, and materials designed to stimulate discussion of historical and current events.

APPENDIX 4

Who said that?

SOURCES & ACKNOWLEDGMENTS

ISSUE 1

Cohen, Michael Lee. *The Twenty-something American Dream: A Cross-Country Quest for a Generation*. New York: Dutton, 1993.

Moore, Martha. "They're Like Us, Only They're Rich" *USA Today*. 22 May 1987, 1.

Phillips, Kevin. *The Politics of Rich and Poor – Wealth and the American Electorate in the Reagan Aftermath*. New York: Random House, 1990.

Stewart, Thomas A. "The New American Century." *Fortune*. 1991.

Terkel, Studs. *American Dreams – Lost and Found*. New York: Pantheon Books, 1980.

"The Twentysomething Generation." *TIME*. 15 August 1992, 61.

Zinn, L. "Move Over Baby Boomers – A Portrait of Generation X." *Business Week*. 14 December 1992, 74-79.

Zuckerman, Mortimer B. "The Glass is Half Full." *U.S. News and World Report*, 27 February 1995, 80.

ISSUE 2

Greene, Mark R. and Dince, Robert R. *Personal Financial Management*. Cincinnati: South-Western Publishing, 1987.

"IBM Cuts Global in Scope" *Poughkeepsie Journal*. 28 March 1993, 2E.

ISSUE 3

Beard, Charles and Mary. *Rise of American Civilization*. Place: NY: Chas. Scribners, 1927.

Brimelow, Peter. "Why the Deficit is the Wrong Number." *Forbes*. 15 March 1993, 79-82.

Cook, Peter D. *Start and Run Your Own Successful Business*. New York: Beaufort Books, Inc., 1982.

Fallek, Max. *How to Set Up Your Own Business*. Mineapolis: American Institute of Small Business, 1990.

Greene, Mark R. and Dince, Robert R. *Personal Financial Management*. Cincinnati: South-Western Publishing, 1987.

Henderson, Nancy. "Personal Finances." *Kiplinger Personal Finance Magazine*. March 1992, 112.

"IBM Cuts Global in Scope" *Poughkeepsie Journal*. 28 March 1993, 2E.

Marx, Karl and Friedrich Engles. *The Communist Manifesto*. Indianapolis, IN: Liberty [1986 Edition].

Smith, Adam. *Wealth of Nations* Indianapolis, IN: Liberty [1986 Edition].

ISSUE 4

Bureau of Economic Analysis. *Business Statistics: 1963-91*. U.S. Department of Commerce, Washington DC 1992.

Cohen, Michael Lee. *The Twenty-something American Dream: A Cross – Country Quest for a Generation*. New York: Dutton, 1993.

Moore, Martha. "They're Like Us, Only They're Rich" *USA Today*. 22 May 1987, 1.

Terkel, Studs. *American Dreams – Lost and Found*. New York: Pantheon Books, 1980.

ISSUE 5

Cook, Peter D. *Start and Run Your Own Successful Business*. New York: Beaufort Books, Inc., 1982.

Fallek, Max. *How to Set Up Your Own Business*. Minneapolis: American Institute of Small Business, 1990.

Greene, Mark R. and Dince, Robert R. *Personal Financial Management*. Cincinnati: South-Western Publishing, 1987.

U.S. Bureau of the Census. *Statistical Abstract of the United States*. U.S. Department of Commerce, Economics and Statistics Administration. Washington DC, 1992.

ISSUE 6

Fierman, Jaclyn. "What Happened to the Jobs?" *Fortune*. 12 July 1993.

Magnet, Myron. "Good News For The Service Economy." *Fortune*. 3 May 1993.

Malone, Michael. "The Search for Jobs that No Longer Exist." *New York Times*. 5 September 1993.

Quinn, Jane Bryant. "A Generation Topped Out." *Newsweek*. 20 September 1993, 42.

Rowland, Mary. "Temporary Work: The New Career." *New York Times*. 12 September 1993.

Saltzman, Amy. "1994 Career Guide: The Changing Professions." *U.S. News and World Report*. 1 November 1990.

Sookdeo, Ricardo. "A Brave New Darwinian Workplace." *Fortune*. 25 January 1993.

Sullivan, Scott. "Economic Highlights" *Newsweek*. 14 June 1993, 46-47.

Zuckerman, Mortimer. "The Glass is Half Full." *U.S. News & World Report*. 27 Feb. 1995, 80.

ISSUE 7

American Express Co. *Getting Started*. World Financial Center, New York: 1993.

American Express Co. *Women's Credit Rights*. World Financial Center, New York: 1993.

Bankcard Holders of America. *Low Rate List*, Box 920 Herndon VA 22070 ($1.00); also, informational pamphlets: "How to Choose a Credit Card," "College Students and Credit, Getting Out of Debt," and "Secured Credit Cards: Selecting the Best for You."

Consumer Action. *Saving Money on Credit Cards*. Suite 233. San Francisco CA 94105: 1992.

Consumer Federation of America. *Student Consumer Knowledge*. Suite 604.1424 Sixteenth Street NW, Washington DC 20036: 1992.

Cruz, Humberto. "Credit Cards, Even Unused, Can Cost You." *Poughkeepsie Journal*. 31 January 1994, B1.

Steinbeck, John. *The Grapes of Wrath*. Viking Press, NY: 1939.

ISSUE 8

Bureau of the Census. *Statistical Abstract of the United States 1992* U.S. Department of Commerce: Washington DC 1992

Smith, Adam. *The Wealth of Nations*. Indianapolis, IN: Liberty [1986 Edition].

ISSUE 9

Bureau of Economic Analysis. *Statistical Abstract of the United States 1992*. Washington: U.S. Department of Commerce. 675.

ISSUE 10

Bureau of Economic Analysis. *Business Statistics, 1963-1993*. Washington: U.S. Department of Commerce. A-106, 107.

Bureau of Economic Analysis. *Statistical Abstract of the United States 1992*. Washington: U.S. Department of Commerce. 675.

Dentzer, Susan. "Exporting the Truth on Trade." *U.S. News & World Report*. 4 April 1992, 47.

Kennedy, Paul. *Preparing for the Twenty-First Century*. New York: Vintage, 1993.

Martin, Tom, and Greenwood, Deborah. "The World Economy in Charts." *Fortune*. 26 July 1993, 82-96.

Rowen, Henry. "Cheer Up, Troubled World." *Wall St. Journal*. 31 August 1993, 5.

ISSUE 11

Allen, Michael. "Eco Systems for Industry," *New Scientist*, 5 February 1994, 21-22.

Alper, Joe. "Protecting the Environment With the Power of the Market" *Science*. 25 June 1993, 1884-85.

Appenzeller, Tim. "Environment and the Economy." *Science*. 25 June 1993, 1883.

Conner, Charles H., Jr. "Mergers and Acquisitions in the Environmental Age," *Chemtech*, November 1989, 662-663.

Gore, Albert. *Earth in the Balance – Ecology and the Human Spirit*. NY: Houghton Mifflin, 1992.

Hammond, Allen L. [editor] *World Resources, 1992-93*. New York: Oxford University Press, 1992.

Himelstein, Linda and Mary Beth Regan. "Legal Affairs, *Business Week*. 29 November 1993, 138.

Johnson, Timothy, et.al. [editors]. *World Resources, 1992-93*. New York: Oxford University Press, 1992.

Kotin, Ilana and Joseph E. Daniel, [editors]. *1993 Earth Journal*. Boulder CO: Buzzworm Books, 1992, 169-171

Rice, Faye. "Next Steps for the Environment." *Fortune*. 19 October 1992, 98-100.

ISSUE 12

Crandall, Robert. "Has the AT&T Breakup Raised Telephone Rates?" *The Brookings Review*. No. 5, Winter 1987.

McCall, James R. *Consumer Protection: Cases, Notes, and Materials*. St. Paul MN: West Publishing Company, 1977, 478-486.

Passell, Peter. *N.Y. Times*. 9 June 1994, D21.

Spanogle, John A. and Ralph J. Rohner. *Consumer Law: Cases and Materials*. St. Paul, MN: West Publishing Company, 1978, 191-195.

Ziegler, Bart. *The Wall Street Journal*. 14 June 1994.

ISSUE 13

Fierman, Jaclyn. "What Happened to the Jobs?" *Fortune* 12 July 1993, 41.

Gallagher, Jay. "Pataki May Pay Price For Spending Reductions." *Poughkeepsie Journal*. 6 March 1995, 2B.

Isaac, Katherine. *Civics For Democracy*. Washington DC: Essential Books, 1992.

Klein, Joe. "Labor's Leverage Lost." *Newsweek*. 6 December 1993, 25.

Lappé, Frances M. and Paul DuBois. *The Quickening of America* San Francisco CA: Josey-Bass, 1994.

Priven, Frances Fox and Richard A. Cloward. *Why Americans Don't Vote*. New York: Pantheon Books, 1988.

Samuelson, Robert J. "R.I.P.: The Good Corporation." *Newsweek*. 5 July 1993, 41.

Sergeant, Jacqueline and Michelle Leder. "4,500 Jobs to Region: State Taking IBM Kingston, East Fishkill Space. Deal Adds $175M to Economy" *Poughkeepsie Journal*. 17 February 1995, 1.

ISSUE 14

"Balanced Budget Amendment Battle Heats Up" *The Concord Courier*. Winter 1994, 1-3.

"Clinton Budget holds No More Deficit Reduction" *The Concord Courier*. Winter 1994, 2-3.

Job Service New York. *Guide to Preparing A Resume*. Albany, NY: New York State Dept. of Labor, 1990.

Kennedy, Paul. *Preparing for the Twenty-First Century*. New York: Random House, 1993.

Lappé, Frances Moore and Paul Martin Du Bois. *The Quickening of America*. San Francisco CA: Josey-Bass, 1994.

L'Heureux, Dave. "Forging the Skills for the Future: New Standards Being Demanded for the Workplace." *Poughkeepsie Journal*, 27 March 1994, 1E.

Schmidt, Peggy. *The 90 Minute Resume*. New York: Petersen, 1989.

Zuckerman, Mortimer. "Who Does Feel Your Pain?" *U.S. News & World Report*. 26 Dec. 1994, 126.

APPENDIX 5

How do I find information?

GLOSSARY & INDEX

A

AARP 266-267, 283 American Association of Retired Persons – powerful lobby speaks for interests of older Americans.

ABC 275 American Broadcasting Co. – entertainment, communications.

Ability-to-pay principle 167, 168 Idea of calculating taxes (especially income taxes) on individual's income.

Absolute advantage 211 Extreme competitive edge one country has over others when it can produce something with the highest efficiency.

Acceleration clause 252 Credit arrangement in long-term loans in which creditor can ask for entire balance in response to a single instance of default.

Acceptance (legal) 250-251 Written or spoken authorization of buyer to seller to proceed.

Affirmative action 120-121 Government sponsored programs to eliminate hiring discrimination.

AF of L (AFL) 117 American Federation of Labor – late 19th c. national organization of craft unions – later merged with CIO.

Age Discrimination in Employment Act 123 federal law prohibits job discrimination against older workers (1967).

Agenda 21 224 June 1992 United Nations Conference on Environment and Development document which sets social goals (elimination of poverty and ecological management of human settlements).

Aggregate (Supply, Demand, Income) 36, 180, 186 total complete, as in aggregate demand in a market.

Agreement on Forest Principles 223 June 1992 United Nations Conference on Environment and Development document which seeks protection of forests – resisted by rain forest countries especially those in South Asia.

Alger, Horatio 95 19th c. U.S. writer of popular industrial success stories.

Allentown 110, 113 Billy Joel song about the eastern PA coal/steel town which went into serious economic decline in the 1950-70 period.

American Bar Association 284 National organization representing interests of attorneys.

American Dream 30-40, 48, 49, 53, 59, 63, 68, 73, 86, 91, 95, 105, 110, 112, 123, 144, 162, 195, 196, 204, 215, 219, 232, 268, 272, 287, 291, 292, 293-294, 307, 309-311 Aspiration for a successful, comfortable life with home and other property.

American Express 130, 134, 135, 136 Major U.S. charge and credit card issuer.

American Revolution 65, 150, 212 Political break with England 1776-1783 fostered by taxation and trade regulations.

American work ethic 299 Set of attitudes and principles of proper behavior about employment recognizing the proper relationship between employer and employee.

Anheuser-Busch 273 Major U.S. conglomerate (MO) brewing – snack foods – entertainment parks; dominates beer oligopoly; Miller and Coors other two major competitors.

Antitrust Division 104, 257-261, 320 U.S. Dept. of Justice agency prosecutes monopolies.

Apartheid 284 Former government system of racial separation in Republic of South Africa.

APEC 205-207 See Asian Pacific Economic Conference.

Appreciate 97, 195 Gain in value.

Asian Pacific Economic Conference 205, 206, 207 Ongoing attempt to eliminate trade barriers in Pacific Region, long-range goal of some sort of "Common Market" arrangement.

Assets 43, 251 Individually owned property, financial product, or resources.

AT&T 130, 259-260 American Telephone and

Telegraph Corp. – major communications firm broken up by government antitrust suit in 1984.

ATM 308 Automated Teller Machines – electronic technology streamlining consumer transactions.

Attachment 255 Court award of a lien on a debtor's property and allows the collection and sale of it in order to satisfy a debt.

Attorney General's Office 241, 337-339 Chief law enforcement officer in federal gov't. and most state governments; usually in charge of consumer protection/fraud investigations.

Automatic fiscal policy 154-155 Permanent government systems that forestall or ease serious economic declines (e.g., unemployment compensation, minimum wage).

Avon 247 Direct sale (in-home) cosmetics franchisor.

B

Balance of payments 195, 213 Statements measuring a nation's export-import relationship (surplus/equilibrium/deficit).

Balanced Budget Amendment 310 (BBA) Proposal to amend the U.S. Constitution to place limits on government spending by requiring the outlays equal to the revenues.

Balloon payment 252 Credit arrangement in long-term loans in which borrower accepts a large payment late in the loan in exchange for lower initial payments.

Banc One Corp. 142 One of the top 10 U.S. banks – 1994 (OH); see Figure 7.9.

Bank 133, 136-144, 307-308 Any institution providing financial services, chief among them the receipt of money for deposit and profits from lending the deposits at interest.

BankAmerica 142 One of the top 10 U.S. banks – 1994 (CA); see Figure 7.9.

Bank Holiday 143 Closing of banks (1933) for inspection by President Roosevelt to calm down panic runs on banks by public.

Bank of the United States 150-151, 154 Officially chartered independent financial clearing house for government revenues created for stability by Hamilton during the Washington Administration (1790s); lapsed during the War of 1812, recreated in 1816, veto of renewal in 1836 by Jackson caused harsh depression; no other central financial agency until Federal Reserve created in 1913.

Bankers Trust 142 One of the top 10 U.S. banks – 1994 (NY); see Figure 7.9.

Bankruptcy 255 Legal action placing all of a debtor's assets at risk (except for her/his home and necessary clothes). All other assets can be sold by the court in order to pay back what is owed.

Barter 131 Making transactions by direct exchange of goods or a series of indirect exchanges until the item needed is available.

Beard, Charles A. 65 20th c. American economic historian.

Benefits-received principle 168 Persons pay this kind of tax based on their frequency of use of a service (ex. toll on highways and bridges).

Better Business Bureau 241 National association of firms which keeps records of business affairs (e.g., complaints).

Big Blue 258-259 Nickname for IBM (International Business Machines Corp.).

Bilateral trade agreement 212 Two-sided arrangement for lower tariff rates and import quotas.

Biodiversity Convention 223 June 1992 United Nations Conference on Environment and Development document which proposed funding for protection of all plant, animal and marine species; international sharing of biotechnology.

Blue collar 294 Base industry, assembly line, factory jobs.

Blue pages 243 Public service agency listings in telephone books.

BMW 212, 268 Bavarian Motor Works – German-based automotive multinational.

Board of Governors 138-142, 322 Central management agency of the Federal Reserve.

Boesky, Ivan 261 Wall Street financier convicted of insider trading violations of SEC rules; implicated in billion-dollar bond market trading scandal in 1980s.

Bonds, corporate 99 Interest bearing certificate; holders lend money to corporation over specified time, money is paid back with interest; see diagram, Figure 7.7.

Bonds, government 140 Interest bearing certificate; holders lend money to government over specified time, money is paid back with interest; interest earnings are usually tax-free; see diagram, Figure 7.2.

Boycott 119, 209, 284 Organized sanction campaign to stop buying products from a particular country or manufacturer; see Figure 10.4.

Budget 55-56 Statement of financial status showing income and expenses; federal budget see Figure 8.5.

Bureau of Economic Analysis, U.S. 212, 320 Division of U.S. Commerce Dept. gathers information on international trade.

Burger-King 100 Burger-King Corp. – fast food/restaurant franchisor.

Bush, George Herbert Walker 38 41st President of U.S., 1989-93; struggled with national debt and tax reduction, recession, and Gulf War.

Business consumption 181 Spending for plants, equipment, supplies, overhead, labor, etc. by commercial enterprises; see investment.

Business cycle 152, 180 The pattern of the economy's "ups and downs," (also demand cycle) measured according to many technical indexes (primarily GDP); four key phases: Prosperity, Recession, Depression, Recovery; the "ups" are defined by high employment and high spending, while the "downs" are defined as low employment and low spending; see Figure 9.1.

Business incubator 274, 275 Community sponsored agencies and facilities to help infant businesses grow; see Figure 13.3.

C

Capital 52, 63, 99 Financial resources (money or goods) that can be invested to produce more wealth; also financial assets.

Capital account 213 Portion of the balance of payment statements measuring long-term financial and investment arrangements to and from other nations.

Capital gains tax 166 federal tax on profits from sales of assets by individuals and corporations.

Capital goods 52 Resources such as tools, property, factories, vehicles, machines, offices, or investment money used to produce wealth.

Capitalism 65, 68, 69 Market economic system in which nearly all productive resources are privately owned; see chart 65.

Career 295-300 Whole-life work environment, includes many jobs and levels of responsibility in a field.

Career clusters 296 Groups of related jobs requiring similar skills.

Carson, Rachel 225 American author whose *Silent Spring* about pesticide poisoning is credited with accelerating the late 20th century environmental movement.

Carter, James Earl ("Jimmy") 279 39th U.S. President, 1977-1981; plagued by rapid inflation ("energy crisis") and mounting budget deficits.

Caveat emptor 240 "Let the buyer beware" – Latin phrase indicating seller is not liable for a product once transaction occurs.

Cellar-Kefauver Act 257 (1950) Strengthened *Clayton Antitrust Act* with respect to mergers and buyouts.

CEO 38, 96 Chief Executive Officer – person chosen by a board of directors to operate and hire managerial staff of a corporation.

Chadwick's 83 Catalog – direct mail clothing merchandising corp.(MA).

Chamber of Commerce 241 Association of firms which promotes a region's business climate; also keeps some records of business affairs (complaints, etc.); has national network of local chapters; lobbies for business interests in political capitals.

Character 251 In lending, creditors look at the life records of a borrower for stability of behavior.

Charge card 128-130 (story), 133-136, 252-54 Certificate (usually plastic) of an individual's creditworthiness issued by a creditor; allows purchase of goods to be repaid over short period; often called a "regular credit card" – terms require full payment for all transactions at end of the billing period.

Charles River Bridge v. Warren Bridge. 256 Case (1837) in which Supreme Court ruled that a corporation's right to protection of their private property rights and freedom to do business could not be absolute in nature.

Chase Manhattan Corp. 142 One of the top 10 U.S. banks – 1994 (NY); see Figure 7.9.

Chattel 166 Personal moveable property (not real estate – autos, boats, RVs stocks, jewelry, etc.) taxed in some states.

Checking accounts 132-133, 136, 307-308 A written order to a bank to pay money out of an account to the person or firm noted on the order; see also "demand deposits."

ChemDry 100 Carpet/upholstery cleaning franchisor.

Chemical Banking Corp. 142 One of the top 10 U.S. banks – 1994 (NY); see figure 7.9.

Chevron 97 Chevron Oil Corp. – petroleum refining and distribution; see chart, Figure 5.2.

China 206, 209.

Choice Hotels 100 Hotel, motel/travel accommodations franchisor.

Chrysler 91, 212, 268 Chrysler Corp. – multinational automotive firm. (MI)

CIO 117 Congress of Industrial Organizations – 1930s national federation of industrial unions, later merged with AFL.

Citicorp 142 One of the top 10 U.S. banks – 1994 (NY); see Figure 7.9.

Civil cases 243 Litigation involving dispute between two parties of noncriminal nature.

Civil Rights Act of 1964 122 Congressional act (1964) prohibited gender, religious, sexual, ethnic, income, and race discrimination.

Civil Rights Act of 1968 254 Congressional act (1968) prohibited gender, religious, sexual, ethnic, income, and race discrimination in credit application.

Clayton Antitrust Act 104, 257 Congressional law (1914) strengthened the *Sherman Act*; forbid certain business combinations which restricted a market (monopolies and near monopolies); see Figure 12.9.

CleanNet 100 CleanNet Corp. – commercial cleaning franchisor.

Climate Convention 223 June, 1992 United Nations Conference on Environment and Development document which aspires to reduce or hold greenhouse gas emissions to 1990 levels.

Clinton, William J. ("Bill") 38 42nd President of U.S., 1993-; struggled with national debt reduction, Haitian democracy, and White Water – SNLs scandle.

Closed corporation 96 Form of corporation in which shares are privately held among a limited number of individuals.

Closed shop 122 Contractual rule for an establishment requiring only union members be hired; outlawed by the *Taft-Hartley Act*.

Coca-Cola 102, 104, 212 Coca-Cola Corp. – U.S. based (GA) beverage/foods/general merchandise multinational conglomerate.

Coincidental indicators 196 Statistical data used to measure and assess the economic conditions that reach peaks or troughs when economy is in a particular condition (Industrial Production Index, Personal Income, etc.; see Figure 9.13).

COLAs 192 Cost of Living Adjustments – contractual or legislative arrangements increasing wages or transfer payments to reconcile purchasing power with inflation.

Collateral 251 Something of value offered to secure a loan.

Collective bargaining agreements 118 Contracts relating to working conditions between employer and groups of employees.

Command systems 64, 65 Economy in which central authority attempts to control resources and decision-making; see communism; see chart 65.

Commercial Revolution 64 14th c. - 18th c. speedup and globalization of trade; led to changes in feudal system and helped capitalism develop.

Common Cause 283 Powerful lobby speaking out against abuse of governmental power.

Communism 65, 67, 69 Command economy in which central authority attempts to control resources and decision-making. Modern communism rests on 19th c. writings of Karl Marx and Friedrich Engels; see chart 65.

Communist Manifesto 67 Marx and Engels' 1847 work which outlined the modern worker controlled socialist state from which communist systems evolved.

Comparable worth 122-123 Demand by women for equal pay for equal work.

Comparative advantage 211 Favorable competitive edge one country has over others when it can produce something with the higher efficiency.

Compensatory damages 251 Court financial award to plaintiff for direct losses suffered because of a breach of contract.

Competition 102-105, 257 Rival firms seek to win consumers for their products, often basis for keeping prices low.

Concord Coalition 283, 284 Powerful lobby speaks out against growing national debt and for fiscal responsibility in federal government.

Conglomerate merger 101-102 A business combines with another in an unrelated industry; example, chain of hamburger stands buys an insurance company.

Consent decree 258-259 An out-of-court settlement that establishes a contract in which the company agrees to stop behaving in a particular manner.

Conservative 69, 151, 156, 255-256 In 20th c. U.S., those who seek to reverse strong government role in economic life; seek to cut gov't. role and promote individual laissez-faire atmosphere.

Consideration (legal) 250-251 Offering of some form of partial payment in exchange for service (deposit).

Constant dollars 184-185 Use of a standard base year to make statistical comparisons to factor out inflation and deflation results in Real GDP or Real GNP measurements; see Figure 9.4.

Constitution, U.S. 150-151, 163 (box) Economic roles of government grew from interpretations of powers assigned to Congress in Art. I, Sec. 8.

Consumer goods 52 Products made for the general public.

Consumer periodicals 241 Consumer Reports, Money magazine, Kiplinger's Personal Finance Magazine (formerly Changing Times), Consumer Digest.

Consumer Price Index 189-191 CPI measures the difference in prices paid for goods and services purchased by consumers over time.

Consumer Product Safety Commission 241 (Figure 12.1), 260, 320 Federal regulatory agency inspects and tests products for safety (1972).

Consumer protection 240 Government acts to ensure fairness and truth with regard to advertising, pricing, labeling, safety, quality, reliability, substance, and grade; see Figures 12.1, 12.8.

Consumer Reports 73, 74, 76, 88, 241, 269 Non-profit, neutral publication of the Consumers' Union (NY).

Contract 243, 247, 250-251 Legally binding promise to perform a service or deliver a good.

Contract with America 256 Republican Congressional campaign platform (1994) aimed at curtailing federal government economic regulation and interference.

Contraction 154 Slump, downturn, recession; phase of business cycle characterized by economic decline (low demand, rising unemployment); see Figure 8.1.

Coors 273 Dominant U.S. brewer (CO); major competitor to Anheuser-Busch and Miller in U.S. beer oligopoly.

Corporation 96-102 Form of business organization in which many share ownership and divide profits, but operation decisions are delegated to a few professional managers.

Correction phase 34 Change in the pattern of economic growth (slowdown or speedup) as in a change in the business cycle.

Cost of Living Adjustments 192 see COLAs.

Cost-push inflation 192 Increased production costs (wages, raw materials, services, etc.) force producers to raise prices in order to maintain reasonable profit margins.

Coverall 100 Coverall North America Corp. – commercial cleaning franchisor.

Credit 128-130 (story), 133-136, 251-256 Goods or money given in belief of another's ability to pay at a later time.

Credit bureau 135 Agency that keeps financial records on individuals and sells the information to lenders determining creditworthiness of borrowers.

Credit card 128-130 (story), 131, 133-136, 251-255 Certificate (usually plastic) of an individual's creditworthiness issued by a creditor; allows purchase of goods to be repaid with interest over extended period of time.

Credit counseling service 255 An agency which helps debtors restore their financial solvency.

Credit history 251 Record kept by creditors or credit clearing houses on individuals and firms as to payment of debt; used to determine creditworthiness for loans.

Credit union 136 Financial cooperative set up by employees or labor union members to pool savings and lend money at lower rates than commercial banks; see Figure 7.4.

Creditor 251 Person or firm that provides the merchandise or money to a borrower/debtor.

Creditworthy, creditworthiness 135 Determination of ability to repay; extension of credit based on an individual's prior experience with loans; trustworthiness.

Criminal fraud 243 Legal action which alleges a party fully intended to victimize another through misrepresentation and failure to perform a service or deliver a good.

Current account 213 Portion of the balance of payment statements measuring merchandise, service, tourism, and short-term finance exports-import relationship.

Current dollars 184 Reporting figures in terms of the present purchasing power of the dollar at the time (no adjustment for inflation); sometimes called raw, or money GDP; see Figure 9.4.

Customs duty/tariff 164-166, 209-210 A tax on imports; see Figure 10.4.

Cyclical unemployment 189 Unemployment stemming from a number of people being between jobs.

D

Damages (civil case) 243 In civil litigation, a plaintiff may ask for compensatory payments equivalent to time or convenience sacrificed because of a wrongful act.

Debt reorganization 255 Chapter XIII of the Federal Bankruptcy Law allows a debtor to meet with the creditors with a court appointed referee to work out a plan for debt repayment.

Debtor 251, 254-255 Person that makes purchases without the use of money or borrows money.

Default 251-252 Nonpayment of a loan.

Defendant (civil case) 243-245 In civil litigation, an accused party being sued by another (plaintiff) for a wrongful act.

Deficit spending 34, 155 Intentionally going into debt beyond means of income; usually government action taken to stimulate the economy.

Deflation 34, 193 Unbalanced condition resulting from too little money in circulation allowing supply to exceed demand and causing unnatural drop in prices.

Demand 78, 81, 82, 84, 86, 114, 191 The aggregate amount of goods consumers are willing and able to buy.

Demand curve 83 A graph line showing relation between price and quantity consumers are willing and able to buy; also see graphs on 80, 81, 82, 85, 86, 114, 115, 116, 117, 121, 271.

Demand deposits 132 Checking accounts which function as the most frequently used type of money.

Demand, Determinants of 81 Underlying factors motivating consumers.

Demand, Law of 79 As P increases, Q will decrease and vice versa.

Demand schedule 82 A chart or list showing relation between price and quantity consumers are willing and able to buy.

Demand-management economics 34, 153, 156 School of thought which seeks to stimulate economic growth through fiscal policy of raising spending levels, providing wages and service payments to consumers (also known as Keynesian economics or demand-side economics).

Demand-pull inflation 191-192 Increased demand without offsetting increasing supply pulls equilibrium prices up.

Democratic-Republican Party 151 Farming interests and followers of Jefferson's state/local power with smaller role for central government in the early history of the U.S. (1790s through 1830s); evolved into modern Democratic Party after the Civil War.

Depository Institutions Deregulation and Monetary Act 143 1980 federal reform to make banking industry more competitive; allowed savings institutions to offer checking.

Depreciate 98, 194 To lose value.

Depreciation 185 The loss of value as equipment wears out; also the cost of replacing machines, buildings, and other productive capital.

Depression 180 Phase of economic activity in market economies in which there is severe and prolonged aggregate decline (high unemployment, business closings, unfavorable trade, little building, very low consumption, deflation, etc.); measured by Real GDP decrease.

Derived demand 114, 115 Demand for labor depends on aggregate demand in a market; see Figure 6.2.

Desert Storm 182 Persian Gulf conflict with Iraq (1991-1992); example of effect of even short war on global economic affairs.

Direct action 284 Groups employ specific movements (demonstrations, marches, rallies, boycotts) to confront injustice in public affairs.

Direct investment 207, 212 Multinationals' outright purchasing of plants and productive properties in another nation; see Figure 10.2; (By contrast, an indirect investment would be buying stock in foreign firms.)

Direct mail merchandising 83 Selling through catalogs rather than retail or wholesale outlets; mail-order catalog sales.

Direct sale 247 Individual seller deals straight away with consumer, eliminating middle seller, wholesaler, distributor, etc.

Disclaimer 250 Statement limiting the legal liability of the seller.

Discount merchandising 83 Offering goods at lower cost to consumers usually through selling large enough volume that makes up for lower profits.

Discount rate 140, 142 FED's interest rate on loans to member banks to keep proper amounts on reserve; changes can alter the money supply.

Discouraged workers 189 Persons who give up job searches but do not count in official unemployment statistics because they do not apply for compensatory programs.

Discretionary fiscal policy 154-155, 181 Immediate and intentional acts by Congress to ease or avoid serious declines or inflation.

Disinflation 193 A slowing down or decline in the rate of price increases during an inflationary period.

Disposable Personal Income 186, 187 Aggregate personal income less taxes; purchasing power; what people have to spend or save; see Figure 9.6.

Diversification 101 A business or investor that has assets in a number of different kinds of businesses to diminish risk.

Dividends 97 Stockholder's share of profits of a corporation.

Division of labor 52 Separating production into smaller, easily mastered tasks to speed the entire operation.

Domino's 100 fast food/pizza franchisor.

Downsizing 45 (news article), 46-47 (story), 102, 110 (story), 112, 113 (side bar), 182, 269-270 Late 20th c. moves by major corporations to reduce costs by reducing and consolidating operations and labor forces.

Dunkin' Donuts 100 fast food/coffee shop franchisor; see chart, Figure 5.5.

DuPont 97, 162 E. I. DuPont Corp. – U.S.-based (DE) chemicals manufacturing multinational; see chart, Figure 5.2.

E

Earned income 185 Wealth gained from direct work by the individual.

Earth Summit 220, 222-224, 225, 231 Unofficial name for the June 1992 United Nations Conference on Environment and Development in Rio de Janeiro, Brazil; also "Rio Summit."

Easy money policy 140 FED actions which expand the money supply to offset recession and increase employment; see Figure 7.8.

EC or EU 116, 205-206 European Community or European Union – ongoing attempt to unify Western European markets into a single unit; phases out tariffs and other barriers; also called "Common Market."

Econometrics 196 Application of mathematical and statistical methods to study economic and financial data.

Economic indicators 196 Statistical data used to measure and assess the economic conditions (Real GDP, money supply, installment credit debt, building starts, etc.).

Economic model 51-52 Controlled hypothetical small-scale plan for an economy (or portion of an economy) allowing study of interaction of basic elements.

Economic Recovery Act of 1981 37, 158 Reagan Era legislation of 1980s; supply-side stimulation attempt that cut taxes, especially for wealthy and corporations.

Economics 50 Study of how people and societies use scarce resources.

Education 33, 35, 116, 297-298 Relationship to career and to the efficiency of the aggregate workforce.

Efficiency 68 Economic value that calls for production which optimizes use of resources.

Elastic clause 150-151, 154, 159 Constitution's Art. I, sec. 8, clause 18 allows Congress the flexibility to broaden the interpretation of its powers; the Elastic Clause conflicts with 10th Amendment, reserving powers not mentioned in the Constitution for the states.

Elasticity, price 82 Dramatic behavior (high % of change) of Q demanded or supplied when there is only slight change in price.

Electrolux 247 Direct sale (in-home) vacuum franchisor.

Embargo 209 Government sanction making it illegal to trade with a particular country; see Figure 10.4.

Emergency Banking Act of 1933 143 Glass-Steagall Act; banking reform led to federal deposit insurance (FDIC) and regular examination of banking records by federal government.

Employee benefits 118 non-wage compensation (medical, dental insurance, vacation, sick days, etc.); also "fringe benefits;" see Figure 6.7.

Employee empowerment 272-273 Business management approach which consciously and formally involved workers in decision-making, usually through production teams.

Employee ownership 271-272 Management and majority stock holdings in hands of workers of a corporation.

Employment Act of 1946 156 Set up agencies and committees which legitimized the Keynesian role of federal government as a stabilizer of the economy's performance.

Entitlement programs 310 Government programs usually involving transfer of funds to groups because of certain legal status (e.g., payments to dependent children, disabled individuals, widows, veterans).

Entrepreneur 92-94, 273-276 Organizer or promoter of a business enterprise (brings together the basic resources of land, labor, capital, management).

Environmental Protection Agency 228, 229, 260, 321 federal agency regulates activities of firms in relation to environmental matters.

Equal Credit Opportunity Act 254 Congressional act (1977) deepened and clarified 1968 *Civil Rights Act* ban on prejudicial discrimination in credit applications.

Equal Pay Act of 1963 122 Congressional act prohibited gender discrimination in employment.

Equilibrium price 78, 83, 84 Average point of balance where interaction of forces of supply and demand meet to clear the market.

Estate and gift tax 167 Government collects a percentage on inheritances.

European Union 205-206 Multilateral trade and economic agreements among Western European nations (formerly the European Community or the Common Market).

Excise taxes 166 Government levies on certain commodities often considered luxuries or nonessentials (leather, jewelry, furs).

Expectations 181-182 Taking actions (raising prices, making purchases) which alter supply and demand based on hunches and beliefs of what may occur.

Expressed warranty 248 A written or spoken statement of what the seller will do if the product does not perform as it should.

Extended warranty 248 A credit card company may grant an additional year of coverage beyond the manufacturer's normal warranty's time limit.

Externalities 226 Costs outside the measurable cost of economic activity, such as pollution, often paid by persons not involved in the production or even the consumption of a product or service.

Exxon 97, 211, 284-285 Exxon – petroleum products; see chart, Figure 5.2.

Exxon Valdez 284-285 Tanker caused major oil spill leading to considerable environmental damage in 1989; led to boycotts and direct action against Exxon Corp.

F

Fair Credit Billing Act 135, 254 Congressional law (1971) outlining consumer rights in relation to access and correction in credit records; see Figure 12.8.

Fair Credit Reporting Act 135, 254 Congressional law (1971) outlining consumer rights in relation to access and correction in credit records; see Figure 12.8.

Fair Deal 35 Late 1940s economic program of Pres. Harry S Truman; reinforced large number of New Deal programs; stimulated consumption and expanded security for workers.

Fair Debt Collection Act 254 Congressional law (1977) deals with the proper and legal means for a debt to be collected from a debtor; see Figure 12.8.

Farmer Labor Party 280 Early 20th c. U.S. political group in mid-west sought labor and social reform.

FDIC 34, 143-144, 155, 321 Federal Deposit Insurance Corporation – 1930s federal agency insures bank deposits and inspects banks; see Figure 8.2; (FSLIC, also created by Congress to oversee Savings & Loan institutions collapsed in 1987 during the S&L Crisis.)

FED, The 37, 38, 136, 138-142, 193, 205, 322 see Federal Reserve System – popular name used by economists and media for the Federal Reserve Bank and its management agencies, most commonly, the Board of Governors.

Federal Budget 158 Division of government expenses; see Figure 8.5.

Federal Communications Commission 241, 260, 321 Federal agency regulates activities of firms in stock, bond, and other financial markets.

Federal Insurance Contribution Act 164 FICA – 1935 Congressional act created a three-part payroll deduction to fund retirement, disability, death benefits under the Social Security system.

Federalist Party 151 Commercial interests and followers of Hamilton's strong government role in the early history of the U.S. (1790s through War of 1812.)

Federal Reserve System 37, 38, 136, 138-143, 193, 205, 322 (The FED); independent central bank of the U.S. – controls money supply.

Federal Revenue Act of 1932 152 Doubled taxes in the early years of the Great Depression to balance federal budget; curtailed demand and worsened conditions.

Federal Trade Commission 104, 241, 260, 322 (FTC) Investigative body created by Congress in 1914 to ensure fair competition in markets prone to monopolistic growth and regulate activities of firms in relation to fair treatment of consumers and marketplace ethics.

Federal Unemployment Taxes 166 (FUTA) Employer-paid taxes per employee for protection of workers against layoffs and other reasons for losing jobs.

Fiat money 132 Money which a government decrees must be accepted as payment for goods and services; also legal tender.

FICA 164 See *Federal Insurance Contribution Act.*

Financial institution 136 An intermediary such as a bank or credit union which functions as a depository for, and lender of, money and other fiscal services.

Fiscal policy 34, 35, 152-158 Actions by Congress to alter (stimulate or slow down) economic growth usually through adjusting spending levels or tax rates.

Fixed exchange rate 214-215 Value relationships among national currencies set by a central authority or agreement such as the gold standard or the Bretton Woods system.

Floating exchange rate 214-215 Value relationships among national currencies set by interaction of supply and demand in foreign exchange markets.

FOMC 140 Federal Open Market Committee of the Federal Reserve System decides FED actions in buying and selling of government securities to maintain proper level for the money supply.

Food and Drug Administration 241 (Figure 12.1), 260, 322 Federal agency (1906) tests and approves drugs, cosmetics, food additives and inspects preparation.

Ford 91, 130, 268, 270 Ford Motors – U.S. based (MI) automotive multinational.

Foreign exchange rate 194, 214-215 Value of a national currency in relation to others; set in world exchange markets such as London, Tokyo, New York.

Forfeit judgment 245 Court decision in favor of one party because the other does not appear.

Four Dragons, The 206-207 Hong Kong, Singapore, South Korea, and Taiwan make up the aggressive, surging NIEs of the Pacific Rim.

Franchise 99-100 License to market and earn profits on products produced by another business as if an independently owned outlet for another company.

Franchisee 99-100 A proprietor, partnership, or corporation which purchases a license to market and earn profits on products produced by another business.

Franchisor 99-100 A company which sells licenses to proprietor, partners, or corporations to market and earn profits on products it produces.

Frictional unemployment 189 Unemployment stemming from a number of people being between jobs.

Frontier (Work) Ethic 152 Strong 19th c. attitude of self-reliance and independence in sustaining oneself and family with no help from outside sources when problems arose.

FSLIC 143 Federal Savings and Loan Insurance Corporation – 1930s federal agency insured savings institutions' deposits and inspected banks; collapsed in 1987 during the S&L Crisis.

Full employment 189 Ideal economic conditions allowing everyone who wants a job to find one.

Fuller Brush Co. 247 Direct sale (in-home) home care products franchisor.

Functions of money 131-132 Money's primary uses as medium of exchange, standard of value, store of wealth.

G

G-8 nations 182 (picture) Called G-7 prior to admission of Russia in 1997; major global industrial powers (Britain, Canada, France, Japan, Germany, Italy, U.S.); involvement in Desert Storm; G-8 nations meet frequently on common economic and currency matters.

Garnisheed 255 Court action ordering a troubled debtor's employer to take part of her/his income and send it directly to creditors.

GATT 205, 206, 207, 209, 212 General Agreement on Trade and Tariffs; 1947 U.N.-sponsored treaty organization to minimize trade barriers.

GDP – Gross Domestic Product 34, 39, 176, 178, 181, 183-185, 206, 207, 208, 224 Statistical measurement of value of all goods and services produced inside a country in a given year. Real GDP is adjusted for inflation and reported in constant dollars; see Figures 9.2, 9.4, 10.3.

G.E. 39, 97, 113 (side bar) General Electric - U.S. based (NY) consumer and industrial electronics, appliance manufacturing multinational conglomerate; see chart, Figure 5.2.

General Motors 91, 97, 268-269, 272 see GM.

General partner 96 One of several business owners actively involved in operations and decisions of a partnership.

G.I. Bill 35 *Servicemen's Readjustment Act of 1944* – Congressional program to aid military personnel and economy as a whole in making transition to post-WW II economy; gov't. mortgages, business loans, education grants, etc.

Gift tax 167 Government collects a percentage on transfer of property or money to another individual.

Global Commons 223 June 1992 United Nations Conference on Environment and Development principle that held certain resources (e.g., oceans, atmosphere)are so vital to the world that they do not belong to any nation.

Global economy 268-269 Growth of free trade (GATT), regional trade agreements (EU, NAFTA), and multinational corporations in late 20th c. changed world economic structure.

Globalized manufacturing 268-269 In late 20th c., multinational corporations response to changed world economic structure by forming alliances such as those in auto industry (e.g., Mazda + Ford to build Probes, Explorers).

GM 91, 97, 130, 268-269, 272 General Motors Corp. – U.S. based (MI) multinational automotive firm; see chart, Figure 5.2.

GNP – Gross National Product 183 Statistical measurement of value of all goods and services produced by firms of country (at home and overseas) in a given year. Real GNP is adjusted for inflation and reported in constant dollars.

Gold standard 214 Monetary system (up to mid 20th c.) in which value relationships among national currencies were locked into the supply of gold (as opposed to today's free floating currency markets); see Figure 10.9.

Goldstar 207 South Korean electronics/home appliance multinational – high imports to U.S.

Gompers, Samuel 117 Founder of AFL (1886).

Good Corporation, The 269 Concept of the paternal and highly ethical corporation that dutifully guarded workers' welfare, behaved scrupulously in regard to the law (e.g. pollution regulations) and sought to promote the good of the community.

Gore, Albert, Jr. 231, 232 U.S. Senator, TN and Vice President (Clinton Admin.); Author: *Earth in the Balance – Ecology and the Human Spirit*, 1992.

Government Expenditures (G) 183 Spending by government for goods and services is the third largest component = "G" of (C+I+G+X) calculation of GDP and GNP. The government spending which is added to consumer, business, and net export spending.

Great Crash 34, 152, 187 Wall Street collapse of October 1929, signalled the beginning of the Great Depression of the 1930s in the U.S.

Great Depression 34, 152-154, 180, 189, 209, 268, 307 Collapse and protracted period of economic decline and paralysis in U.S. (and global) economy from 1929-1940.

Great Safety Net 159, 161 Controversial idea that government's major role is to create a base of security for citizens; that tax revenues should be devoted to a massive welfare structure to insure citizens against economic hardship.

Great Society 36, 69, 193 Pres. L.B. Johnson's 1960s expansion of Kennedy economic program; large number of gov't. programs to stimulate consumption and render greater security.

Gross Income 185 Total amount of wages, salaries, and other financial gains from investment (earned and unearned) in the nation.

Growth 38, 68 Net increase in production, jobs, standards of living.

H

Habib, Peter 275-276 Entrepreneur, owner and operator of Madison Media (MD).

Hamilton, Alexander 150-151, 154, 256 President Washington's first Secretary of

Treasury; believed in active gov't. role in promoting business and industry; founder of Federalist Party which sought broader economic power for central government.

Haymarket Riots 117 1886 Chicago labor protests led to the downfall of the Knights of Labor.

Honda 212 Honda Corp. – Japan-based automotive multinational.

Hoover, Herbert 34, 152 31st U.S. President (1929-1933) retained laissez-faire approach to government role in early part of the Great Depression.

Horizontal merger 100 A business combines with another in the same industry. (Chain of hamburger stands buys another chain of hamburger stands.)

Hudson Valley 282 Southeastern region of NY saw extensive economic repercussions from IBM downsizing.

Hughes, Langston 268 20th c. American poet.

Human resources 49 Essential factor of production that entails processes done by people; most commonly called "labor."

Hyperinflation 36, 192 Extremely rapid increase in prices, usually in double digits (rate above 10% per annum) devastating incomes and making growth unpredictable. Also called "galloping inflation."

Hyundai 207 South Korean automobile multinational.

I

IBM 45, 46-47, 48, 52, 97, 258-259, 269, 282 International Business Machines Corp. (NY) – major multinational computer manufacturer; see chart, Figure 5.2.

ILGWU 117 "The I.L.G." – International Ladies' Garment Workers Union – most powerful of the U.S. textile industry unions.

IMF 214, 326 International Monetary Fund of the U.N. (NY); managed post-WWII fixed currency exchange system; now oversees international loans to nations with currency difficulties.

Imperfect competition 102-104 Market structure with many buyers and sellers, with similar products, some nonprice competition, usually intensely price competitive.

Implied powers 151 Idea that Congress can expand the scope of government by using the elastic clause to broadly interpret its enumerated (specified) constitutional powers.

Implied warranty 248-249 An unwritten or spoken promise that the product will perform for the purpose advertised.

Indicators 196 Statistical data used to measure and assess the economic conditions (real GDP, money supply, installment credit, building starts, etc.).

Industrial Revolution 113, 268 Conversion from hand and animal power to machine power; late 18th c. in Europe; later 19th c. in U.S.

Inelasticity, price 82 Sluggish behavior (low % of change) of Q demanded or supplied even with dramatic changes in price.

Inflation 36, 191-193 Unbalanced condition resulting from too much money in circulation allowing demand to exceed supply and causing unnatural rise in prices.

Initiative and referendum 287 Formal state governmental procedures that allow individuals and groups to place reform measures on ballots in general elections, often bypassing state legislatures.

Insider trading 261 Violation of Federal Securities and Exchange Commission's rules against brokers or corporate financial officers seeking to profit by making transactions on information not yet made public.

Interdependence 211, 219 Reliance of nations and people on each other for goods and services.

Interest 251-254 Amount of money charged by a creditor to a borrower for the principal.

International Business Machines Corp. v. United States 258-259 First of a series of U.S. gov't. antitrust prosecutions of IBM (1936).

Interstate Commerce Commission 260, 323 Federal agency regulates activities of firms in interstate transportation markets (1887).

Investment Expenditures (I) 183 Second largest component ("I") of (C+I+G+X) calculation of GDP and GNP in which business spending is added to consumer, government, and net export spending.

J

Jani King 100 Jani-King Corp. – commercial cleaning franchisor; see Figure 5.5.

Japan 38, 39, 168 (Figure 8.13), 187, 194, 195, 202, 204-206, 212, 215, 268, 294.

J.P. Morgan and Co. 142 One of the top ten

U.S. banks in 1994 (NY); see Figure 7.9.

Jefferson, Thomas 150-151, 154 George Washington's Secretary of State; opposed Hamilton's view of active gov't. role in promoting business and industry; also 3rd President of the U.S. (1801-1809), embargo on European trade to avoid being drawn into Napoleonic Wars.

Job search 300-306 Strategic steps to guide an individual seeking employment.

Justice, economic 68 Basic economic value seeks to insure fairness and equal opportunity.

K

K-Mart 83, 207 U.S.-based (MI) clothing, general merchandising corp.(Waldenbooks, Payless Drugs); multinational chain store.

Katz Broadcasting Co. 275 Independent television production firm (U.S.).

Keiretsu 206 Large, powerful corporations in Japan – usually multinationals.

Keynes, John Maynard 152, 153, 156 20th c. British economist – proponent of governmental demand-side management policies.

Keynesian economics 152, 153, 156 School of thought championed by John Maynard Keynes c. Great Depression; seeks to stimulate economic growth through fiscal policy of raising spending levels, providing wages and service payments to consumers; (also, demand-side economics).

Kiwi Airlines 271 Employee-owned airline emerged during downsizing of 1990s.

Knights of Labor 116-117 Mid-19th c. nationwide labor union.

Kuznets, Simon 183 Awarded Nobel Prize in Economics (1971) for his method of determining Gross National Product and National Income.

L

L.L. Bean 83 Catalog – direct mail clothing merchandising corp. (ME).

Labor force 115 All the people over 16 years of age who have employment or are seeking it.

Labor productivity 114 How much profit a worker creates for an employer.

Labor union 116-122, 269 Organization of workers for purpose of collective bargaining with employers.

Lagging indicators 196 Statistical data used to measure and assess the economic conditions that reach peaks or troughs later than others, but confirm conditions (Av. Prime Rate, Change in CPI, Change in Business Loans, etc.).

Laissez-faire 34, 66, 69, 152, 153, 157, 255, 256 Economic concept in which government minimizes its economic activity.

Lands' End 83 Catalog – direct mail clothing merchandising corp. (WI).

Law of demand 79 Market economy behavior occurs when a product's market price rises, consumers will desire less; there is an opposite effect: if prices decline, consumers will demand more.

Law of supply 79 Market economy behavior occurs when a product's market price rises, producers will produce more; there is an opposite effect: if prices decline, producers will supply less or even drop out of the market.

LDCs 179, 204, 207-209, 215, 220, 222, 223, 224, 226 Less Developed Nations (also "Third World"); poor nations of Asia, Africa, Middle America (especially Caribbean) troubled by overpopulation, food shortages, and weak industrial development.

Leading indicators 196 Statistical data used to measure and assess the economic conditions that reach peaks or troughs earlier than others, indicating business cycle trends (building permits, common stock price index, initial unemployment claims, etc.).

Lewis, John L. 117 United Mine Workers leader in 1930s and 1940s; founder of CIO (1938).

Liability 97, 99 Having legal or financial responsibility for something.

Liberal 69, 151, 156, 255-256 In 20th c. U.S., those who endorse strong government role in economic life; seeks programs to stimulate consumption, render greater security, monitor competition.

Lien 250-251 Legal claim to the property of another; see Figure 12.7.

Limited partner 96 One of several business owners passively involved a partnership;. share profits but are basically financial backers; also 'silent partners."

Limited warranty 250 A promise made by the seller that guarantees the quality and performance of the purchased product for a specific time (e.g., 90 days).

Lincoln, Abraham 265, 276 16th U.S. President (1861-1865); *Gettysburg Address* principles applied to citizen involvement in public policies.

Liquid (liquidity) 133 Ease with which a financial asset can be converted into money.

Liquidate 97 Dispose of; sell assets to pay debts or obtain capital.

Little Caesar's 100 Leading U.S. fast food (pizza) franchisor.

Lobbying 285-286 Formal attempts to influence public policy; usually by organized groups with professional agents.

Low-end manufacturers 207 Producers of cheaper, lesser quality goods.

M

M-1, M-2, M-3, L 132-133 Various measurements of the money supply, from narrowest *M-1* (currency and checks) to the *L* (broadest inclusion of all possible types of money and near money); see Figure 7.2.

Ma Bell 259-260 Nickname for AT&T (American Telephone and Telegraph Corp.).

MAD 283 Mothers Against Drunk Driving – powerful lobby speaks out against crimes related to intoxication.

Madison Media Co. 276 Advertising venture (1995) in Maryland of entrepreneur Peter Habib.

Mail Boxes Etc. 100 Shipping/receiving services franchisor.

Margin 79 Percentage of income or profit to make a venture worthwhile; lowest acceptable level of performance.

Market clearing price 83 Same as equilibrium price.

Market price 77, 78 Same as equilibrium price.

Market system 65 Buyers and sellers come together to make transactions and determine prices; also private enterprise system.

Marshall Plan 36 Formally called the *European Recovery Act* (1947); Congress authorized massive aid to Western European nations to aid in rebuilding after WWII; named after U.S. Sec'y of State Gen. George C. Marshall; also stimulated U.S. economic growth after WWII because most of supplies for Europe were manufactured by U.S. corporations.

Marshall, John 151 Chief Justice of U.S.

Supreme Court (1801-1835); landmark decisions interpreted the *U.S. Constitution* in broad sense to allow more federal power in economic questions.

Mary Kay 247 Direct sale (in-home) cosmetics franchisor.

MasterCard 130, 134-135 Major issuer of international bank credit cards.

Mazda 191-192, 211, 268, 269 Mazda Automotive Corp. – Japanese based automotive multinational.

McCulloch v. Maryland 151 One of Chief Justice Marshall's landmark decisions (1819) allowed broad interpretation of Congress' implied power (setting up the Bank of the United States); other decisions (e.g., *Gibbons v. Ogden*, 1824) laid groundwork for more federal power in interstate economic questions.

McDonald's 100 McDonald's Corp. – fast food/restaurant franchisor.

Mechanic's lien 250-251 Legally binding agreement giving claim to title on a vehicle wherein it becomes security until full payment of service is rendered; see Figure 12.7.

Medicare 164 Extension of Social Security system which taxes workers to pay for health care of the elderly.

Medium of exchange 131 Money's use as a simple, neutral instrument for making transactions (as opposed to barter).

Mercedes 212 Mercedes-Benz Corp. – German-based automotive multinational.

Metropolitan 97 Metropolitan Life Insurance – financial products and securities; see chart, Figure 5.2.

MGM 258-259 Metro-Goldwyn-Mayer Studios – accused of being a monopoly by federal government (1956); motion picture studio accepted a consent decree to sell all of its theaters throughout the country.

Military expenditures 183 Extensive purchase of war matériel can have an effect on economic growth patterns, often overstimulation and causing distribution problems during the action, and withdrawal at end can trigger recession as plants close and jobs disappear; see illustration 182.

Milkin, Michael 261 Wall Street financier convicted of insider trading violations of SEC rules; implicated in billion-dollar bond market trading scandal in 1980s.

Miller Brewing 101-102, 273 One of the top

three U.S. brewers; part of the Philip Morris tobacco-food conglomerate; dominant competitor to Anheuser-Busch and Coors in U.S. beer oligopoly.

Miracle Ear 100 Leading franchisor of hearing aid devices.

Mitsubishi 268, 269 Japanese-based automotive multinational.

Mixed economy 64, 67, 69 Economic system combining elements of tradition, market, and command; see chart 64.

MNCs 202-203, 206, 212, 215 see multinational corporations.

Mobil 97, 211 Mobil Oil Corp. – petroleum refining and distribution.

Monetary policy 139-142 FED actions which change the money supply to deal with unfavorable economic conditions.

Money 131-132 Objects commonly accepted for transactions in markets; medium for exchange.

Money GNP or GDP 184 Raw GNP or GDP figures in current dollars without any adjustment for inflation.

Money supply 132-133, 181 Aggregate amount of money available in the nation (see *M-1*).

Monopoly 102, 103, 104-105, 257-260 Only one seller in a market (absence of competition).

Monopsony 310 Market in which there are many sellers but only one buyer (e.g., U.S. defense department for restricted military weaponry).

Motor-Voter reforms 279-281 Attempts to raise the percentage of those who participate in public affairs by registering to vote when registering for driver's licences.

Most favored nations 212 U.S. trade agreements which minimize legal restrictions and tariffs for trading partners.

Multinational corporation 202-203 (story), 206, 212, 215 (MNC) Firm owning and operating substantial business facilities and having direct investments in many countries.

Mutual savings bank 137 Financial institution for small consumer savings and loan services (especially home mortgages) not originally available in commercial banks; see chart, Figure 7.4.

N

NADA book 73, 75 National Association of Automobile Dealers Association publishes this monthly regionalized list of used car/truck/and RV prices.

NAFTA 116, 205, 206, 212, 228, 295 North American Free Trade Association – 1993 Canadian-Mexican-U.S. trade agreement unifies their markets into a single unit; phases out tariffs, other barriers.

National debt 38-39, 155, 310-311 Total of all unpaid financial obligations of the federal government; see Figure 1.3.

National Income 186 Total amount of wages, salaries, and other financial gains from investment (earned and unearned) in the nation less business taxes (but *including* personal taxes).

Nationsbank Corp. 142 One of the top ten U.S. banks – 1994 (NC); see Figure 7.9.

Natural monopoly 259 Market in which a single firm supplies a product or service such as electricity or water for which no substitutes and no other sources; the natural monopoly is allowed because it is much more efficient (cheaply) and safer to be provided by one regulated supplier.

Naugatuck Valley 282-283 Economic recovery project in Connecticut in 1980s and 1990s trained leaders for participatory role in political processes.

NBC 275 National Broadcasting Co. – major television broadcasting network.

NEA 118 National Education Association – largest U.S. employee/labor organization.

Near money 133 Valued assets that can be converted to money with relatively simple processing such as savings accounts.

Net Exports (*X*) 183, 213-214 "*X*" component C+I+G+*X* calculation (of GDP and GNP) in which gross imports are subtracted from gross exports; trade surplus (positive yield) contributes to aggregate growth; a negative yield indicates a trade deficit.

Net National Product 185 Refined statistical measurement of national economic production which discounts cost of replacing worn out productive equipment by subtracting depreciation from the Gross National Product.

New Deal 34, 69, 152-155, 156, 159, 276 Economic program of Pres. F.D. Roosevelt (1930s); initiated large number of gov't. programs to stimulate consumption and render security; see Figure 8.2.

New Frontier 36, 69 Economic program of Pres. J.F. Kennedy (1960s); number of gov't.

programs to stimulate consumption and render greater security.

Newly Industrializing Economies 206, 207, 215, 228, 294 (NIEs) Nations such as Hong Kong, Singapore, South Korea, and Taiwan that are breaking out of the less developed stages.

NIEs 206, 207, 215, 228, 294 see Newly Industrializing Economies.

Nissan 212 Nissan Automotive Corp. – Japanese based automotive multinational.

Nixon, Richard M 36 37th President of the U.S. (1969-1974) Vietnam War inflation, oil crises, imposed wage-price freeze, 1973.

Non-Partisan League 280-281 Early 20th c. U.S. political group in mid-west (ND) sought labor and social reform.

Nonprice Competition 102-104 Rival firms seek to win consumers for their products by advertising, promotions, packaging, event, team, and media program sponsorship, etc.

NOW 283 National Organization of Women – powerful lobby in interests of women's rights.

NRA 283 National Rifle Association – powerful lobby in interests of gun owners and hunters.

O

Occupational Safety and Health Administration 260, 324 (OSHA) federal agency regulates activities of firms in relation to working conditions and consumer products safety.

Oligopoly 103, 104 Market structure characterized by limited competition; only a few sellers in a market; usually national or international corporations; see chart, Figure 5.7.

OPEC 36, 183 Organization of Petroleum Exporting Countries – a cartel of Middle East, African, Asian, and Latin American oil countries which attempts to fix crude prices and production levels on global scale.

O.P.E.N. 100 O.P.E.N. Cleaning Systems – commercial cleaning franchisor.

Open market operations 140 Federal Reserve's FOMC (Federal Open Market Committee) actions that change the money supply through government security transactions.

Open shop 122 Employment of both union and nonunion members.

Opportunity cost 50-52 Value of resources expended in making a choice.

P

Pacific Rim 38, 205, 207 Rising economies of the region around the Pacific Ocean, especially East and Southeast Asia and Oceania (Taiwan, S. Korea, Hong Kong, Singapore, Australia, New Zealand).

PACs 161, 285-286 Political Action Committees subgroups formed by industrial and private interest groups and lobbies to influence election of individuals sympathetic to their cause; see Figure 13.9.

Partnerships 96-99 Form of business organization in which several owners operate and divide profits.

Pataki, George 277-278 Governor of New York, 1995-, attempted to apply corporate downsizing principles to state government.

PATCO Strike 119 Organized job action in 1981 by federal air traffic controllers, shut down airports; Pres. Reagan dismissed participants and broke the strike.

Pay equity 122 Compensation without discrimination.

Peak 154 Phase of business cycle characterized by economic growth and prosperity (high demand, low unemployment); see Figure 8.1.

PepsiCo 102, 104, 120 PepsiCo Corp. – beverage/foods/restaurant/general merchandise U.S.-based (NY) multinational conglomerate.

Perfect competition 102, 103 Market structure with many buyers and sellers, with identical products; completely price competitive; little advertising, very sensitive to supply and demand (e.g., farm products); also called monopolistic competition.

Personal capital 97 Individual using savings or income to invest in business ventures.

Personal consumption (C) 183 "C" is the largest component of C+I+G+X calculation in which consumer spending is added to business, government, and net export spending to determine GDP and GNP.

Personal Income 185-186 Aggregate amount of spending power before business and personal taxes are deducted from wages, salaries, and other financial gains from investment in the nation; gross (earned + unearned) income.

Pete's Brewing Co. 273 Minnesota microbrewery; newly competitive nationally in a market dominated by a few companies.

Philip Morris 97, 101 Diversified tobacco, food

processing, brewing conglomerate; U.S.-based (NY) multinational; see charts, Figures 5.2 and 5.6.

Picket line 119 Organized line of workers to publicize a disagreement with employer. Sometimes used to stop substitute workers or customers from entering a business firm.

Pillsbury (Green Giant Div.) 268-269 Major employment layoffs after 1990s buyout by Grand Met, a British multinational conglomerate.

Plaintiff (civil case) 243-247 In civil litigation, an aggrieved party who brings suit accusing another (defendant) of a wrongful act.

PNC Bank Corp. 142 One of the top 10 U.S. banks – 1994 (PA); see Figure 7.9.

Pre-legal actions 241-243 Consumer recourses to rectify disputes prior to using court action.

Price ceiling 84-86 Maximum price sellers can charge by government decree; see graph, Figure 4.7.

Price Elasticity/Inelasticity 82 The degree of change in quantity (Q) demanded or supplied in relation to changes in price (P); high degree of change = elastic; small degree of change (little or no change in Q)= inelastic; see Figure 4.4.

Price floor 84-86, 121-122 Minimum price sellers can charge, or the minimum wage employers can pay, by government decree; see graphs, Figures 4.7 and 6.8.

Price system 84 Money value on a good or service; in market system, interaction of forces of supply and demand create equilibrium price.

Primary Resources 208 Raw materials – ores, minerals; most basic natural substances used to manufacture goods.

Prime rate 142, 252 Benchmark interest rate for big banks offering large commercial loans; usually 3-4% above FED's discount rate; influences almost every kind of bank and credit transaction.

Principal 251 Amount of money borrowed in a loan transaction; interest is computed on this base amount.

Probable cause 243 In litigation, for prosecutors to have enough evidence to justify the consumer's complaint of criminal fraud.

Proctor and Gamble 112, 270 U.S.-based (OH) personal care, household cleaning multinational conglomerate; major layoffs and downsizing in early 1990s.

Producer Price Index 190-191 PPI measures the difference in prices paid for goods and services purchased by producers over time.

Production possibilities curve 50-52 Graph representing the array of choices for using resources in an economic situation.

Productivity 52 Measurement of the output resulting from applying economic resources in a certain situation; sometimes a synonym for efficiency; see page 68.

Profit 64, 68, 79, 115, 192 The amount by which revenue (sales income) exceeds production cost. (Revenue minus costs of production equals profits.)

Profit motive 81 Producers are enticed to produce more by the chance for greater profits.

Progressive Era 104, 225, 256 Late 19th and early 20th c. reform period began strong role for federal government in antitrust and consumer protection.

Progressive tax 162 Tax that has escalating rates; rising with income levels (ability-to-pay principle).

Property tax 166-167 State, municipal, and school taxes on real estate and sometimes personal possessions.

Proportional tax 163 Tax that has same rate for all.

Proprietorship 96-99 Form of business organization in which one owner operates and receives all profits.

Prosperity 180 The "peak" in the pattern of the economy's "ups and downs," characterized by aggregate expansion, high employment and high spending. Measured by Real GDP increase.

Protectionism 209-210 National policy uses rules and regulations to shield domestic market from foreign competition.

Prudential 97 Prudential Insurance – financial products and securities multinational; see chart, Figure 5.2.

Psychological (or "Psychic") rewards 99 Psychological benefits derived from owning and operating a business (independence, satisfaction, ego gratification).

Public assistance 189 tax-supported government social programs to help the unfortunate (unemployment compensation, medical subsidies, and welfare).

Public corporation 96 Form of corporation in which shares are publicly bought and sold on open stock markets.

Public Service Commission 259 State agencies that regulate electric, cable, water companies, and other natural monopolies.

Punitive damages 251 Court orders financial awards to plaintiff beyond direct losses from a breach of contract as punishment for the defendant's violation.

Purchasing power 186 Extent of consumer's ability to buy goods and services.

Q

QVC Network 83, 247 Television direct selling market arrangement.

R

Rationing system 86 Sharing or distributing goods in equal quantities; government controlled certain strategic products (e.g., tires, meats, dairy products, gasoline) in WWII by an elaborate coupon system over and above price.

Reagan, Ronald 37-38, 119, 142, 156, 157, 279 40th U.S. President (1981-1989) adopted "supply-side" stimulation policies; cut taxes but failed to reduce gov't. deficits.

Reaganomics 37-38, 156 1980s supply-side stimulation policies; cut taxes and reduce gov't. spending.

Real GNP, Real GDP 181, 184-185 Statistical measurement of value of all goods and services produced that is adjusted for inflation and reported in constant dollars of an official base year; used to make statistical comparisons to factor out inflation and deflation results in Real GDP or Real GNP measurements; see Figures 9.2 and 9.4.

Real growth 38 Net increase (adjusted for inflation) in economic activity over previous period; increased jobs, higher productivity.

Real property 166 Land or buildings that are subject to property tax.

Real wages 294 Net increase in pay over a previous period, adjusted for inflation; changes in real wages indicate growth or decline in standard of living and purchasing power; see Disposable Personal Income.

Recession 180 Phase of economic activity in market economies in which there is aggregate decline for three consecutive months or more (unemployment, less factory activity, unfavorable trade, little building, low consumption, etc.); measured by Real GDP decrease.

Reciprocation 210 One government raises or lowers tariffs and trade policies in response to another.

Recovery 154, 180 The point in the pattern of the economy's "ups and downs" after a recession or depression characterized by improving business activity, growing employment and increased spending; measured by Real GDP increase; see Figures 8.1 and 9.1.

Redress 249 Legal right of compensation under law; also remedies.

Reebok 104, 269 U.S.-based (MA) athletic footwear multinational.

Regressive tax 163 A tax that takes a larger percentage of poorer persons' income than from richer persons' income.

Regulation 259-261 Government commands, rules, restraints, and limitations placed on business that contradict Smith's concept of laissez-faire in market systems.

Rehabilitation Act 123 Federal law prohibits job discrimination against the handicapped (1973).

Related goods 81 Goods used with others or substituted for others; changes in prices of one will affect the other.

Remedies 243 Legal right of compensation under law; also redress.

Remington Rand 258 Former computer competitor of IBM; later merged with Sperry to form Unisys (PA-based multinational); involvement with gov't. antitrust suits against IBM.

Repossession 252, 255 Creditor takes back goods rendered on credit in response to nonperformance (default).

Representative money 132 Money (often paper) that symbolizes some valuable wealth (gold or silver) held in storage.

Rescission (civil case) 243 In civil litigation, a plaintiff may ask for the cancellation of a contract and restitution of a situation prior to a transaction.

Reserve 137, 142 In banking, a percentage of deposited funds not to be used for loans and kept as a stockpile to cover withdrawals; also a legal minimum banks must keep as a safety margin against excessive lending.

Reserve requirements 142 State and FED restrictions on amounts banks must store (and not use for loans). FED alteration of reserves that change the money supply.

Résumé 300-306 Written summary of one's career and qualifications.

Revenue 38, 160, 162-168 Income; usually refers to government income from taxation and fees.

Revolving credit (card) account 252 Credit card arrangement in which debtor need not pay total liability at end of billing period, but creditor can charge interest on unpaid balances.

Right-to-Work laws 122 State laws providing for open shop employment (union and nonunion employment). Outlaw exclusive union shops; see map, Figure 6.9.

Rio Declaration 223 June 1992 United Nations Conference on Environment and Development document which promotes twenty-seven principles on rights and obligations concerning the environment; cites international responsibility for "Global Commons."

Rio Summit 220, 222-224, 225, 231 June, 1992 United Nations Conference on Environment and Development in Rio de Janeiro, Brazil; also known as the "Earth Summit."

Robinson-Patman Act 257 (1936) Prevention of unfair preferential volume discounts in business.

Roosevelt, Franklin D. 34, 143, 152 32nd U.S. President (1933-1945); New Deal program attempted Keynesian approach to stimulating economy during the Great Depression.

S

S & L Crisis 137, 143-144 Collapse of many Savings and Loan Association banks in the U.S. during the 1980s; bailout by federal government exceeded $600 billion.

Salary caps 256 Earning limits defined in an employment contract.

Sales tax 167 State and local government collects a percentage on nonessential items at point of sale.

Samuel Adams Brewing Co. 273 Boston-based microbrewery reestablishing competitive market in oligopolistic U.S. brewing industry.

Sanctions (trade sanctions) 209 Embargoes, boycotts, high tariffs, and other regulations used to punish trade rivals.

Saturn 120, 272, 300 New, semi-independent automotive firm launched by GM.

Savings and loan association (S&L) 136-137 Financial institution for small consumer savings and loan services (especially home mortgages) not always available in larger commercial banks; see Figure 7.4.

Savings rate 186-187 Percentage of Personal Disposable Income stored in various savings accounts.

Say, Jean-Baptiste 156, 157, 158 Late 18th - early 19th c. economist believed that supply created its own demand. Became base for supply-side school of thought in 20th c.

Scarcity 48-52 Lack of sufficient resources to meet needs and wants (demand exceeding supply); shortage.

Schmidt, Peggy 301-303 Author, The 90 Minute Résumé.

Sears 83, 97 Sears, Roebuck – Chicago-based clothing, general merchandising corp., national chain store (formerly catalog direct mail); see chart, Figure 5.2.

Secured loan 251-252 A loan which is covered by some collateral; usually offered at lower interest rate than nonsecured loans.

Securities and Exchange Commission 34, 256, 261, 325 Federal agency regulates activities of firms in stock, bond, and other financial markets.

Security 67-69 Economic value of providing individuals with basic needs and a means to maintain a decent standard of living.

7-Eleven 100 Southland Corp. – convenience store franchisor.

Service Corps of Retired Executives 276 S.C.O.R.E.; volunteer organization of business managers help entrepreneurs.

Service Merchandise 83 Large chain of discount jewelry and household merchandise catalog showroom – volume selling.

Shell 130, 211 Major multinational petroleum firm.

Sherman Antitrust Act 104, 162, 256-257 Congressional law (1890) forbade certain business combinations which restricted a market (monopolies and near monopolies).

Shift in demand 84, 85 General change in the total amount of goods that producers are willing to provide at all price levels (shift to right = more, shift to left = less).

Shift in supply 84, 85 General change in the total amount of goods that consumers are willing to buy at all price levels (shift to right = more, shift to left = less).

Shortage 84, 86 Too few goods available – gap between quantity demanded and quantity supplied.

Simple machines 52 Wheels, levers, screws, inclined planes when adapted to implements to mechanize them and make work efficient.

Small Business Administration 274-275 (Figure 13.3), 276, 325 U.S. Dept. of Commerce; agency helps entrepreneurs with advice and funding arrangements with banks.

Small claims court 239, 240, 243-246 Inferior civil court or lower court operates on a local level [village, city, or town] usually handling cases involving disputes of under $3000.

Smith, Adam 52, 64, 66, 104, 147, 157, 211, 255 18th c. Scots political economist whose *Wealth of Nations* (1776) articulated the basic philosophy of the classical market structure.

Sovereignty (economic) 223 Independence of decision-making and control over available resources; troublesome when resources and problems stretch beyond national borders.

Spanish Peaks Brewing Co. 273 One of many microbreweries (MT) challenging the U.S. beer oligopoly.

Specialization 52 Becoming adept at performing a particular job or phase of an operation.

Specific performance 243 Beyond compensatory damages, plaintiff in civil litigation may ask court to order that a defaulted contract be fulfilled.

Stability, economic 68 Basic economic value: even growth so that planning can occur.

Stabilization 154, 156-158 Government actions to avoid serious declines or inflation; see monetary and fiscal policy.

Stagflation 36, 193 Unbalanced condition resulting from combination of inflation and no real economic growth.

Standard and Poor's Register of Corporations 242 Reference for obtaining corporate information; source for consumer complaints.

Standard Directory of Advertisers 242 Reference for obtaining corporate information; source for consumer complaints.

Standard of value 131 Money's use as a measure of an item's worth.

State office on consumer fraud 241, 249, 337-339 State agencies dealing with consumer affairs (some states include as a bureau under the state prosecutor's or attorney general's office); see state government

appendix for specific agencies.

Steinbeck, John 127 American writer, c. 1930s – Depression stories; quote on banks from *The Grapes of Wrath*, 1935.

Stocks 96-99 Certificates of shared ownership in a corporation without liability; can be traded; earn dividends.

Store of wealth 131 Money's use as a consistent reserve of resources for future use.

Strike 117-120 Organized refusal of employees to work, usually in protest of some action by employer.

Strong, Maurice 222 Canadian businessman diplomat; Gen. Secretary of the U.N.'s 1992 Earth Summit in Rio de Janeiro, Brazil.

Structural unemployment 189 Unemployment stemming from basic changes (technological) which throws people out of work for lack of skill and training.

Subway 100 Subway Sandwich Corp. – fast food franchisor.

Subpoena 245 A court order to appear and give testimony.

Subsidiary 101 A corporation wherein the majority of stock is owned by another corporation; usually allowed to operate under its own name.

Subsistence level 64 All the energy of the society devoted to producing bare essentials (no surplus to trade elsewhere).

Substitute goods 81 Goods used in place of others, ex. coffee v. tea.

Superfund 229-230 *Comprehensive Environmental Response, Compensation, and Liability Act* (1980) amended the *Superfund and Reauthorization Act* (1976) to help clean up abandoned toxic waste sites; see Figure 11.8.

Supply 78-79. 81, 82, 84, 86, 116, 191 Aggregate amount of goods producers are willing and able to produce.

Supply curve 83 Graph line showing relation between price and quantity producers are willing and able to provide; see graphs on 80, 81, 82, 85, 86, 114, 115, 116, 117, 271.

Supply, Determinants of 81 Underlying factors motivating producers.

Supply, Law of 79 As P increases, Q will increase and vice versa.

Supply schedule 82-83 Chart or table showing relation between price and quantity producers are willing and able to provide.

Supply-side economics 37, 156, 157, 158 School of thought which seeks to stimulate economic growth through fiscal policy of tax cuts and reduction of government spending levels, providing incentives for the private sector.

Surplus 52, 83, 86 Too many goods available; overproduction – a gap between quantity demanded and quantity supplied.

Sustainable development 222-225 Programs of environmentally sound economic improvement; see map, Figure 11.4.

T

Taft-Hartley Act 119, 122 Congressional act of 1947 gave President power to intervene in job actions which threatened national security; also outlawed closed (union only) shops.

Tariff 164, 209-210 A tax on imports (also customs duties); see Figures 10.4 and 10.5.

Tax withholding system 163-164 Employers reduce employees' gross pay by taking out income tax owed on the gross and send to government.

Taxes 160, 162-168, 229-230, 309-311 Revenues collected by governments to fund activities; also fiscal policy tool to remedy adverse economic conditions; see Figures 8.6, 8.7, 8.8, 14.9.

Tax Independence Day 160 Facetious May celebration by anti-tax groups as the day when the past 5 months of earnings would equal the average American's tax burden.

Teachers' Insurance 97 Teachers' Insurance Corp. – financial products and securities; see chart, Figure 5.2.

Teamsters 117, 120 International Brotherhood of Teamsters, Warehousemen, and Helpers of America – 1.4 million members, in many fields, began as transport drivers.

Technology 52, 115, 230 Application of scientific, electronic, and mechanical processes to production.

Tenth Amendment 151 Last of the *U.S. Constitution*'s *Bill of Rights* amendments reserves powers not assigned to federal government for states and localities; conflicts with the "Elastic Clause."

Texaco 97, 211 Texaco Oil Corp. – petroleum refining and distribution multinational; see chart, Figure 5.2.

Thomas Register of American Manufacturers 242 Reference for obtaining corporate information; source for consumer complaints.

Tight money policy 38, 140 FED actions which

constrict the money supply to offset inflation; contractionary actions.

Town meeting concept 278 Idea of using localized community meetings to get people participating in public policy reform.

Trade barriers 209-210 High tariffs, quotas, licenses, and other regulations used in protectionist trade policies.

Trade deficit 195, 213-214 Balance of payments statements show a nation spends more on imports than it sells to other countries.

Trade Names Directory 242 Reference for obtaining corporate information; source for consumer complaints.

Tradeoff 224 Scarcity necessitates economic choices that entail a sacrifice of alternatives and opportunities as well as optimum gain.

Trade proficiency certificates 298 Documentary evidence that an individual has met a level of standards for an occupation by a recognized authority (professional organization).

Trade surplus 195, 213 Balance of payments statements show a nation exports more than it buys from other countries.

Traditional system 63-64, 65, 67 Economic decision-making based on past practices, or cultural or religious beliefs; see chart 65.

Transaction 131 Exchange of goods and services.

Transfer payments 161 Government payment of revenues to individuals (pensions, welfare, unemployment compensation, etc.).

Trough 154 Slump, depression; lowest phase of business cycle characterized by economic stagnation (low demand, rising unemployment); see Figure 8.1.

Truman, Harry S 35 33rd President of U.S. after WW II (1945-1953), involved with economic conversion, G.I. Bill, and Fair Deal.

Truth in Lending Act 135, 254 Congressional law (1968) outlining consumer rights to be apprised of finance charge, APR, and all pertinent details regarding loans and credit arrangements; see Figure 12.8.

U

Underemployed 34 When a person is working, but for fewer hours and at lesser pay than needed for survival.

Unearned income 185 Wealth gained from indirect sources such as gifts, investments, rents, etc.

Unemployment rate 187-189 Percentage of workforce not actively engaged in wage-earning activity.

Union shop 122 A firm agrees to hire only union members (outlawed by right-to-work laws in some states).

Unionism 116-122 Drive to organize workers for collective bargaining purposes.

United Airlines 271 Employee-ownership launched in 1990s.

United Nations Environmental Programme 225 Chief monitoring and implementing unit for the Earth Summit agreements.

Unsecured loan 252 A loan which is not covered by some collateral; usually offered at higher interest rate than secured loans; bank credit card transactions are nonsecured, merchandise purchased is not considered collateral, and therefore the card transactions bear very high interest rates.

Usury 134, 252, 253 Lending money at excessive interest rates.

Utility tax 168 Government collects revenue on electric, telephone, CATV, water, etc.

V

Venezuela 211 Comparative advantage in petroleum production.

Vertical merger 100-101 A business combines with another in the a different phase of same industry (e.g., chain of hamburger stands buys a beef cattle ranch).

VISA 130, 134 Major issuer of international bank credit cards.

Volume selling 83 Large-scale sale of items at lower profit margin.

Voter participation reforms 278-281 Attempts to raise the percentage of those who participate in public affairs by increasing traditionally low numbers that vote on all levels of government.

Voting Rights Act 279 (1965) Congressional legislation forbade discrimination in federal elections.

W

Wage floor 121 minimum wage; either legislated or agreed to in a contract negotiation; see graph, Figure 6.8).

Wage rate 114 Amount one gets paid for one's labor (usually per hour).

Wagner Act 117 Congressional act (1935) upheld workers right to hold elections to select bargaining agents (unions).

Wall Street 34, 38 Site of the New York Stock Exchange.

Wal☆Mart 83, 97, 207 U.S.-based (AR) clothing, general merchandising corp.; multinational chain store; see chart, Figure 5.2.

Warranty 248-250 A promise made by the seller that guarantees the quality and performance of the purchased product for a specific time.

Warranty of merchantability 249 Protection that a product will meet the reasonable criteria of most people to be at the very least, a good that is of average quality.

Washington, George 150-151 1st President of the U.S. (1789-1797); accepted a basic financial plan for making the new U.S. government solvent and stable; divisions in cabinet led to formation of first political parties.

Wealth of Nations, An Inquiry into the 52, 64, 66, 153, 157, 255 Adam Smith's classic outline of the philosophy and structure of market economic systems (1776).

Wells Fargo Co. 142 One of the top 10 U.S. banks – 1994 (CA); see Figure 7.9.

White collar 294 Managerial level office jobs.

Work ethic 299 Set of attitudes and principles of proper behavior about employment recognizing the proper relationship between employer and employee.

Workingmen's Party 280 19th c. U.S. political group sought labor reform in 1830s at dawn of industrialization era.

World Bank 207 U.N.-associated financial agency makes development loans, especially in Third World LDCs.

World War I 33, 192 U.S. role changed global economic status; hyperinflation in Germany.

World War II 34-36, 118, 154 U.S. emerged as predominant economic power.

XYZ

Xerox 300 Major U.S.-based (CT) multinational office equipment/printing conglomerate; downsizing layoffs in early 1990s.

Zaibatsu 206 Huge, powerful monopolistic corporations of Japan in the pre-1980s era.